EVENT-CITIES
(PRAXIS)

Third printing, 1996
© 1994 Massachusetts Institute of Technology
All rights reserved. No part of this book may be reproduced in any form by any electronic or mechanical means (including photocopying, recording or information storage and retrieval) without permission in writing from the publisher.

This book has been prepared on the occasion of Bernard Tschumi's exhibition at the Museum of Modern Art in New York from April 21 to July 5, 1994. It is an expanded version of Praxis: *Villes-Événements*, produced in French in November 1993 (Le Fresnoy and Massimo Riposati Editeur, Paris.)

Book Design and Production: Bernard Tschumi, Yannis Aesopos, Henning Ehrhardt and Massimo Riposati with the assistance for the American edition of Stephen Perrella, Lois Nesbitt and Keena Suh.

ISBN # 0-262-70052-2
Library of Congress Catalog Card Number 94-75566

The MIT Press, Cambridge, Massachusetts/London, England
Carte Segrete, Rome, Italy
Printed and bound in Italy

BERNARD TSCHUMI

EVENT-CITIES
(PRAXIS)

The MIT Press
Cambridge, Massachusetts
London, England

Acknowledgements

Bernard Tschumi would like to thank all whose assistance and collaboration have been essential, specifically, Jean-François Erhel for the Parc de la Villette and Le Fresnoy and Luca Merlini, associated architect for the Tokyo Opera and the Lausanne Bridge-City projects.

Colin Fournier, Robert Young, Tom Kowalski, Mark Haukos, François Gillet, Véronique Descharrières, Ko Yasuda, Yannis Aesopos and Marie-Line Le Squer have played an equally important role in the elaboration of various projects. Peter Rice and Hugh Dutton have also contributed to the overall concepts of several schemes through their structural engineering suggestions.

Also to be thanked are the public representatives whose support, patience and persistence permitted some of these projects (and others not presented here) to be realized, particularly François Barré and Serge Goldberg for the Parc de la Villette, Alain Fleischer for Le Fresnoy and Marcel Linet, new president of the Établissement Public du Parc de la Villette.

The university is a context for many contemporary debates. The late Alvin Boyarsky at the Architectural Association in London; Jonathan Cole, Michael Sovern and George Rupp at Columbia University in New York deserve acknowledgement for their tacit support and encouragement.

Roger Conover, Pierre Keller, Terry Riley and (last but not least) Kate Linker have given generously of their valuable advice.

This book is made possible in part by the generous support of the Office Fédéral de la Culture, Pro Helvetia Fondation Suisse pour la Culture, Fondation Nestlé pour l'Art, Obayashi Corporation, YKK and the Ministère de la Culture de la Francophonie.

Contents

Introduction   **11**

A. Planning Strategies
Parc de la Villette, Fireworks, 1992: *Cities of Pleasure*   **16**

Chartres, Business Park, 1991–: *Edge City*   **38**

Rotterdam, Railway Tunnel Site, 1988: *Continuous/Discontinuous Lines*   **86**

B. Architectural Urbanism
Kansai, International Airport, 1988: *Linear Cities*   **102**

Lausanne, Bridge-City, 1988–: *Typological Displacements—Crossprogramming*   **154**

Kyoto, Center and Railway Station, 1991: *Disprogramming*   **220**

C. Urban Architecture
Tokyo, Opera, 1986: *A Mode of Notation—Programmatic Dissociations*   **266**

Strasbourg, County Hall, 1986: *Old and New—The Logic of Fragments*   **302**

Paris, Library of France, 1989: *Transprogramming*   **326**

Karlsruhe, Center for Art and Media (ZKM), 1989: *Unstable Images*   **364**

Tourcoing, Le Fresnoy, 1991–: *Strategy of the In-Between*   **390**

The Hague, Villa, 1992–: *Domesti-City*   **524**

D. Transient Events
Groningen, Glass Video Gallery, 1990: *Immaterial Representation*   **556**

Paris, Pompidou Center, "Art et Publicité" Exhibition Design, 1990: *Mediation I*   **576**

Tourcoing, Le Fresnoy, "BTA" Exhibition, 1993: *Mediation II*   **594**

Project Teams   **608**

Project List   **610**

Bibliography   **612**

Biographical Notes   **620**

Introduction
The works presented in *Event-Cities* are a selection of recent projects. The argument of *Event-Cities* is three-fold:
- it is about "praxis" insofar as it documents the elaboration of a conceptual process that is inseparable from the actual making of architecture.
- it is about "cities" insofar as it argues that all architecture is inextricably linked to our urban condition and that each of the projects featured here is first and foremost a constituent element of our global system of cities.
- it is about "events" insofar as it constantly affirms that there is no architecture without action or without program, and that architecture's importance resides in its ability to accelerate society's transformation through a careful agencing of spaces and events.

Praxis
Event-Cities aims to be a "different" kind of book about architecture. While in the past few years theoretical texts on architecture have received proper in-depth treatment, accumulating into a body of serious contributions to textual discourse, the projects and the spaces of architecture have generally been the object of glossy picture books, in which projects receive only a cursory treatment.

With *Event-Cities* we have tried to show that a "project" discourse potentially can be as accurate and extensive as important theoretical texts of recent years. The result is a precise documentation of a number of recent projects, some of which are built or under construction, some of which are competition entries or feasibility studies.

Using different modes of notation from rough models to sophisticated computer images, and using different means of inscribing the unfolding of events in architectural space, we have attempted to show the complexities of the architectural process. The relentless accumulation of plans (for example, in the section including the Le Fresnoy construction documents) may irritate those for whom architecture should be first a "media bite," to be consumed instantly and uncritically. These pages attempt to indicate the patient elaboration of any architectural project: often several hundred plans, sections, elevations and details are necessary to inform the making of buildings. Because these documents represent an inevitable stage in the final materialization of architectural concepts, they also need to be scrupulously exact. Their relation to the immediate reality of users and contractors makes them different from the theoretical projects developed in *The Manhattan Transcripts*[1] or from the positions argued in *Architecture and Disjunction*,[2] in which the logic of concepts was my primary concern. In *Event-Cities*, realism is what counts, but only the sense of something that is realizable: every praxis is an action towards a result. If theory is only responsible to theory, a praxis can only project itself towards the constructed, social, economic and political reality. A praxis is constantly responsible to others, precisely because it has to render an account: to those who, by their use of the spaces, will create the event; to those who will finance and support the work, whether as an identifiable political and economic body or society as a whole.

The dryness of the system of notation used in *Event-Cities* — going from ideograms to construction drawings of projects — is voluntary. The notions of form and style play a negligible role. These pages are nothing but accounts: they render an account of, and they account for. Indeed, the goal of these projects is neither abstract theory nor design (whatever reading one would like to make, these projects are, in general, indifferent to the notion of style) but, on the contrary, a series of conceptual strategies aimed at establishing conditions for new urban events. This book starts in the middle of this strategic process, like a text that would start in the middle of a phrase. It is a "work-in-progress," in transition.

What in most architectural books is the object of abbreviation is documented here in minuteness. We have also included some detail drawings. In opposition to the absolute of a theoretical project, the construction detail, with its joints, screws and bolts, appears nearly obscene. The construction detail calls things by their names; it describes what one ordinarily makes. Sometimes prosaic and dirty, but also lively and luminous, this detail is part of the conditions of the city-event. If architecture is the materialization of concepts, then the most absolute part of such concepts may occasionally correspond to the most advanced construction technology.

Cities
Each of the projects developed in this book is a history of a city. The city, as their object, is presented here as synonymous with architecture. From the organizational strategies of the territory developed for the city of Chartres to those established for the project of Le Fresnoy, the subject is always the urban effect: there is no architecture without the city, no city without architecture.

We can distinguish four types of projects in *Event-Cities*. The first type (exemplified by La Villette, Chartres and Rotterdam) involves projects of urban planning, in which the organization of the territory precedes the definition of any specific program. If we have shown in these pages the fireworks realized at La Villette in the summer of 1992 instead of the Park itself, it is in order to emphasize the "event" dimension, the dimension of action, in what makes up a city. (The Park would also require a book in itself.)

In the second type (the architectural urbanism of Kansai, Kyoto and Lausanne), we have tried to demonstrate the hypothesis of urban generators, or architectural systems that are actual catalysts for every kind of activity or function, independent of the form they may take. In such city-generators, functions and programs combine and intersect in an endless "disprogramming" or "crossprogramming." The linear airport-city of Kansai, the inhabited bridges of Lausanne, the "skyframe" or programmatic extractor of Kyoto — each organizes the city in space and time. Urban operations in large scale, these projects cannot be conceived other than as constructions that extend in time, in which the notion of multiple and heterogeneous programs inevitably substitutes for a homogeneous and unitary one. If the linear Kansai Airport is literally a city created *ex-nihilo*, the architectural urbanism of Kyoto or Lausanne is confronted with the historic city. On one level, the scale and unprecedented density of the new center-station of Kyoto is enough to create an "event." However, it is in the montage of attractions, or programmatic collision, that the importance of the project resides. What concerns Lausanne in particular is the *détournement* or displacement of a typology (the bridge) that provides the conditions for a new urban act.

In the third type (the Tokyo Opera, the Strasbourg County Hall, the Karlsruhe Center for Art and Media, the Paris Library of France as well as Le Fresnoy), we are confronted with specific programs, defined in space and time. Through their cultural and political ambition, these urban architectures suggest a new type of city, in which the notion of the event that happens in them is as important as that of a street or a square. The fragments of the Strasbourg project, the autonomous strips of the Tokyo Opera, the linear core of the Karlsruhe Media Center, the circuits of the Library of France and the electronic roof of Le Fresnoy propose, to different degrees, a new relation between space and event, in which the "in-between" or programmatic interstice plays an essential role. The project for an urban villa at The Hague brings the notion of the in-between from the public realm to the smaller scale of the private.

In the fourth and final type — the transient architectures of the city — one particular reading of events is discussed. At the Glass Video Gallery, spatial definition changes constantly following the unstable images of video displays. At the exhibitions designed for the Centre Pompidou or for Le Fresnoy, space is activated by electronic, as much as by architectonic, artifacts: cut apart equally by media images and by suspension cables, the dense interiority of a city space expands to the dimension of an urban event.

Events

Each of the projects described in *Event-Cities* begins with some form of a program, from organizing large metropolitan territories to providing a functional enclosure for the most common uses.

What distinguishes these projects, however, is the manner in which their programmatic dimension becomes as much a part of their architecture as of their use. "Architecture is as much about the events that take place in spaces as about the spaces themselves." I will elaborate this little, as I have done so at length elsewhere. Here it suffices to say that the static notions of form and function long favored by architectural discourse need to be replaced by attention to the actions that occur inside and around buildings — to the movement of bodies, to activities, to aspirations; in short, to the properly social and political dimension of architecture. Moreover, the cause-and-effect relationship sanctified by modernism, by which form follows function (or vice versa) needs to be abandoned in favor of promiscuous collisions of programs and spaces, in which the terms intermingle, combine and implicate one another in the production of a new architectural reality.

This point should be placed in the context of considerable changes taking place in architecture today. Rather than questioning the technology of construction, architects will be involved increasingly in the construction of technology, including the new computerized processes already altering building and design. But it is also through a new attitude to programs that architecture will find its role. "Crossprogramming," "transprogramming," "disprogramming" are some of the concepts *Event-Cities* seeks to explore.

In our contemporary world in which railway stations become museums and churches are turned into night-clubs, the old, stable coordinates cease to apply. And, in this world in which airports incorporate amusement arcades, cinemas, churches, business centers and so on, the "city," as a complex and interactive web of events, becomes the relevant point of reference. These imbrications of elements lead, potentially, to new social relations, altering the once stable contours of institutions and accelerating the process of change on the way. They disrupt and disfigure but, simultaneously, reconfigure, providing a rich texture of experiences that redefine urban actuality: city-events, event-cities.

Bernard Tschumi
25 January 1994

[1] *The Manhattan Transcripts.* London and New York: Academy Editions/St. Martin's Press, 1981
[2] *Architecture and Disjunction.* Cambridge and London: The MIT Press, 1994

A.
Planning Strategies

La Villette, Chartres and Rotterdam are projects of urban planning, in which the organization of a territory precedes the definition of any specific program. If we have shown here the fireworks realized at La Villette in the summer of 1992 instead of the Park itself, it is to emphasize the "event" dimension in what makes a city.

Parc de la Villette, Fireworks, 1992

Cities of Pleasure

The fireworks at Parc de la Villette in Paris in 1992 expanded the theme of the fireworks as a manifesto for architecture (see Bernard Tschumi, *Architectural Manifestoes*, exhibition catalog [New York: Artists Space, 1978]):

Good architecture must be conceived, erected and burned in vain. The greatest architecture of all is the fireworkers': it perfectly shows the gratuitous consumption of pleasure.

The fireworks at La Villette were a three-dimensional version of the organizational principles of the park: the superimposition of systems of points, lines and surfaces. A system of notation (like a partition) defines the event in space and time. The fireworks, lasting half an hour, took place on June 20, 1992 in front of more than one hundred thousand people.

Phase I
First minute: points 250 meters high
Rhythm: every seven seconds
Phase I
Second minute: lines 250 meters high
Rhythm: every seven seconds
Phase I
Third minute: surfaces 250 meters high
Rhythm: every seven seconds
Phase I
Fourth minute: superimposition, points, lines, surfaces 250 meters high
Rhythm: every seven seconds
Phase II
First minute: points 50 meters, 150 meters, 250 meters high
Rhythm: every seven seconds
Phase II
Second minute: lines 50 meters, 150 meters, 250 meters high
Rhythm: every seven seconds
Phase II
Third minute: surfaces 50 meters, 150 meters, 250 meters high
Rhythm: every seven seconds
Phase II
Fourth minute: superimposition, points, lines, surfaces 50 meters, 150 meters, 250 meters high
Rhythm: every seven seconds
Phase III
First minute: points
Rhythm: every seven seconds
Phase III
Second minute: lines
Rhythm: every seven seconds
Phase III
Third minute: surfaces
Rhythm: every seven seconds
Phase III
Fourth minute: superimposition, points, lines, surfaces
Rhythm: every seven seconds

Vue perspective depuis le sol	→						
Plan	→						
Elevation	→						
Couleur Points Lignes Surfaces	→						
Intensité sonore	▭▭▭▭▭ →	▭▭▭▭▭	▭▭▭▭▭	▭▭▭▭▭	▭▭▭▭▭	▭▭▭▭▭	▭▭▭▭▭

250
150
50

250

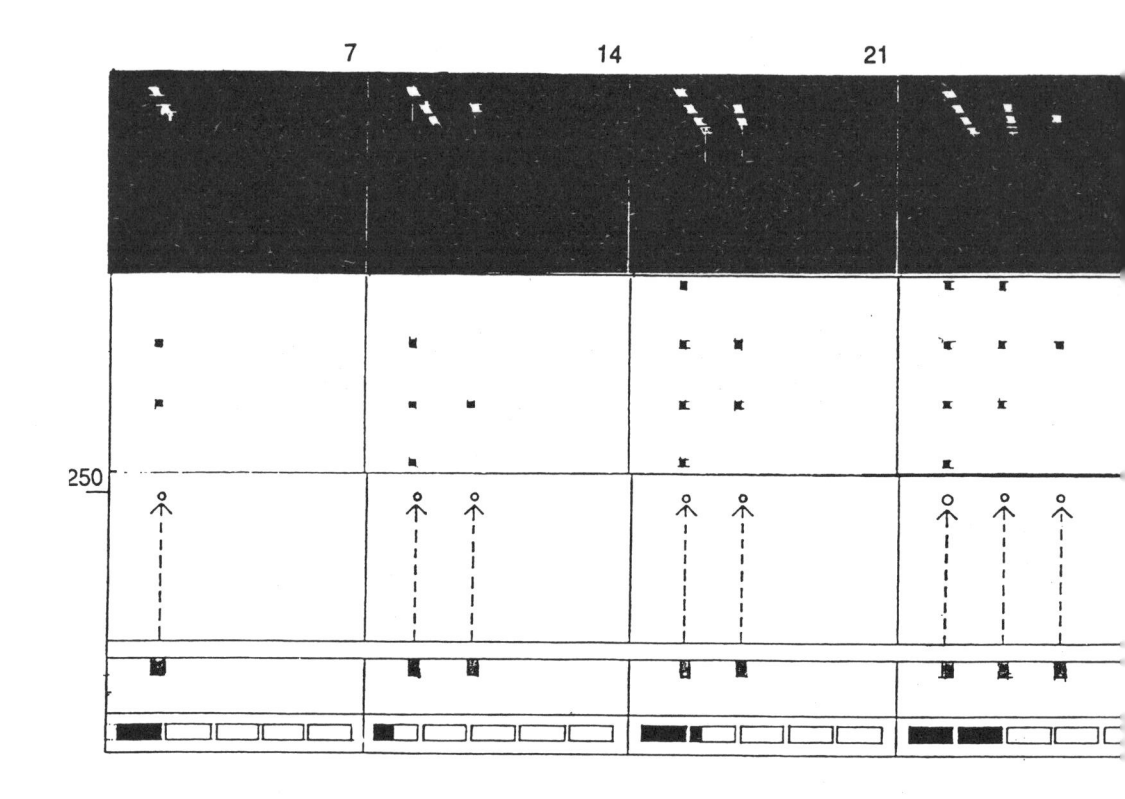

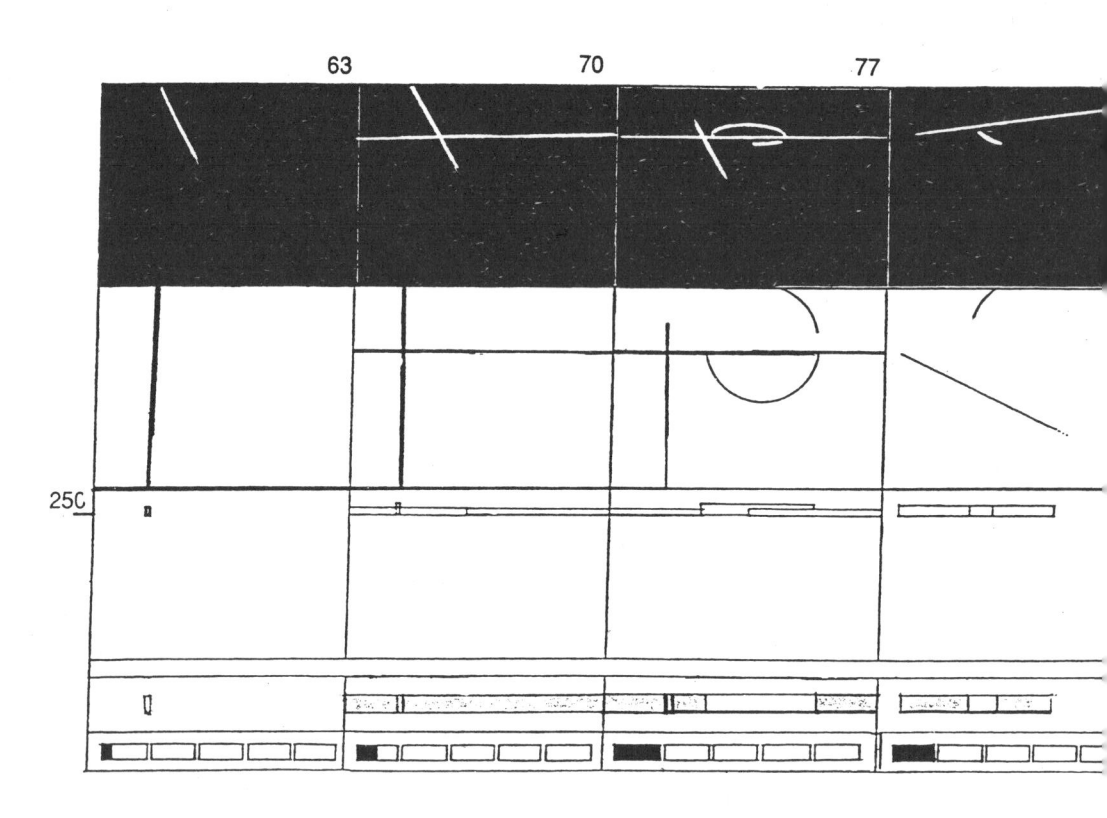

250

35 42 49 56

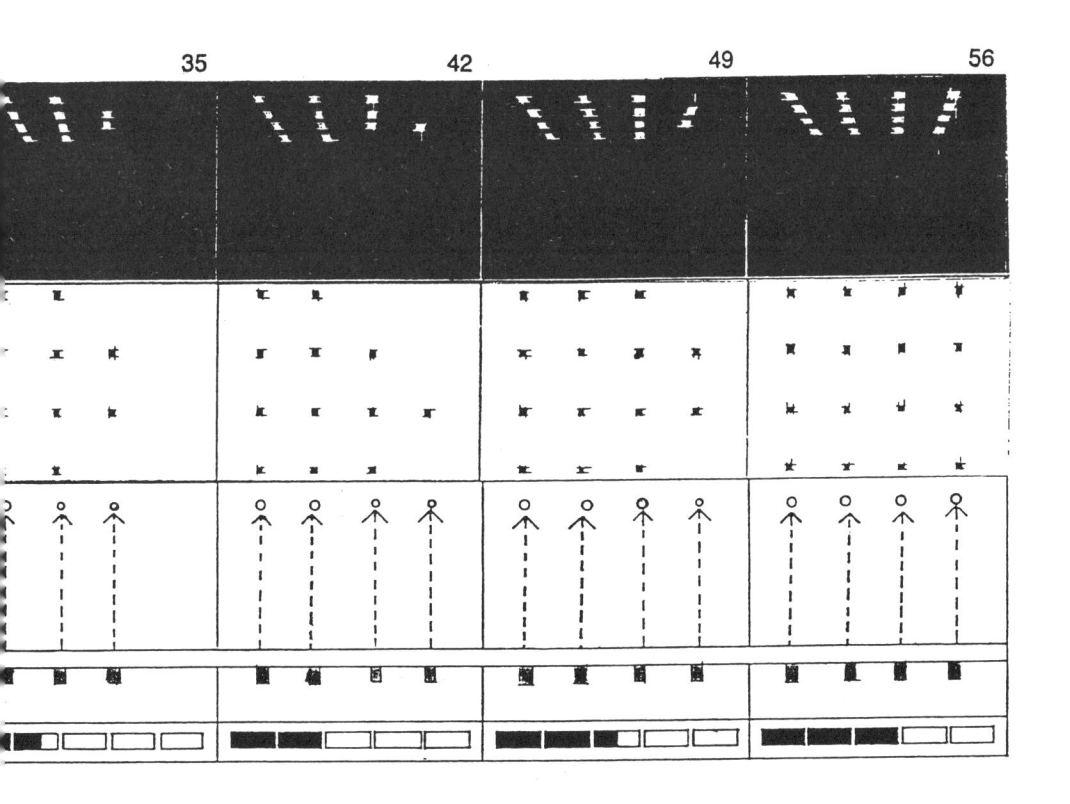

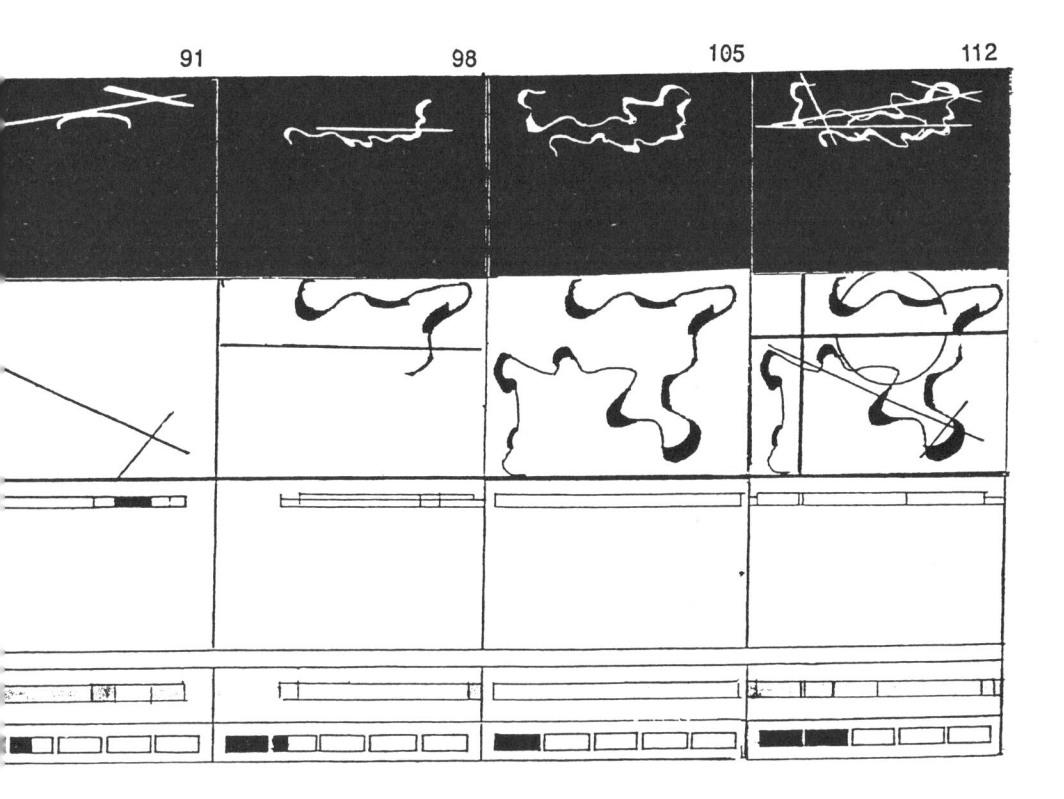

91 98 105 112

250

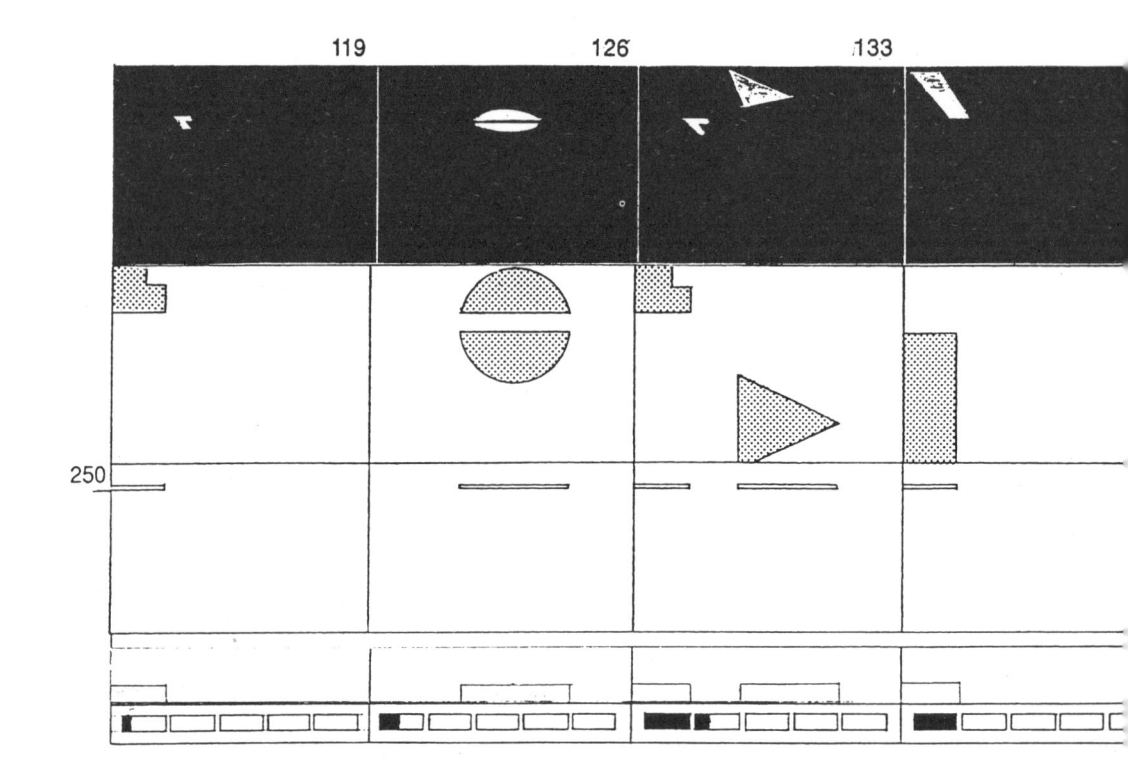

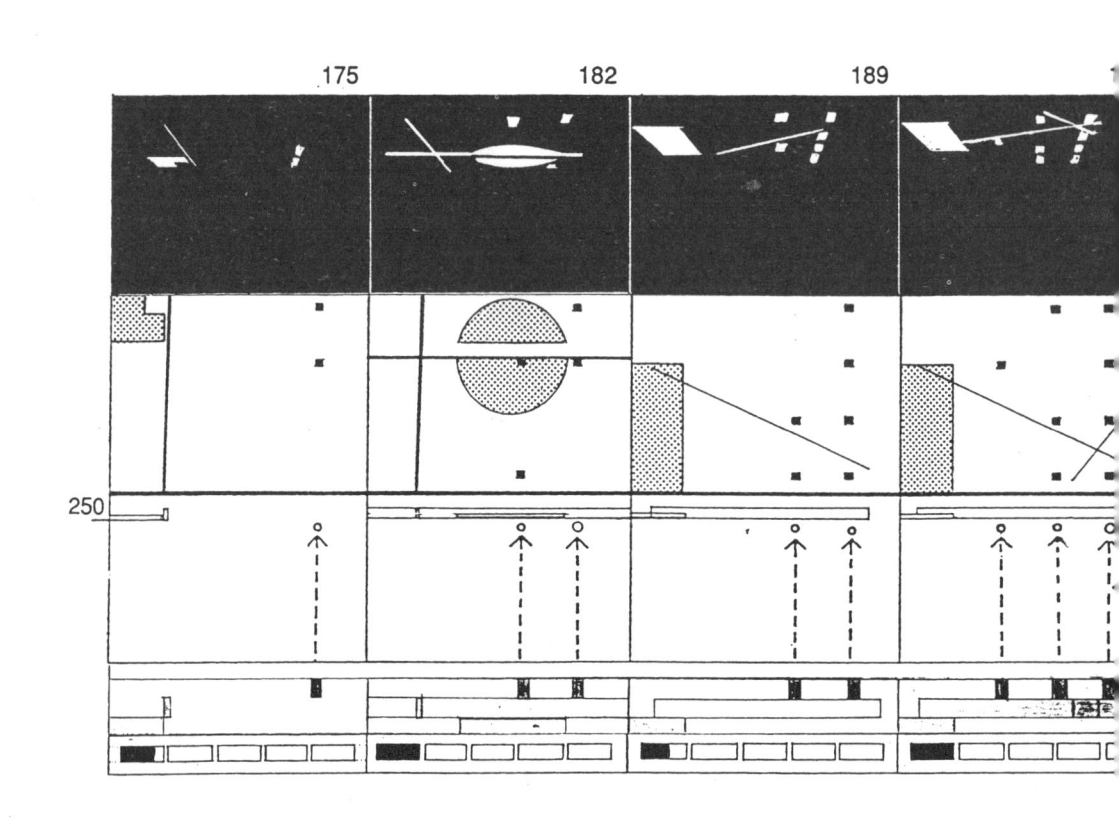

175 182 189
250

147 154 161 168

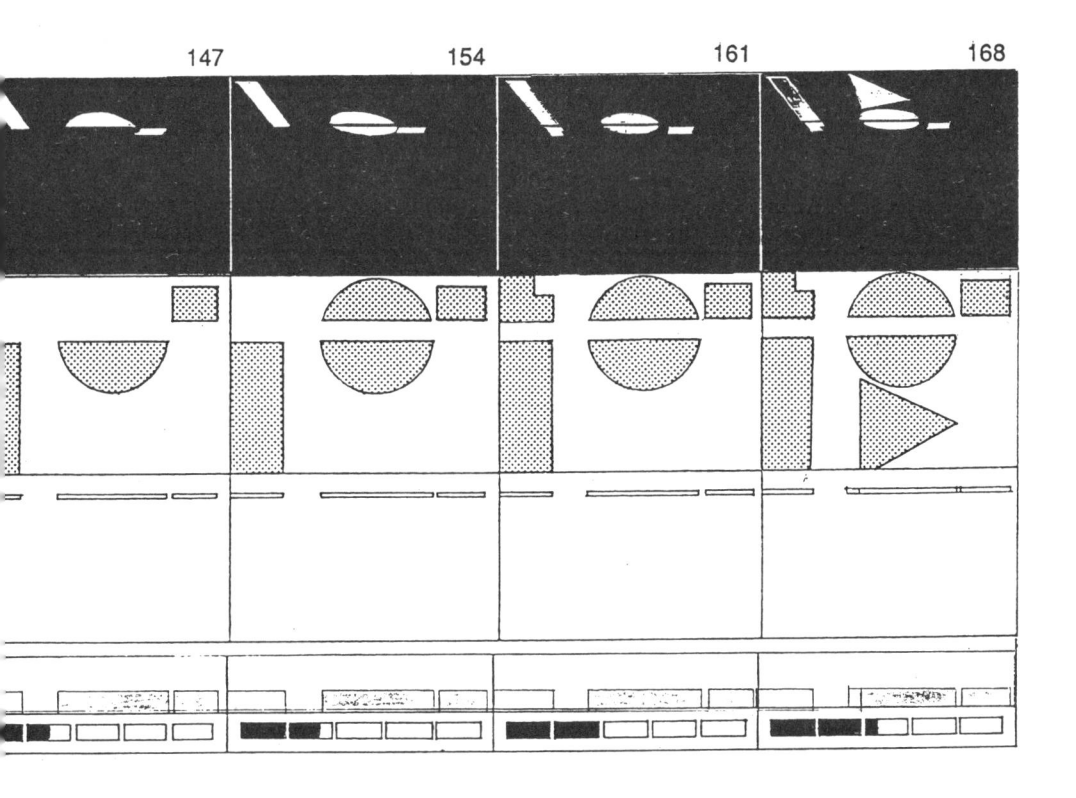

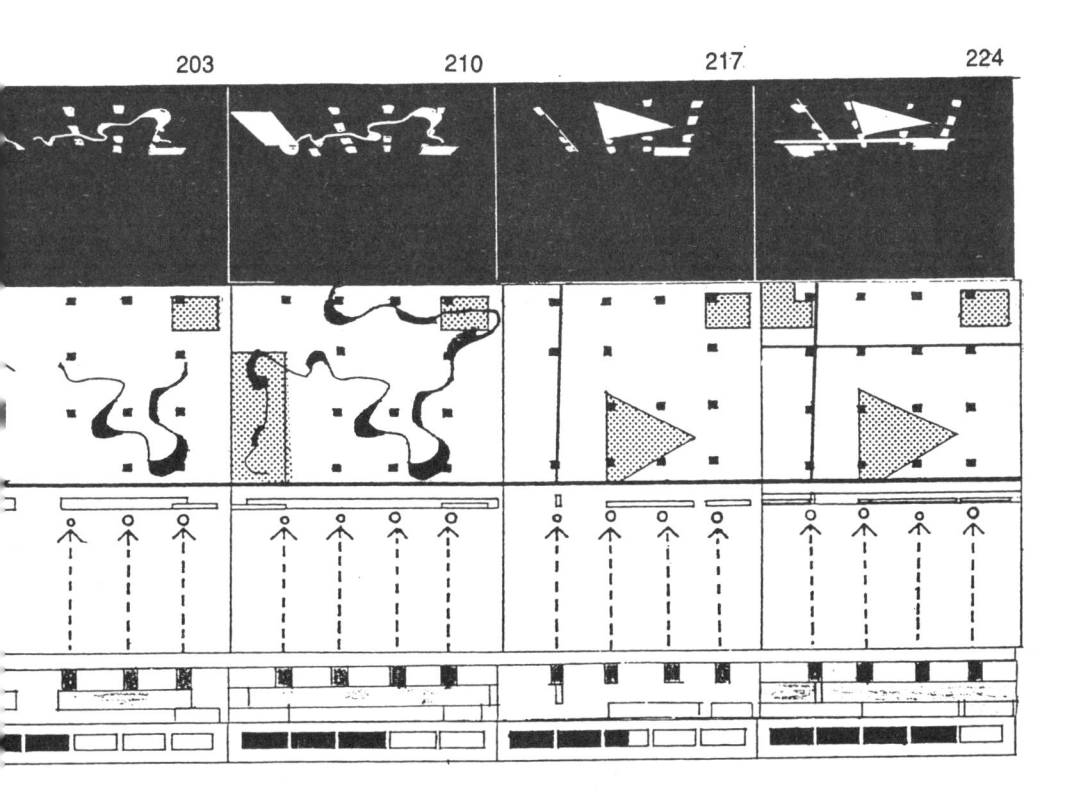

203 210 217 224

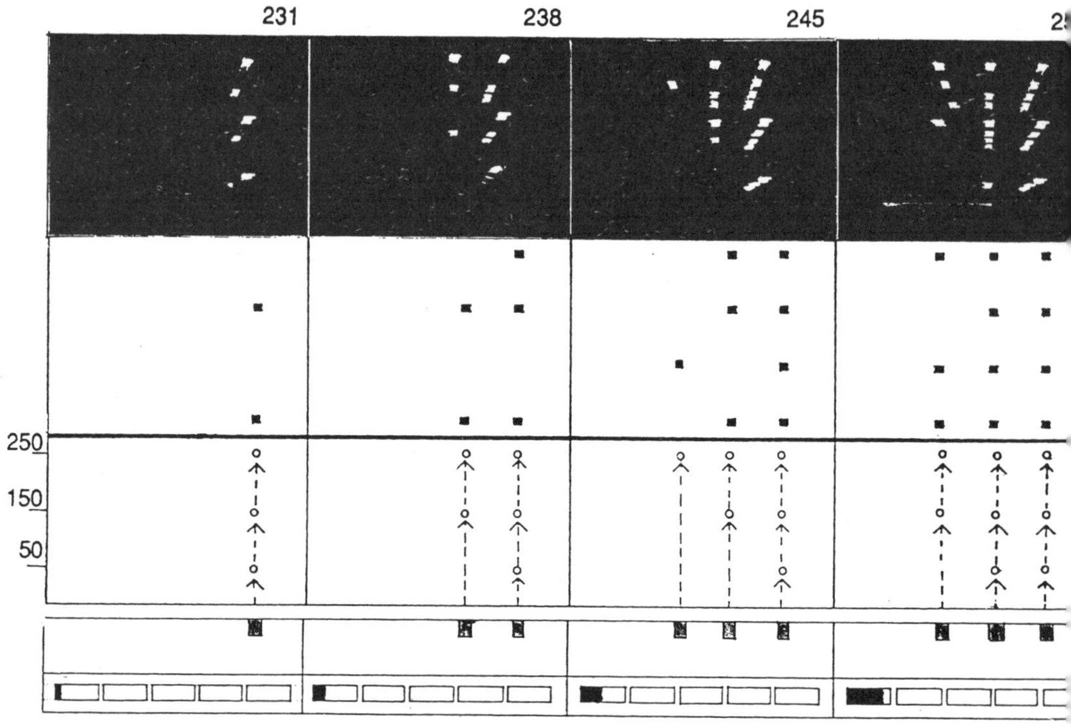

231
238
245
250
150
50

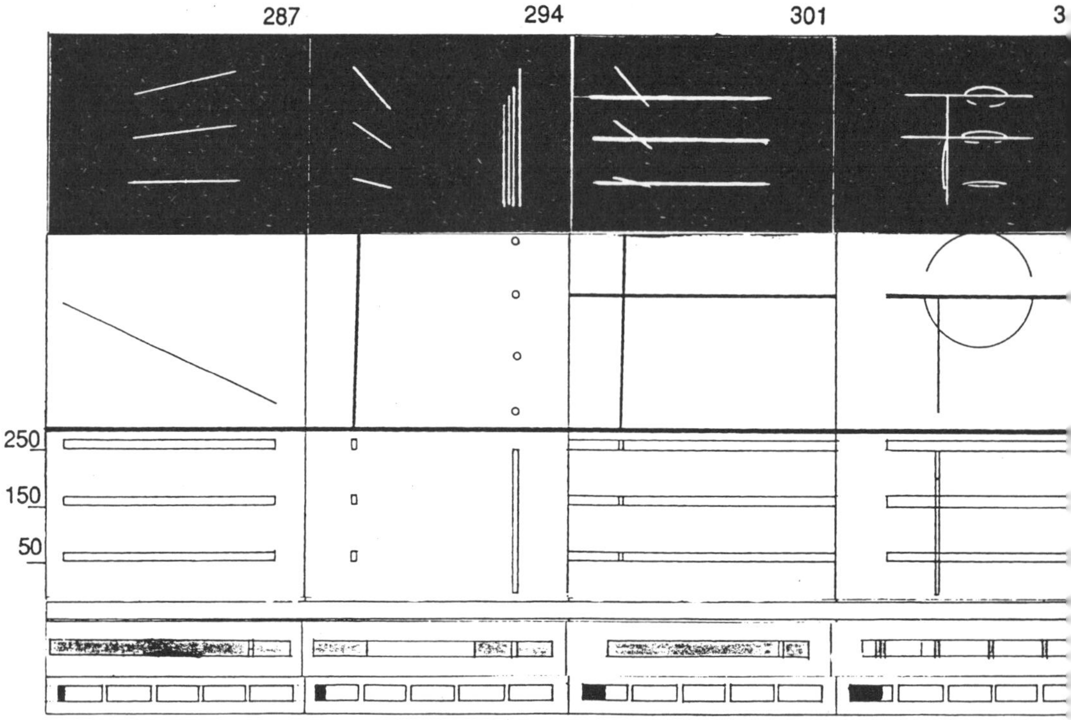

287
294
301
250
150
50

259 266 273 280

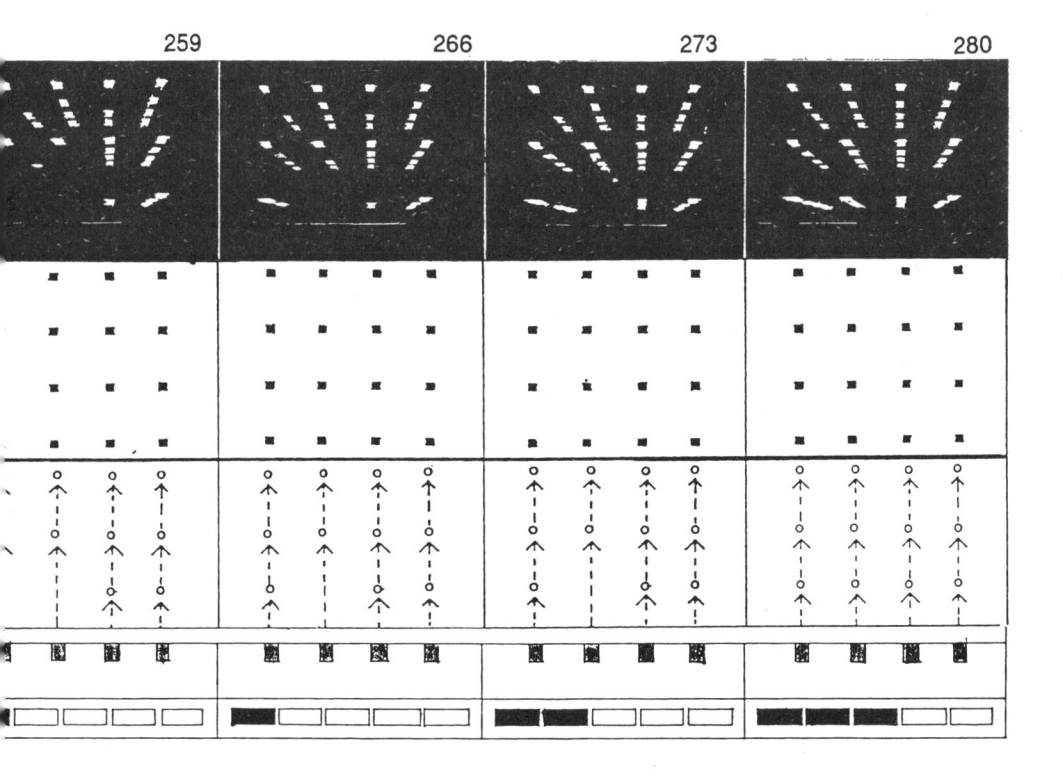

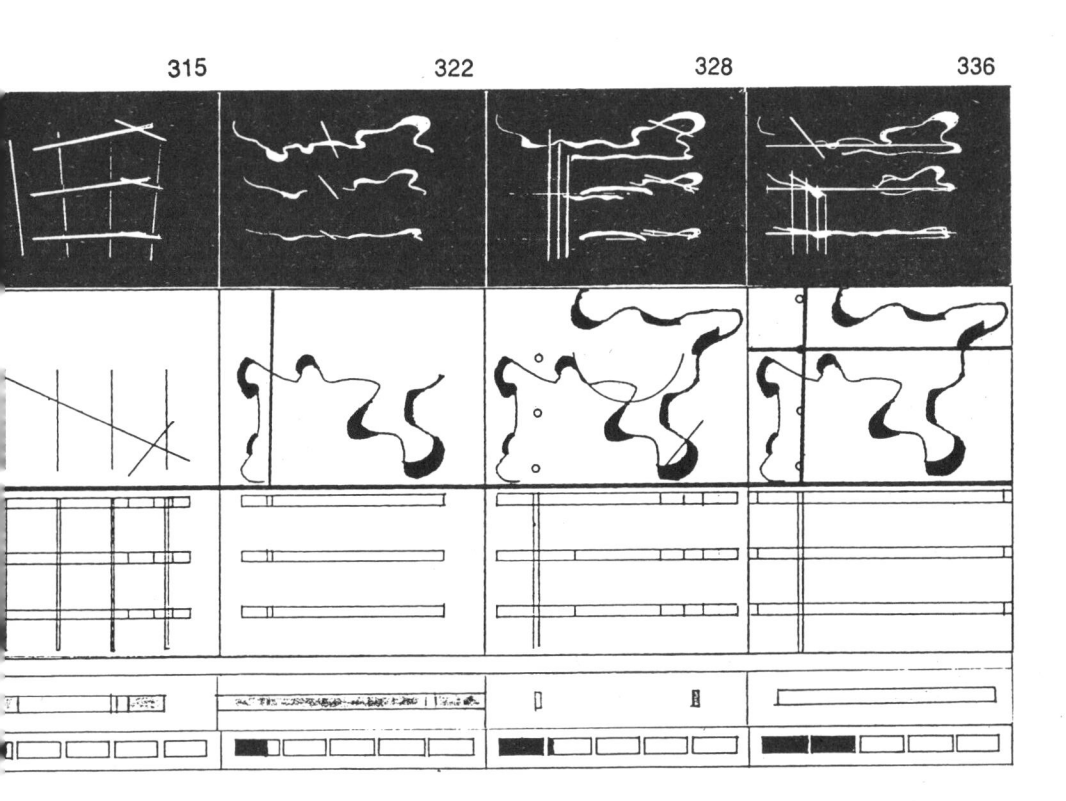

315 322 328 336

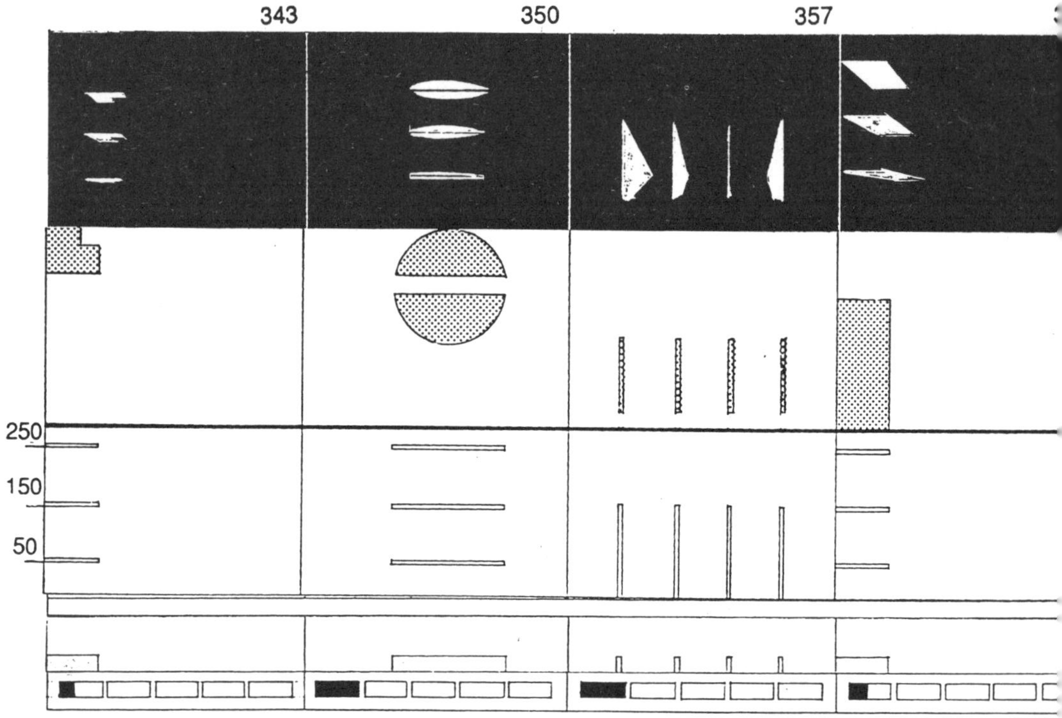
343
350
357
250
150
50

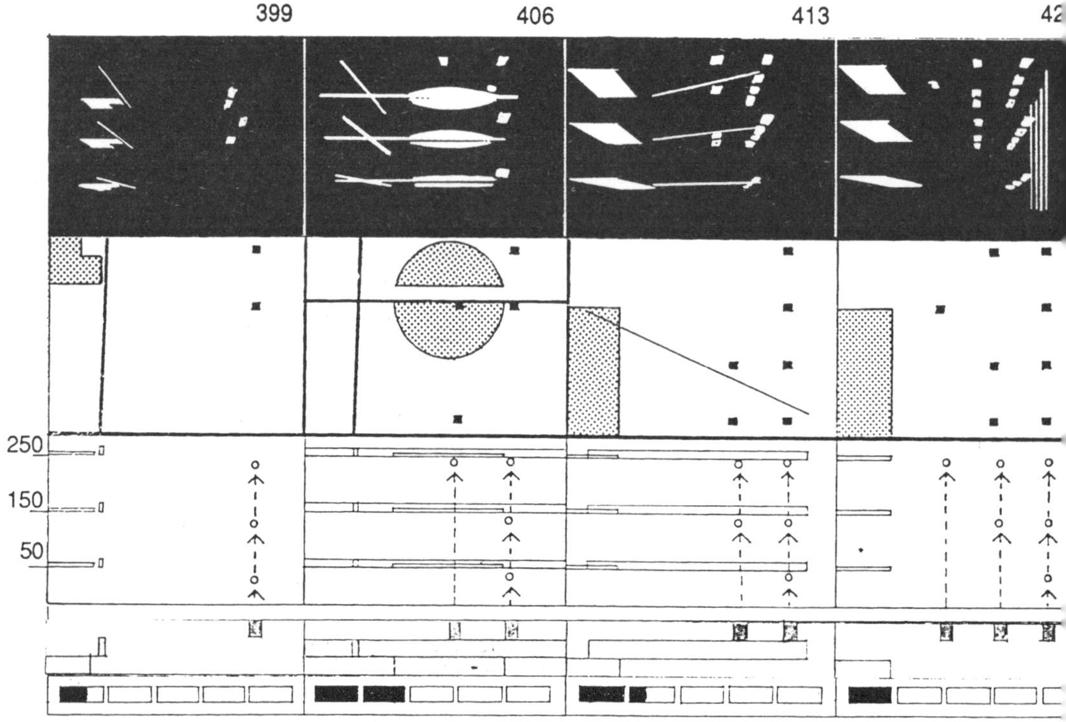
399
406
413
250
150
50

371　　　　　378　　　　　385　　　　　392

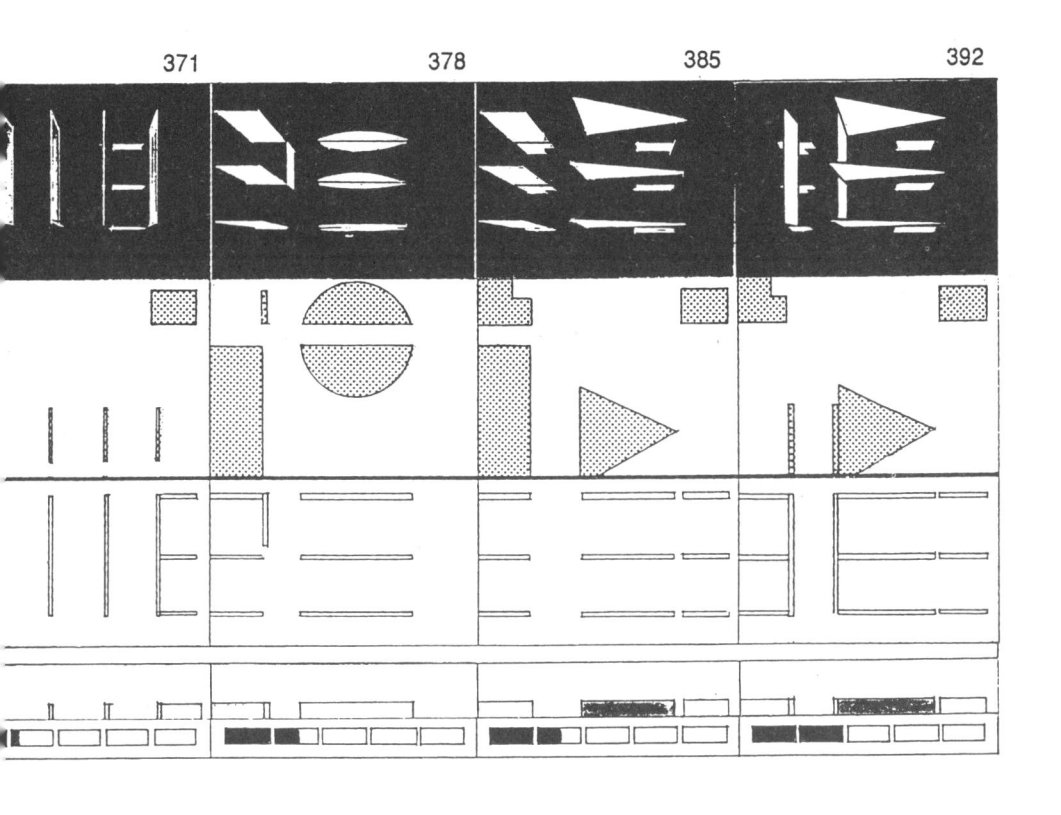

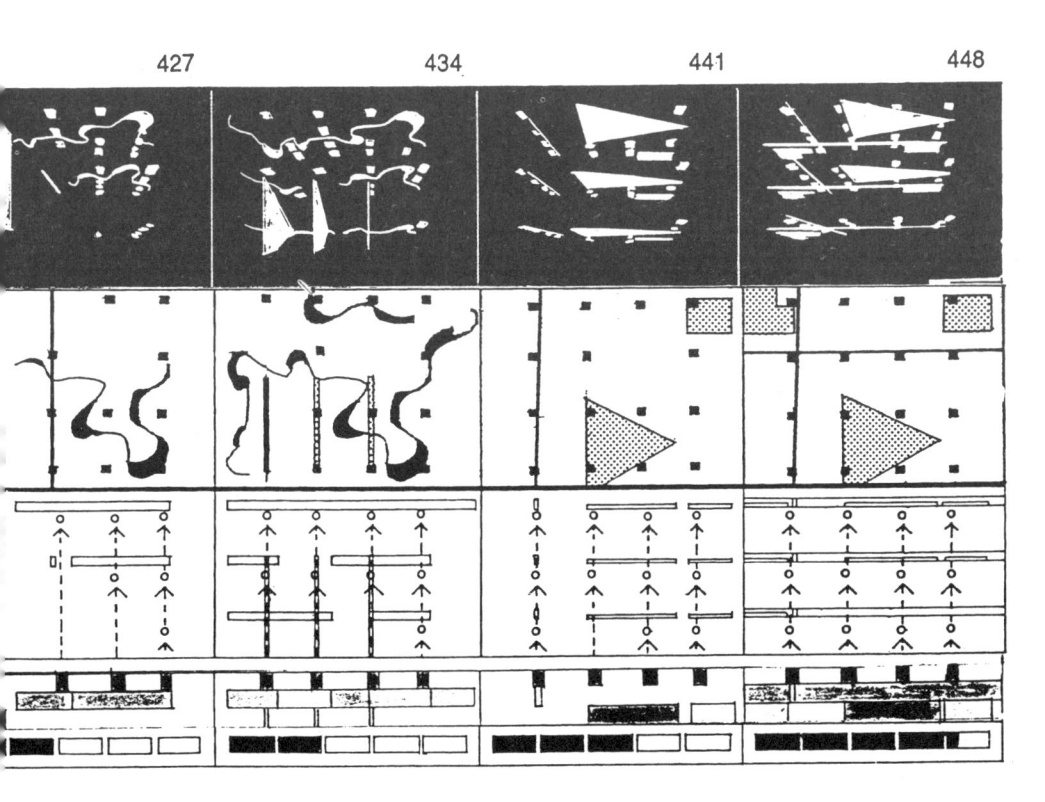

427　　　　　434　　　　　441　　　　　448

455 462 469

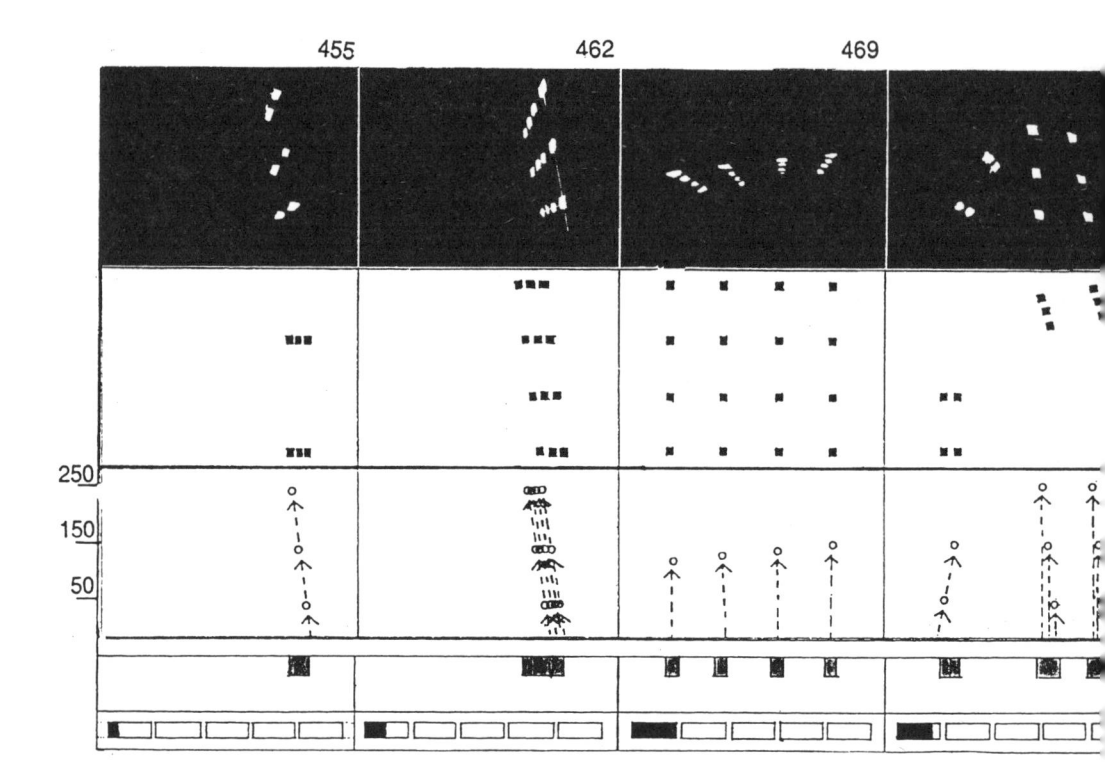

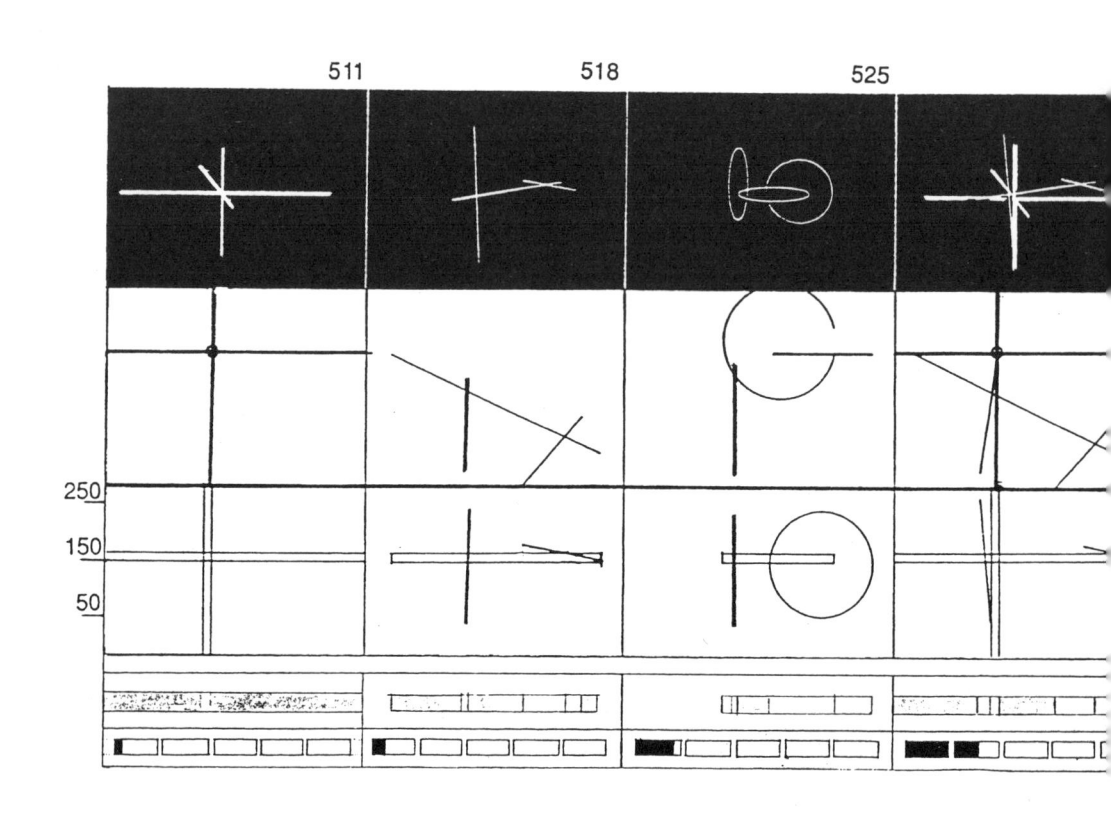

511 518 525

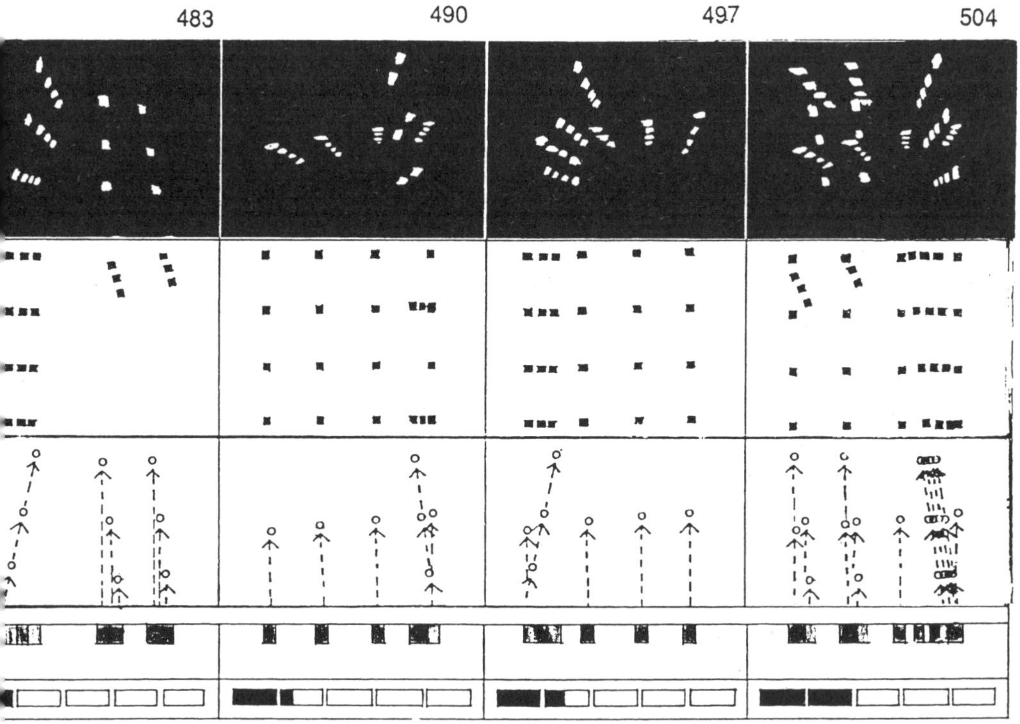
483
490
497
504

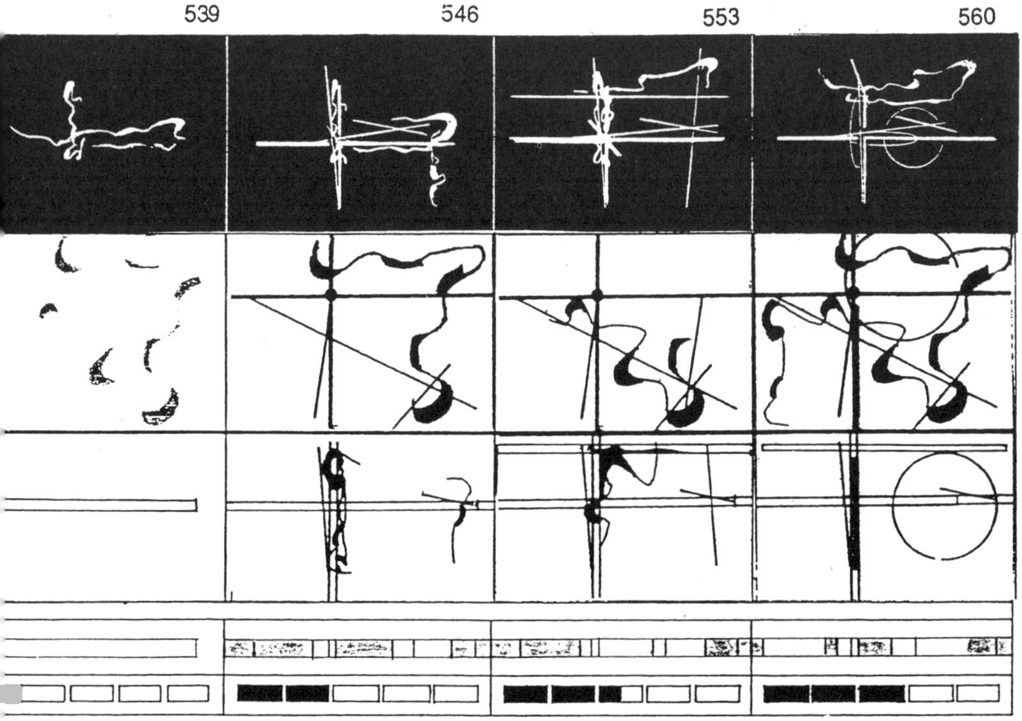
539
546
553
560

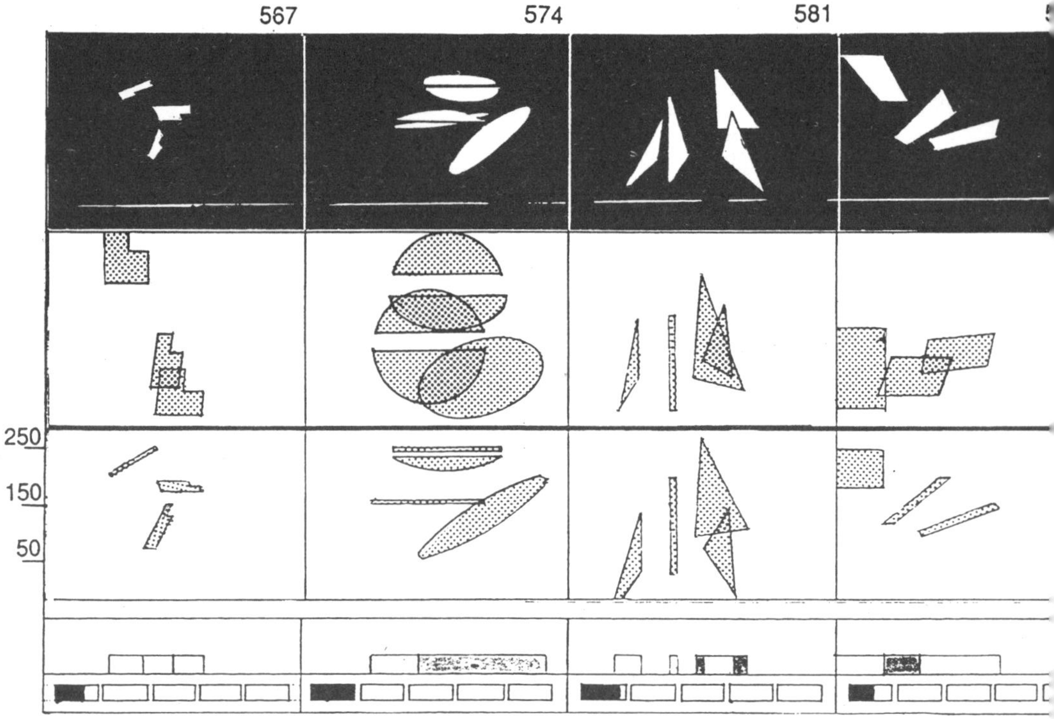
567
574
581
250
150
50

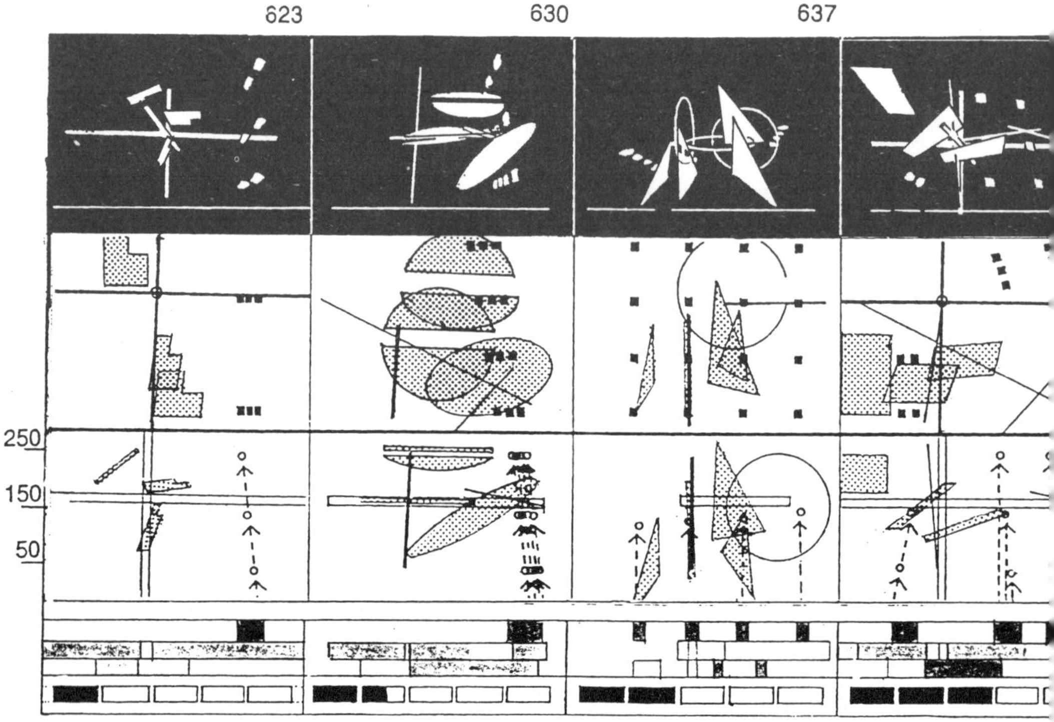
623
630
637
250
150
50

595 602 609 616

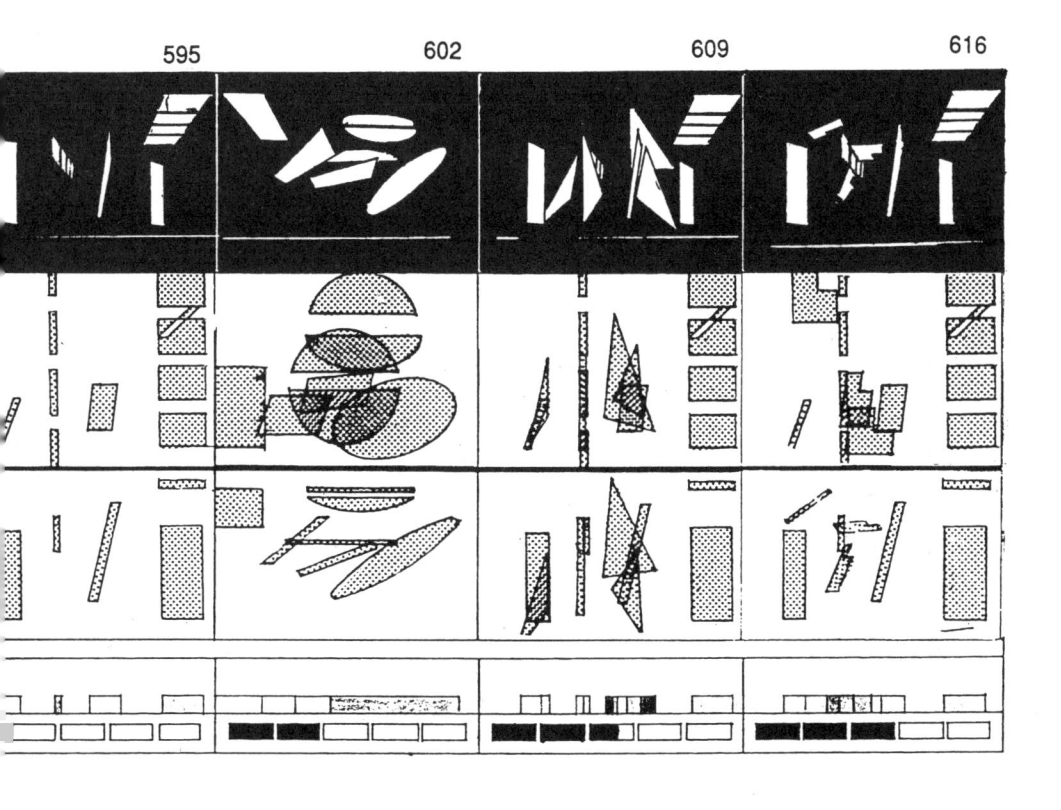

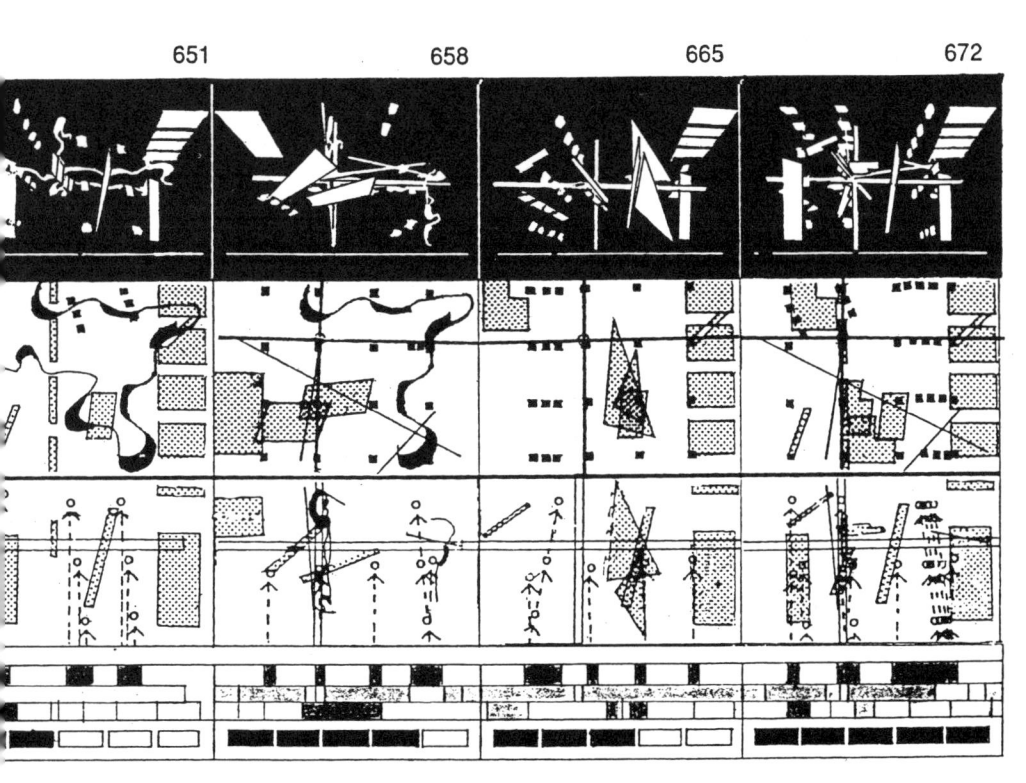

651 658 665 672

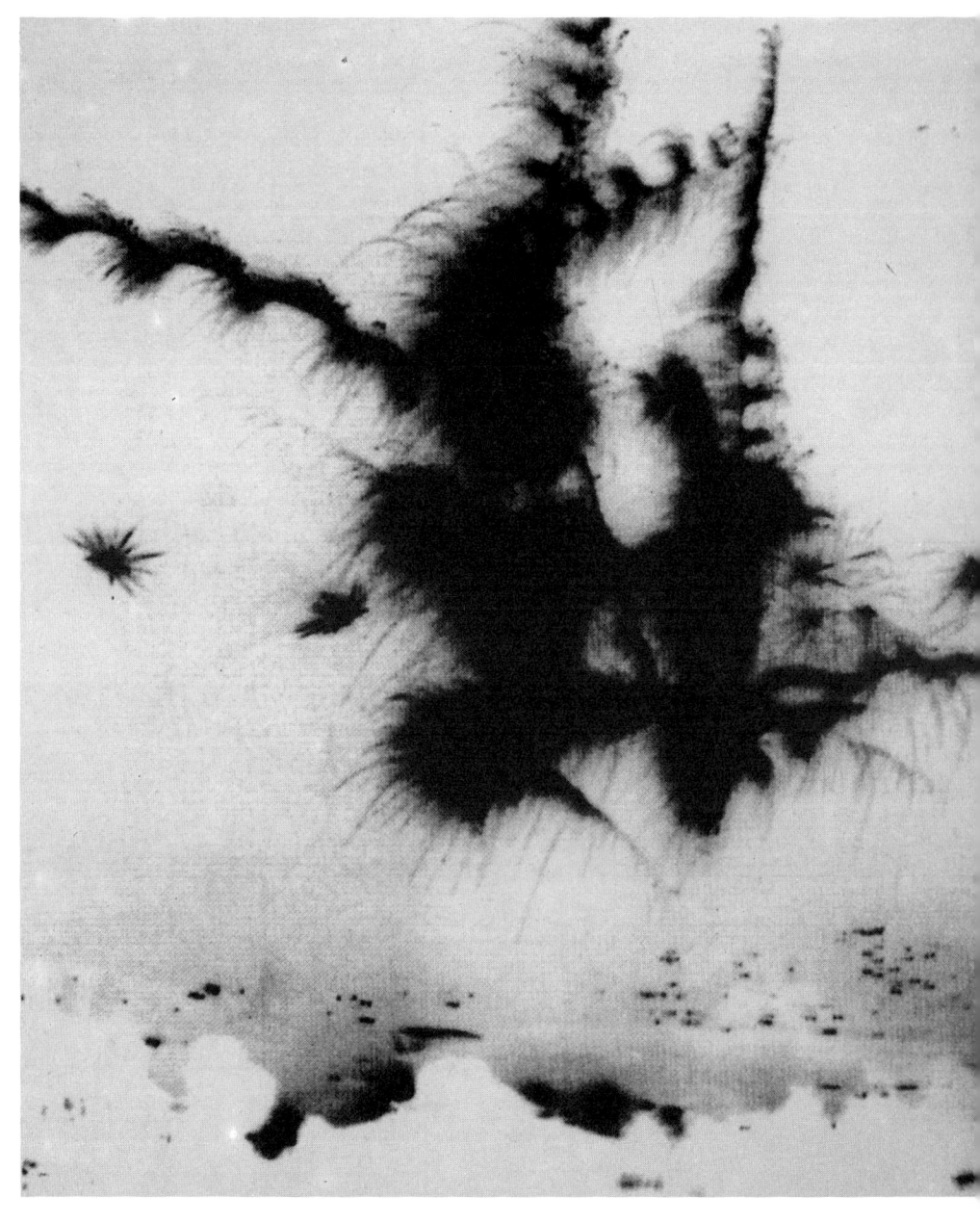

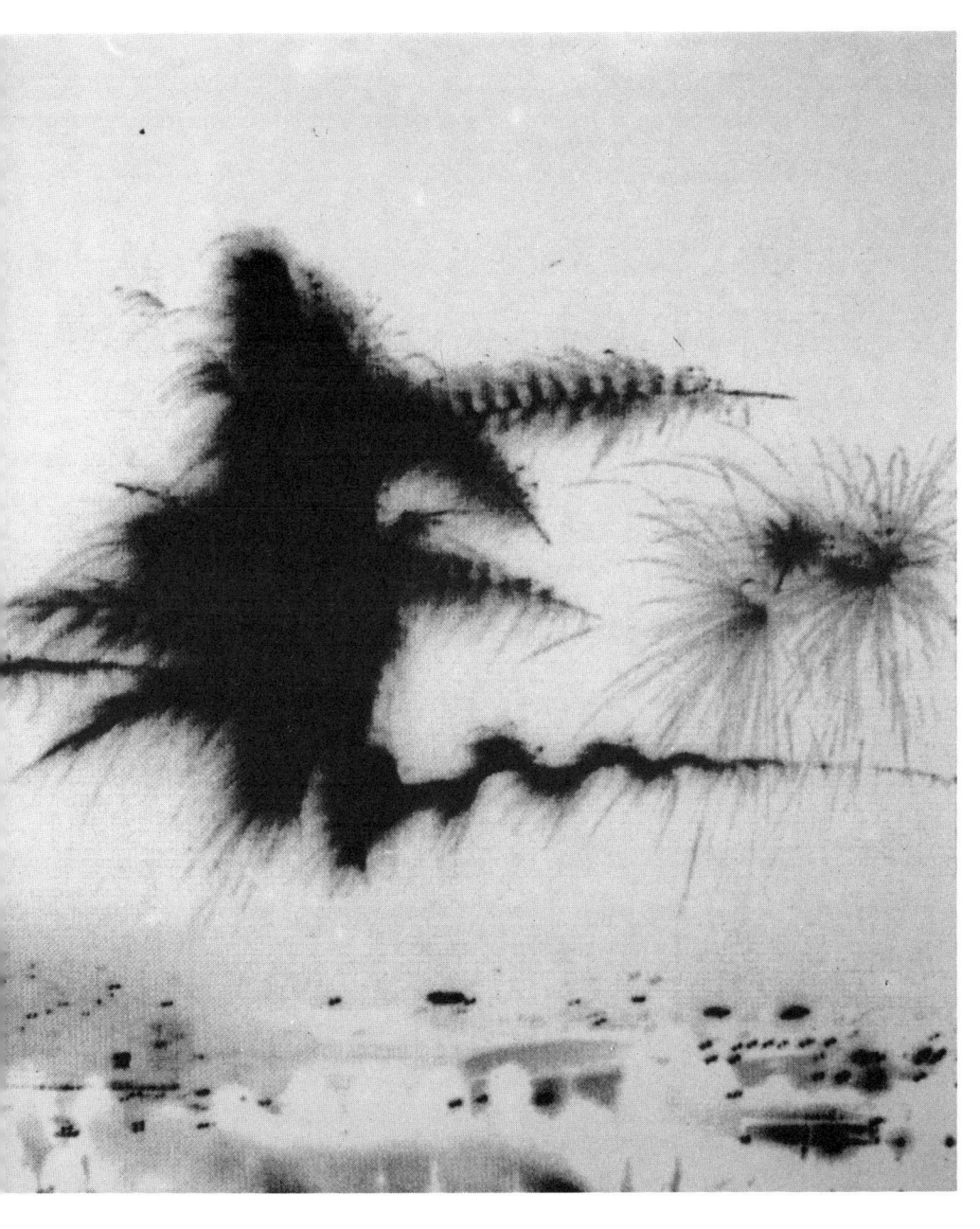

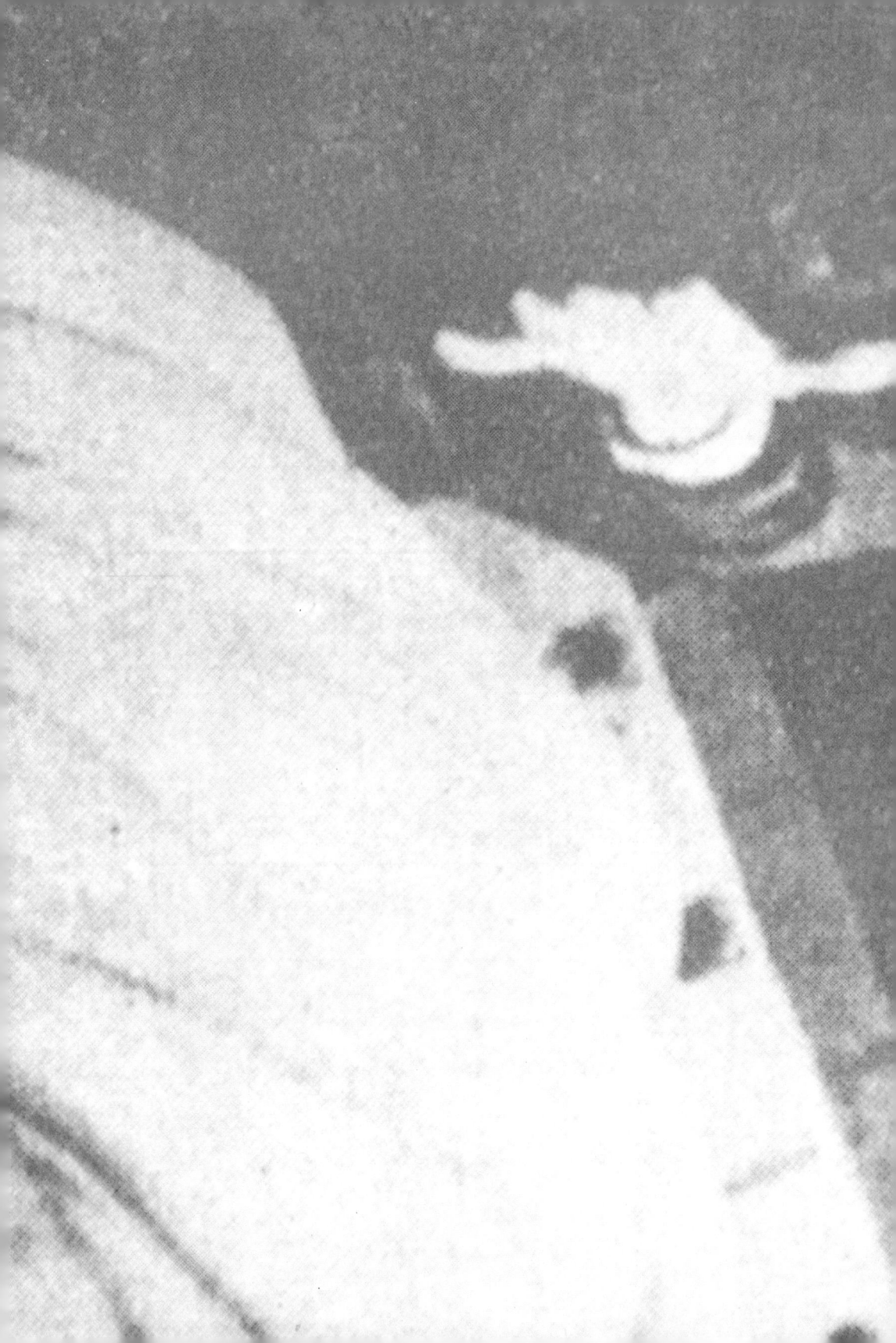

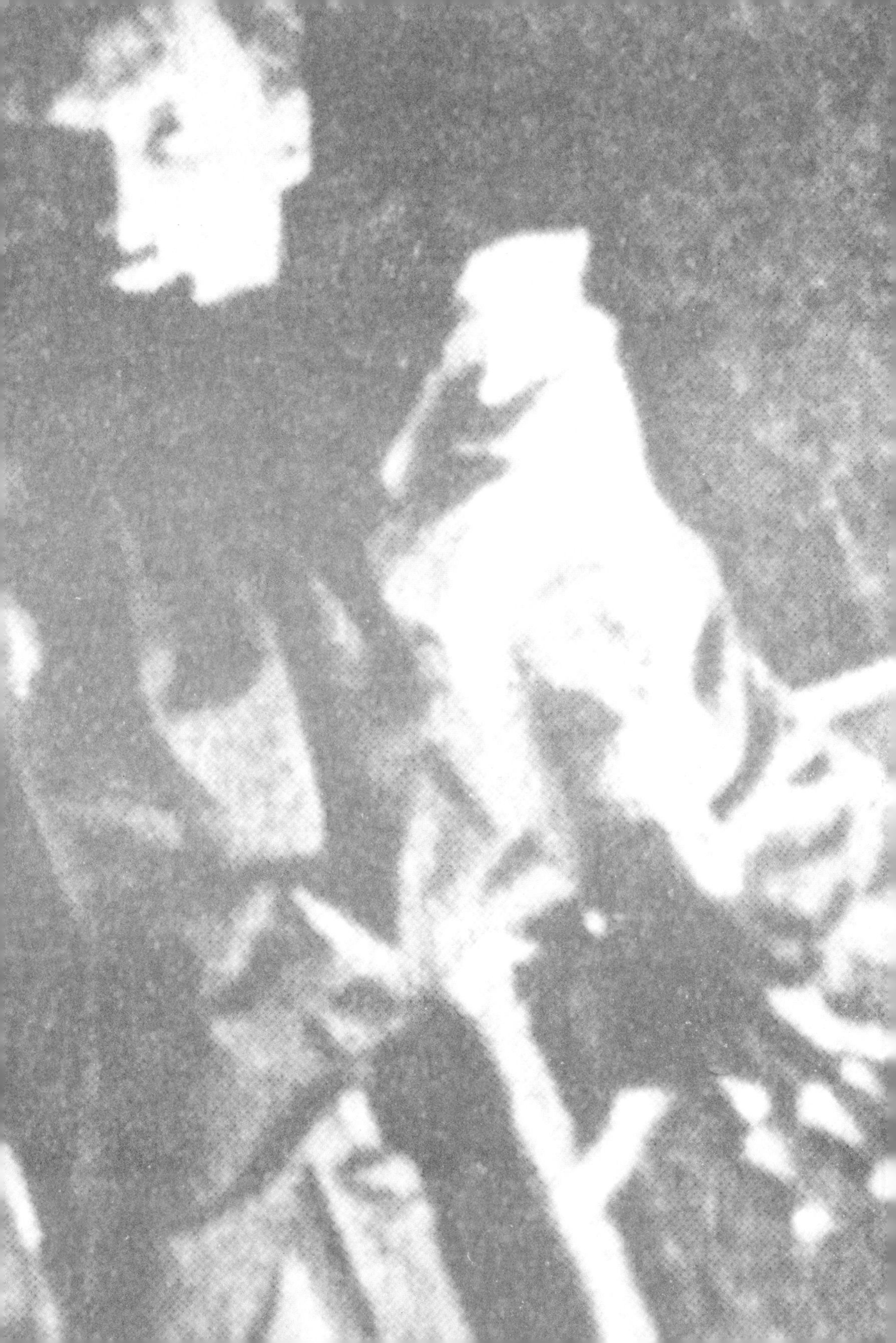

Chartres, Business Park, 1991–

Edge City

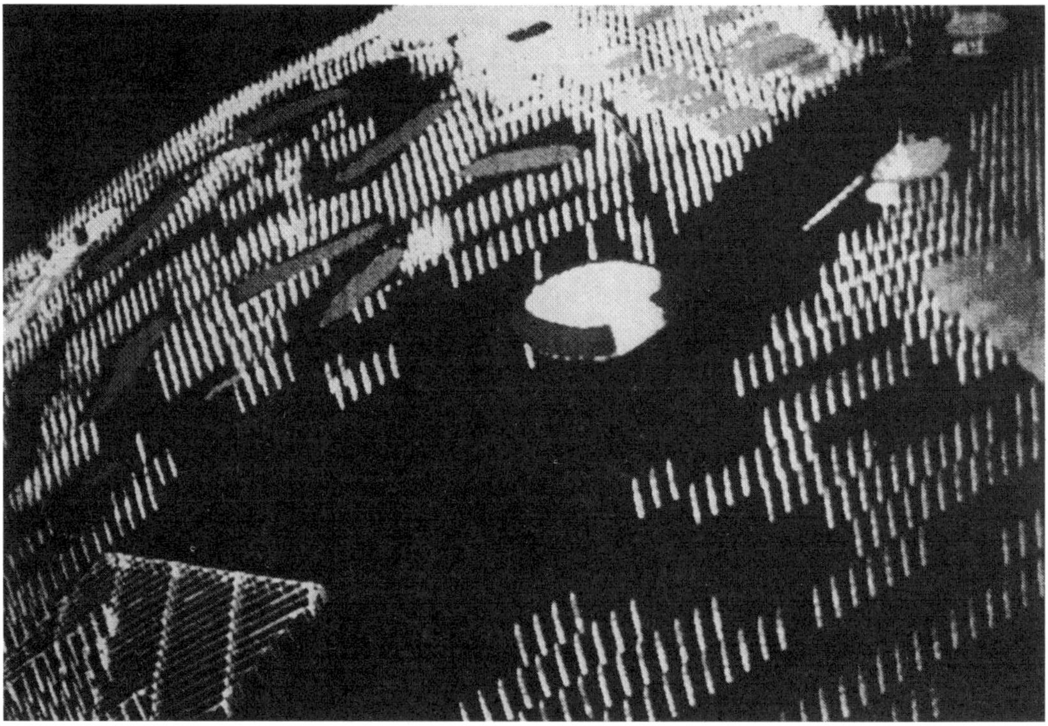

Can a new urban strategy encourage a new type of architecture? Reciprocally, can one invent an architecture capable of generating a new urban lifestyle?

The project for a 450-acre extension of the city of Chartres, France, with an office park, indoor leisure facilities, sports fields and a housing complex proposes a new type of relationship between work and leisure, based on intersection and superimposition rather than on segregation. We tried to develop such a strategy for a site facing the city and its cathedral, on agricultural land (the Beauce) along a national highway.

We first established a strong link with the city through an "attractive" element: the *long-cours*, a vector leading from the center of Chartres and the cathedral. The *long-cours* gathers together leisure facilities, a clubhouse, meeting halls, shops and so forth, in curved halls. Each construction is partially suspended and acts as a shelter for diverse public events. The *long-cours* can accommodate other facilities such as an open-air cinema, a swimming pool and tennis courts. It extends west over the highway (acting as a bridge to Chartres) and east towards the countryside.

We then proposed a second vector, parallel to the highway and gridded to accommodate numerous plots of land, each defined by lines of trees extending into the countryside. Inside these plots light factories and office buildings can be built freely. Office spaces are also located in straight halls (shiplike buildings scattered across the countryside). The rectangular grid also divides cars from heavy industrial vehicles. Neon signs are proposed.

Finally, perpendicular to the gridded office vector, we planted long parallel rows of trees that articulate a new landscape. Between these lines we placed sports facilities and playgrounds, as well as various entertainment centers.

The whole scheme is conceived as a strategy, a game, so that concept and realization, function and finance interact in such a way that the complex programmatic mechanisms coincide with the conceptual clarity of the built image.

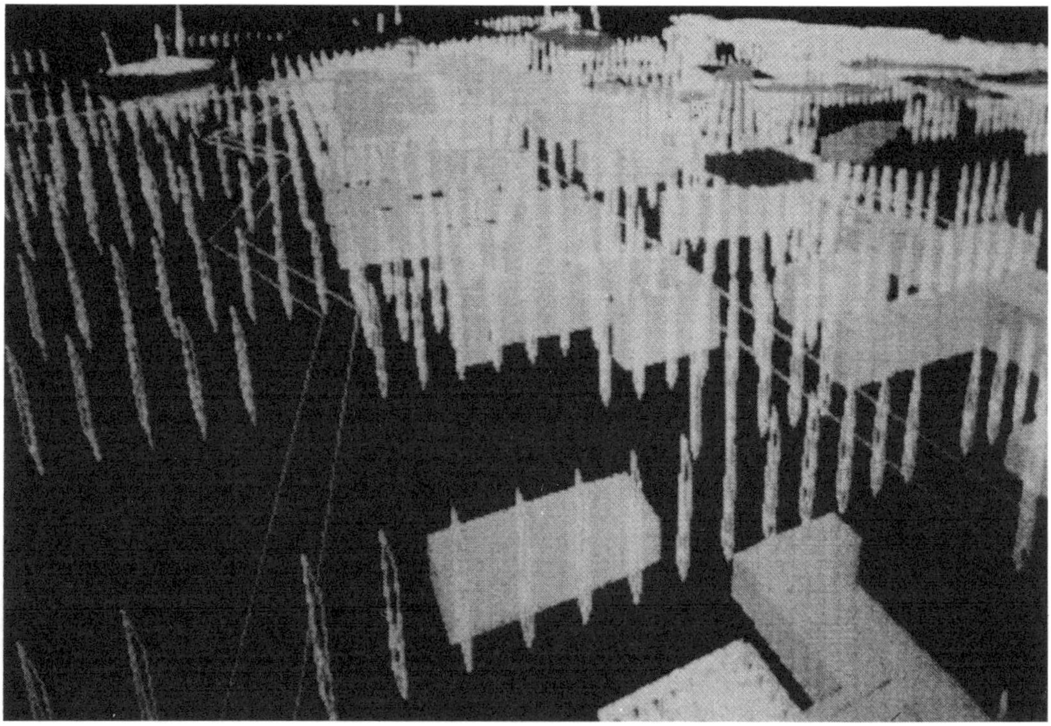

CHARTRES
043

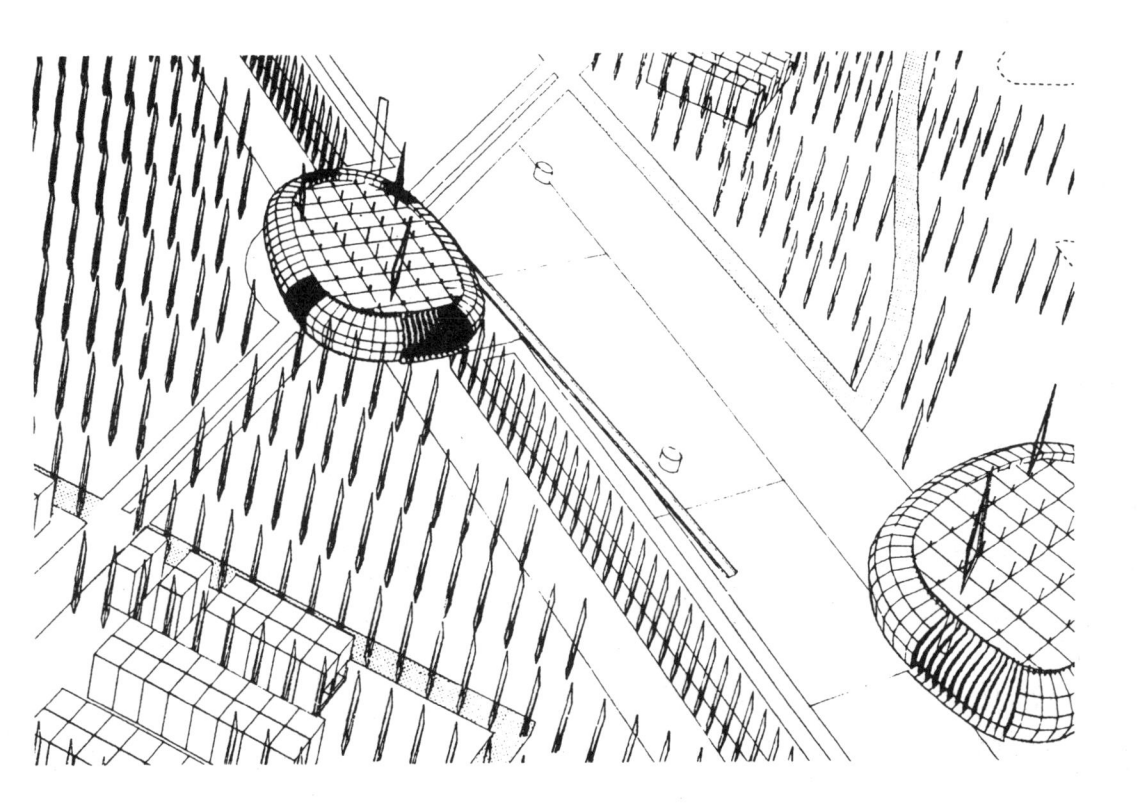

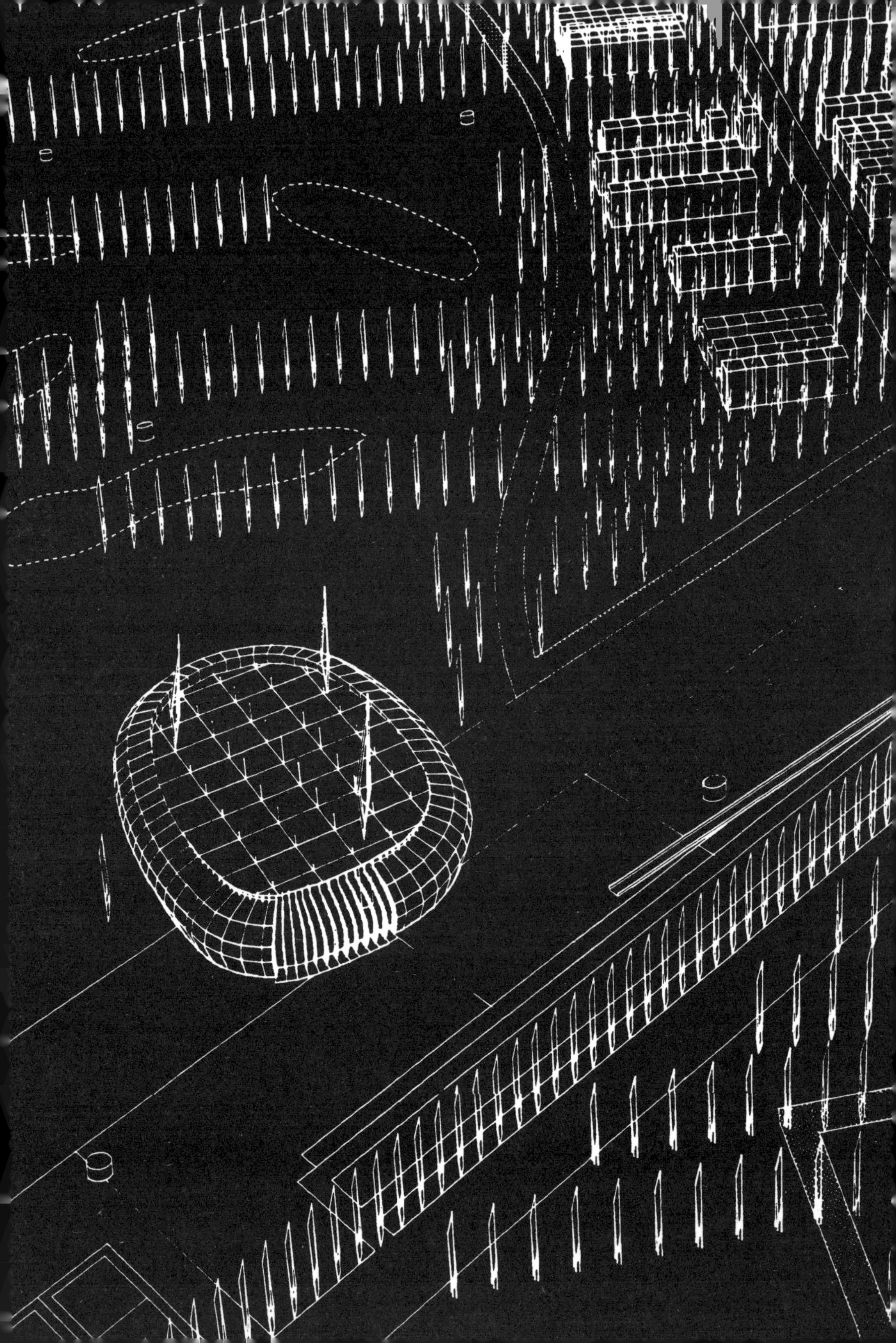

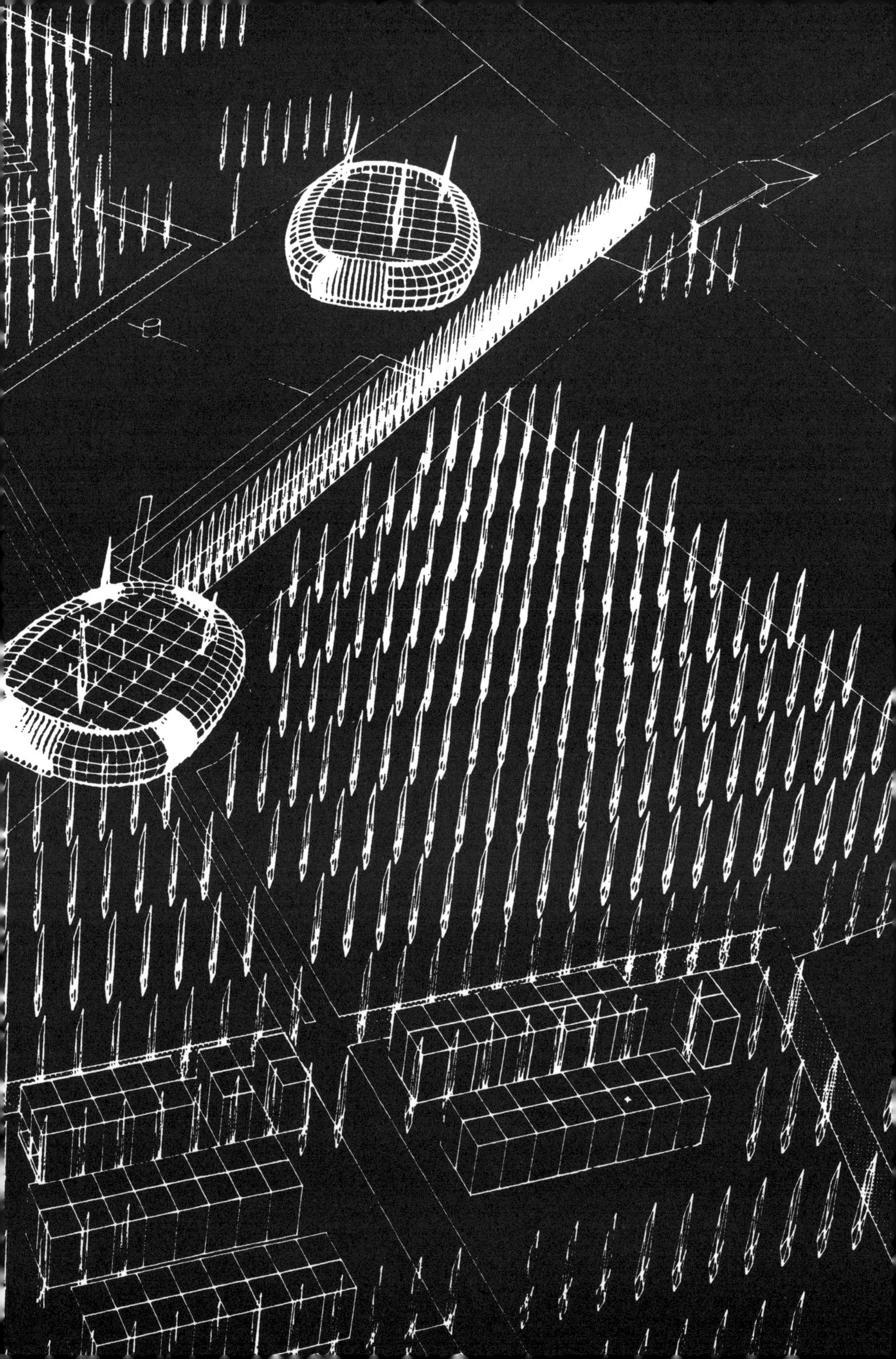

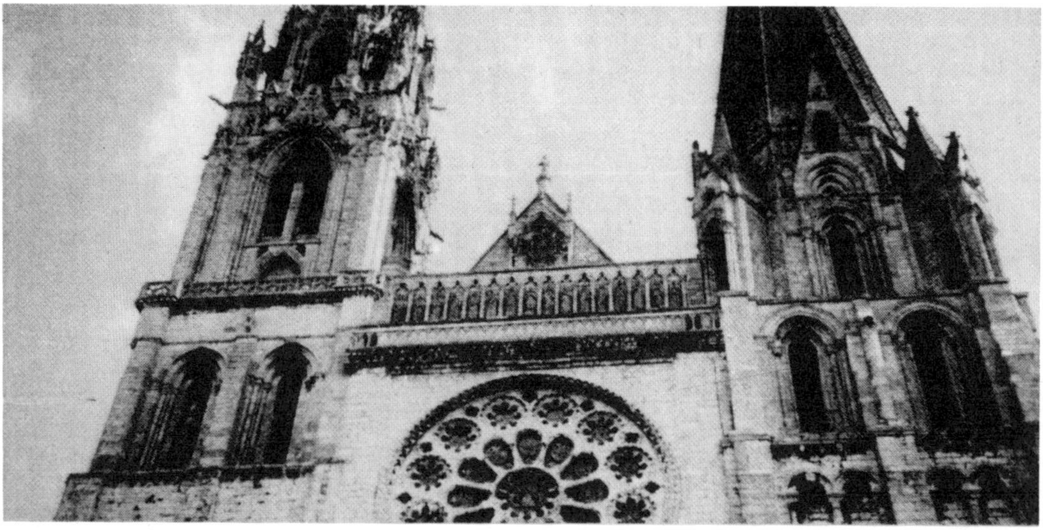

CHARTRES
047

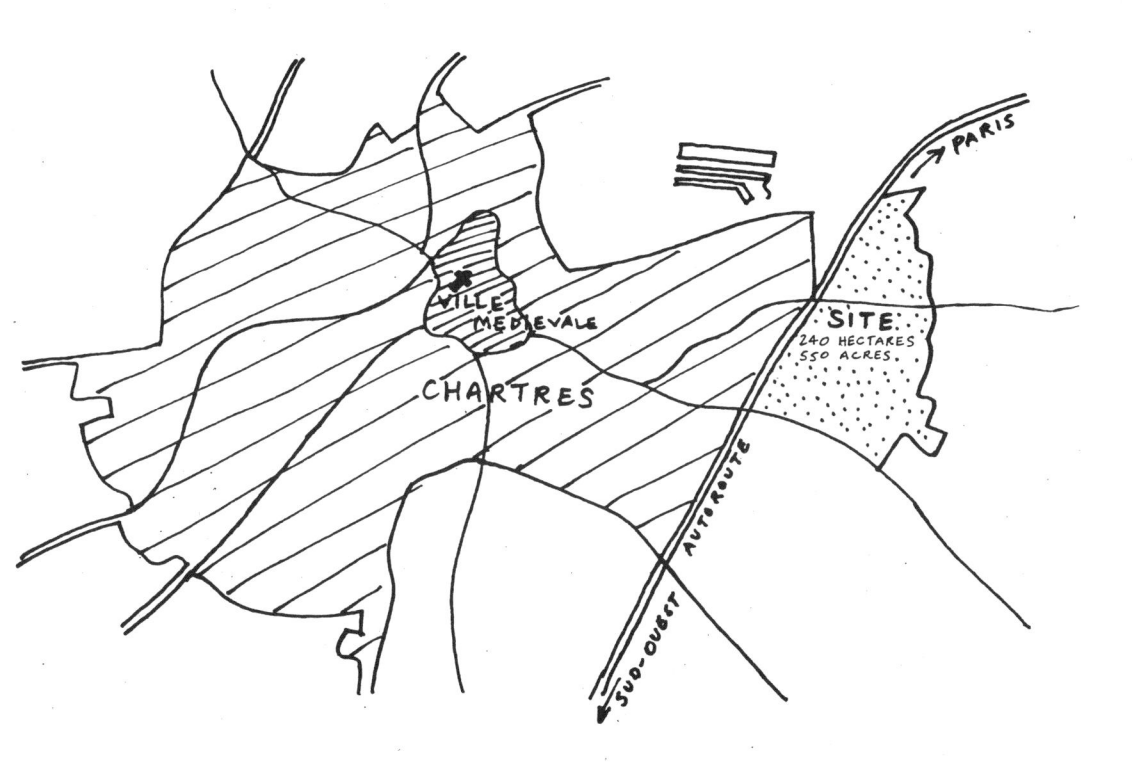

From the historical center to the edge of the city: new territories along the major highways

The edge of the city: a deregulated universe

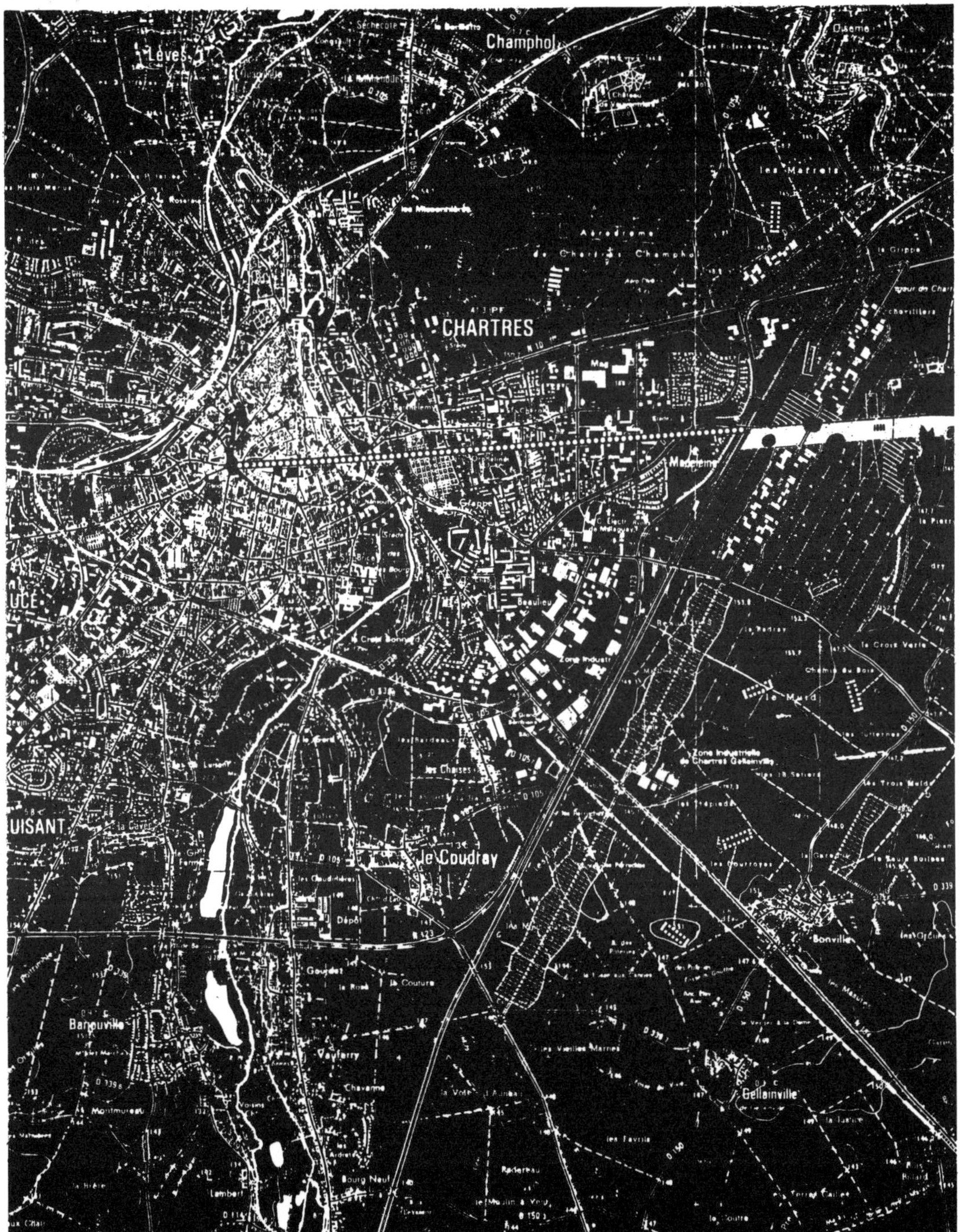

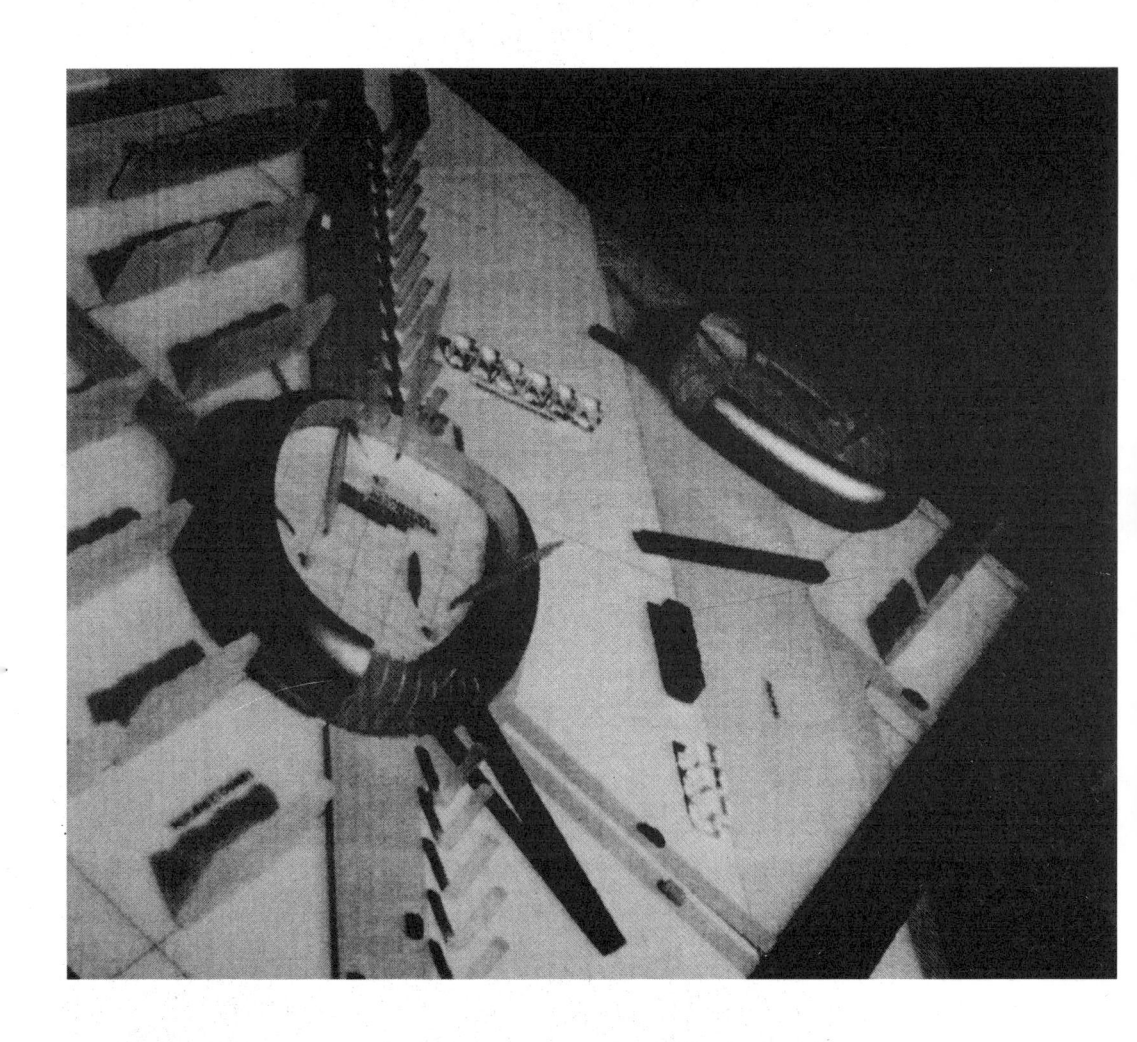

Programming the edge: the 21st century cathedrals

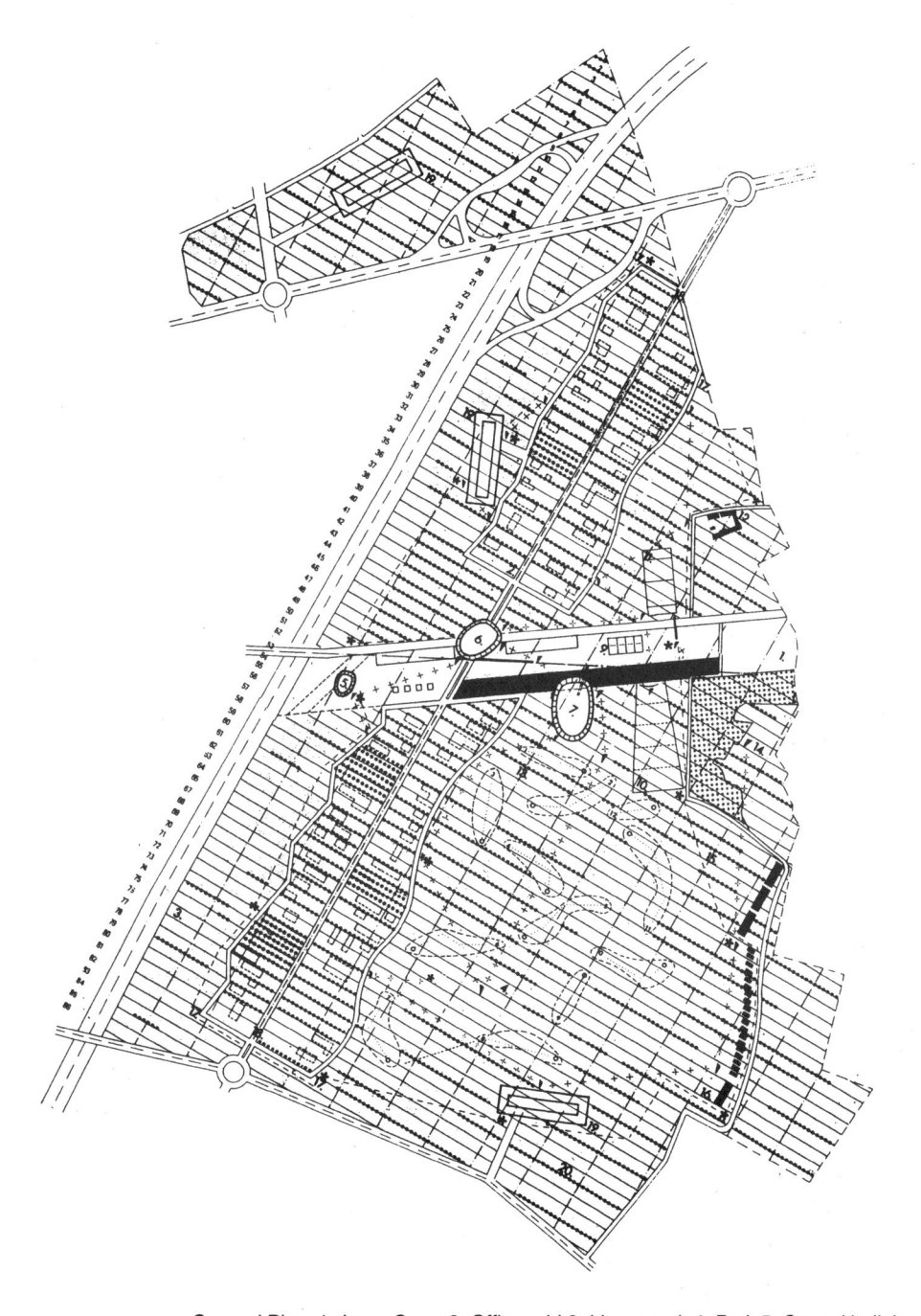

General Plan: 1. *Long-Cours* 2. Office grid 3. Linear park 4. Park 5. Curved hall: business and meeting center 6. Curved hall: restaurant, services, commerce 7. Curved hall: clubhouse, squash courts, tennis courts, leisure facilities 8. Lake 9. Tennis courts 10. Putting range 11. Sports field 12. Farm 13. Golf course 14. Police station 15. Cycling track 16. Housing (blocks or individual units) 17. Visitor access 18. VIP access 19. Manufacturers' rental spaces 20. Lines of elms and poplars, points of attraction

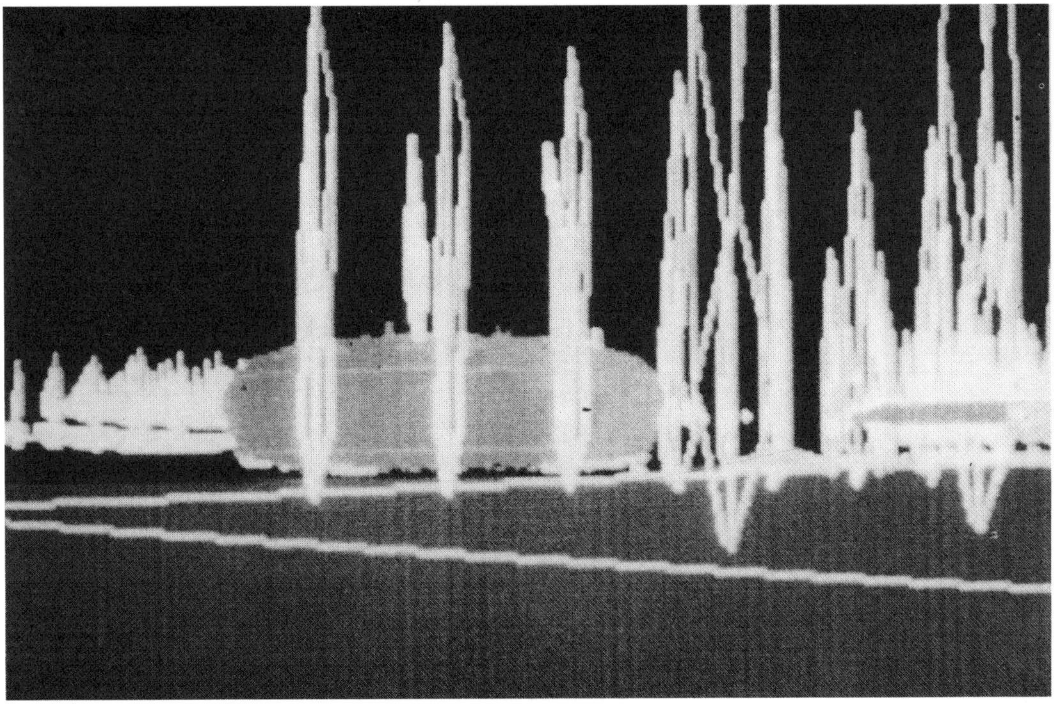

CHARTRES
053

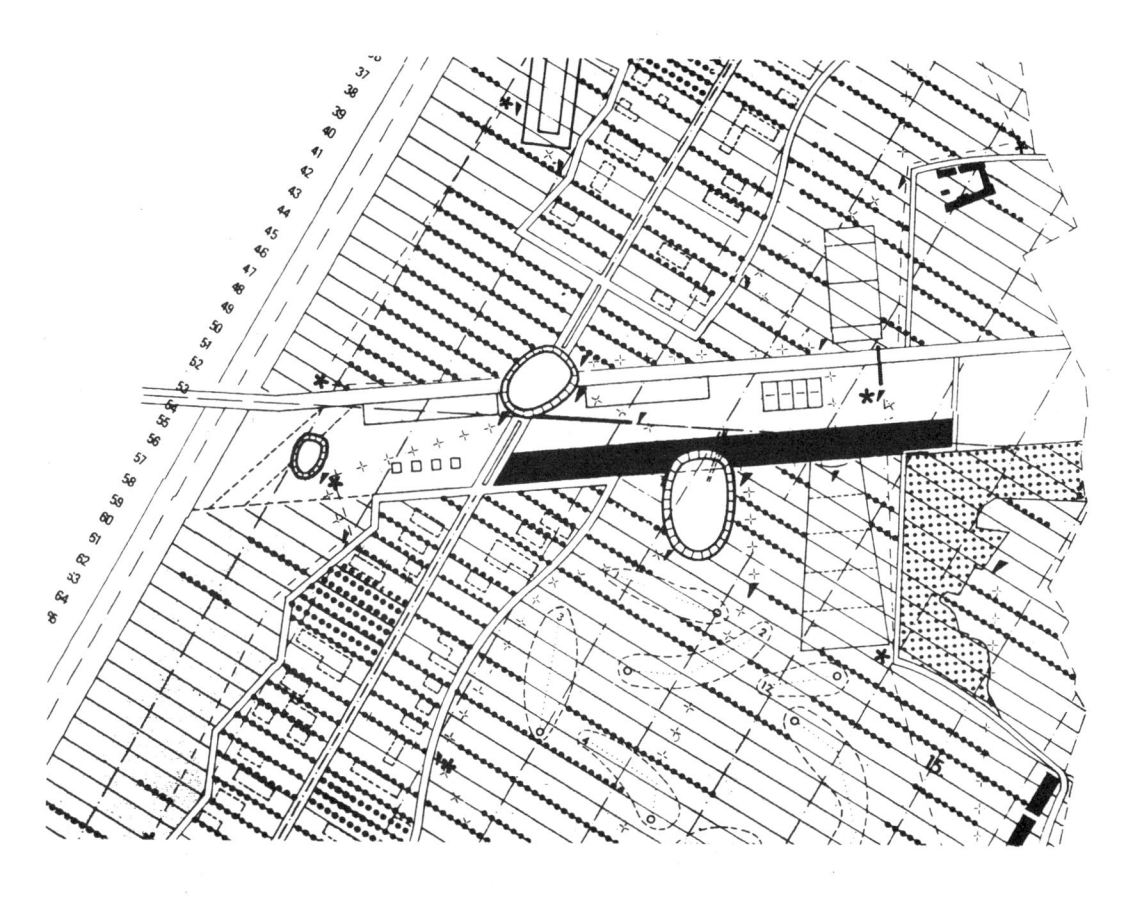

The *Long-Cours*: no historicist contextualism but decontextualization

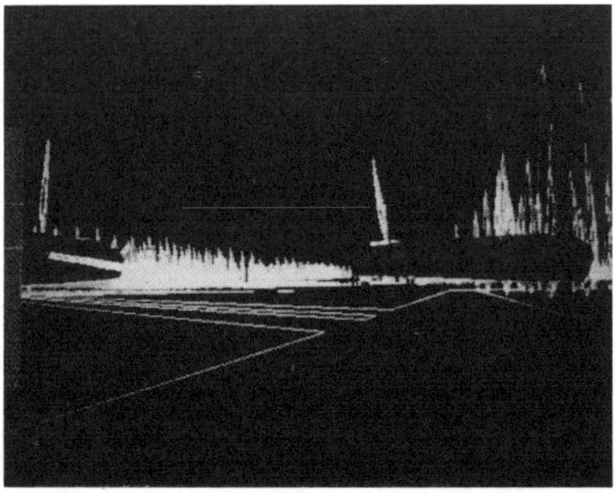

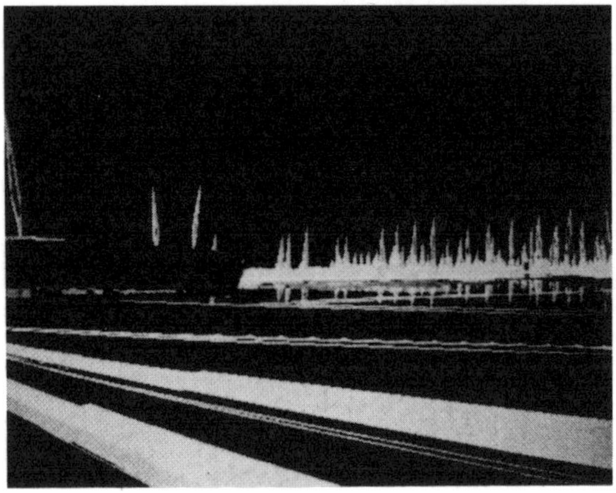

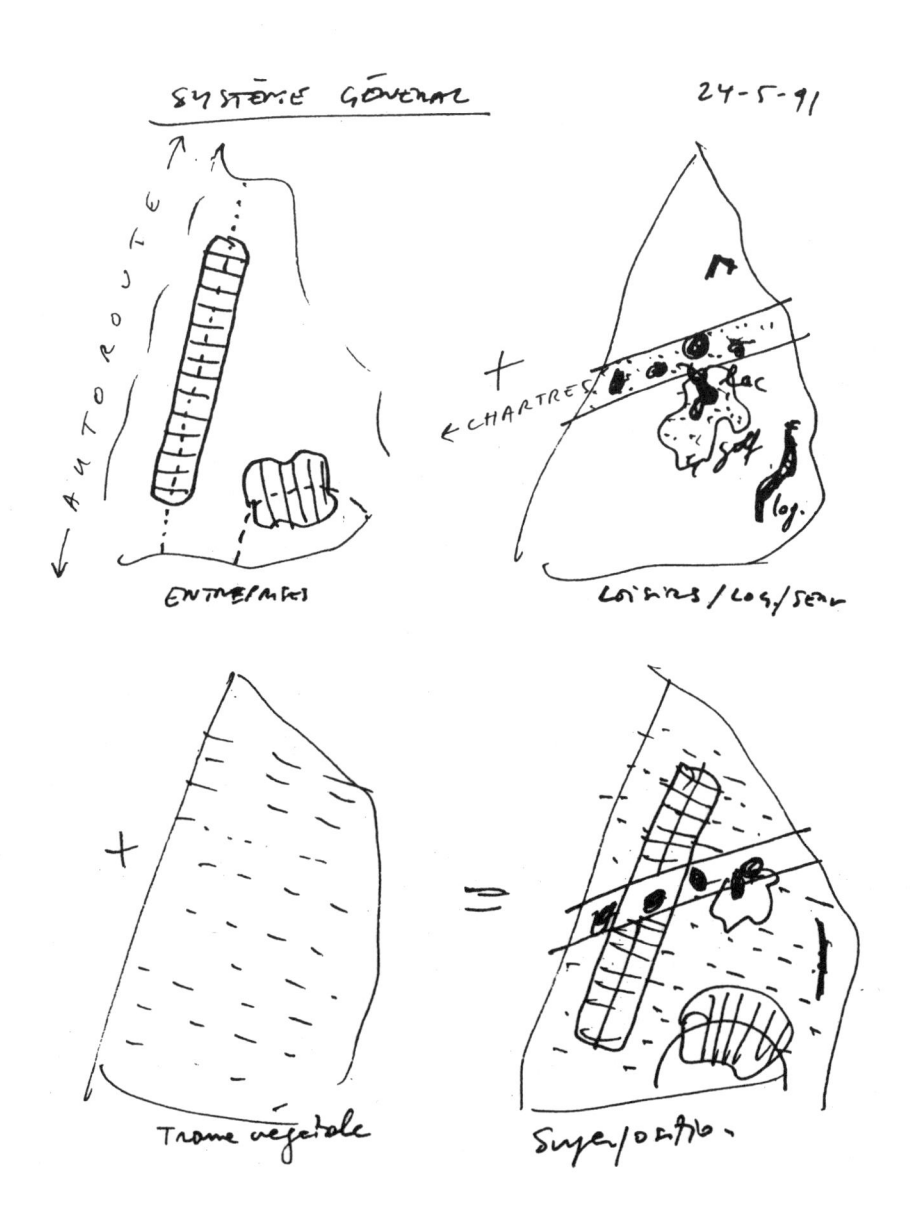

The first sketches: superimpositions of autonomous systems

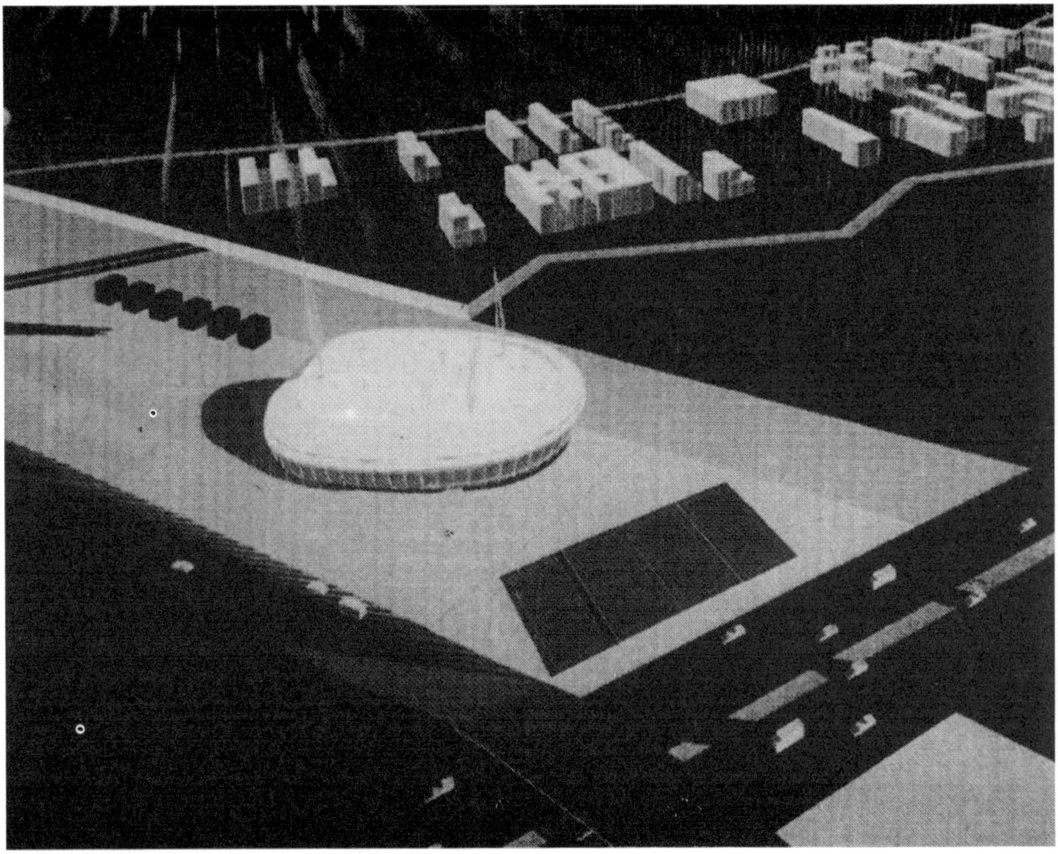

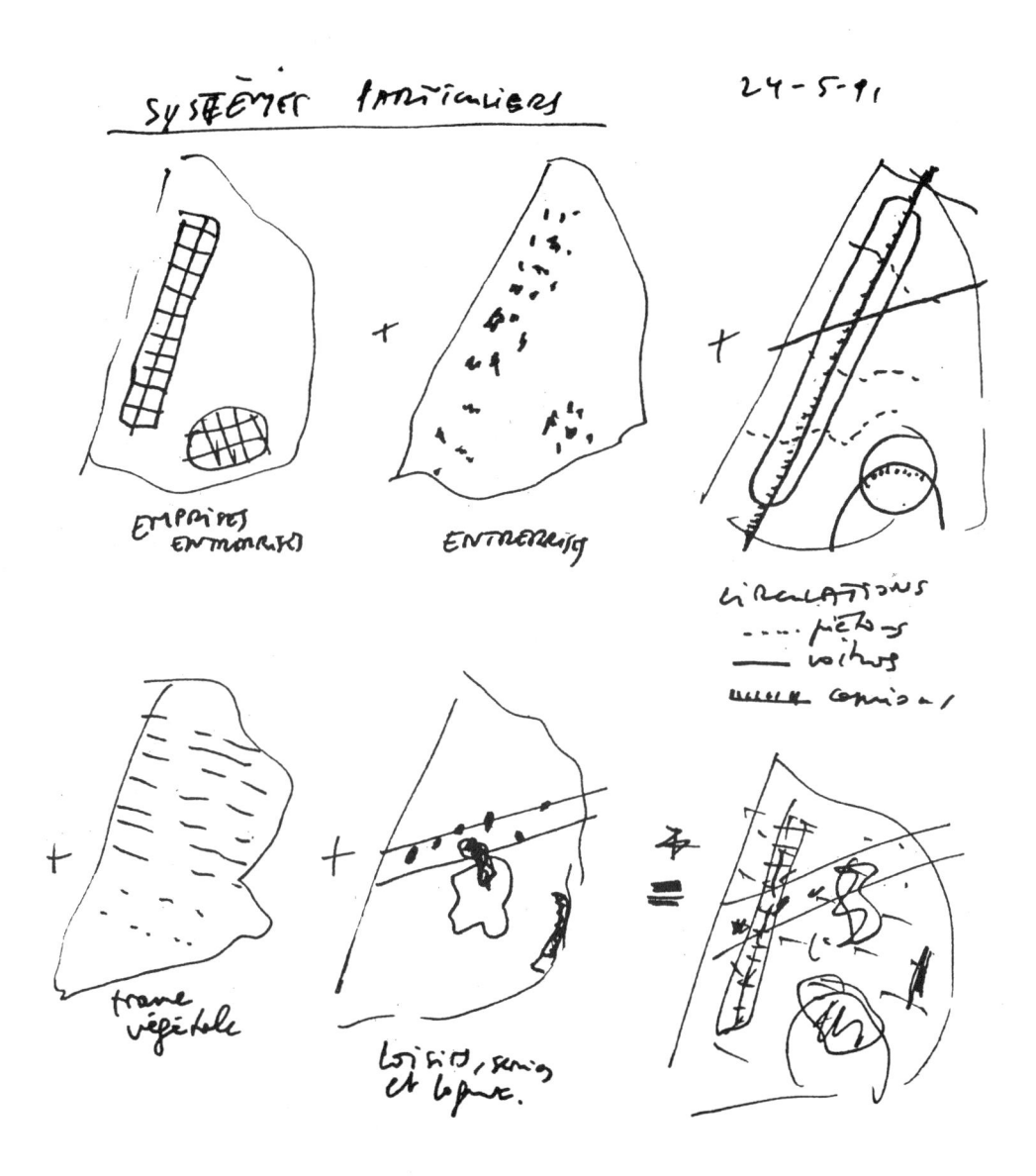

Dismissing the binary oppositions of traditional architecture:
a strategy of multiple systems

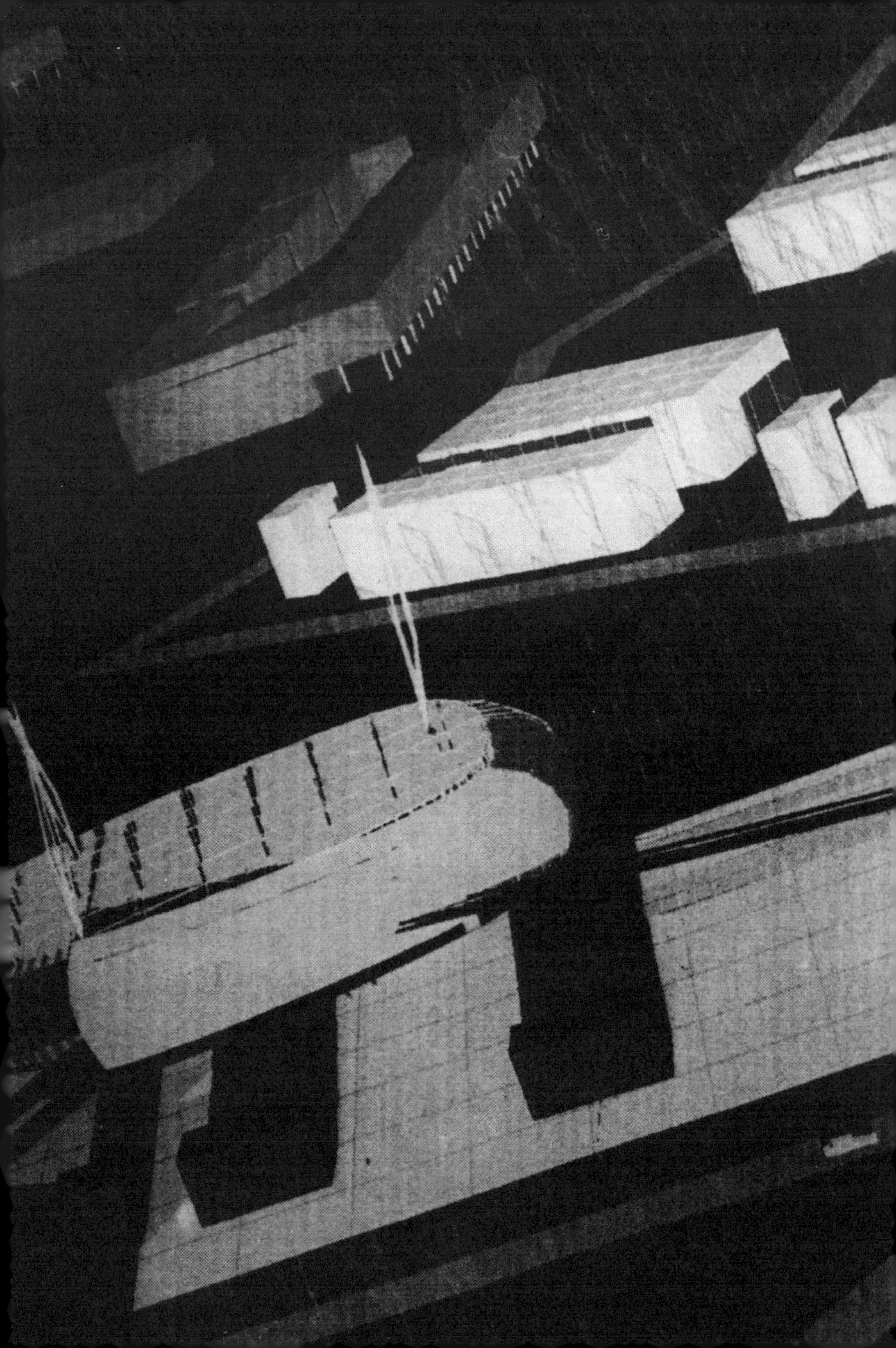

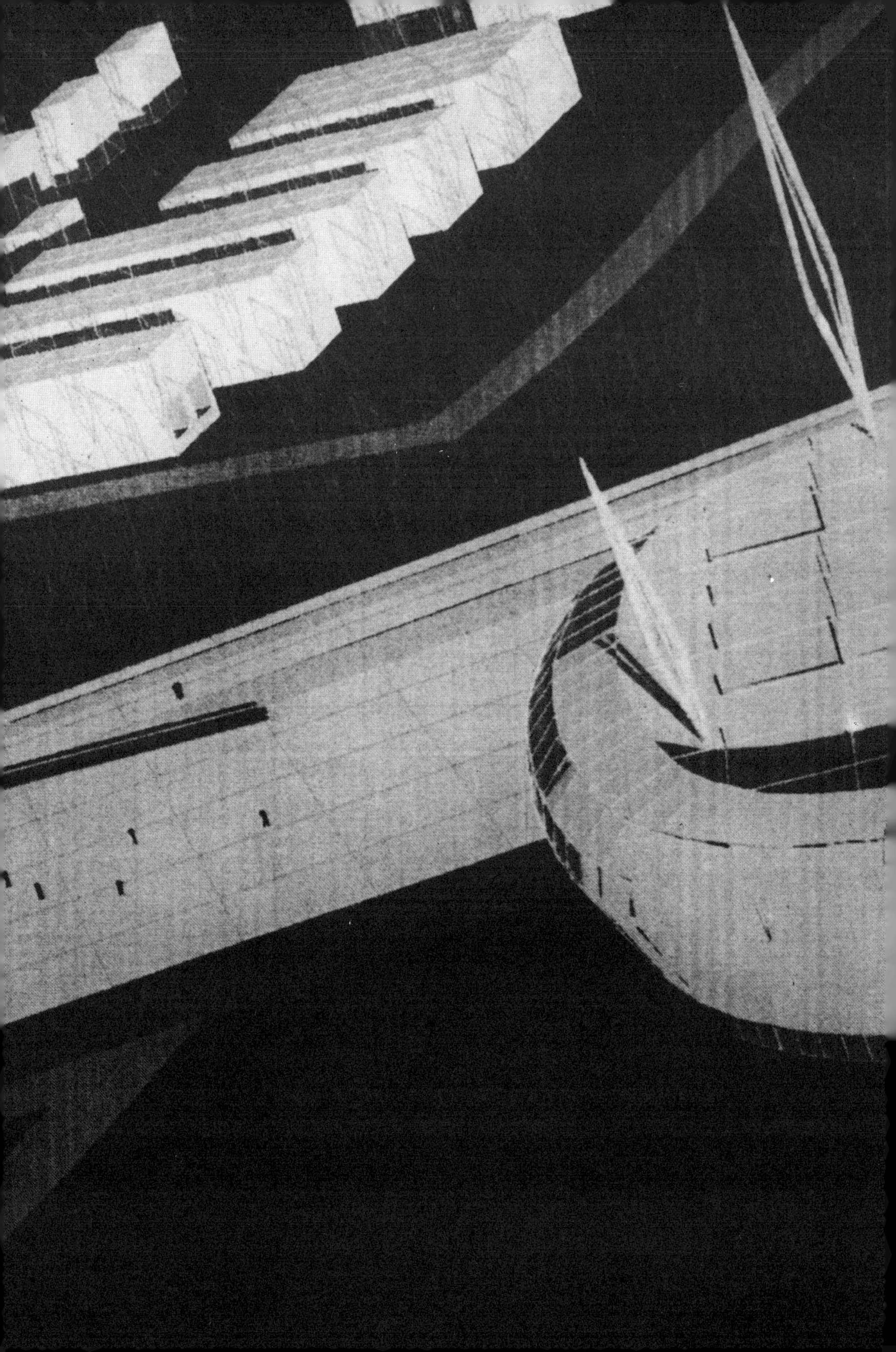

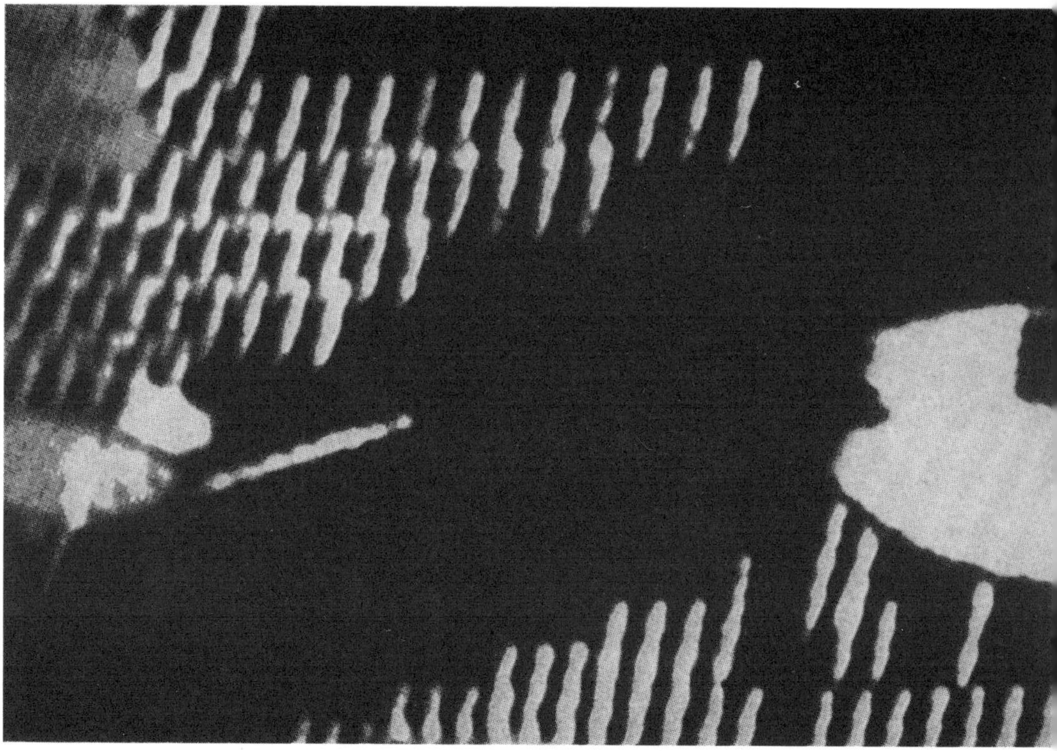

CHARTRES
061

Landscape strategy: planting as a mode of defining spaces and new land distribution

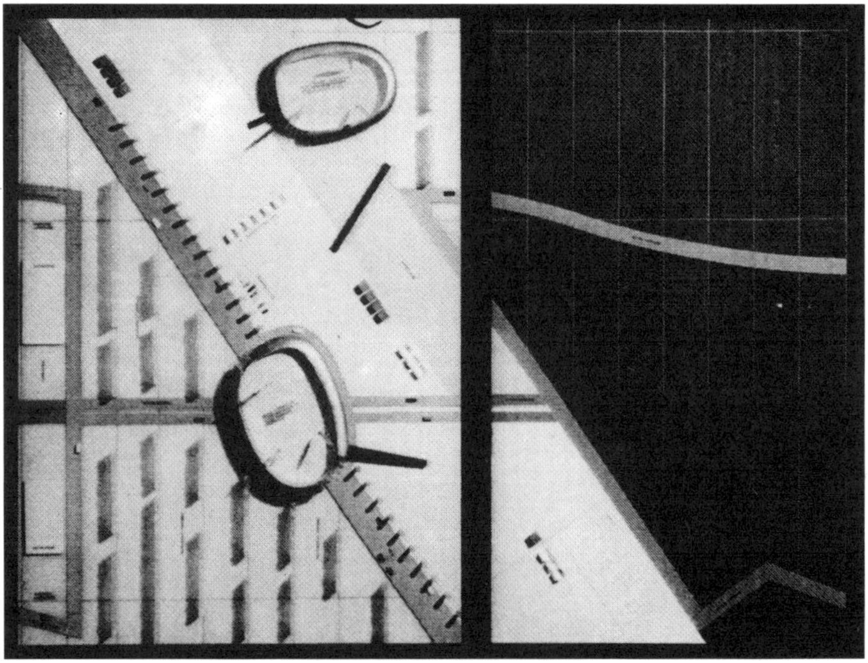

CHARTRES
063

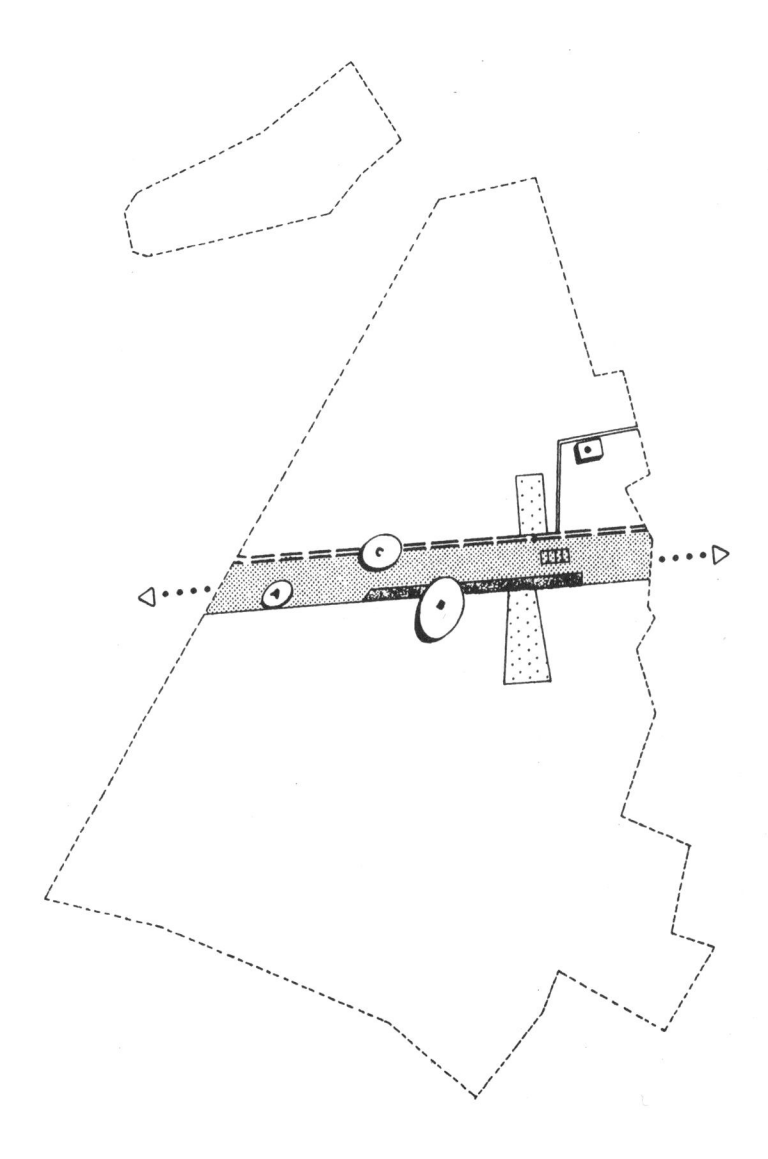

Programmatic strategy: public amenities on a vector from the core of the old city

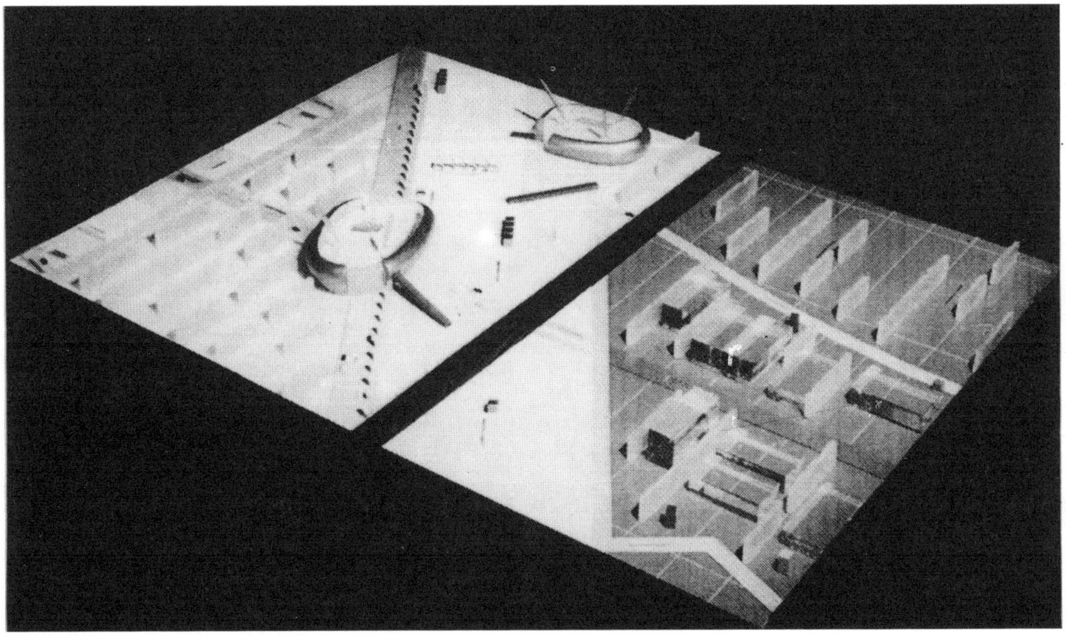

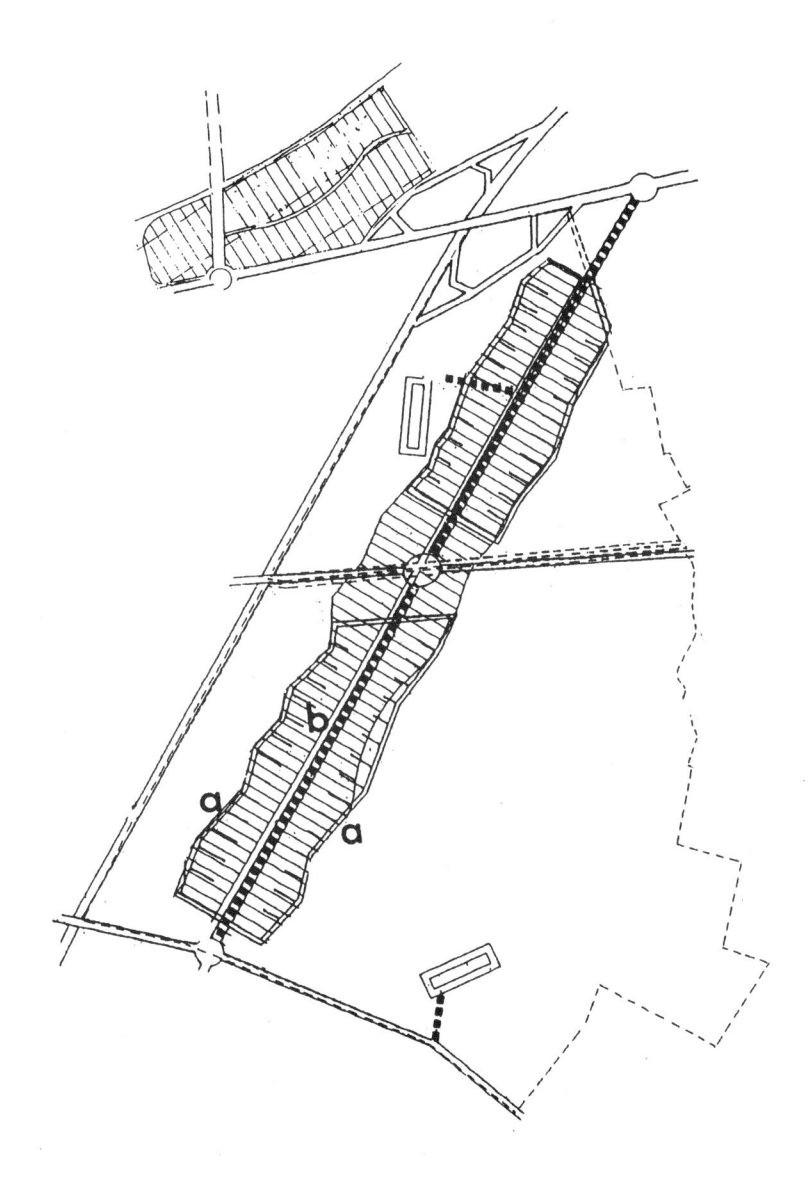

Movement strategy: road networks expanding parallel to the major highway

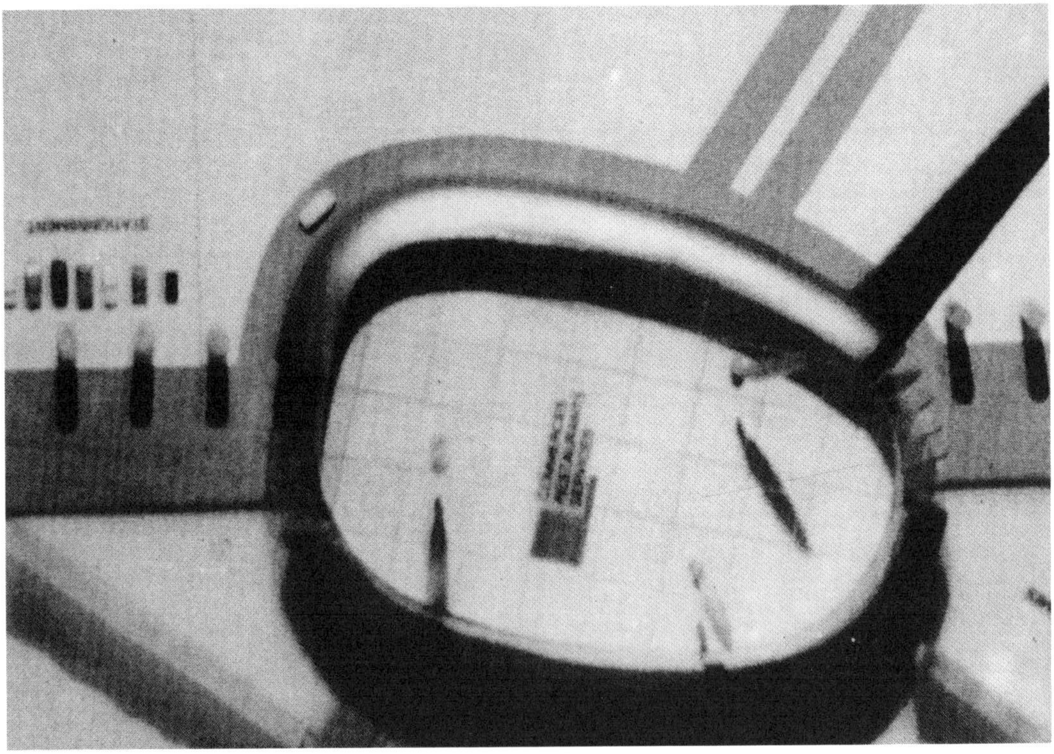

CHARTRES
067

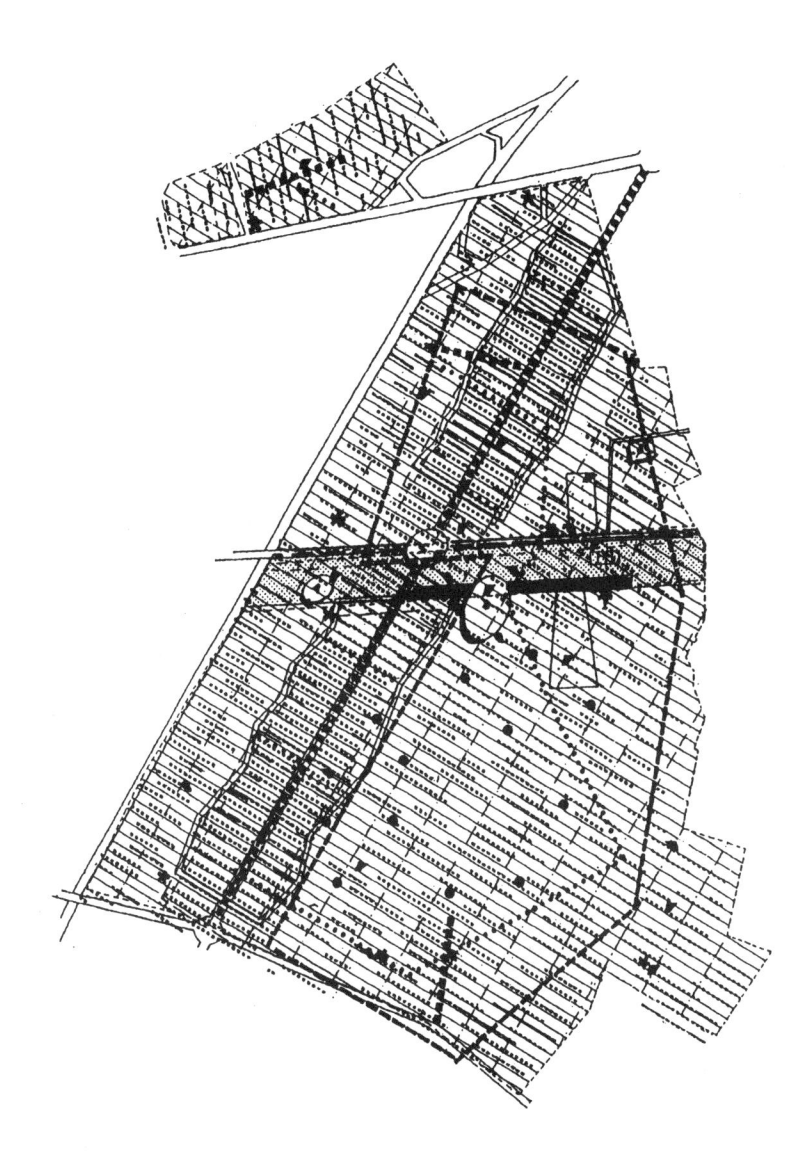

Superimposition 1+2+3: no more boundary delineating a coherent and homogeneous whole, but instead superposition, parcellization, atomization

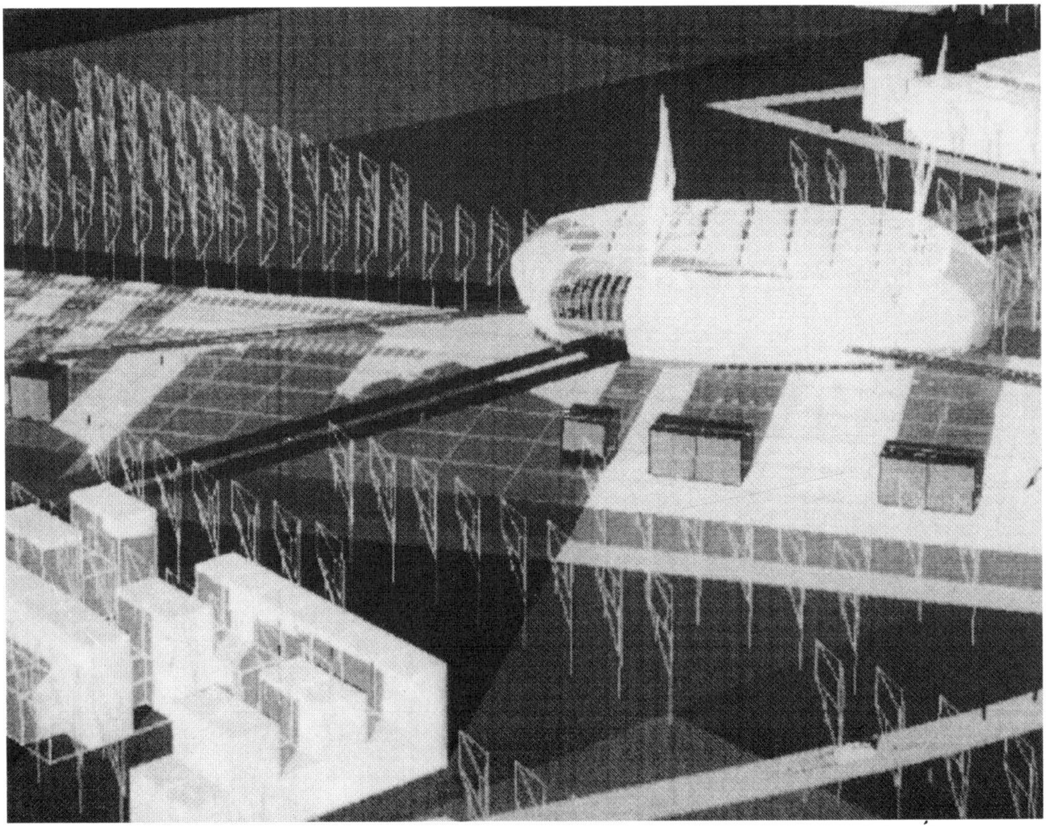

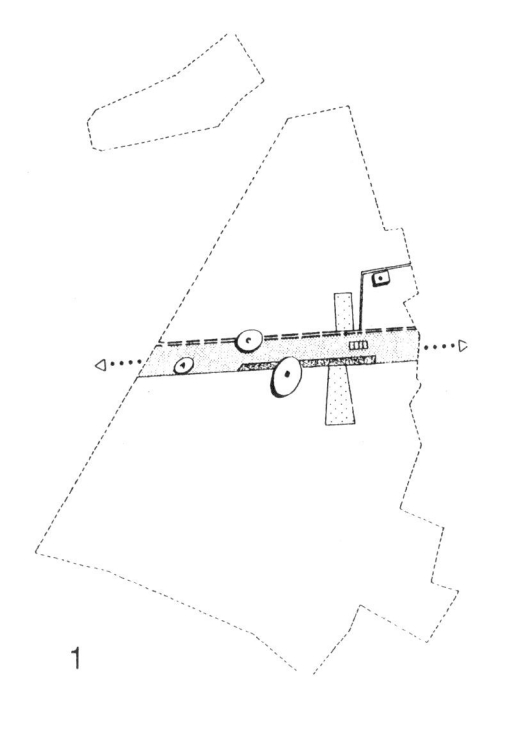

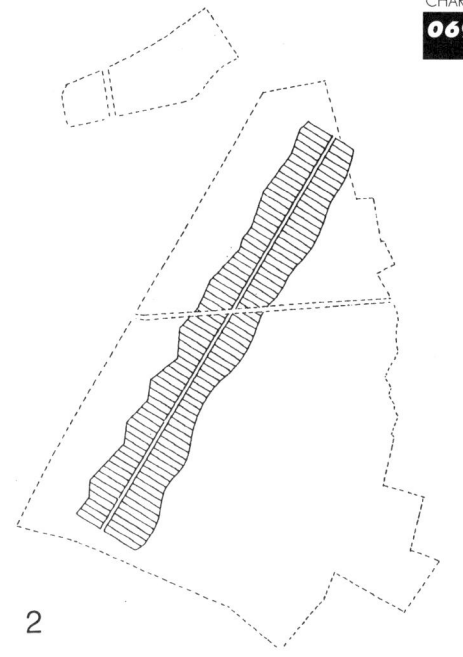

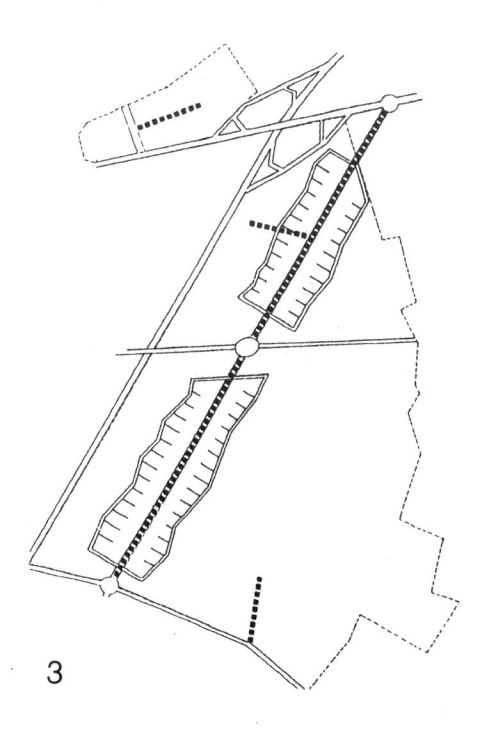

1. *Long-Cours* 2. Office grid 3. Access 4. Planting grid

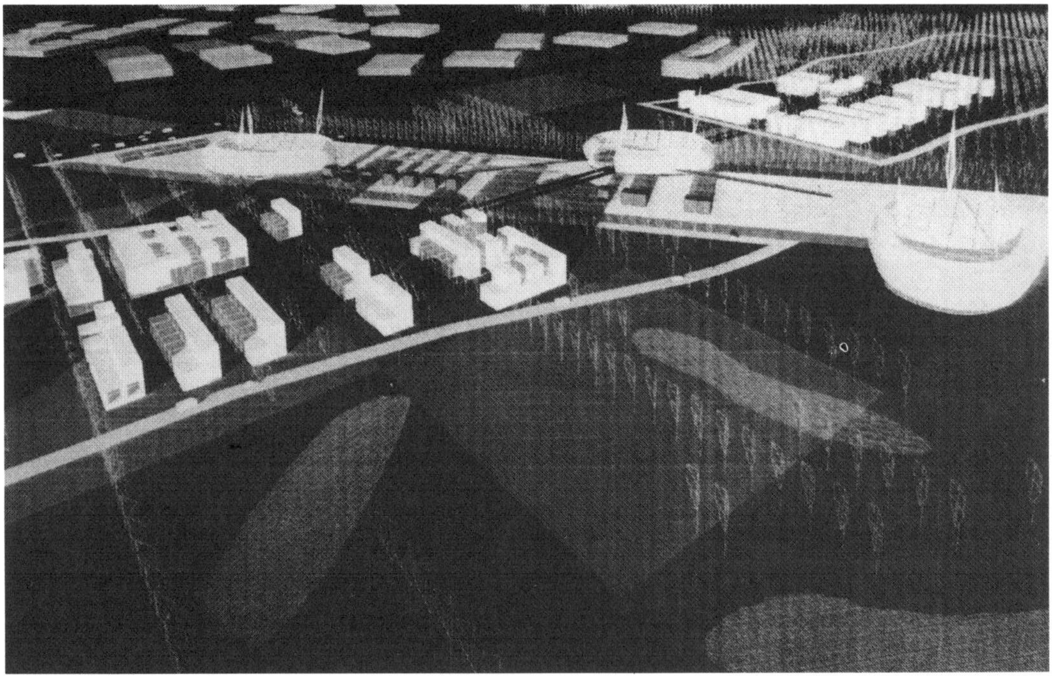

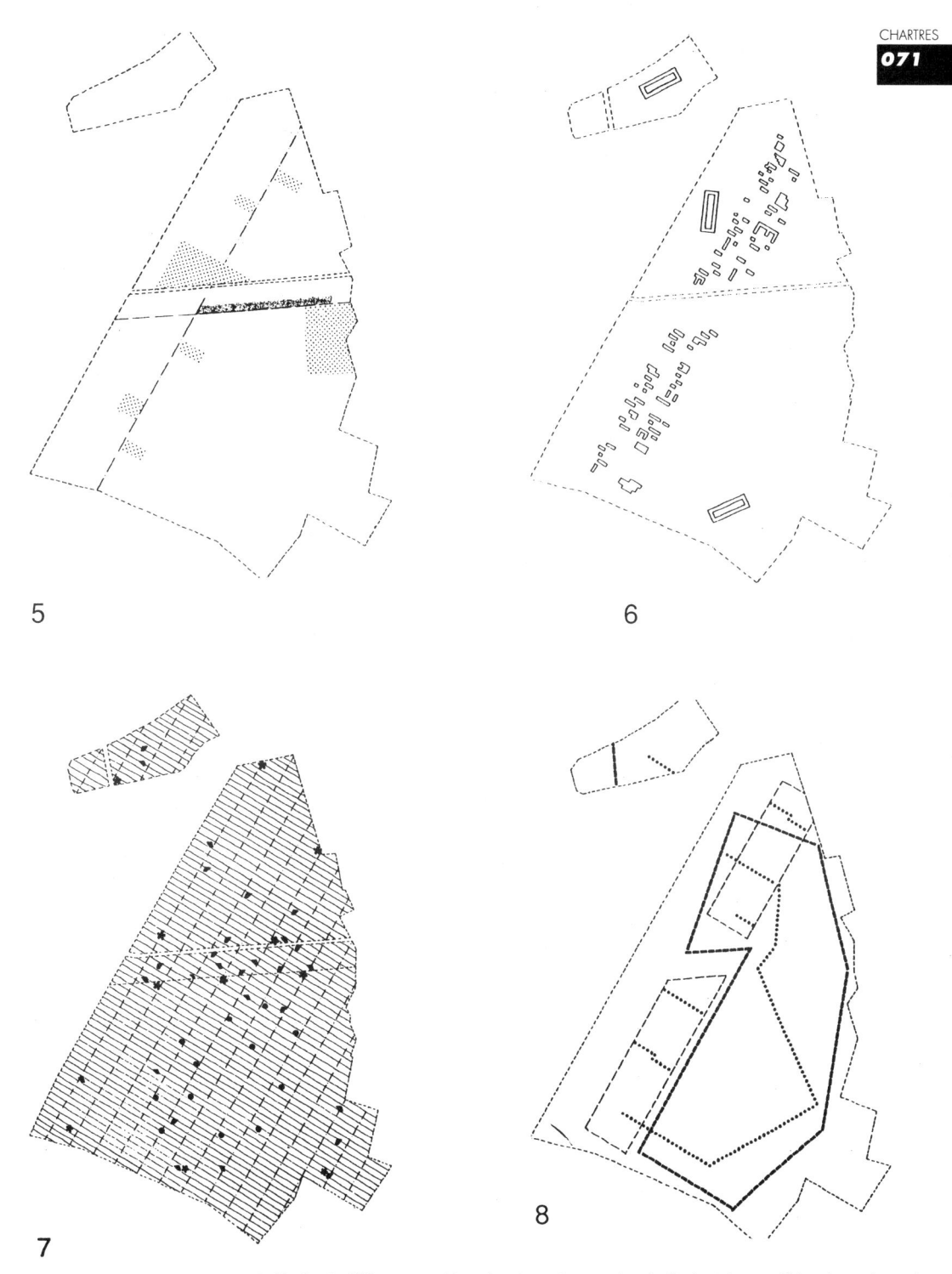

5. Parks 6. Offices 7. Grid and points of attraction 8. Pedestrian and bicycle path

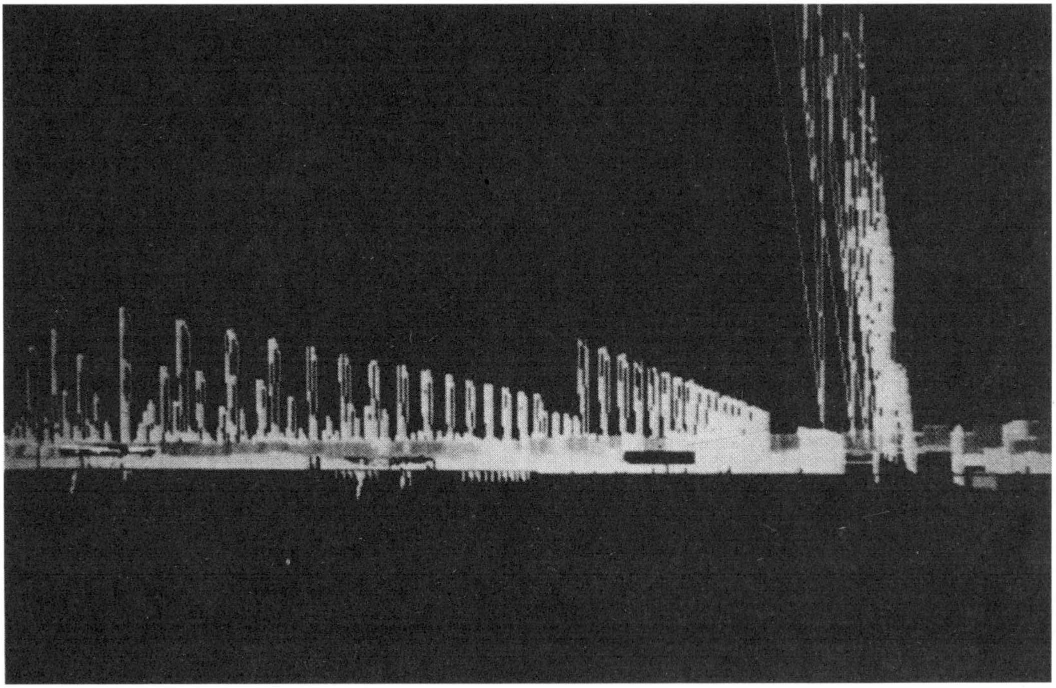

CHARTRES
073

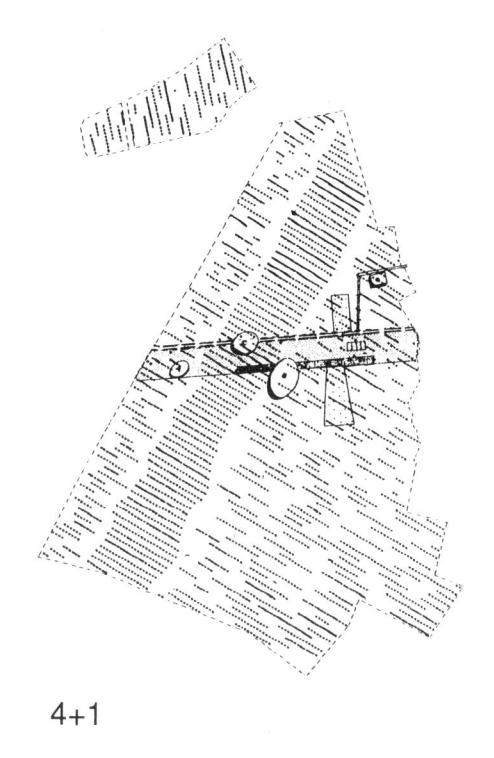

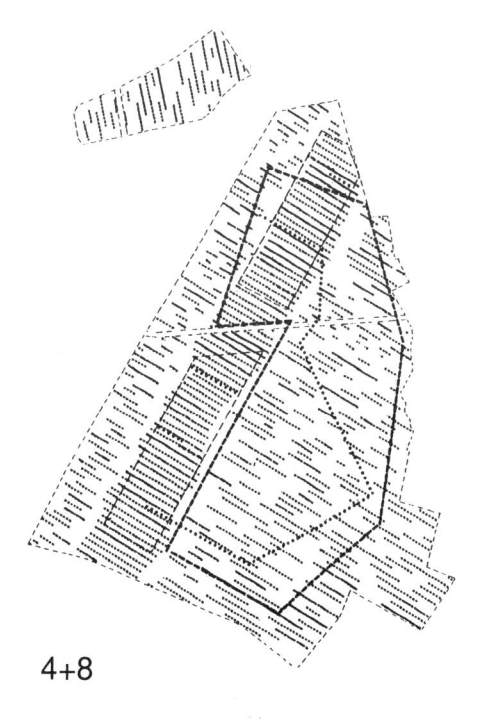

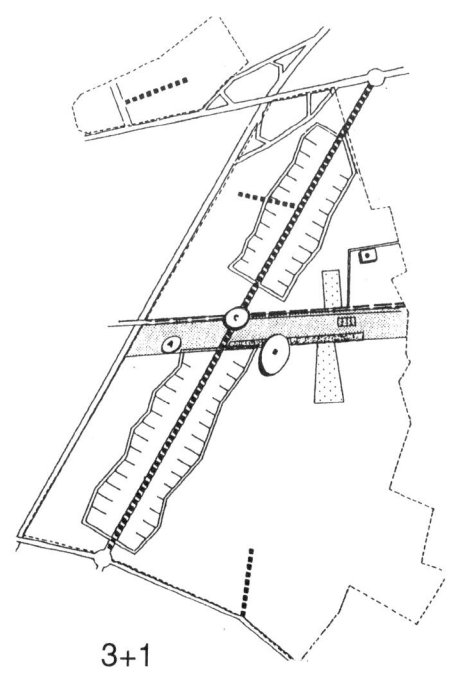

4+1

2+5

4+8

3+1

Combinations

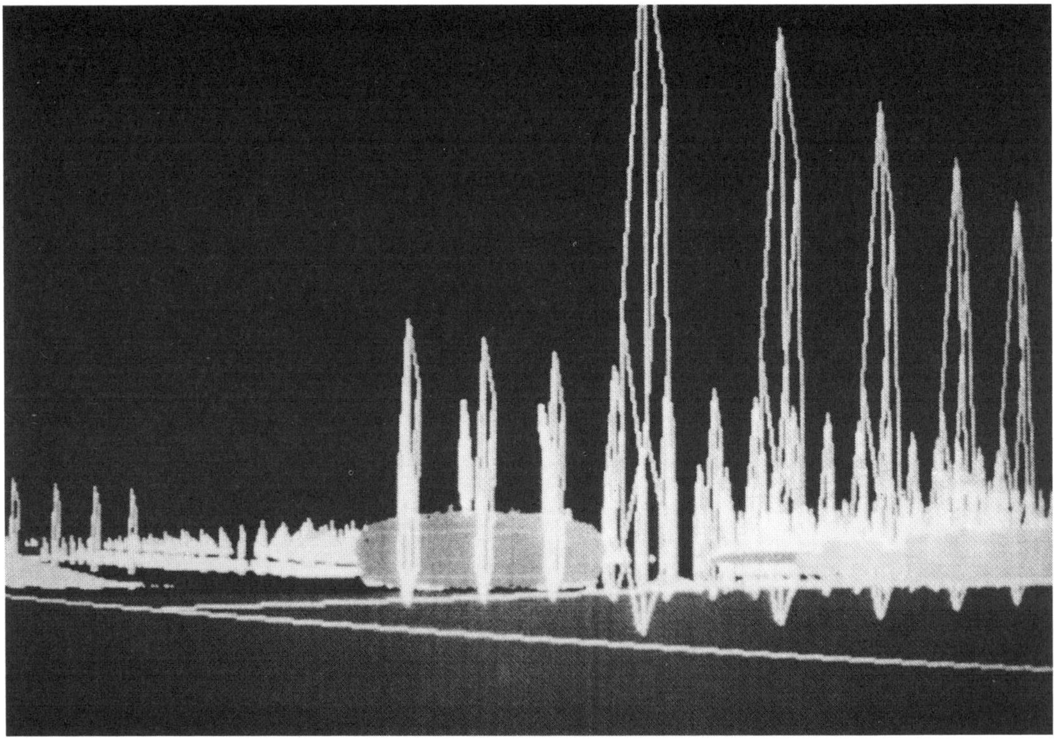

CHARTRES
075

3+5

1+2+5

4+6

7+1

Combinations

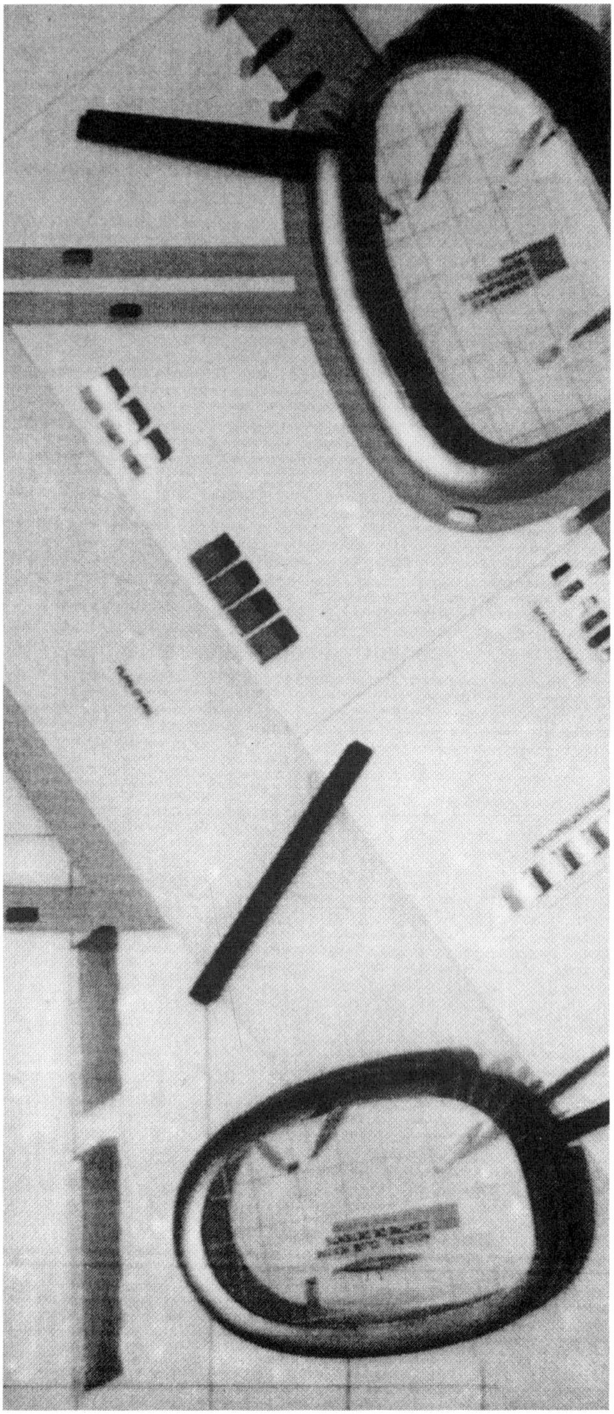

CHARTRES
077

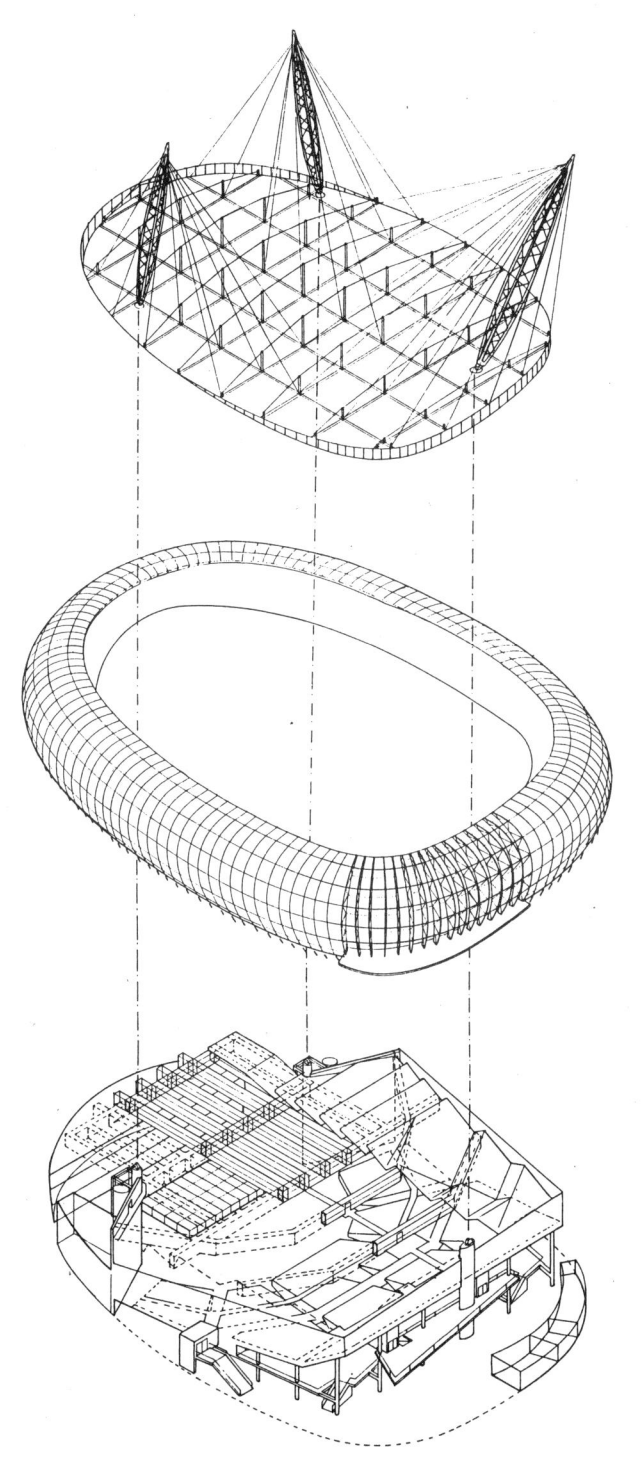

Three curved halls (similar in construction) accommodate varied amenities: (1) conferences and concerts (2) indoor sports facilities (3) shopping center and restaurant

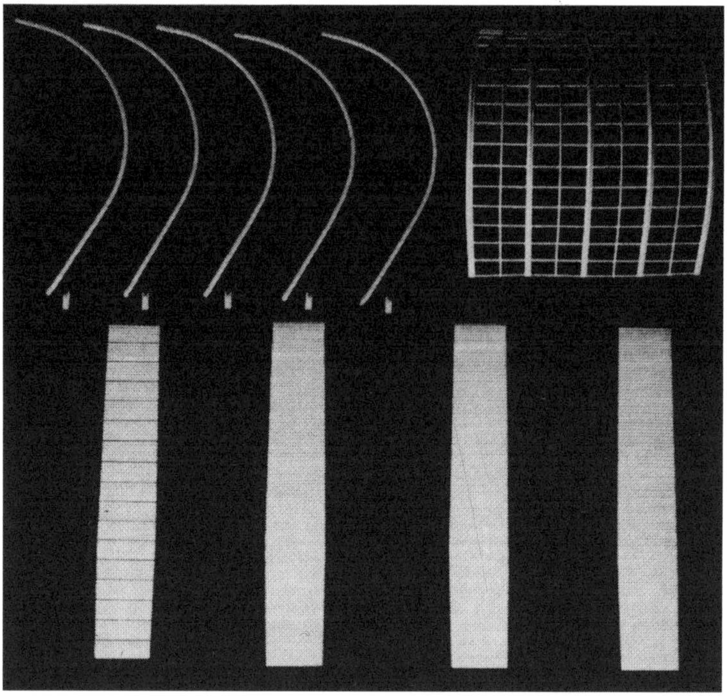

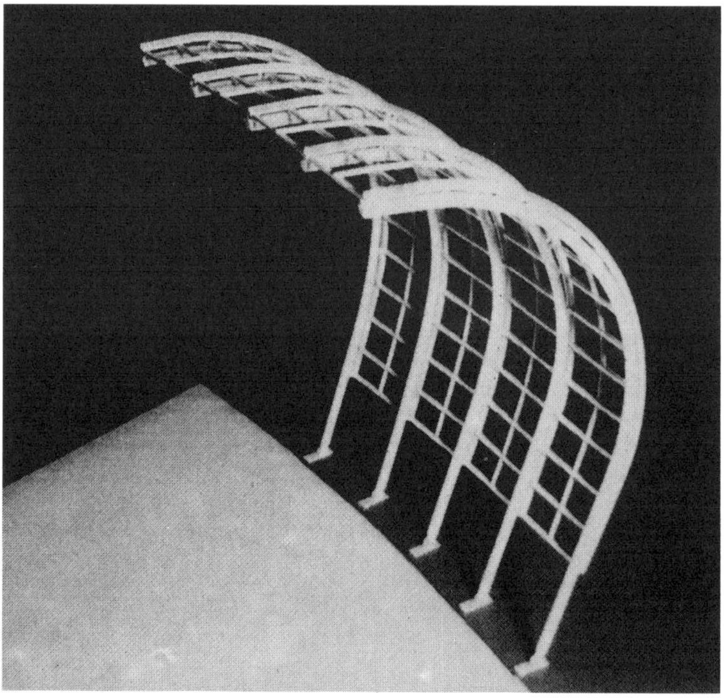

CHARTRES
079

One of the curved halls: conference and concert hall

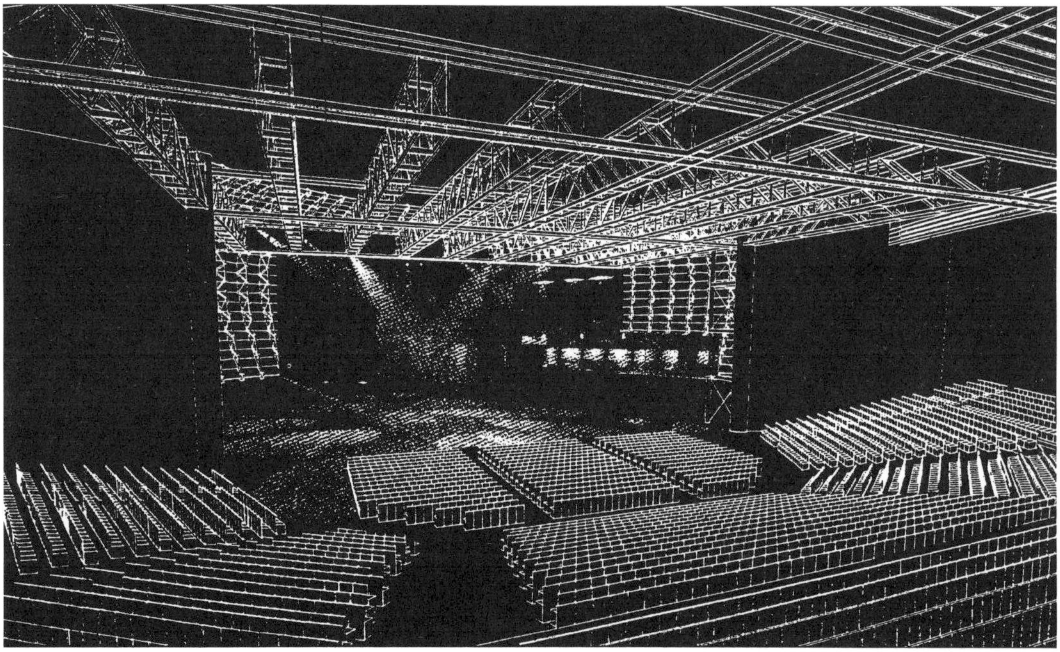

CHARTRES
081

The curved halls. Constants: a horizontal roof suspended from three masts, a thin aluminum outer skin. Variables: the inner skin (according to thermal or acoustical demands), interior volumes according to program

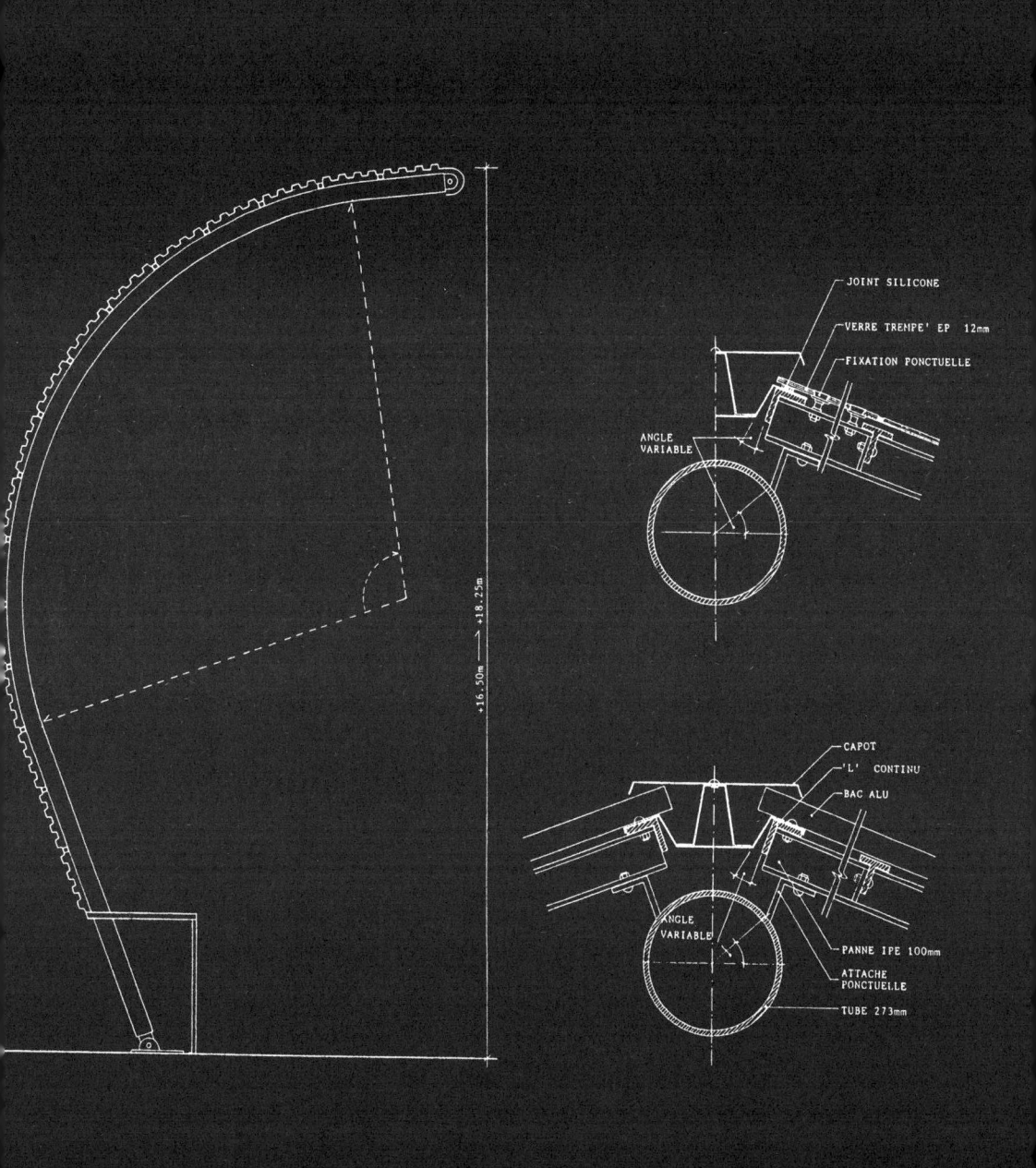

- JOINT SILICONE
- VERRE TREMPE' EP 12mm
- FIXATION PONCTUELLE

ANGLE VARIABLE

+16.50m → +18.25m

- CAPOT
- 'L' CONTINU
- BAC ALU

ANGLE VARIABLE

- PANNE IPE 100mm
- ATTACHE PONCTUELLE
- TUBE 273mm

Rotterdam, Railway Tunnel Site, 1988

ROTTERDAM
087

Continuous/Discontinuous Lines

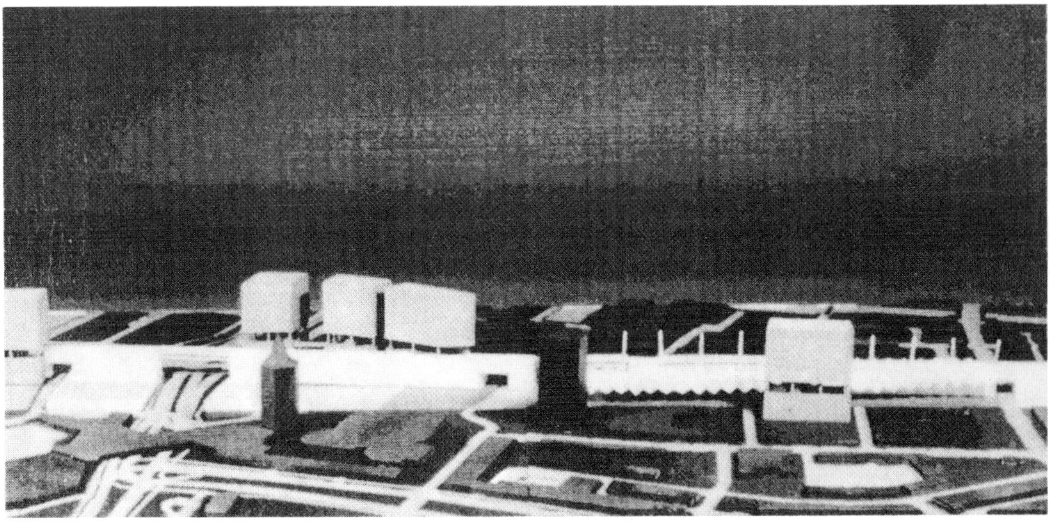

What should be done with a major but now obsolete elevated railway line cutting through the city of Rotterdam in The Netherlands?

The Triple Line

We made no attempt to perform cosmetic or rehabilitative surgery by establishing an illusion of contextual continuity between the areas on the left and right of the railway tunnel site. On the contrary, just as the elevated railway acted as a common denominator between various Rotterdam neighborhoods, so our new "railbuilding" becomes the origin of a linear development for twenty-first-century Rotterdam. This future system, the Triple Line, is made of three interwoven lines:

1. The *railbuilding*, on the exact location of the old railway, is a linear, five-story continuous/discontinuous construction that can accommodate offices, housing and commercial facilities according to programmatic demands. Its roof provides a walkway and bicycle path from the suburbs to the urban center. Archaeological remnants of the old railway (bridges, for example) can be partly preserved and turned into fragments of the railbuilding.

2. The *groundstrip* sits on ground level, above the new underground railway system. It contains park pockets, seasonal markets, children's playgrounds, swimming pools and other recreational and cultural facilities.

3. The *double-deck slab*, located anywhere along the linear system, consists of vertical fragments of an almost endless curvilinear high-rise slab, with a public deck on the fifth floor that connects with the roof of the railbuilding. The double-deck slab contains residential and office facilities. The conceptual presence of this near-endless four-kilometer curvilinear slab pervades the system. We "edited out" the slab wherever it was not necessary. The slab marks high-density development areas on the Triple Line.

The Triple Line expands upon the linear cities envisioned by Soria y Mata, Leonidov and Le Corbusier.

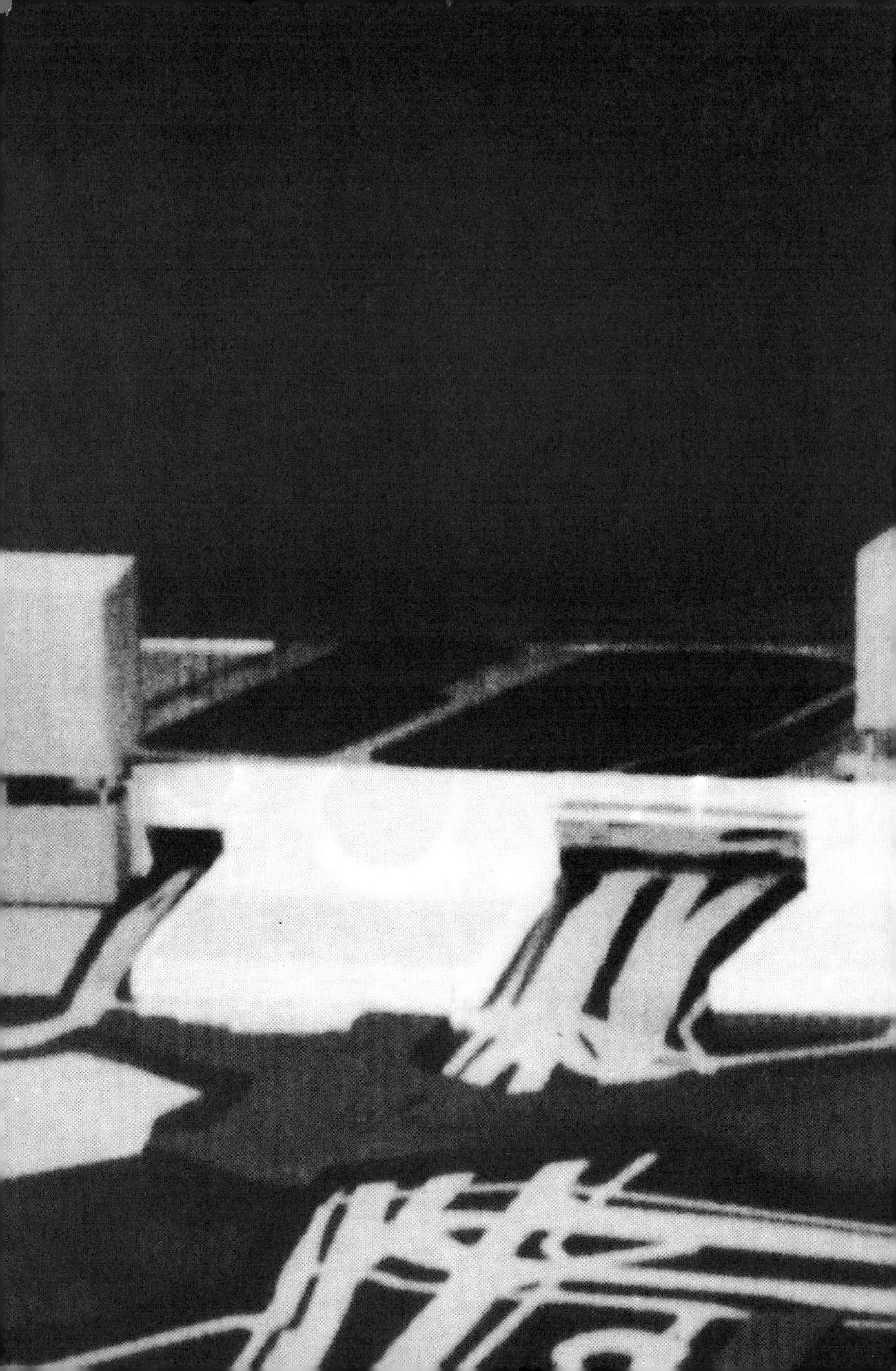

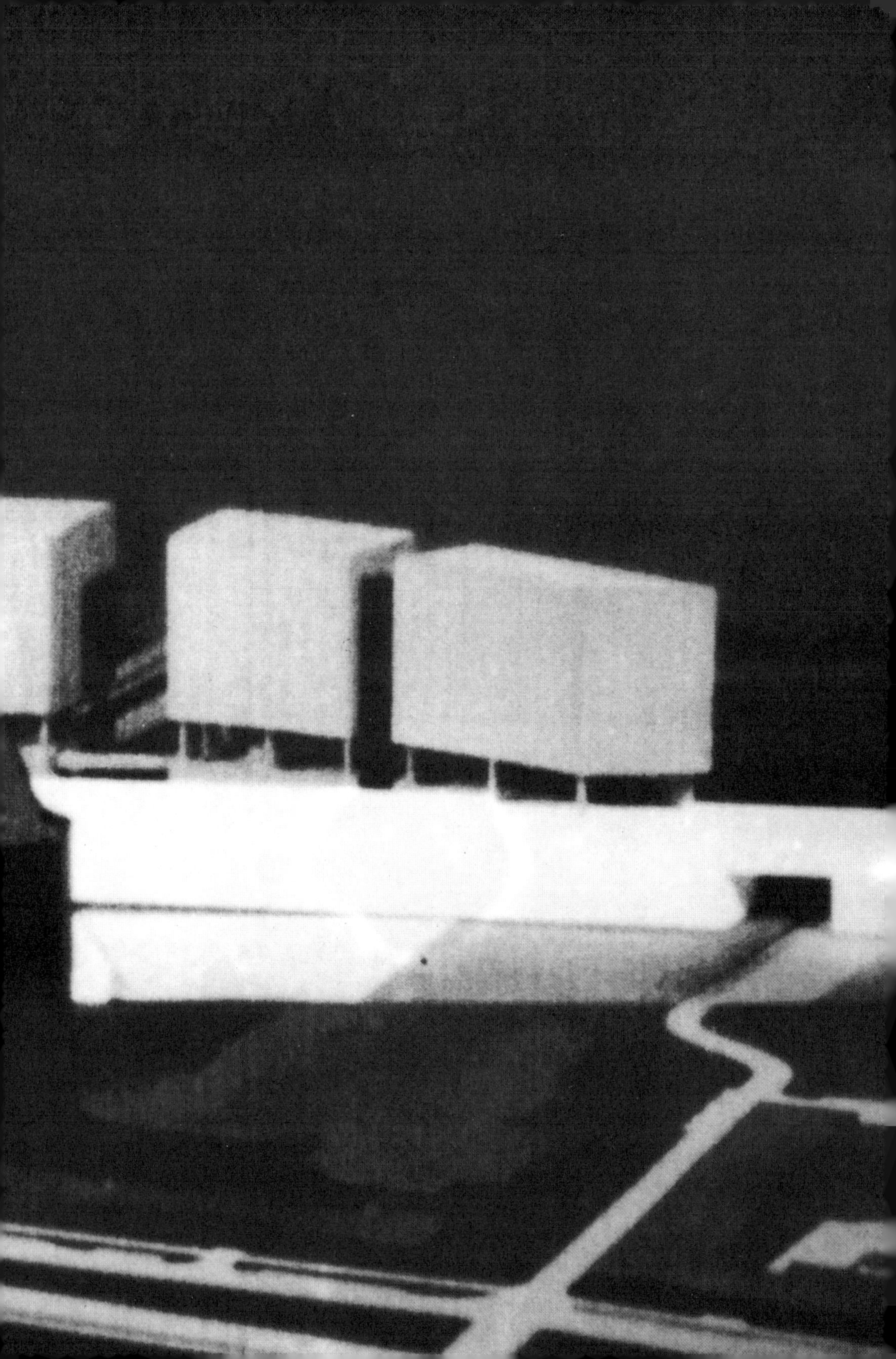

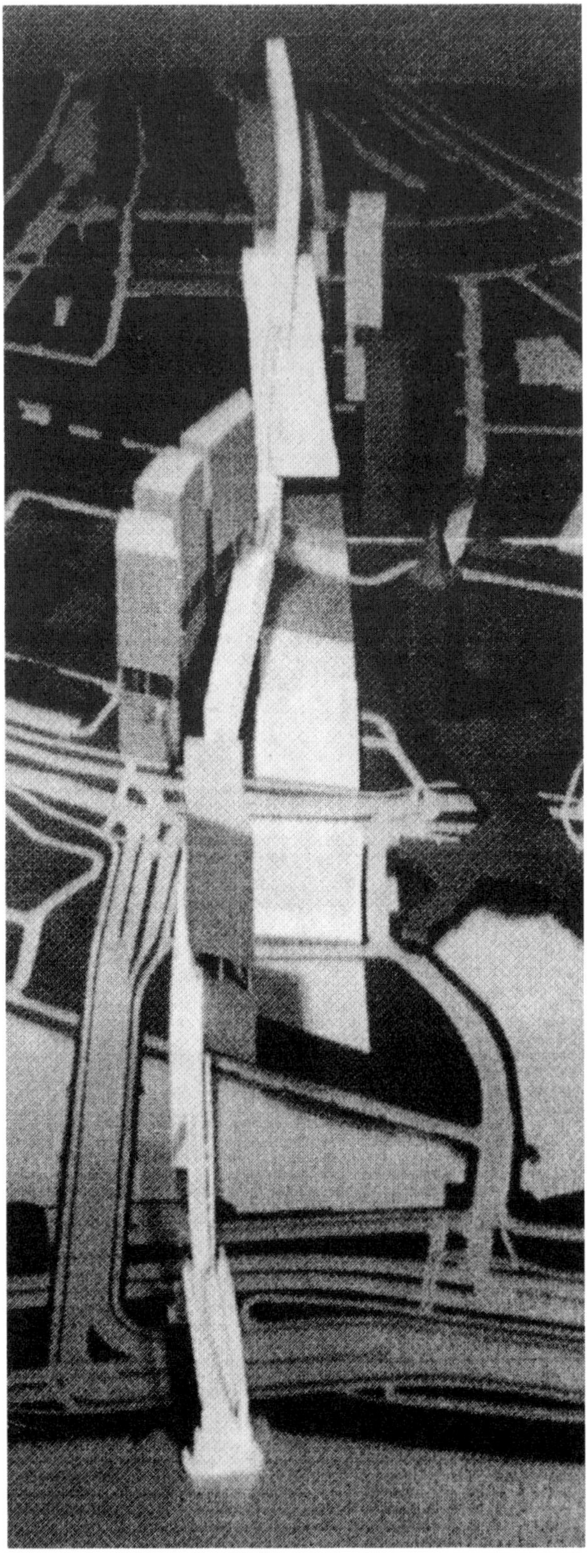

ROTTERDAM
093

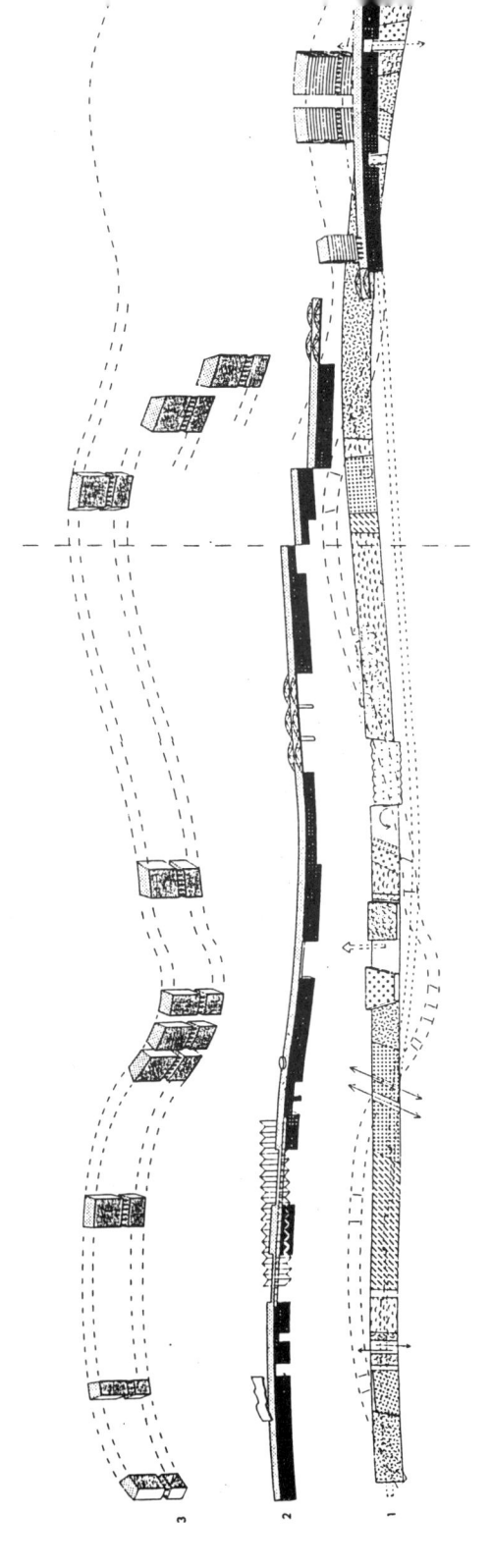

Triple Line: 1. Recreation 2. Housing 3. Offices

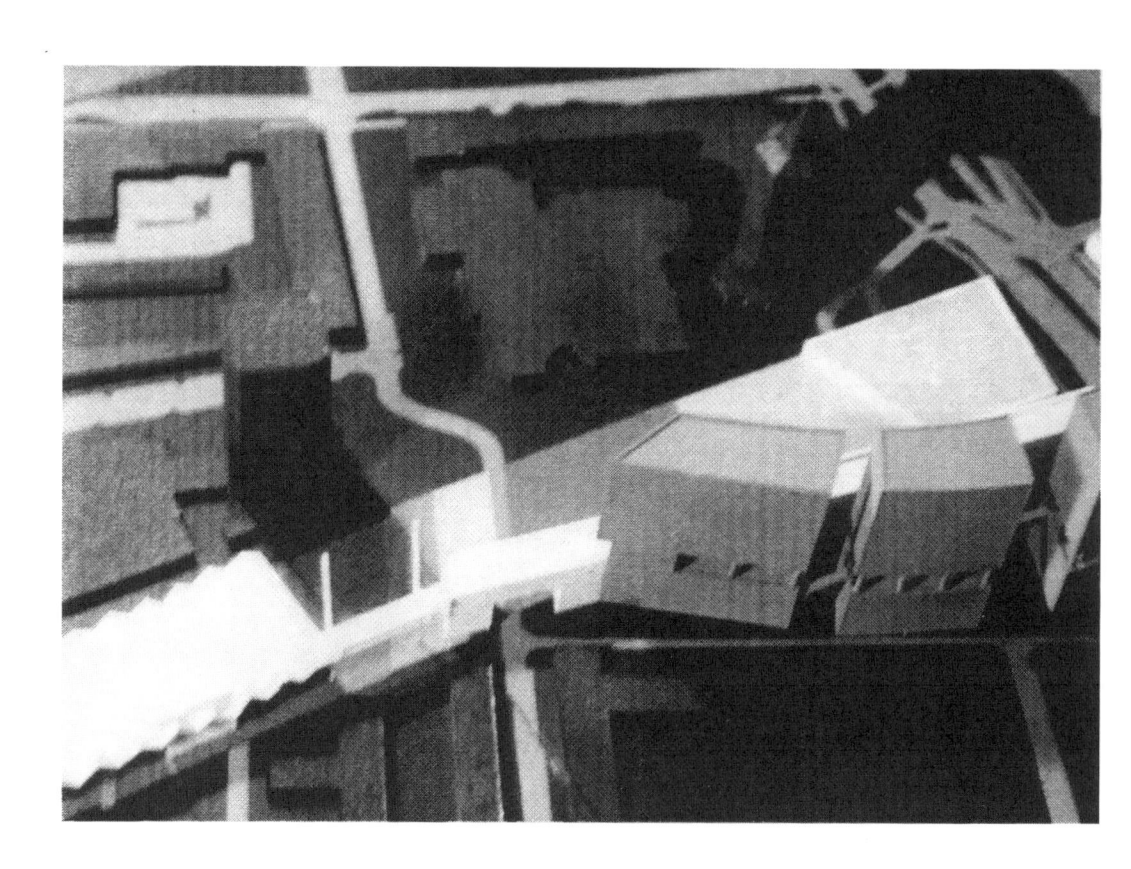

Deformable geometries: lines of activities, of programs, of events

ROTTERDAM
095

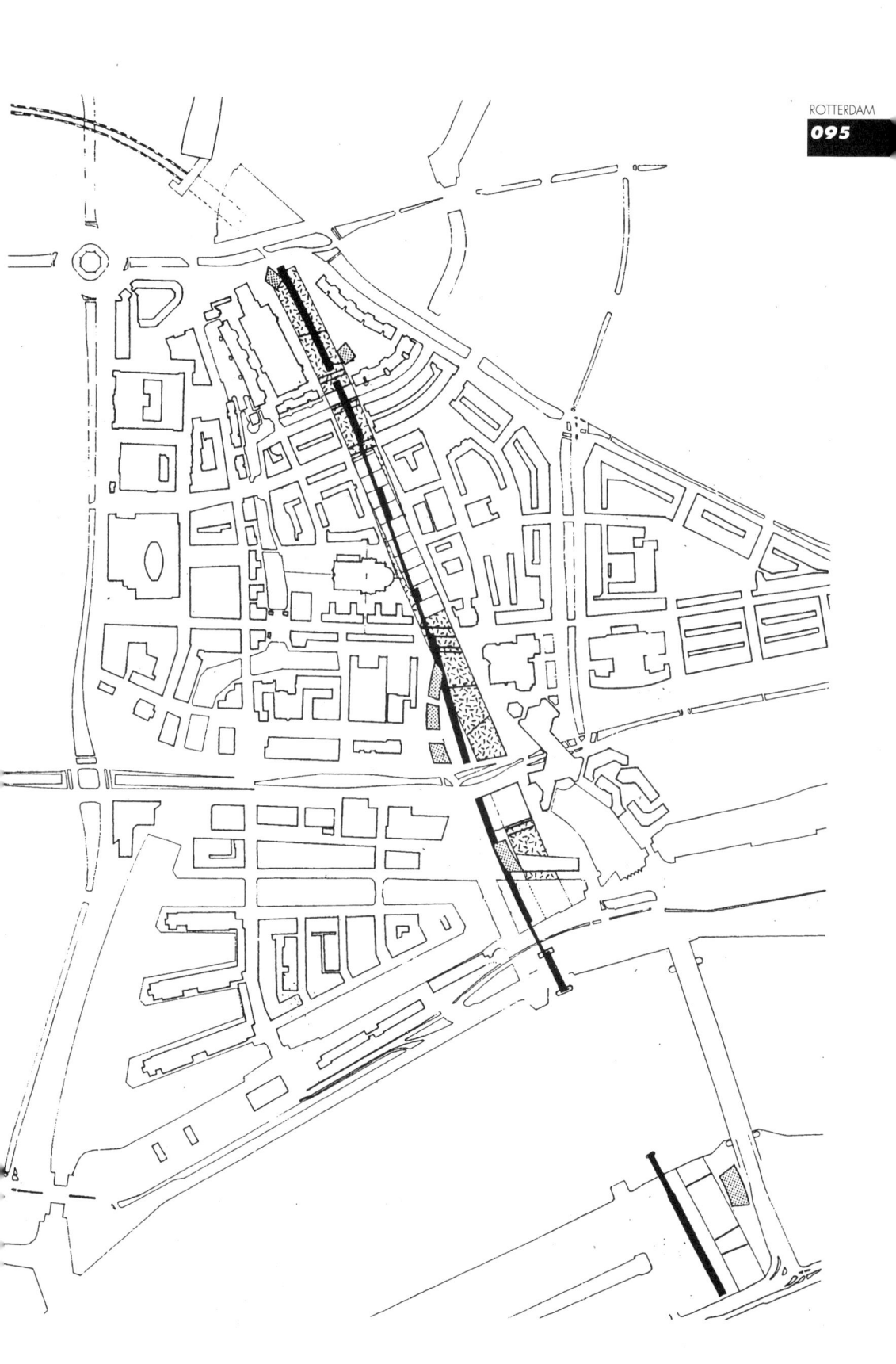

Integration of programmatic differences into a continuous system

ROTTERDAM
097

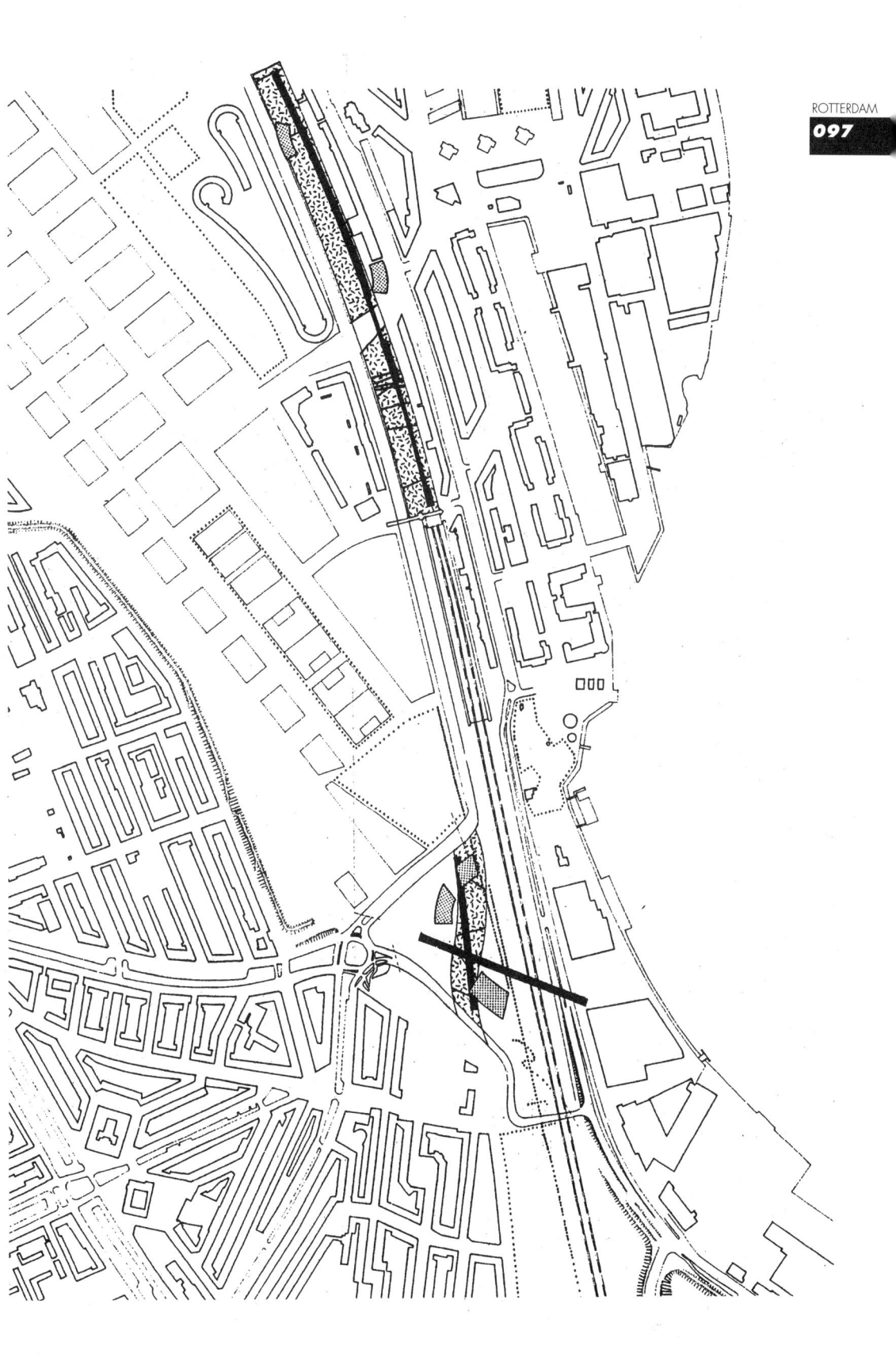

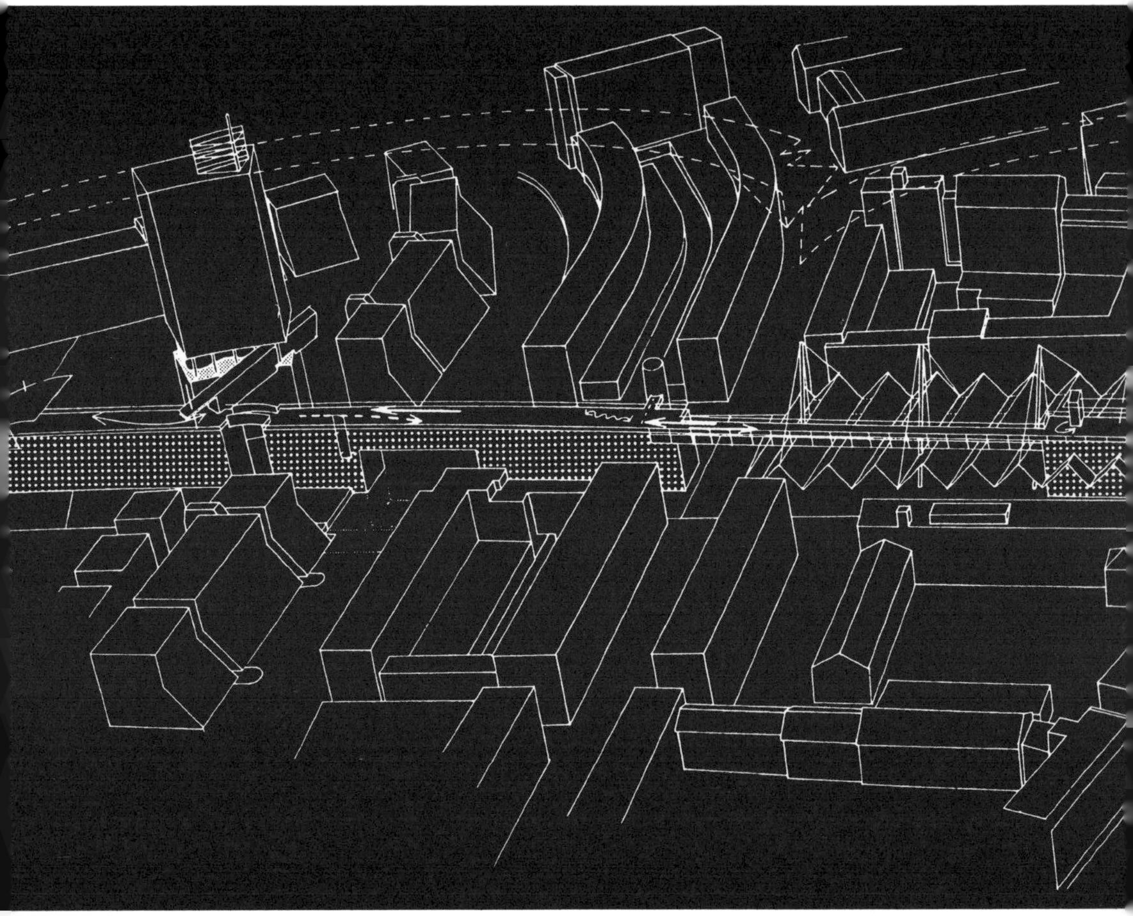

ROTTERDAM
099

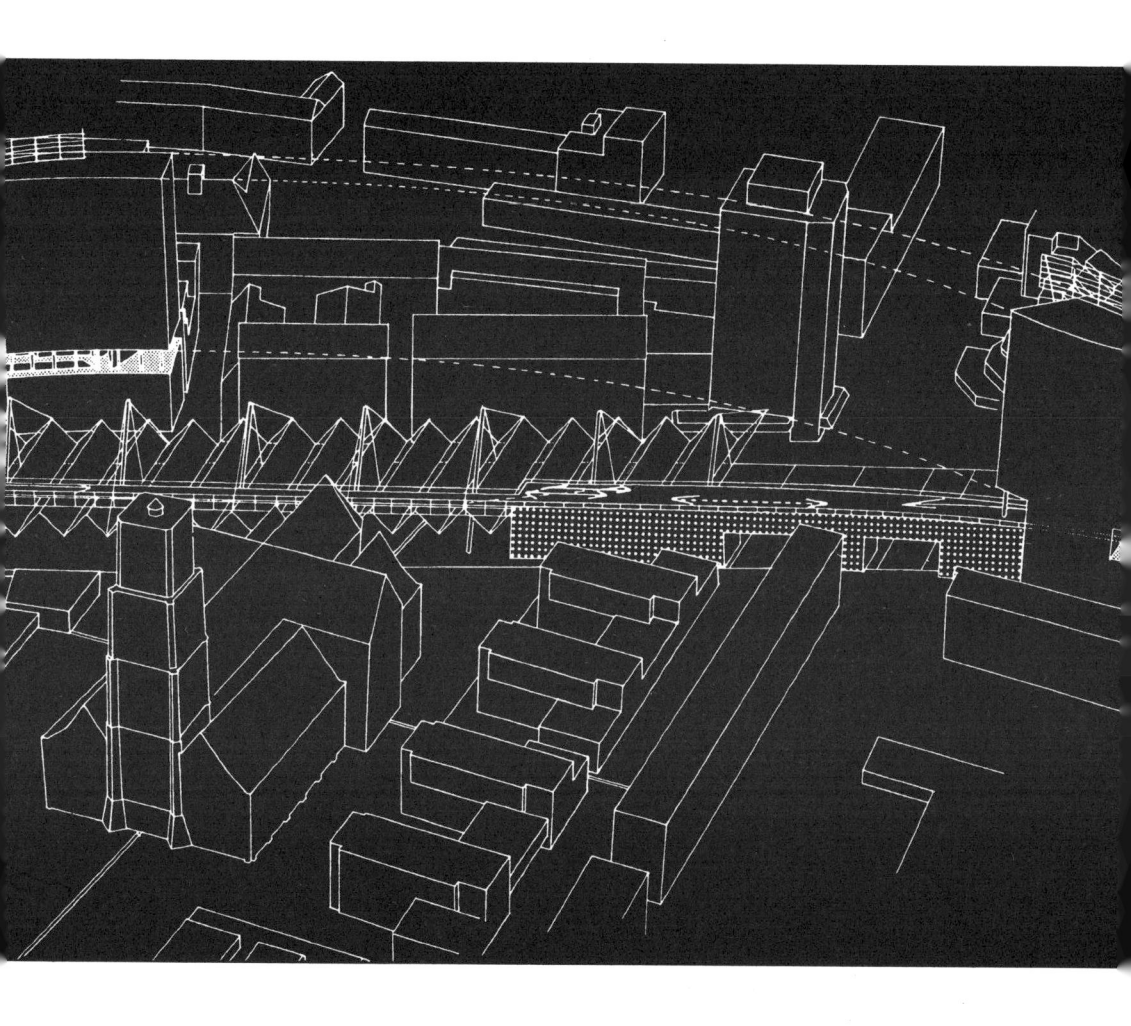

Continuity and dissociation. The three interwoven lines are lines of intensity:
the place of city events

B.
Architectural Urbanism

The architectural urbanism of Kansai, Kyoto and Lausanne demonstrates the hypothesis of urban generators, or architectural systems in the city that act as catalysts for every kind of activity or function, independent of the form that they may take. In these city-generators, functions and programs combine and intersect in an endless "disprogramming" or "crossprogramming."

Kansai, International Airport, 1988

Linear Cities

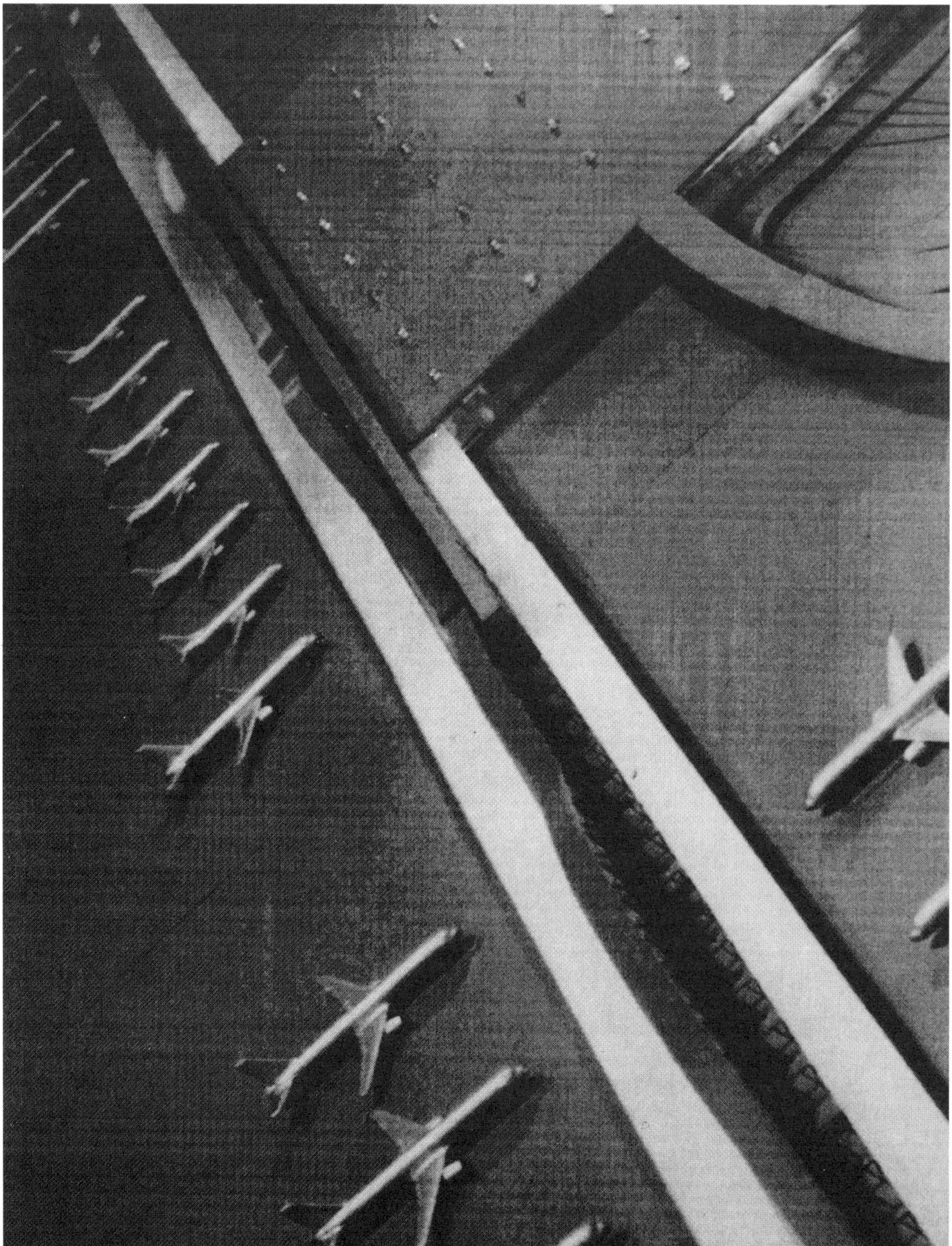

Will the major world airport on an artificial island in Osaka Bay be another transfer facility, comparable to dozens of others around the globe, only larger and more efficient? Or will it be something else, something unprecedented, which will turn the very idea of the airport into a new form of international life? Such a project could make Osaka and Japan forerunners of the most intense mode of city life, in which people would fly to Kansai International because it is the place to be.

Airports no longer serve isolated functions: they are not unitary buildings. They now extend—and redefine—the metropolis. They explode boundaries and limits. They are also one of the fastest growing industries, attracting entrepreneurs of all sorts.

Program
We chose to turn Kansai International Airport into a new type of metropolis, to enlarge the airport into an event, a spectacle, a new city of interchange and exchange, of business, commerce and culture—a twenty-four-hour-a-day continuous invention that acts as an extraordinary counterpoint to the city of Osaka. Our ambition is for Kansai International not only to address world travelers but to act as a new urban segment for culture and recreation, superstores and great hotels.

Site
The unusual location on an artificial island (created specially for the occasion) five miles offshore in Osaka Bay suggested an equally bold move on the part of the architect: we looked at the airport as the generator of the ultimate linear city—a twenty-four-hour line that would conceptually extend around the globe: a 40,000-kilometer-long city, with a relentless sequence of events. Such a program also required a powerful *image* that would challenge all architectural preconceptions about structure and composition.

We started by differentiating the new airport into two distinct parts: the linear city and the deck.

The linear city consists of three lines: the double strip, the wave and the slab. The double strip contains all airport transfer functions: the terminal wings. Between the two layers of the double strip are the wave and the slab, key features of the project. Both are very narrow—approximately twelve meters for the wave and eight meters for the slab. Their respective lengths will be determined after feasibility studies concerning the ever-increasing numbers of potential visitors. Short segments may be built initially and extended according to demand. We project (for the slab) two hotels with a total of 1,000 rooms as well as hourly-rental office space and (for the wave) a mile-long entertainment/cultural/sports center with cinemas, exhibition spaces, swimming pools, golf courses, shooting galleries, and so forth. The hotel rooms (left and right of the deck, along single-loaded corridors) are serviced by *sine-movers*: cabins that combine the functions of elevators and teleferics to service four floors over long horizontal distances. The wave is serviced by travelators that follow the slope of the random wave curve.

The narrowness of the two bands not only reinforces the dominant linearity of the new city but forces an unprecedented density of events.

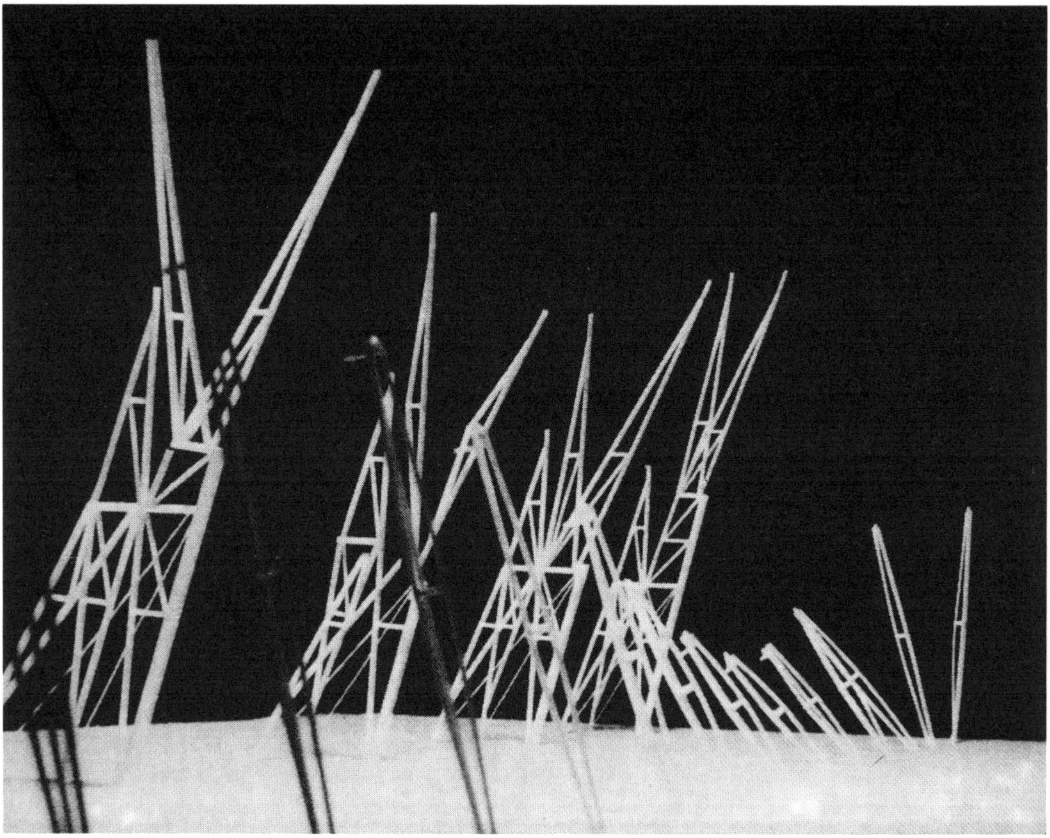

The deck extends all activities taking place in the linear city: offices, trade and commerce, aspects of art and culture. Its nondirectional structure allows for extended tracts of space. It appears as an endless, four-story functional landscape with check-in counters, immigration offices and other related functions.

The bands of the wave, slab, double strip and deck challenge traditional architecture by introducing spectacular parallel disjunctions. Hence the interstices between bands become architecturally as important as the bands themselves. Perceived by the visitor as stunning visual rifts, such linear negative space questions architectural composition by proposing unclassifiable space (it shuns the realm of historical precedent and repetitive typology).

The wave's distortion, as well as its obliquely vertical axis, questions gravity just as airplanes once did: the datum plane ceases to be the ground and becomes a conceptual or technological parameter. The supporting masts become all important since they are the last retaining link between earth and air. Slab and wave already belong to the realm of the sky, as the wave hovers above the new airport city.

The slab is all brushed stainless steel or aluminum. The wave is covered with copper plates; as it oxidizes, it will become an extended blue-green curve.

Structure
The two bands (the copper wave and the steel slab) inserted into the "given" terminal building infrastructure are supported by three independent systems in steel growing out of the two bands.

We have called the three types of supporting masts the "crane," the "pencil," and the "cigar." Each has an independent longitudinal rhythm. The crane supports both bands in taking some of their vertical loads as well as all of the horizontal loads. The height of the "steel" band remains constant while that of the "copper" band varies. Half of the crane and the cigar vary in geometry in response to the changing height of the upper band. The half of the crane supporting the steel band and the pencil remains constant. In several places the band touches the ground. Expansion between the touch-down points concentrates in local expansion joints. The mast systems all hinge in a manner similar to the steel band but in varying places in response to the varying mast configurations. The masts will all be hinged to allow free expansion of the bands.

The entire length of the terminal (double-strip) building is clad in a glass skin. Solar protection is achieved by varying the translucency. The horizontal surfaces are white, becoming clearer as the surface becomes steeper. The external surface is textured to break any reflectivity where glare could present a risk to pilots. The glass skin is supported by an intricate mesh of pretensioned cables. In section two parabolic curves are tensioned one against the other. The levels of prestress in the cables will be designed so that no element is ever required to work in compression. The upper curve of cables is a diagonal mesh while the lower is a simple cross cable that, when tensioned, pulls down the mesh and itself forms a continuous vault.

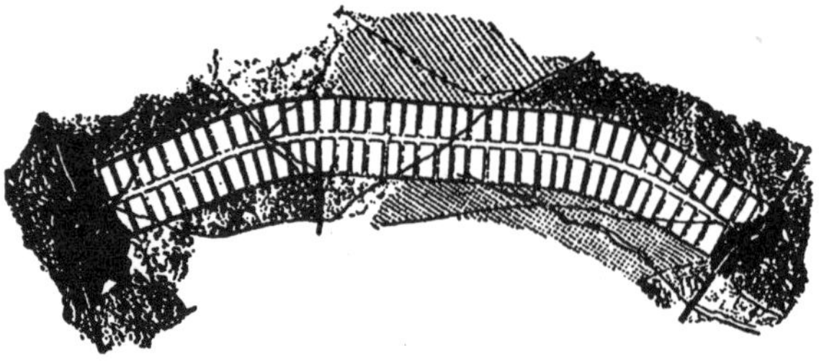

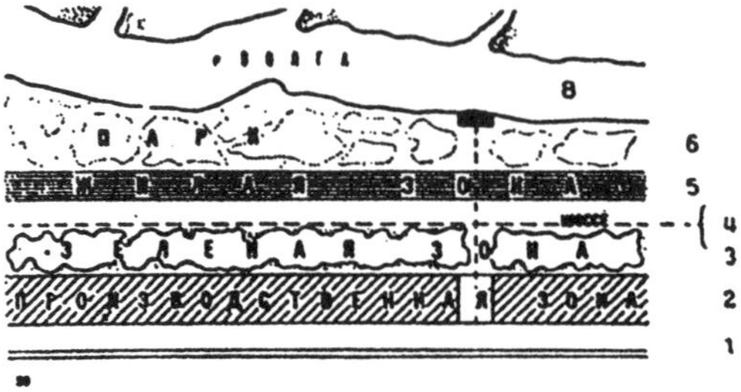

р. ВОЛГА
8
ПАРК
6
ЖИЛАЯ ЗОНА
5
4
ЗЕЛЕНАЯ ЗОНА
3
ПРОИЗВОДСТВЕННАЯ ЗОНА
2
1

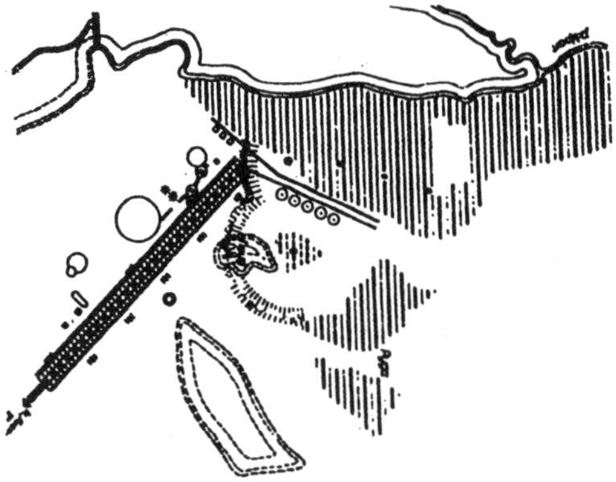

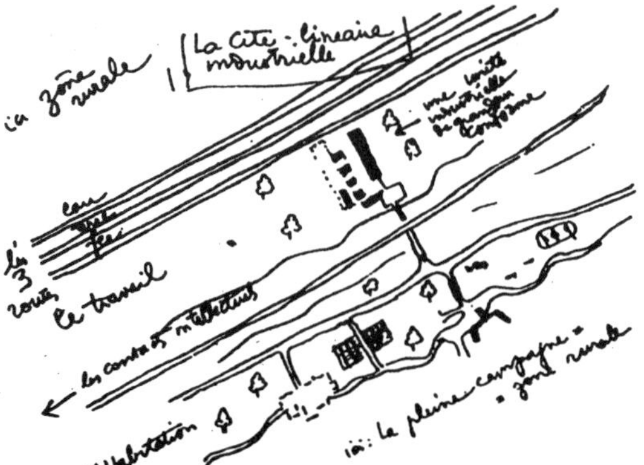

La Cité-linéaire industrielle
ici la zone rurale
une unité industrielle de grandeur conforme
eau
fer
les 3 routes
le travail
les centres intellectuels
l'Habitation
ici: la pleine campagne = zone rurale

KANSAI
109

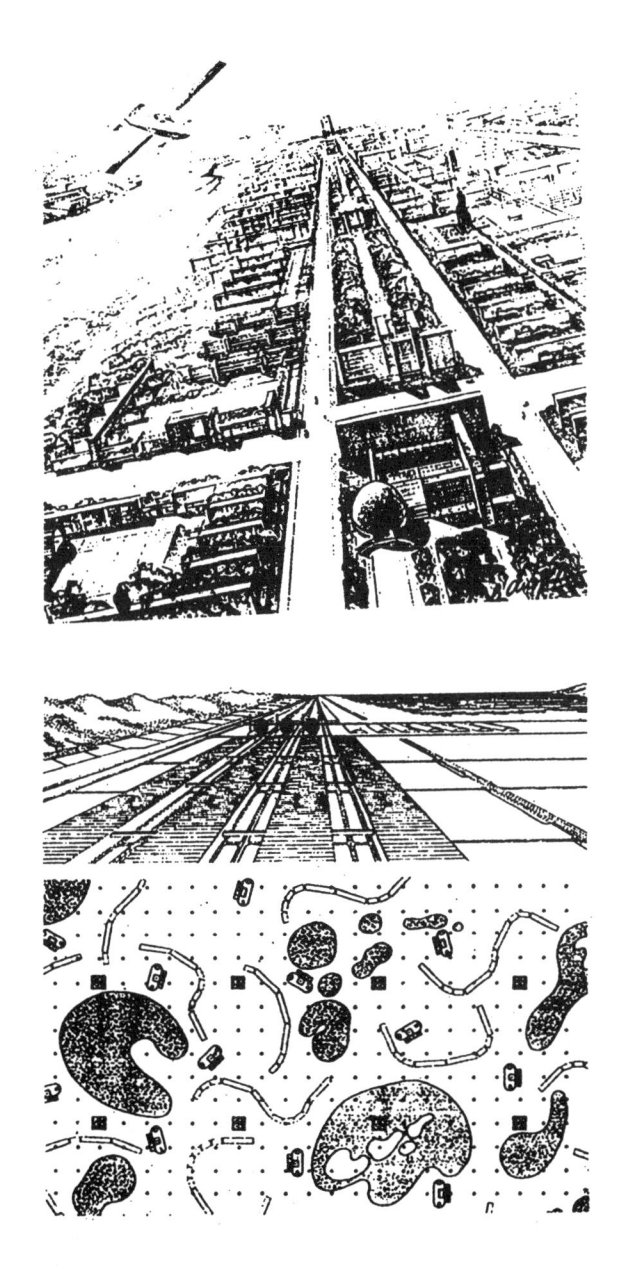

Artificial cities that never end...

HIMEJI   KOBE   OSAKA

OSAKA BAY

AWAJI ISL.

THE KANSAI INT'L AIRPORT

KANSAI
111

THE DECK　デッキ

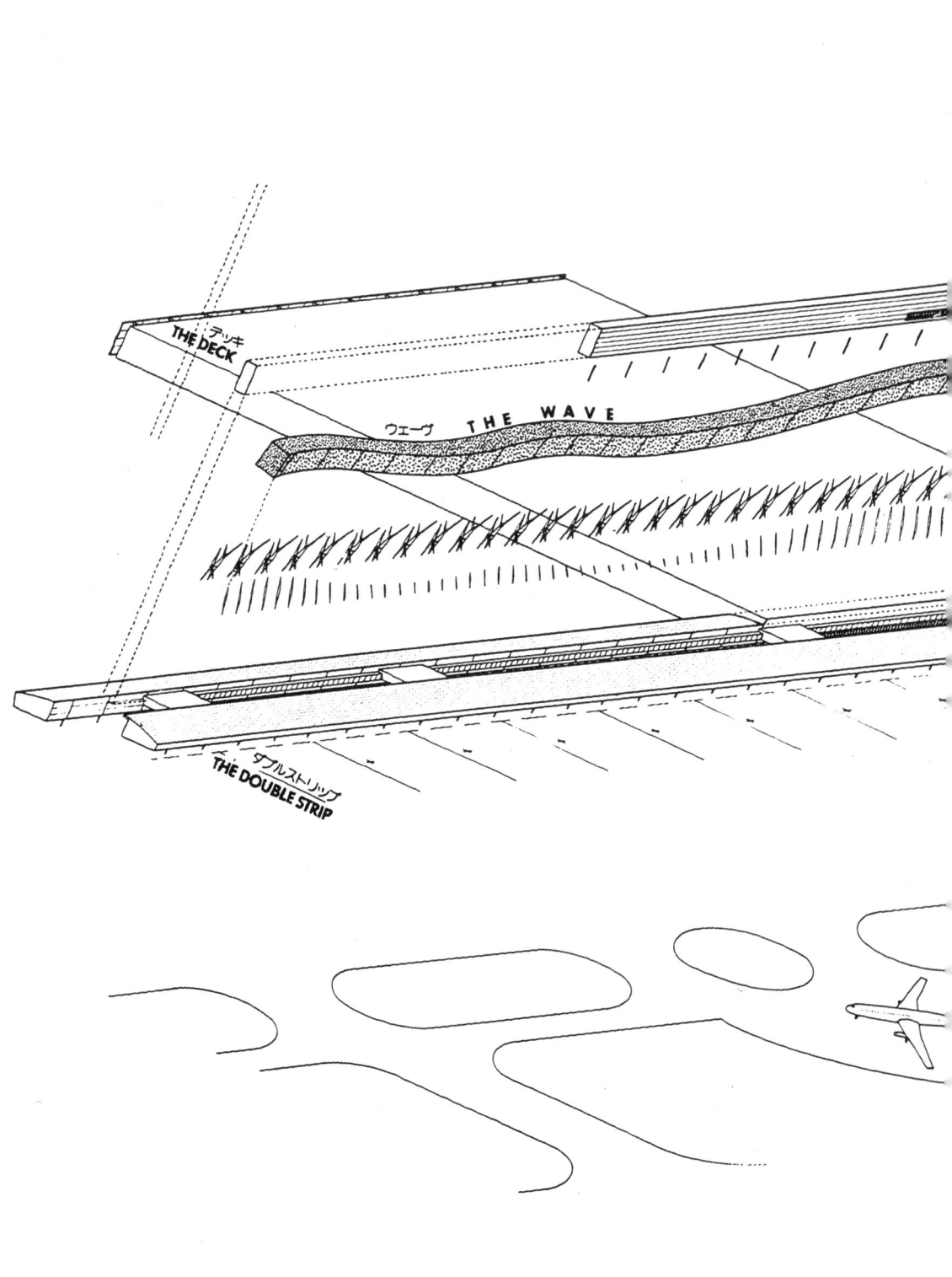

ウェーヴ　THE WAVE

THE DOUBLE STRIP　ダブルストリップ

KANSAI
113

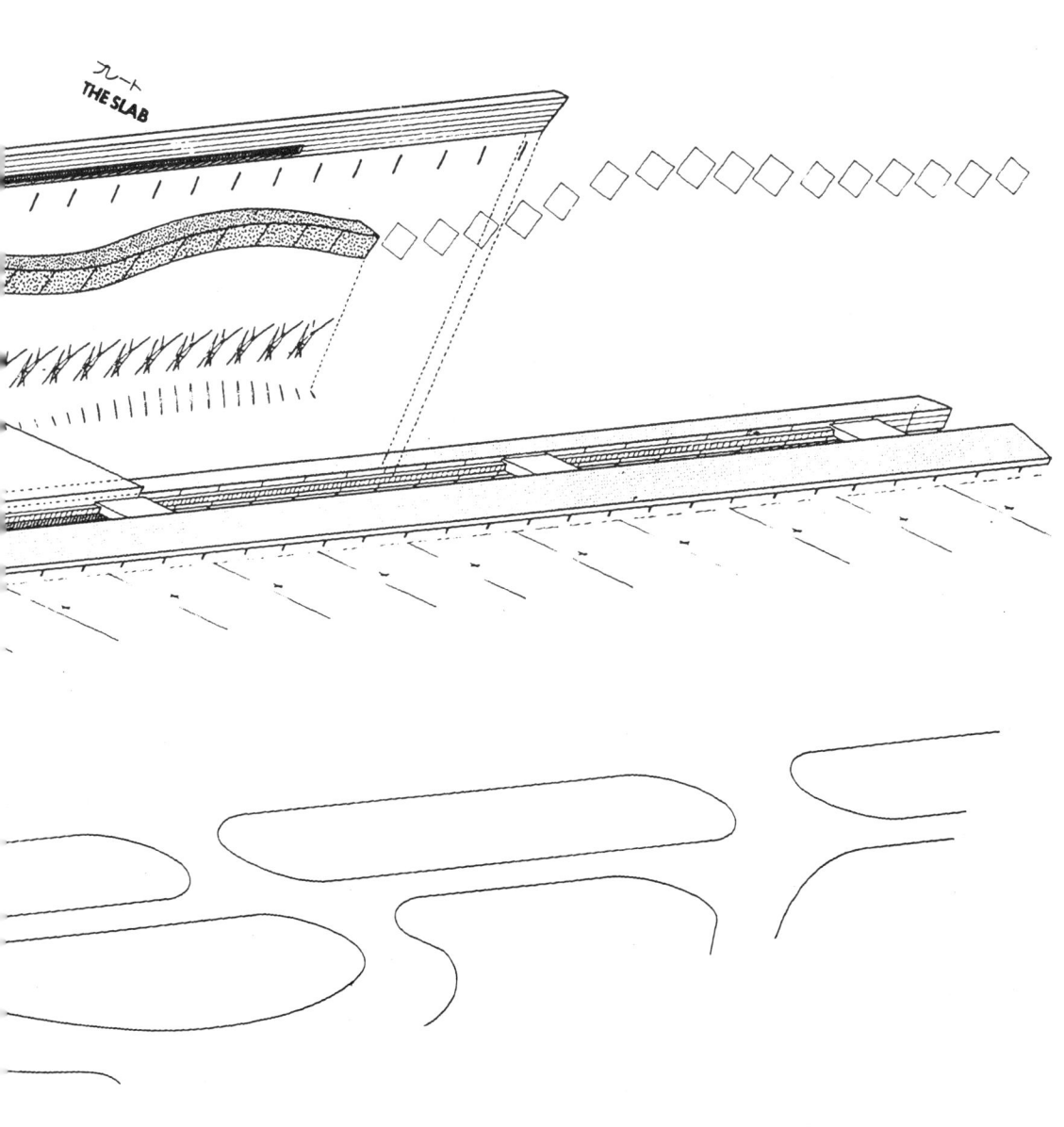

プレート
THE SLAB

Linear city: double strip, wave and slab

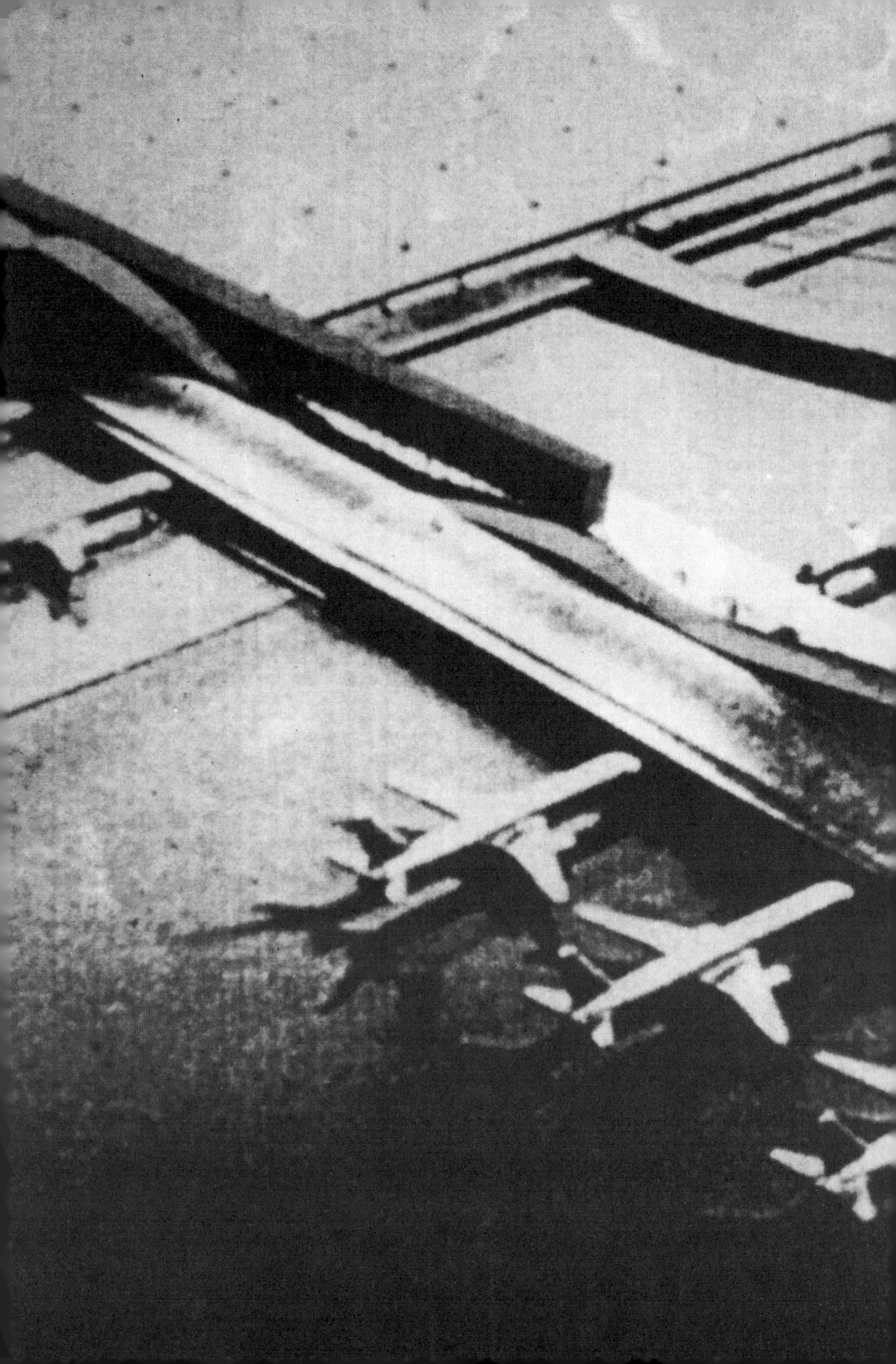

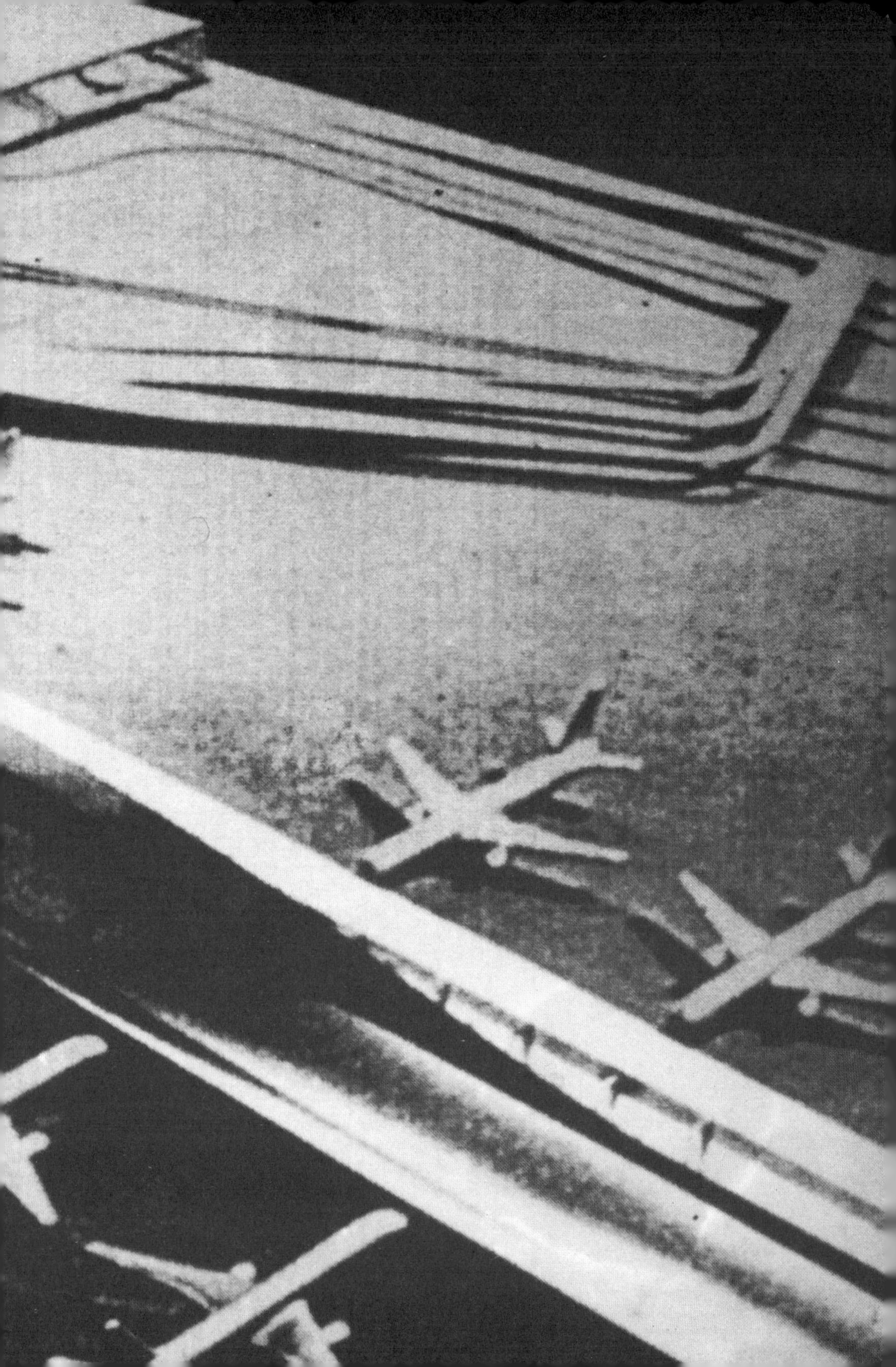

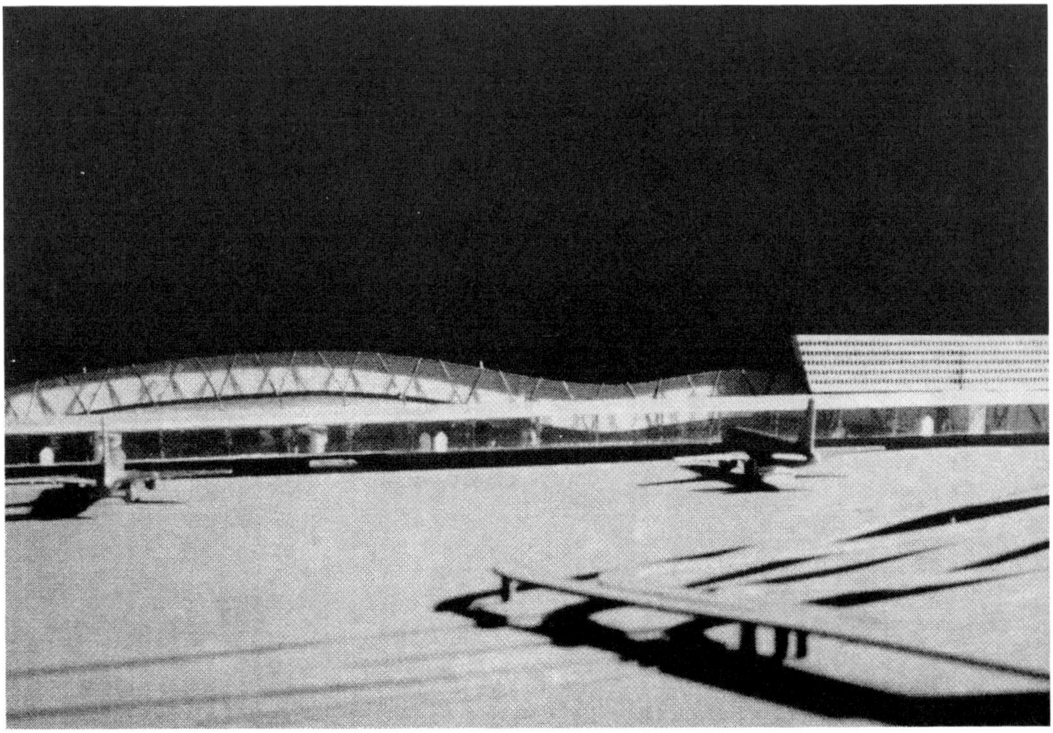

KANSAI
117

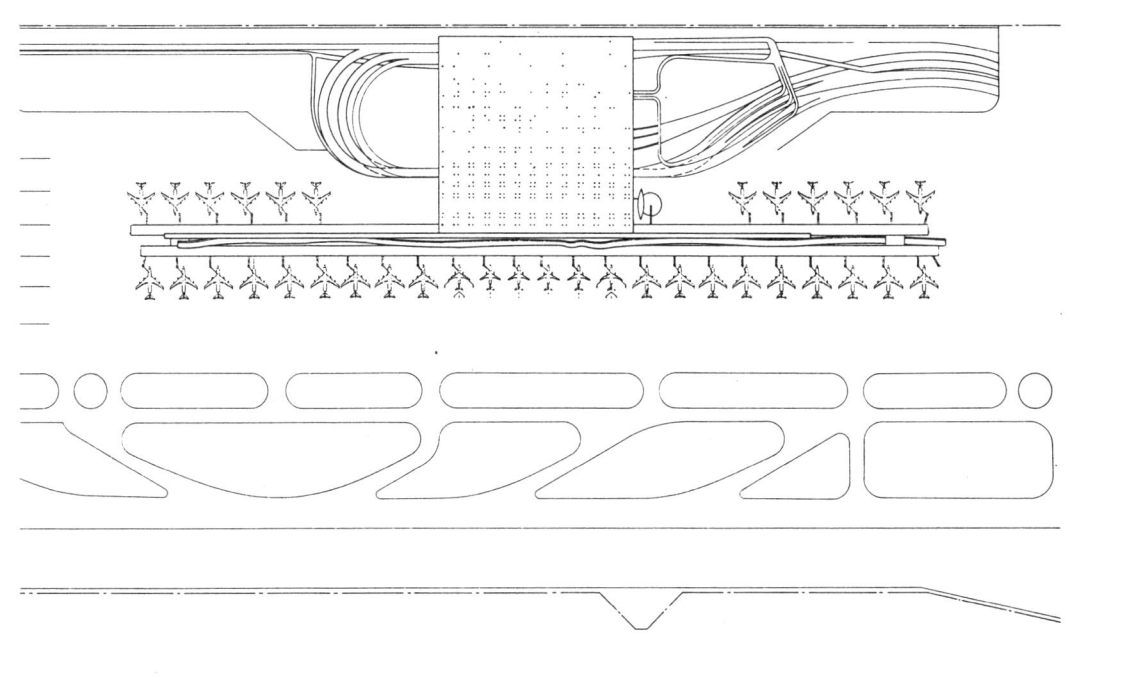

Programs of the future, in which airports are simultaneously amusement arcades, athletic facilities, cinemas, hotels, business centers

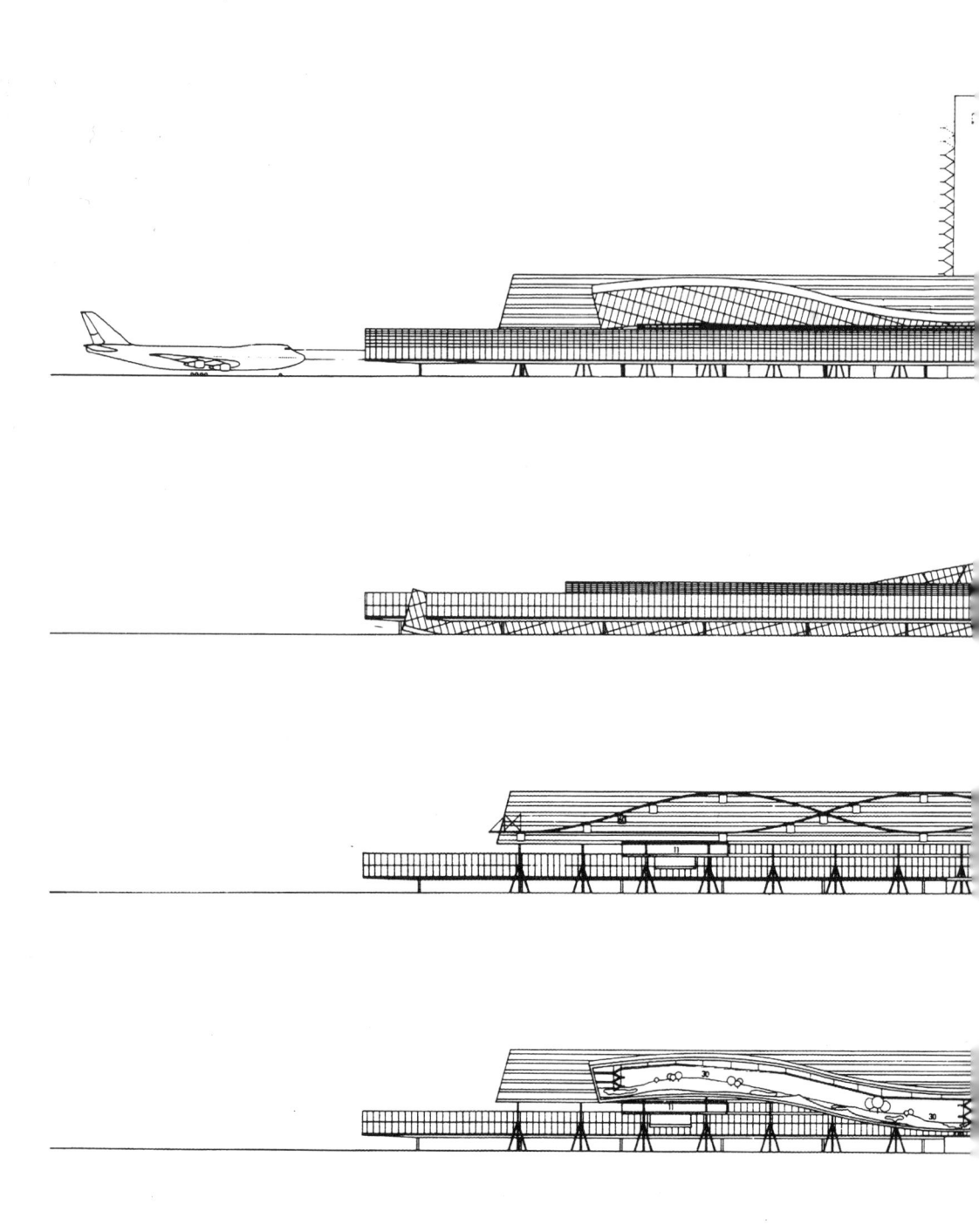

34. Swimming pool 43. Changing rooms 31. Tennis courts 47. Stage 48. Backstage 45. Theater

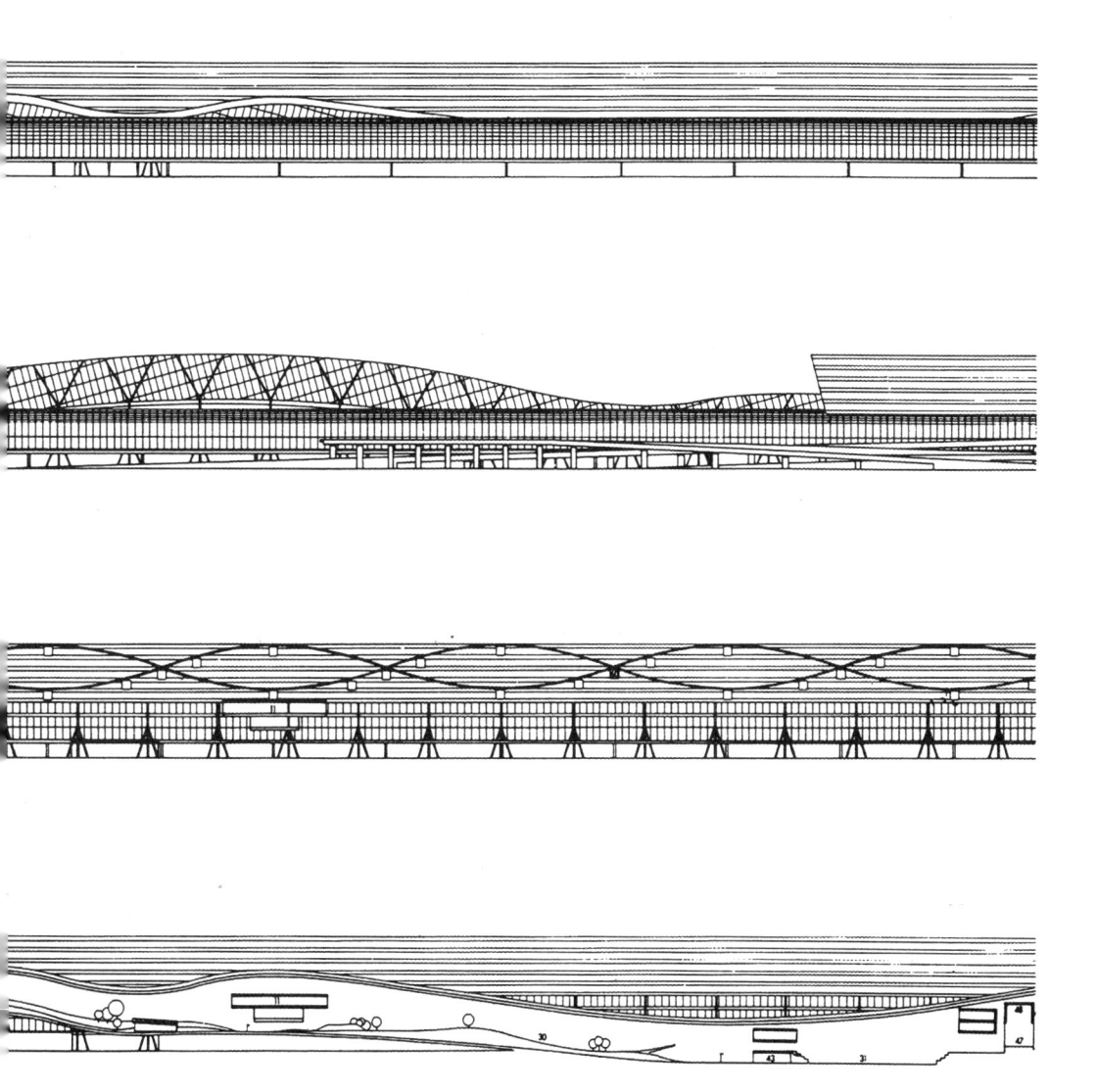

50. Sleeping capsules 51. Shops 52. Bars 53. Restaurants 49. Cinema 46. Theater lobby 105. Café 9.

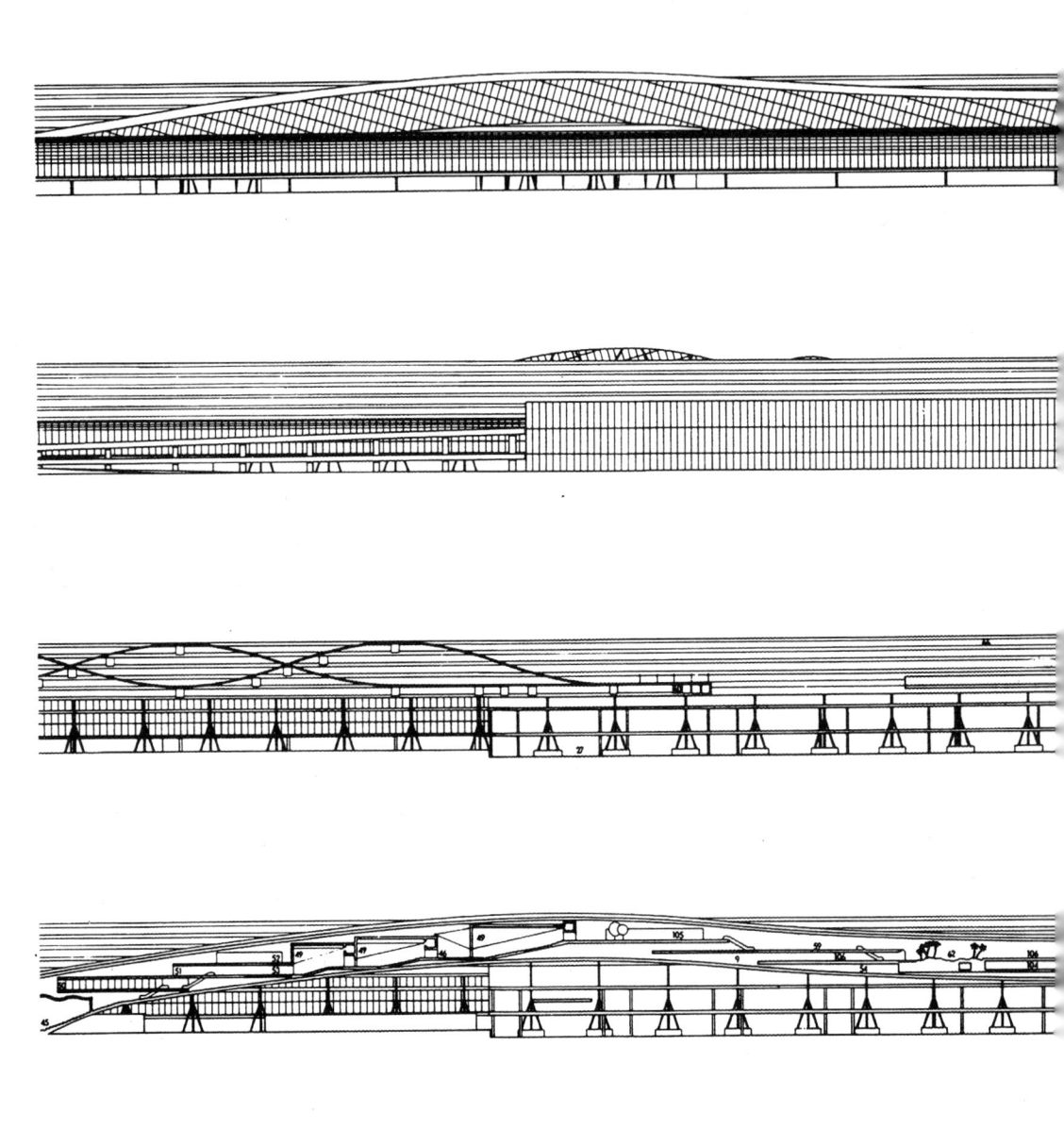

Arrival lobby 59. Departure lounge 106. Restaurant 54. Kitchen 62. Rest area 104. Bar 103. Shops 42.

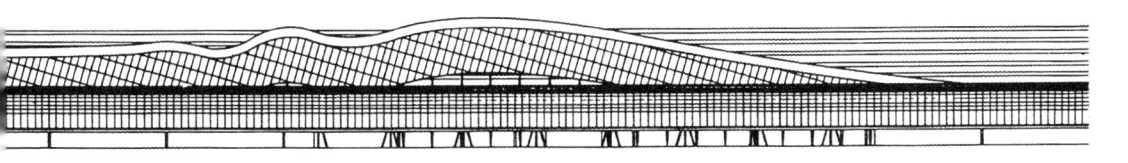

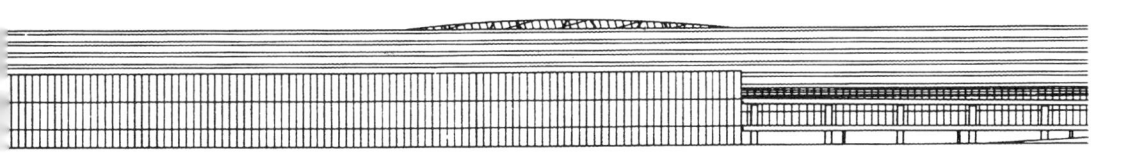

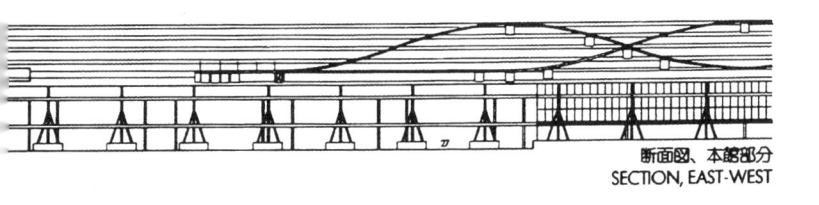

断面図、本館部分
SECTION, EAST-WEST

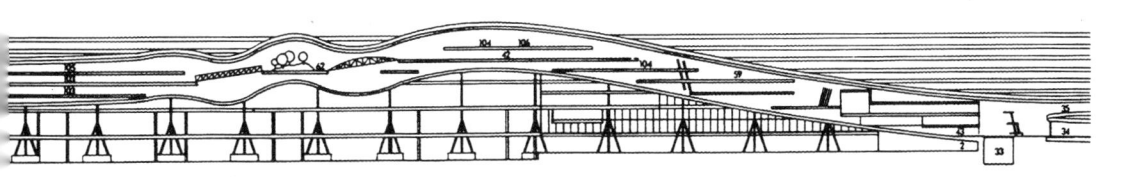

Bowling alley 43. Changing rooms 2. Offices 33. Diving pool 34. Swimming pool 35. Jogging track 38.

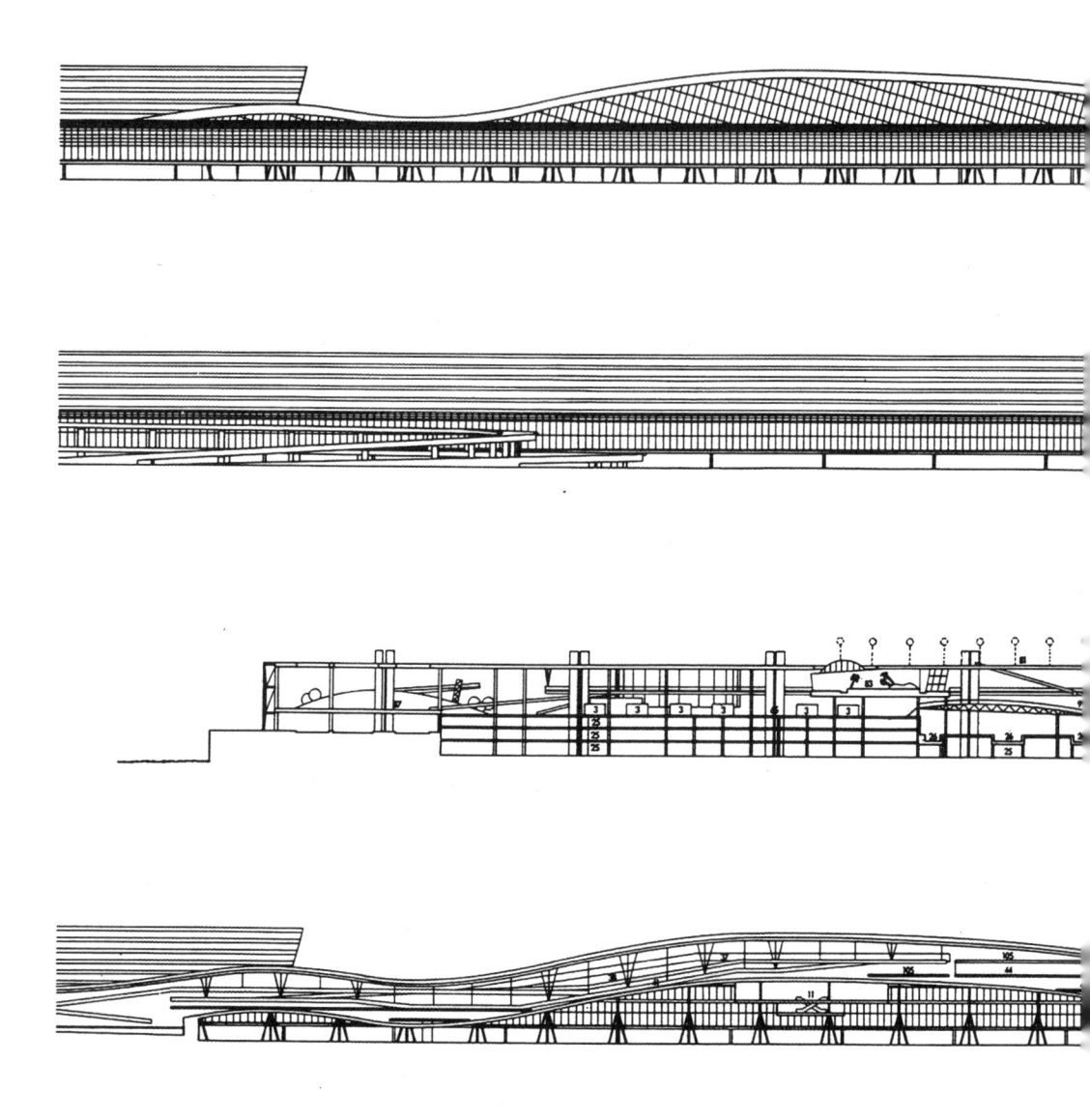

Archery range 41. Skateboarding ramp 37. Rifle range 105. Café 58. Planetarium 19. Garden 34.

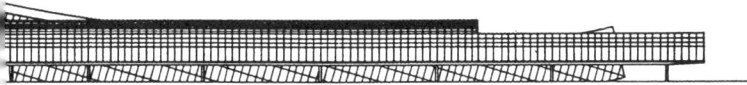

立面図、エアサイド側
ELEVATION, AIRSIDE

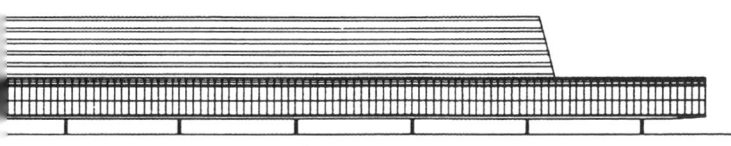

立面図、ランドサイド側
ELEVATION, LANDSIDE

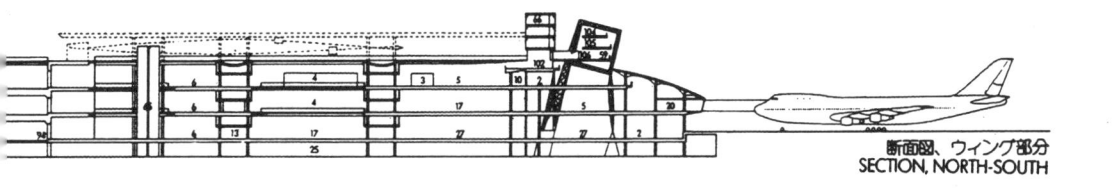

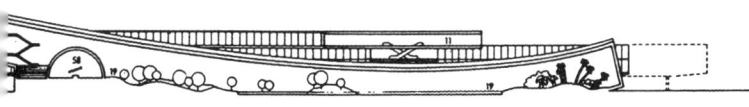

断面図、ウィング部分
SECTION, NORTH-SOUTH

断面図、本館部分
SECTION, EAST-WEST

Swimming pool 43. Changing rooms 31. Tennis courts 47. Stage 48. Backstage 45. Theater 50. Sleeping

A linear but undecidable curve

KANSAI

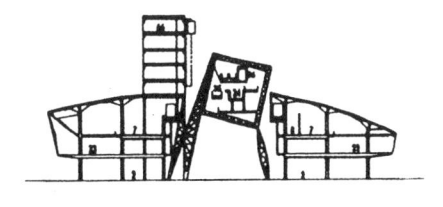

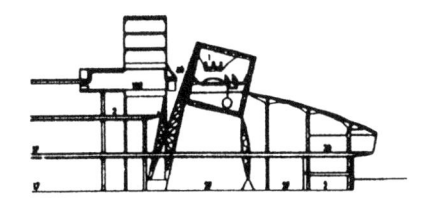

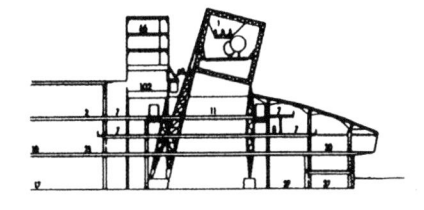

125

Emergence of a disparate multiplicity

Several heterogeneous lines flowing in the same direction

KANSAI

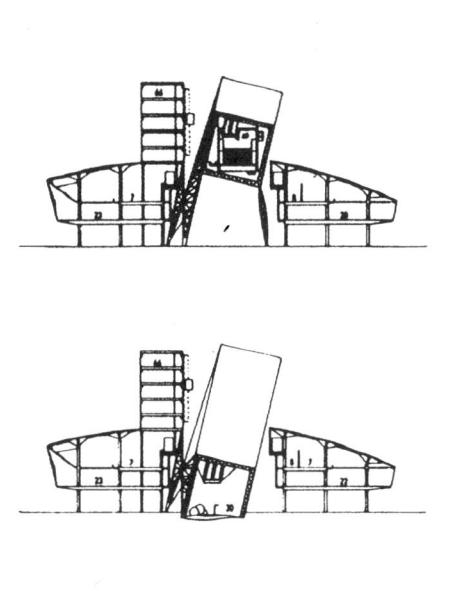

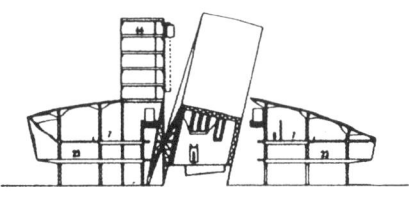

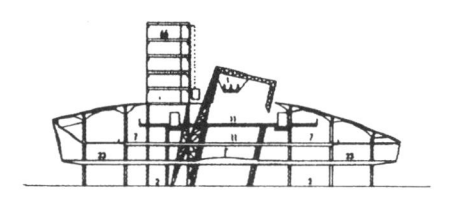

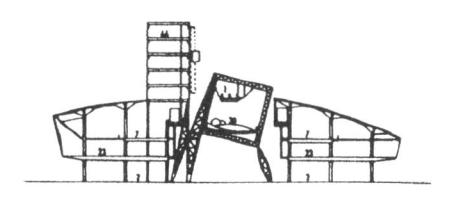

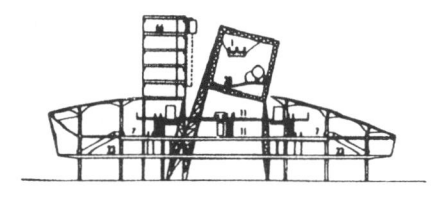

127

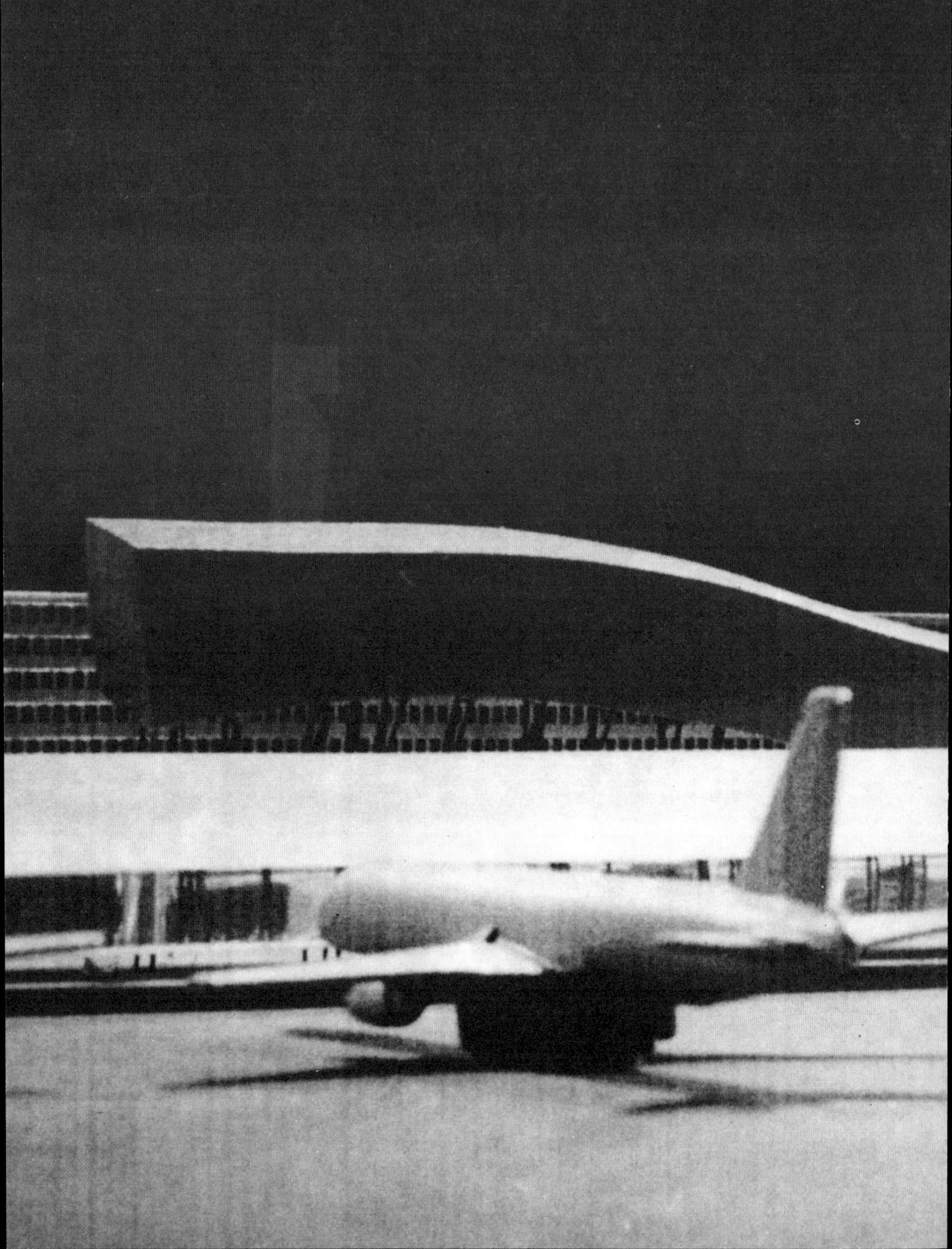

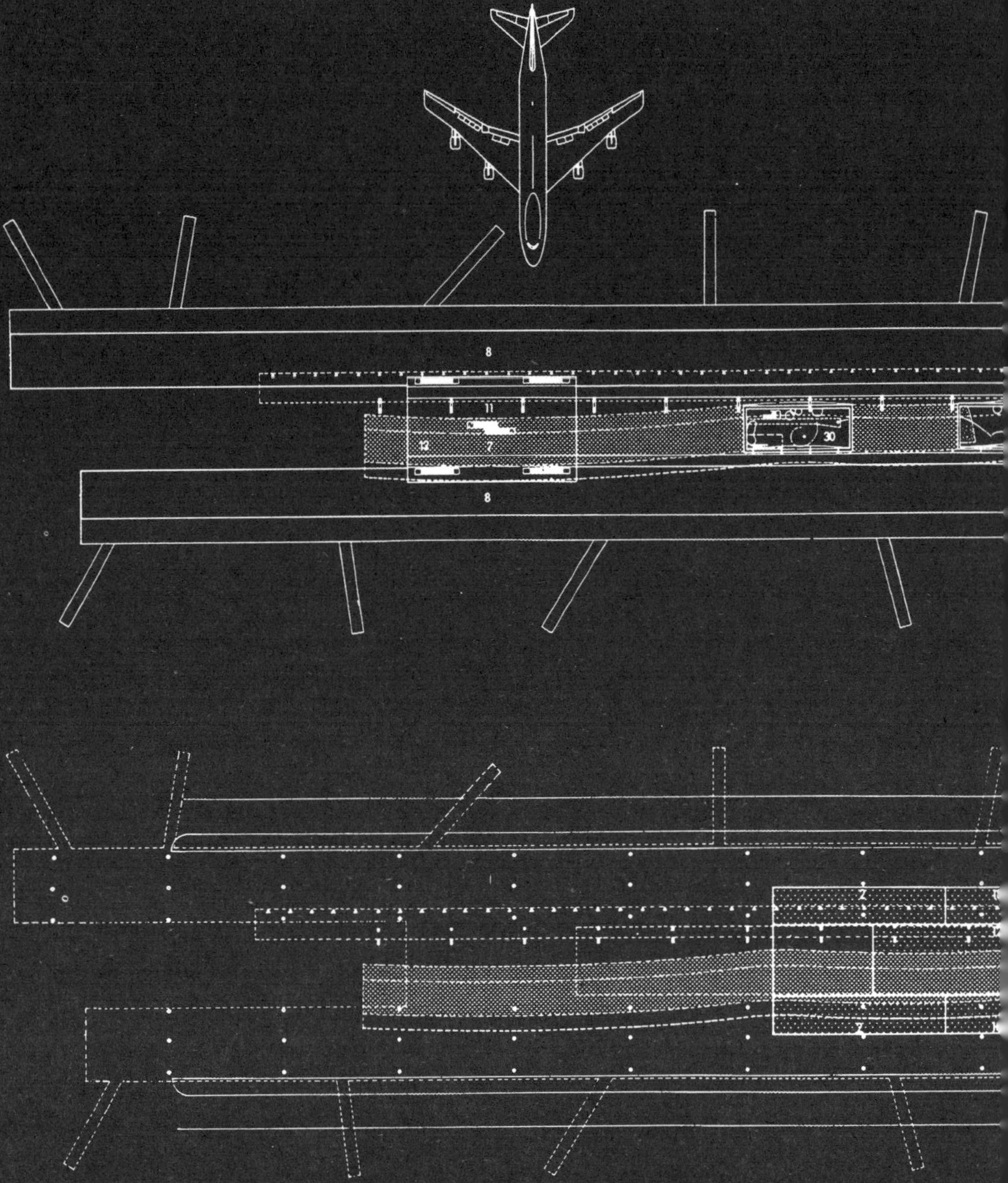
8
11
13
7
30
8

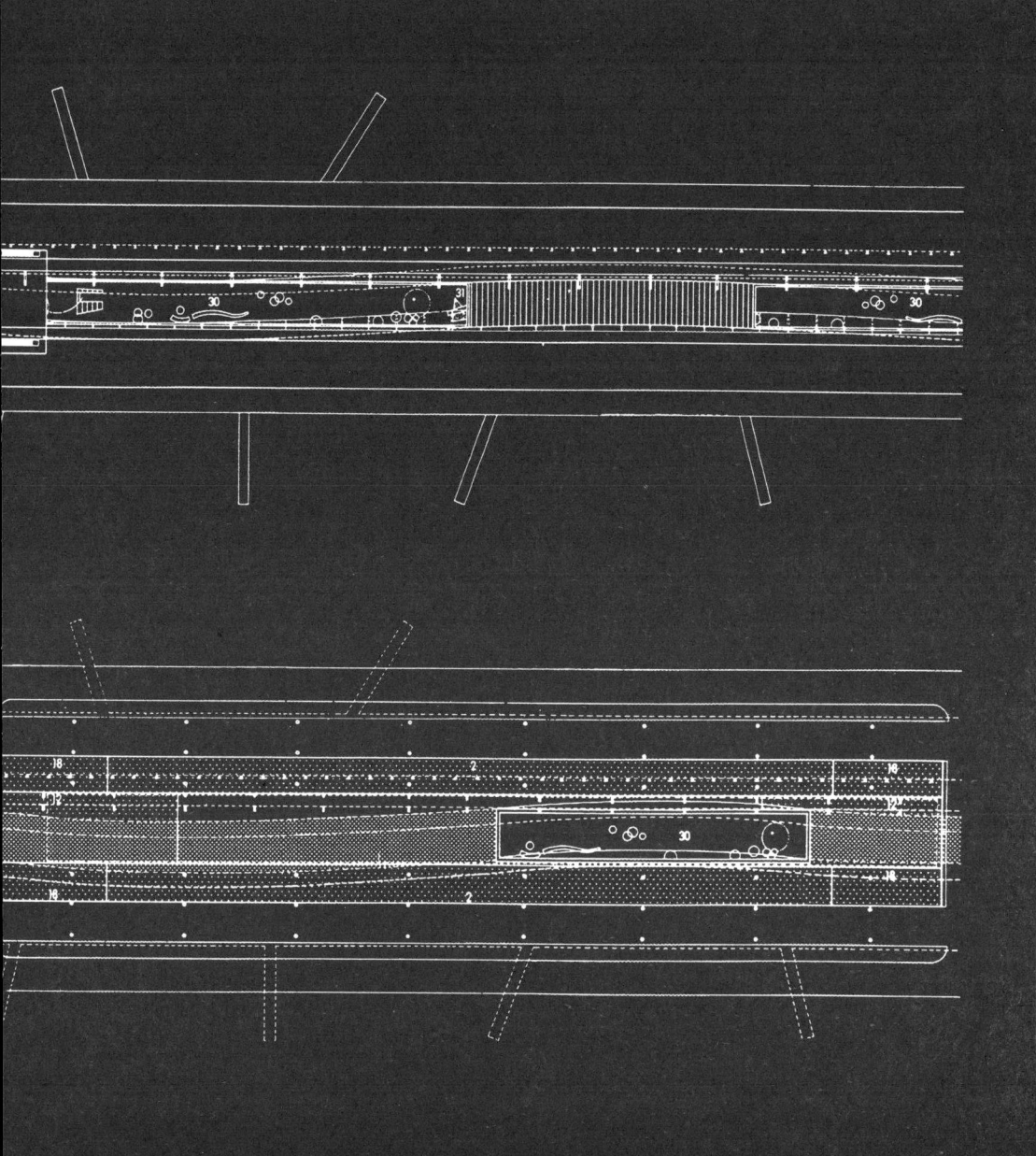

Level 3

Level 1

A continuous yet differentiated plan: the lines and their in-between

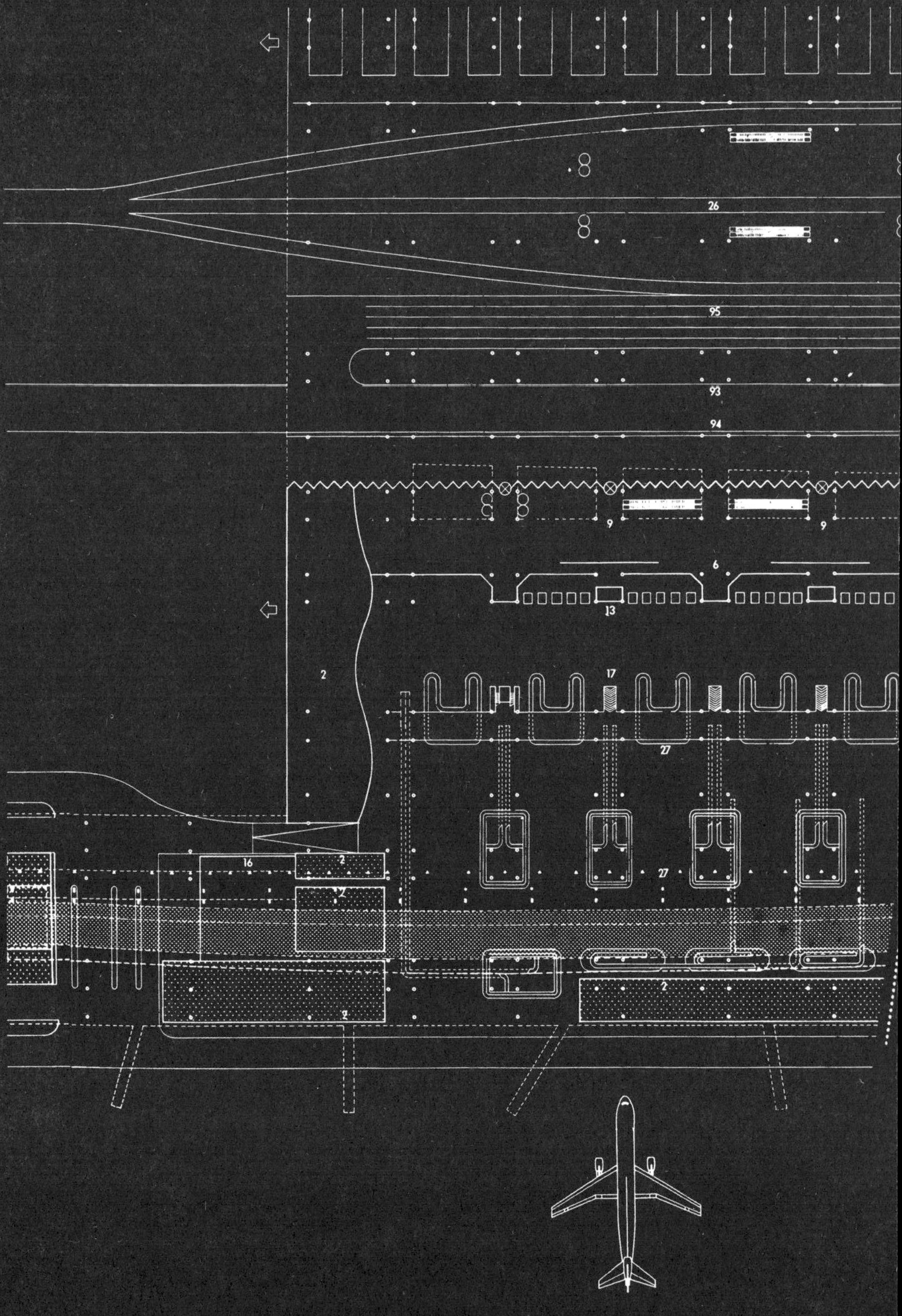
26
95
93
94
9
9
6
13
2
17
27
16
2
2
27
2
2

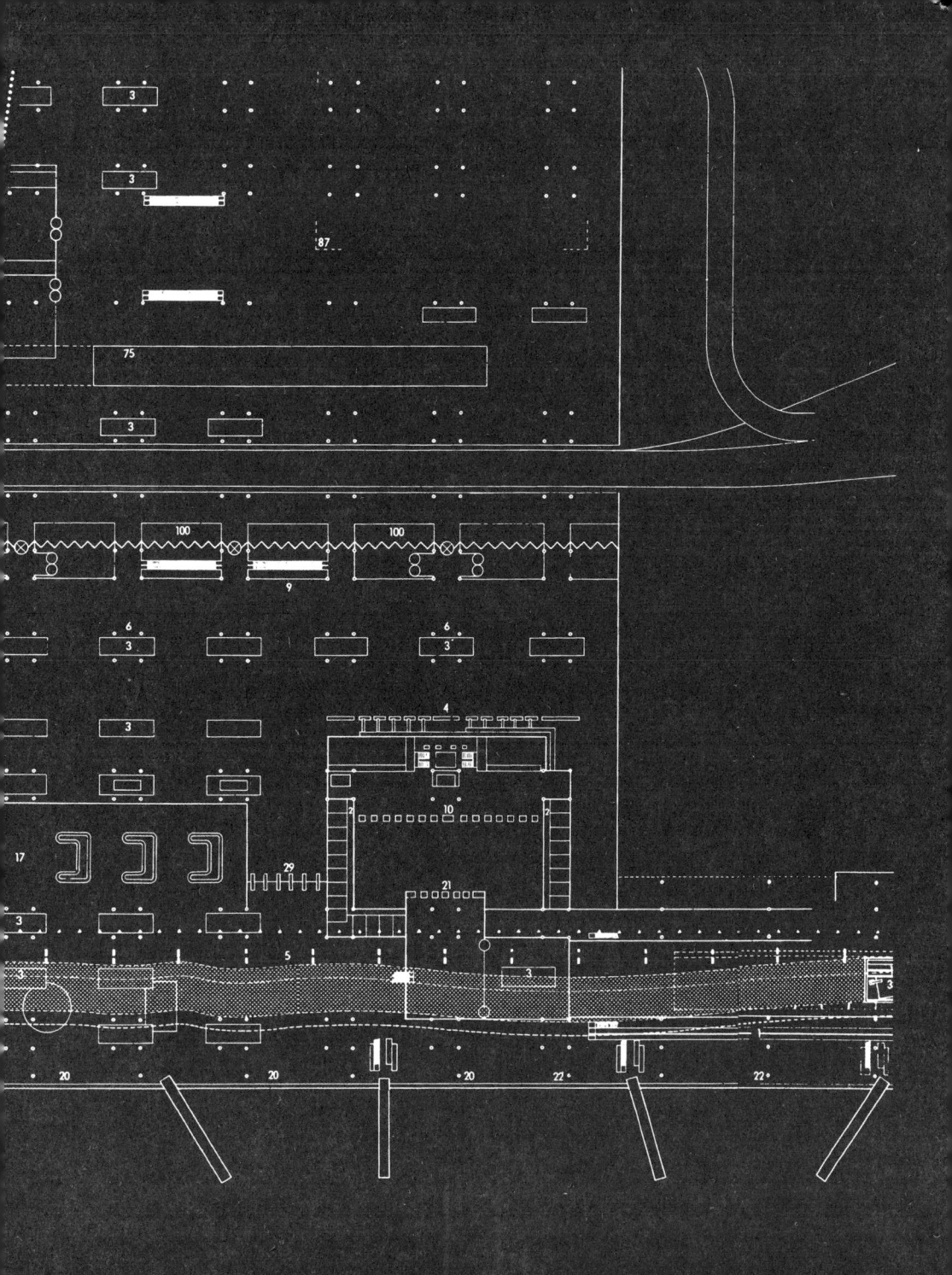

Disparate formal and programmatic elements with a neutral enclosure:
an avoidance of composition

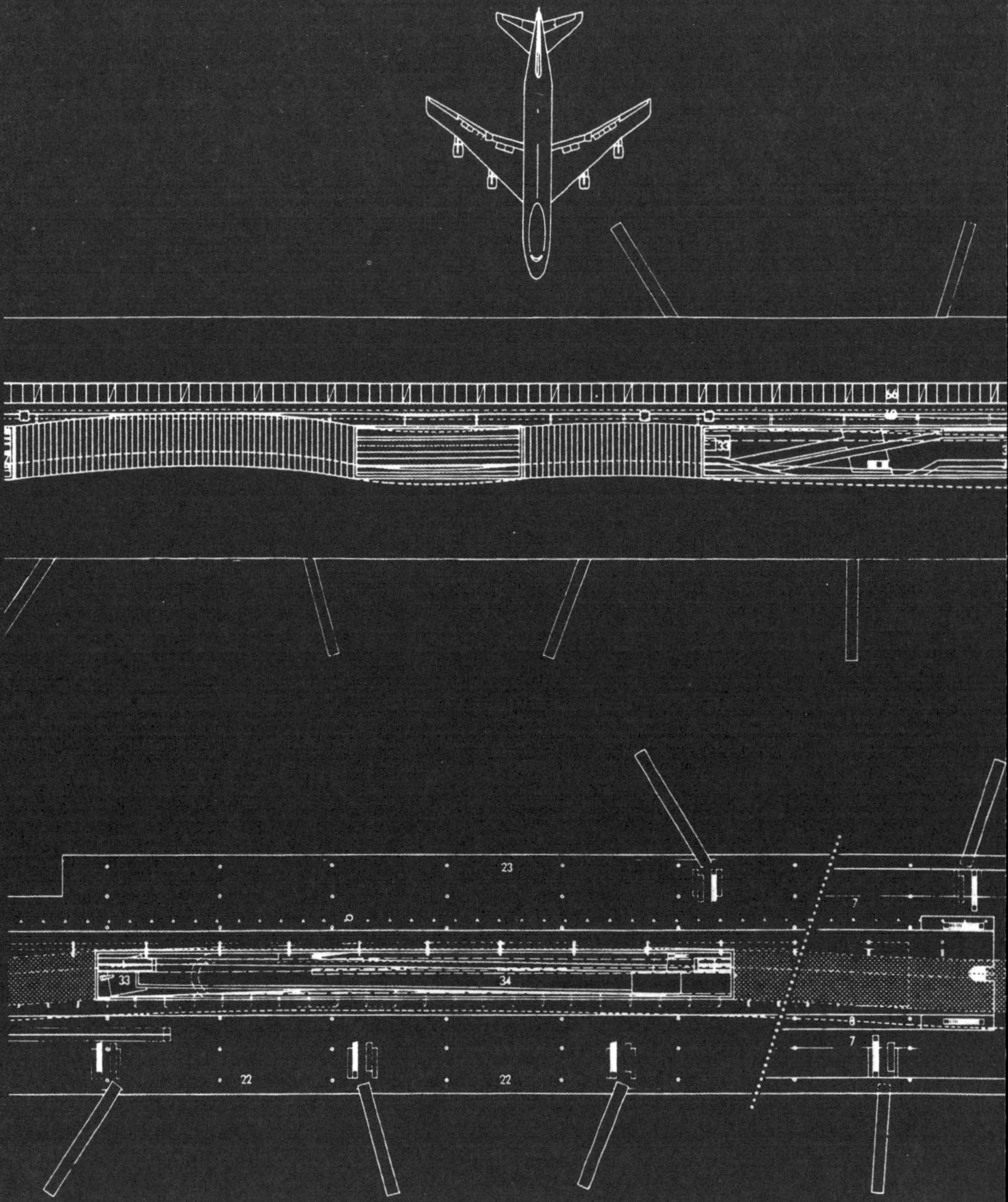
33
23
7
33
34
8
7
22
22

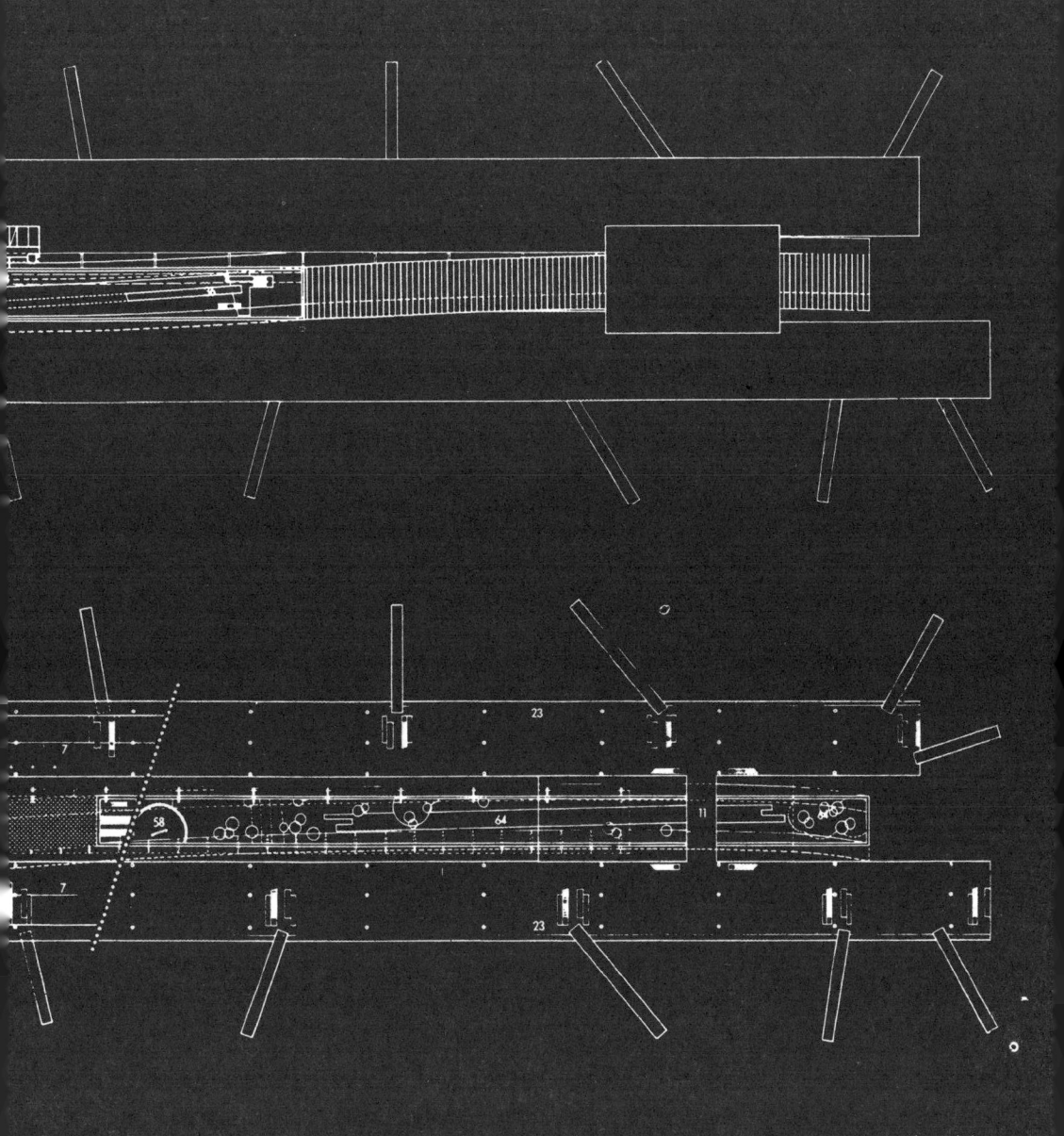

Level 4

Level 2

A fluid, incomplete, indefinite frame for events

Flexible, ever-expanding programs in **space**

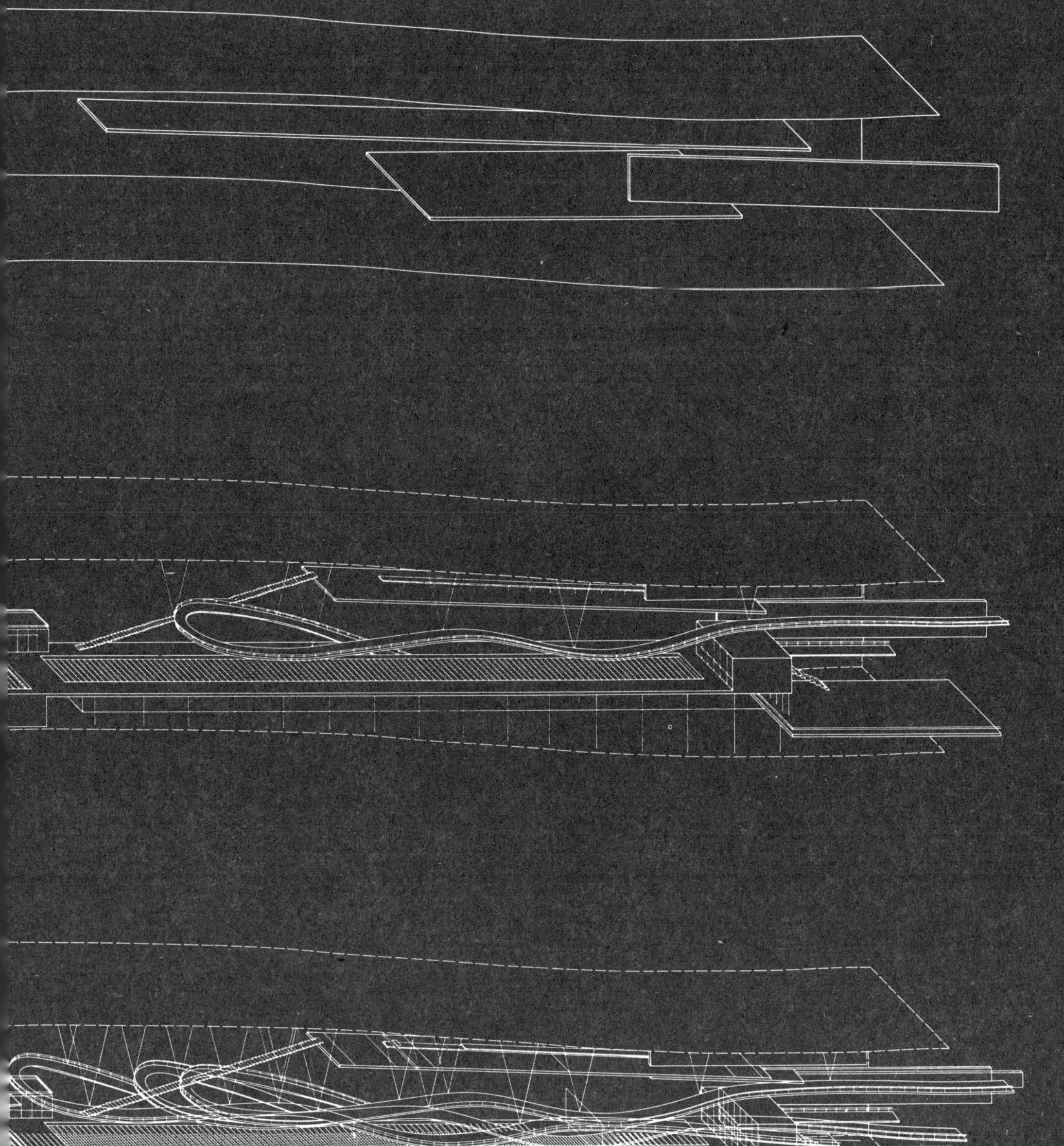

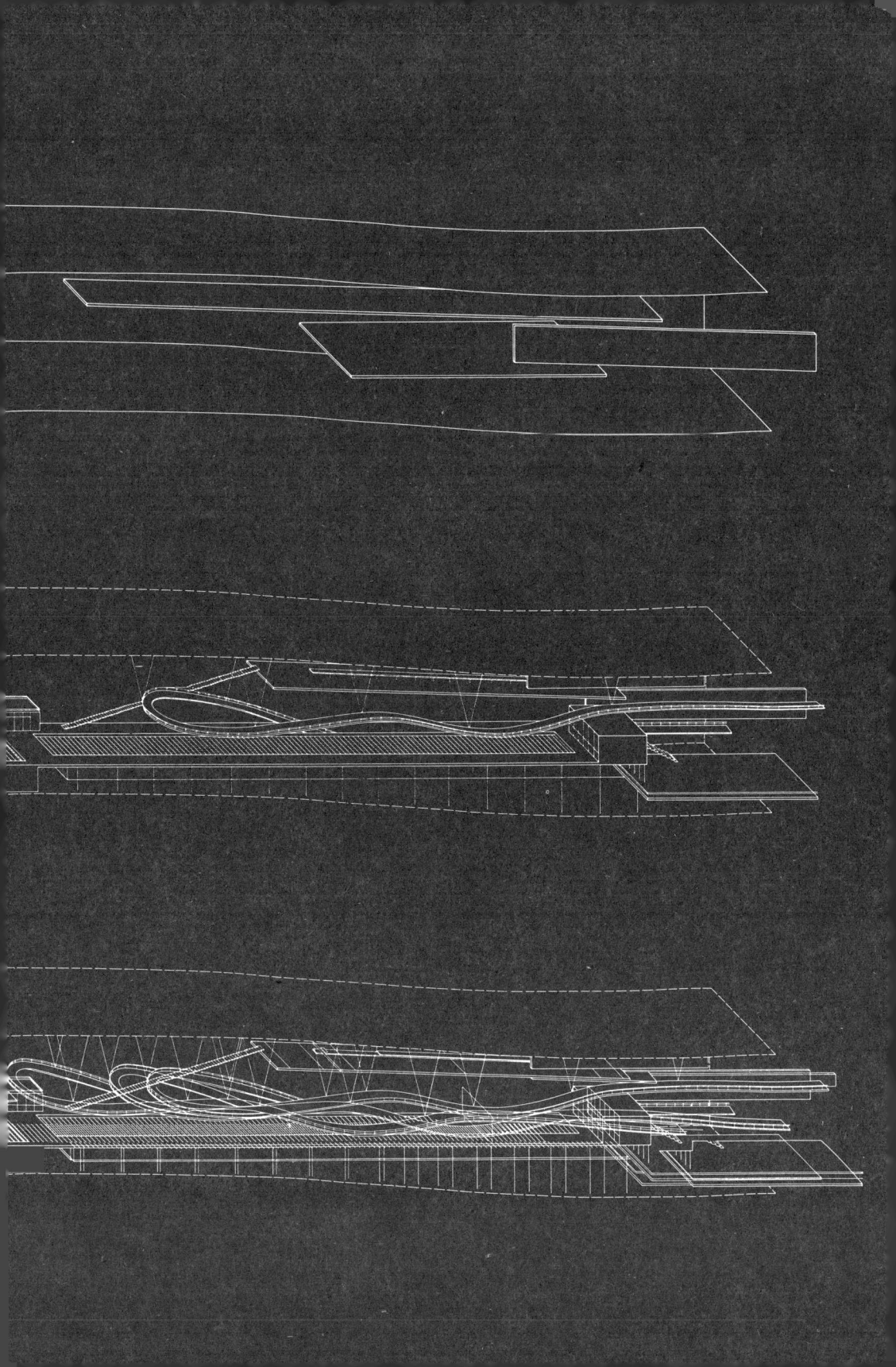

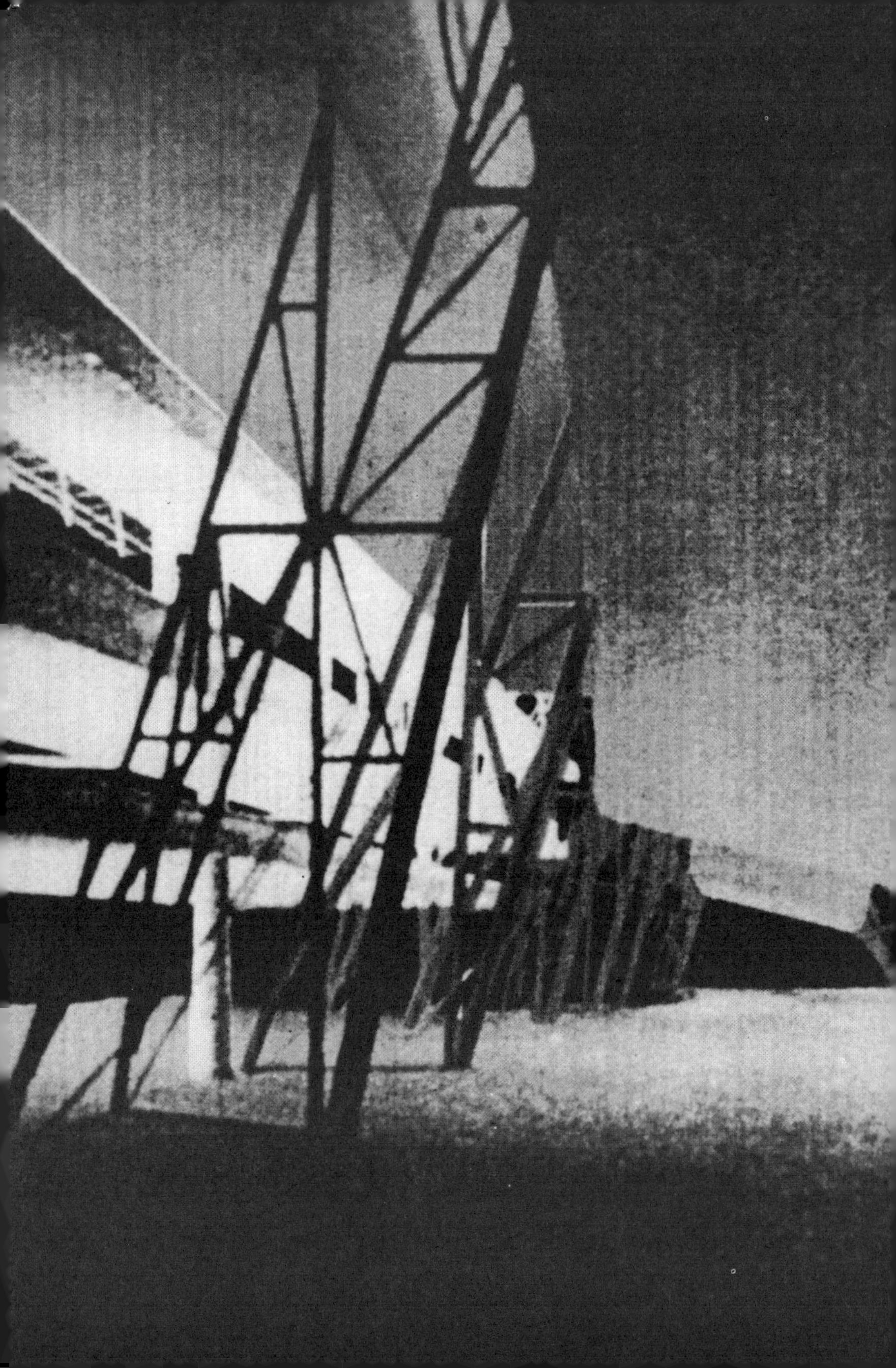

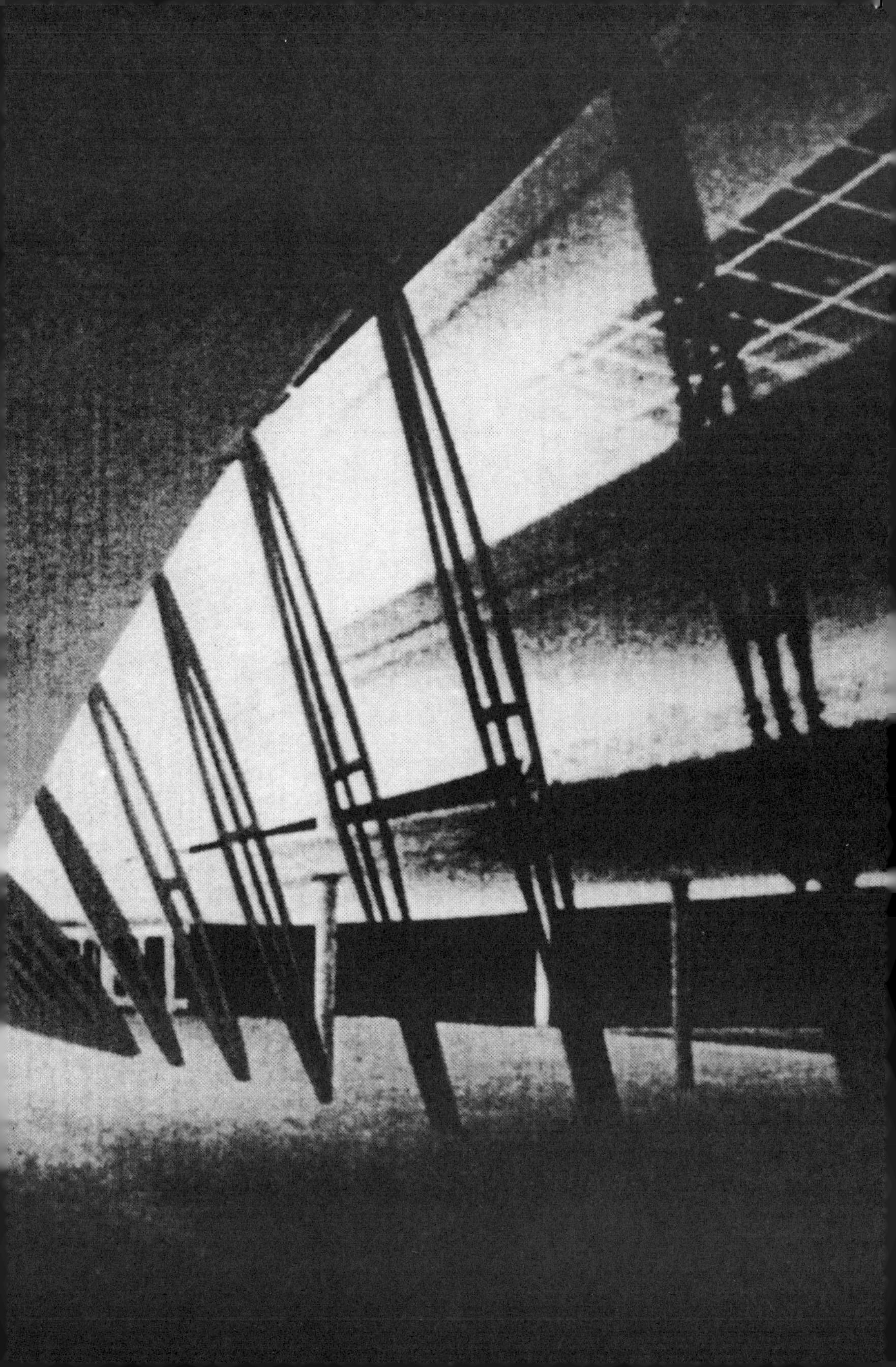

The construction of events: Sine-Mover, suspended pool, bar, art galleries

ヒンジ接合ライン方向
HINGELINE DIRECTION

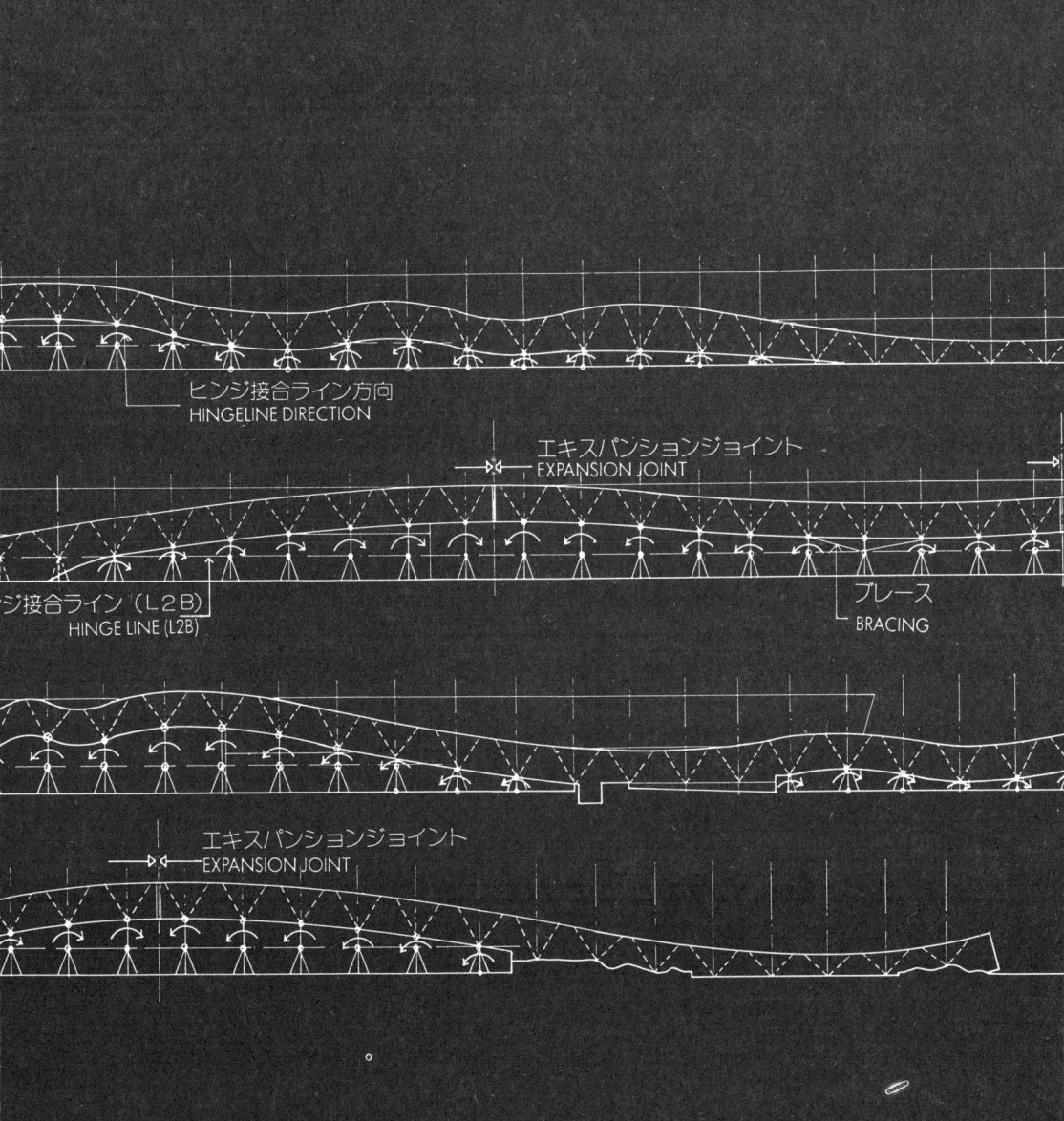

エキスパンションジョイント
EXPANSION JOINT

ヒンジ接合ライン（L2B）
HINGE LINE (L2B)

ブレース
BRACING

エキスパンションジョイント
EXPANSION JOINT

Double strip: no graphics, no interior motive; only structural details

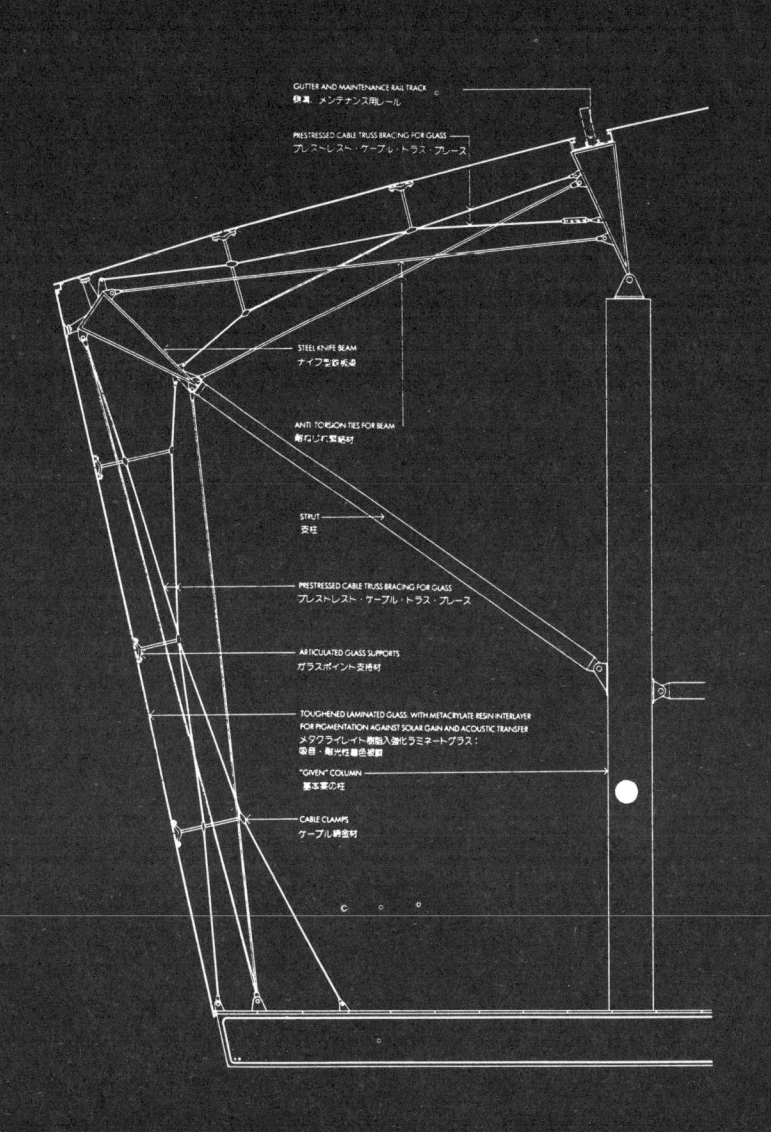
GUTTER AND MAINTENANCE RAIL TRACK
メンテナンス用レール
PRESTRESSED CABLE TRUSS BRACING FOR GLASS
プレストレスト・ケーブル・トラス・ブレース
STEEL KNIFE BEAM
ANTI TORSION TIES FOR BEAM
STRUT
支柱
PRESTRESSED CABLE TRUSS BRACING FOR GLASS
プレストレスト・ケーブル・トラス・ブレース
ARTICULATED GLASS SUPPORTS
ガラスポイント支持材
TOUGHENED LAMINATED GLASS: WITH METACRYLATE RESIN INTERLAYER FOR PIGMENTATION AGAINST SOLAR GAIN AND ACOUSTIC TRANSFER
メタクライレイト樹脂入強化ラミネートグラス：
吸音・耐光性着色被膜
"GIVEN" COLUMN
基本案の柱
CABLE CLAMPS

Gap, seam or in-between

KANSAI
145

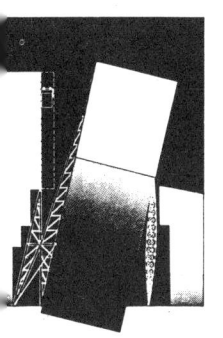

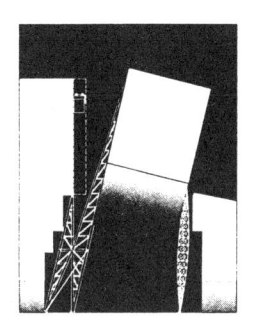

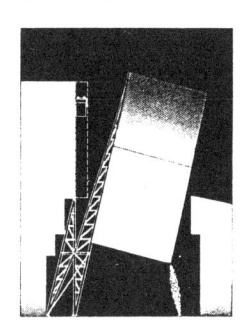

Random sections through the wave

Pulsating space under the wave: servicing the airport-city

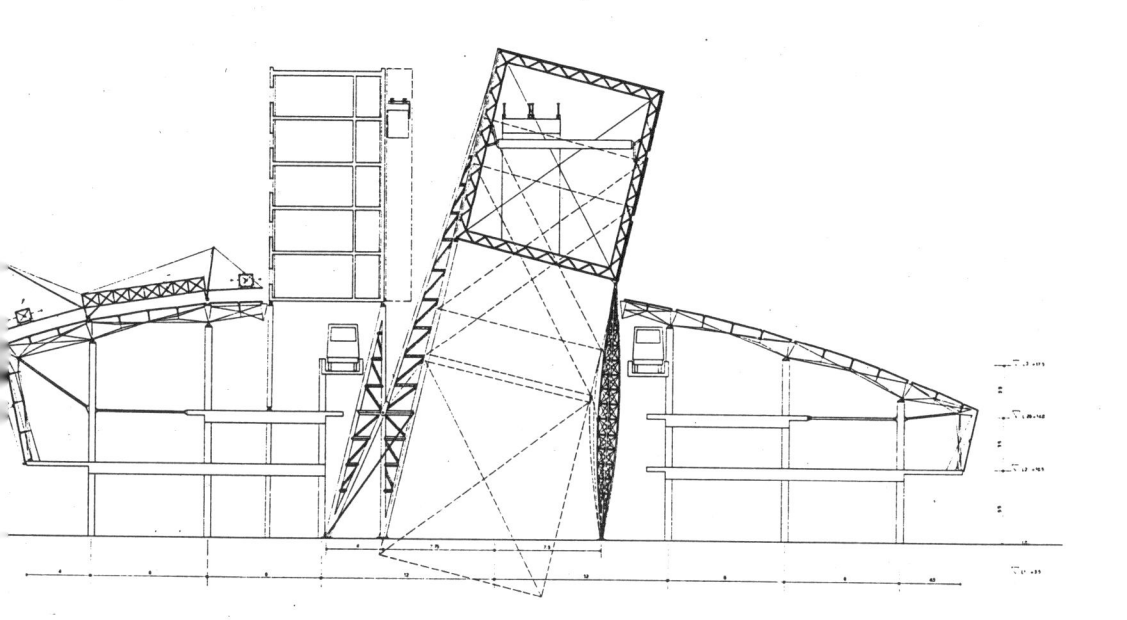

Double strip, slab and wave: the structural and geometric system is totally independent of the functions of the building

Wave to the infinite

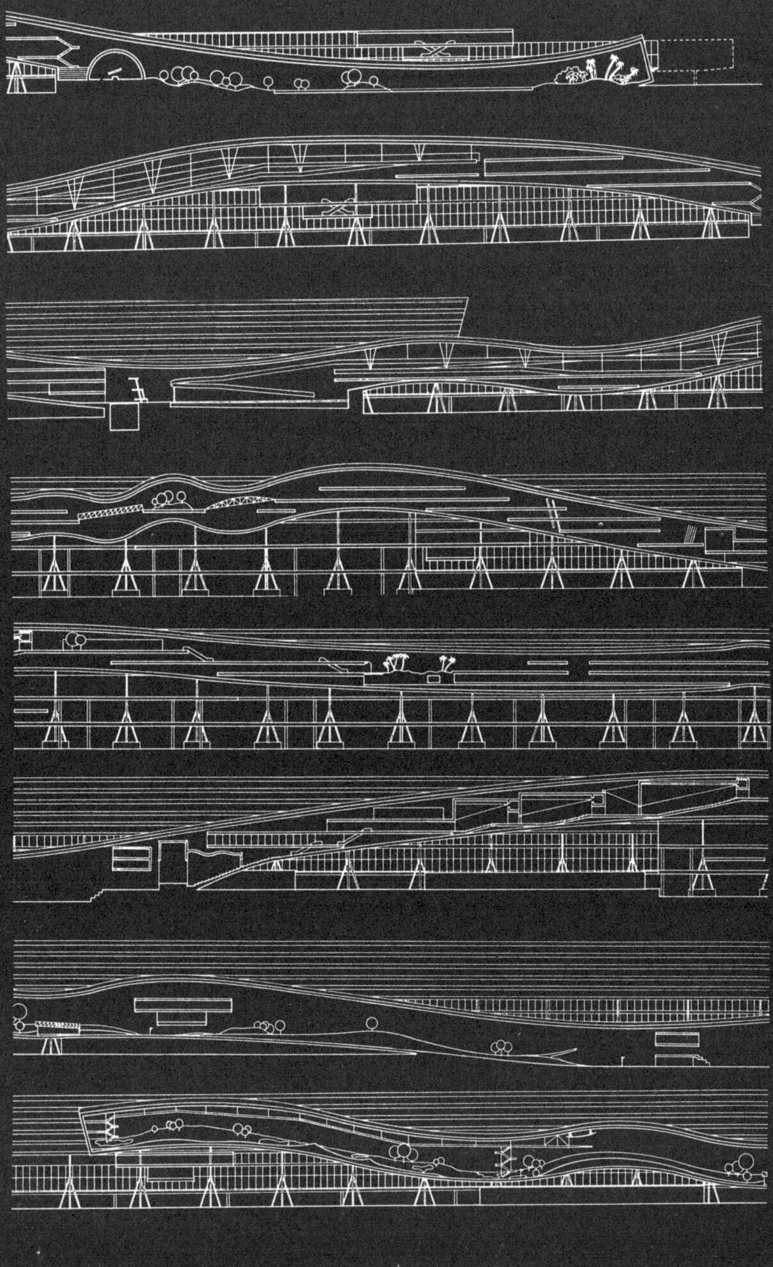

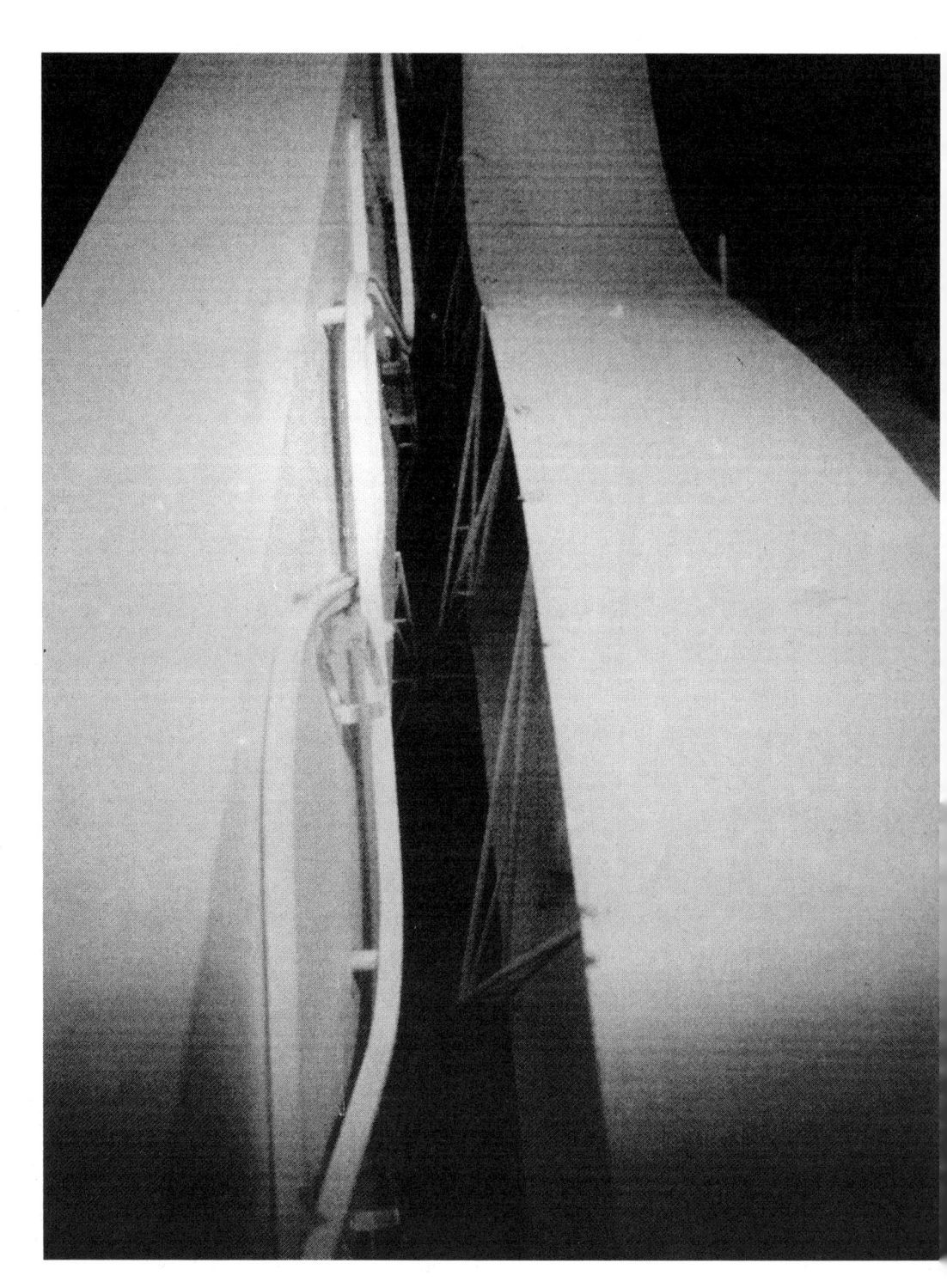

Seam between slab and wave

KANSAI
151

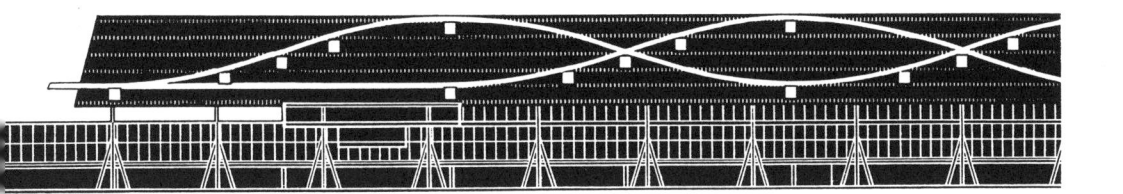

Sine-Mover

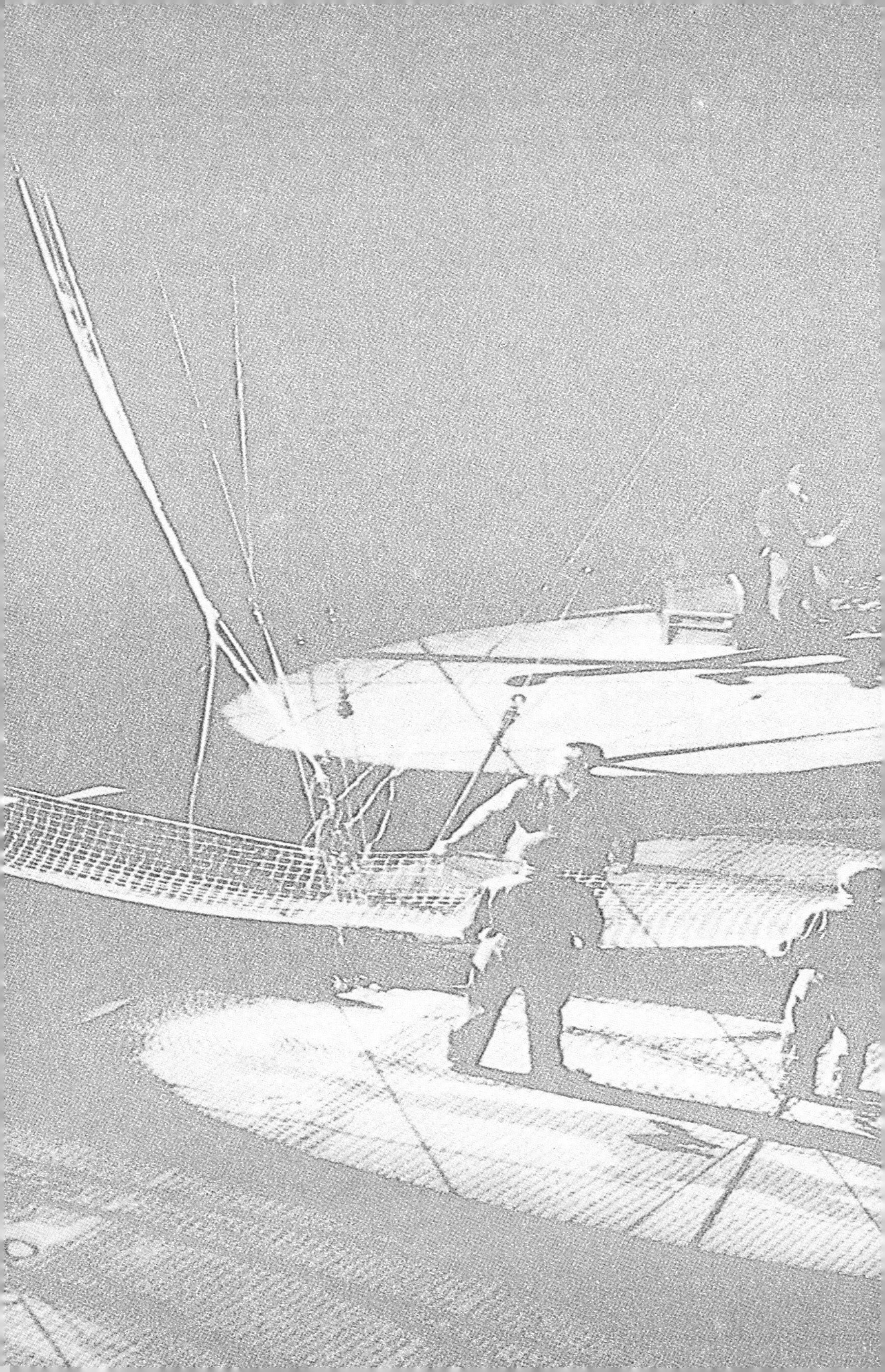

Lausanne, Bridge-City, 1988-

Typological Displacements—Crossprogramming

Crossprogramming: Using a given spatial configuration for a program not intended for it, that is, using a church building for bowling. Similar to typological displacement: a town hall inside the spatial configuration of a prison or a museum inside a car park structure. Reference: crossdressing.

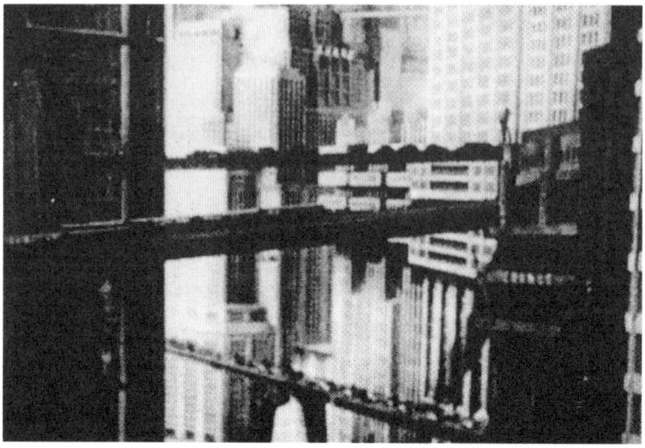

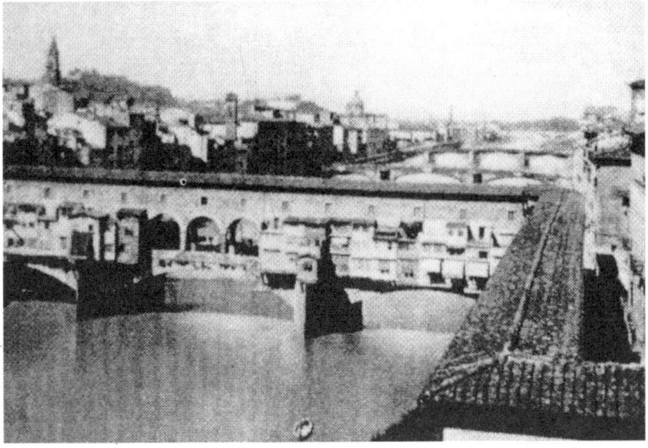

How to assert the character of a city at the very point where it negates itself?
How to reconcile the rugged and picturesque topography of Lausanne, Switzerland with the American-style grid at the bottom of the valley?
How to transform an obsolete industrial site into a live quarter at the very center of the city?
How to reinforce the "unconscious" modernity of this city where, as in the film *Metropolis*, the entrances to the buildings in Place Saint-François are on the sixth floor, while their exits are on the ground floor in the Rue Centrale?

Metropolis
Lausanne's topography has transformed the relation of streets to buildings, indeed the whole notion of urban space. In some parts of the city, streets are suspended and buildings buried in the ground. Rooftops act as ground floors while the *piano nobile* can be found on any level. Buildings function as vertical passageways and bridges as multistory crossings.

The practical irrelevance of a consistent datum plane has also transformed the very concept of urbanism in this city. Moreover, the no-man's-land of obsolete industry that forms a ubiquitous buffer at the periphery of the late-twentieth-century city occurs, instead, in the very center of Lausanne, in the lowlands of the Flon Valley. This unusual condition allows for the implementation of the most contemporary activities in the very heart of the city.

Programmatic and spatial transformation is the basis of our intervention. Instead of adopting the conservative strategy of concentrating only on the lower level of the valley, pretending to preserve the neighborhood's soul while in reality only preserving its warehouses, or of treating it as a delimited sector in need of *ex nihilo* rehabilitation, we took advantage of Lausanne's existing bridge typologies by extending them radically into the project area.

The Bridges
The scheme's primary spatial elements are then the inhabited bridges. As functional supports, the four new structures augment the existing system of bridges and create a new density of spatial relationships and uses. Along the valley's north-south axis, the inhabited bridge-cities use the program to link two parts of the city in conflict in both scale and character.

The inhabited bridges are both horizontal and vertical connectors, as their ramps, escalators and elevators link the lower levels of the valley to the upper levels of the historical city. Each bridge accommodates two categories of use: in the core element, public or commercial use, and at the deck level, pedestrian traffic and related uses.

The individual programs applied to each of the four bridges then give each a specific character, allowing the inhabited bridge to function as an urban generator. The concept of the urban generator not only allows new spatial links with the existing city but encourages unpredictable programmatic factors, new urban events that will inevitably appear in coming decades.

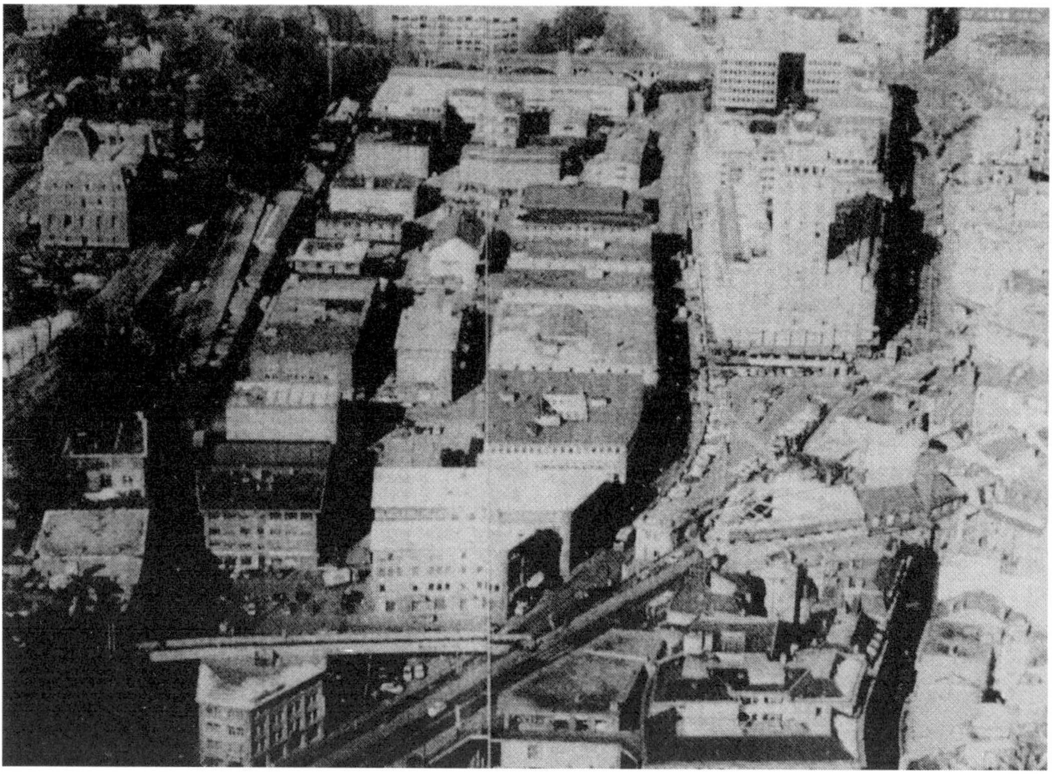

In a valley itself, housing, offices and light industry are situated along the north side, using currently unoccupied, salvageable buildings and adding new construction where necessary. The combination of the inhabited bridge with the new surrounding context enables us to maintain a consistent density, allowing space for a linear park along the south side of the valley. A new network of urban relationships results, without the imbalances of overdensification, supporting an urban center capable of integrating programs of any variety.

The following pages illustrate the various schemes that led to the final plan adopted by the city officials. First, a competition for ideas determined the overall concept. After a second stage of competition, the scheme was articulated into a series of precise planning guidelines for the future growth of the valley.

Studies for two of the bridges were then developed: a feasibility study for a new art center in the southern half of the Pont Montbenon, and the design of the Metropont. Numerous public meetings and media controversies accompanied the project as the resistance of conservationists, claims by a private land-holding company and election strategies added an intricate dimension to a complex process of political approvals.

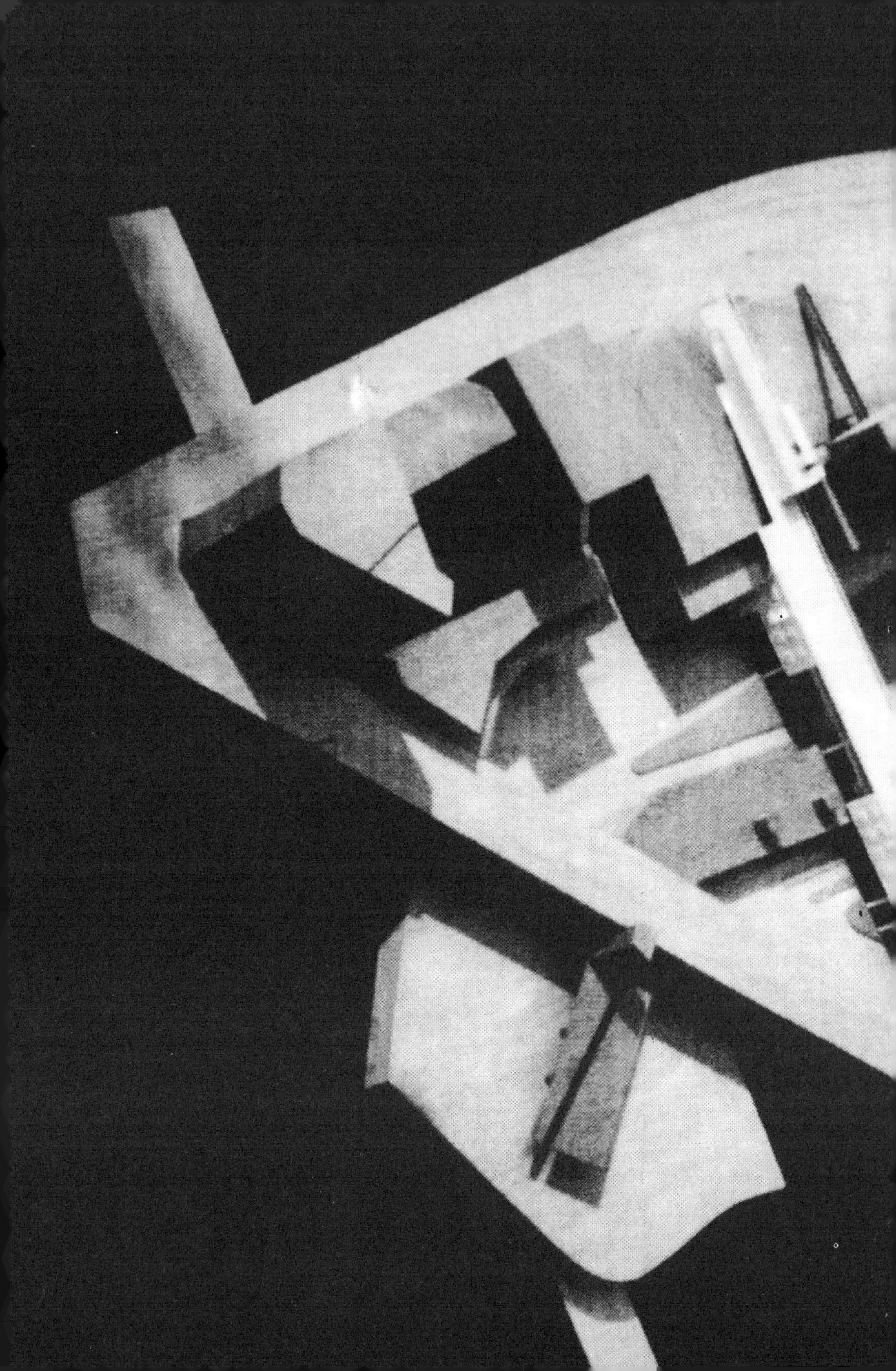

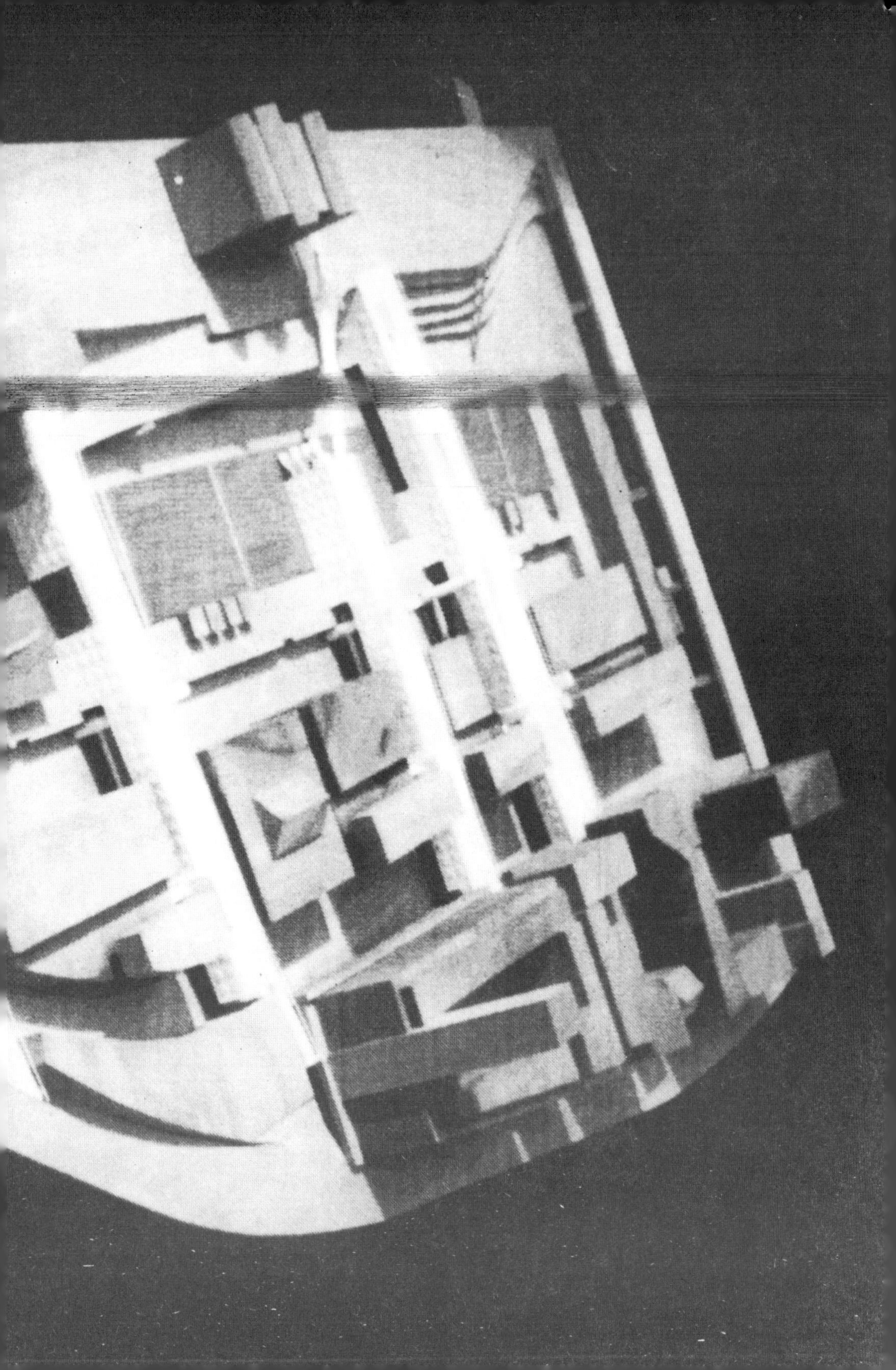

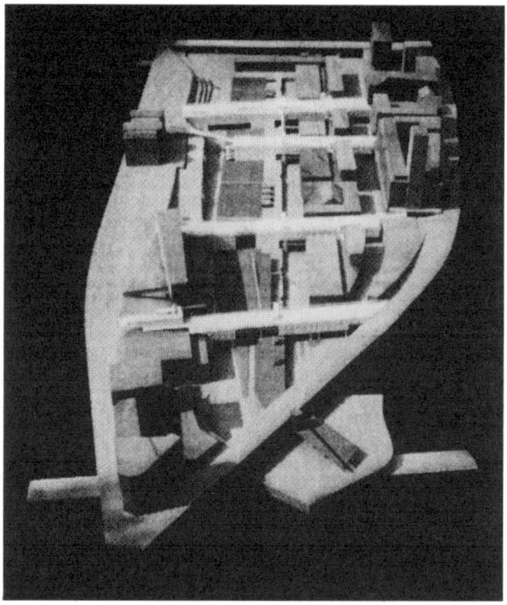

LAUSANNE
163

Multiple and dislocated topographies

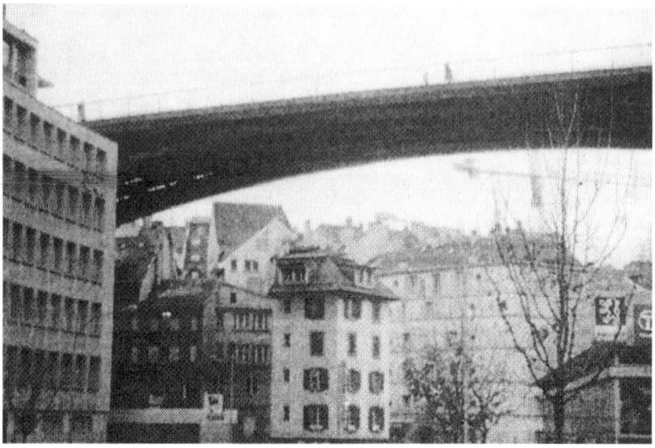

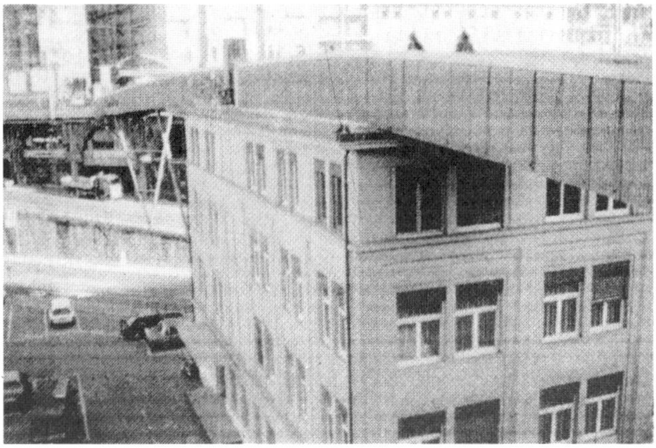

LAUSANNE
165

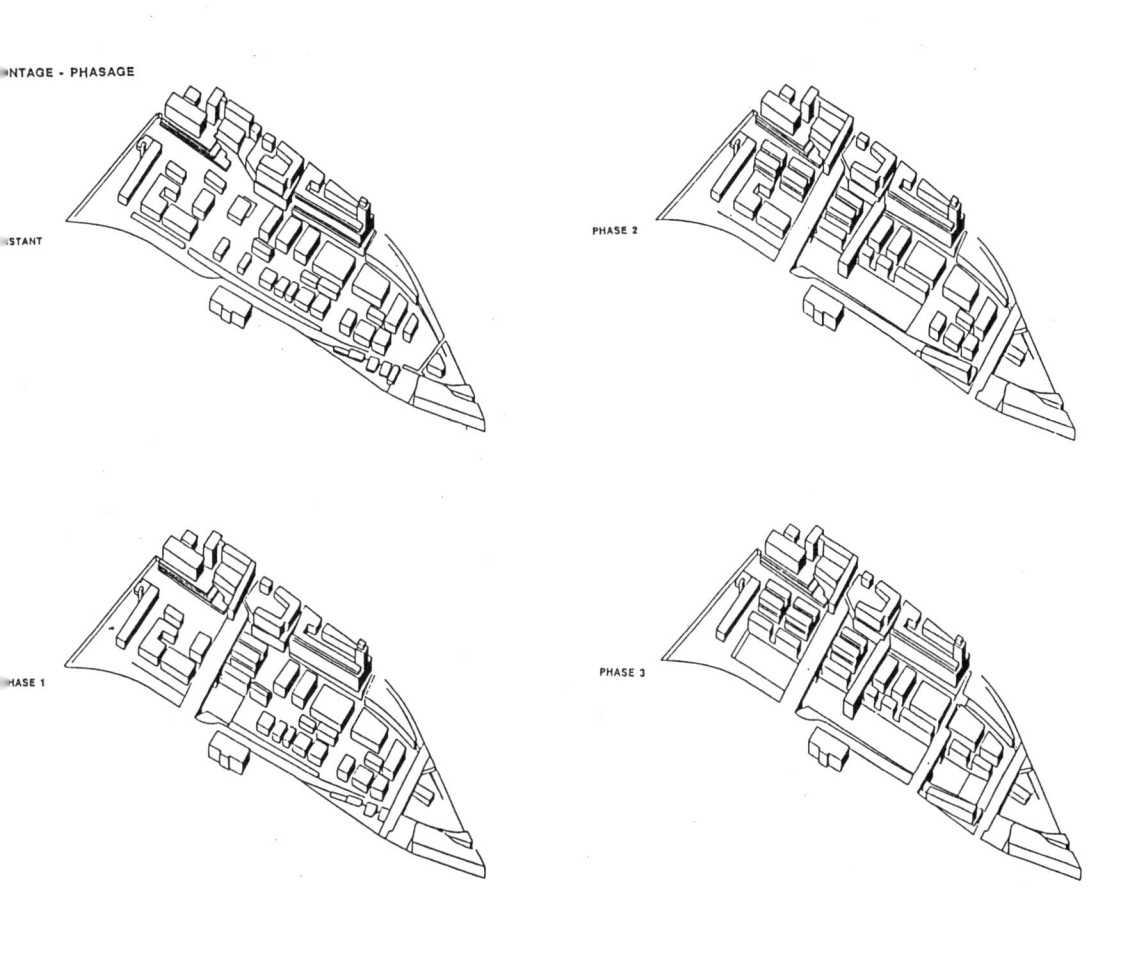

NTAGE - PHASAGE

STANT

PHASE 1

PHASE 2

PHASE 3

Montage-Phasing (first version): programmatic uncertainties

G. PONT DE LA VIGIE

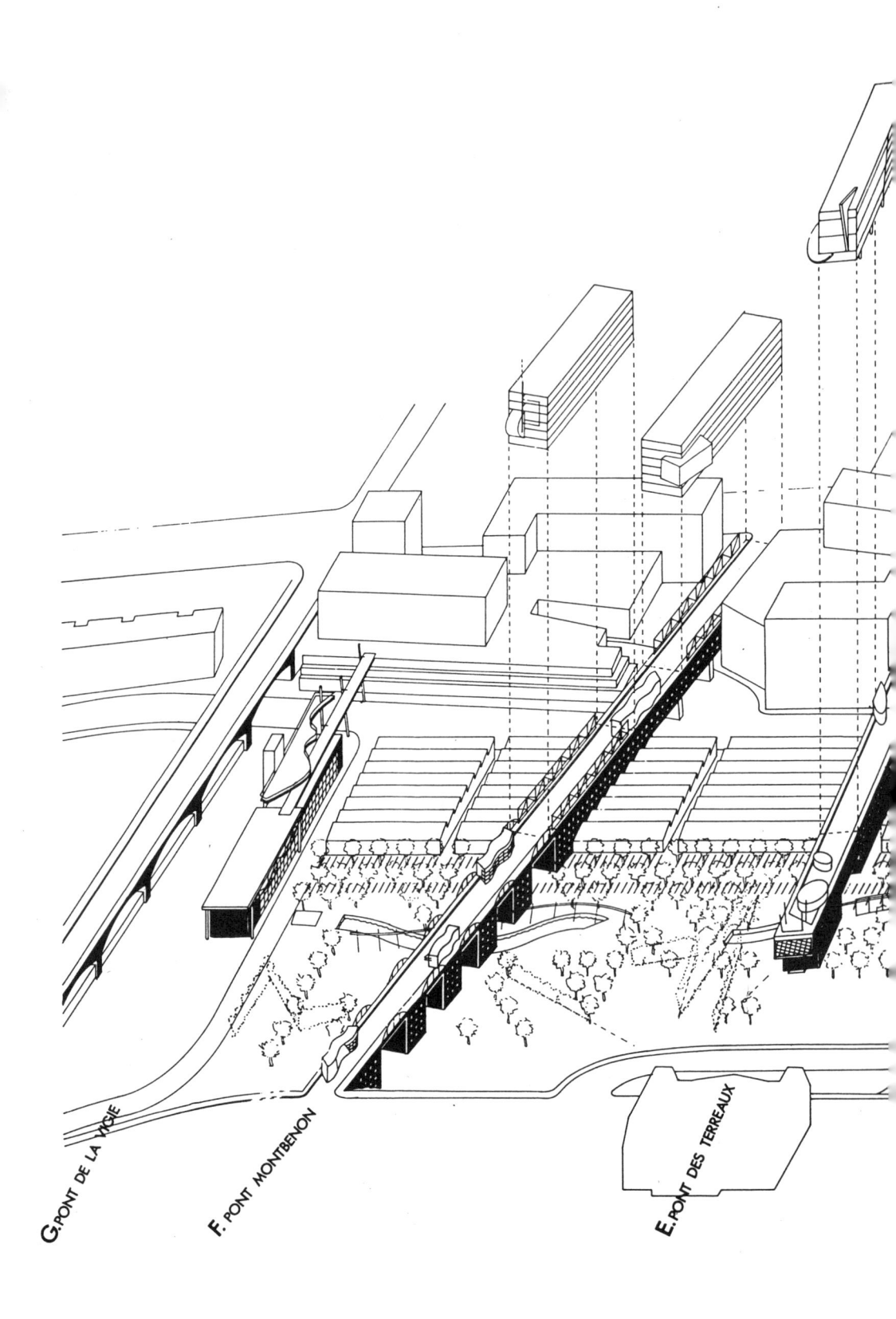

F. PONT MONTBENON

E. PONT DES TERREAUX

LAUSANNE
167

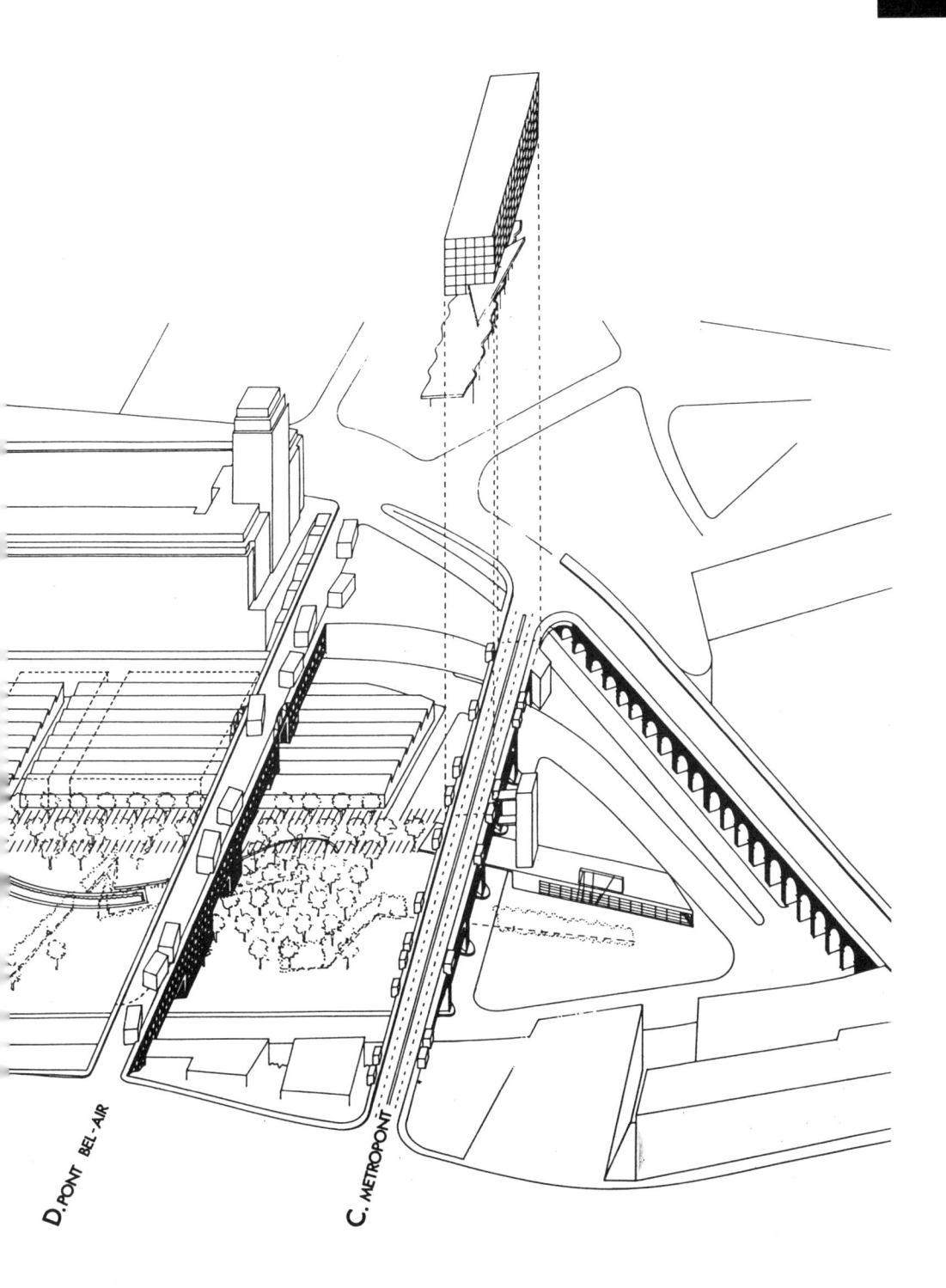

D. PONT BEL-AIR

C. METROPONT

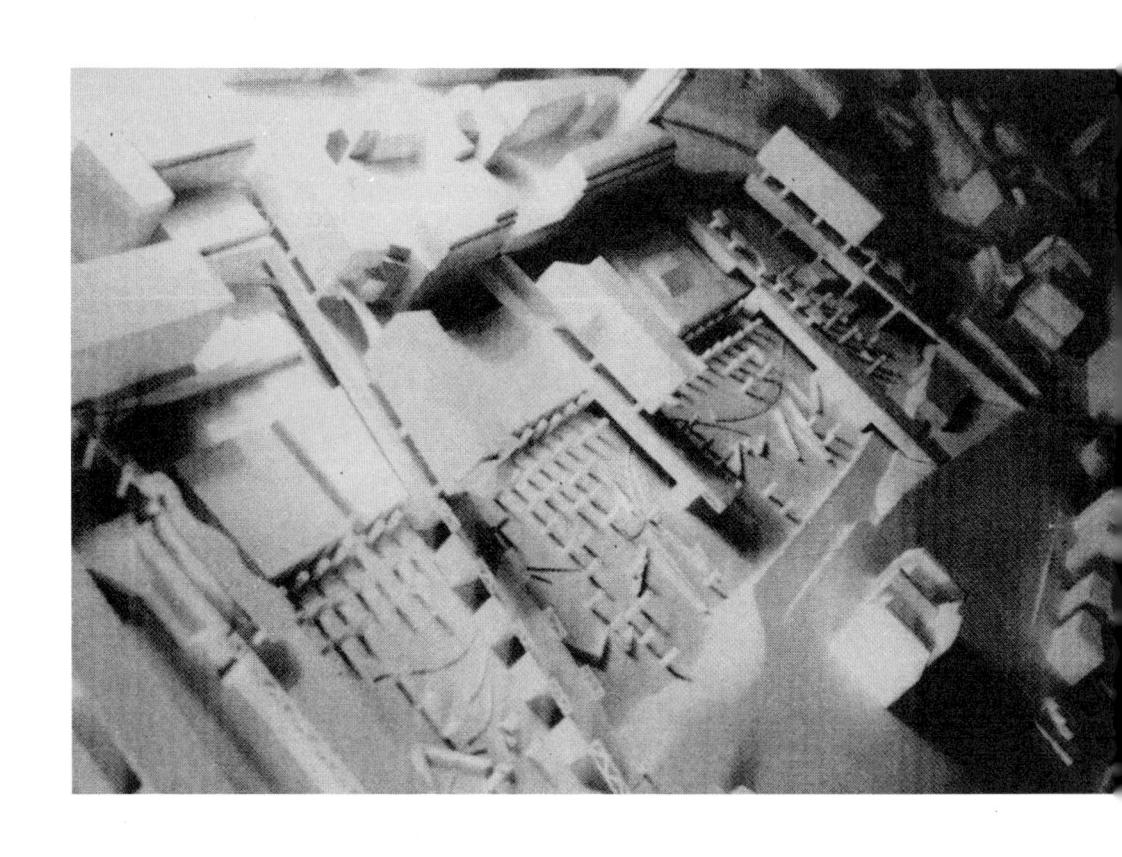

The search for an intermediary: an abstract system to mediate between the site and programmatic demands

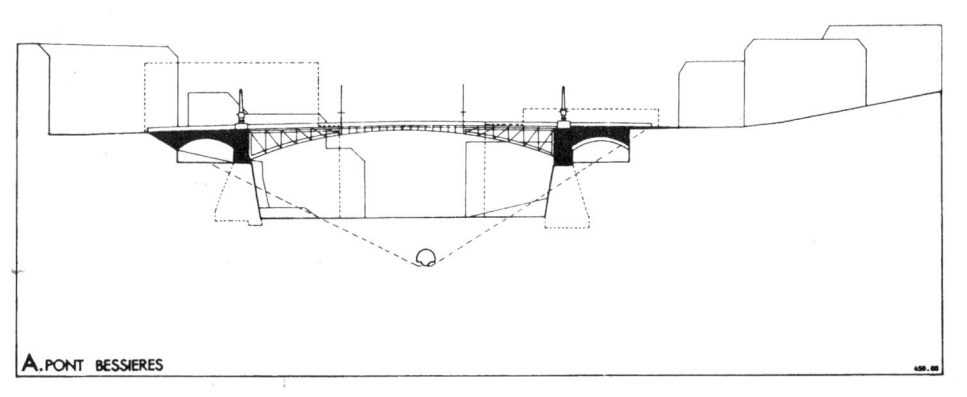

LAUSANNE
169

A. PONT BESSIERES

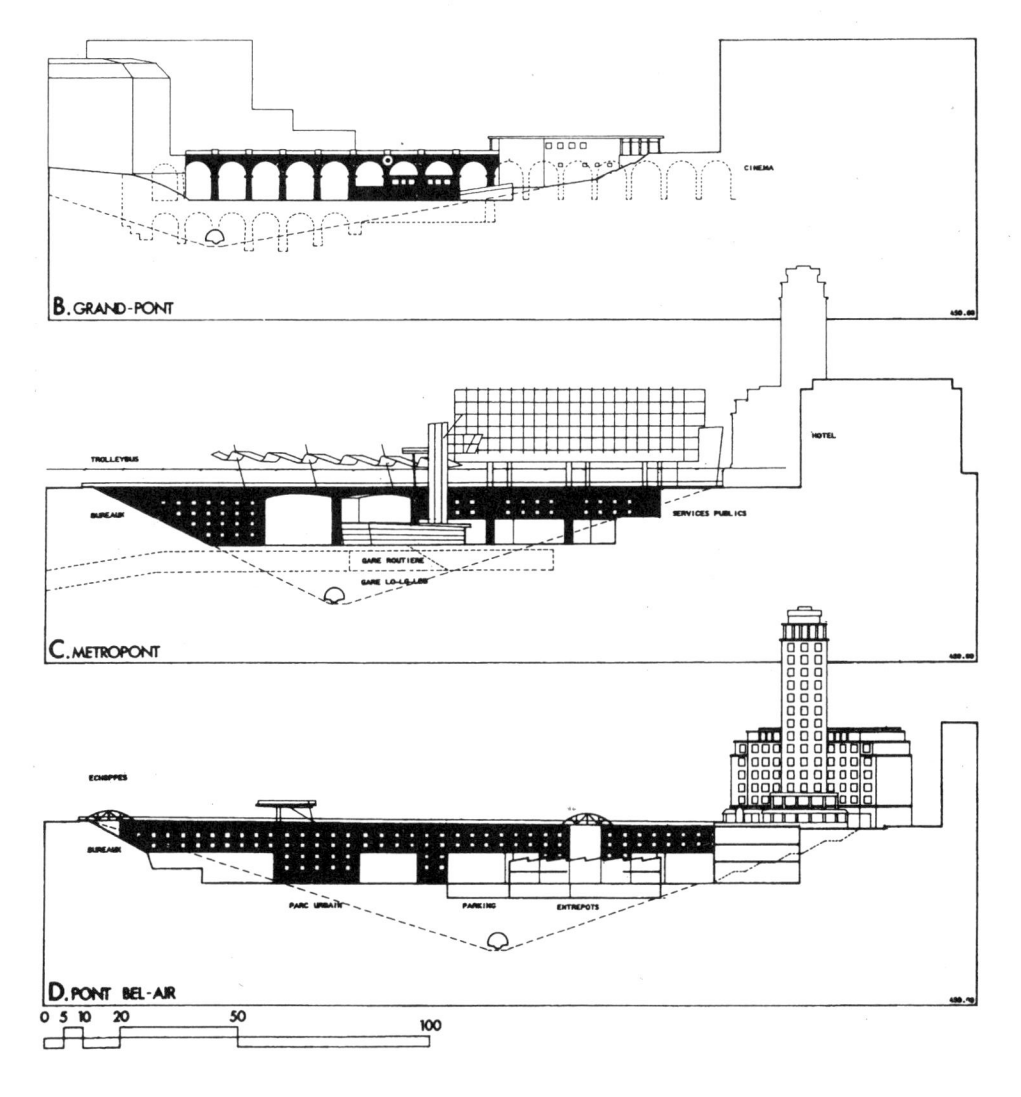

B. GRAND-PONT

C. METROPONT

D. PONT BEL-AIR

0 5 10 20 50   100

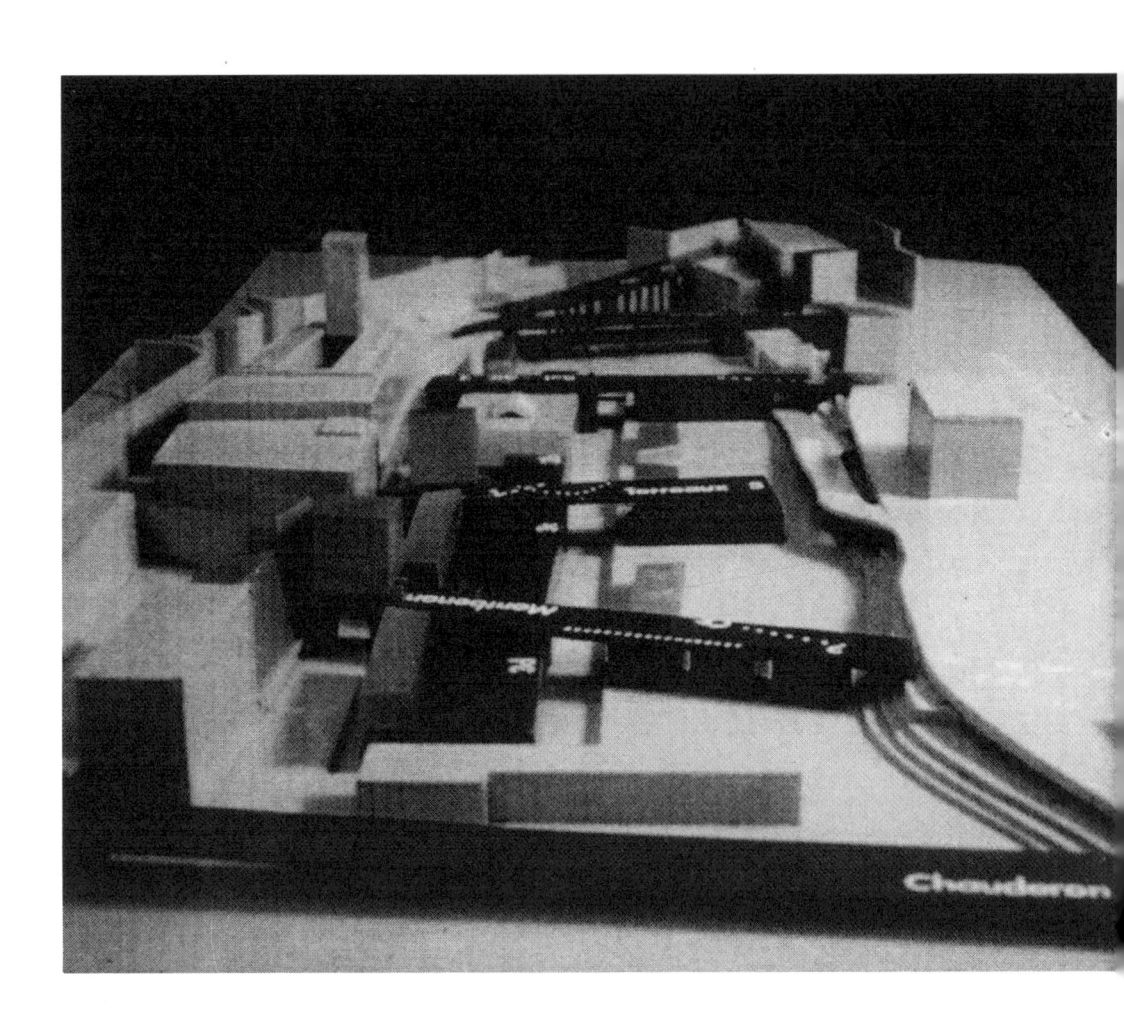

Articulating the in-between: bridges over a valley

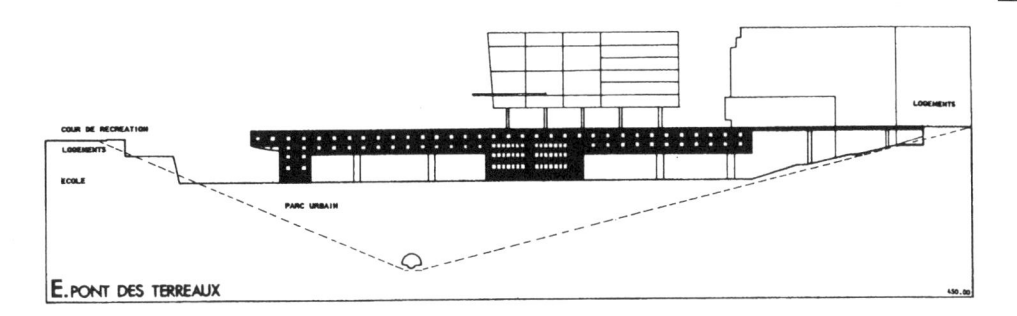

LAUSANNE

171

E. PONT DES TERREAUX

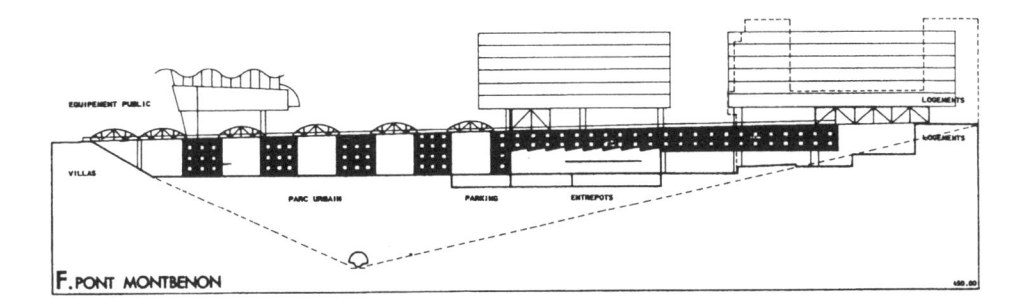

COUR DE RECREATION
LOGEMENTS
ECOLE
PARC URBAIN
LOGEMENTS

F. PONT MONTBENON

EQUIPEMENT PUBLIC
VILLAS
PARC URBAIN
PARKING
ENTREPOTS
LOGEMENTS
LOGEMENTS

G. PONT DE LA VIGIE

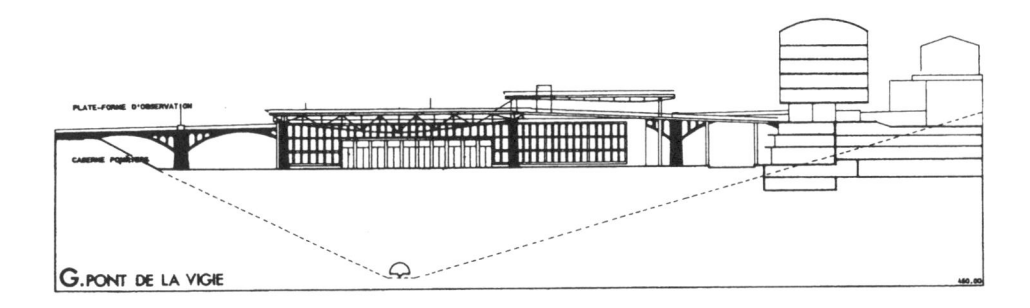

PLATE-FORME D'OBSERVATION
CASERNE POMPIERS

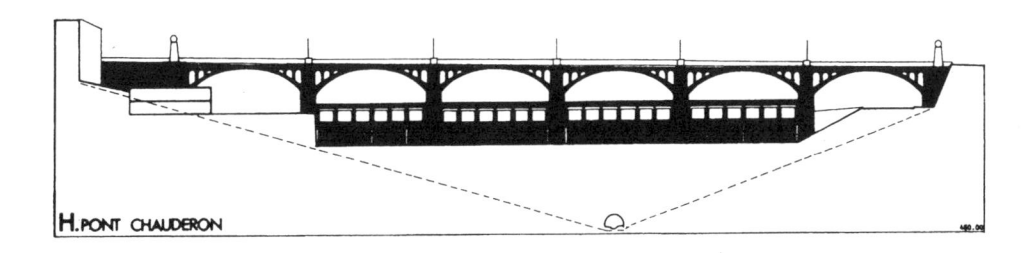

H. PONT CHAUDERON

A programmatic sequence that suggests secret ways and impossible fictions

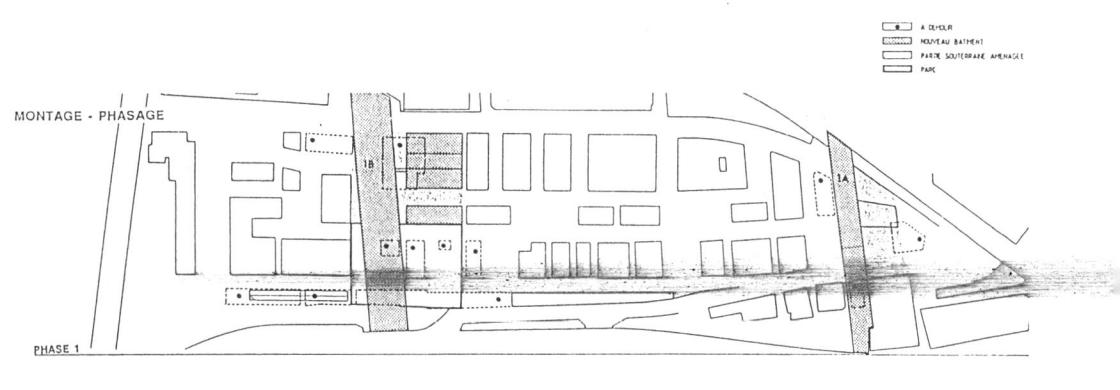

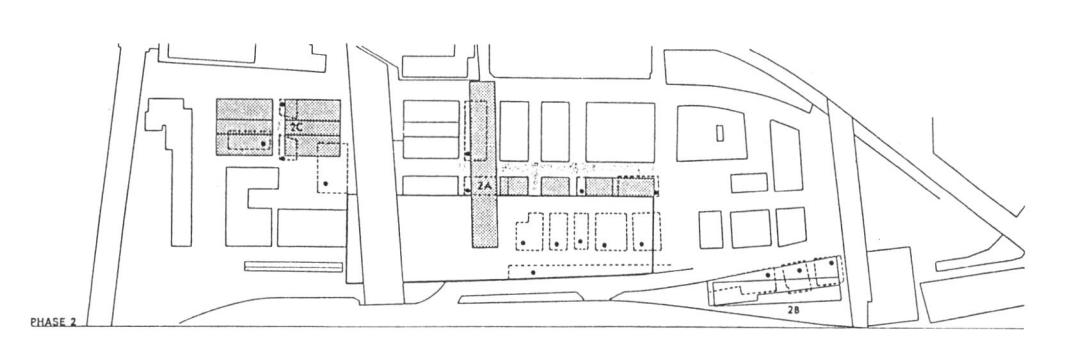

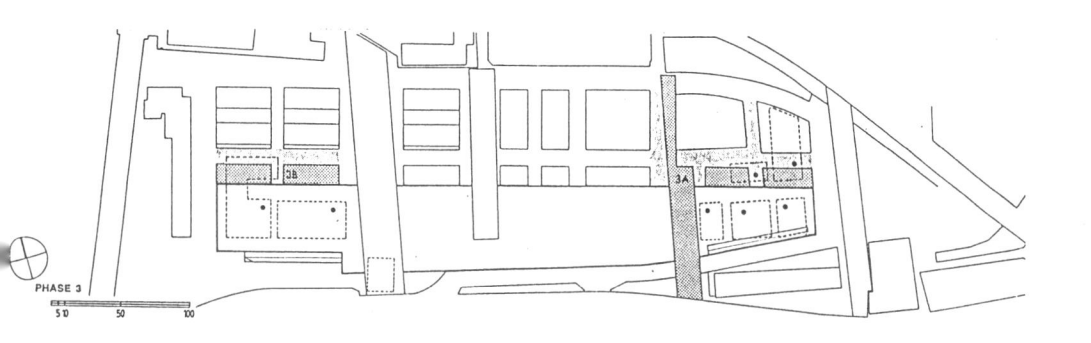

LAUSANNE
173

MONTAGE - PHASAGE

PHASE 1

PHASE 2

PHASE 3

Montage-Phasing (second version): no identification between architecture and program (a distanciation)

Sequences of transformations and sequences of space do not necessarily intersect

LAUSANNE
175

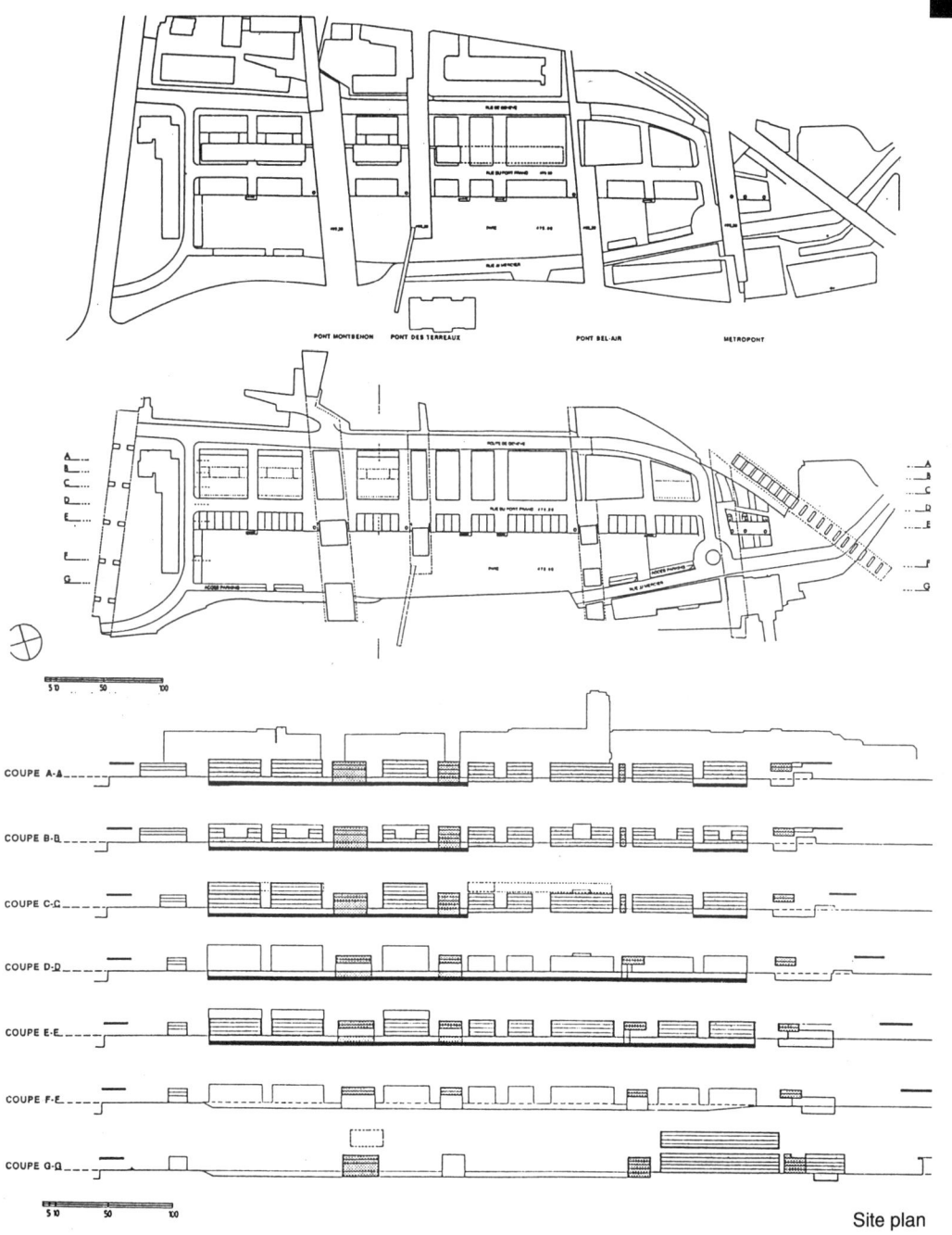

COUPE A-A
COUPE B-B
COUPE C-C
COUPE D-D
COUPE E-E
COUPE F-F
COUPE G-G

Site plan

Level 0

Sections

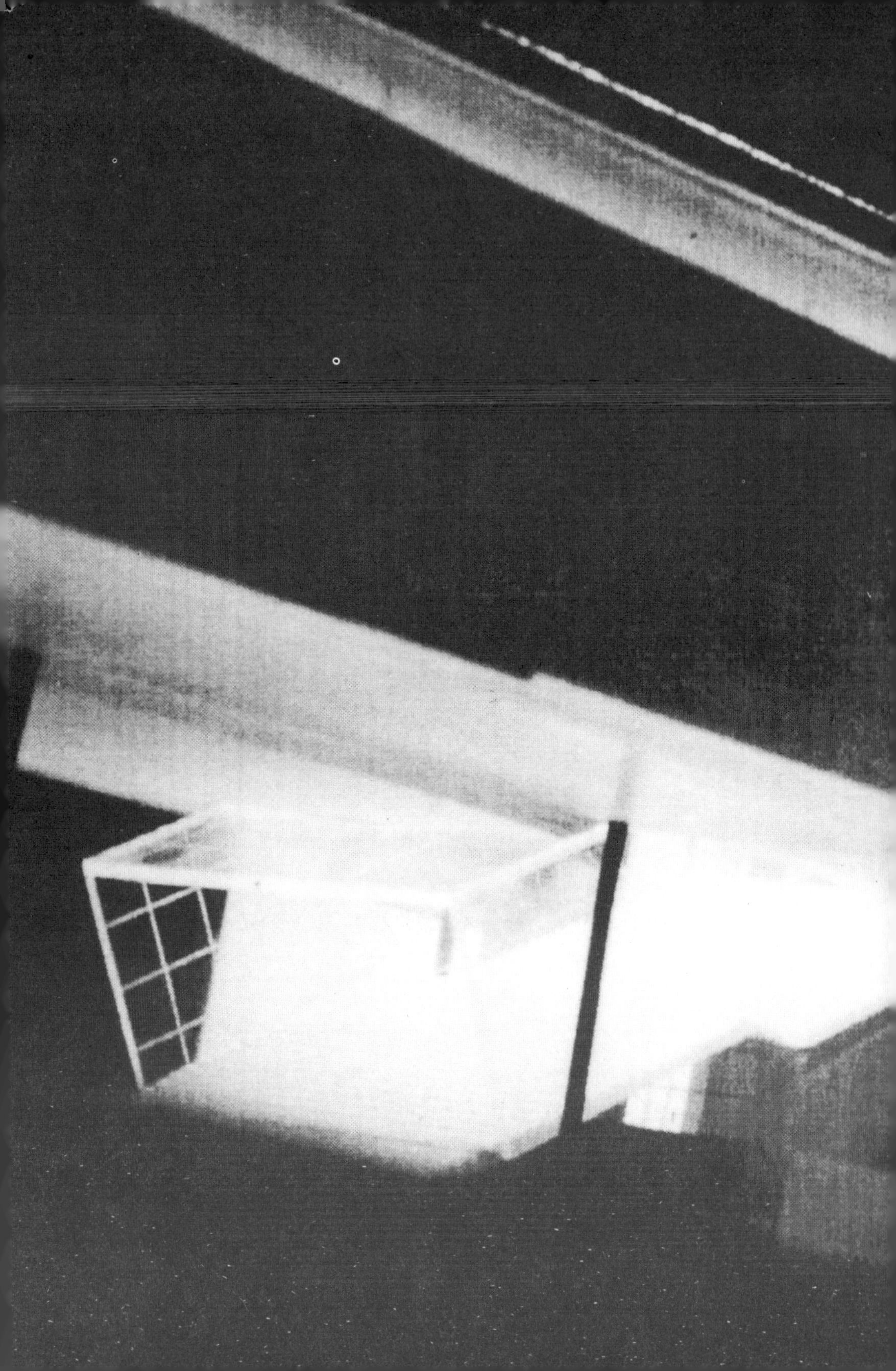

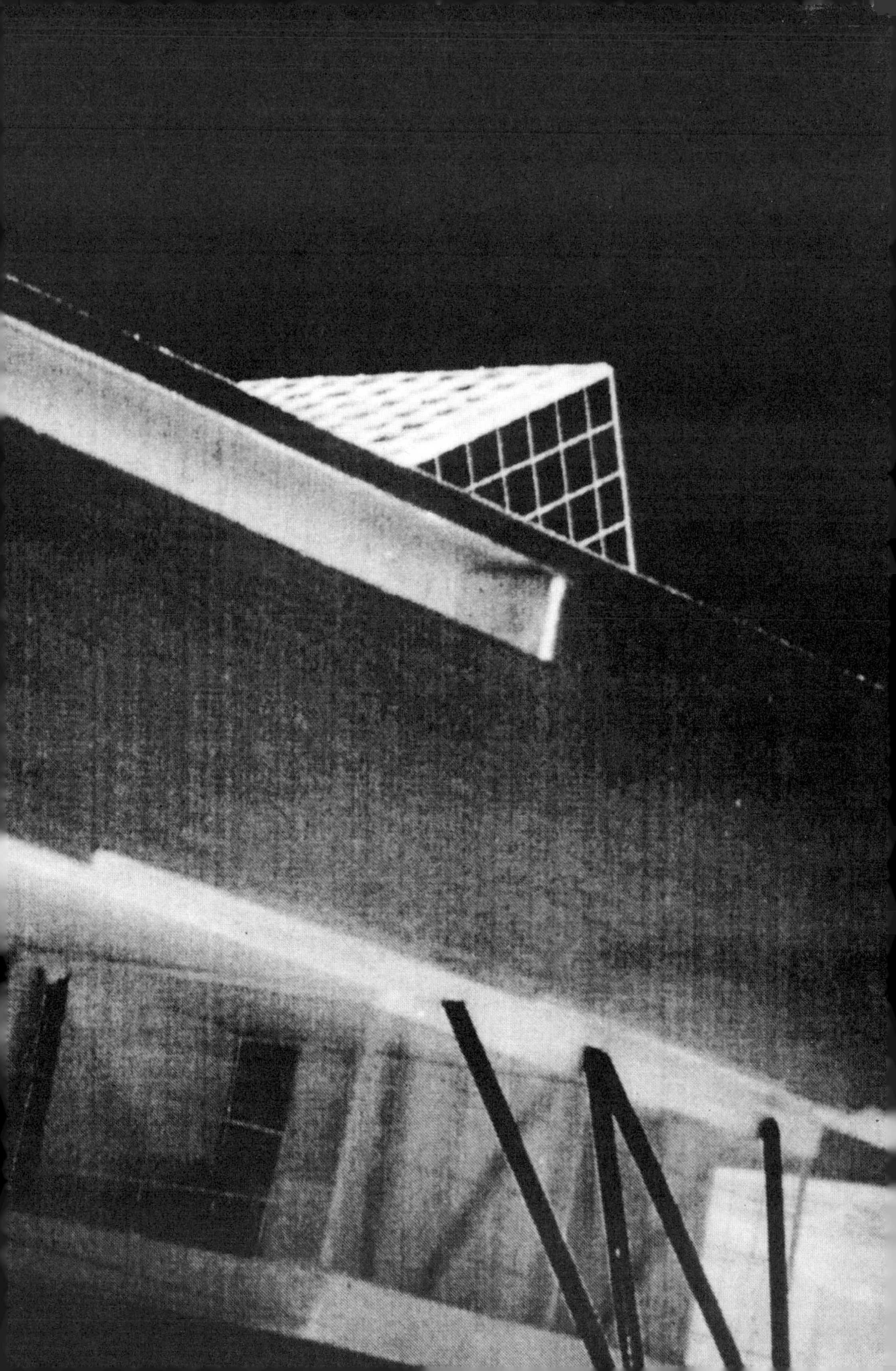

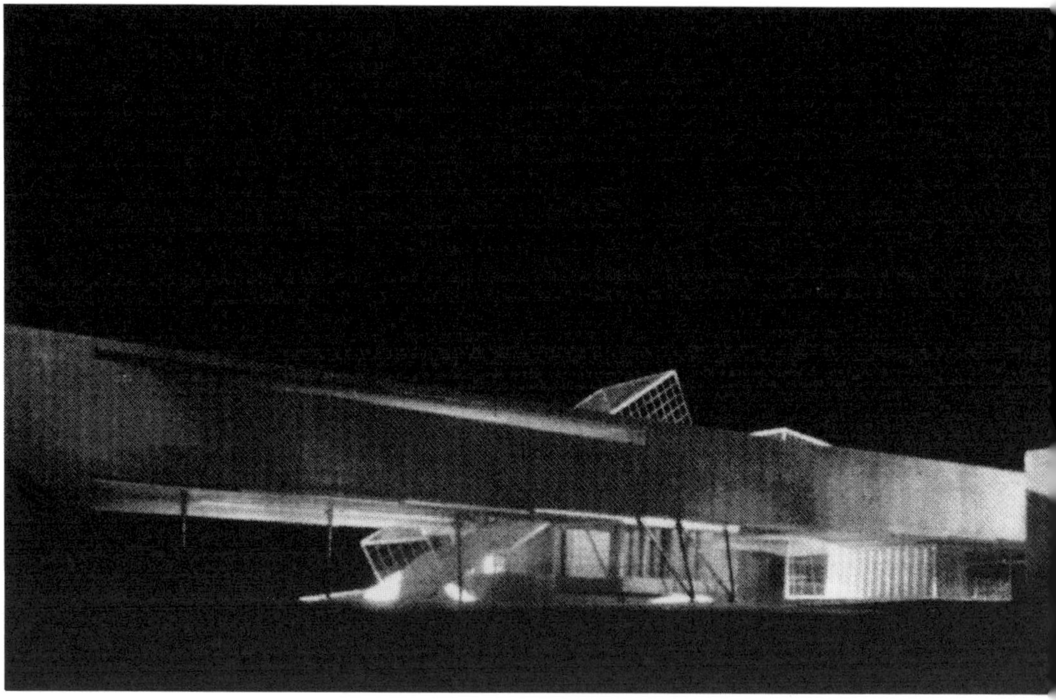

Center for Contemporary Visual Arts (CAPC), Pont Montbenon

Our study locates the new Center for Contemporary Visual Arts in Lausanne in the southern half of the Pont Montbenon. Conceived as a series of parallel spatial strips, each of a different character, the bridge allows for multiple "circuits" of movement for both museum users and pedestrians moving on and through the bridge.

One enters the museum from either north or south. From the north, the main access is by a glass-enclosed staircase intersecting the body of the bridge, with the entrance at the midpoint of the passage from the top of the bridge to the valley below. A narrower, glass-bottomed long stair, running parallel to the main stair, descends from the top of the bridge to the entry lobby, providing access from the southern end of the bridge. Both access strips offer a view into the main exhibition space, the entrance lobby and the bookshop, revealing the sectional nature of the bridge while piercing through it.

Once inside the museum, two more circuits of movement are possible: (1) from the west, through a long, narrow gallery, then reversing direction down a glass-bottomed ramp (directly under the glass-bottomed long stair) into the central exhibition space and finally through a series of smaller stepped exhibition rooms, and (2) from the east, along the same sequence, inverted.

Upon leaving the center for the valley below, one finds conference rooms and curators' offices suspended below the main stair and artists' lofts embedded in the southern wall of the valley.

The structure of the bridge is also conceived as strips, with the majority of the forces handled by two-meter-thick box beams running along the outside walls. All mechanical systems are located in the thickness of the beams. A row of slender columns off-center helps support the main gallery, assisted by the sides of the stair/ramp, which are beams supporting the top surface of the bridge above and suspending the gallery floor below.

The strip configuration, tilted in section, allows for the development of a new spatial type, using movement and program to activate the passage from one side of the valley to the other and from the top of the valley to the bottom.

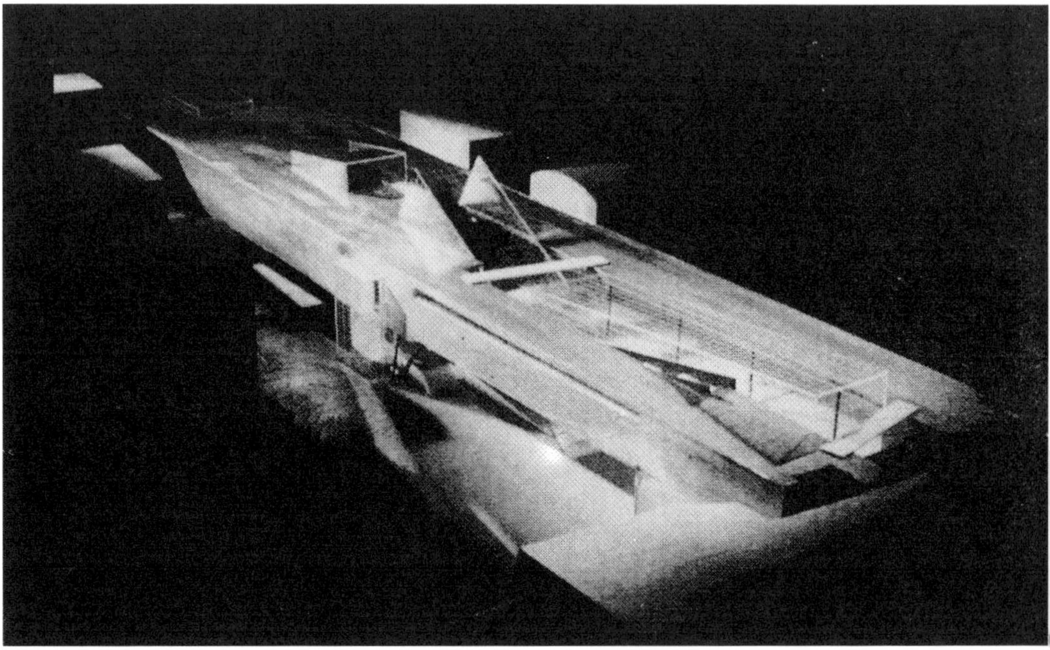

LAUSANNE
181

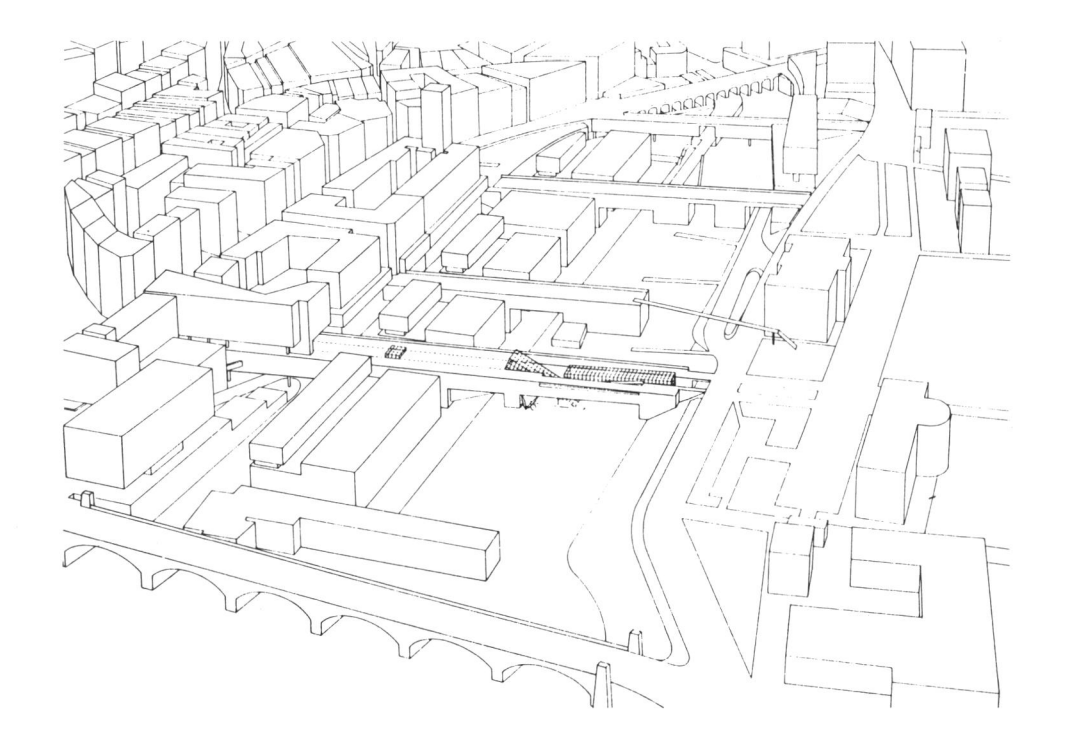

Aerial view of Pont Montbenon: Center for Contemporary Visual Arts (CAPC)

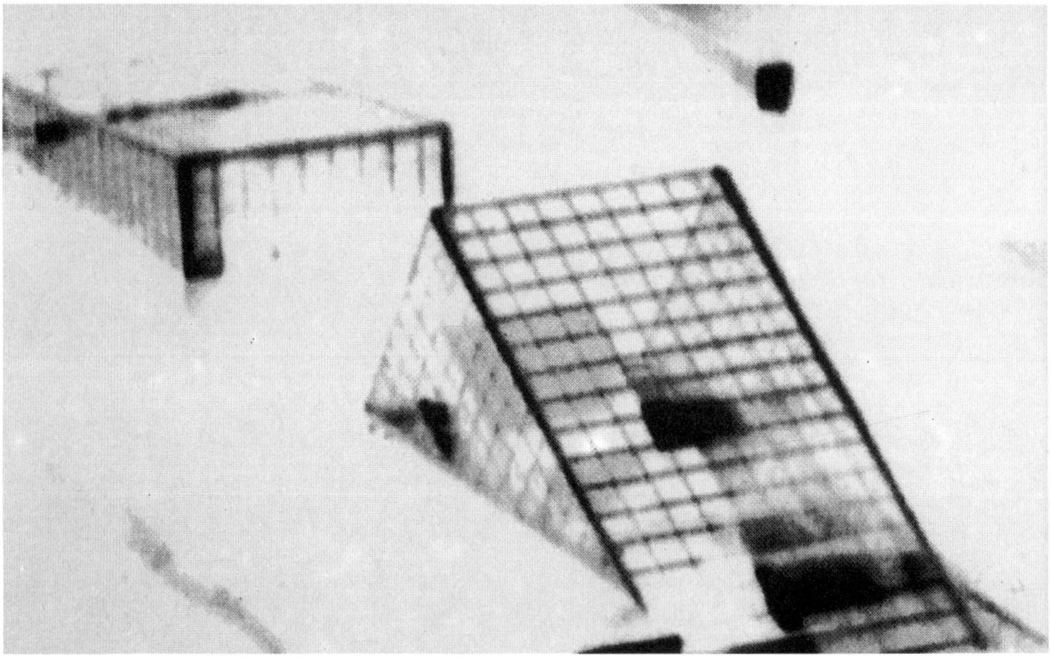

LAUSANNE
183

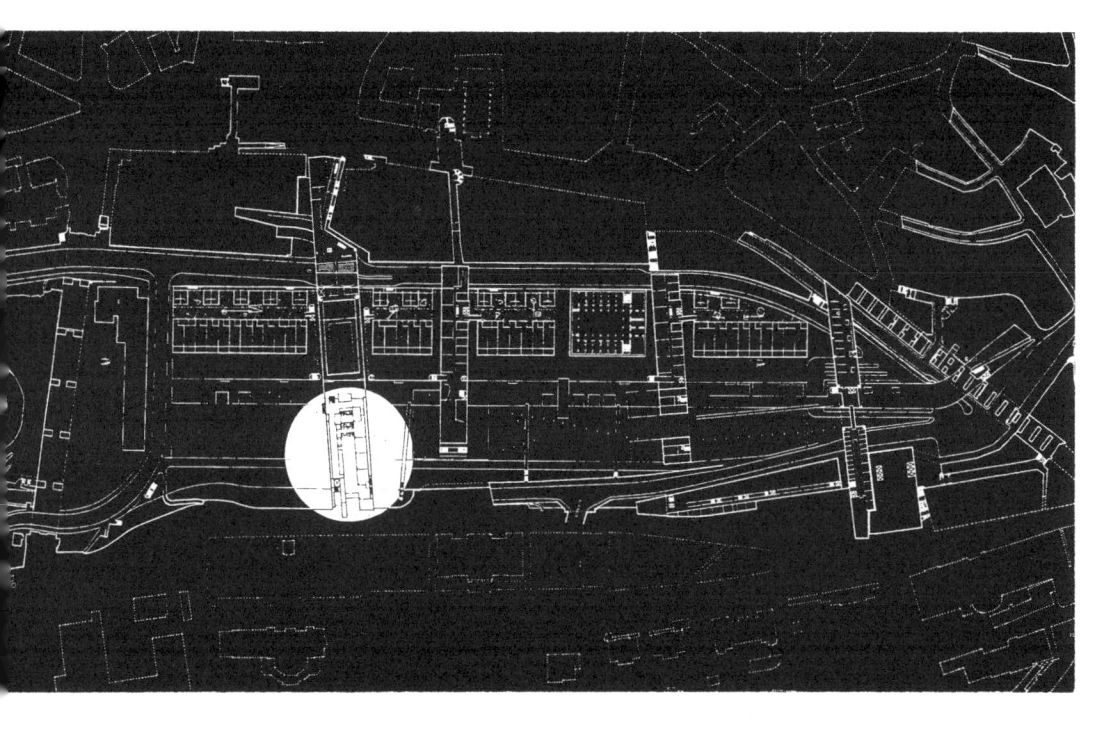

Center for Contemporary Visual Arts

LAUSANNE
185

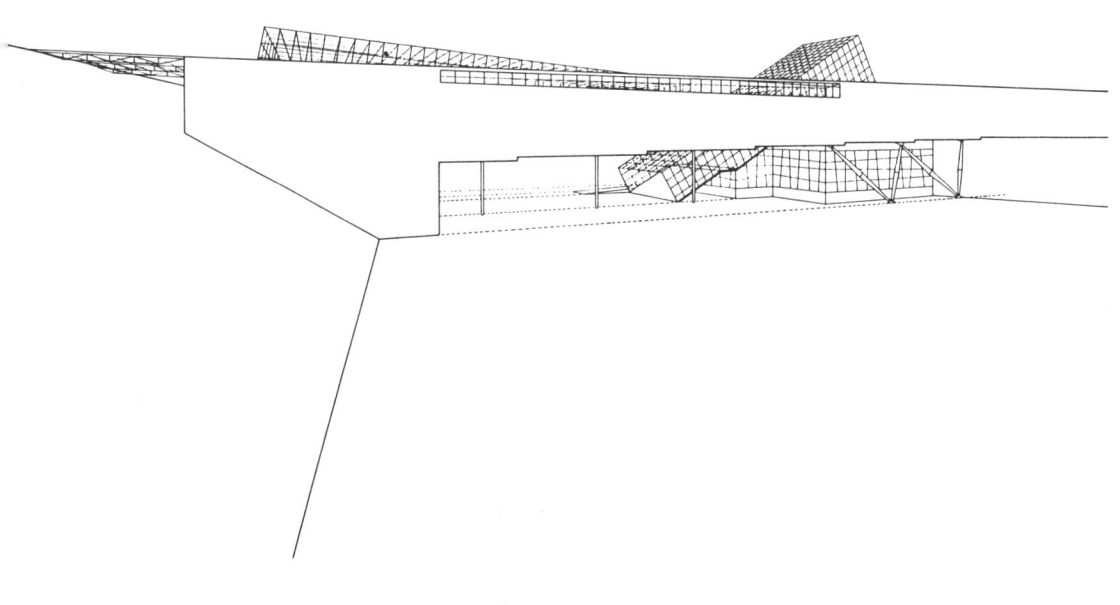

Programmatic content versus urban typology

The inhabited bridges connect the lower and upper levels of the valley

LAUSANNE
187

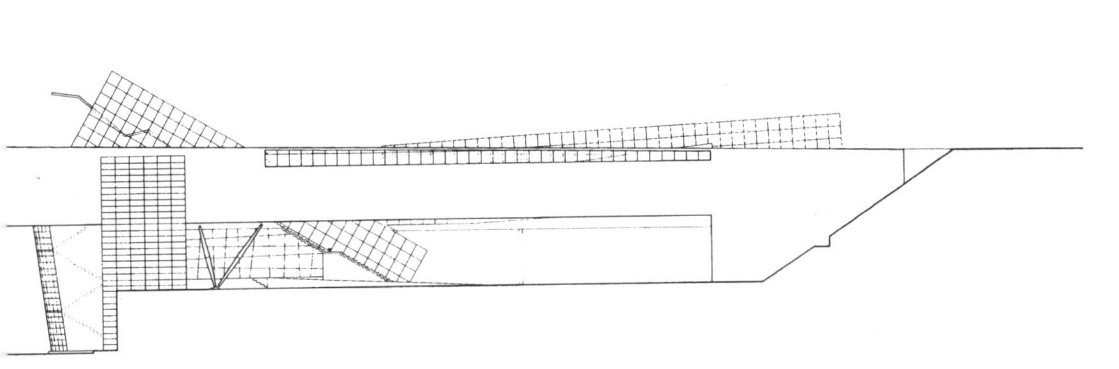

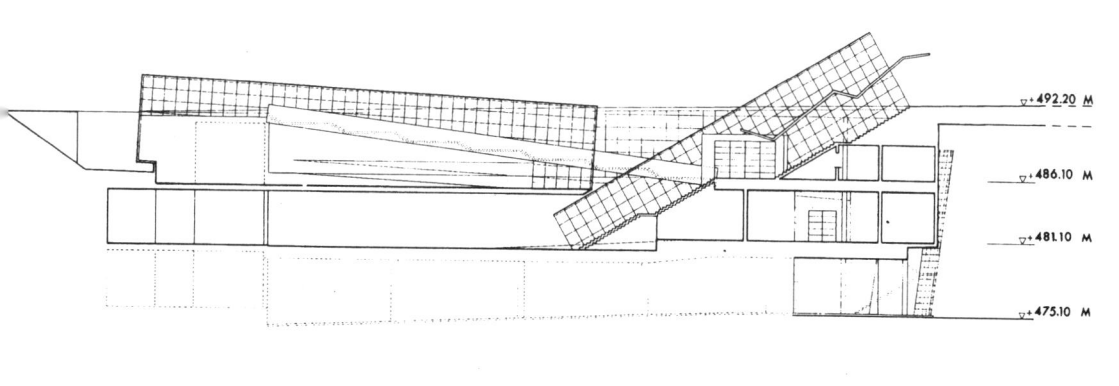

▽ +492.20 M
▽ +486.10 M
▽ +481.10 M
▽ +475.10 M

East and West elevations

Longitudinal section

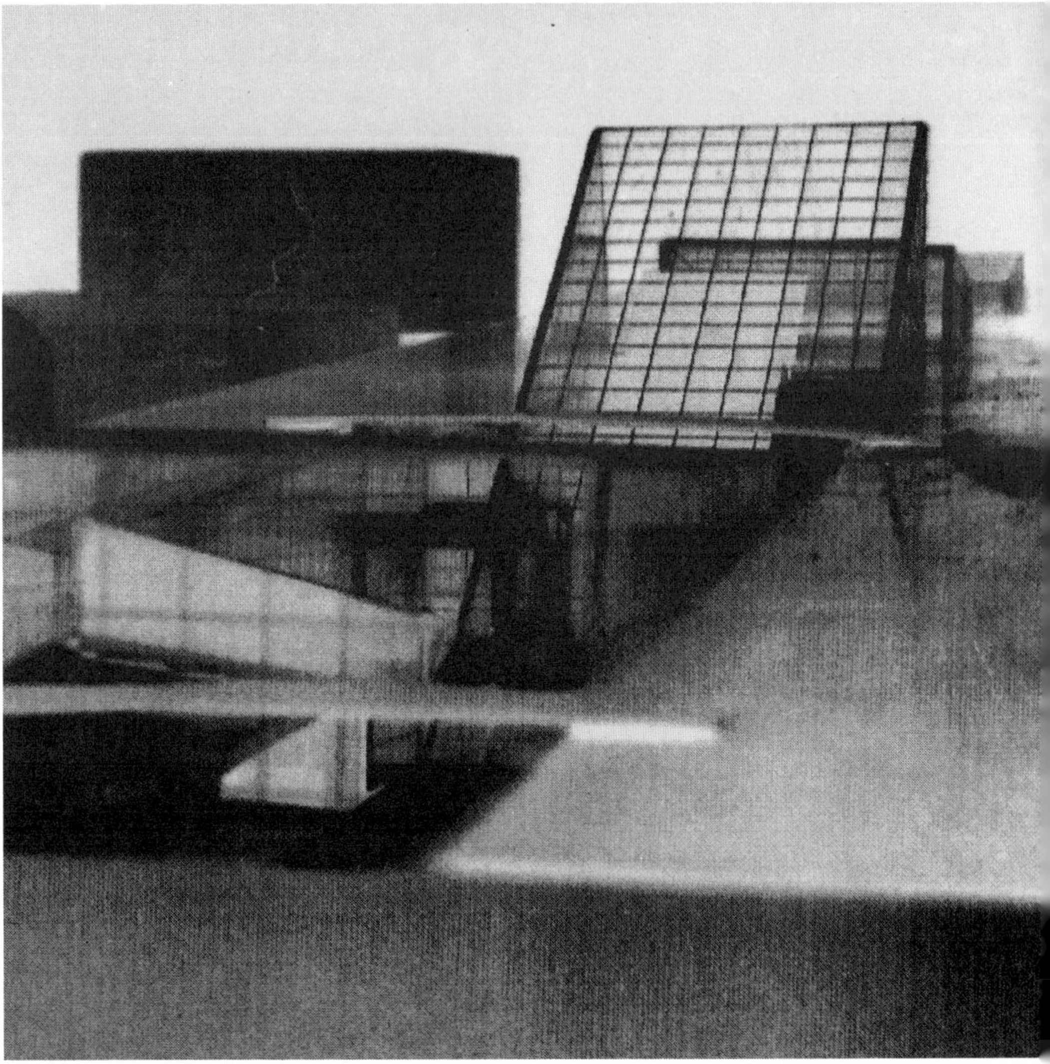

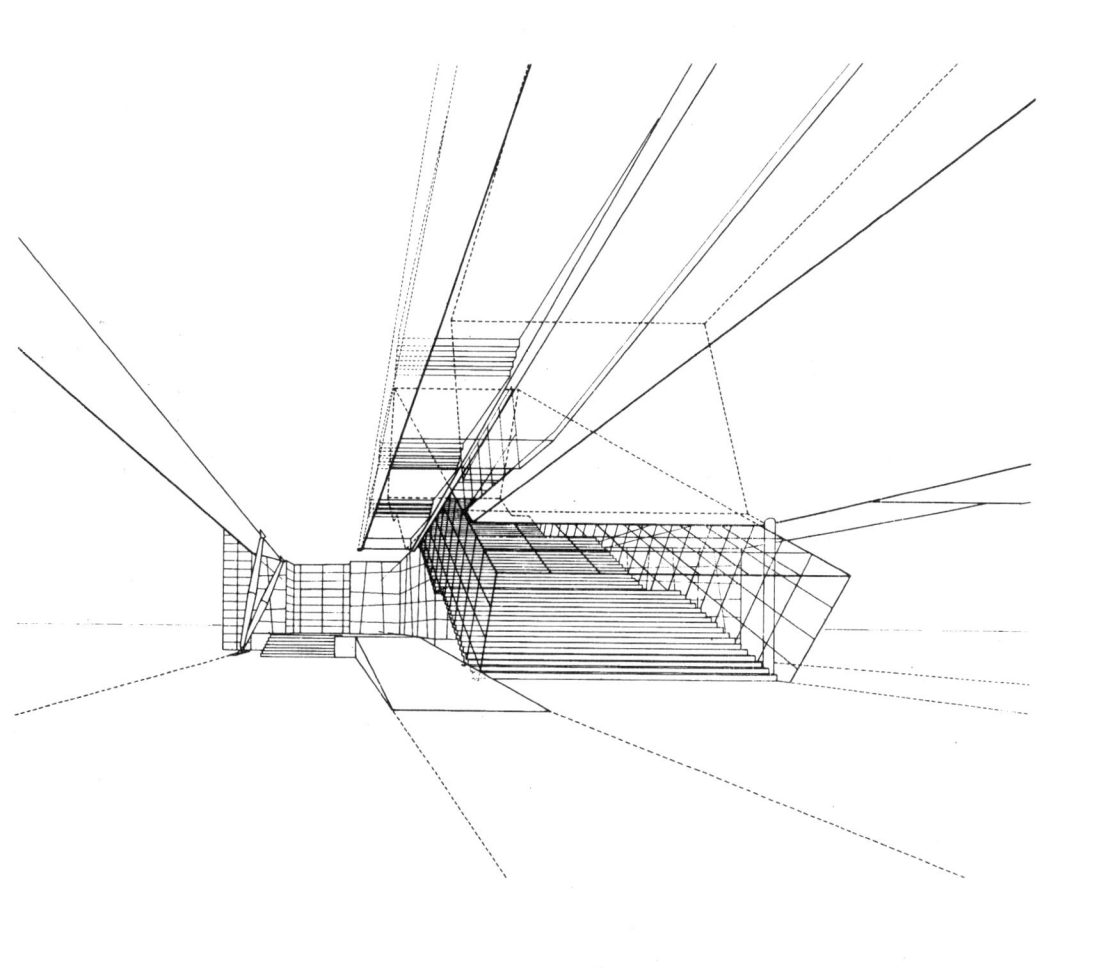

CAPC (entrance from lower level): urban typology versus spatial experience

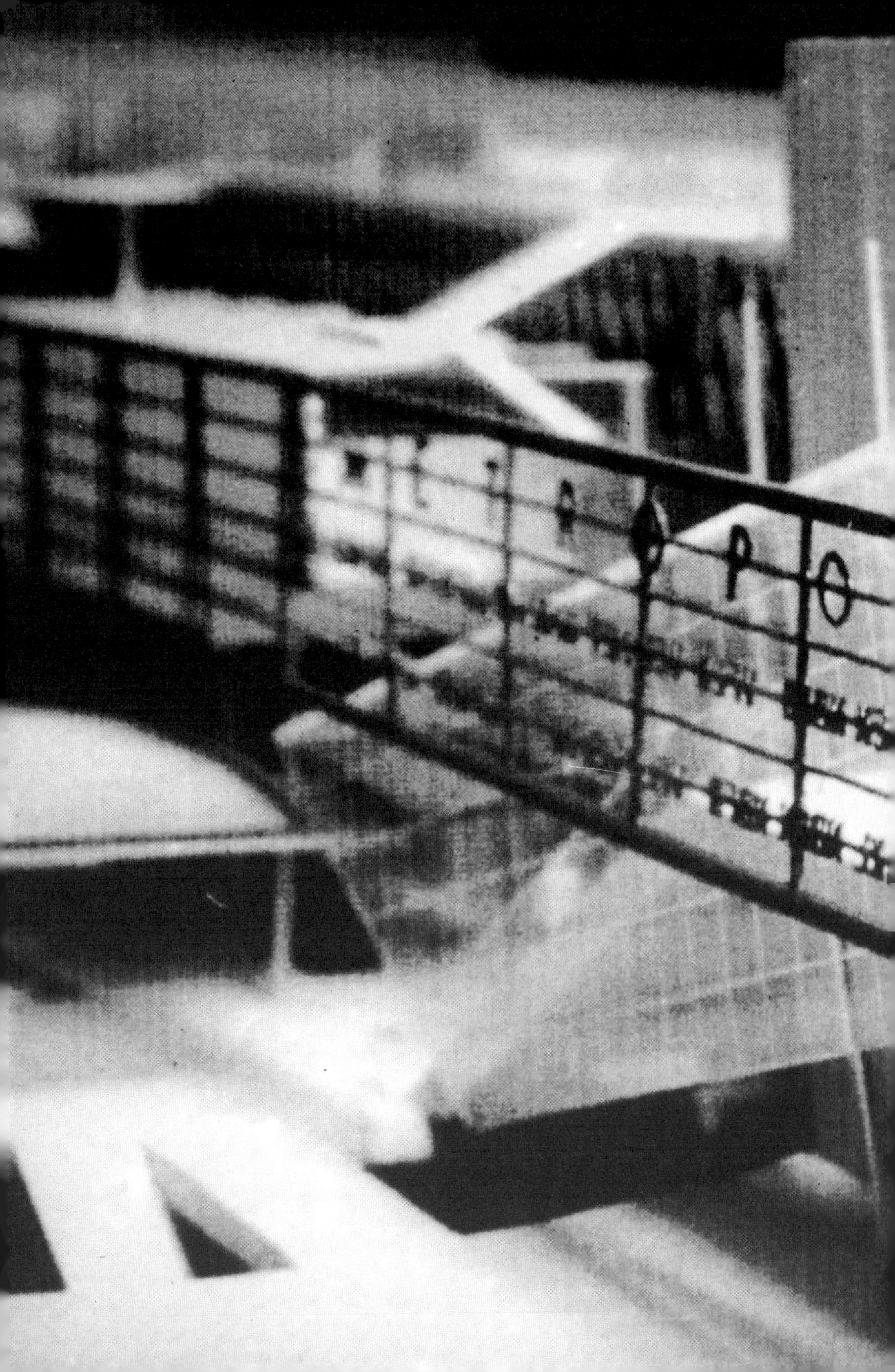

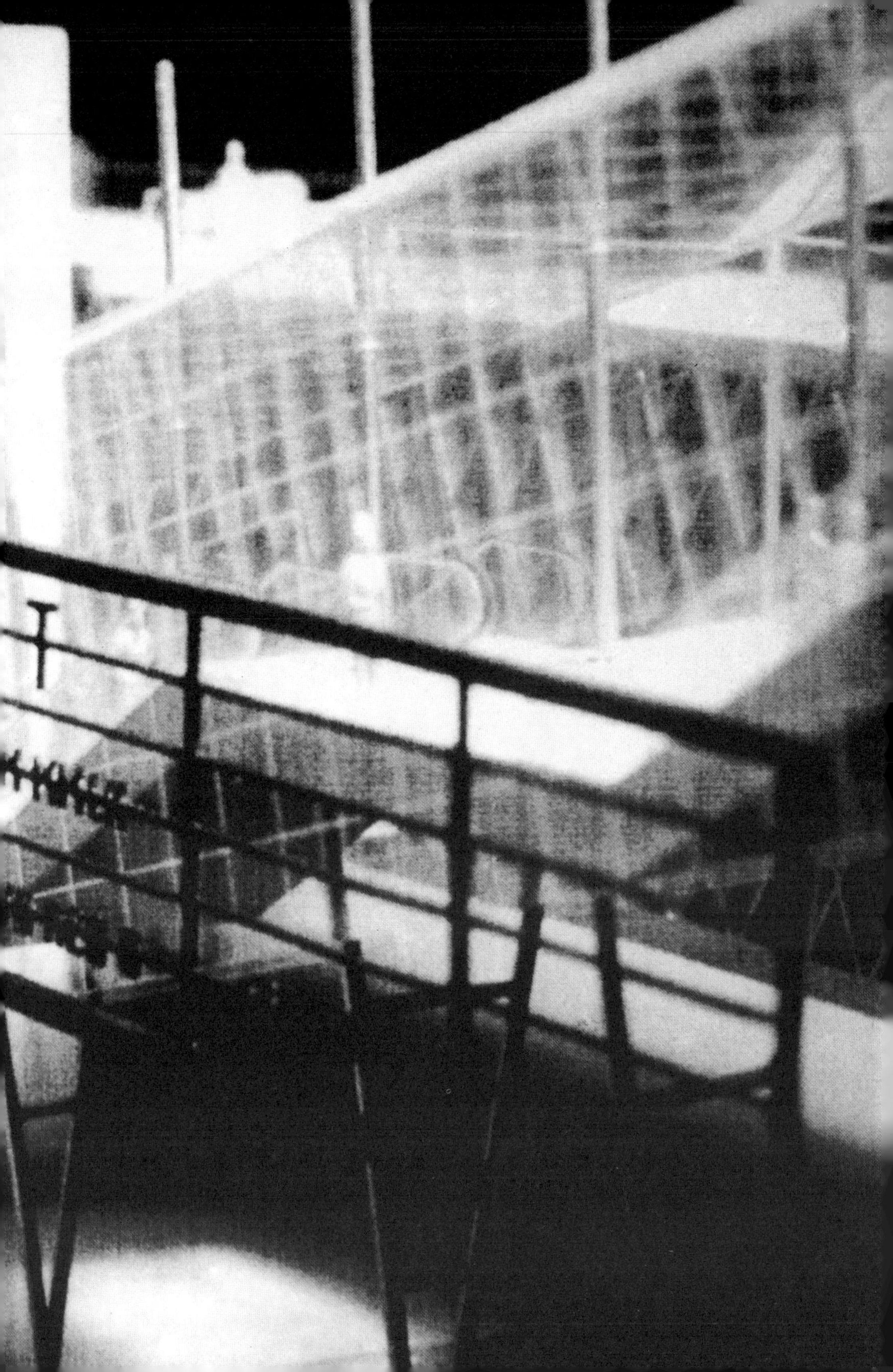

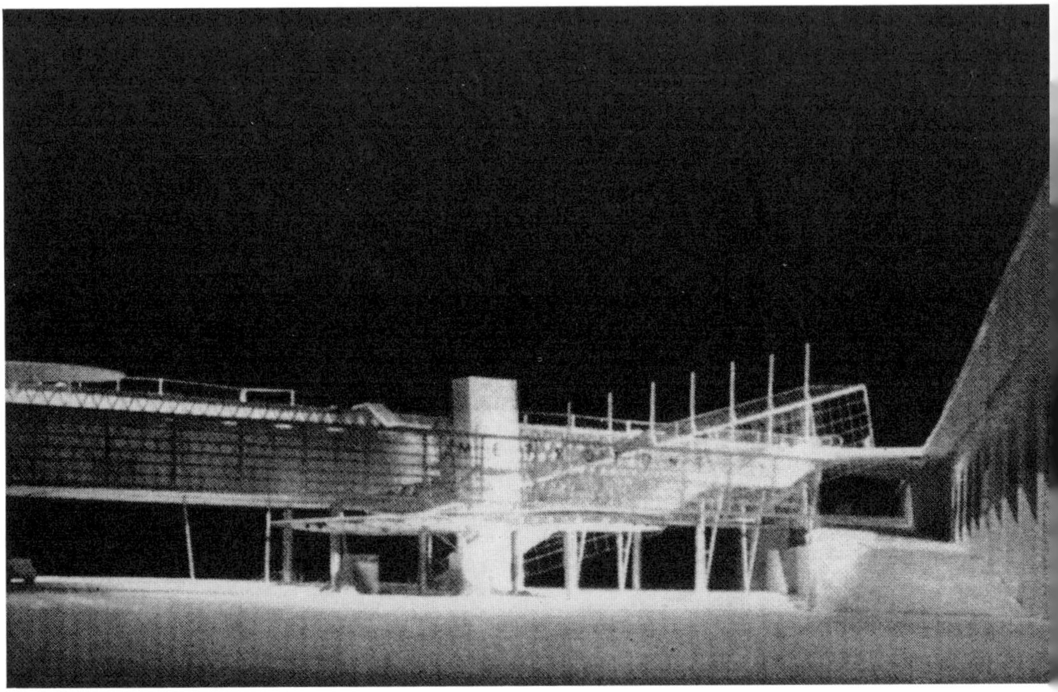

Metropont

The Metropont bridge acts first as a new transportation interchange for the city. Located at the western end of the Flon Valley, it combines three separate train and subway lines on one level and two bus lines on another, with pedestrian traffic coming from four separate stories. Functioning not as an end point but as a momentary pause along multiple routes, the Metropont also generates new events for this part of the city. Programmatic collisions will be encouraged as mass movement intersects other functional requirements.

The Metropont is organized spatially in two parallel bands, each with its own system of organization, function and structure. The western band, spanning the length of the valley from rue Gonin to Grand-Pont, contains two levels of office/commercial space.

Structurally, it is conceived as an enormous hollow beam. An exterior steel trellis forms a structurally continuous unit. The middle floor plate is then suspended from the top surface of the "beam." Pedestrian circulation is both horizontal and vertical, with diagonal transfer occurring in the eastern band.

The eastern band is a series of discrete elements providing vertical movement from the top of the bridge (and the surrounding area) to the floor plates of the "beam," the valley floor and the train platforms below ground. The primary element is the glass box, containing escalators that directly connect all levels. A stepped café is sandwiched between interlevel stairs, and elevators provide rapid transport from either end of the bridge. A wing is suspended from the beam to provide cover for the escalators and stairs leading to the trains below.

Structurally each element is independent, with its own logic, but taking advantage of the adjacent beam to provide horizontal stabilization. The glass box uses the inherent structural capacity of the continuous run of escalators to support a light tension-cable system that holds the glass.

Running the full length of the eastern band is a continuous framework for semitransparent advertisements and media events. Providing a heterogeneous datum of fleeting images and light, the media strip can be seen from the environs of the bridge and from inside the bridge itself. Combined with the constant flow of people through the glass box it becomes a city event. A new urban type results, based not on the static composition of building mass and urban axes but on the condition of the momentary and the constantly moving.

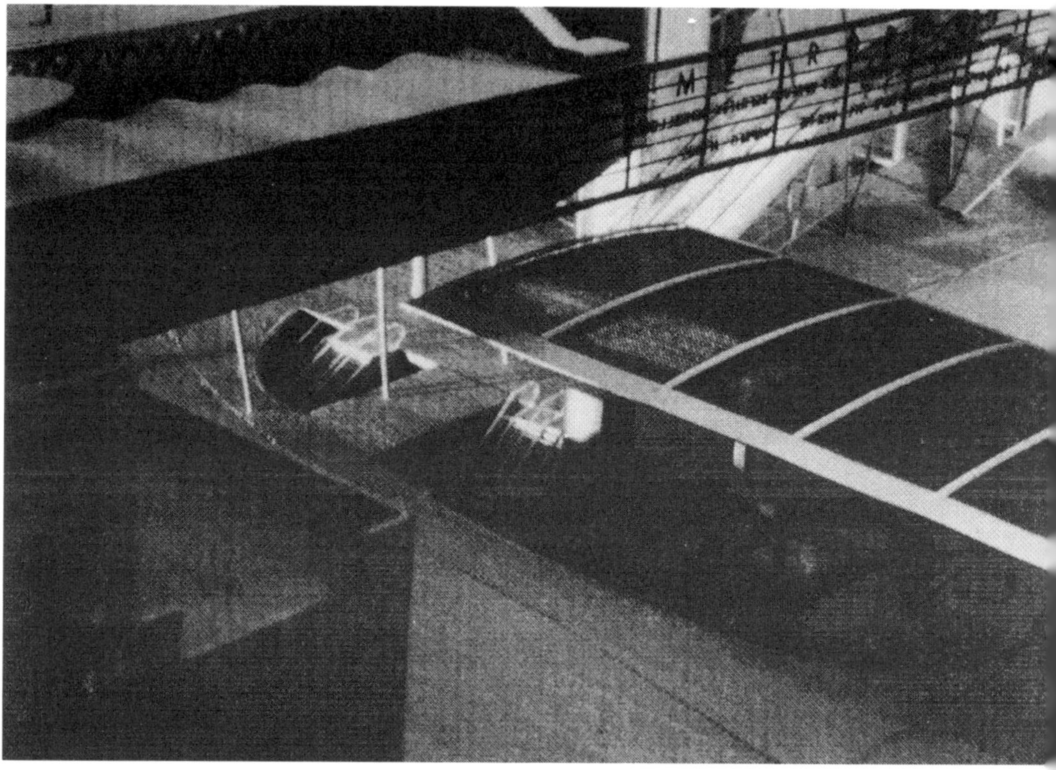
M T R

LAUSANNE
195

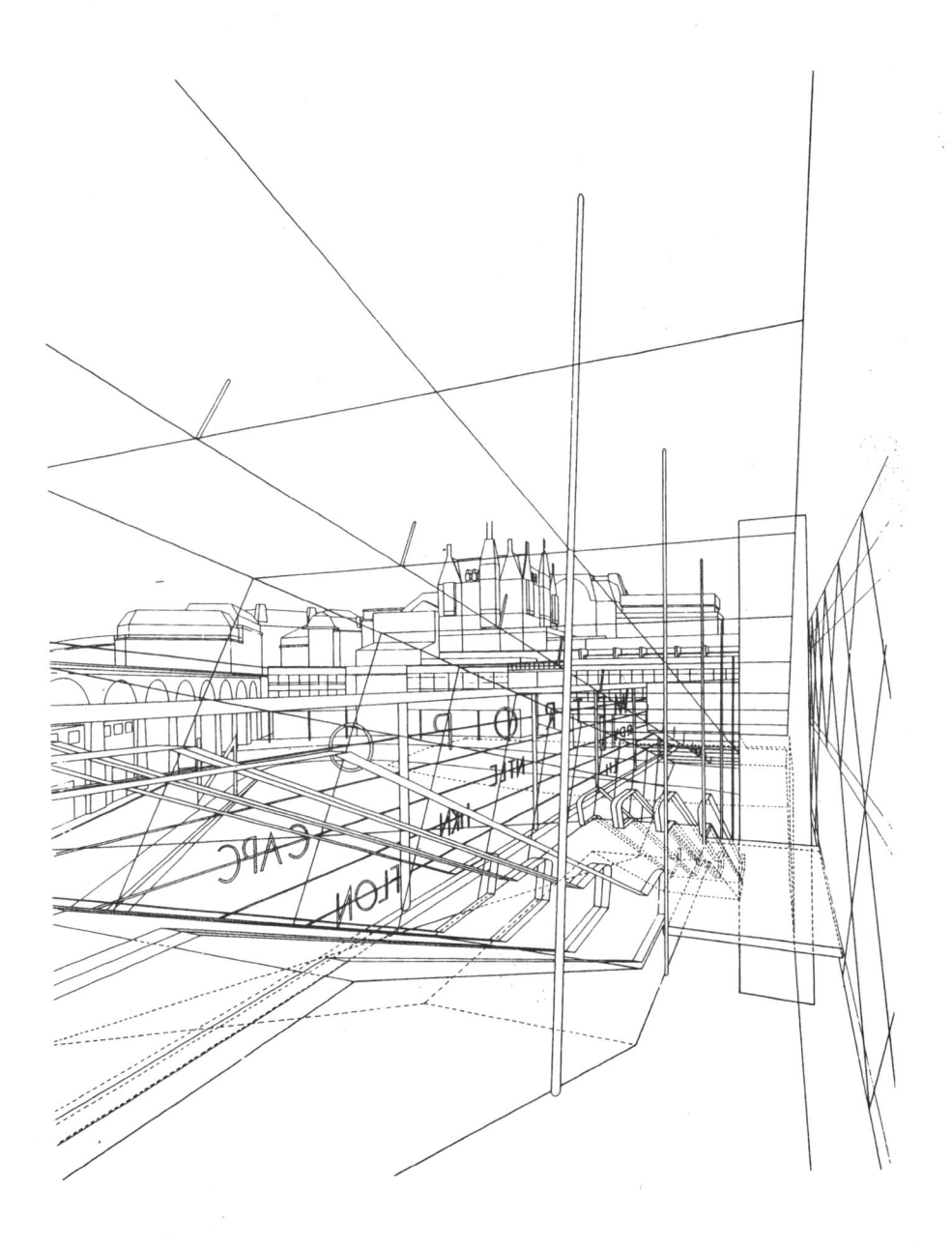

Metropont: a diagonal link to the valley

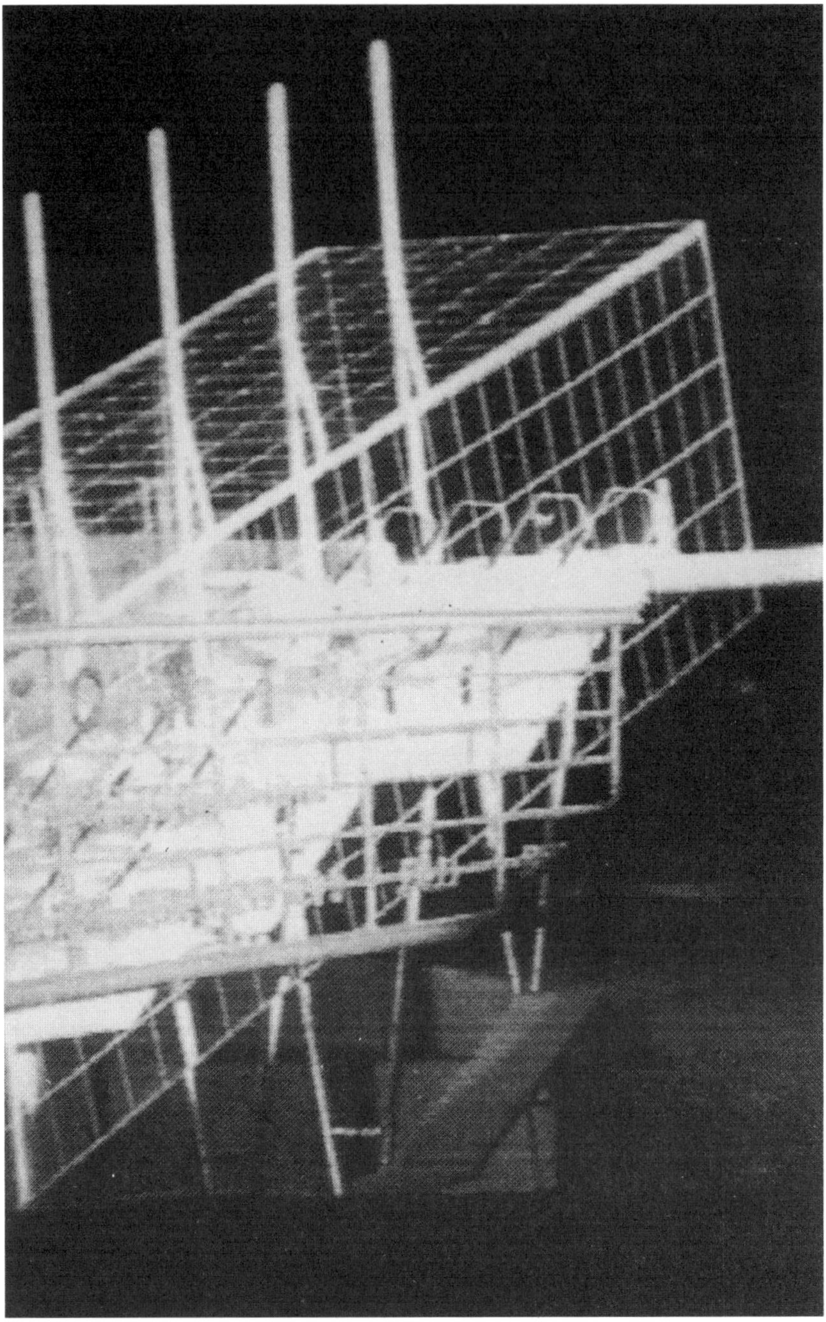

LAUSANNE
197

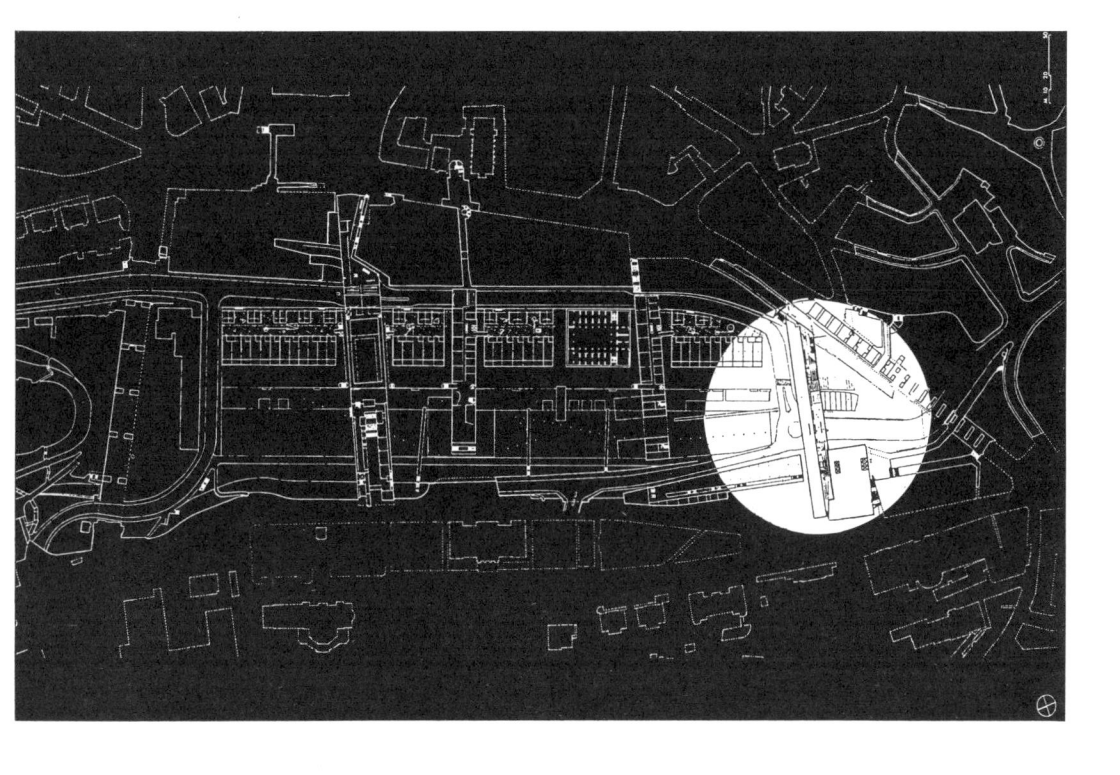

The "electrotecture" beam: a part of the event

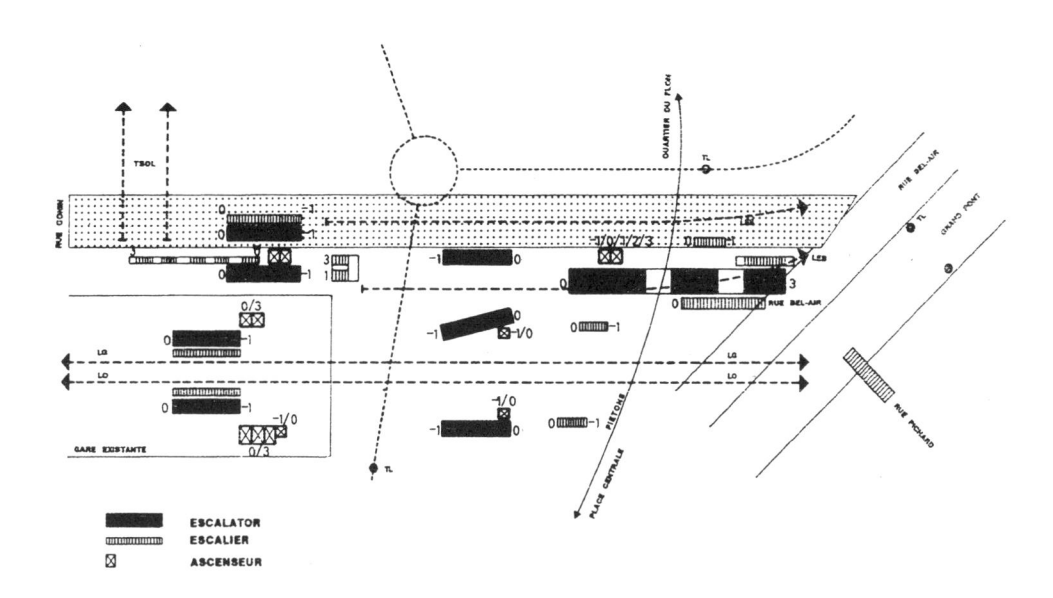

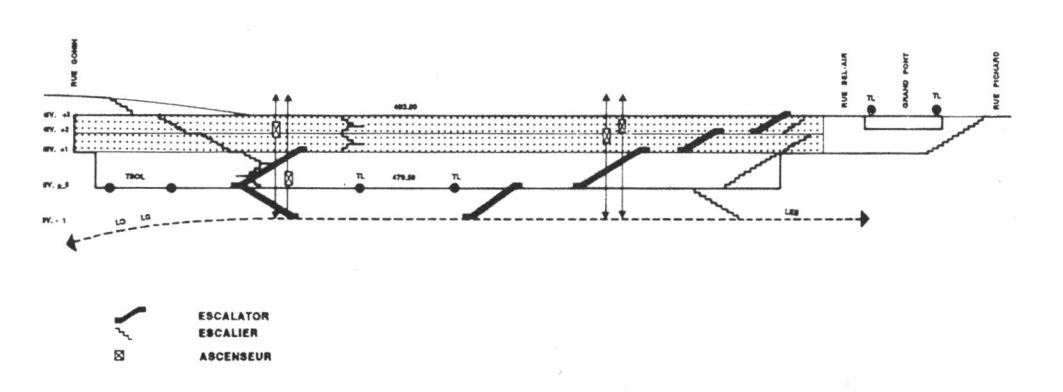

Horizontal circulation: plan

Vertical circulation: section

Glimpse into the underground subway: the event

LAUSANNE
201

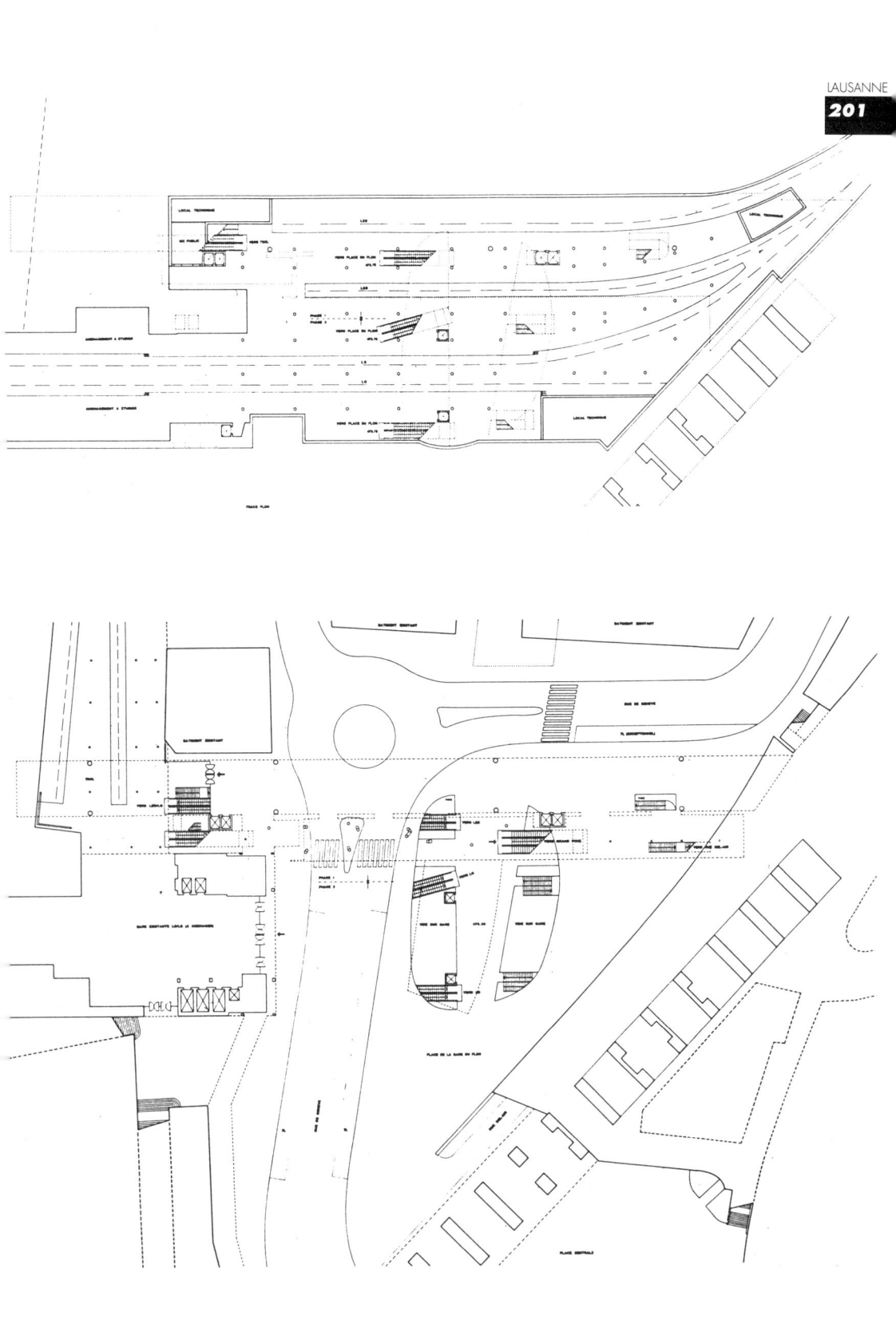

"Electrotecture"

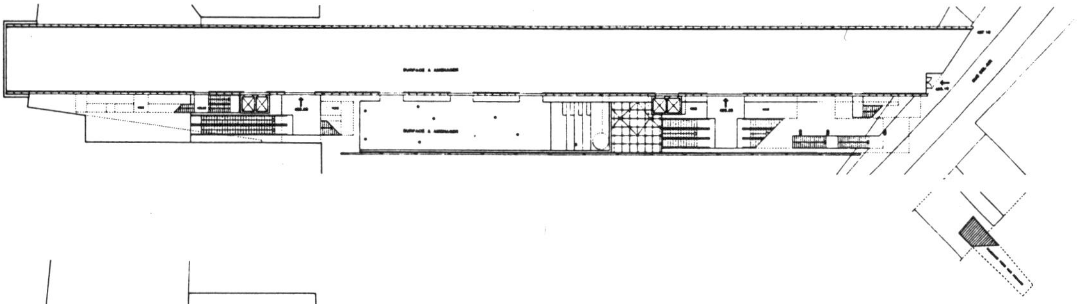

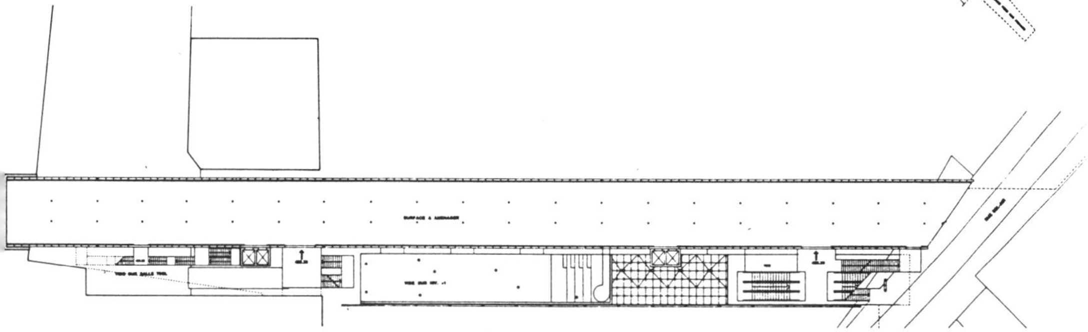

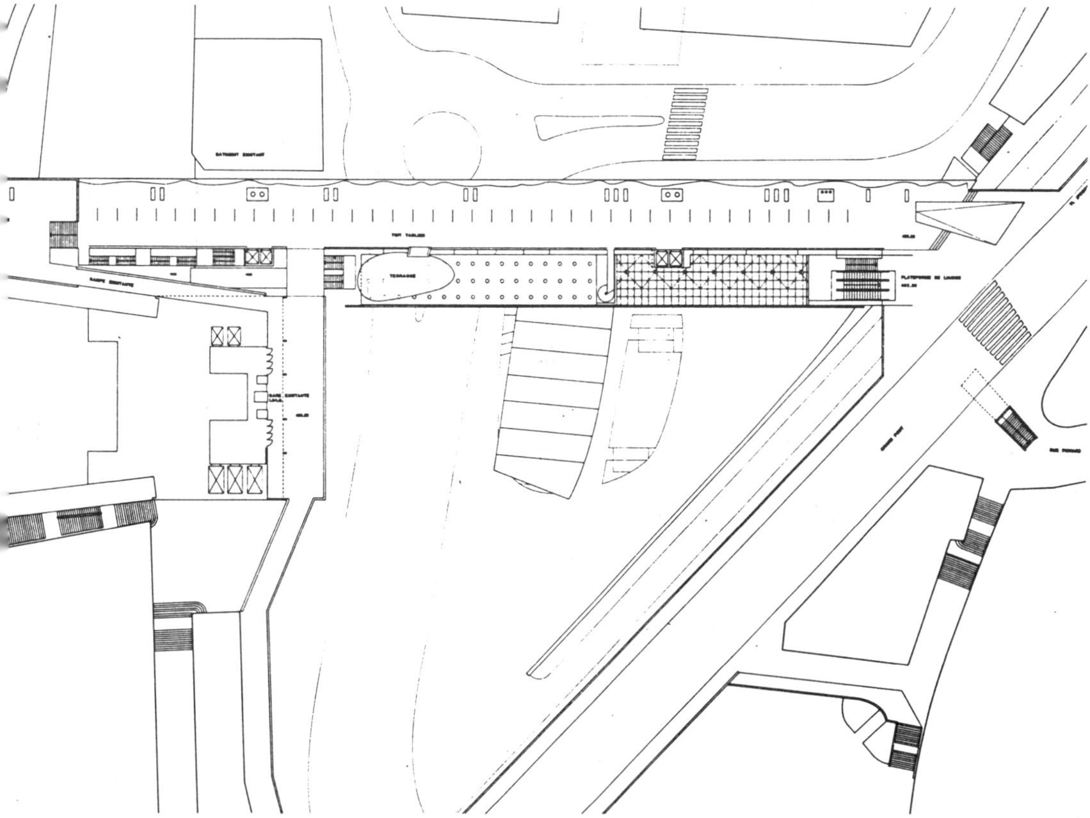

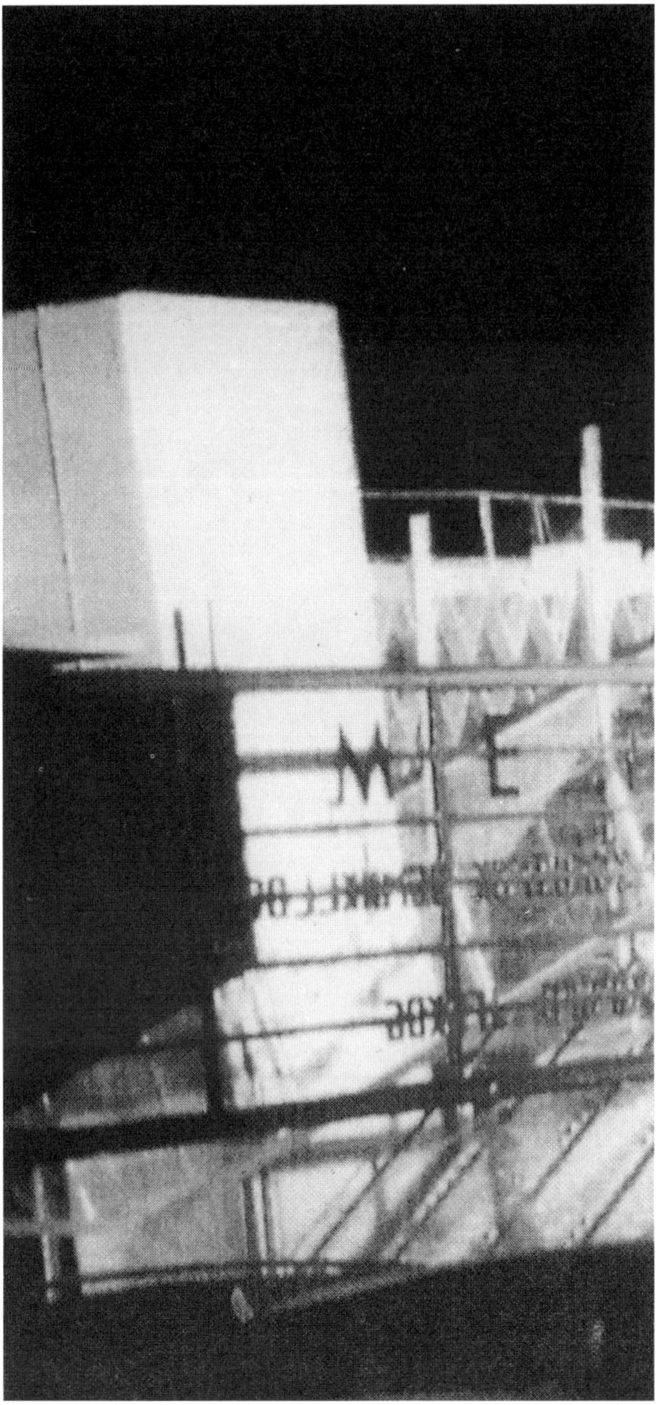

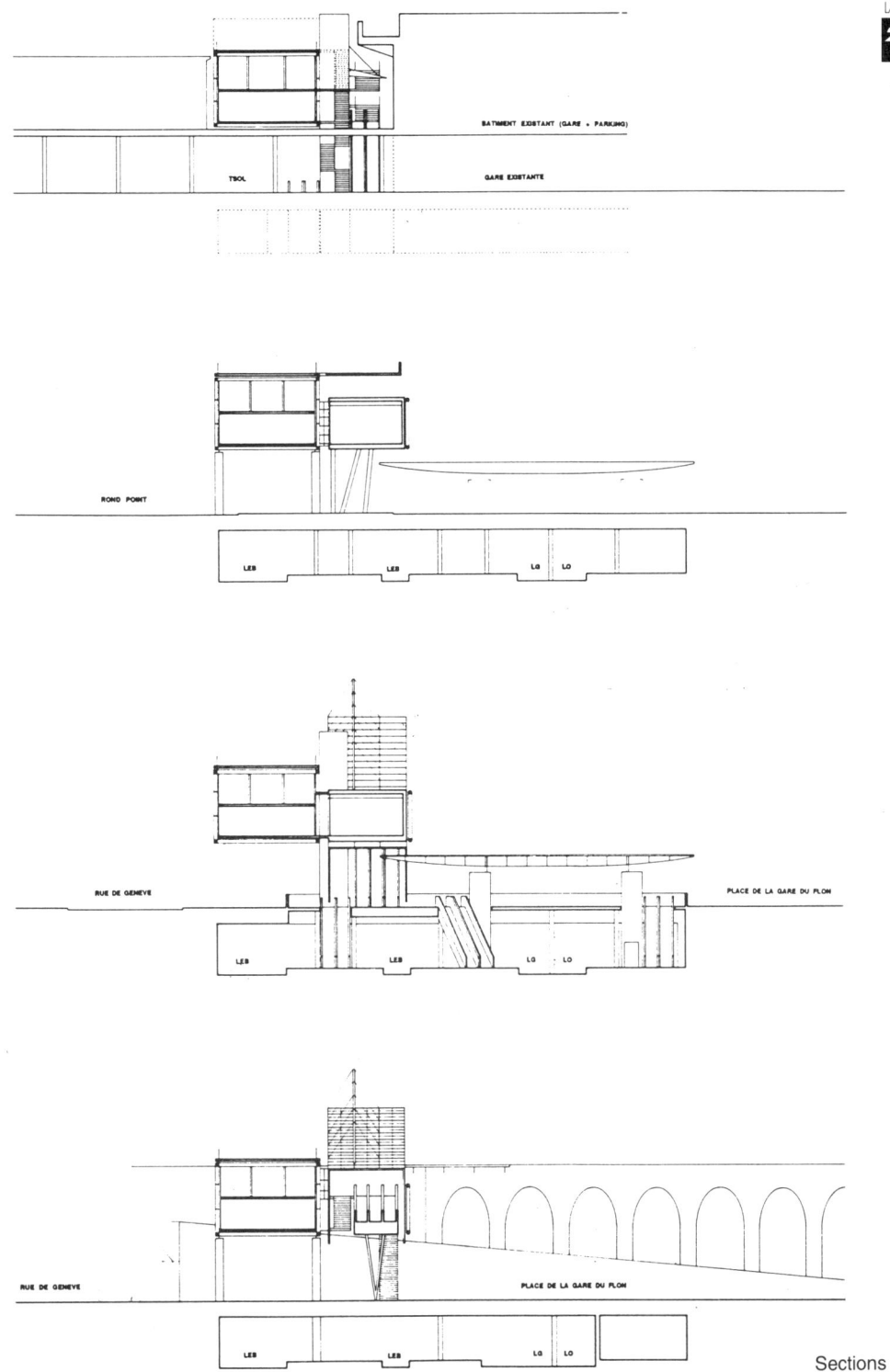

Sections

Intersections: electronic flows and the oblique movement of bodies

LAUSANNE
207

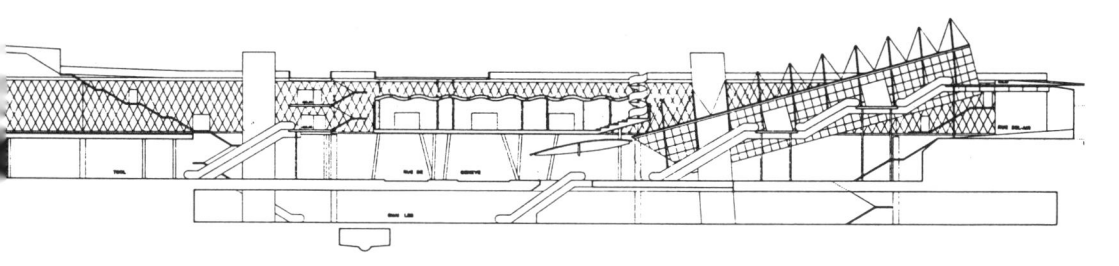

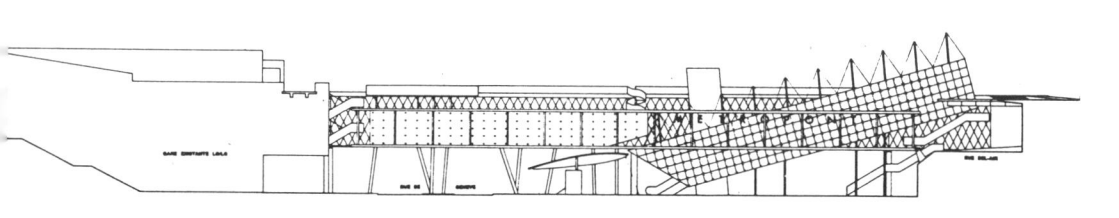

Longitudinal section

East elevation

Bridge structure: a hollow beam

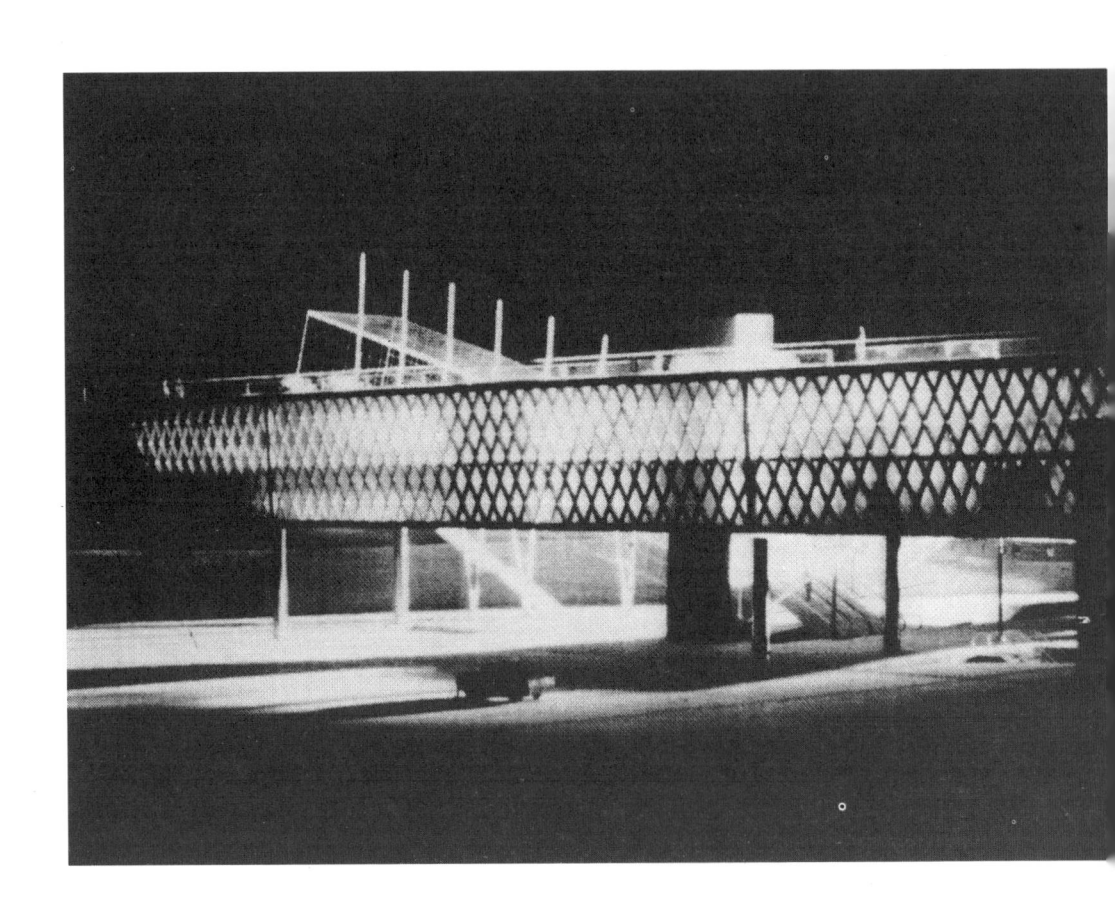

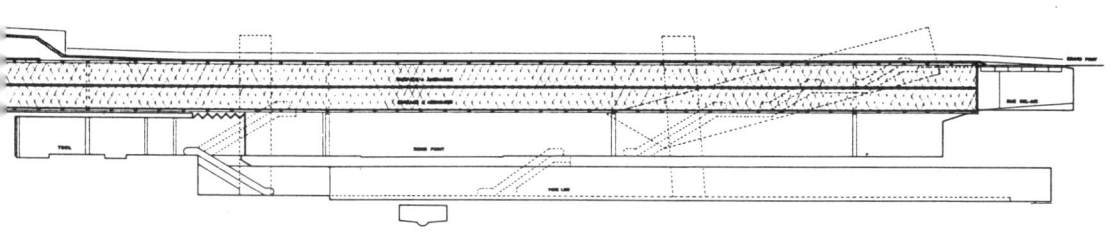

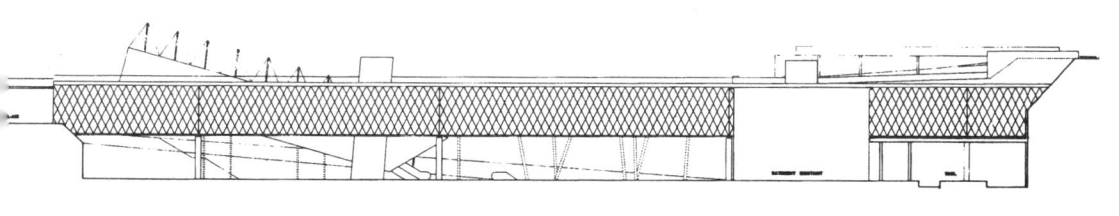

LAUSANNE
209

Longitudinal section

West elevation

COUPE AA

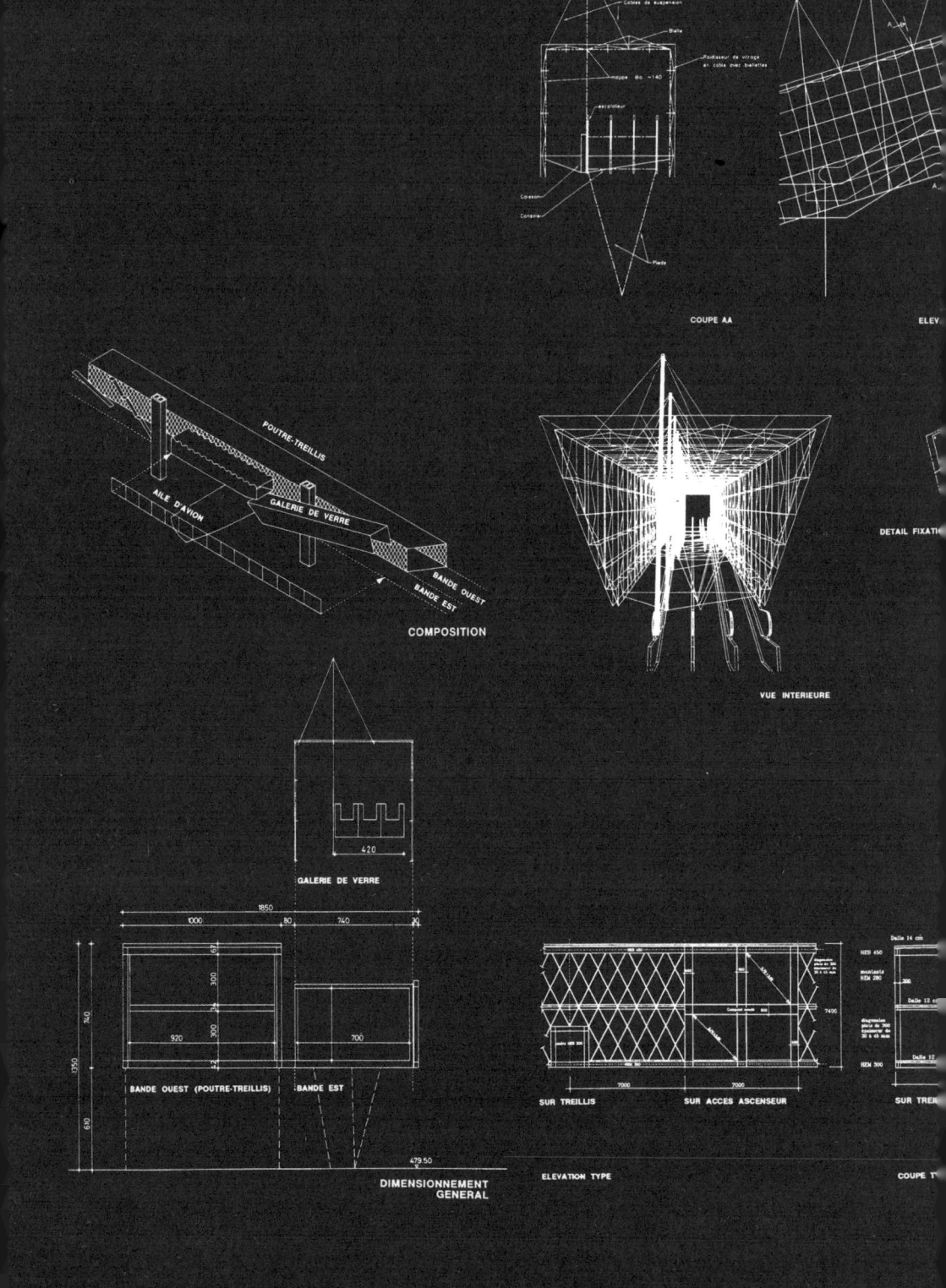

ELEV

DETAIL FIXATI

VUE INTERIEURE

COMPOSITION

GALERIE DE VERRE

BANDE OUEST (POUTRE-TREILLIS)   BANDE EST

DIMENSIONNEMENT GENERAL

SUR TREILLIS   SUR ACCES ASCENSEUR   SUR

ELEVATION TYPE

COUPE T

PLAN

ELEVATION

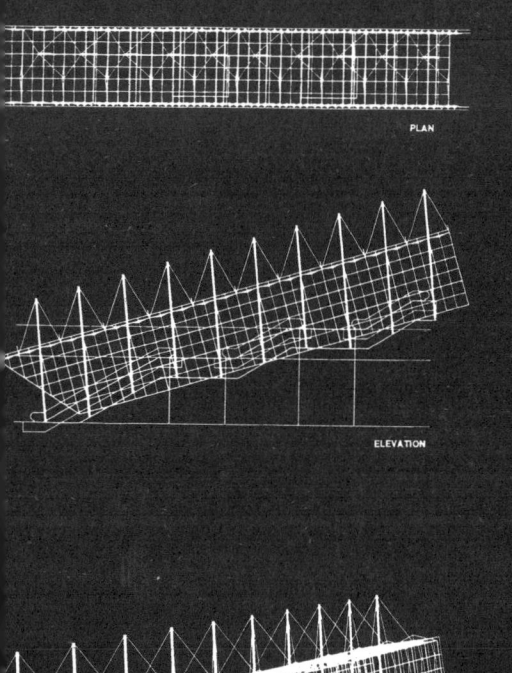

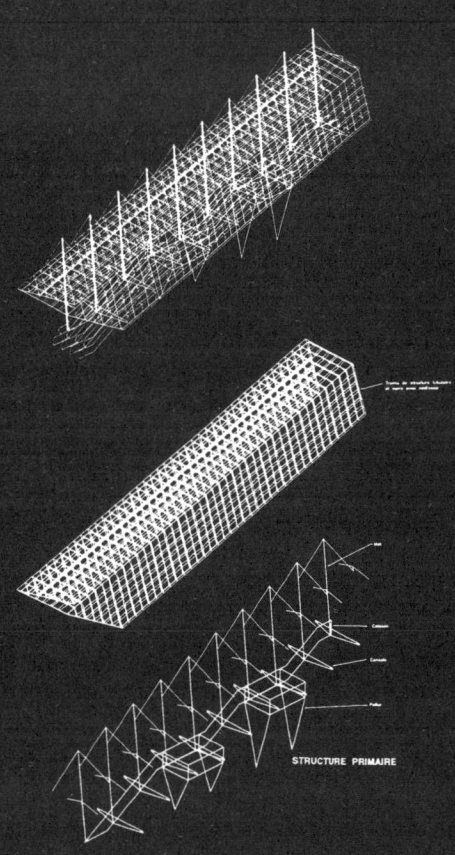

VUE EXTERIEURE

AXONOMETRIE

STRUCTURE PRIMAIRE

STRUCTURE DE LA GALERIE DE VERRE

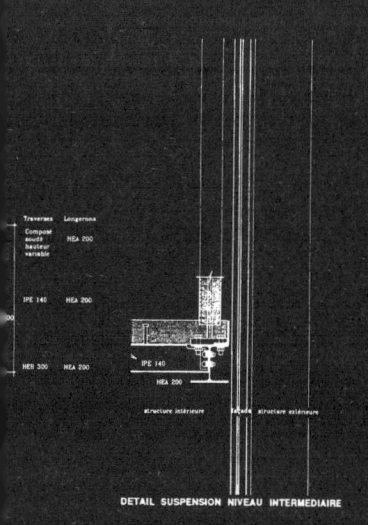

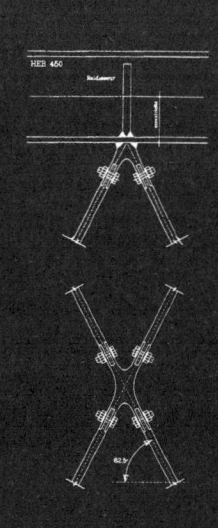

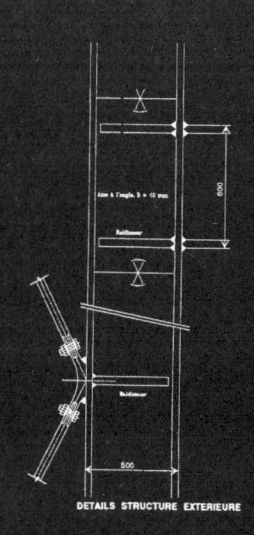

DETAIL SUSPENSION NIVEAU INTERMEDIAIRE

DETAILS STRUCTURE EXTERIEURE

STRUCTURE DE LA POUTRE-TREILLIS

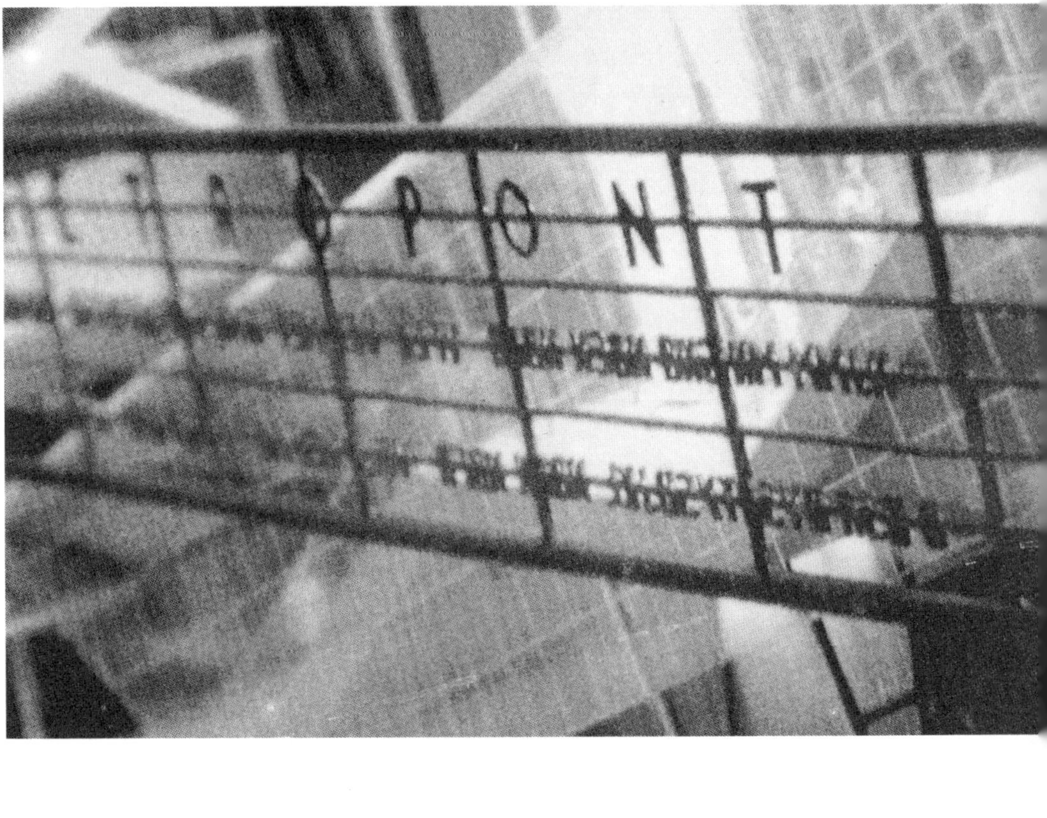

LAUSANNE
213

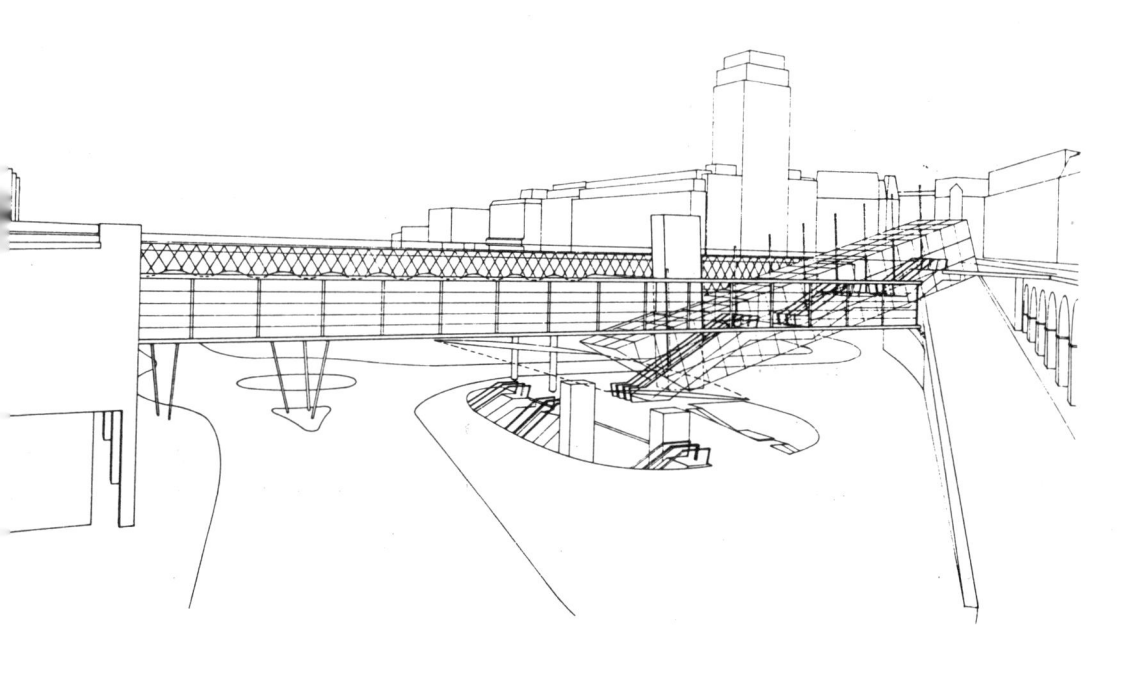

Metropont: view from the Grand Pont

The two disjoined terms: space and events, technology and use

LAUSANNE
215

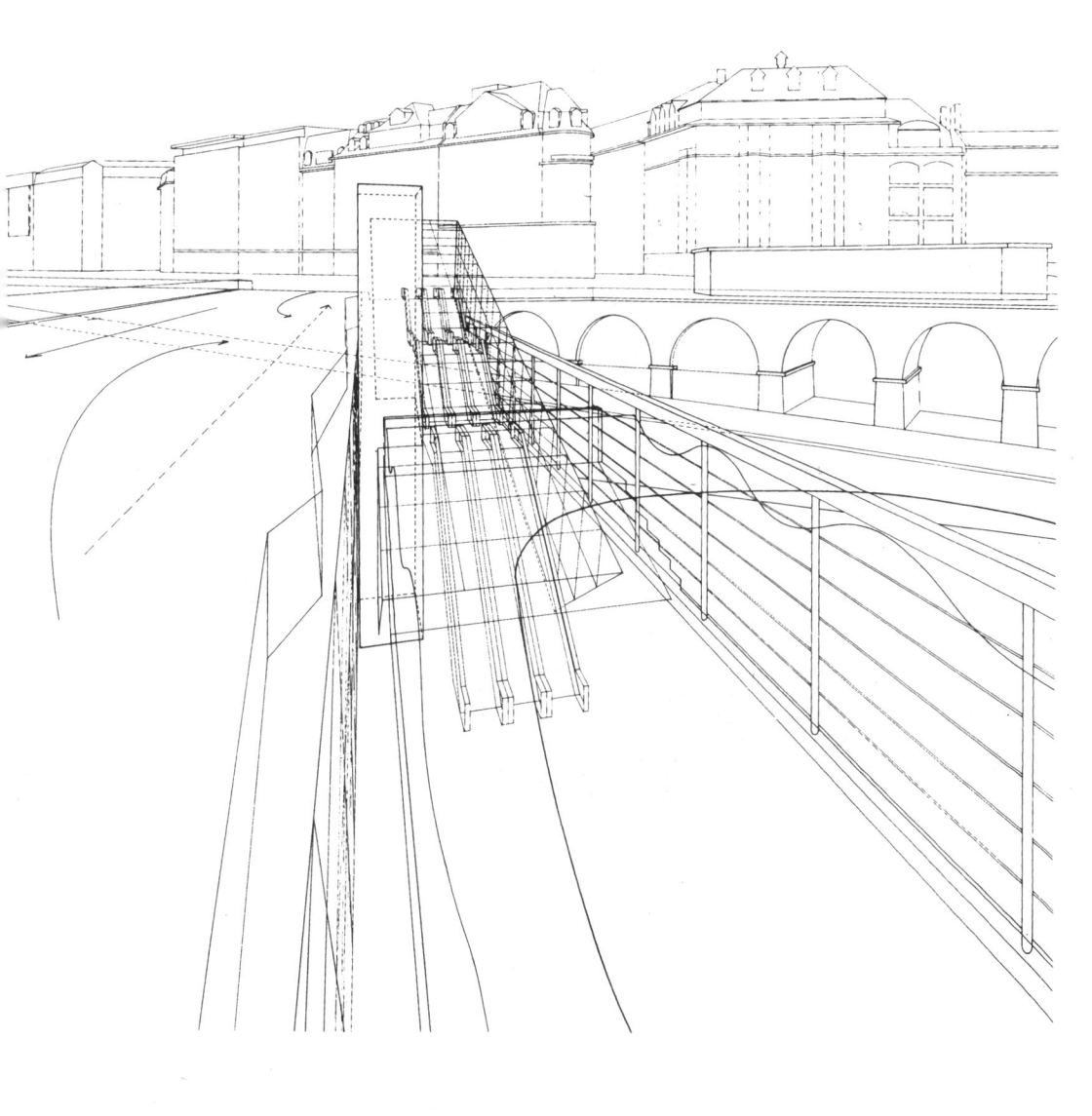

Metropont: glass gallery

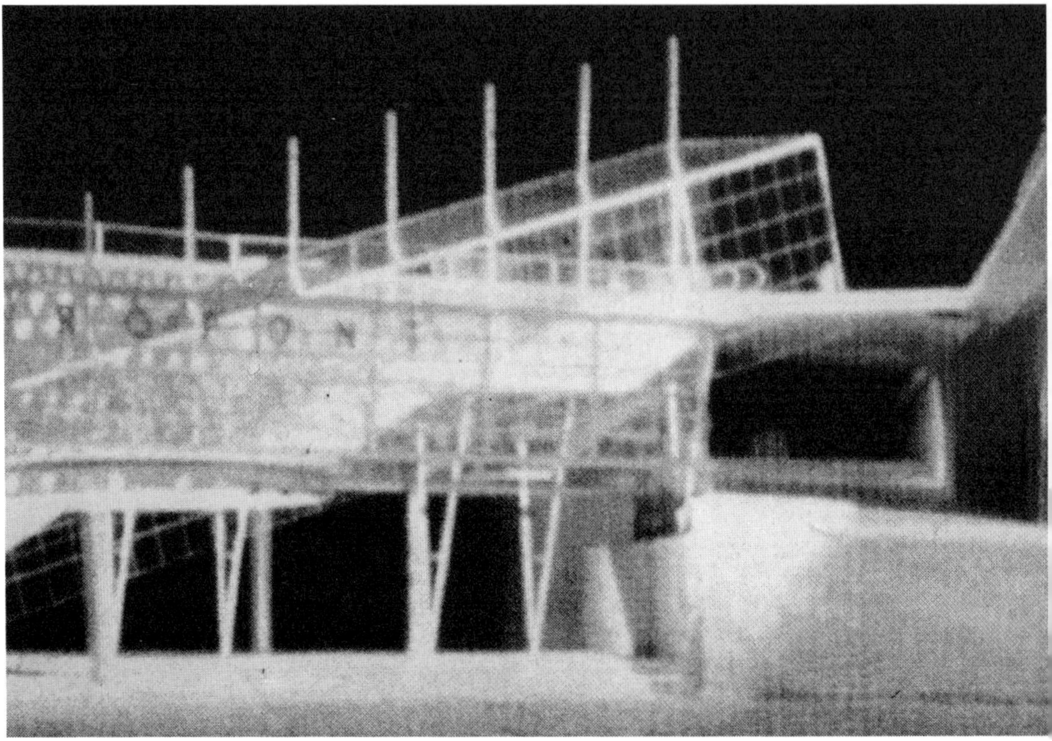

LAUSANNE
217

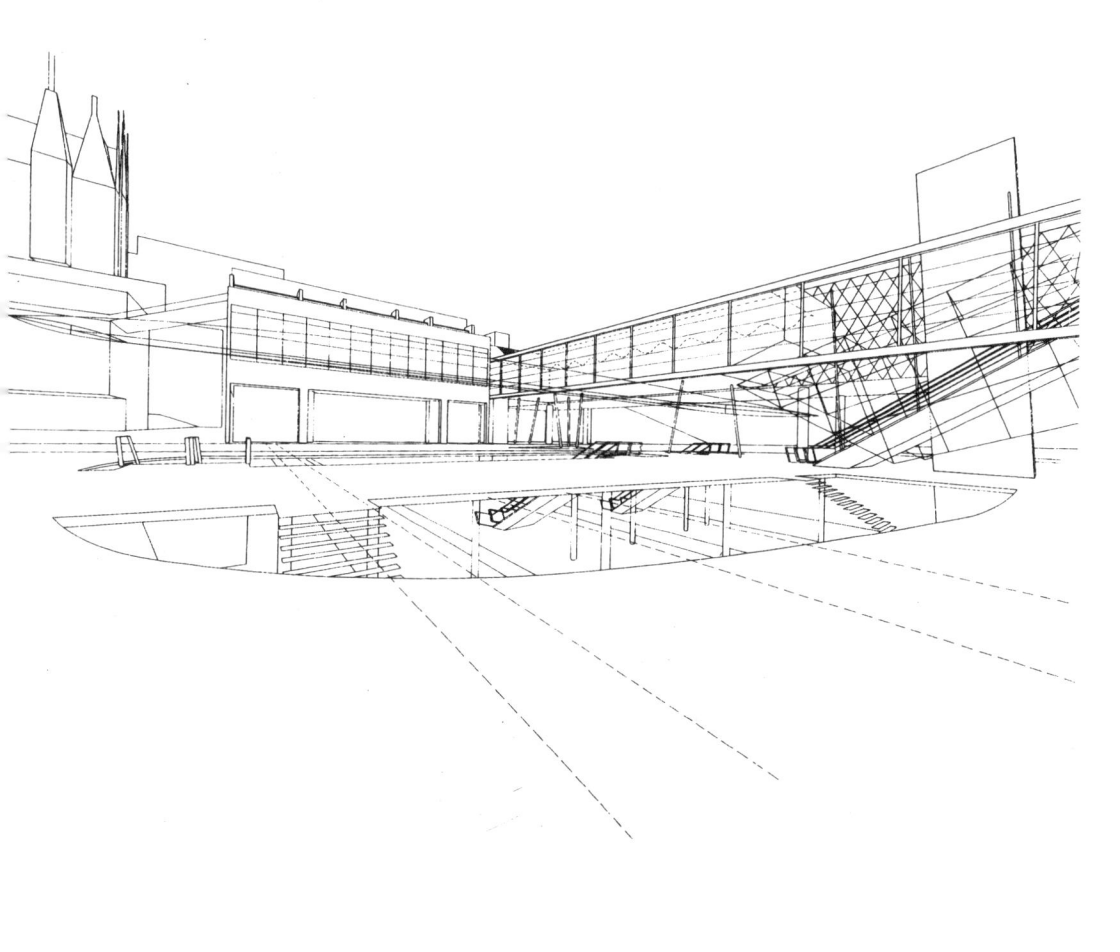

Crossprogramming: displacement and mutual contamination of terms

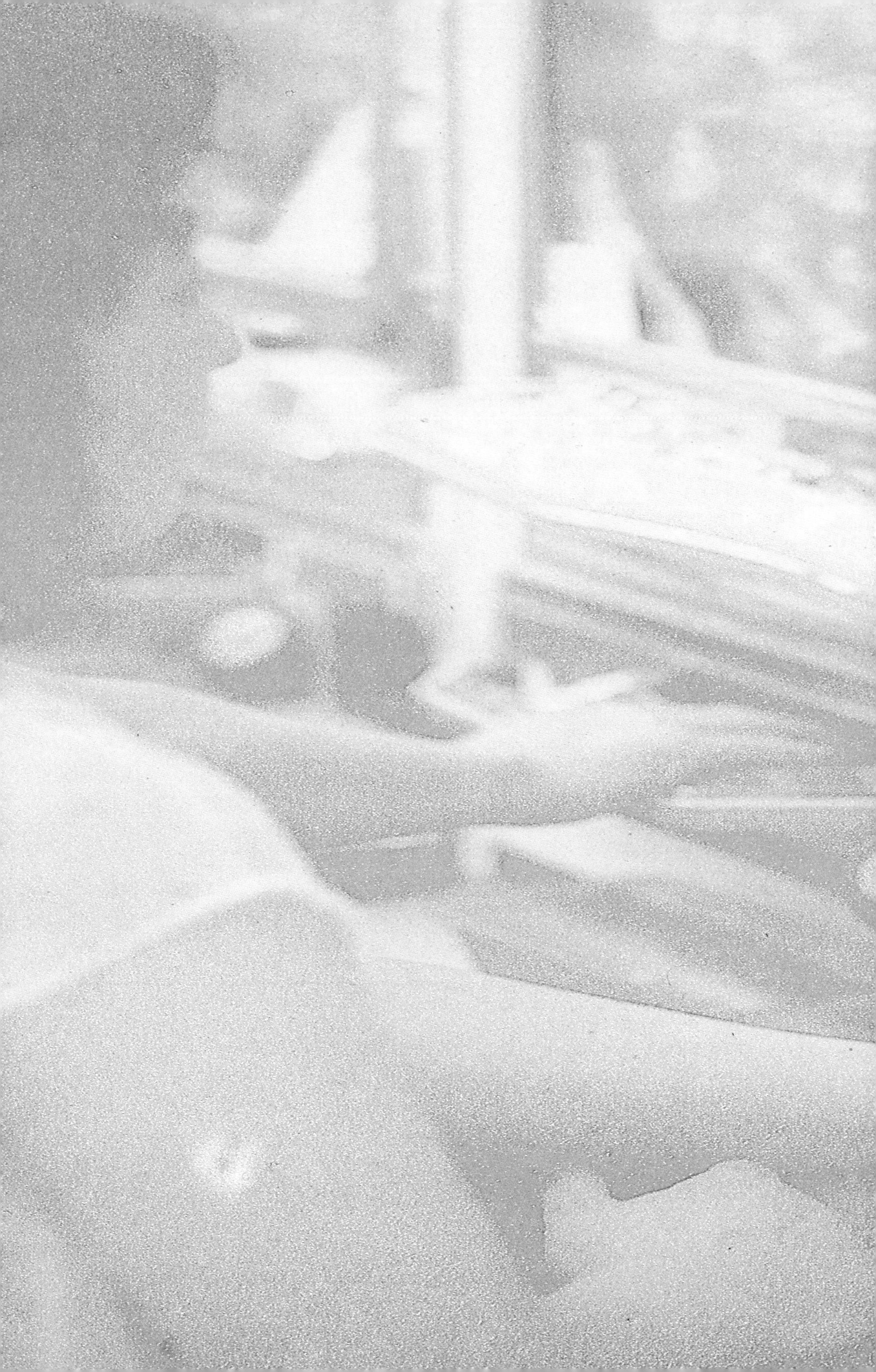

買場

15個賞

HEIWA

Kyoto, Center and Railway Station, 1991

Disprogramming

Disprogramming: Combining two or more programs, whereby a required spatial configuration of program A contaminates program B and B's possible configuration. The new program B may be extracted from the inherent contradictions contained in program A, and B's required spatial configuration may be applied to A.

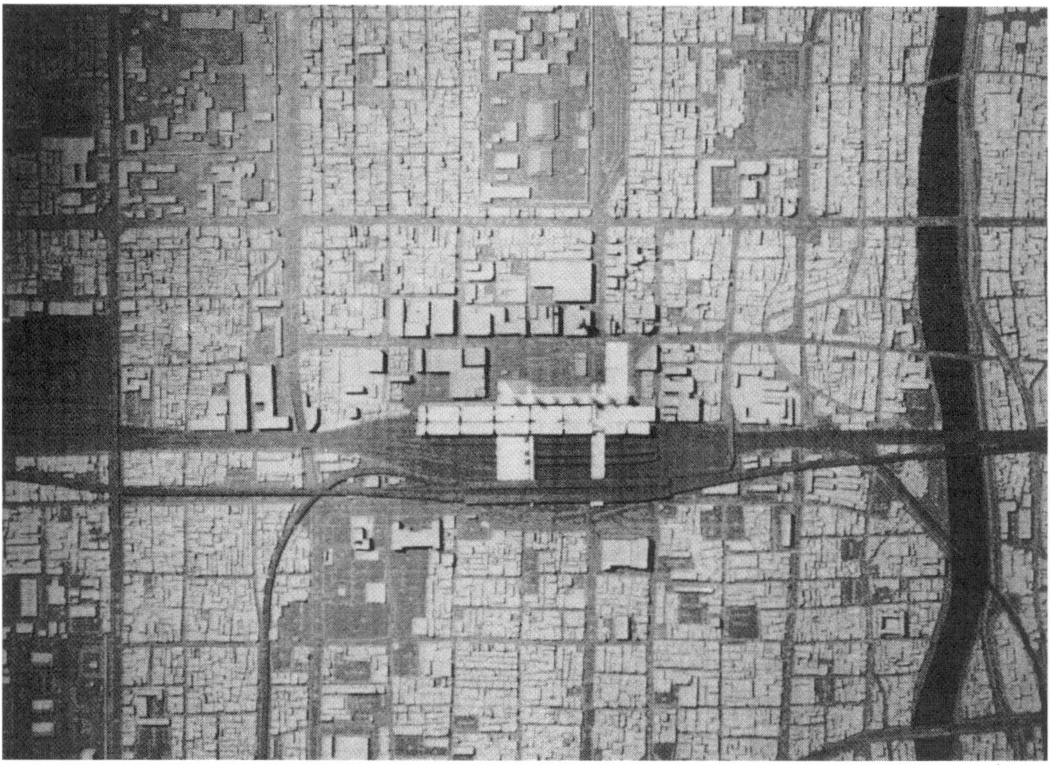

What is a railway station that is simultaneously a cultural center, a hotel, a convention center and a department store?
What do speed, communication and modernity have to do with the ancient civilization of Kyoto?
What does the small scale of the typical Japanese dwelling or *machiya* have to do with today's megablocks?

The juxtaposition of function, scale and historical time in contemporary culture is not a negative phenomenon but belongs to the logic of a new urban society. How, then, could the proposed encounters between disparate activities affect each other positively? How could the juxtaposition of the past and the future influence everyday lives in a constructive and enjoyable manner? How could the alignment of megascale and tatami scale generate a new pleasure in the contemporary city?

The competition for the railway station in Kyoto, Japan is characteristic of hybrid megaprojects at the end of the twentieth century. With over 250,000 square meters of space (1,000 percent more than the site area) and an estimated construction cost of over one billion dollars, such a huge facility with complex functions has no precedent.

To make matters more difficult, this large-scale, concentrated urban facility was not to be located in some booming business district in Tokyo, Paris or Frankfurt but in the heart of traditional Japanese culture, in historic Kyoto with its low density and horizontal landscape.

We began by decomposing the overall program into its main constituent elements and aligning them with the Kyoto grid—one block for the cultural center, two for the hotel and convention center, two for the department store and two for parking, keeping a nine-meter opening between each block at the location of the street grid. This permitted us to avoid building a massive wall and to keep the access points open across the north-south axes which traverse the railroad tracks. We then subdivided the blocks into organizational strips eighteen meters, twenty-seven meters and eighteen meters wide respectively, with a three meter gap between them to allow natural light into the center of the blocks. These strips intentionally reinforce Kyoto's current building height (forty-five meters south of the station, thirty-one meters on the north), so that the new building—despite its mass—would not act as a barrier but as a transition between the old and new parts of the city.

We also extracted from the program the most particular or "eventful" functions or activities, which in combination would produce the "event."

Hence, we "staged" a combination of image theater, sky lounge, wedding chapel, athletic club, amusement arcade, gourmet market and historical museum into a new and composite architectonic element invented by us: the programmatic extractor or "skyframe."

Placed in front of the hotel, convention center, large store and the parking lot blocks, the skyframe is the intersection of a horizontal slab (the 250-meter-long structurally gridded hollow beam) and seven uneven vertical slabs (the supporting towers or *yaguras*, 5.4 meters wide by 15 meters deep and ranging from sixty-two to eighty-three meters high). Besides extreme programmatic intensity, the skyframe, with its long cantilevered space and slender glass towers ("seven gates"), was to give Kyoto a new heterogeneous sign, to be superimposed on the temple landscape without obliterating it.

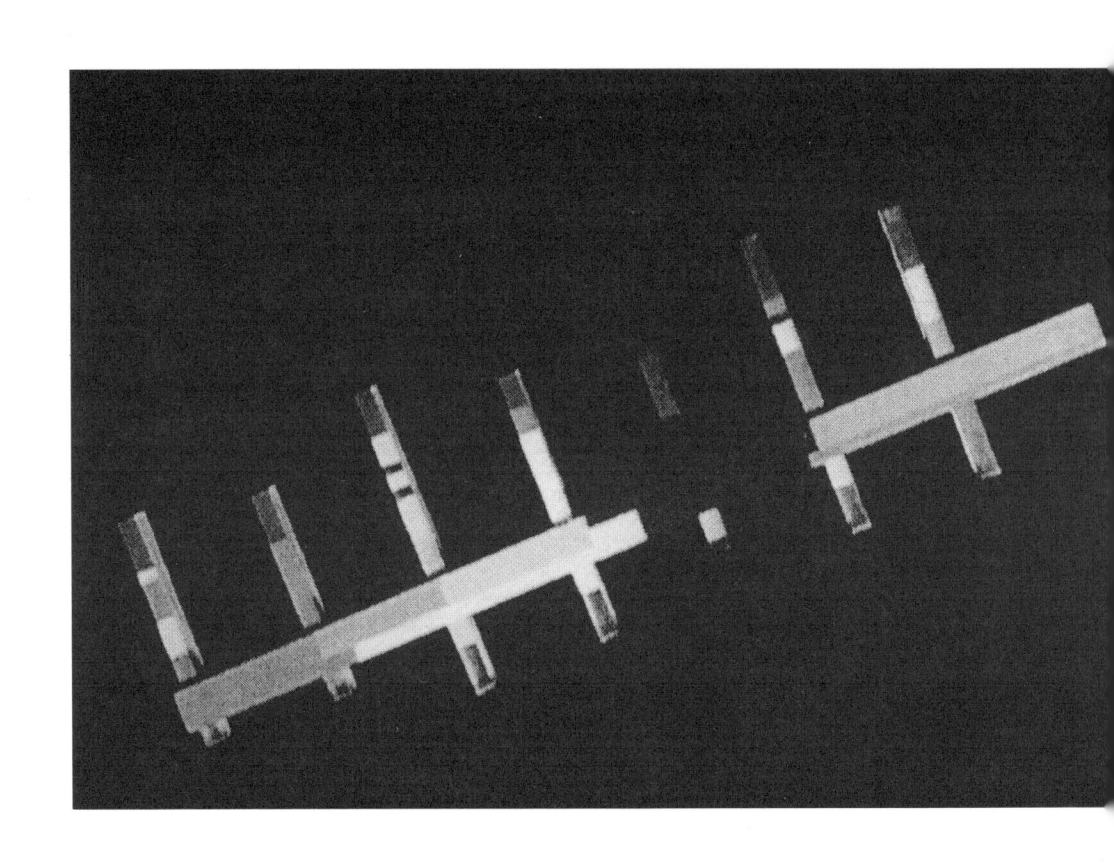

Skyframe: disprogramming the event

The glass towers contain video viewing rooms, video bars, sky lounges, museum displays, small restaurants and private dining rooms, kimono exhibition spaces, wedding waiting rooms, exercise and weight lifting spaces, small amusement halls and, at the top, aviaries, teahouses, greenhouses, banner displays and observatories—all floors being connected through ultrarapid elevators.

The skyframe defines the public space of the station below and the symbolic space of the city above. It frames the sky (an open frame). At ground level, a tilted glass curtain hung from the skyframe marks the great hall—a common denominator among the main functions.

The skyframe concentrates the exceptional aspect of the complex by acting as a program extractor and by transprogramming activities into unusual vertical and horizontal relations. Ultimately, the combination of a new spatial artifact (the skyframe) and a new programmatic mix aims to produce an unprecedented architectural event and suggests a new reading of historic Kyoto.

Structure
The skyframe consists of seven slender towers and a horizontal hollow beam linking them. The towers are situated in the middle of the hollow beam, so that the elements form a structural entity. In the longitudinal direction the towers are columns and the *caisson* a torsionally stiff beam connected to form a portal frame system. In the transversal direction the towers are a simple cantilever from the ground level upwards. The structure of the skyframe is independent of the other blocks in the development. The skyframe is divided into two independent elements with a separation joint between towers 3 and 4, numbering from the east. Towers 2 and 5 do not extend down to the ground; they are vertically supported. The supporting towers (towers 1, 3, 4, 6 and 7) are founded directly at the ground level. They support the hollow beam and the remaining towers. Heights vary between 72.5 and 83 meters from the ground level or between 41.5 and 52 meters from the top of the hollow beam. The towers consist of four vertical circular tubes connected to each other at each floor level by horizontal rectangular tubes. The connections are rigid moment joints permitting the whole to have a vierendeel action for lateral loads. The "supported" towers are identical to the supporting ones, with the exception of the structure below the hollow beam which is not braced diagonally. At the western end of the block, the hollow beam extends thirty meters beyond the last tower as a simple cantilever. The rigid planar nature of the surfaces permits holes to be cut out at certain penetration points, such as for towers, staircases or elevator shafts.

The suspended glass curtain under the skyframe has been made as transparent as possible in order to emphasize the architectural concept. The glass surface is suspended in a vertical wave such that its reflections are fragmented. An attempt is made to minimize the number of times the sky is reflected to a viewer on the plaza. The glass is fixed directly to lozenge-shaped glazing trusses comprised of two prestressed cables, each of which describes a parabola curve, and a central compression strut. The glass plane follows a curve delineated by cables at each row of trusses. Individual panes are fixed to the ends of the spreader arms of the trusses with articulated point support fittings.

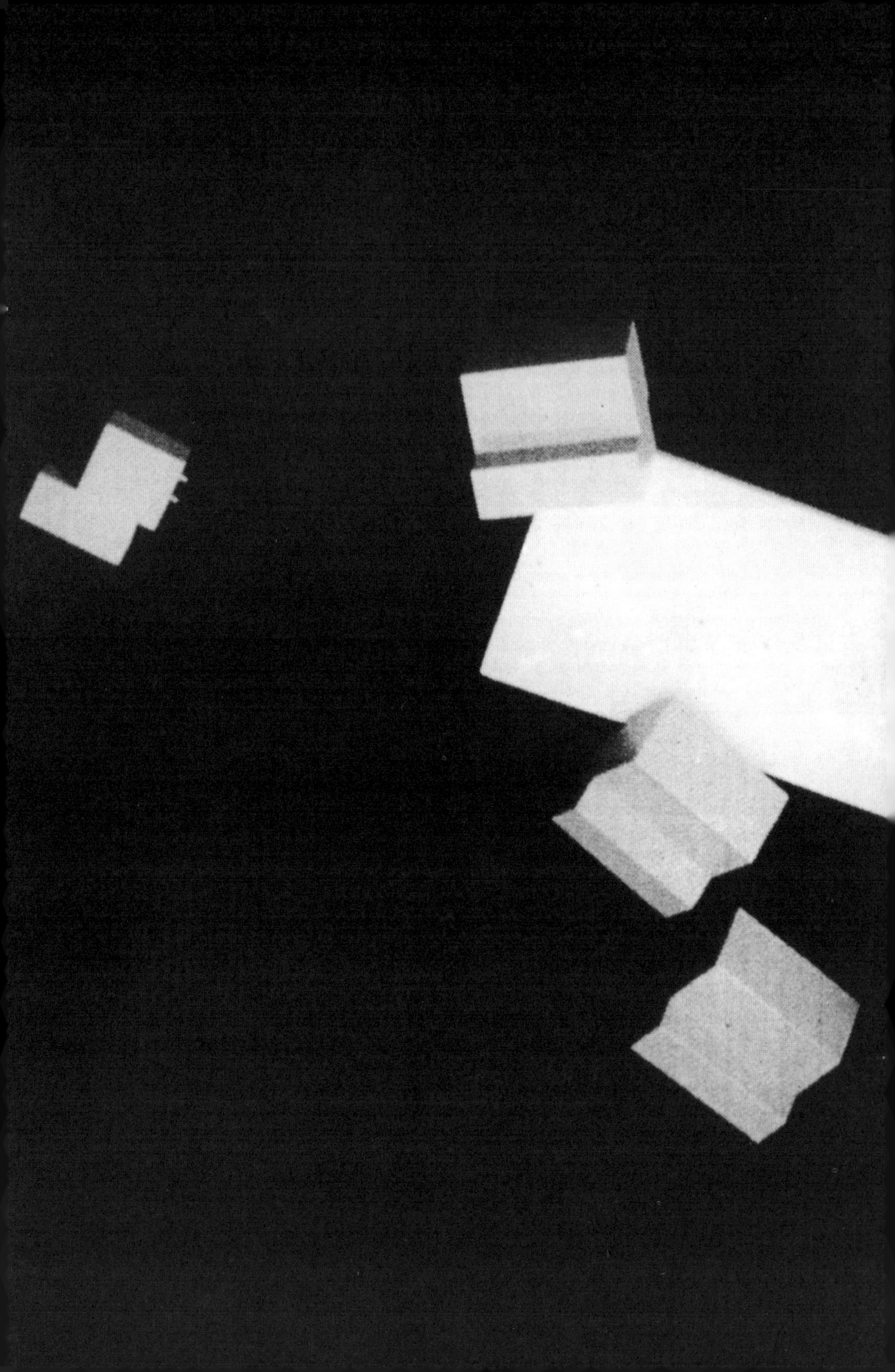

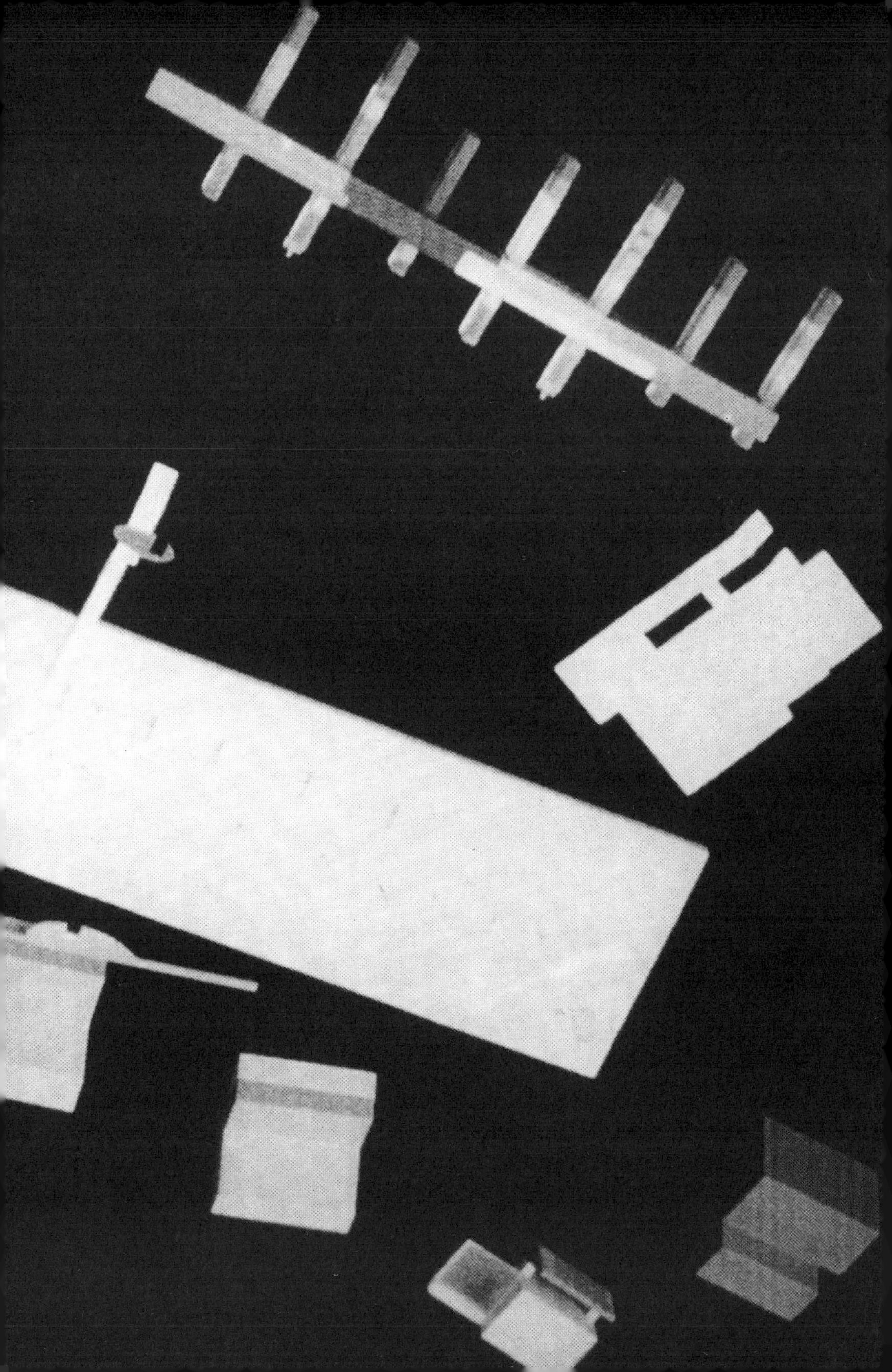

Inserting a vertical programmatic axis into the horizontal grid: the skyframe

KYOTO
229

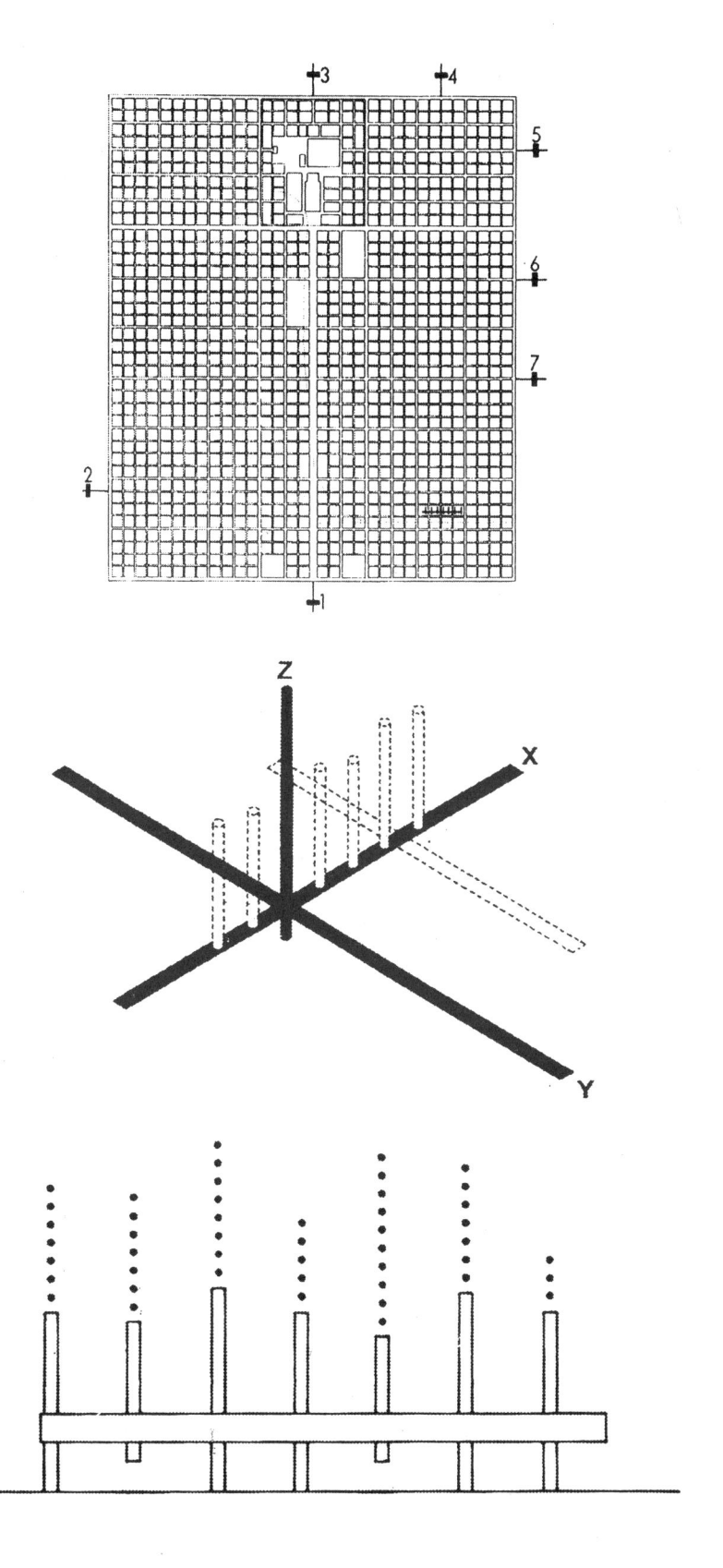

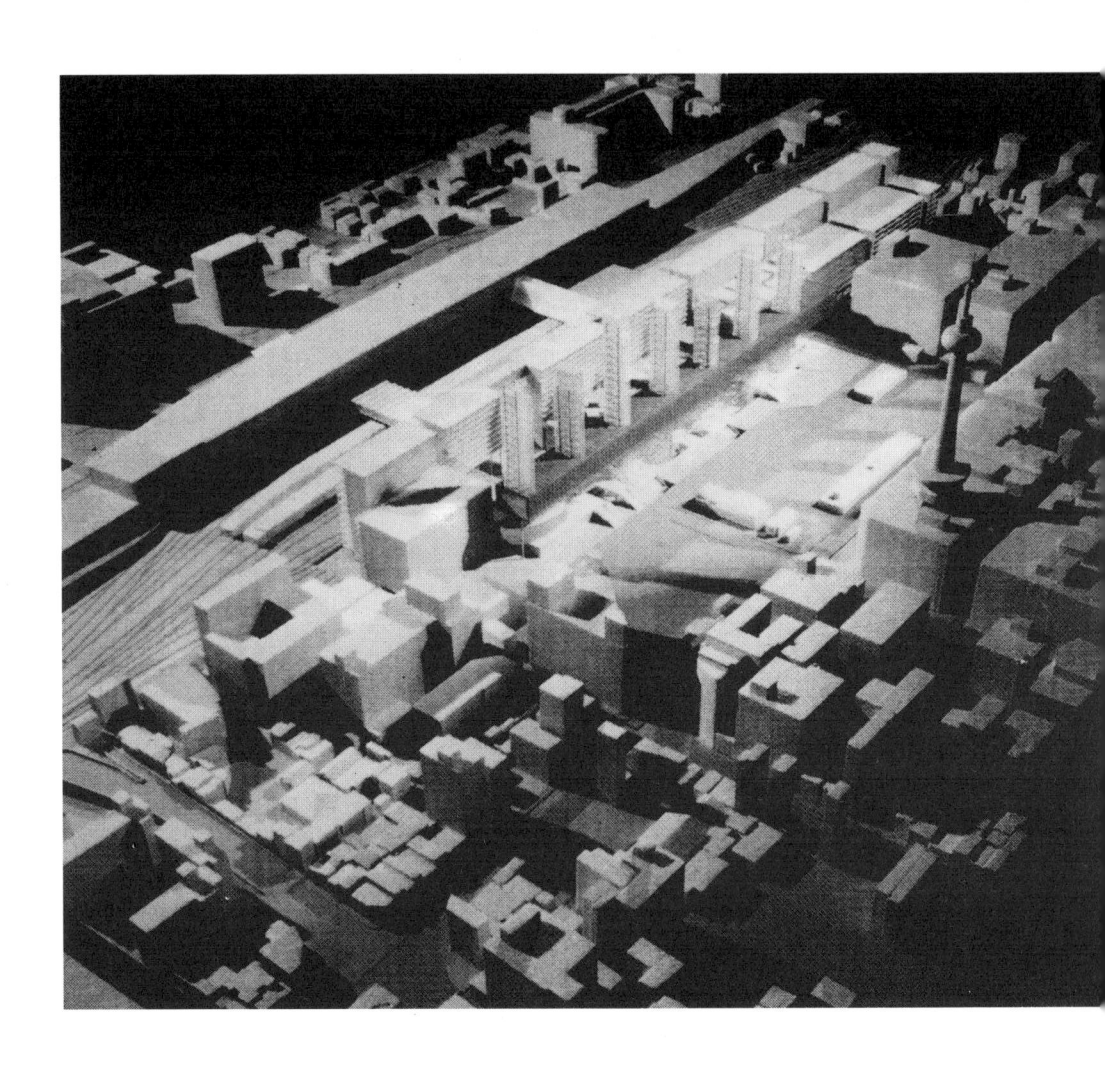

Distribution of the "quantitative" functions

文化施設
CULTURAL CENTER

駅
STATION

ホテル
HOTEL

デパート
DEPT. STORE

駐車場
CAR PARK

文化施設　　　　　ホテル　駅　　　　デパート　　　　駐車場
CULTURAL CENTER HOTEL STATION DEPT. STORE   CAR PARK

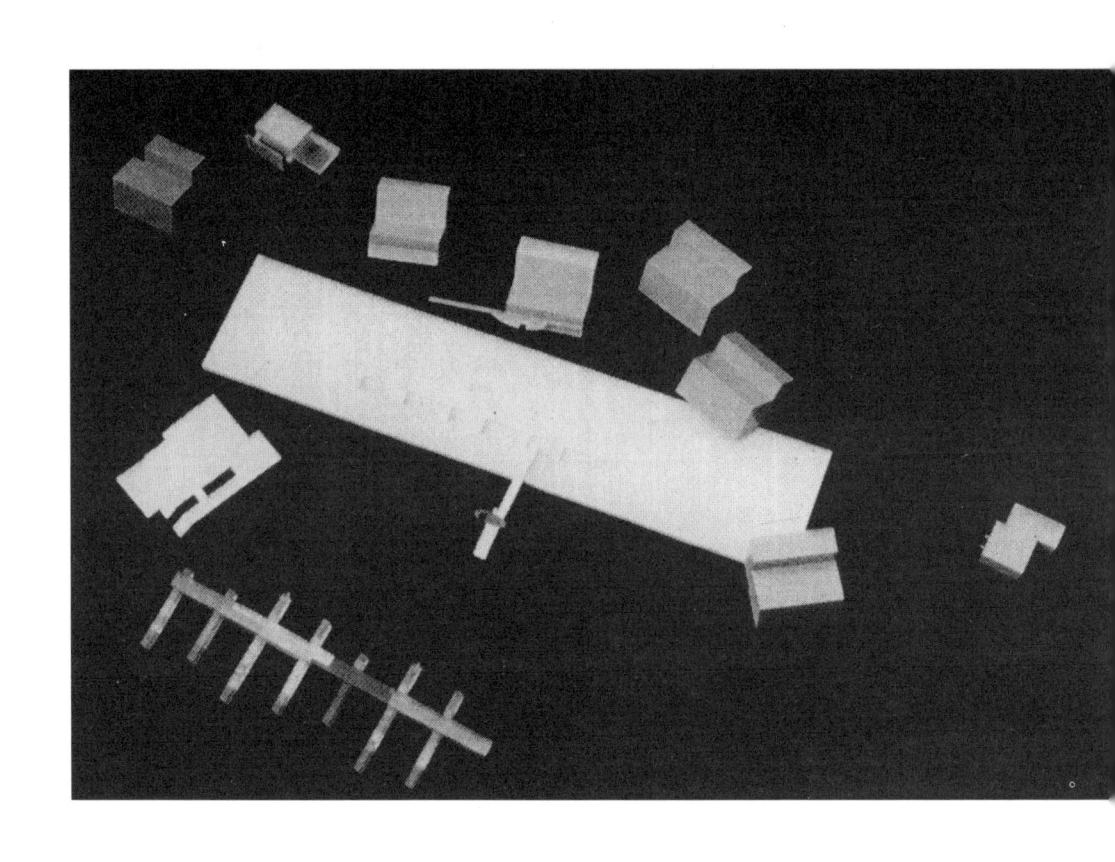

Decomposing the hidden programmatic logic of the event

KYOTO
233

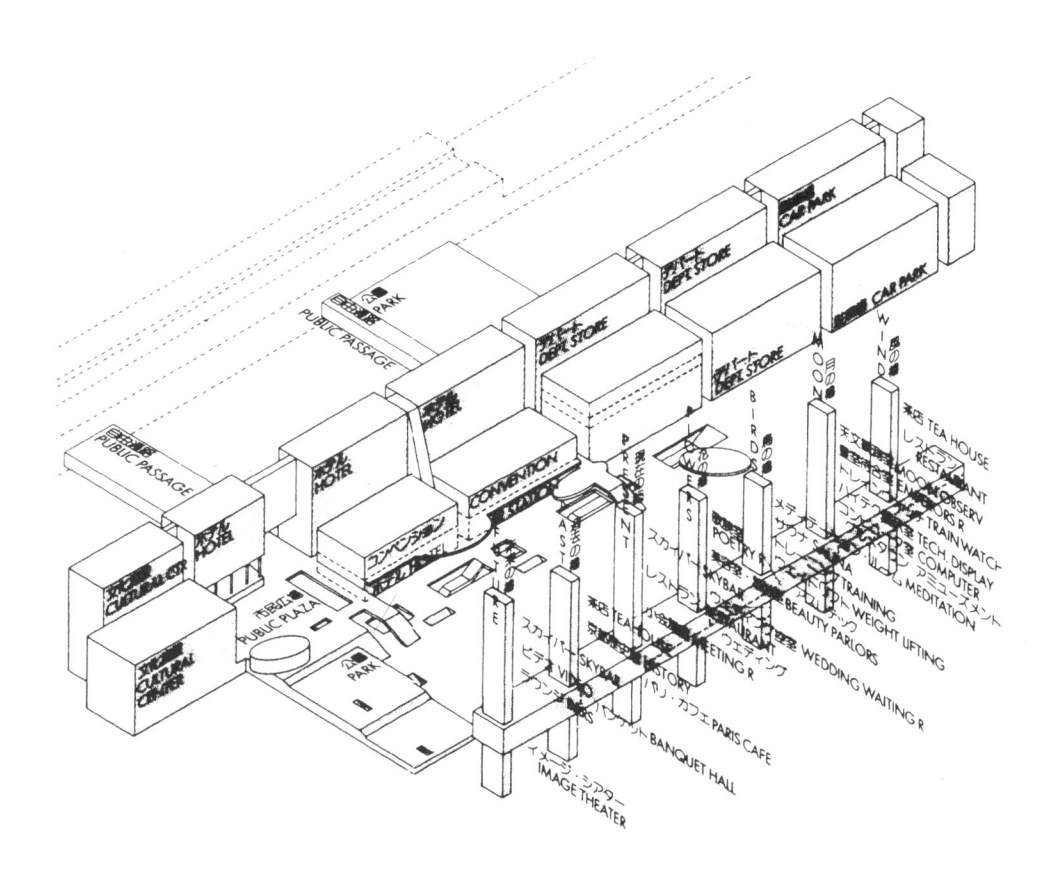

Organization:

Blocks: quantitative functions

Skyframe: qualitative functions

Intensifying and **accelerating** the urban experience

KYOTO
235

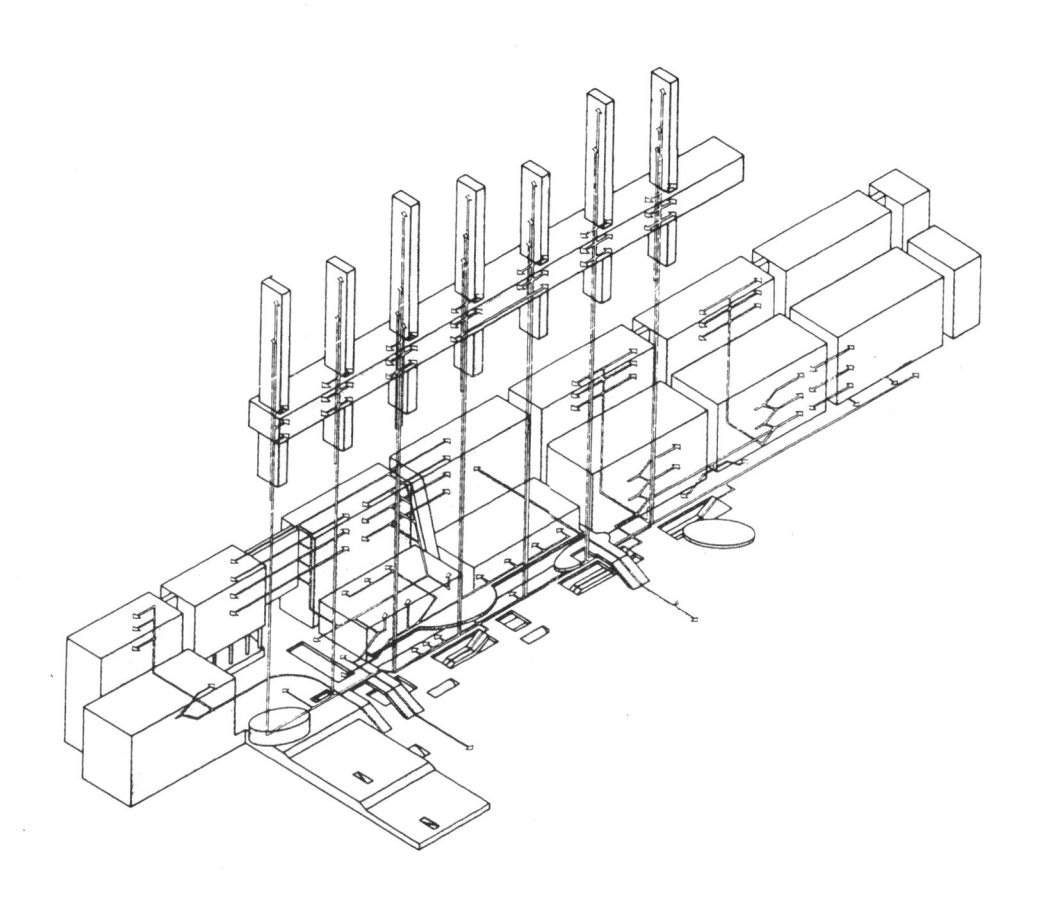

Movement: travelators, escalators, elevators, ramps, stairs, catwalks

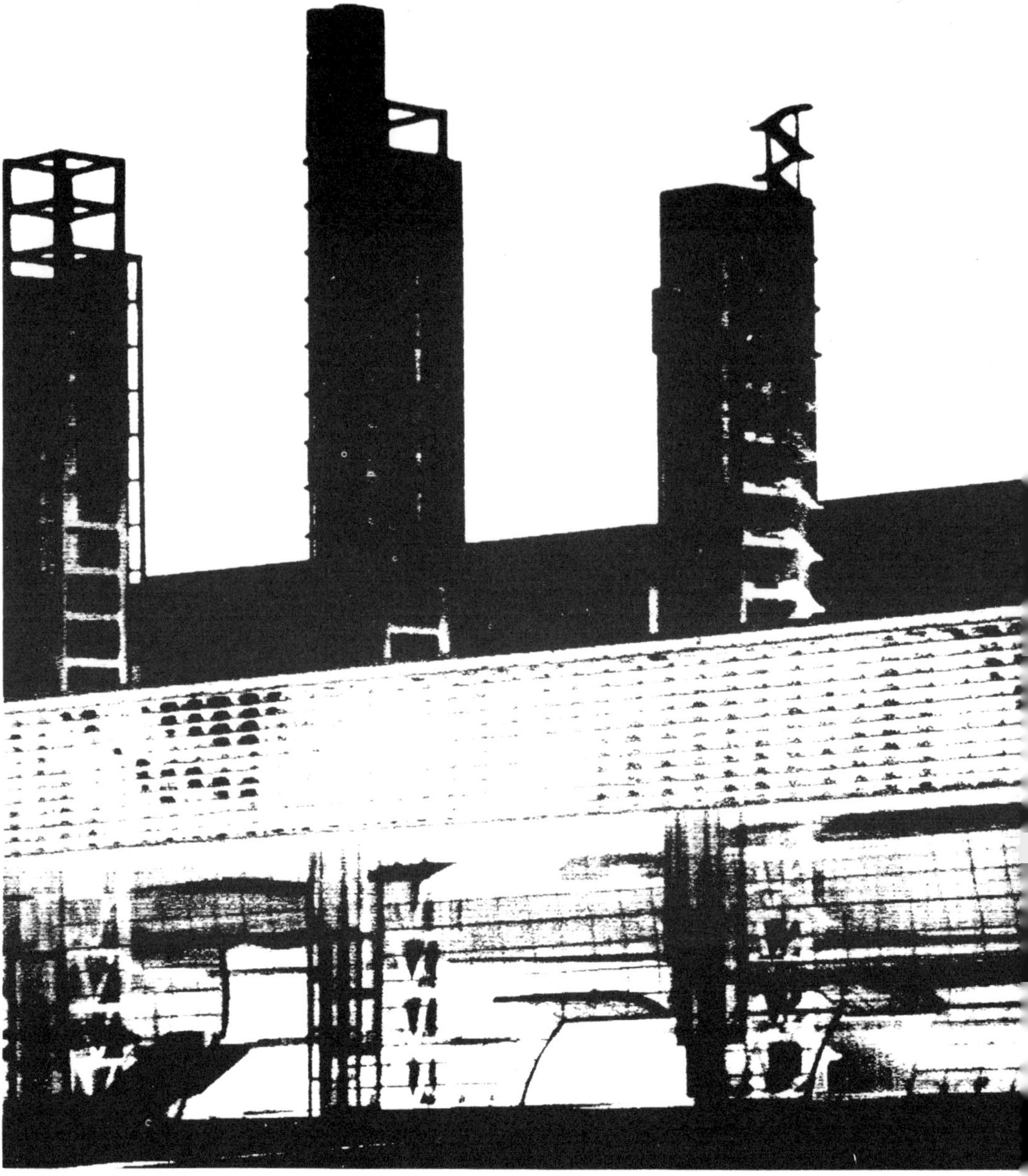

Structure. Blocks (quantitative functions): an endlessly repetitive and neutralized grid; skyframe (qualitative functions): a search for technological invention

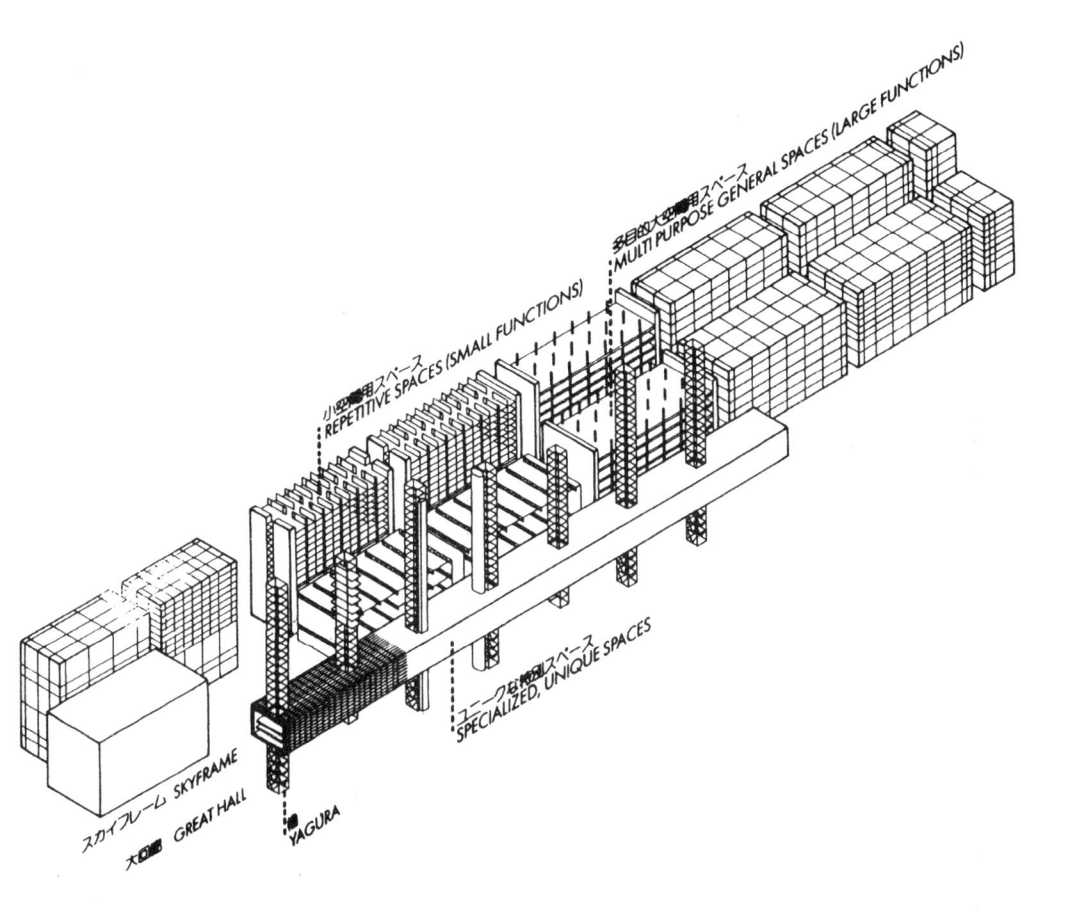

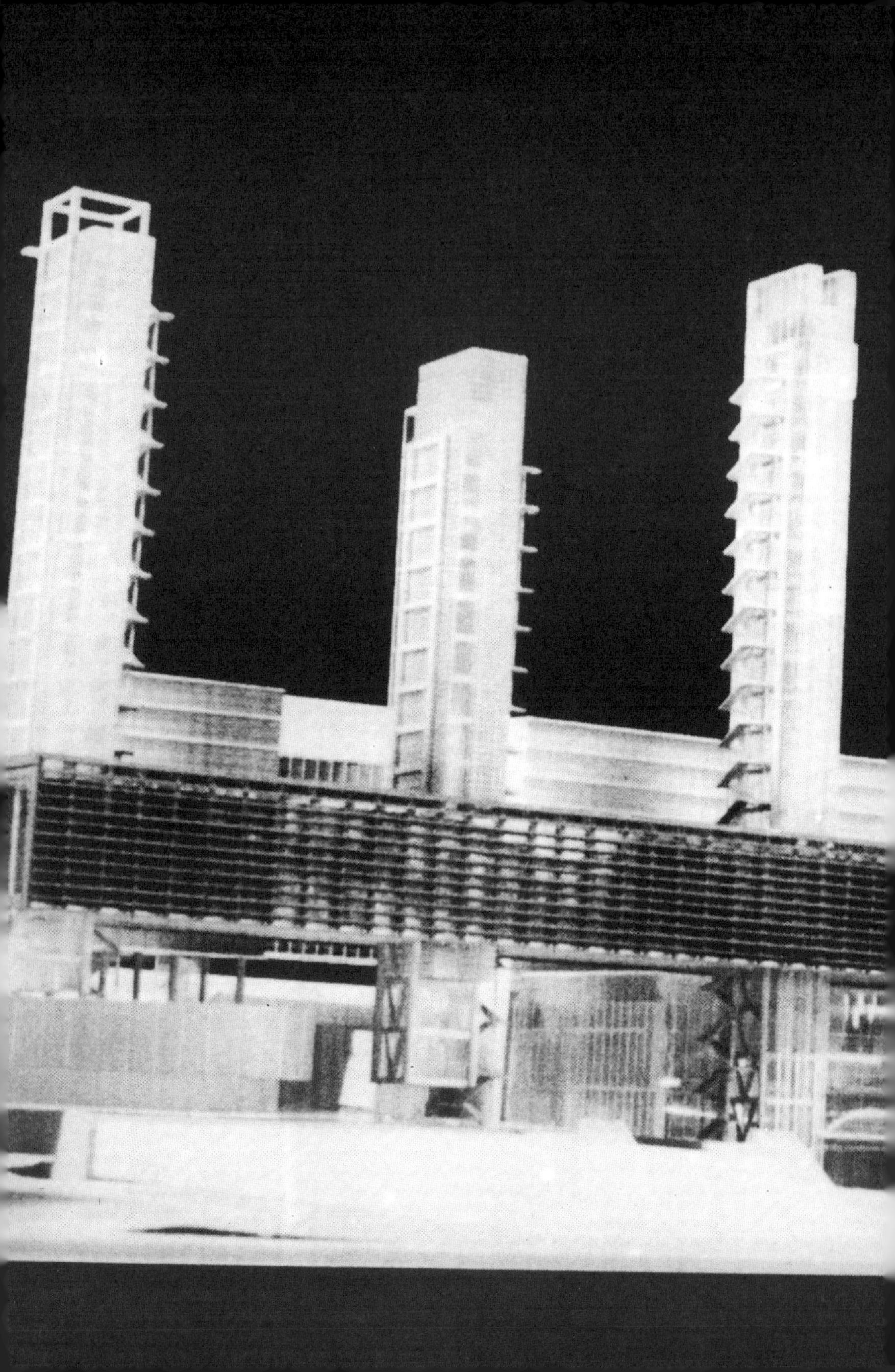

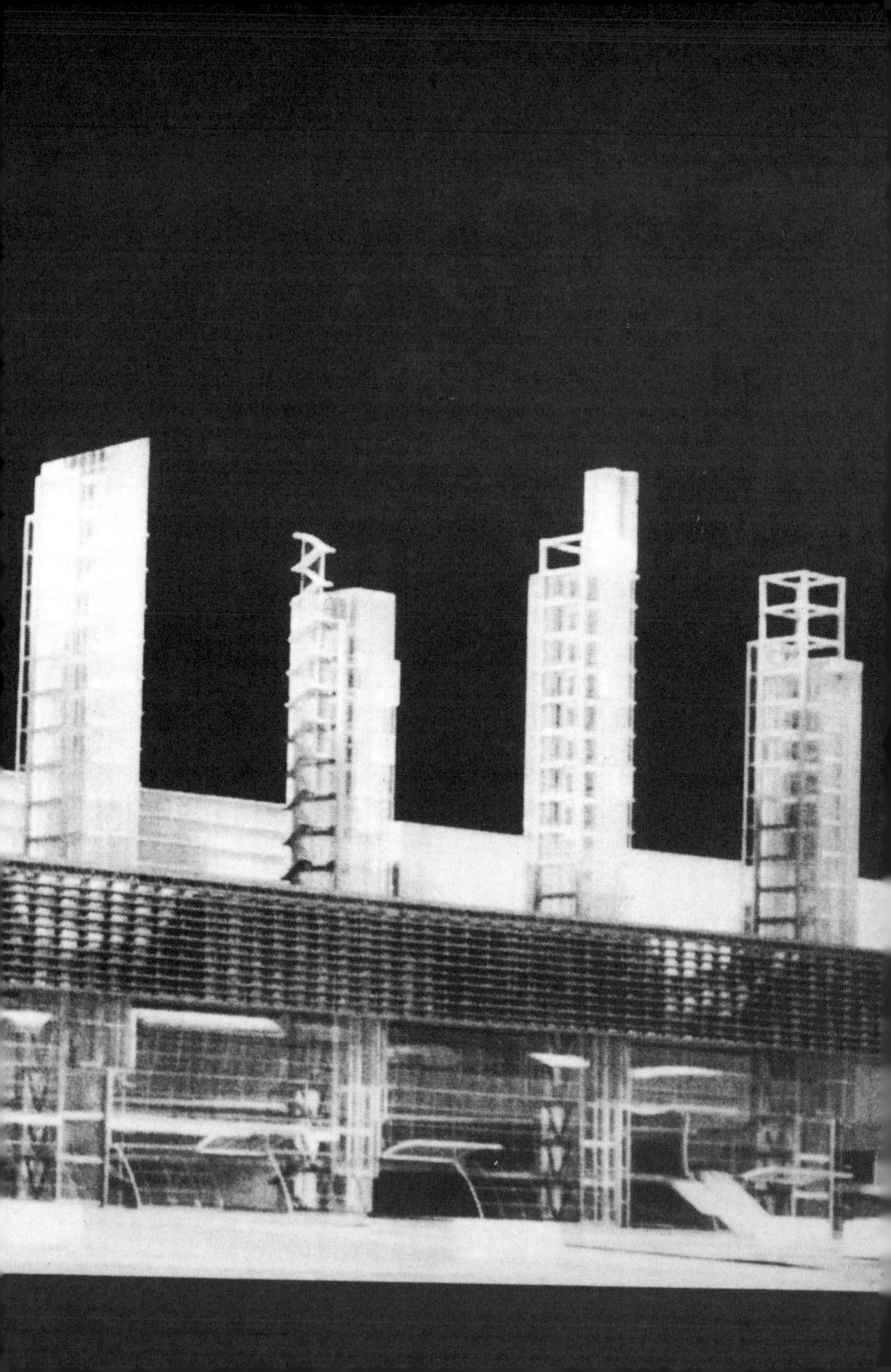

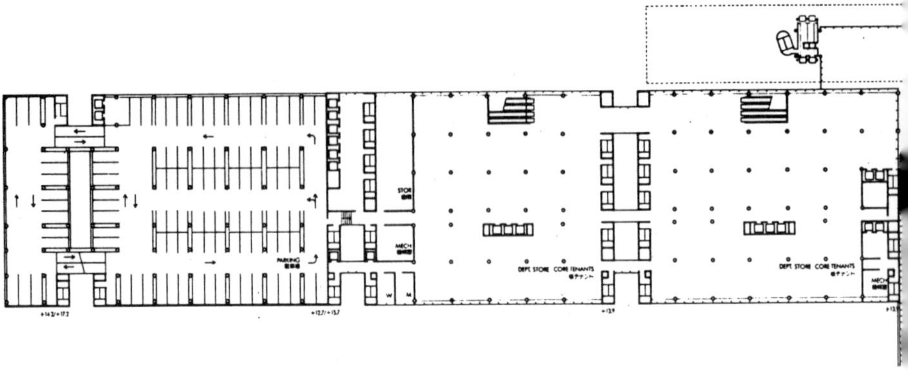
PARKING
STOR
MECH
W
M
DEPT. STORE CORE TENANTS
DEPT. STORE CORE TENANTS
MECH

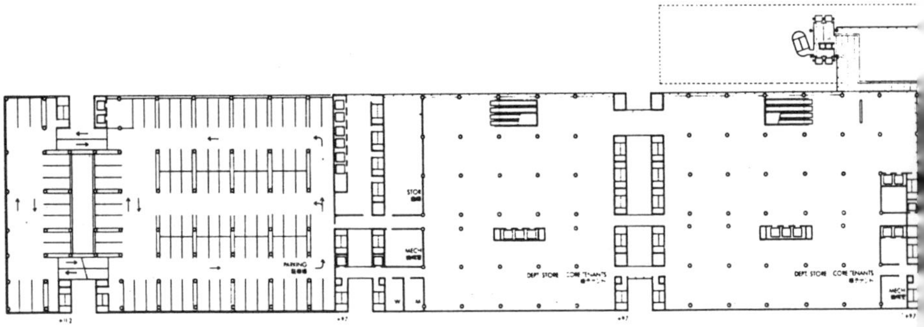
PARKING
STOR
MECH
W
M
DEPT. STORE CORE TENANTS
DEPT. STORE CORE TENANTS
MECH

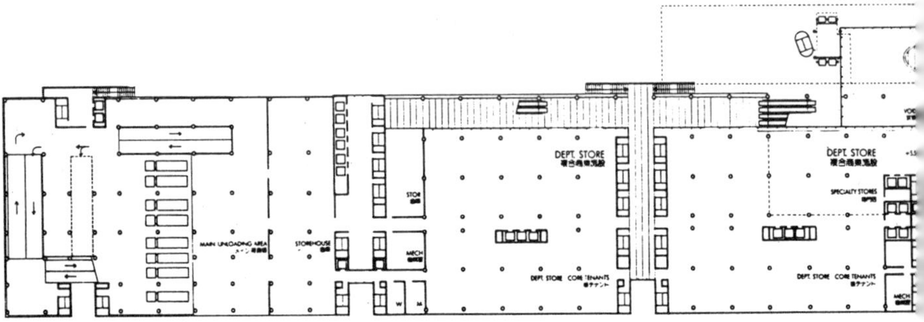
MAIN UNLOADING AREA
STOREHOUSE
STOR
MECH
W
M
DEPT. STORE
DEPT. STORE
SPECIALTY STORES
DEPT. STORE CORE TENANTS
DEPT. STORE CORE TENANTS
MECH

KYOTO
241

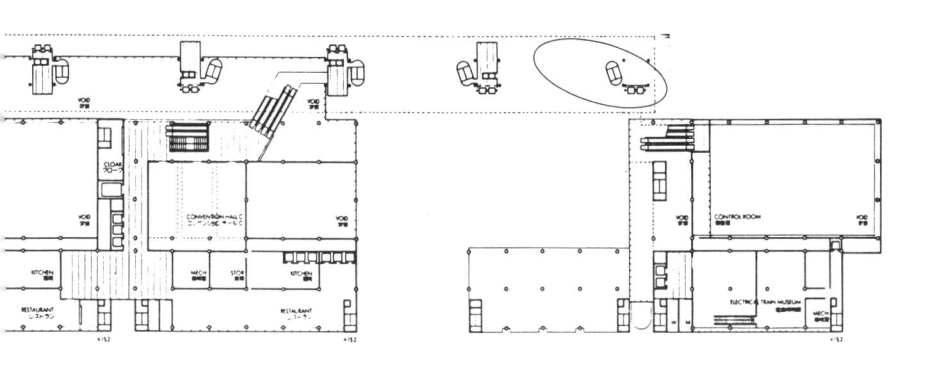

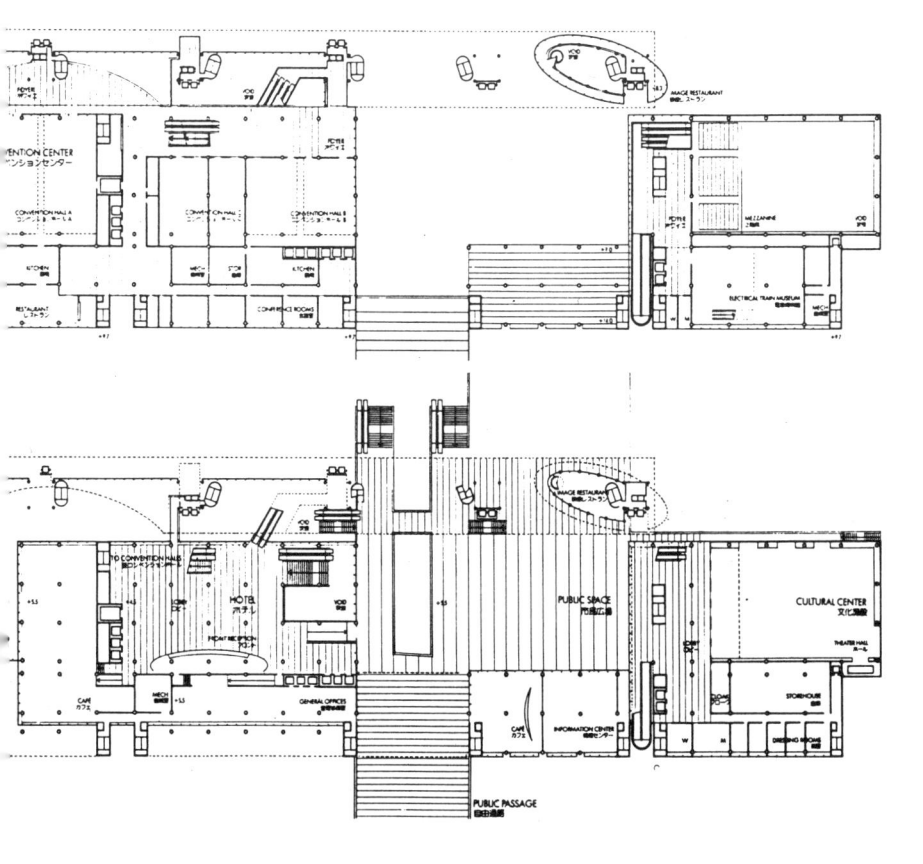

Level 4

Level 3

Level 2

Plans: no composition, but a programmatic abstraction

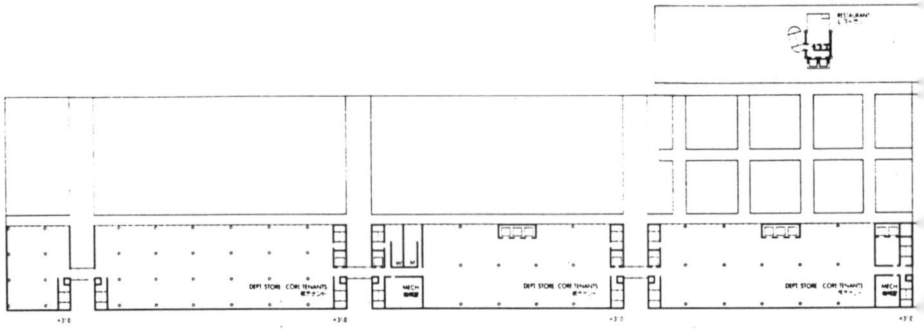
RESTAURANT
DEPT STORE CORE TENANTS
MECH
DEPT STORE CORE TENANTS
DEPT STORE CORE TENANTS
MECH

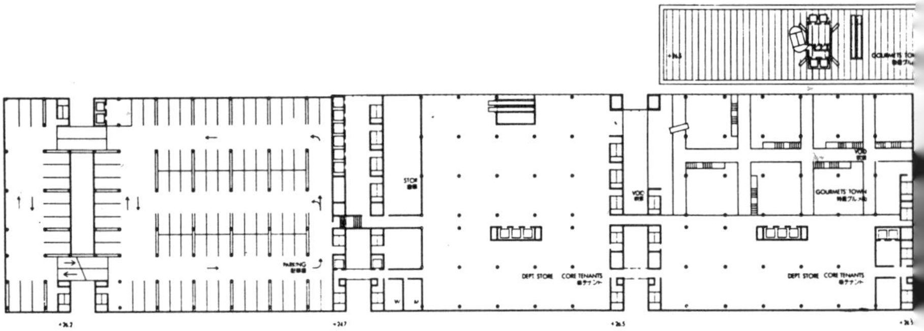
GOURMETS TOWN
PARKING
STOR
VOID
GOURMETS TOWN
DEPT STORE CORE TENANTS
DEPT STORE CORE TENANTS

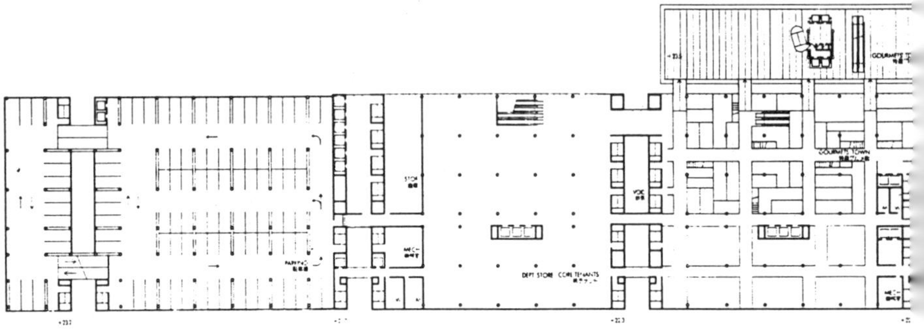
GOURMETS TOWN
STOR
VOID
GOURMETS TOWN
PARKING
MECH
DEPT STORE CORE TENANTS
MECH

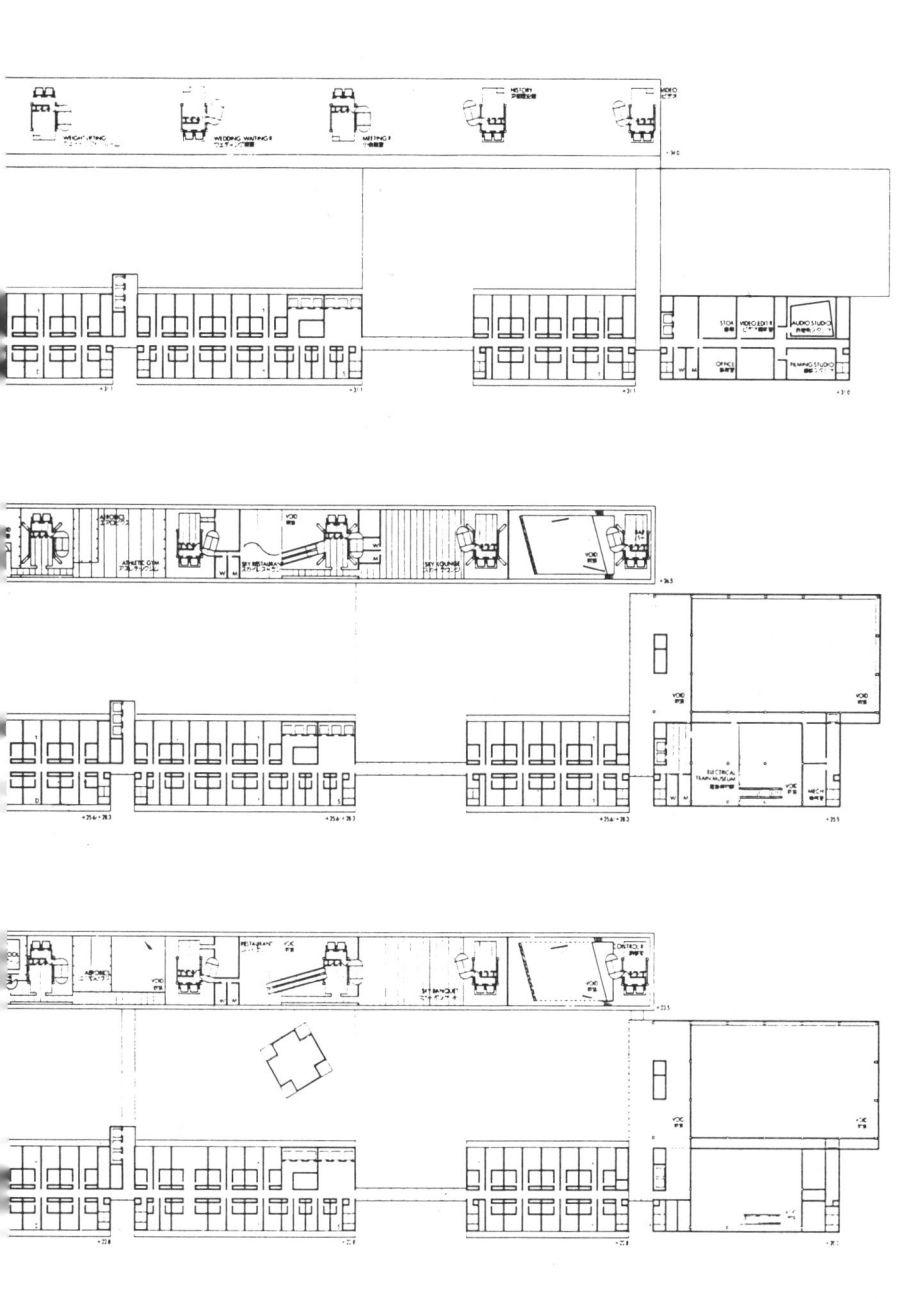

Level 8

Level 7

Level 6

TEA HOUSE
茶屋

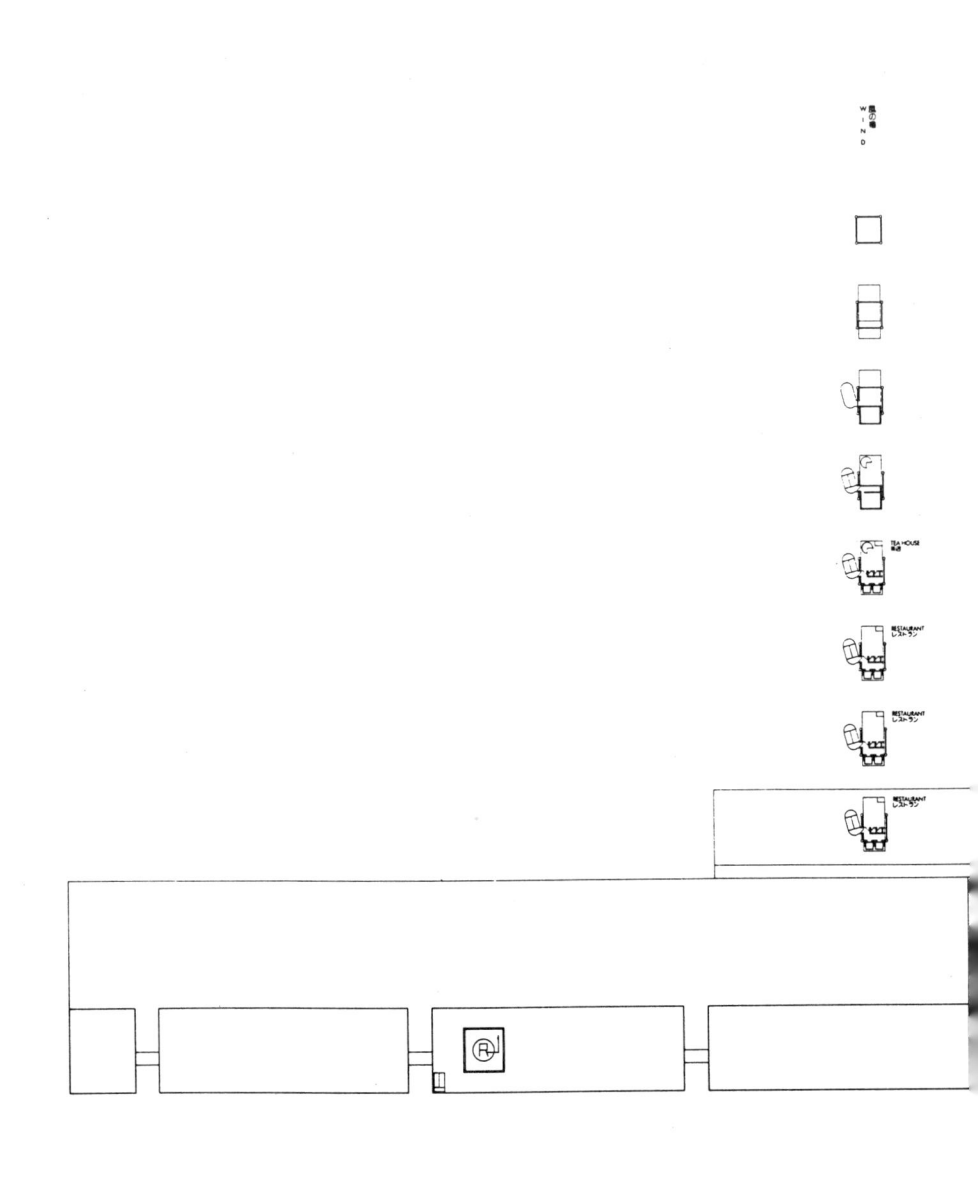

RESTAURANT
レストラン

RESTAURANT
レストラン

RESTAURANT
レストラン

Tower levels

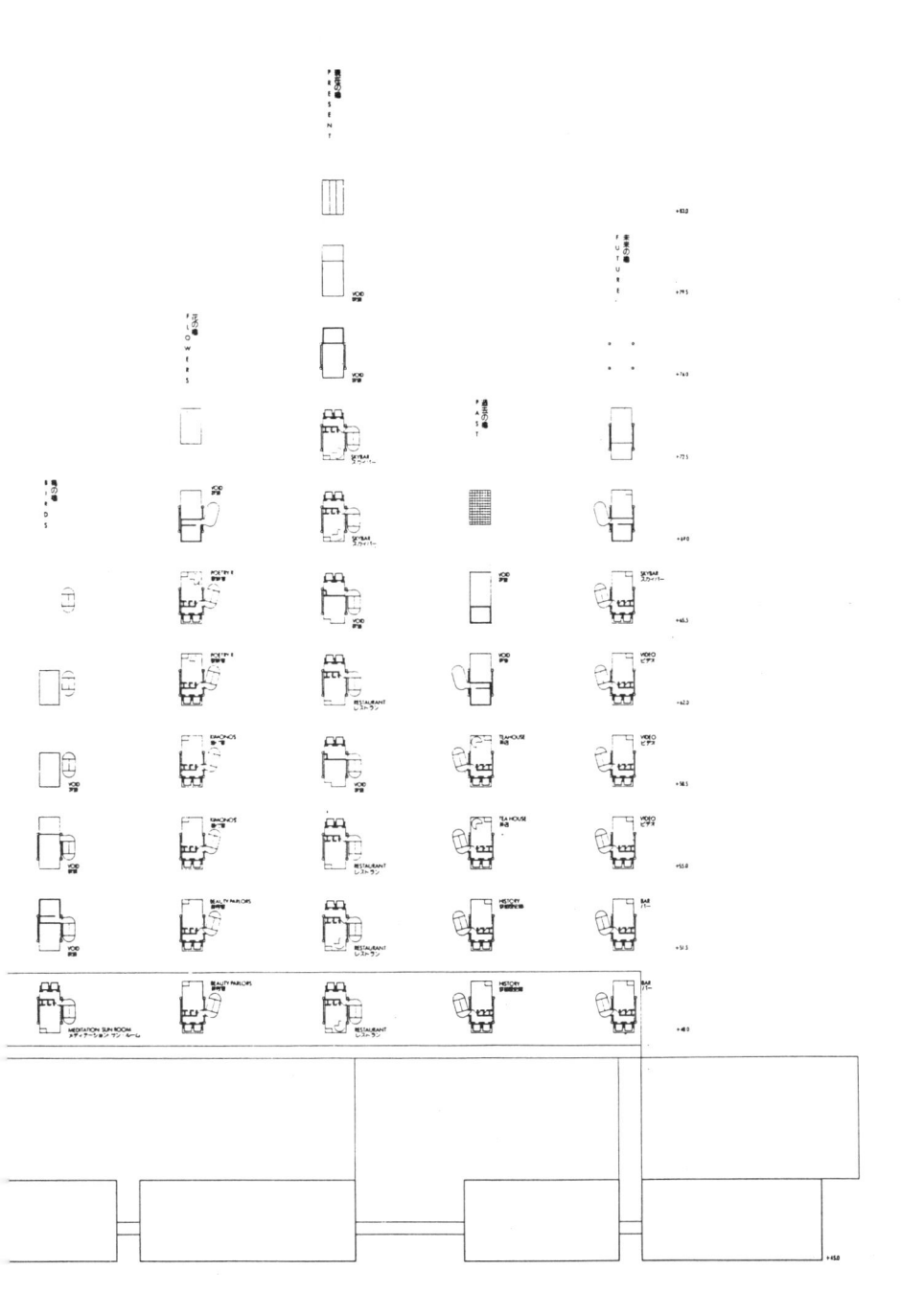

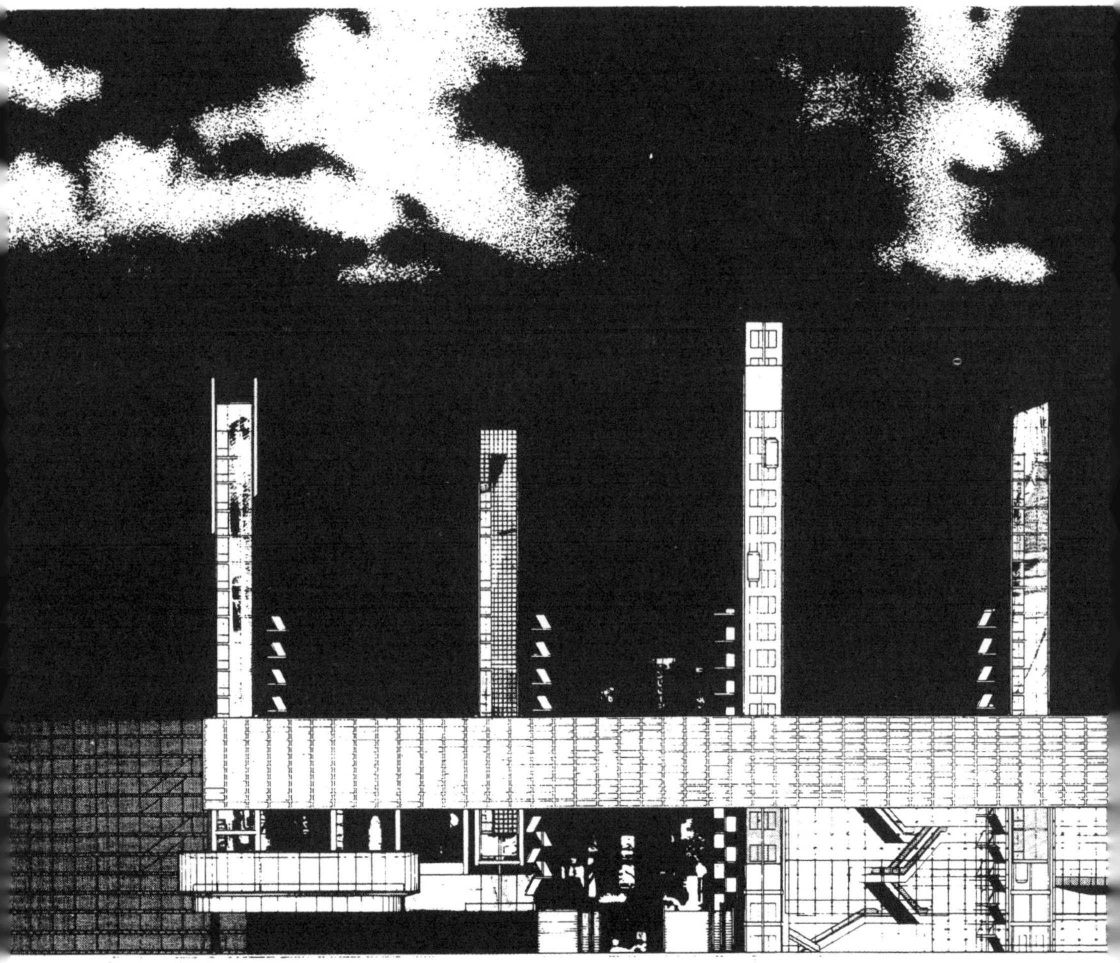

KYOTO
247

+79.5

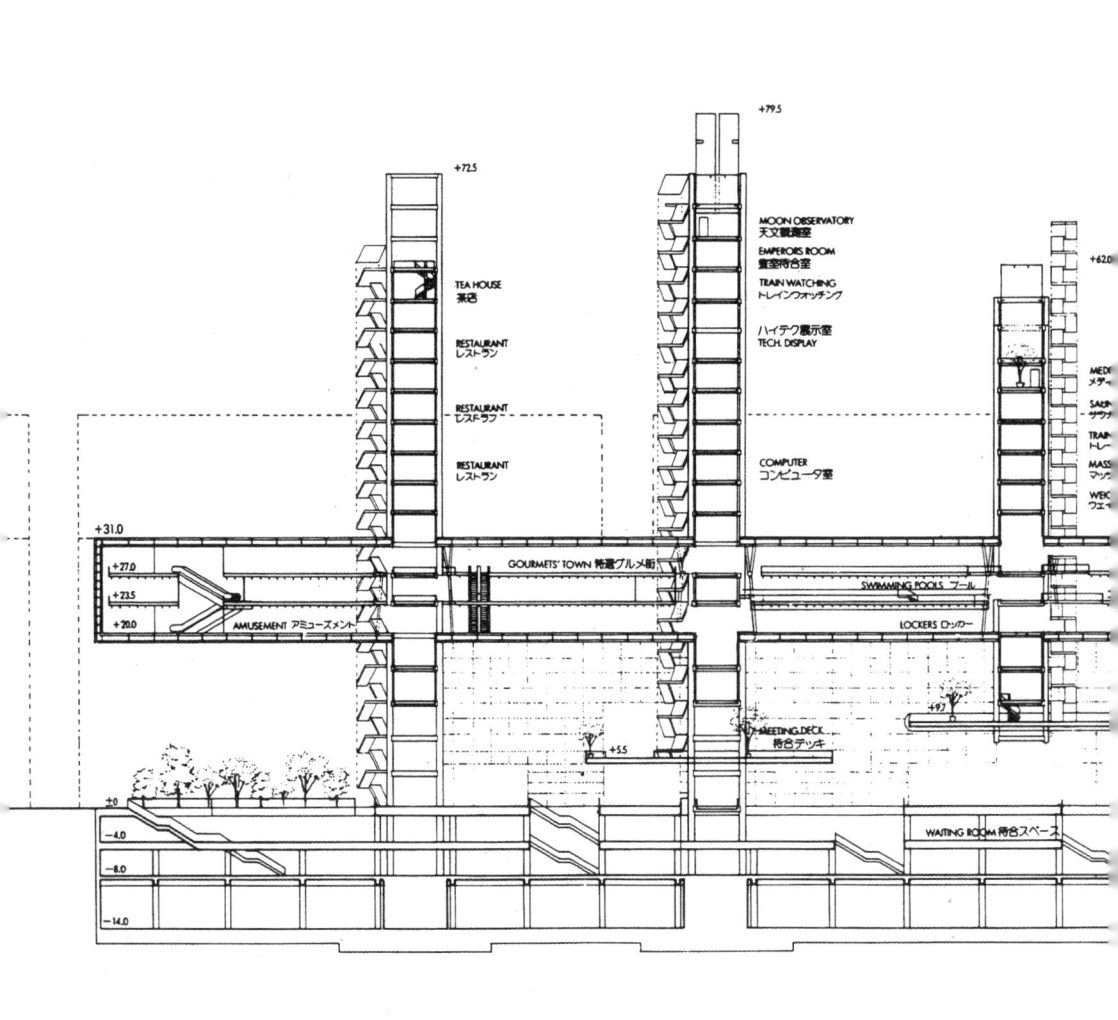

+72.5

MOON OBSERVATORY
天文観測室

EMPEROR'S ROOM
皇室待合室

TEA HOUSE
茶店

TRAIN WATCHING
トレインウォッチング

+62.0

RESTAURANT
レストラン

ハイテク展示室
TECH. DISPLAY

RESTAURANT
レストラン

MEDI
メディ

SAUN
サウナ

RESTAURANT
レストラン

COMPUTER
コンピュータ室

TRAIN
トレー

MASS
マッサ

+31.0

WEC
ウェ

+27.0

GOURMETS' TOWN 特選グルメ街

+23.5

SWIMMING POOLS プール

+20.0

AMUSEMENT アミューズメント

LOCKERS ロッカー

+9.7

MEETING DECK
待合デッキ

+5.5

±0

WAITING ROOM 待合スペース

−4.0

−8.0

−14.0

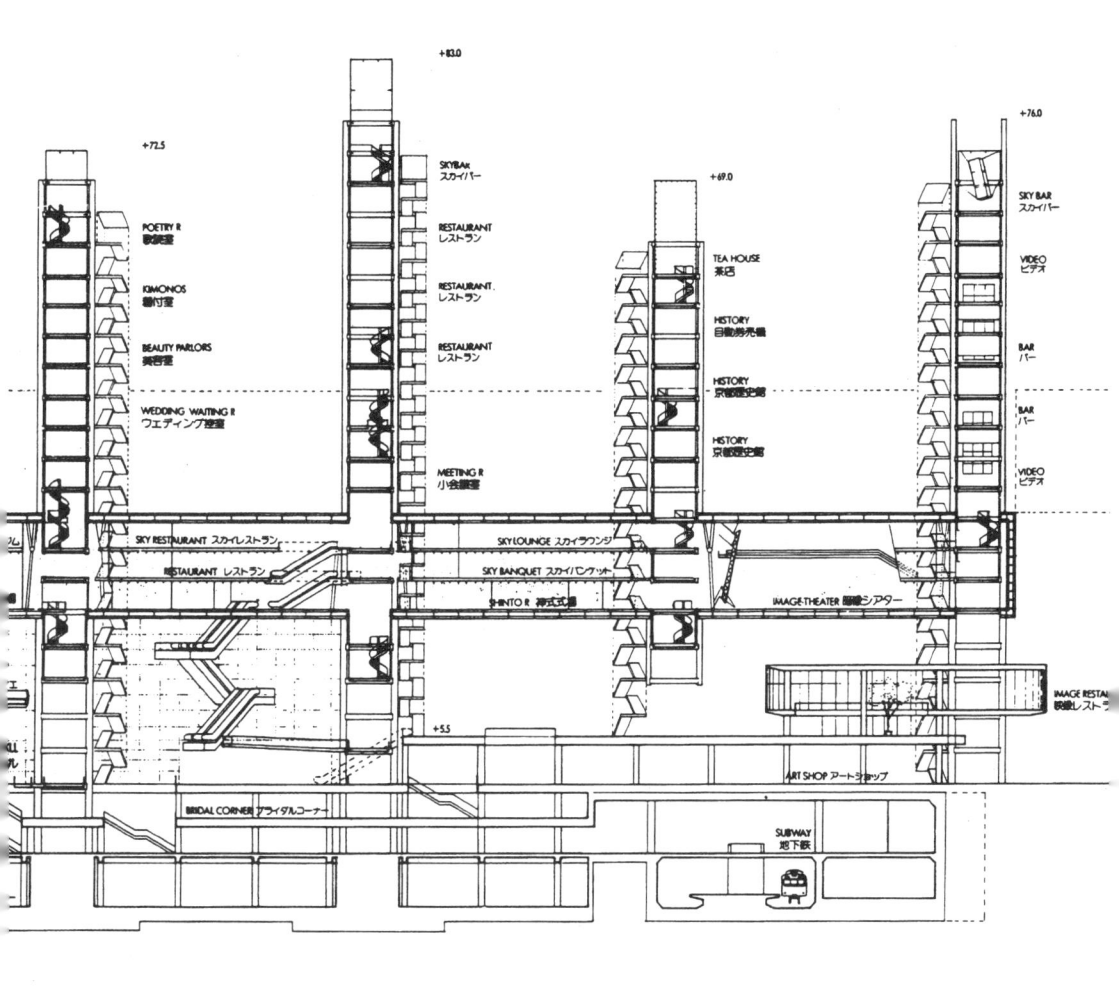

An unprecedented combination of programs and spaces:
a multiplicity of events without classification or hierarchy

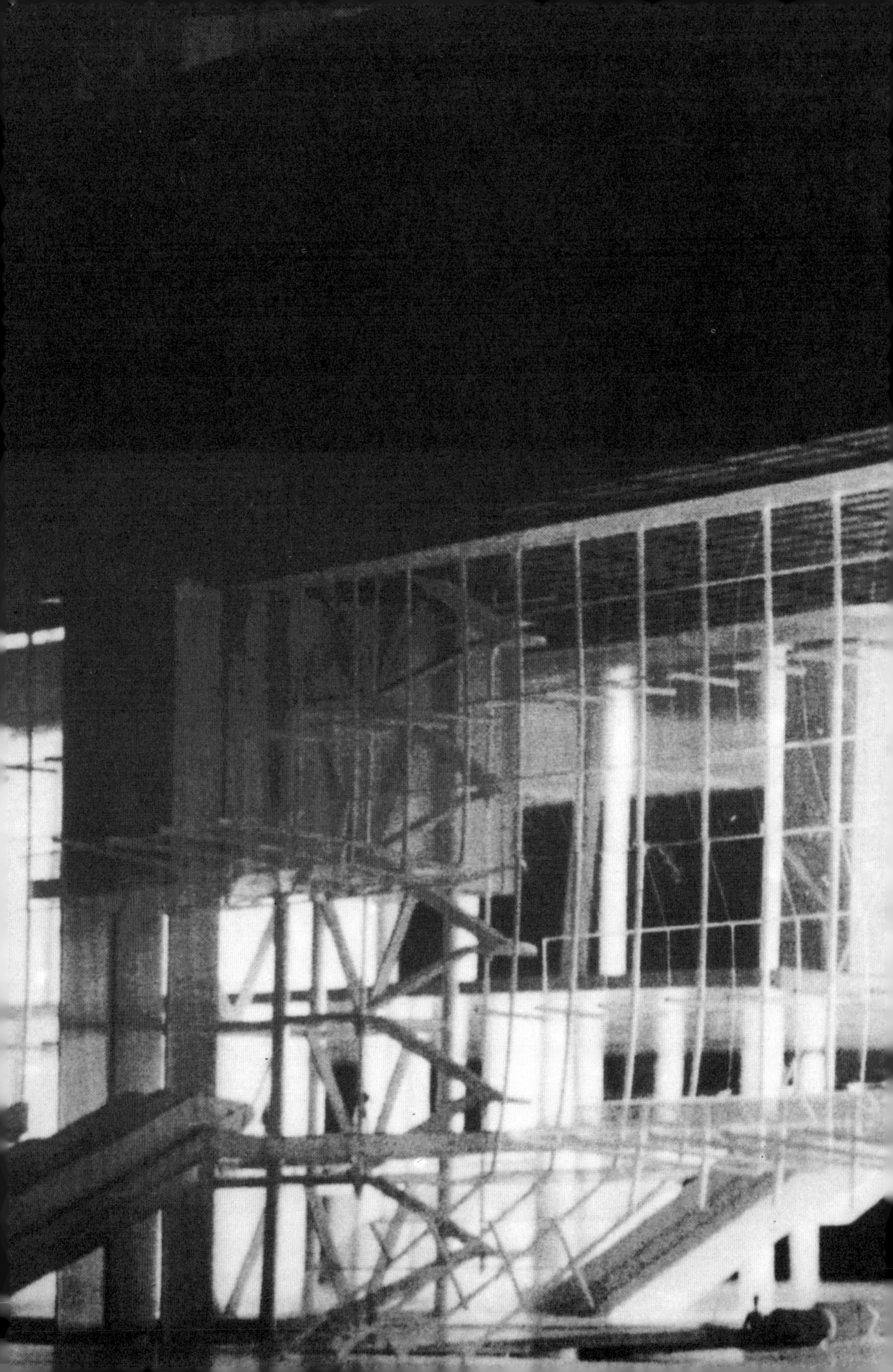

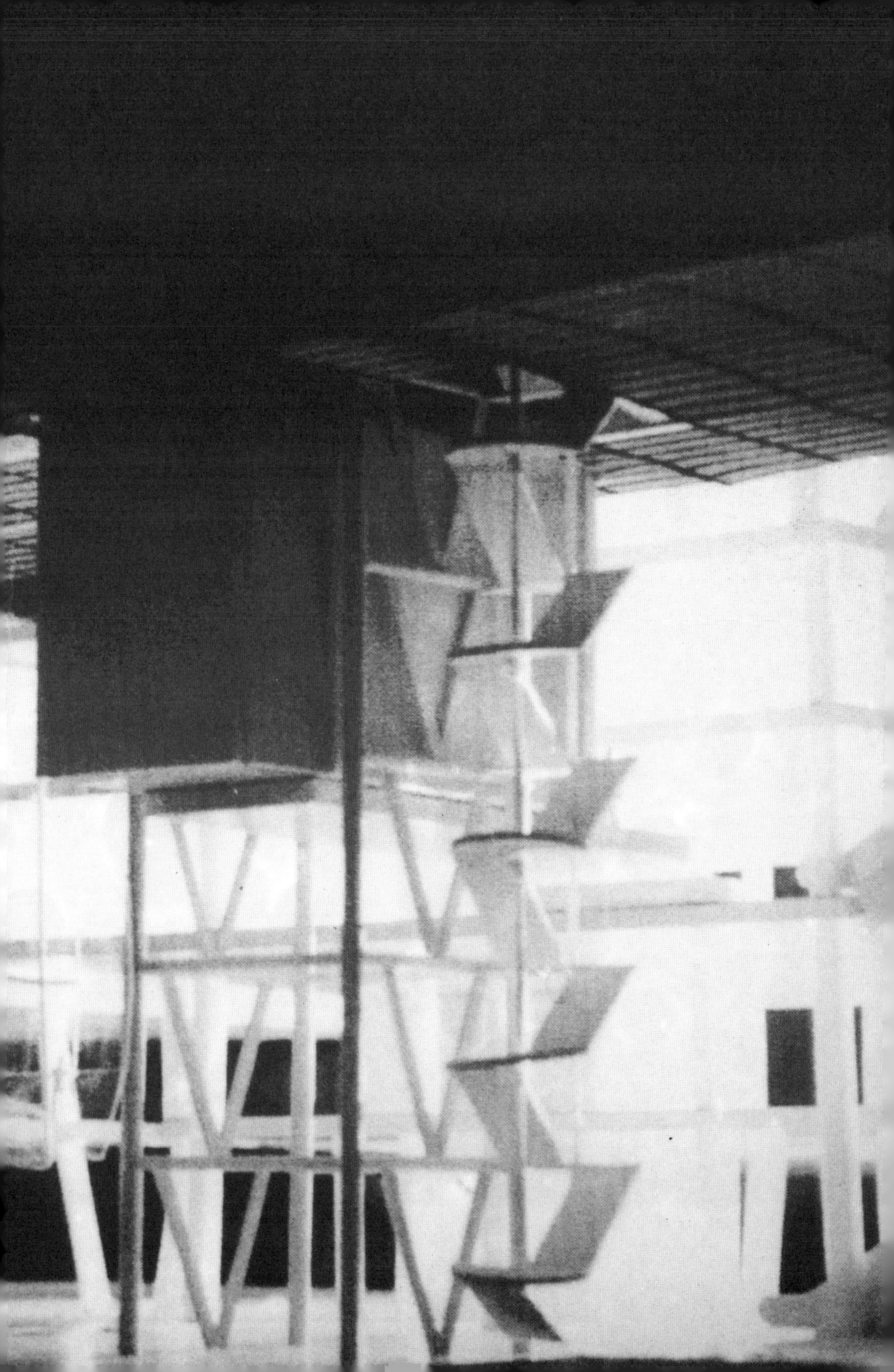

過去の櫓 PAST

スカイバー

ビデオ

ラウンジ

ビデオ

茶店

京都歴史館

映像シアター

スカイフレーム

スカ

パリ・カフェ

現在の櫓 PRESENT

花の櫓 FLOWERS

鳥の櫓 BIRDS

月の櫓 MOON

スカイバー
レストラン

歌読室
着付室
美容室
ウェディング控室
ブライダル

小会議室
スカイレストラン

メディテーション
サウナ
トレーニング
アスレテック

天文観測室
空待合室
トレイン
ウォッチング
ハイテク展示室
コンピュータ

大回廊

ホテル　　　駅　　　　　　　　　　デパ

Spatial sequences are independent of the meaning they evoke

Hanging glass curtain (structural glass and tensile cables)

Skyframe: inside the hollow beam

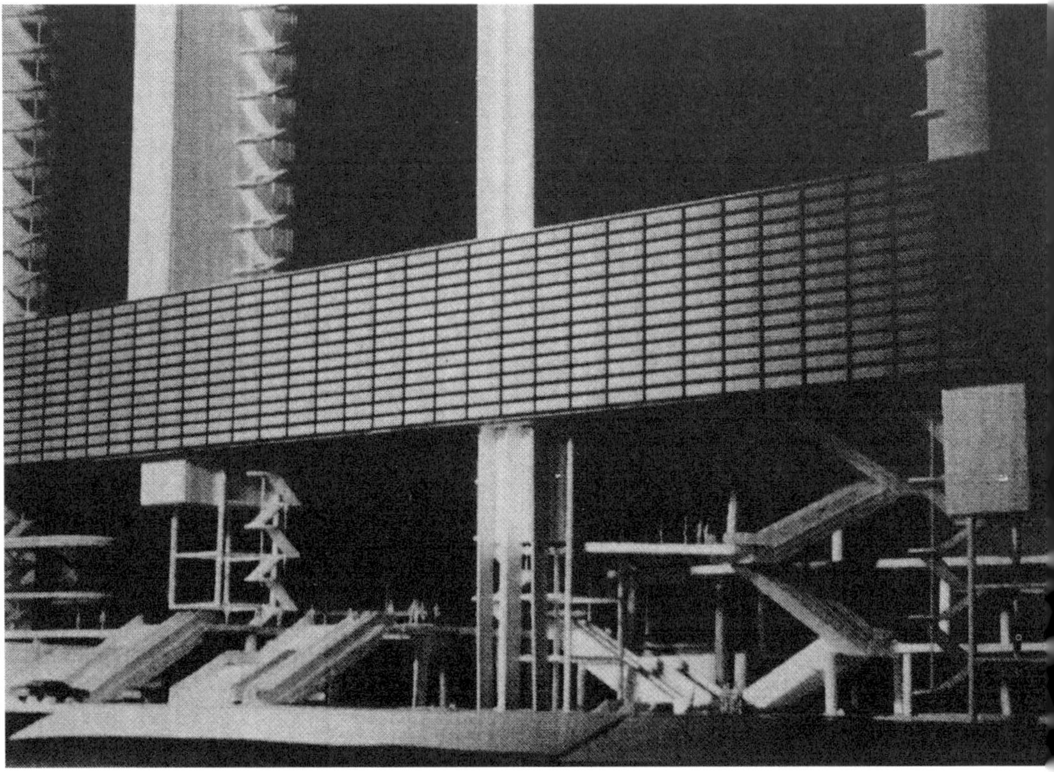

KYOTO
257

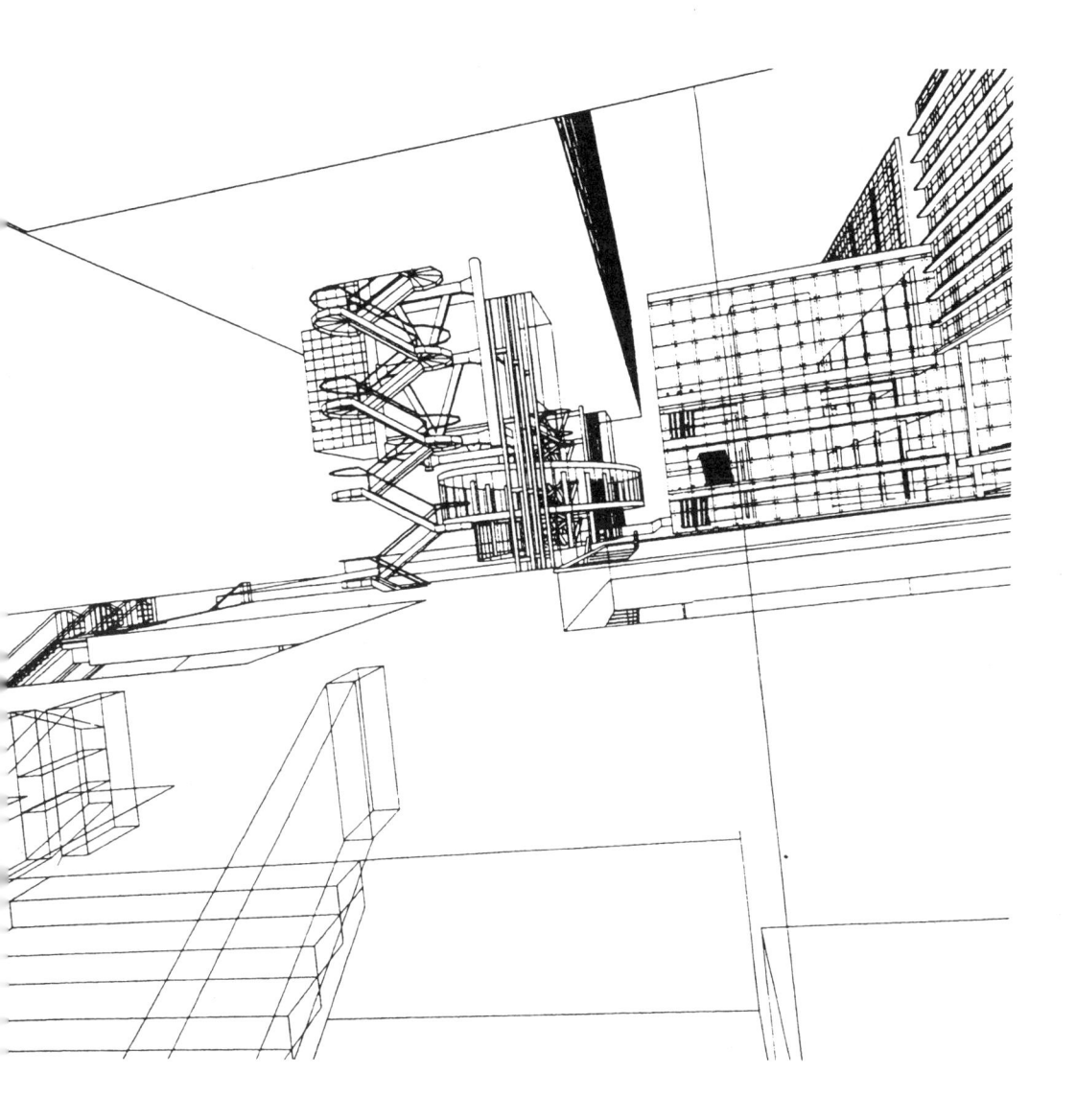

Suspended tower: view towards the cultural center

Emerging from the bullet train and the subway link:
making an event out of the urban shock

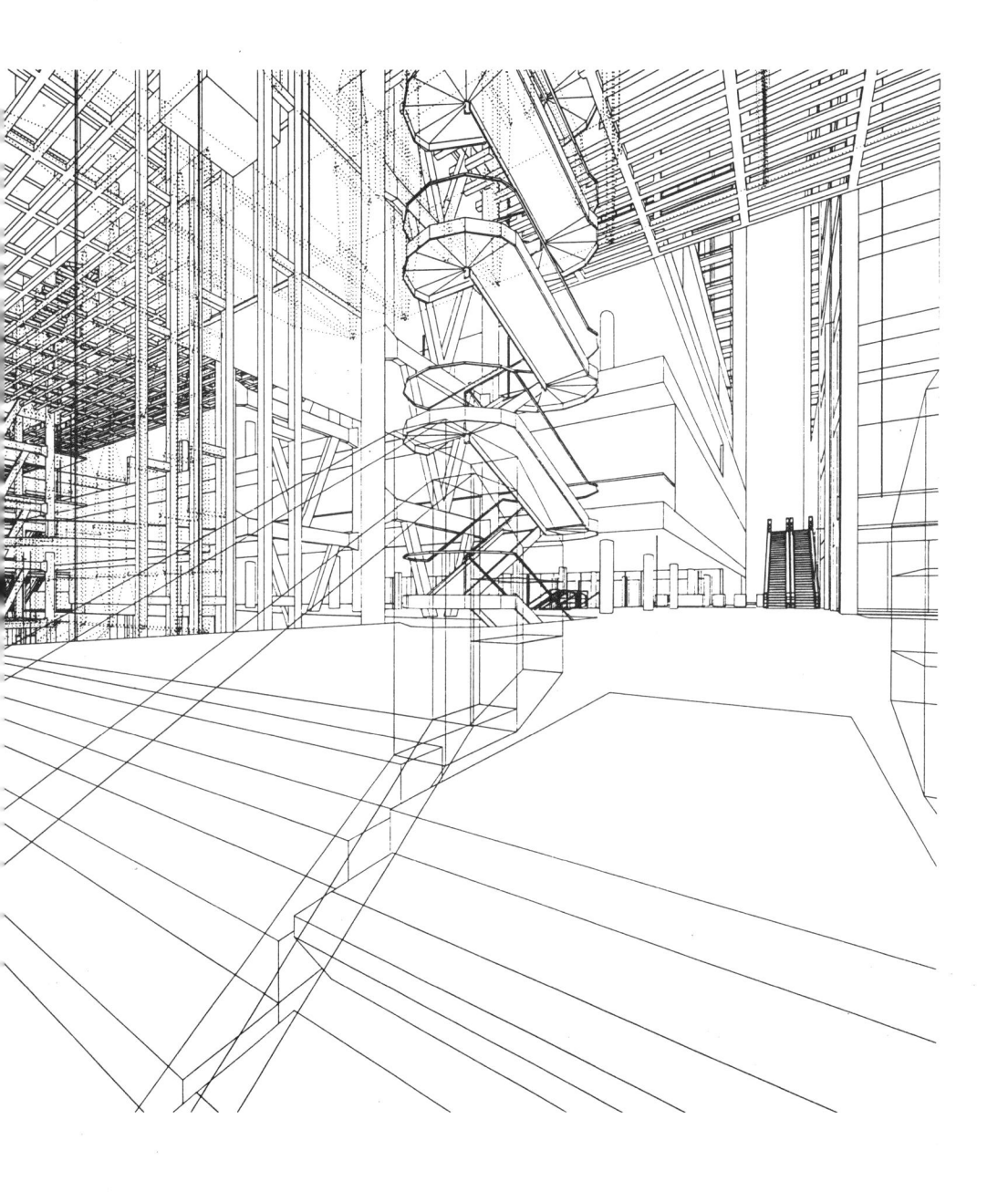

Under the skyframe, towards the interior square

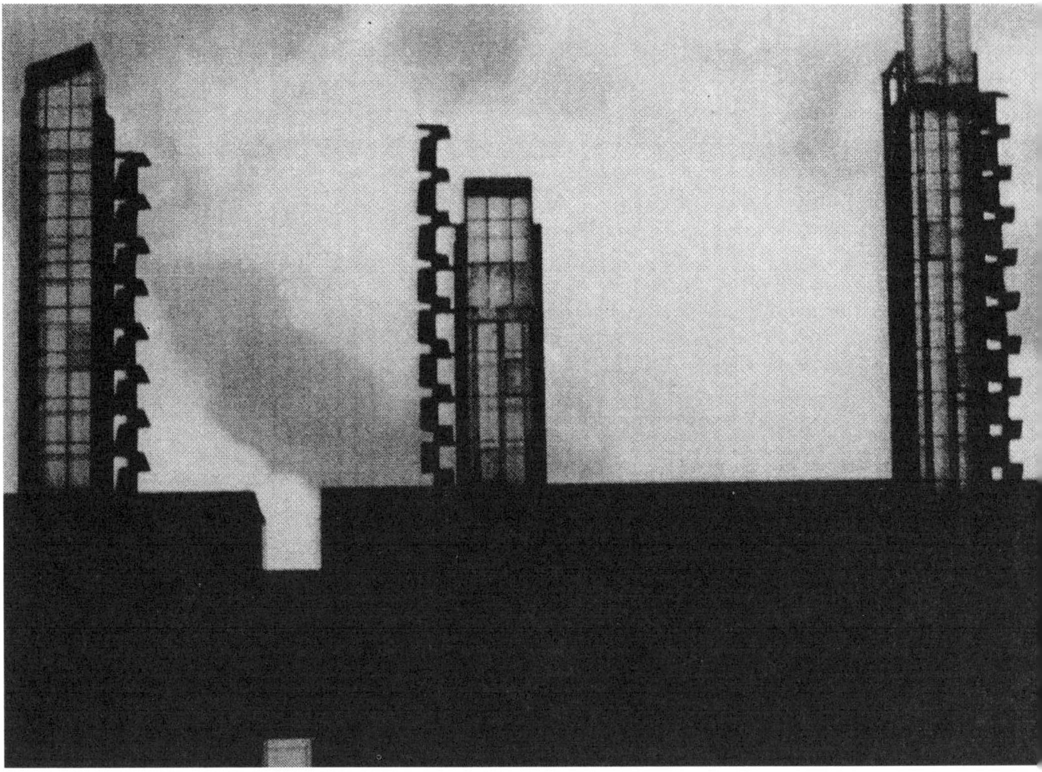

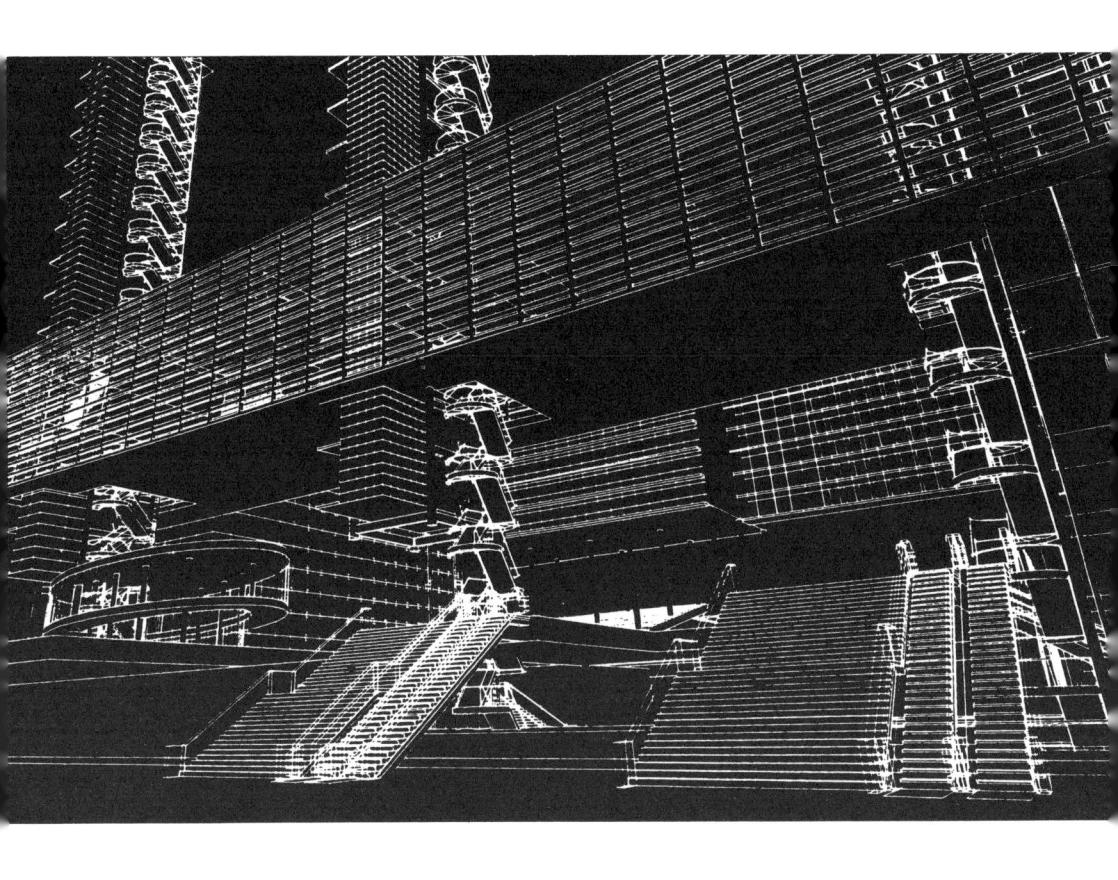

Structural logic taken to excess: a suspended tower

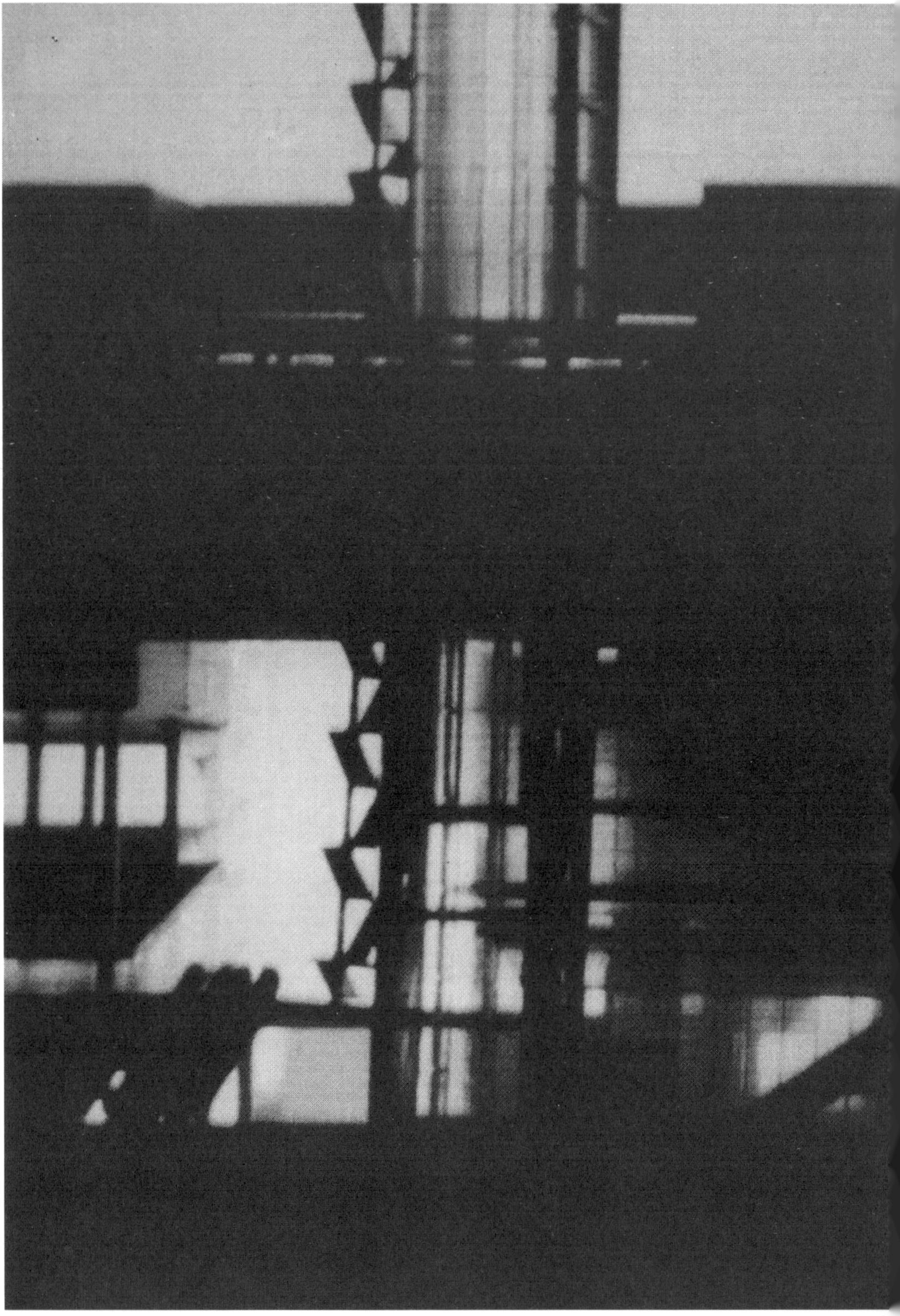

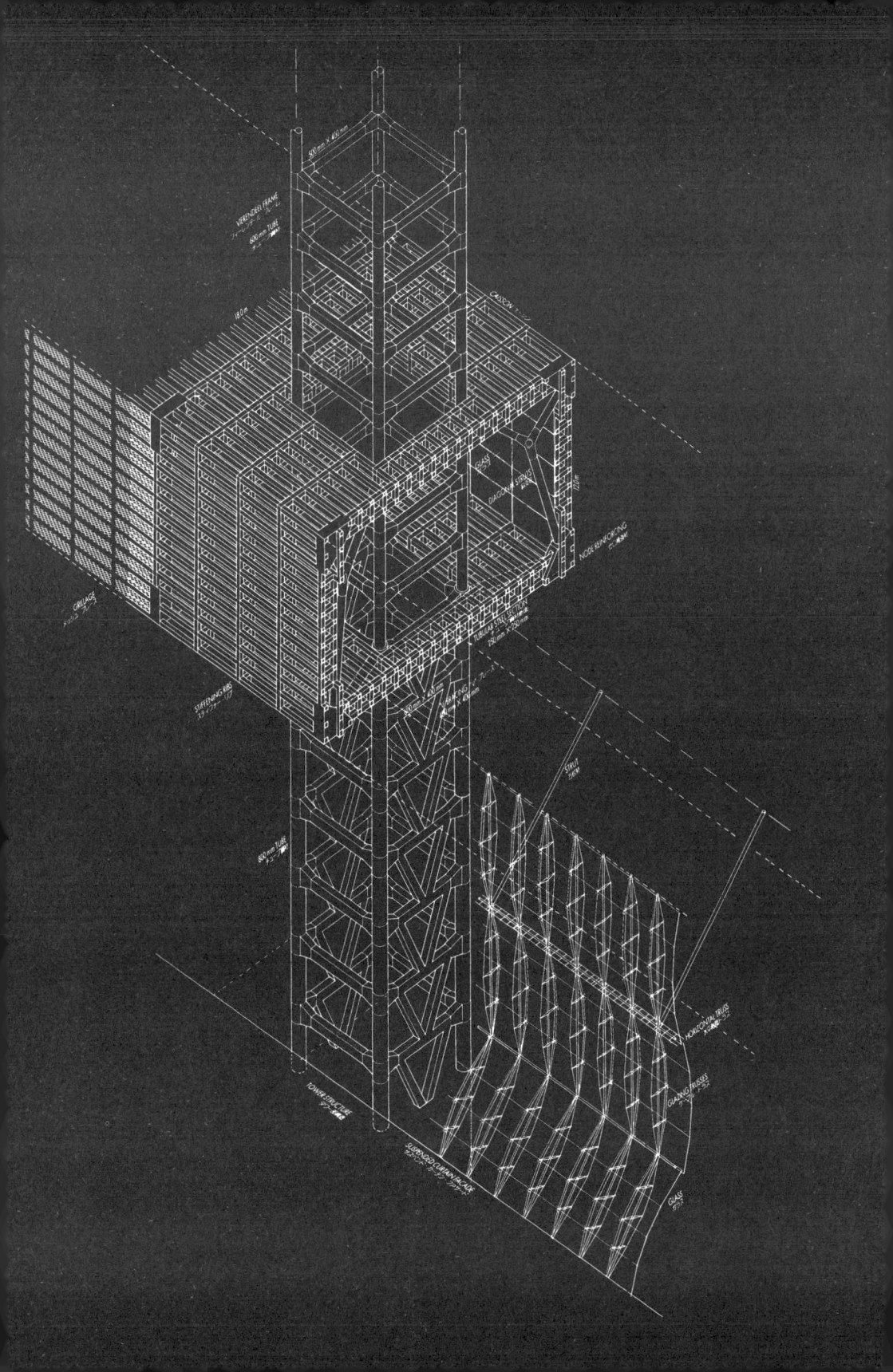

500 mm X 400 mm
VIERENDEEL FRAME
600 mm TUBE
CAISSON
18.0 m
GLASS
DIAGONAL STRUTS
12.0 m
NODE REINFORCING
TUBULAR STEEL SECTION
250 mm X 250 mm
GRILLAGE
STIFFENING RIBS
800 mm X 400 mm
BRACING
STRUT
800 mm TUBE
HORIZONTAL TRUSS
GLAZING TRUSSES
TOWER STRUCTURE
SUSPENDED CURTAIN FACADE
GLASS

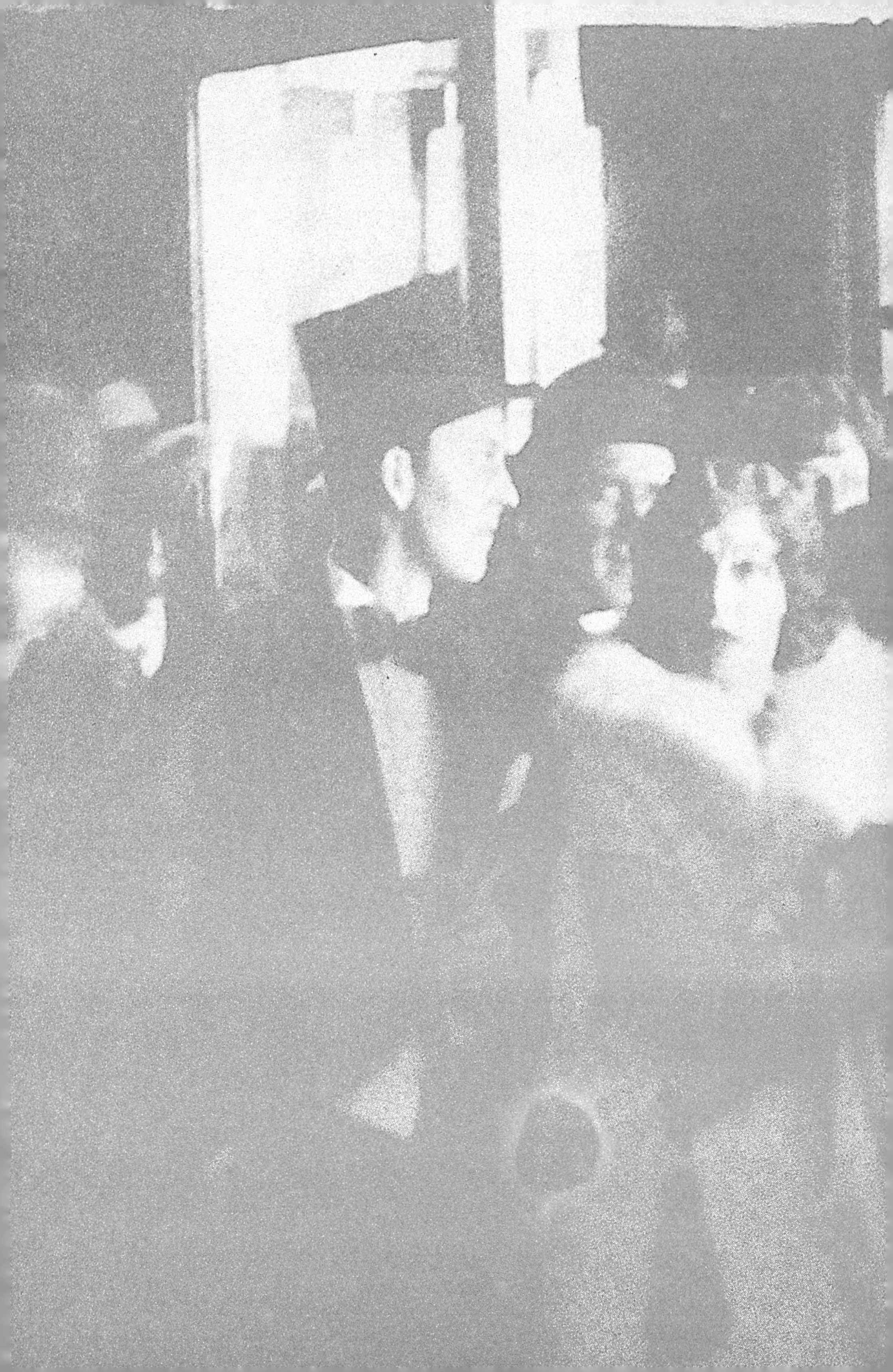

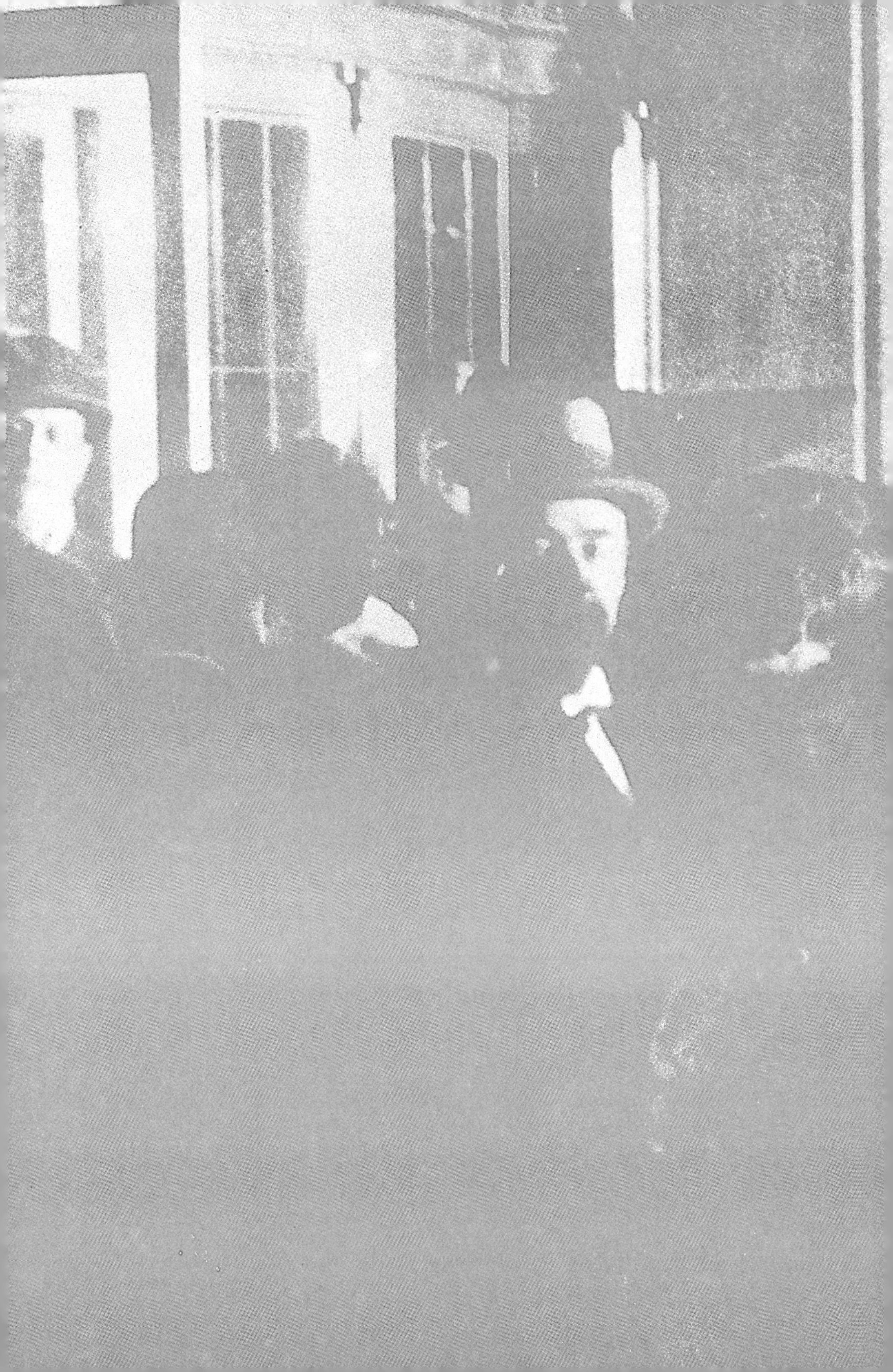

C.
Urban Architecture

In the urban architectures of the Tokyo Opera, the Strasbourg County Hall, the Karlsruhe Center for Art and Media, the Paris Library of France and Le Fresnoy, we confronted specific programs, defined in space and time. Through their cultural and political ambition, these urban architectures become centers of attraction suggesting a new type of city, in which the notion of the event is as important as that of the street or the square.

Tokyo, Opera, 1986

A Mode of Notation—
Programmatic Dissociations

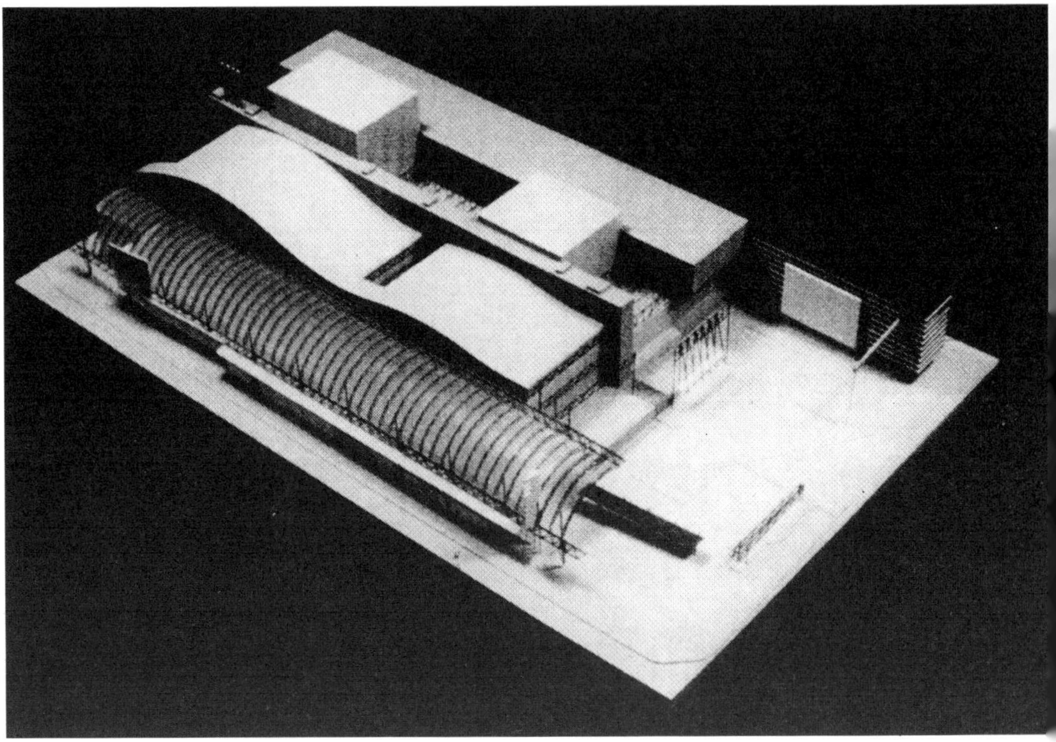

Hypothesis
How to deconstruct opera and architecture so as to think their concepts in the most precise manner possible and, simultaneously, to observe them from an external, detached point of view? How to devise a systematic and irreducible configuration of concepts, such that each concept intervenes at some decisive moment in the work? How to question the unity of a building or a monument without recourse either to a composition of articulated and formalized elements or to a random accumulation of isolated programmatic fragments? To play on limits without being enclosed within limits? To relate to other operas while referring only to one's own?

Juxtaposition
We abandoned traditional rules of composition and harmony, replacing them with a mode of organization based not on "form follows function," "form follows form" or even "form follows fiction" but rather on breaking apart the traditional components of the theater and opera house to develop a new "tonality" or "sound." No more artful articulations among the auditorium, the stage, the foyer, the grand staircase; a new pleasure lies in the parallel juxtaposition of indeterminate cultural meanings, as opposed to fixed historicist practices.

In our project, functional constraints are not translated into a composition of symbolic units but are extrapolated into a score of programmatic strips, each of which contains the main activities and related spaces. The sequence of strips is as follows:

1. The glass avenue provides direct access from the subway, parking lot and buses. Its busy mezzanines (theater lobbies) provide a vertical spectacle while its ground floor gathers crowds employing public services—box offices, shops, bars, press office, reception areas, information, police station and exhibition spaces. A restaurant is located between the glass avenue and the opera's garden.

2. The vertical foyers overlook the glass avenue and encompass coatrooms, box offices, bars or buffets, and suspended gardens. The border between the glass avenue and the vertical foyers is articulated by lighting for the avenue (handrails, stairs, and so forth).

3. The auditoriums act as an acoustical strip accommodating each audience in a minimum volume (for acoustical quality) with maximum visual access. This strip, which also accommodates VIP rooms, lavatories, etc., allows for small, localized future programs at either end.

4. The strip coincides with the proscenium, acting as a central artery servicing the whole complex.

5. The stages provide maximum flexibility and technical potential.

6. This strip contains the backstage area, assembly hall, rehearsal spaces and scenery workshops. Wherever possible, the latter two are provided with daylight.

7. The final strip serves artists and staff. It contains dressing rooms and related spaces—organized along the balconies of a four-story artists' concourse (which avoids the anonymous repetition of corridors)—as well as the administrative offices, which benefit from a direct view of the opera garden.

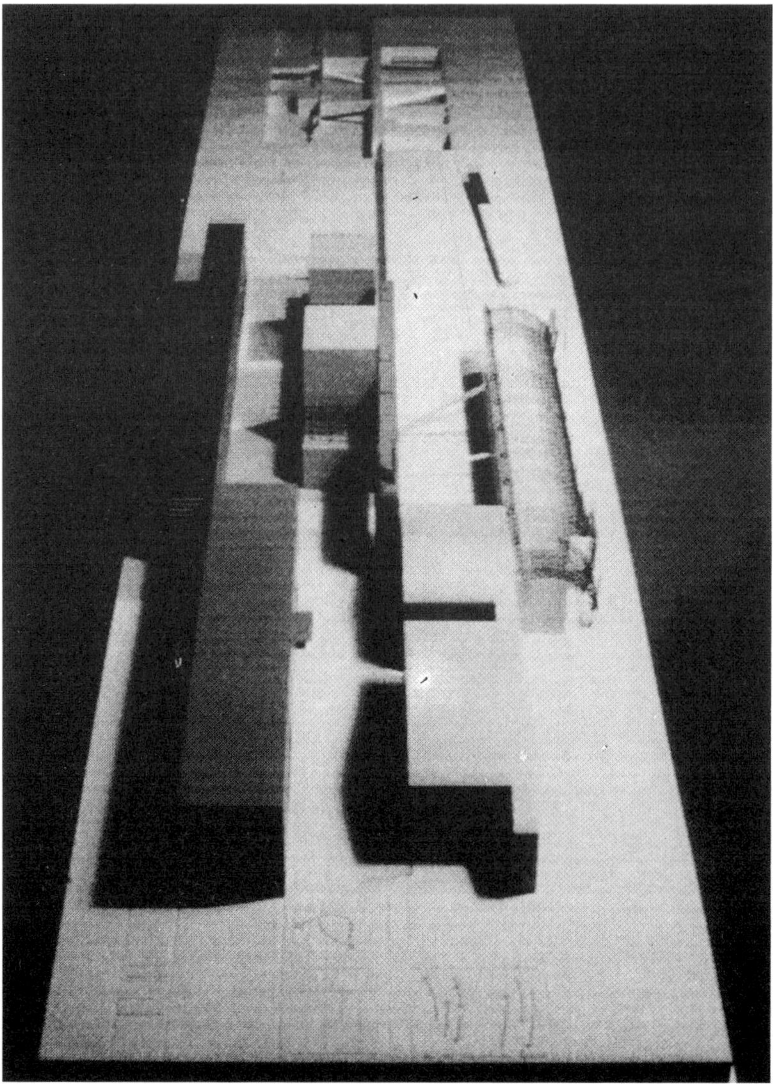

Notation
The bands are analogous to the lines of a music partition that can accept any kind of melody or rhythm. Some are technical or administrative spaces, others are urban spaces, concert spaces where the crowd sits, listens and observes. All are interchangeable.

The Logic of Differences
This organization reflects the dissociation between *langue* and *parole,* the code and the message, that leads to a system of difference: in our project, for example, one can distinguish between the logic of stages, halls and auditoriums. Each logic is different from the others and lies in a different space from the adjacent ones. None of the bands can exist by itself; however, no one must depend on the others in order to exist. They slide on parallel, neutral, independent rails. However, the events (the crowd, the spectacles) cut across them and establish ephemeral relations between them.

A Hypermetropolitan Stage
This project offers a simple tool open to a great variety of theatrical demands, a working instrument, without a preconceived form, whose flexibility allows for the viewing of an opera or of the Elizabethan theater as an electronic or neon spectacle. The stage becomes hypermetropolitan and suggests a new spatial model for the arts of spectacle.

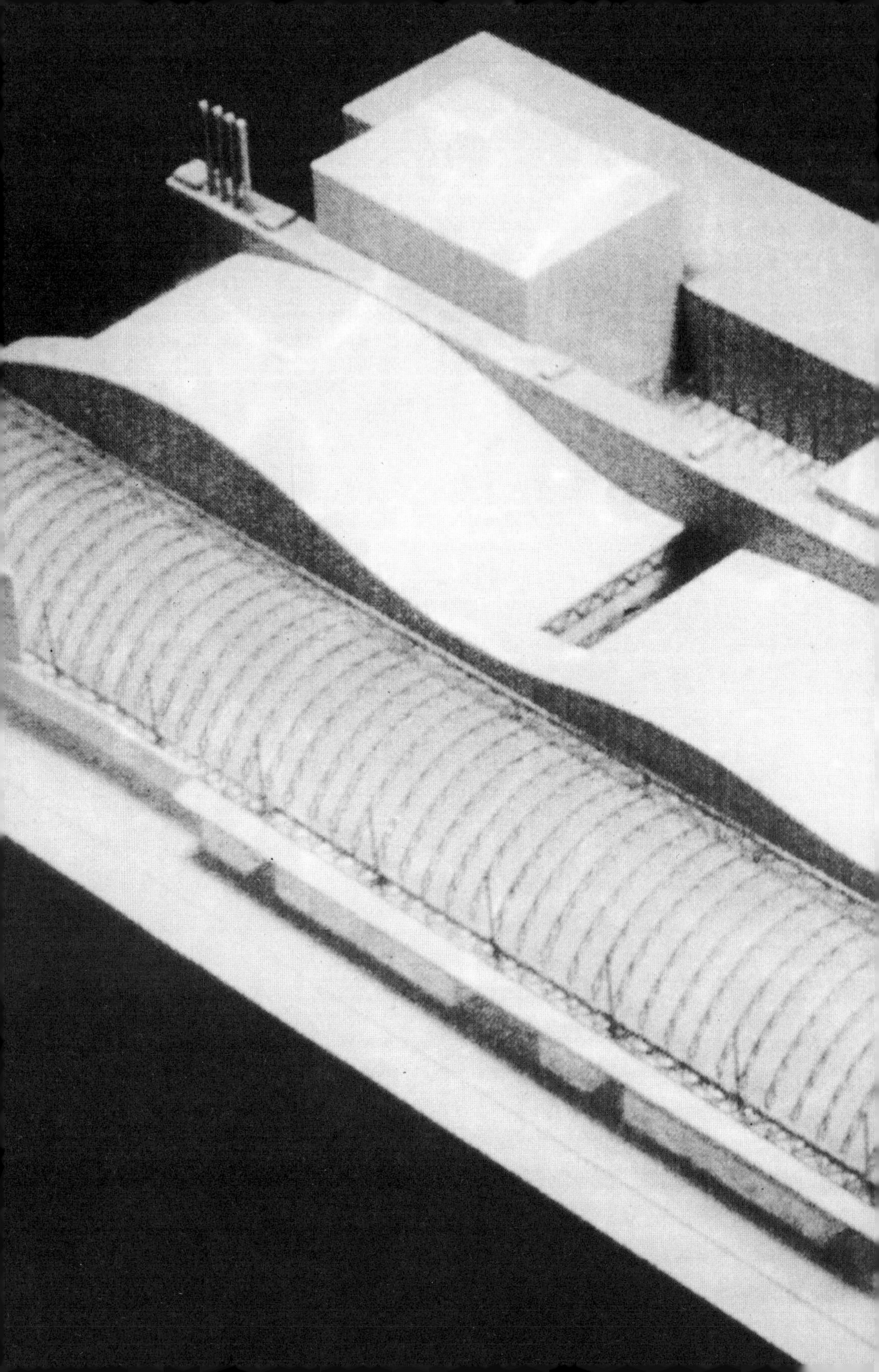

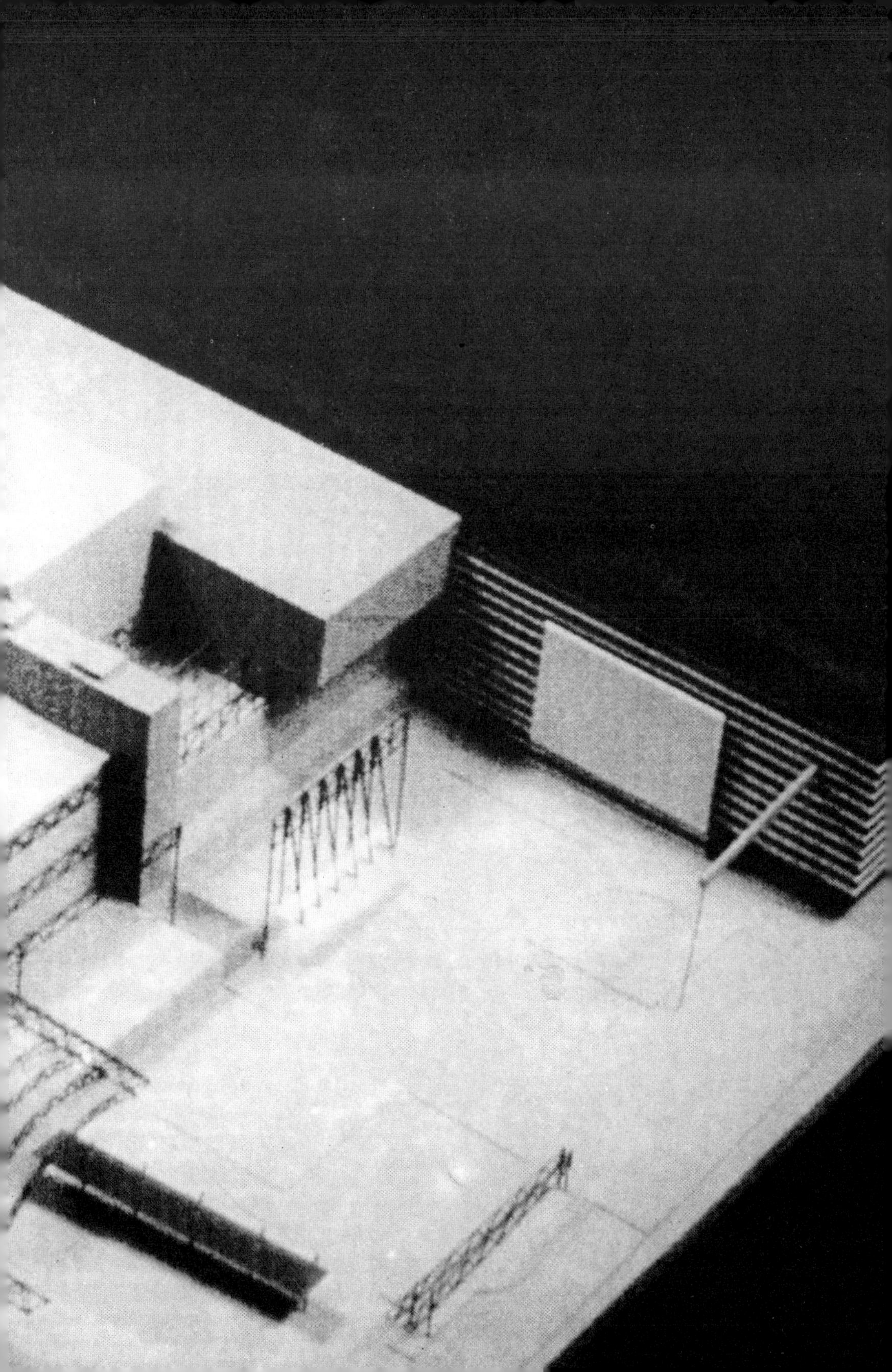

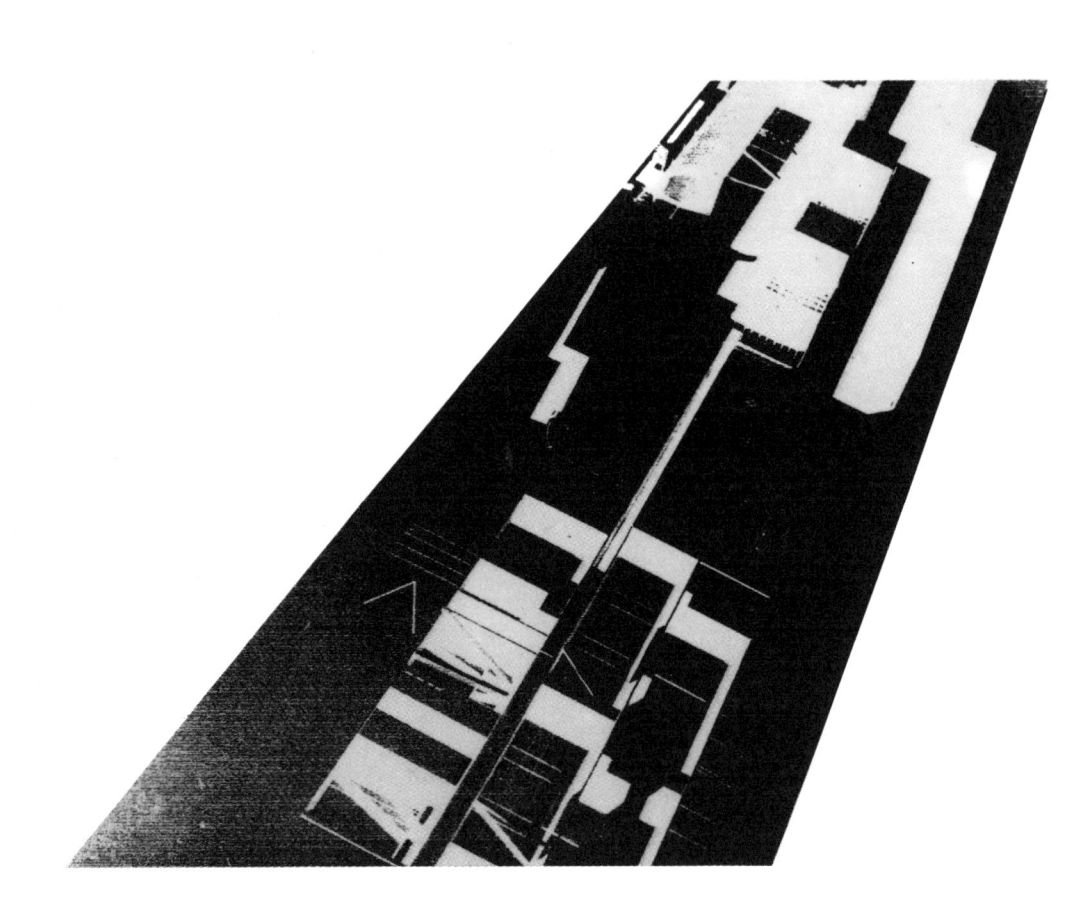

Supplementing the limitations of plans: new modes of notation

TOKYO
275

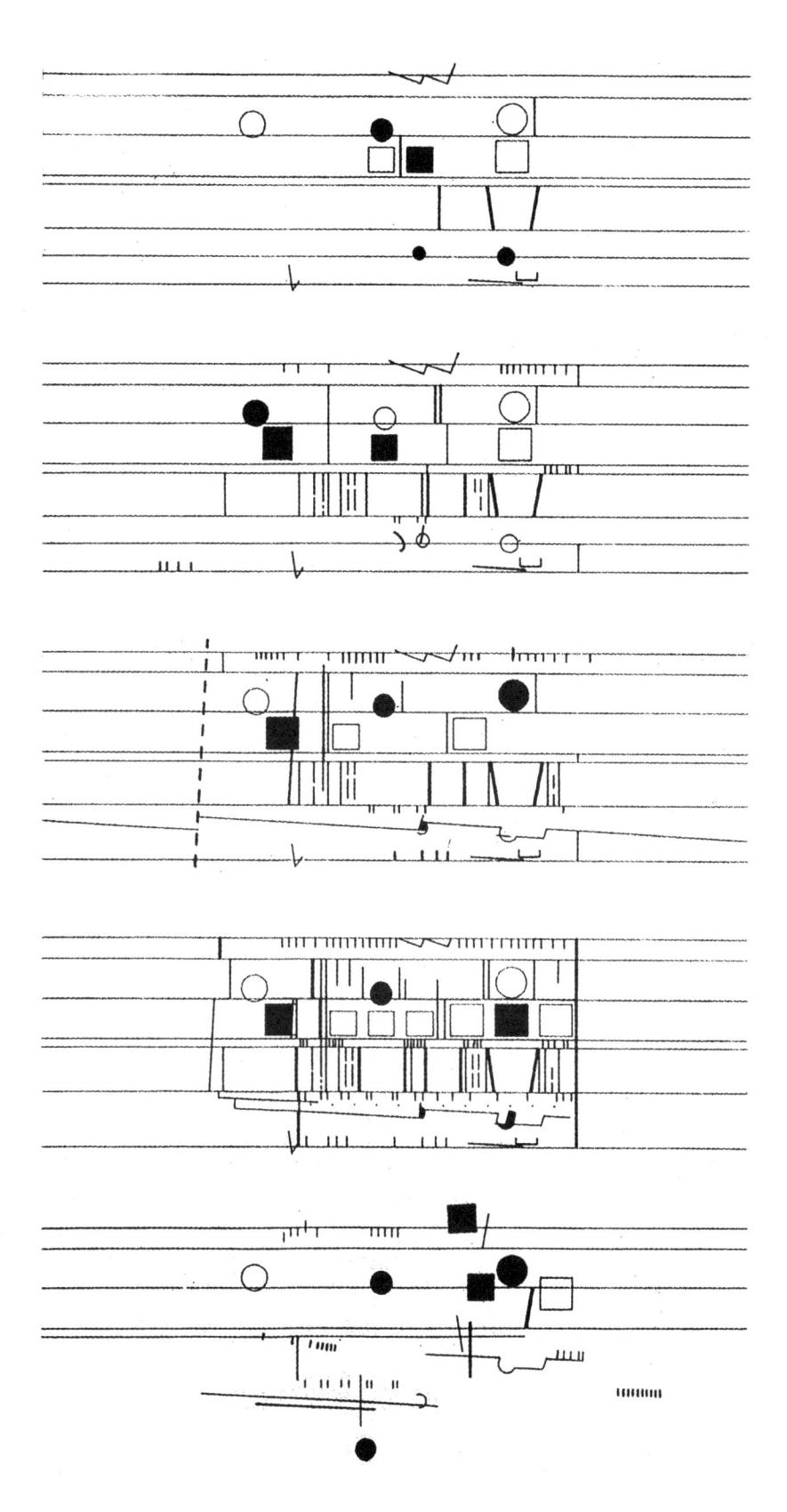

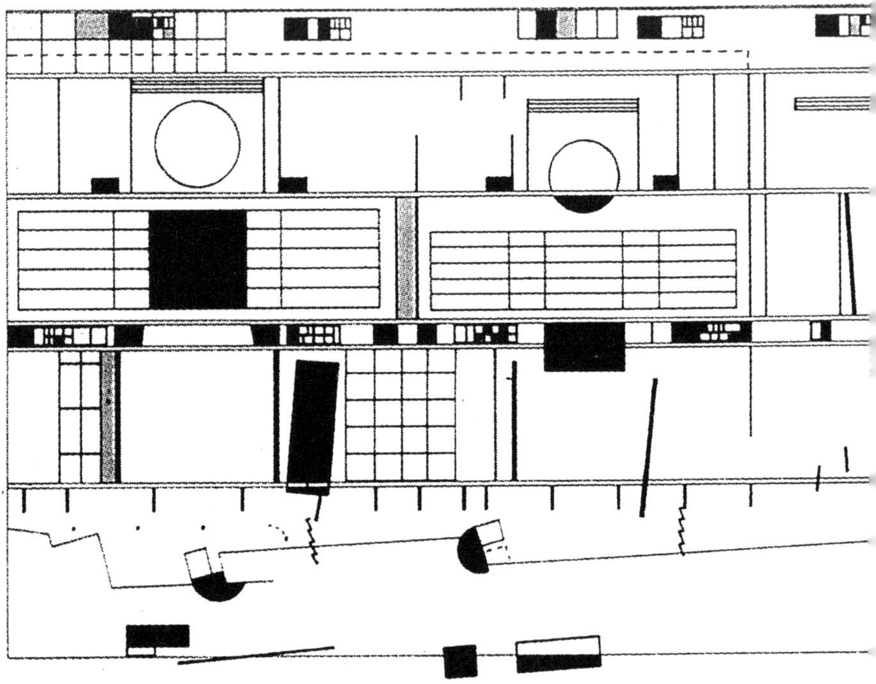

TOKYO
277

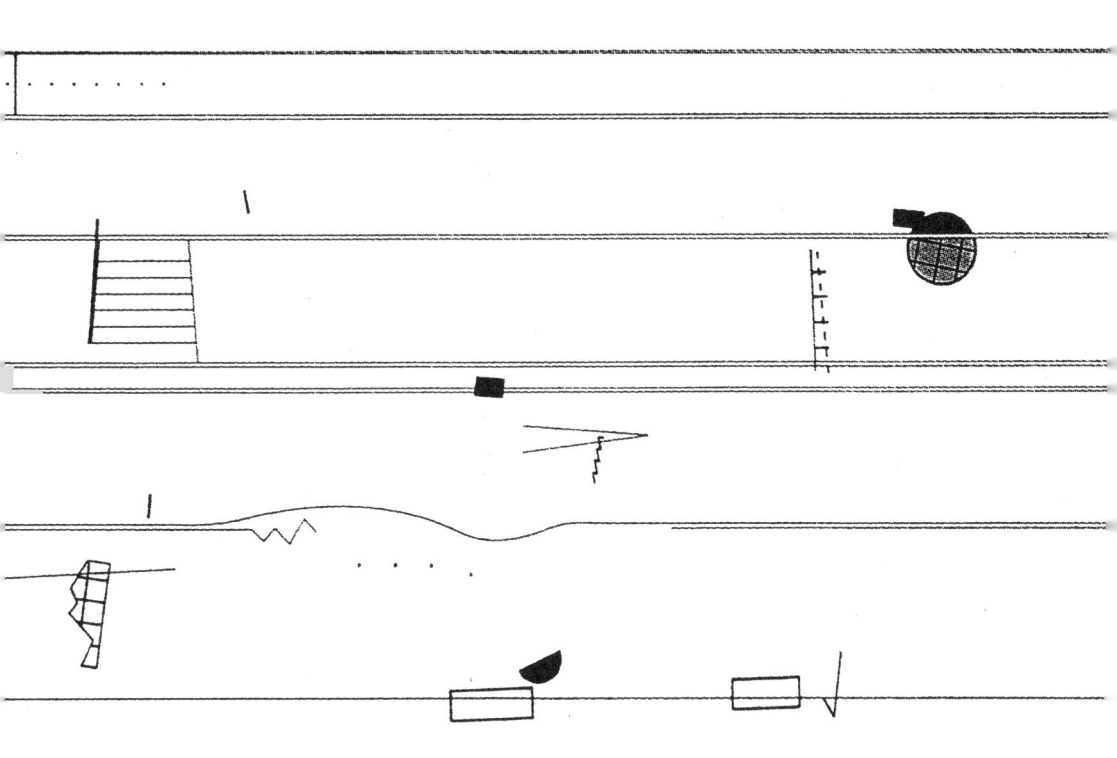

A theoretical concept either can be applied to a project or derived from it: notation of the bands;
linearity, juxtaposition, disintegration

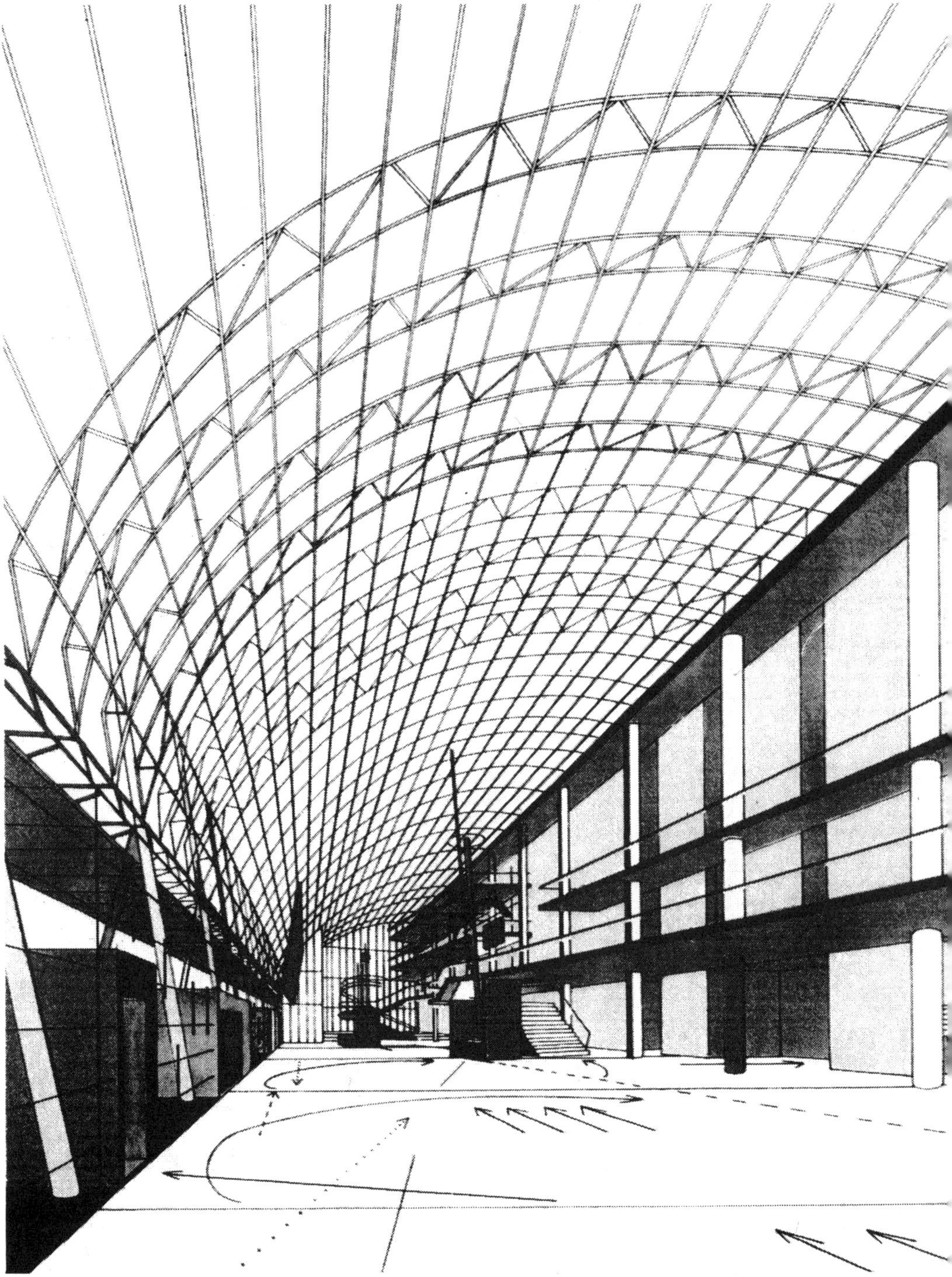

TOKYO
279

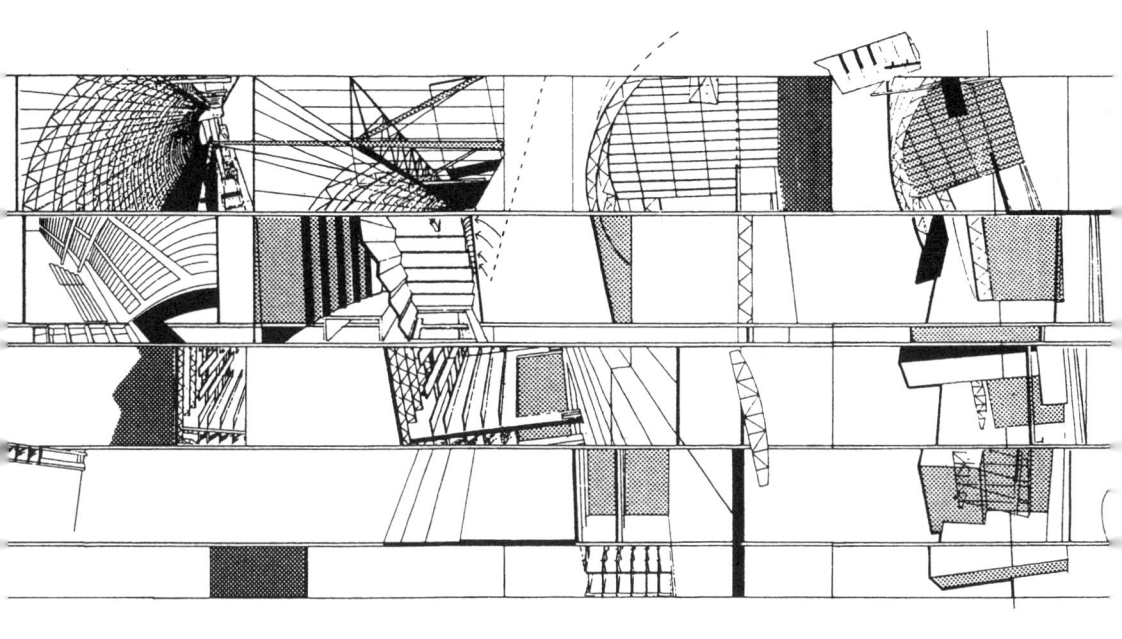

The inherent disjunction of architecture —
between space and event, between buildings and their use

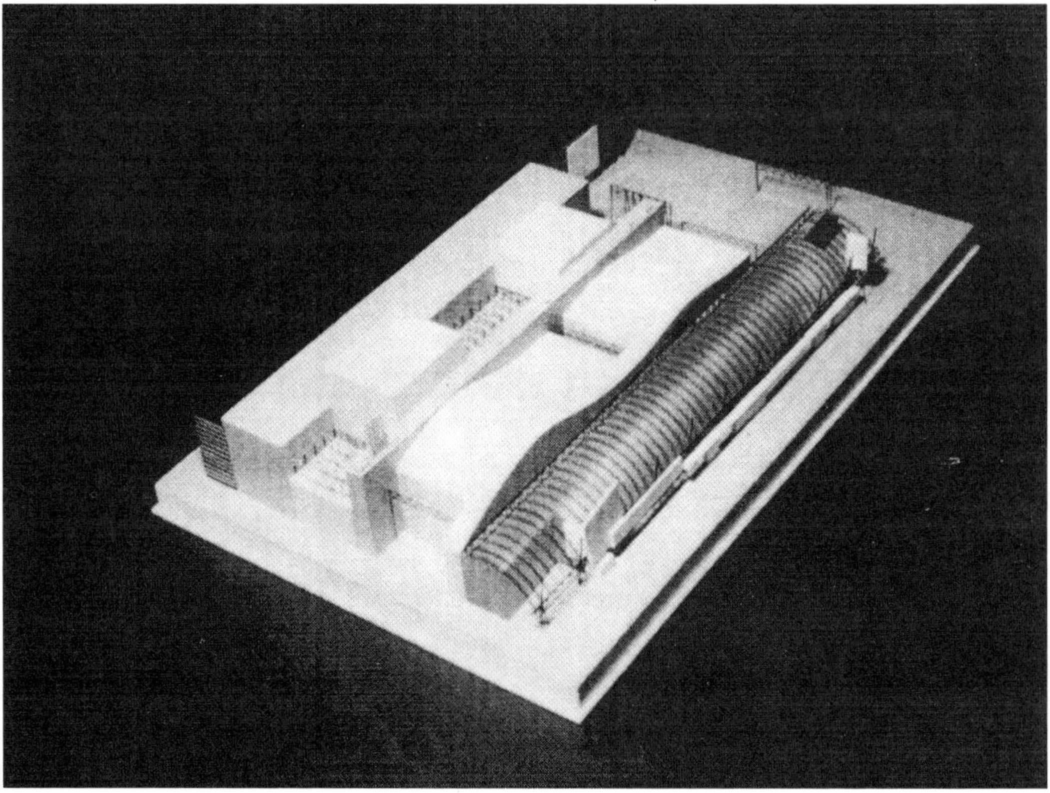

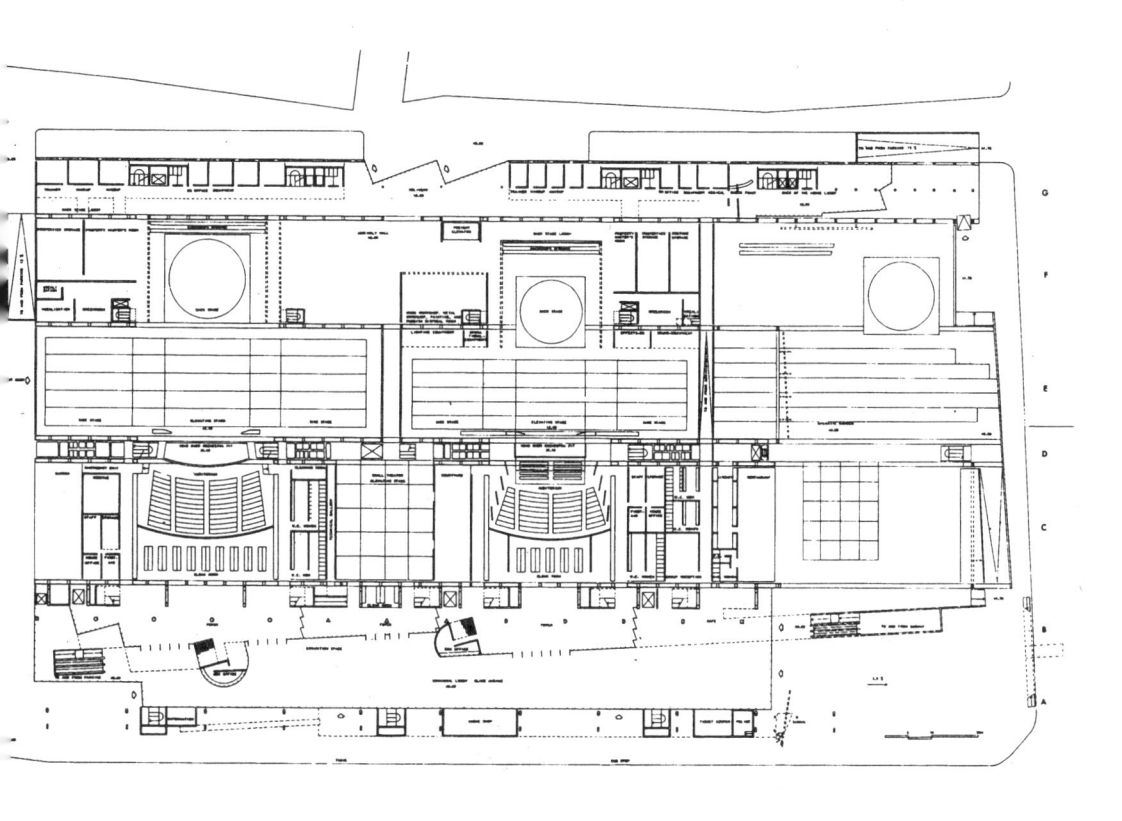

Ground level: required functions are effortlessly inserted into the conceptual framework

Incomplete bands: traces of a concept on the ground

TOKYO
283

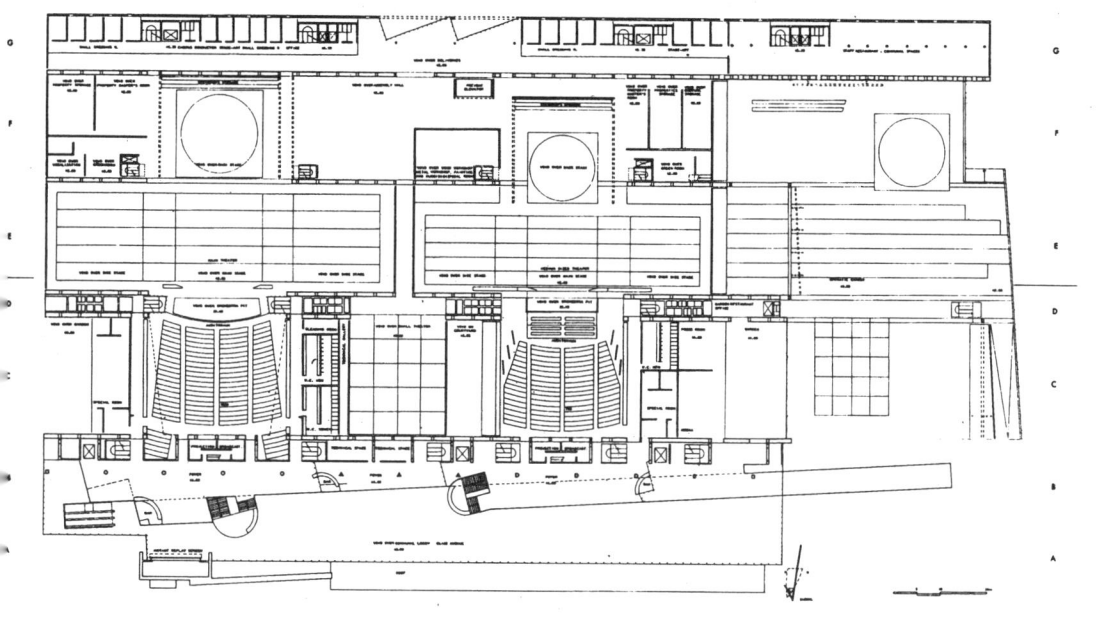

Mezzanine level: within each band are repetition and simplicity.
The only disruptions occur in the most public strip (A)

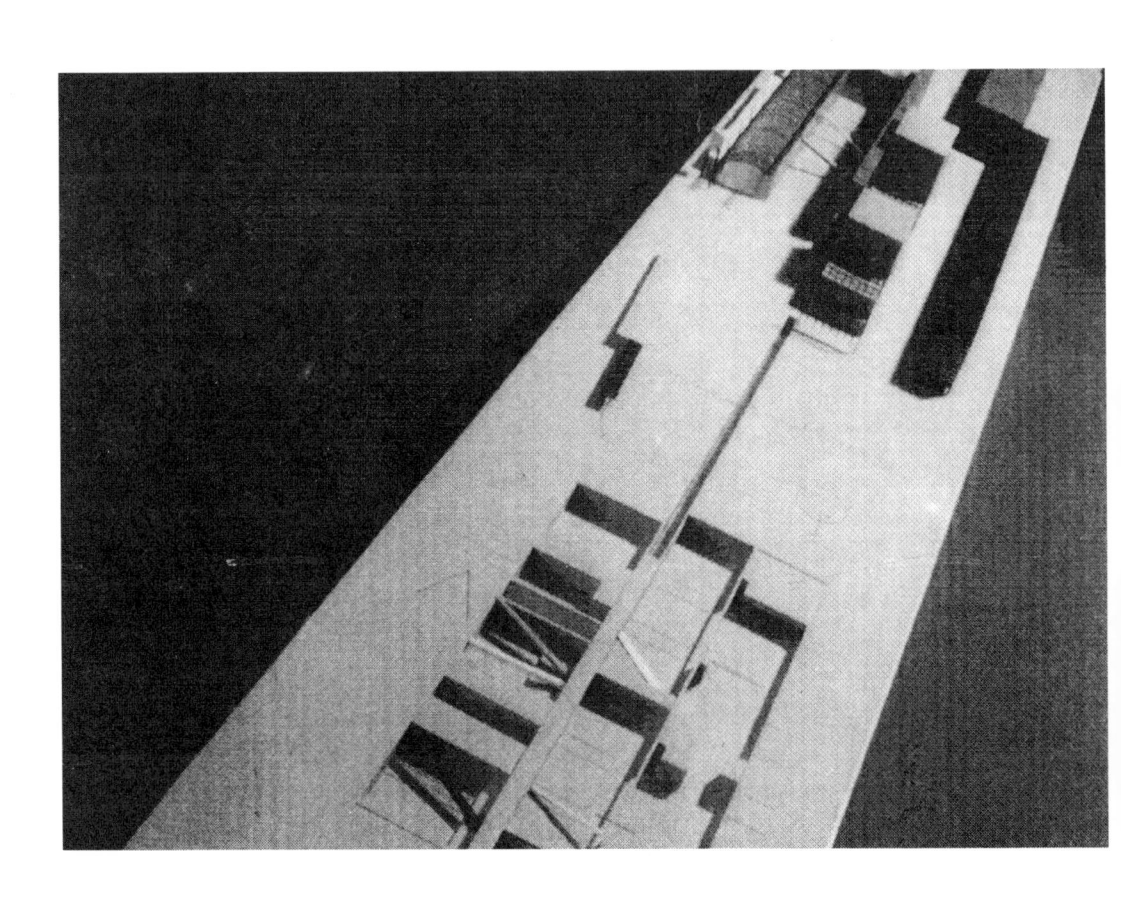

Programmatic bands: A/B. Public arcade, shops and lobbies C. Auditorium and theaters D. Mechanical E. Stages F. Backstages, rehearsal rooms G. Dressing rooms, administrative offices

TOKYO
285

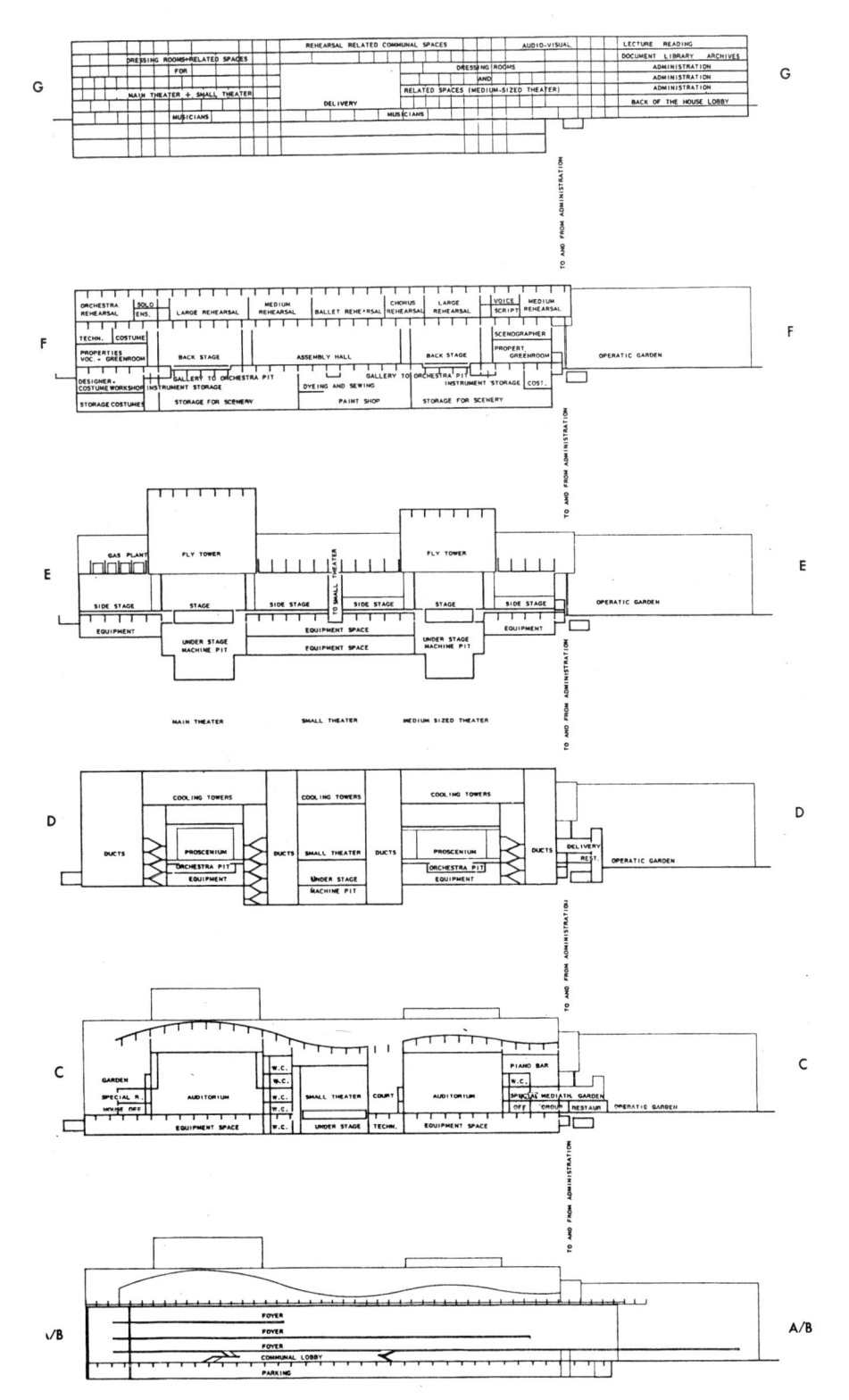

Section G
		REHEARSAL RELATED COMMUNAL SPACES	AUDIO-VISUAL	LECTURE READING
	DRESSING ROOMS+RELATED SPACES		DRESSING ROOMS	DOCUMENT LIBRARY ARCHIVES
	FOR		AND	ADMINISTRATION
G	MAIN THEATER + SMALL THEATER	DELIVERY	RELATED SPACES (MEDIUM-SIZED THEATER)	ADMINISTRATION G
	MUSICIANS		MUSICIANS	BACK OF THE HOUSE LOBBY

TO AND FROM ADMINISTRATION

Section F
ORCHESTRA REHEARSAL	SOLO ENS.	LARGE REHEARSAL	MEDIUM REHEARSAL	BALLET REHEARSAL	CHORUS REHEARSAL	LARGE REHEARSAL	VOICE SCRIPT	MEDIUM REHEARSAL	
	TECHN.						SCENOGRAPHER		
PROPERTIES	COSTUME	BACK STAGE		ASSEMBLY HALL		BACK STAGE	PROPERT.		OPERATIC GARDEN
VOC + GREENROOM							GREENROOM		
DESIGNER +		GALLERY TO ORCHESTRA PIT				GALLERY TO ORCHESTRA PIT		COST.	
COSTUME WORKSHOP		INSTRUMENT STORAGE		DYEING AND SEWING		INSTRUMENT STORAGE			
STORAGE COSTUMES		STORAGE FOR SCENERY		PAINT SHOP		STORAGE FOR SCENERY			

TO AND FROM ADMINISTRATION

Section E
	GAS PLANT	FLY TOWER				FLY TOWER			
E					TO SMALL THEATER				OPERATIC GARDEN E
	SIDE STAGE	STAGE	SIDE STAGE	SIDE STAGE		STAGE	SIDE STAGE		
	EQUIPMENT	UNDER STAGE MACHINE PIT	EQUIPMENT SPACE	EQUIPMENT SPACE		UNDER STAGE MACHINE PIT	EQUIPMENT		

MAIN THEATER   SMALL THEATER   MEDIUM SIZED THEATER

Section D
		COOLING TOWERS		COOLING TOWERS		COOLING TOWERS		
D	DUCTS	PROSCENIUM	DUCTS	SMALL THEATER	DUCTS	PROSCENIUM	DUCTS	DELIVERY D
		ORCHESTRA PIT		UNDER STAGE		ORCHESTRA PIT		REST.
		EQUIPMENT		MACHINE PIT		EQUIPMENT		OPERATIC GARDEN

TO AND FROM ADMINISTRATION

Section C
	GARDEN						PIANO BAR		
C	SPECIAL R.	AUDITORIUM	W.C.	SMALL THEATER	COURT	AUDITORIUM	SPECIAL MEDIATH. GARDEN		OPERATIC GARDEN C
	HOUSE OFF		W.C.				OFF GROUP RESTAUR		
		EQUIPMENT SPACE	W.C.	UNDER STAGE TECHN.		EQUIPMENT SPACE			

TO AND FROM ADMINISTRATION

Section A/B
		FOYER		
A/B		FOYER		A/B
		FOYER		
		COMMUNAL LOBBY		
		PARKING		

Entrance and opera garden: traces on the ground

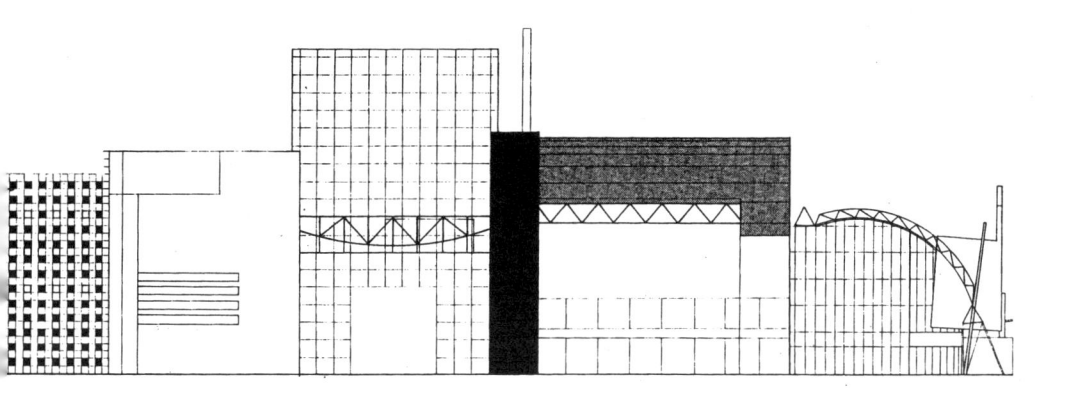

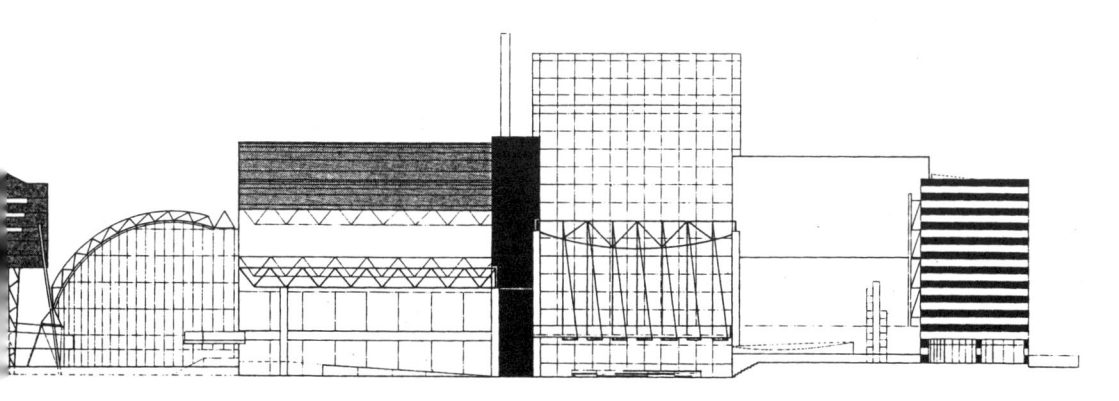

North elevation

South elevation

Elevations: no design, no composition, but materialization of the construction concept

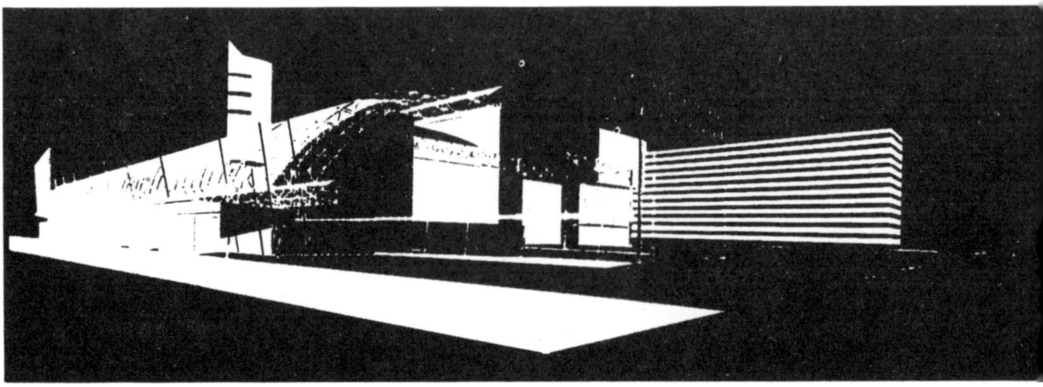

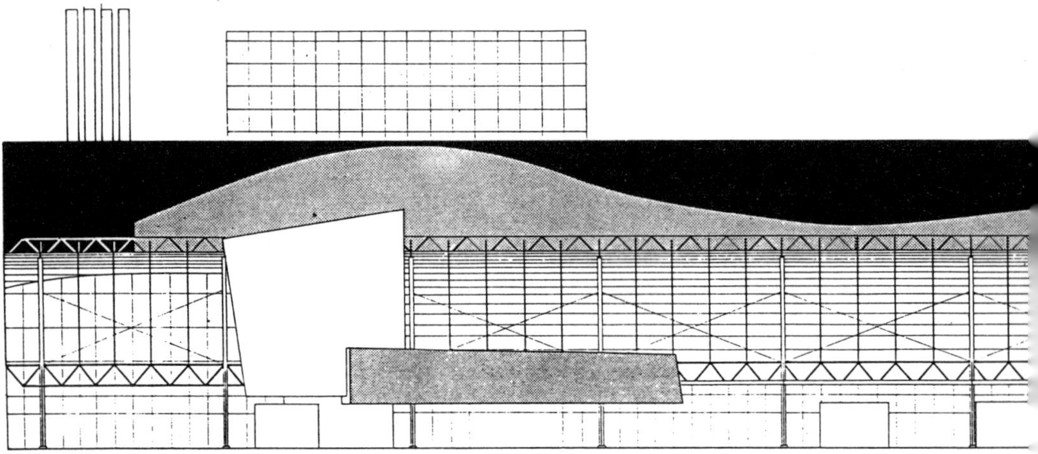

TOKYO
289

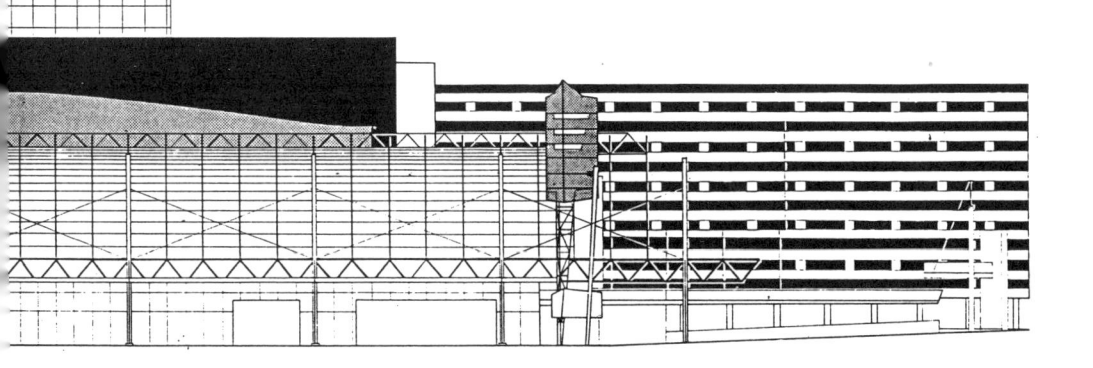

West elevation

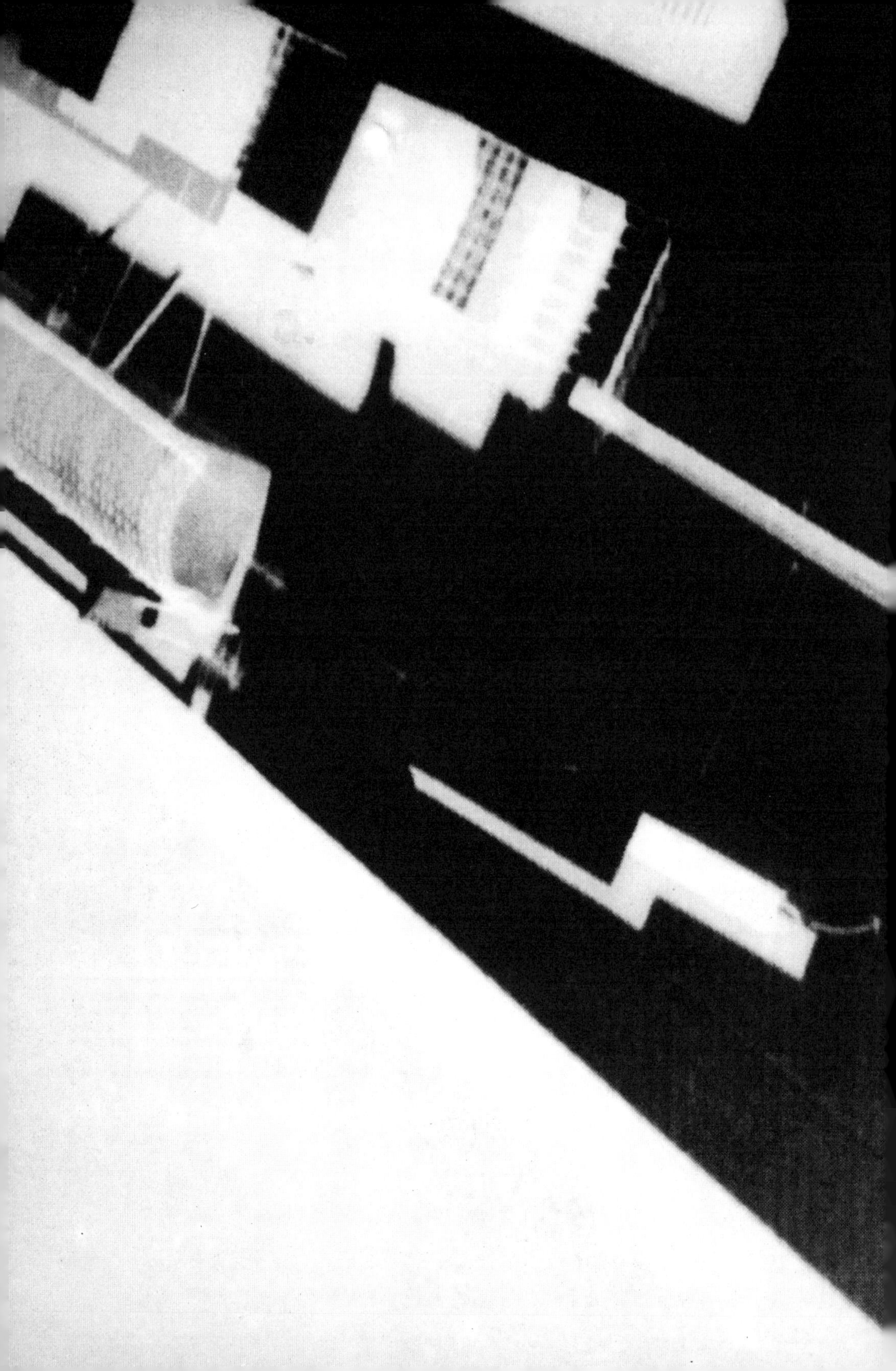

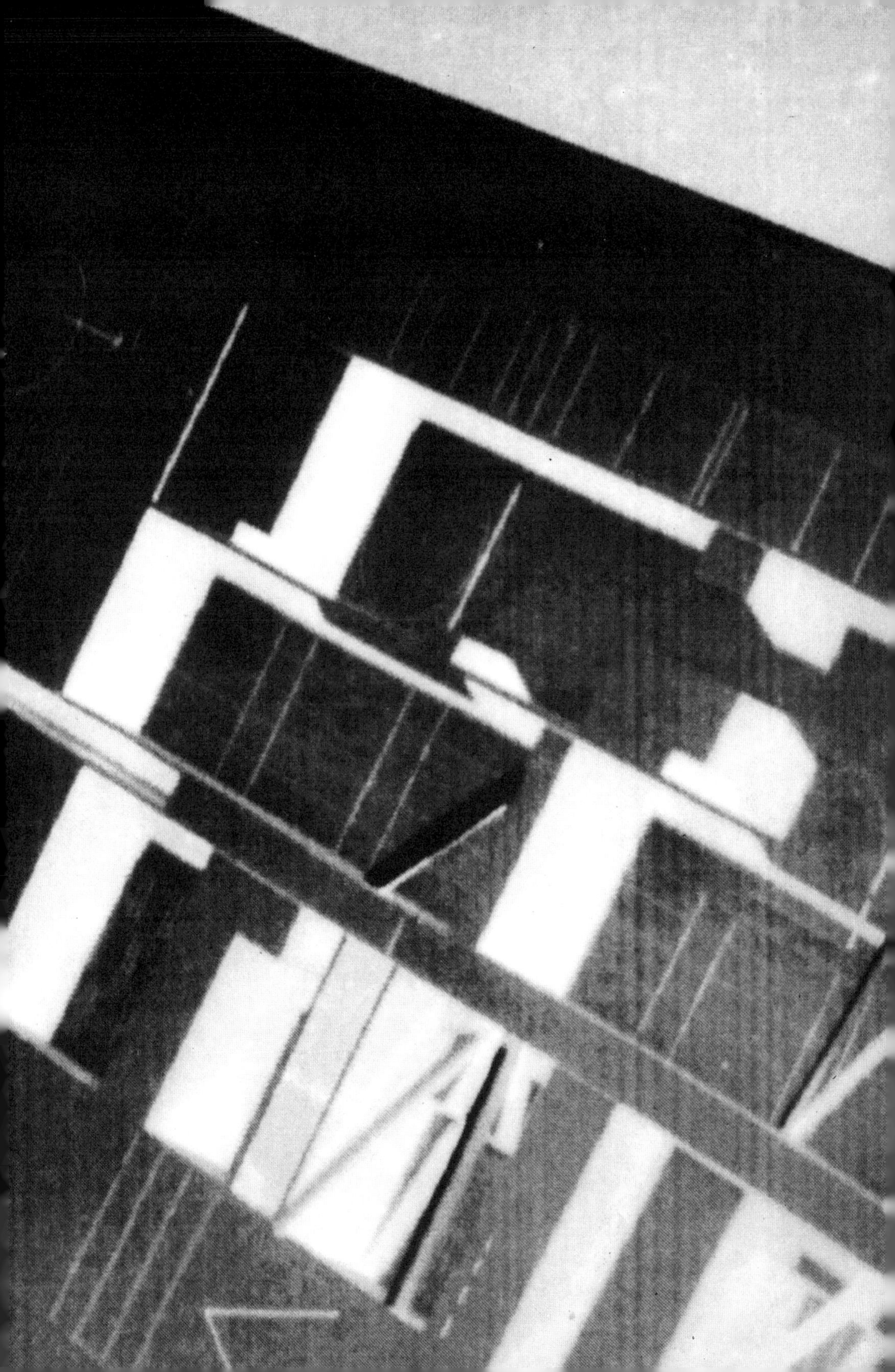

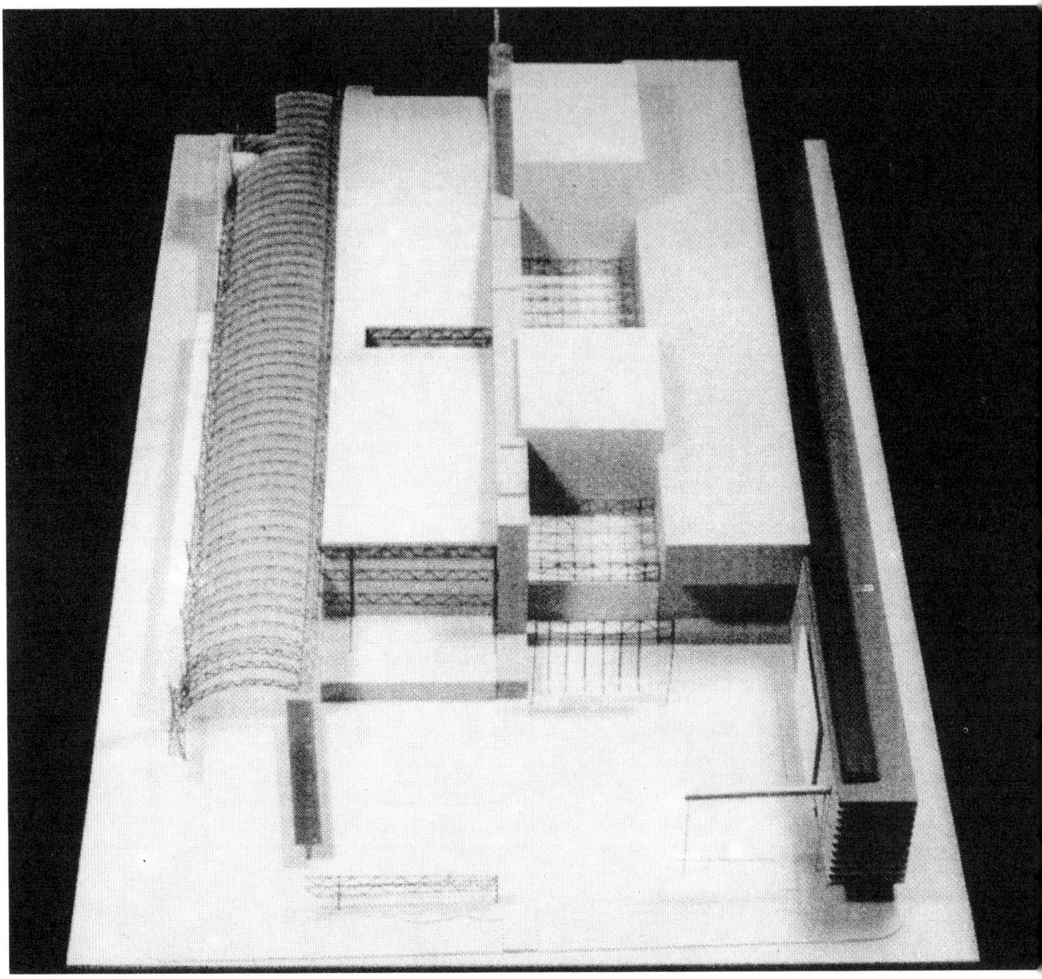

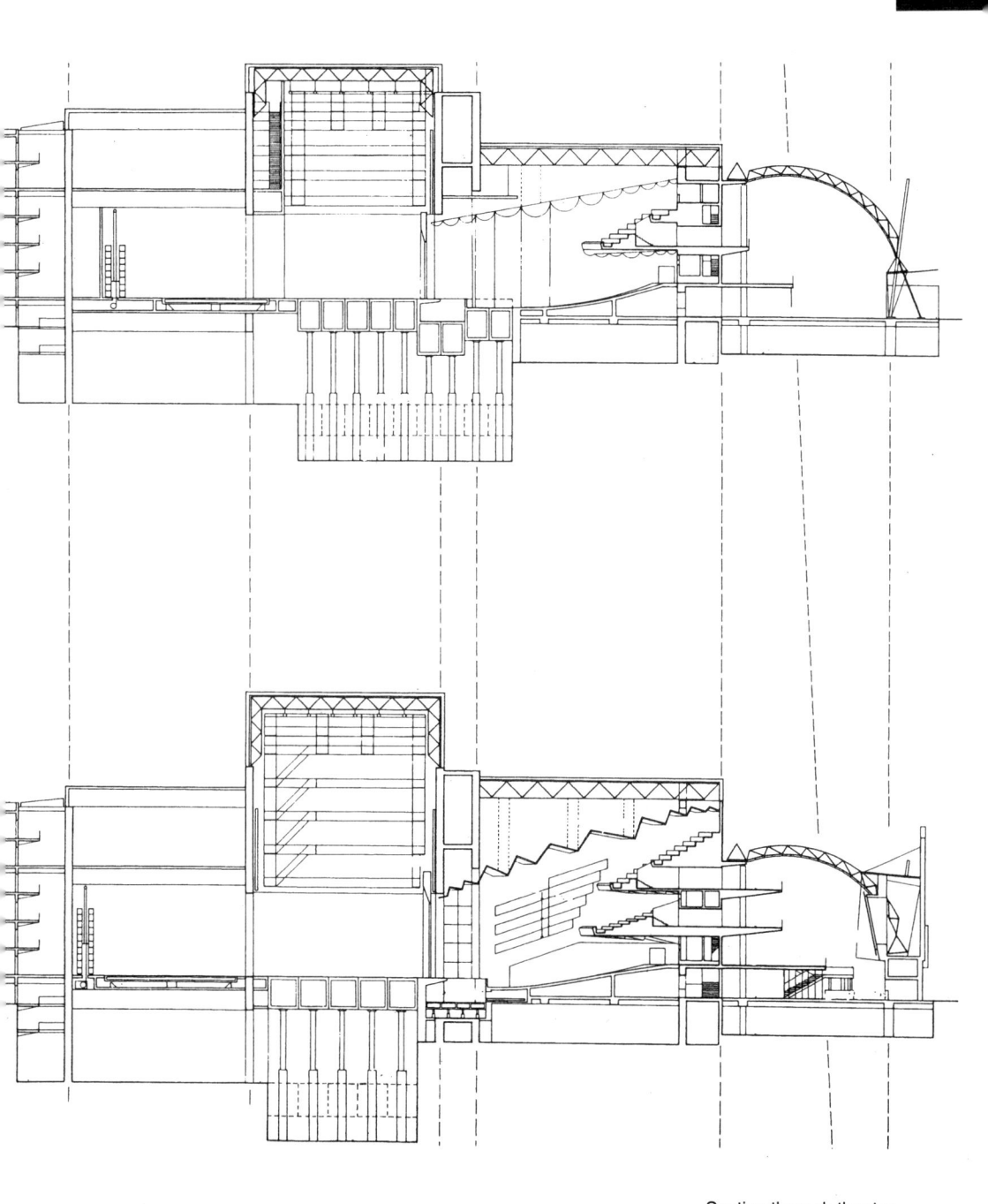

Section through theater

Section through concert hall

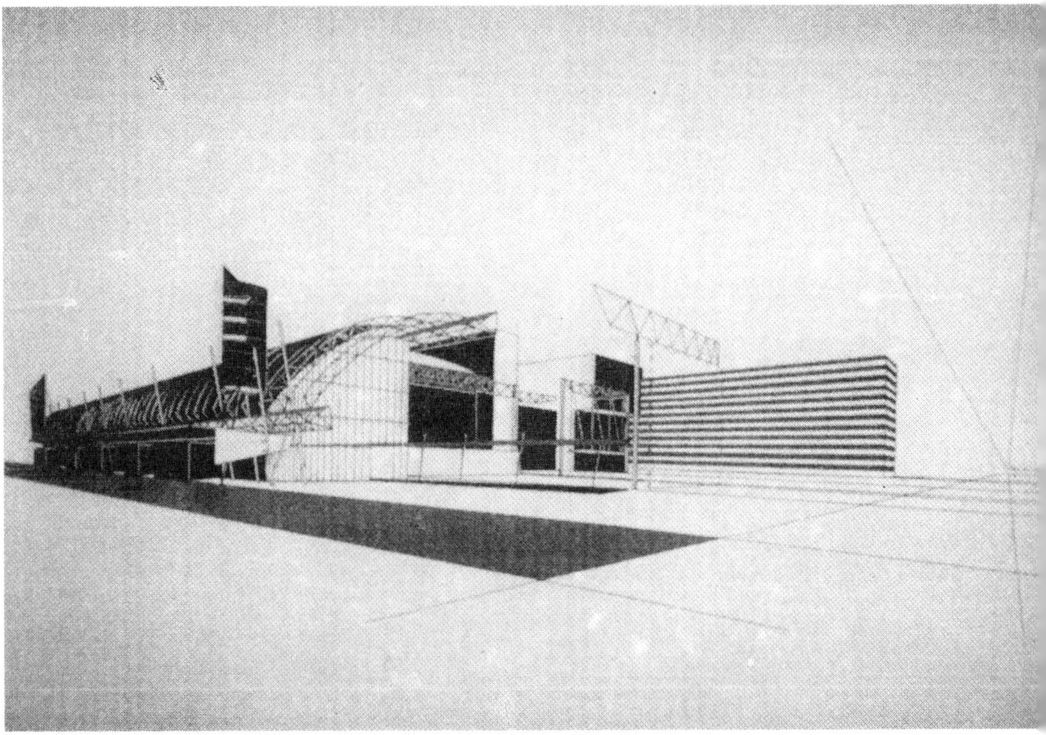

TOKYO
295

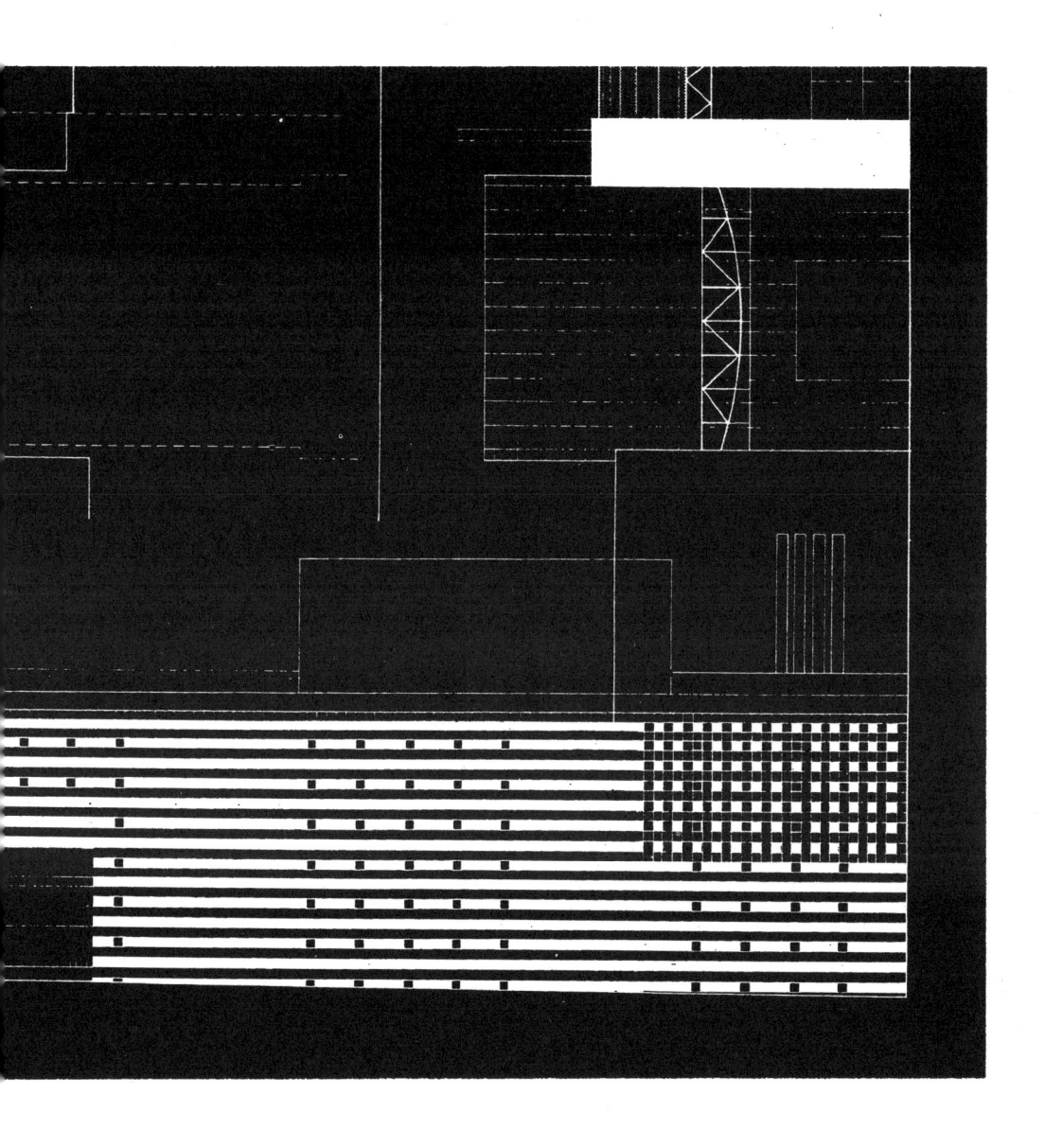

North and west elevations

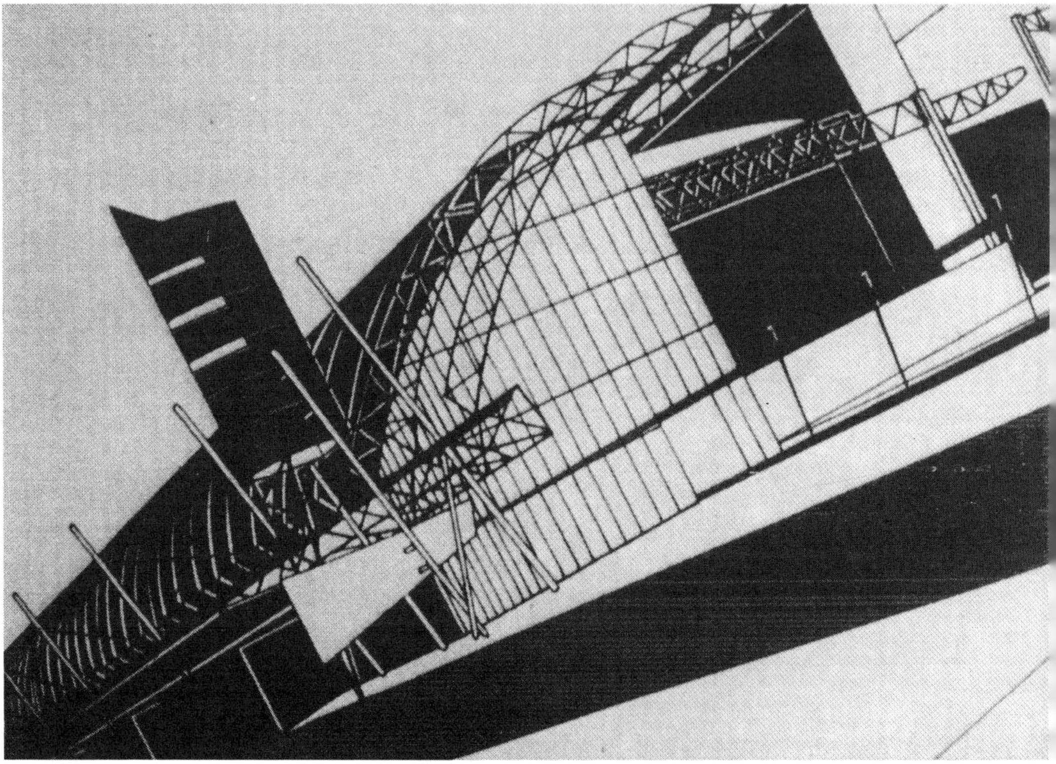

Entrance: de-emphasizing the role of "form"

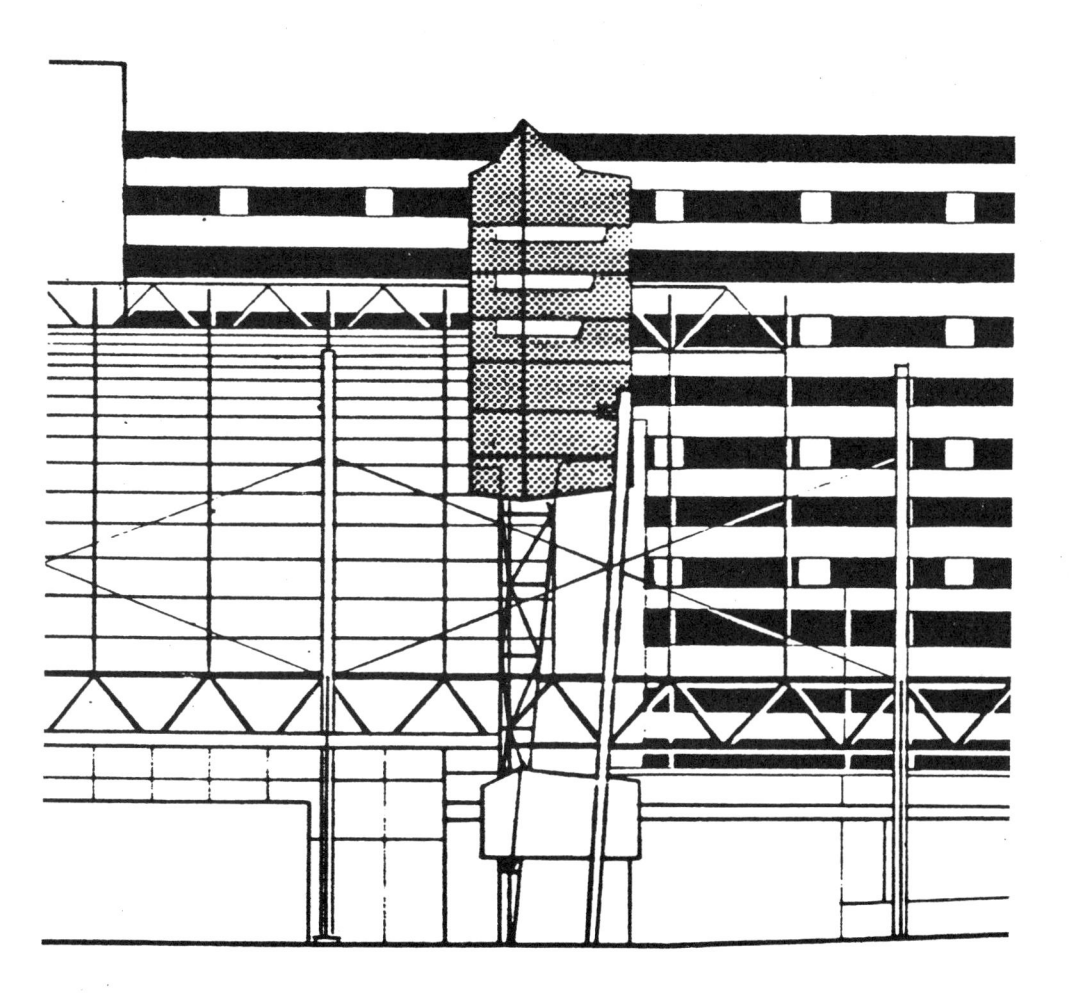

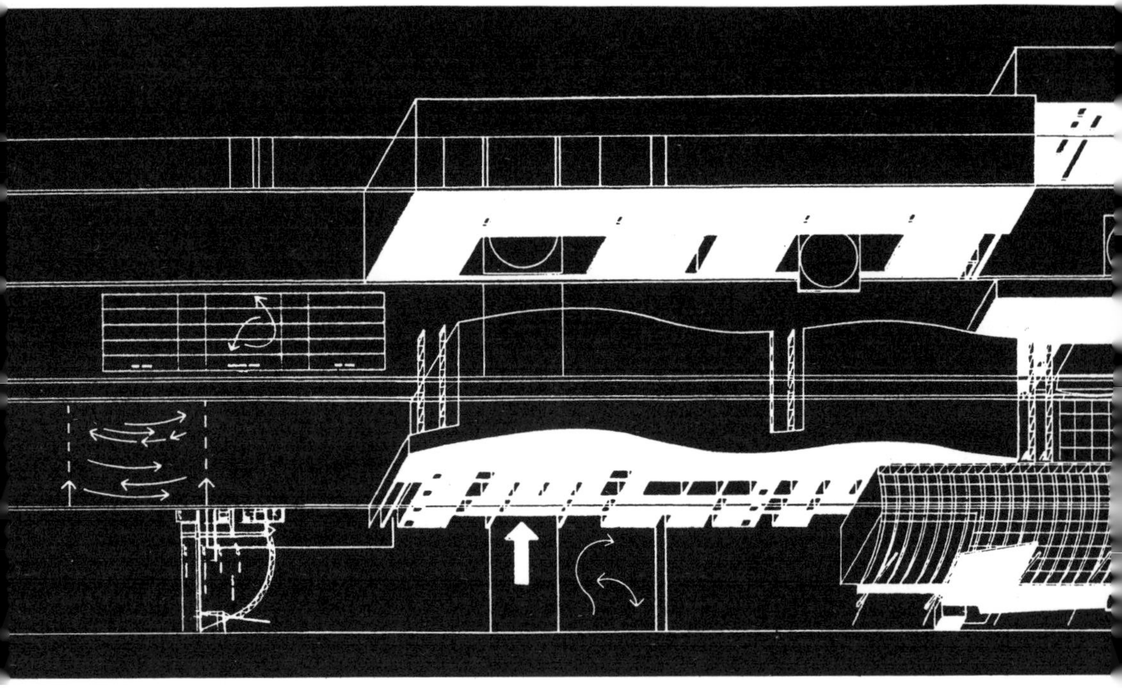

TOKYO
299

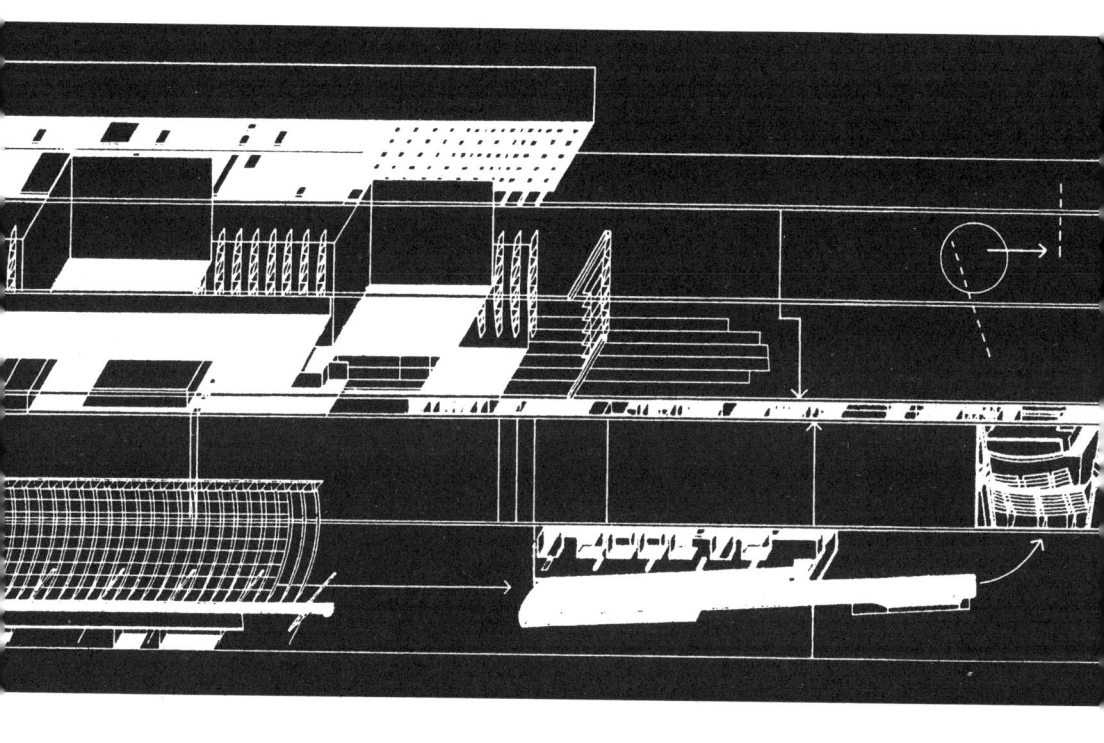

Bands in action: programmatic permutations

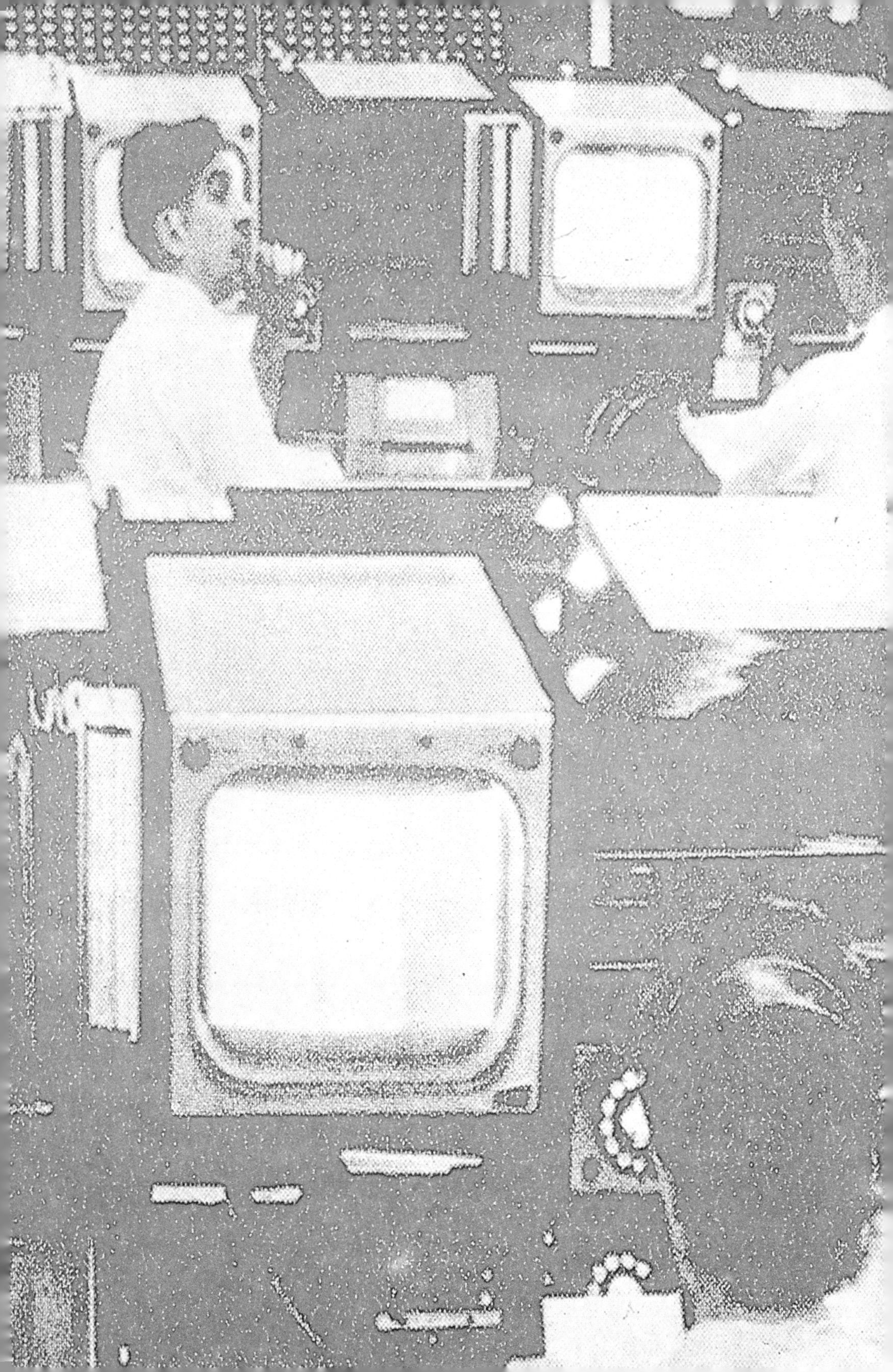

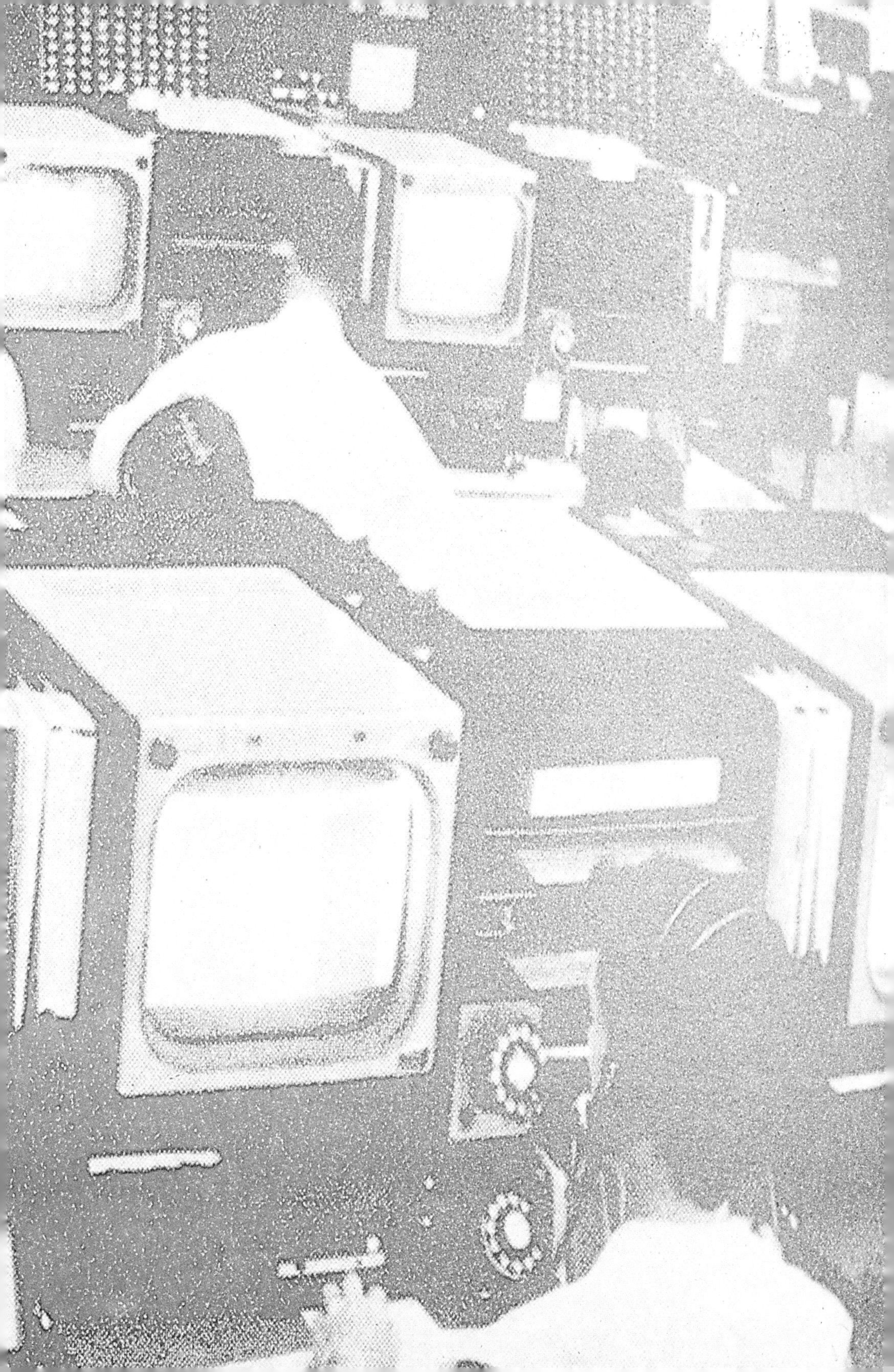

Strasbourg, County Hall, 1986

Old and New—The Logic of Fragments

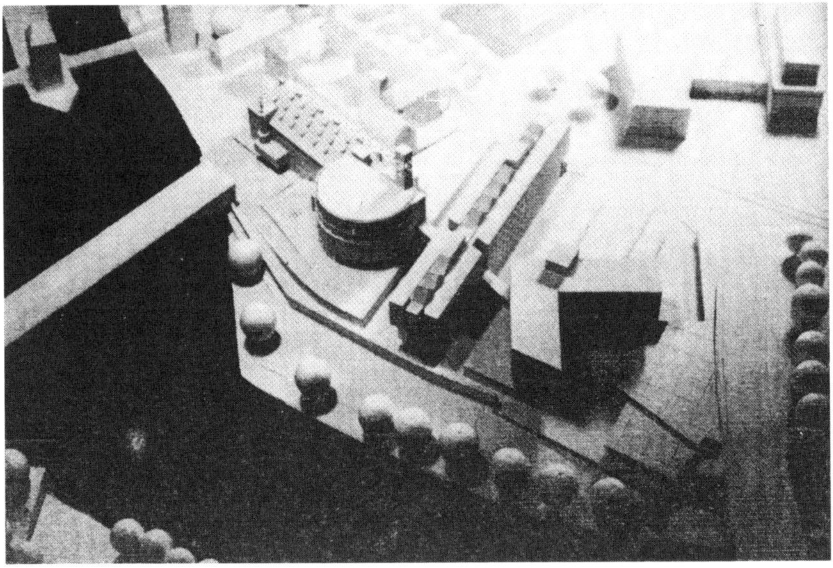

The competition was for a new county hall for Strasbourg, France, a complex consisting of 20,000 square meters of offices, together with spaces accommodating the protocol connected with local administration and visits by important state dignitaries. The proposed location is southwest of the town, on the bank of the river Ill, exactly where historic Strasbourg (the district known as "Little France") meets the twentieth-century Strasbourg (embodied in the slabs housing the medical faculty). A dam built by Vauban fronts the site, and the remains of fortifications are still visible on the site itself. The program asked for a "representative" building and seemed to favor the demolition of an abandoned eighteenth-century building at the entrance to the site, the large mansard roof of which visually links the historic town and the new districts.

The question of demolition was fundamental. To demolish an interesting building, a major landmark of the town, simply to make room for a building whose purpose is essentially administrative, suggests a certain cynicism. Moreover, it seemed to us that a more up-to-date approach would reject the expedient of demolishing the old building while introducing a new concept of urban combination.

The site lies exactly on the boundary between two types of urban planning, one emphasizing the traditional perimeter block, the other reflecting the ideology of large postwar developments, in which each building is treated as an isolated entity. Rather than imitate either of these, we adopted a conceptual framework that would create a new relation between these different architectural types—and offer a strategy that could be applied to similar situations.

Strasbourg has witnessed a variety of urban layouts—the Roman *cardo* and *decumanus*, narrow medieval streets, eighteenth-century neoclassical compositions, nineteenth-century German town planning, and the counter-compositions of Van Doesburg. We decided that the nature of the competition site as a meeting point between old and new would justify rehabilitating the old barracks and suggest a new urban project that would clarify the relation of the historical fragments to today.

The problem, then, was to design a complex of offices linking old and new. Fragmentation seemed appropriate for the following reasons:

1. The fragment enabled us to take into account the specific constraints of each element of the program (for example, the conference hall) without compromising the whole (for example, repetitive office floors).

2. The fragment gives the elements autonomy, while making it easier to perceive their relative importance.

3. The varying scale of each fragment relates to the incoherent space of the historic town.

4. The fragment also allows, through free juxtapositions, a spatial inventiveness, a poetic dimension and a new conception of the site.

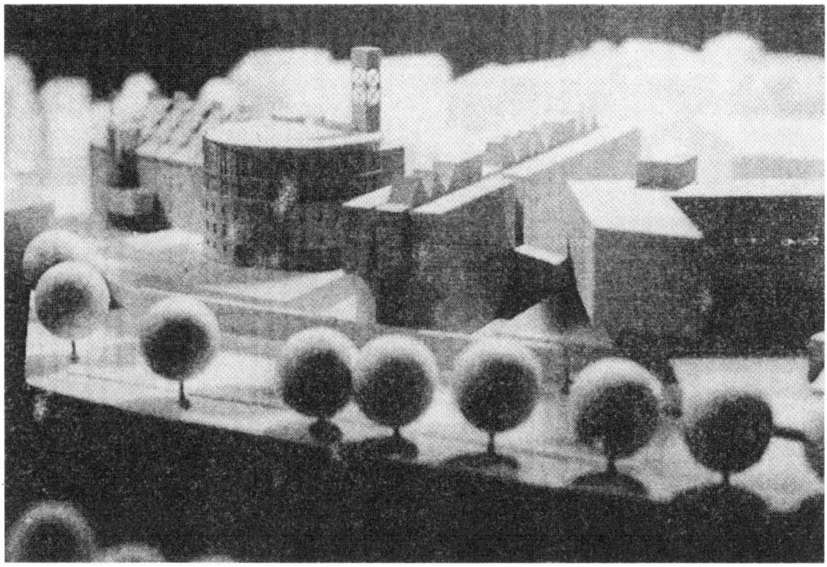

We then elaborated a precise assemblage of volumes based on the program requirements and the particularities of the site:

1. The rotunda, hinge element of the project, immediately perceivable and identifiable, articulates all other functions.

2. The eighteenth-century building, renovated and restructured, houses many of the services as well as the restaurant and faces the old Strasbourg. The addition of contemporary elements (elevators and stairs) on the west and east facades, as well as the glazing of the north gable, effaces the building's military connotations while conserving its essential features.

3. The slab houses most of the administrative services. It lies perpendicular to the island (a major element of Strasbourg), parallel to the existing bridges and floodgate.

The slab, as opposed to the neighborhood's gloomy and scaleless postwar buildings, plays with two distinct facades: the south facade in pink sandstone announces the city center from the exterior avenues, and the north facade in glass announces modernity as seen from the quarters of the old town center.

4. The "right angle" will extend the whole, placed on the twentieth-century grid.

5. The base, which forms an abstract, mathematical landscape, in part treated as a garden, consists of two levels. The first contains underground parking; the second, most of the general services located on the ground floor. The latter profits from natural light.

The five elements clearly define the whole. Each has its own distinct personality; together they offer an image of the departmental reality between the historic city and the new quarters.

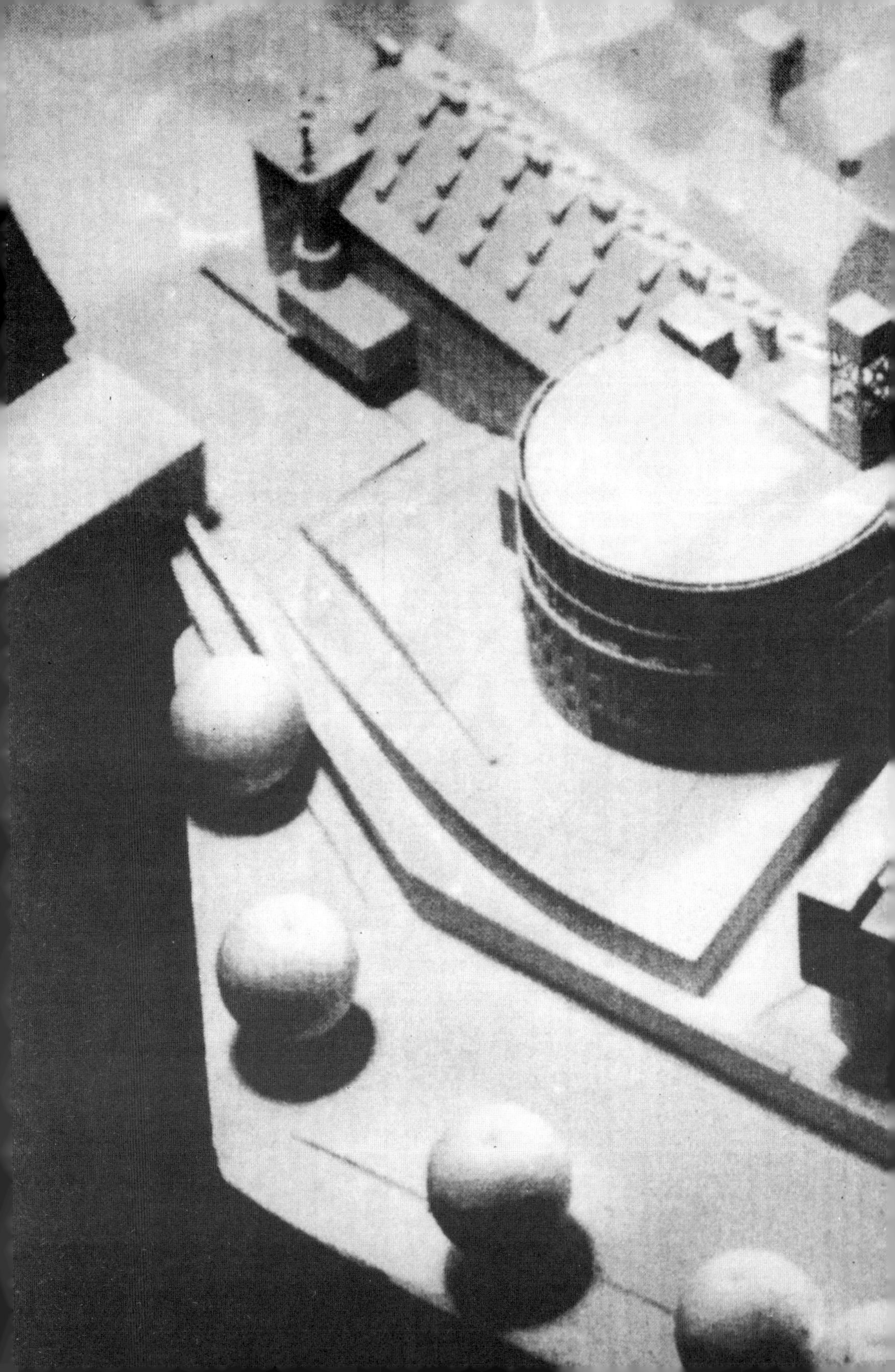

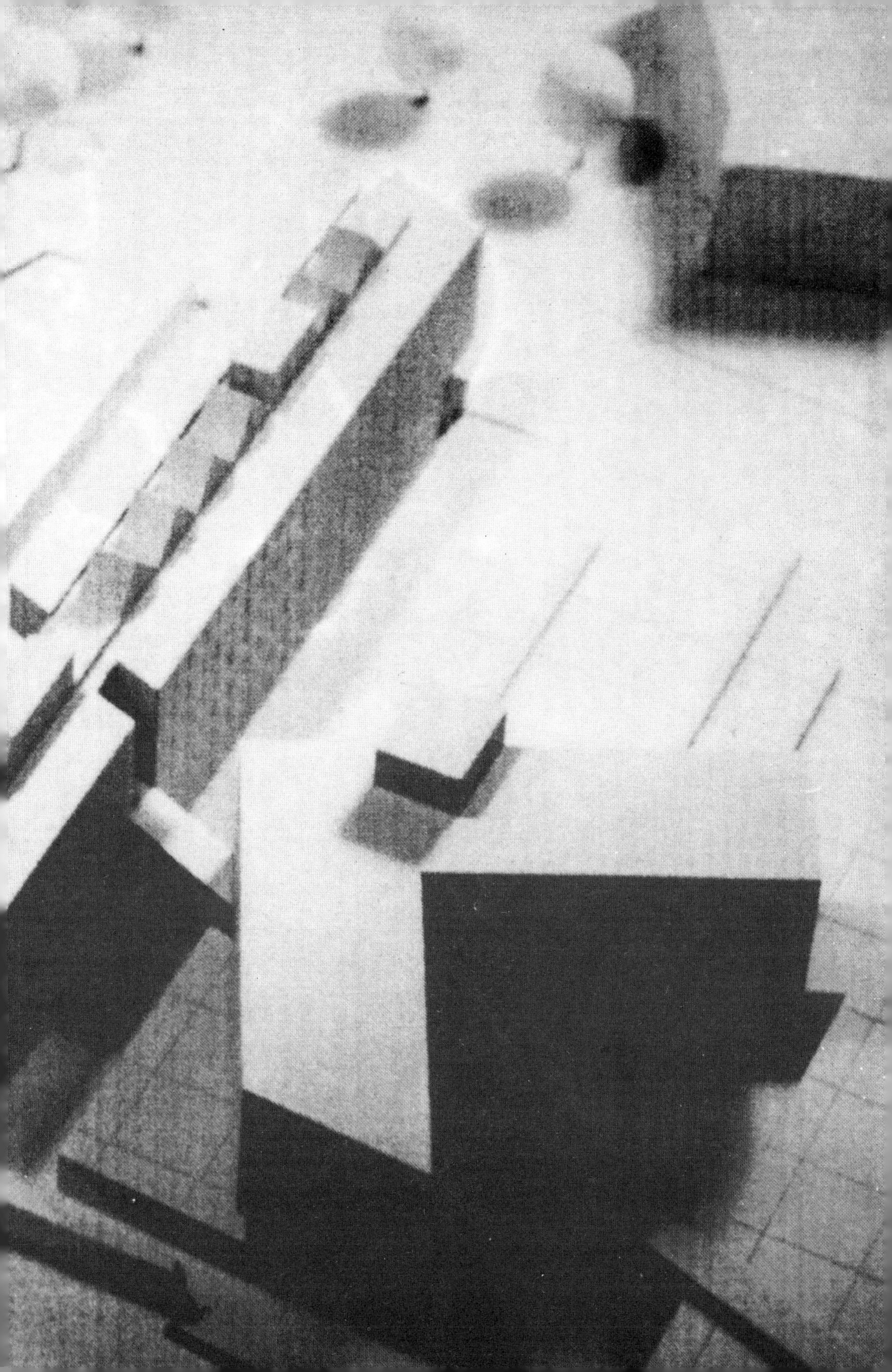

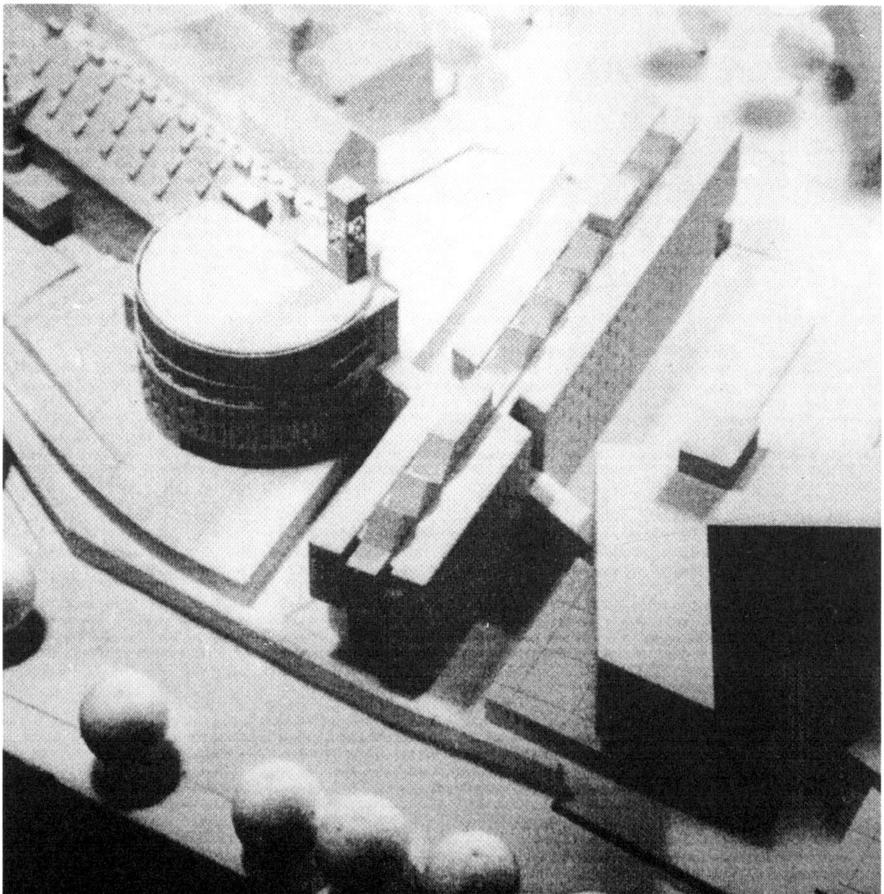

STRASBOURG
311

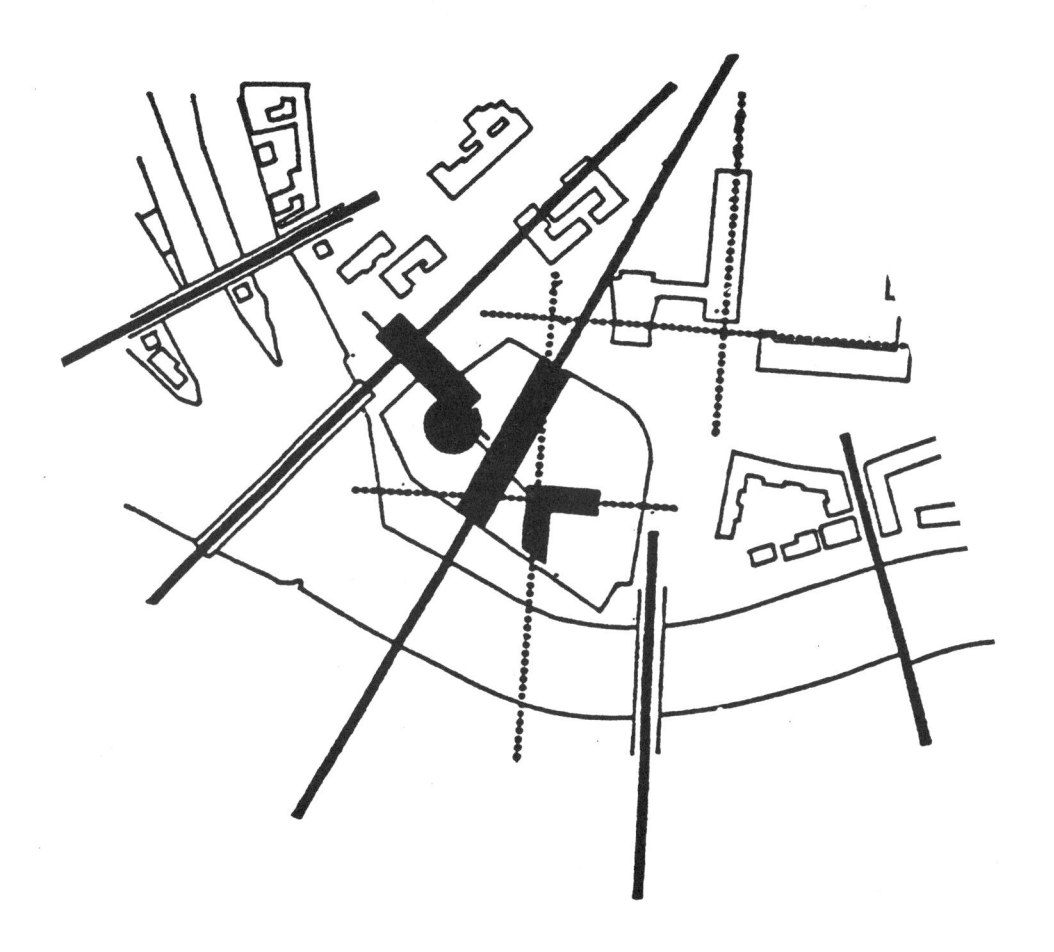

Power lines: abandoning the opposition between the old and the new,
the "authentic" and the "inauthentic"

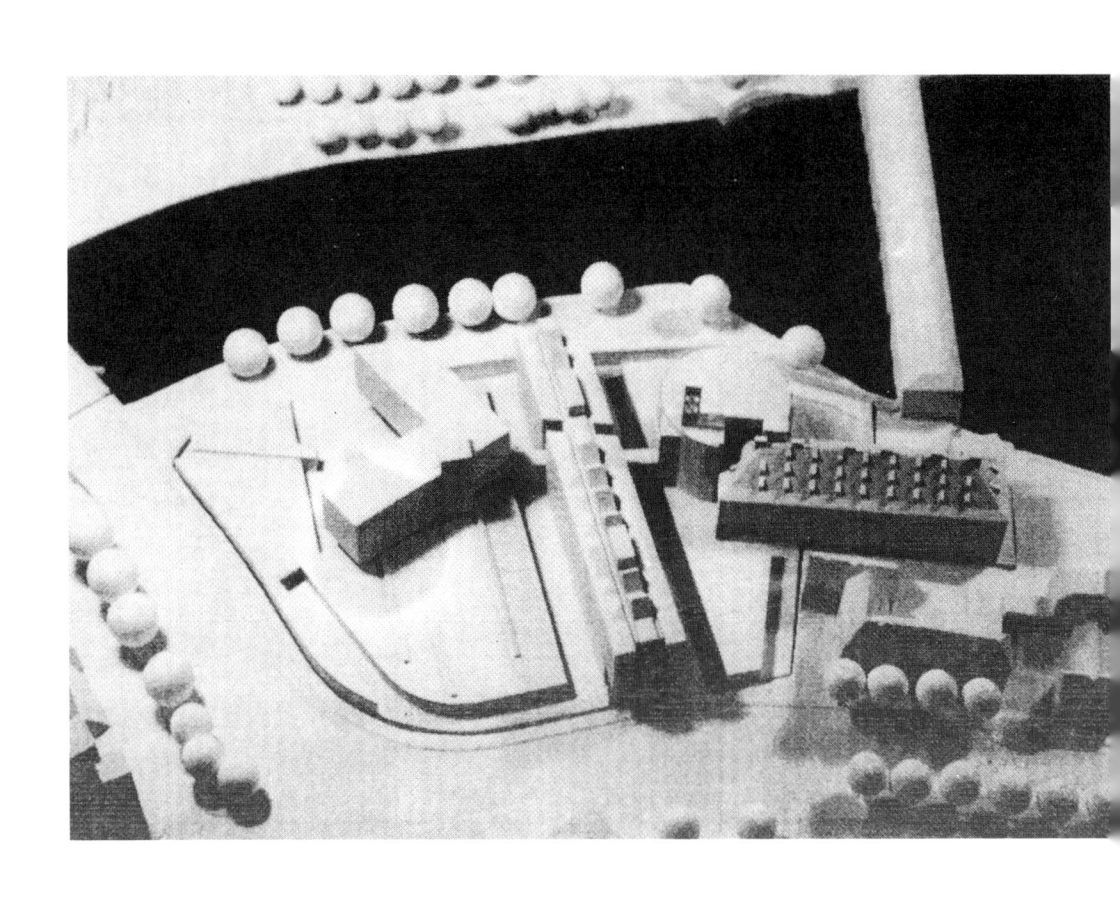

No hierarchy: old and new fragments are of exactly equal importance

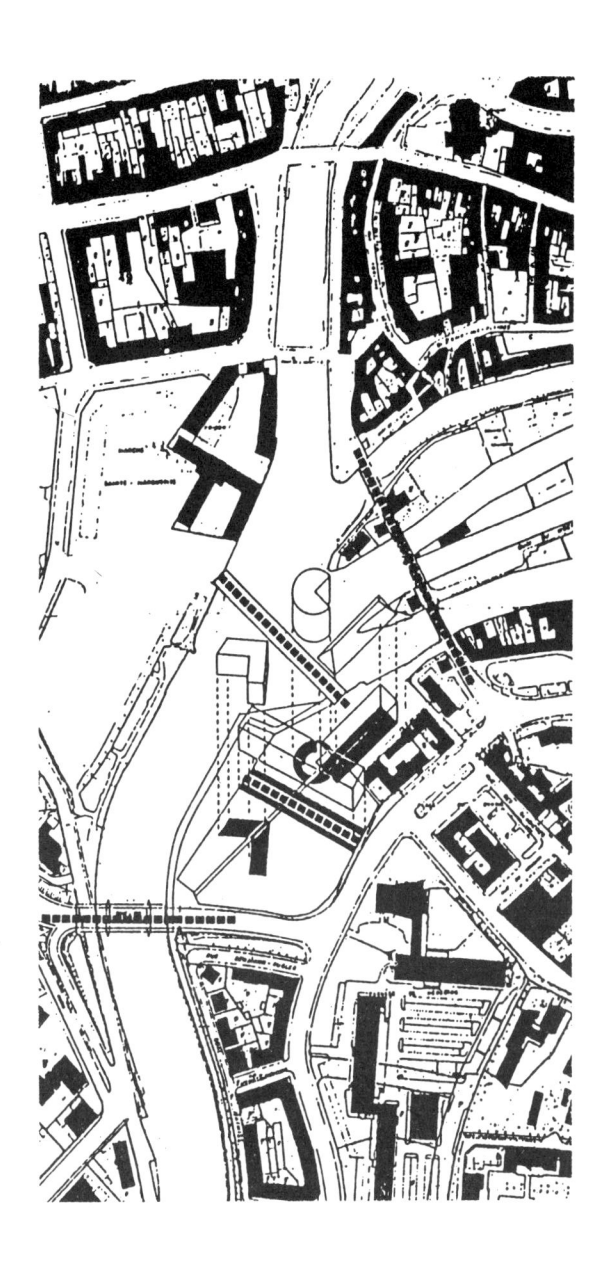

Fragments articulate between the old and the postwar city

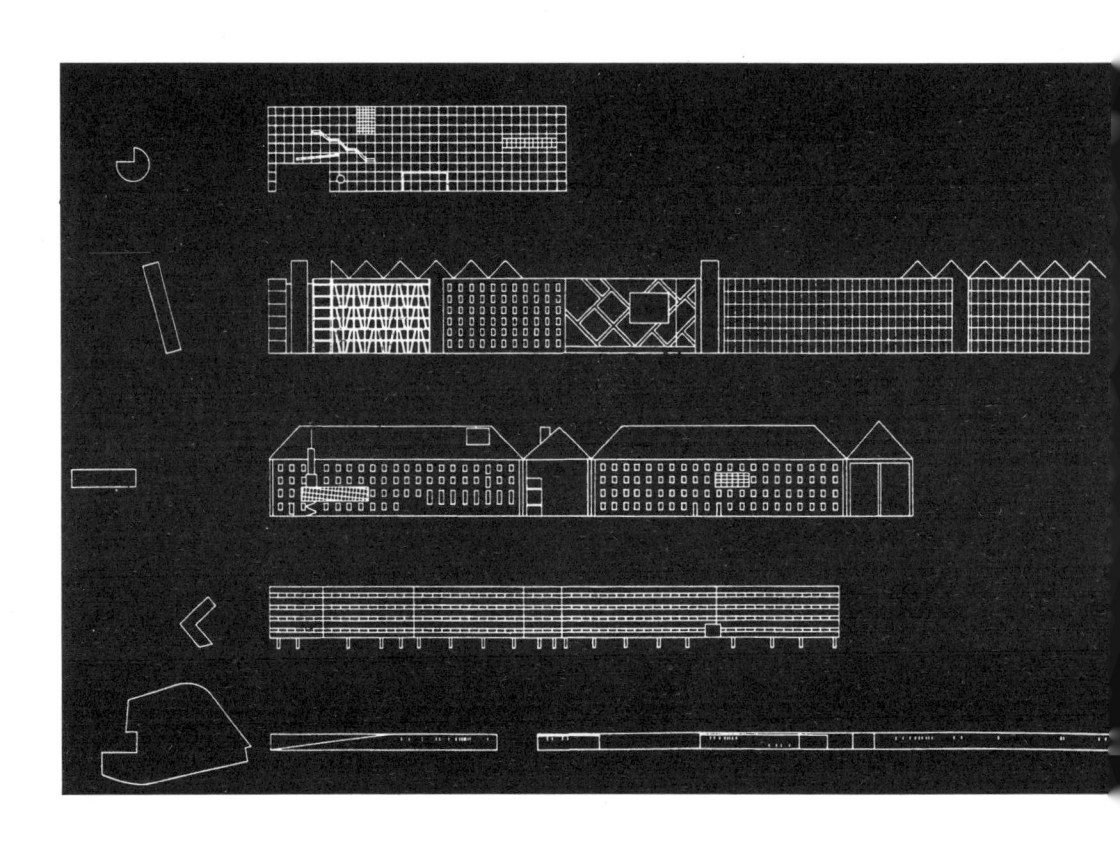

Multiple elevations: celebrating fragmentation by accelerating a culture of differences

STRASBOURG
315

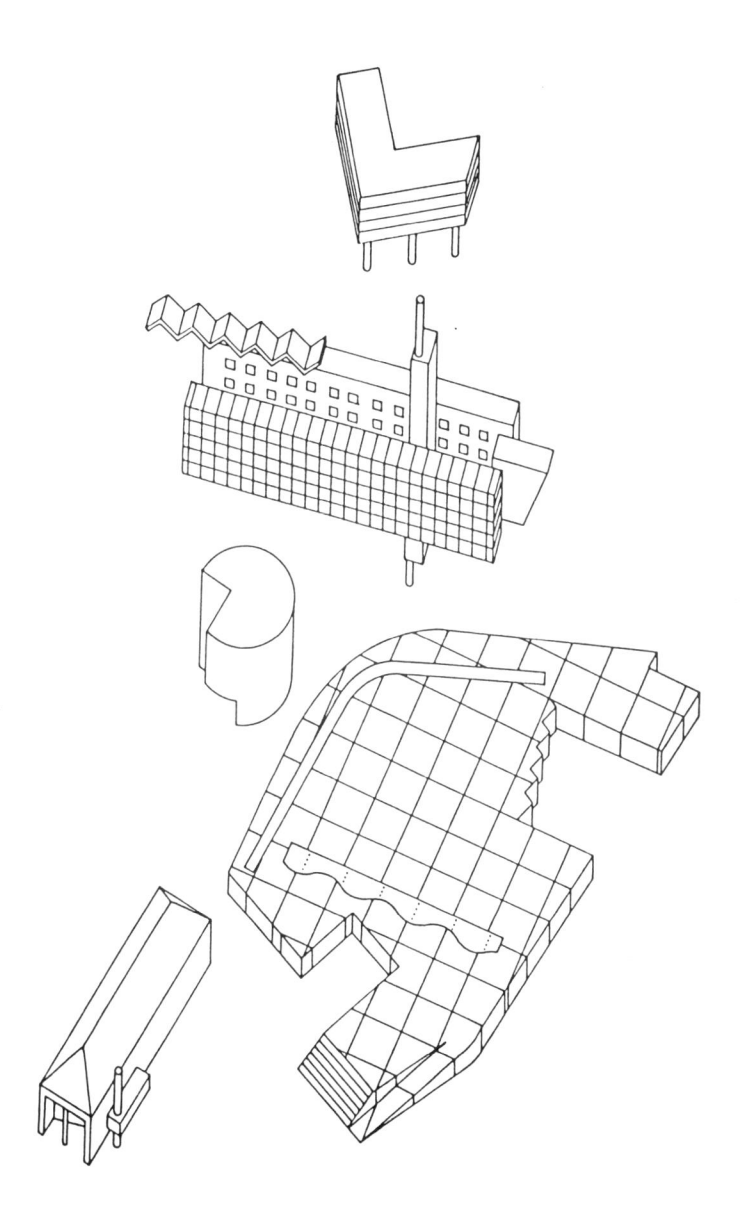

Five fragments: 18th-century barracks, base, rotunda, administration slab
and right angle (extension); combination, permutation, transformation

Accelerating and intensifying the loss of center, of certainty

STRASBOURG
317

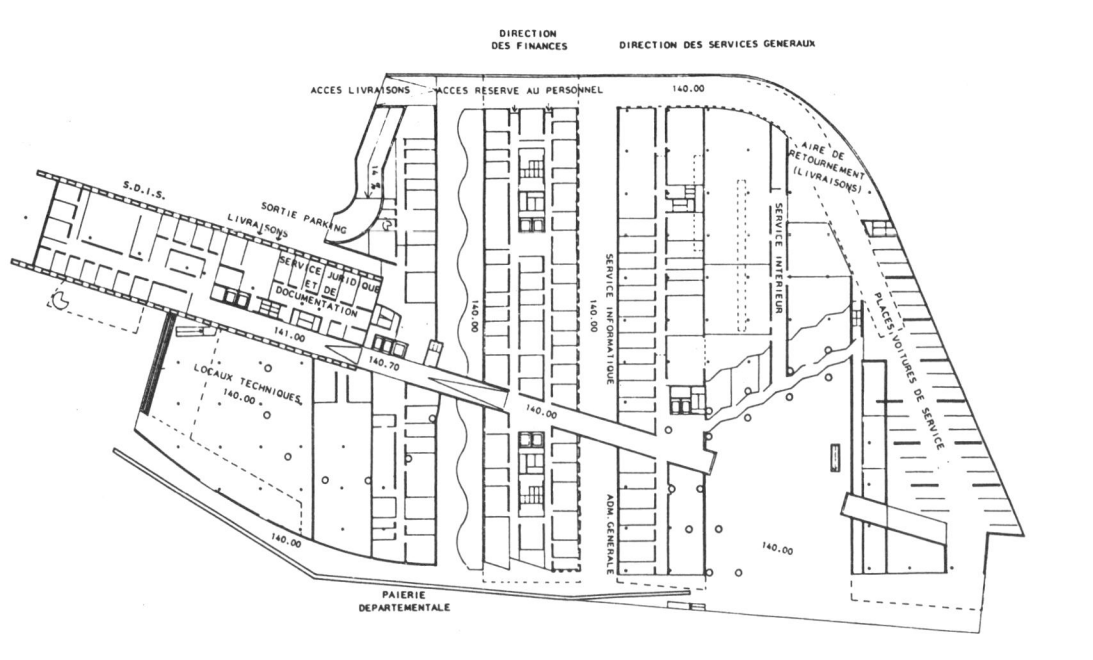

Ground level: base containing general services

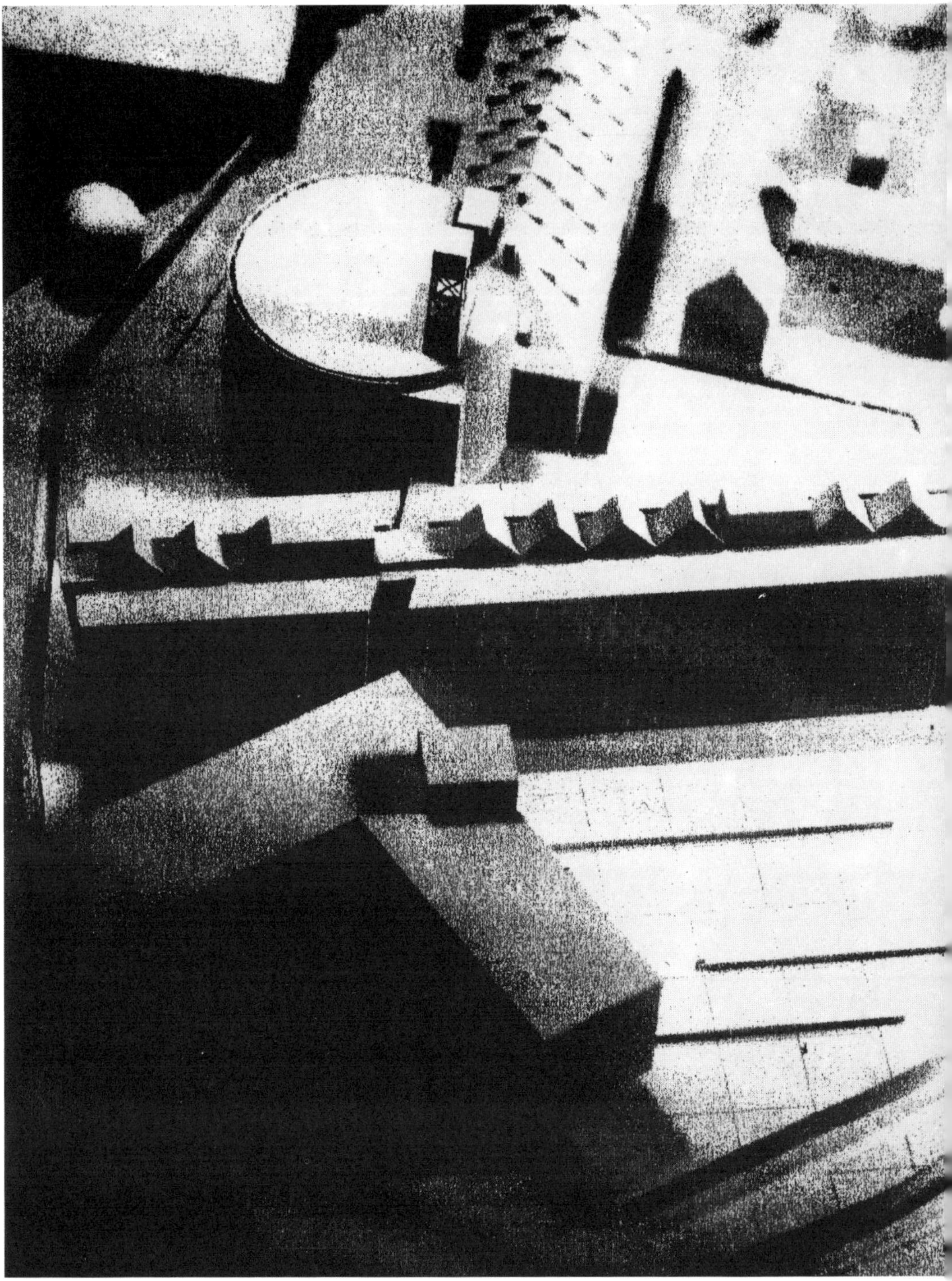

STRASBOURG
319

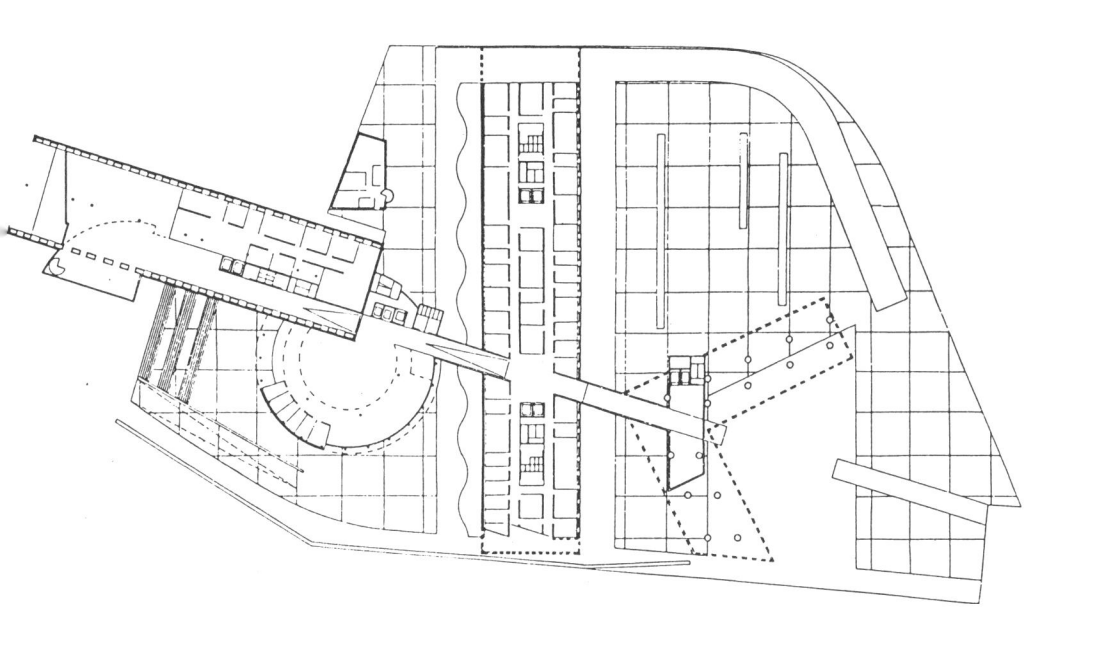

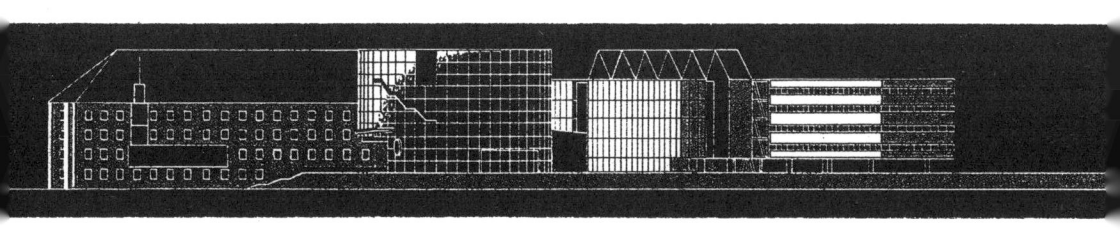

Level 1: rotunda (reception), administration slab and 18th-century barracks

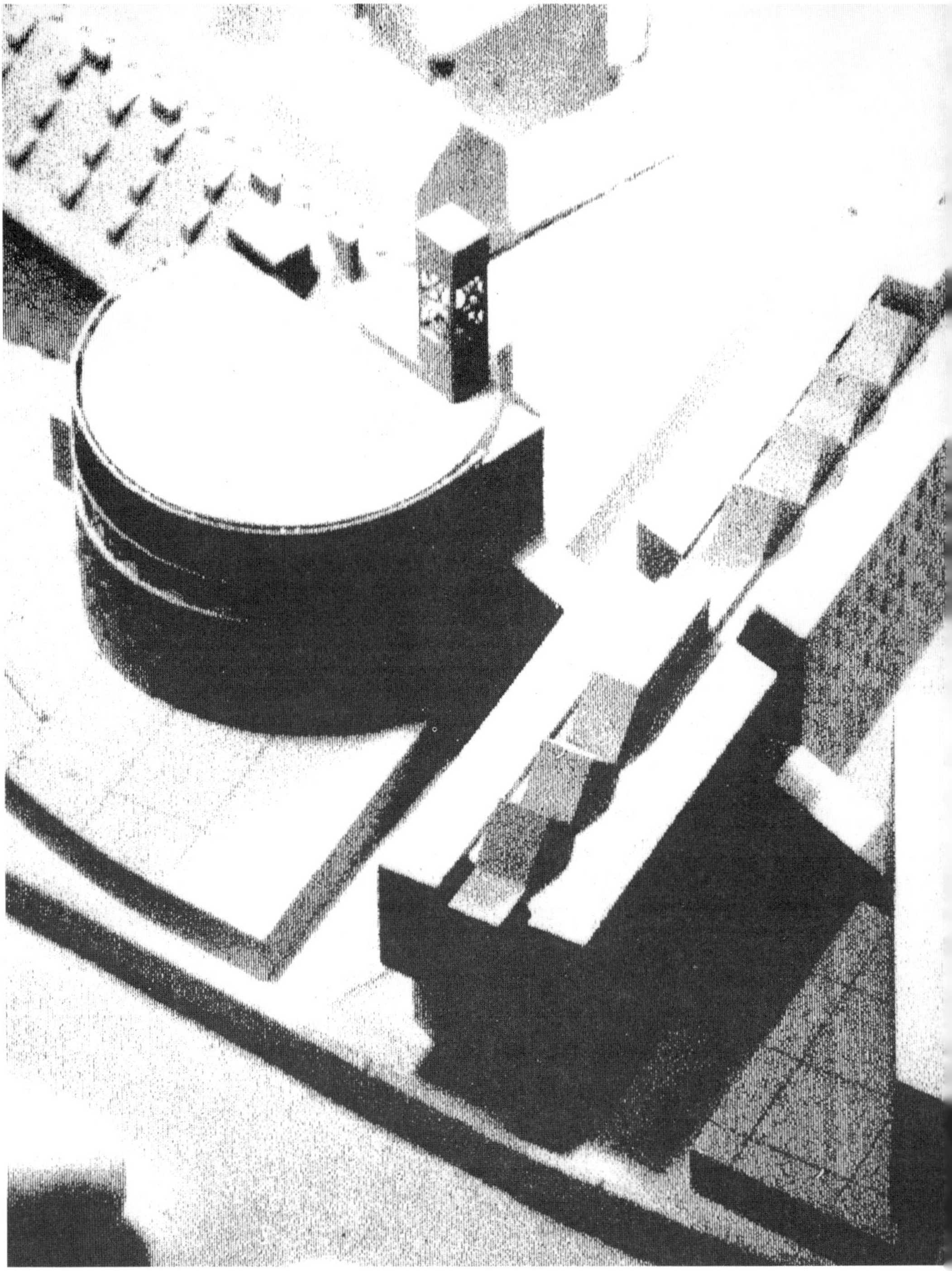

STRASBOURG
321

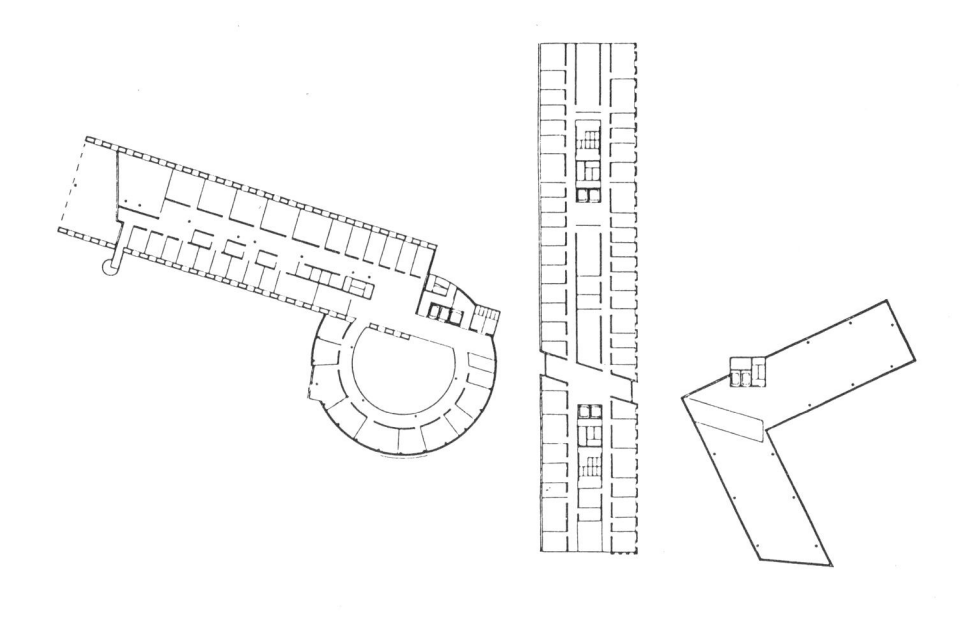

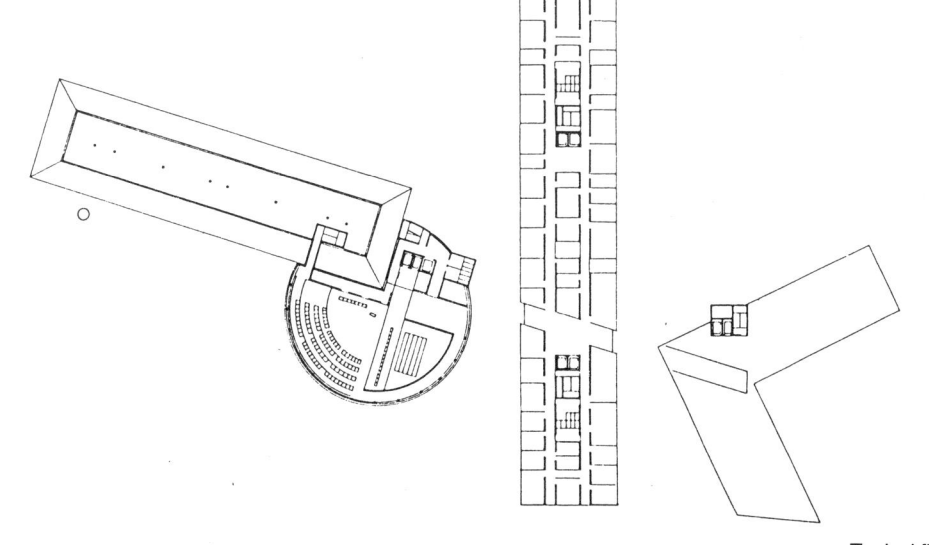

Typical floor

Level 8

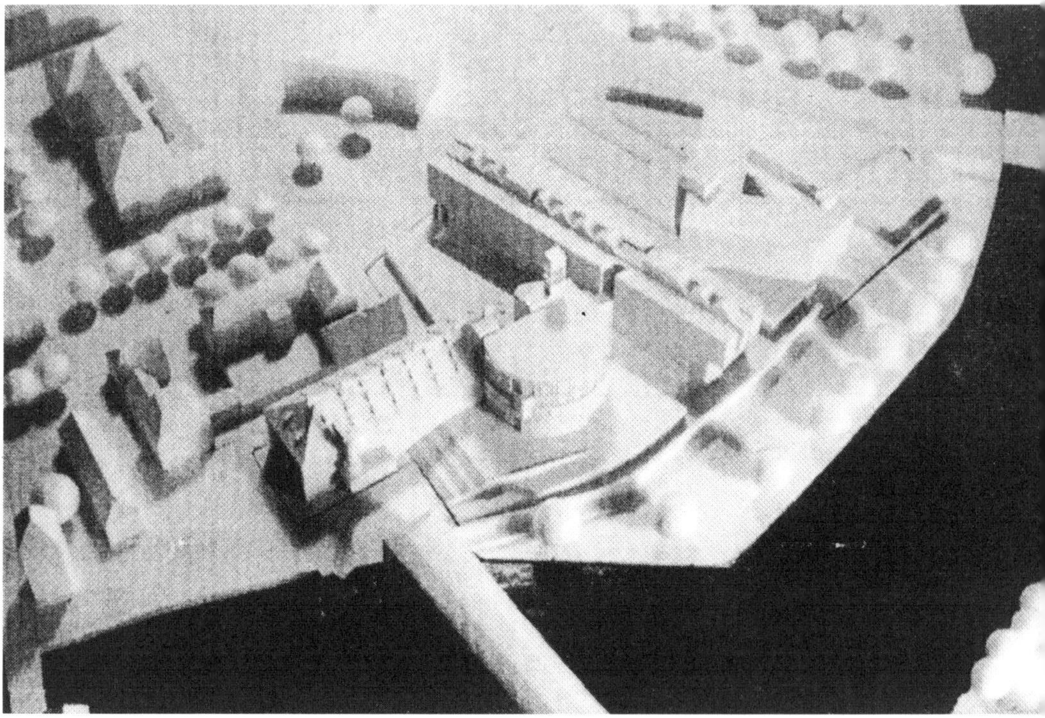

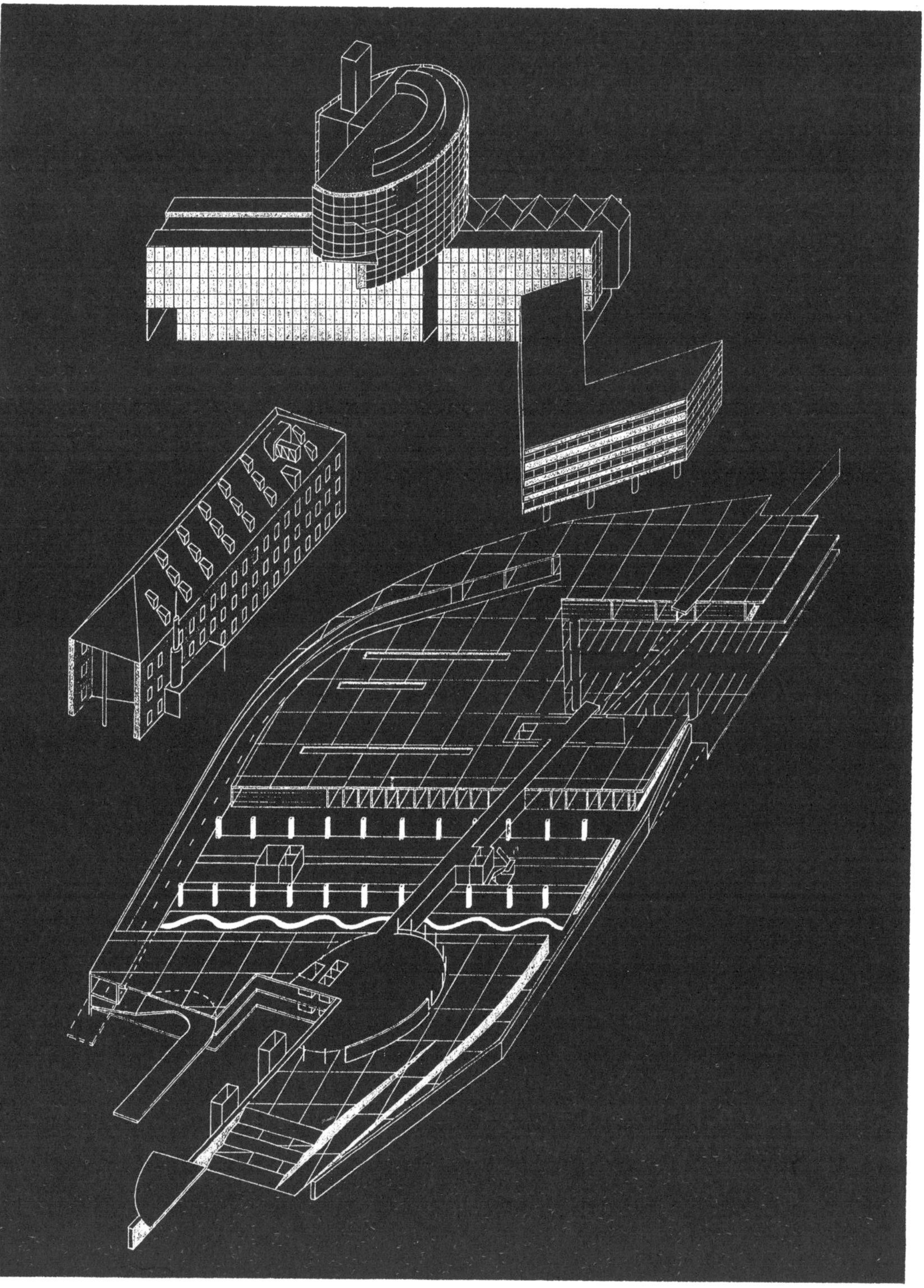

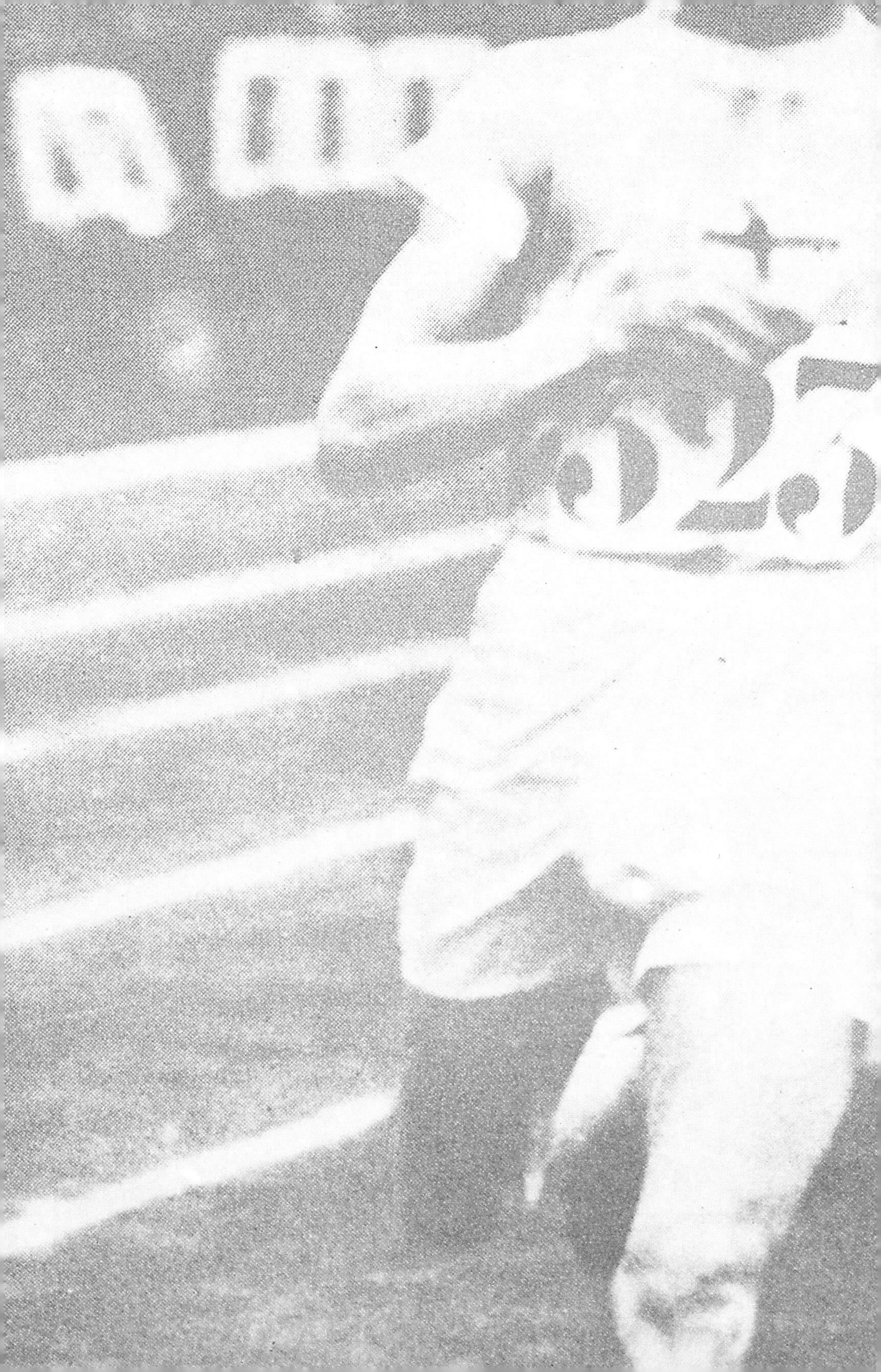

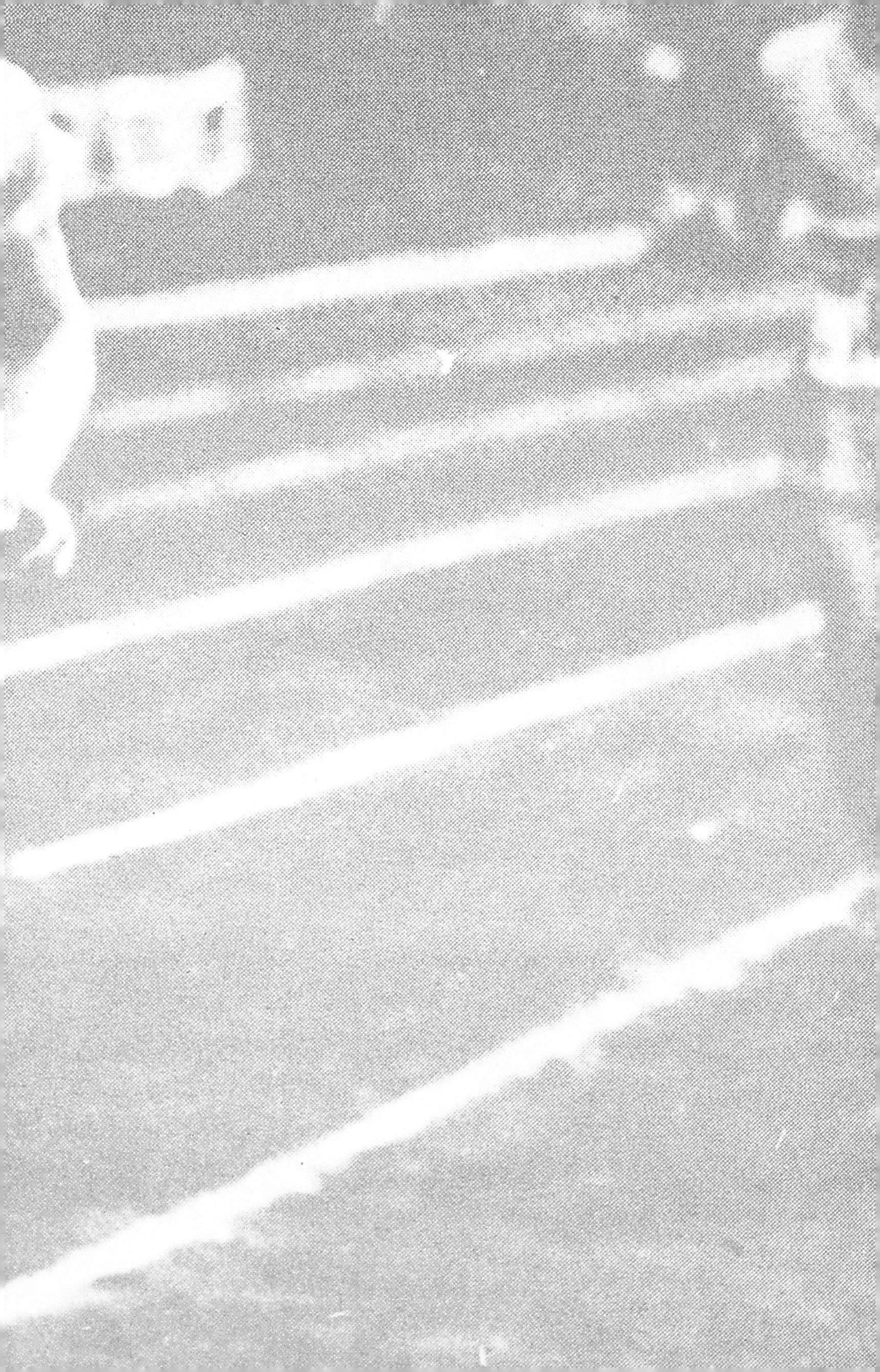

Paris, Library of France, 1989

Transprogramming

Transprogramming: Combining two programs, regardless of their incompatibilities, together with their respective spatial configurations. Reference: planetarium + roller-coaster.

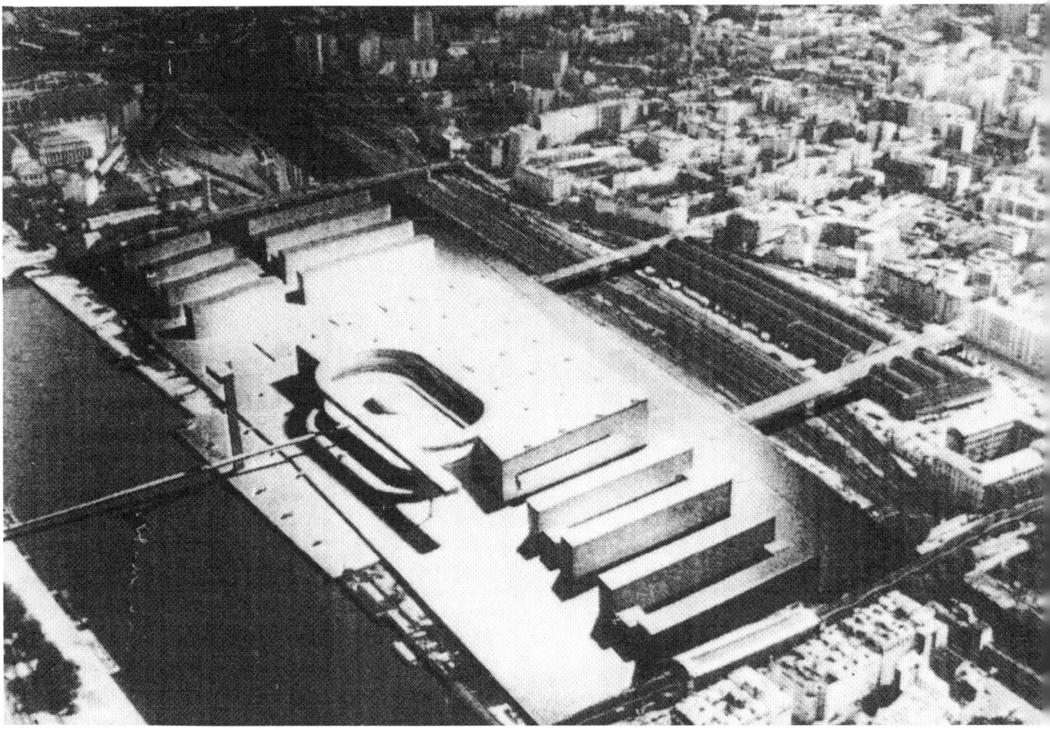

The competition for the National Library of France asked for a new type of library, capable of reconciling the contradictory demands of the traditional institution of the past and the computerized library of the future, the book and the electronic image, timeless scholarship and the contemporary crowd. Its site by the River Seine displays a similar duality, both 2,500 meters from Notre-Dame and within the peripheral industrial land east of Paris.

Such dualities, far from restrictive, suggest unusual possibilities in which disciplines merge and cross-fertilize. Shifting architectural types signal the emergence of a new form of architecture and urbanism.

Concepts:
1. Multiple circuits: a new library combining the pursuit of modernity and the pursuit of knowledge, the athlete and the scholar; multimedia "circuits" for the public, book circuits, visible architectural circuits and invisible circuits for cutting-edge information technology.

2. Transprogramming: combining several types of programs, regardless of incompatibilities, together with their respective spatial configurations (the forum and the reading room, 400-meter races and scholarly pursuits).

Circuits
That the library is not located in the historic center of Paris is an important and positive factor. Its very eccentricity allows it to break away from any static concept of libraries. The library cannot be a frozen monument but must instead turn into an event, a movement. Hence the concept of the open circuit, in which the endless pursuit of knowledge is matched by the pleasure of physical effort. Intersecting a jogging track with the library is more than a dynamic convenience; it embodies the library's complex role as generator of a new urban strategy (the open circuit).

Within the new library are five interrelated sets of circuits.

The Visitors' Circuit
The visitors' circuit, consisting, on the ground floor (lower circuit), of a spectacular, ring-like great hall, offers reception and information facilities, multimedia exhibitions, shops, a conference center and a children's library as well as direct access to the recent acquisitions library. The upper circuit on the top floor features video displays, temporary and permanent exhibitions and a small café and lounge area in an unprecedented setting. Above the upper circuit is the running track for energetic scholars and intelligent athletes.

The Administrators' Circuit
Arriving from the Nouvelle Avenue, administrators and employees enjoy the southern section of the new library. Above the technical services are various administrative offices.

The Book Circuits
Storerooms are sandwiched between the administration and the reading rooms. They are designed to permit all three kinds of storage (traditional, compact, automated) with minimal alterations.

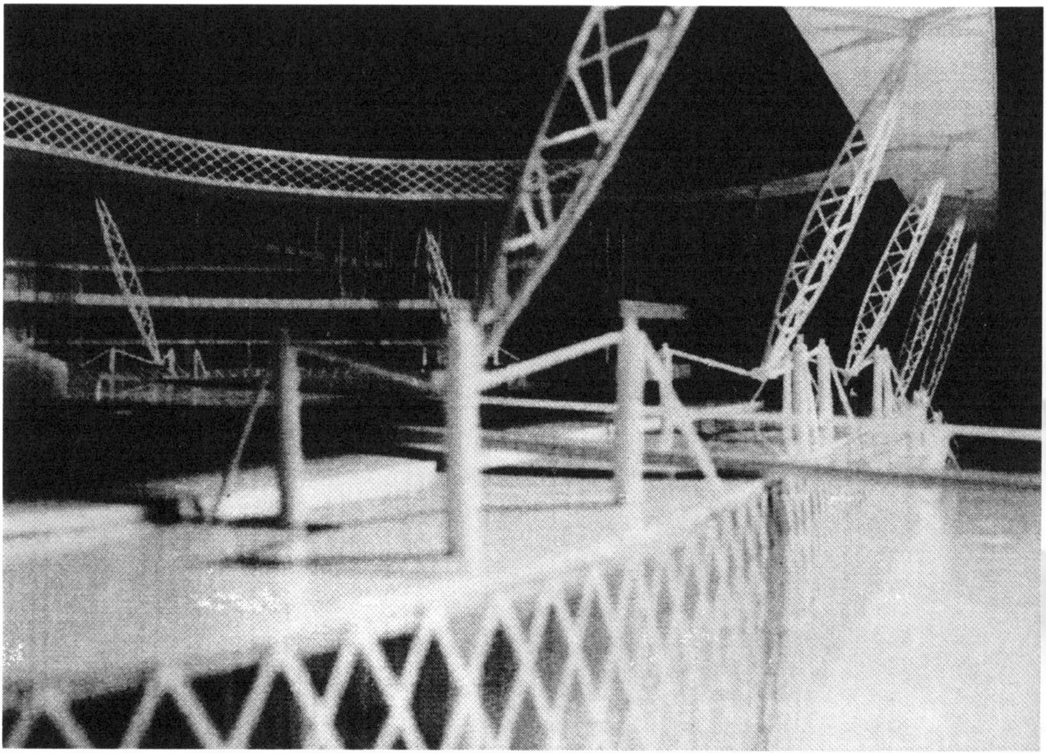

The Electronic Circuits
A fundamental part of the new library, the electronic circuits govern most of the new cataloguing and information retrieval. The role of the library as part of a general network reinforces this priority.

The Mechanical Circuits
The spatial configuration by zones allows for separate handling of the stacks, independent of the administration, the reading rooms and the great hall. Fluids are distributed horizontally in the basement and then vertically on a diagonal point grid for maximum efficiency.

Dynamic Spaces
Library programs have offered architecture some of its most significant works, including those of Boullée, Labrouste, Carrère and Hastings, Asplund and others. Although the new library should be compared to such illustrious precedents, we must avoid nostalgia for outdated spatial forms. Hence, we displaced the great central reading room of the past toward the exterior: eccentricity of the central space, exteriority of space that once was interiorized. Simultaneously the great hall inside and the esplanade outside, this space is the project's revolving circuit.

Eschewing the static spaces of the historical past, we searched for dynamic circuits for the future. Our concept of the library revolves around movement—of people, of ideas. Visitors circulate around circuits giving access to a variety of events and information.

Structure
The ring structure is a stiff torsional box supported at forty-meter intervals against vertical loads. The box, which forms an oval ring, is restrained horizontally in at least four places by the main building. The box, 10 by 3.6 meters deep in cross section (9.5 by 3.2 meters center line to center line), has diaphragms, at least four in the curved section and an additional one in the straight part, which stabilize the torsional shape and guarantee that the cross section does not deform under the asymmetrical torsional load. The box has concrete top and bottom surfaces that act as the floor and the rooftop jogging track and also provide horizontal beams that ensure that the shape does not distort in the horizontal plane. The vertical facades are treated structurally as a series of overlapping V trusses, four meters deep and spanning an average sixty meters, that also provide the vertical sides of the torsion box. The combined effect of the torsional strength and the horizontal bending resistance means that the box can carry eccentric horizontal and vertical loads. It can transfer the horizontal component back to the main building and span between the eccentrically placed inclined columns. The horizontal load generated by the inclination of the columns will be transferred as tension and shear to the main building.

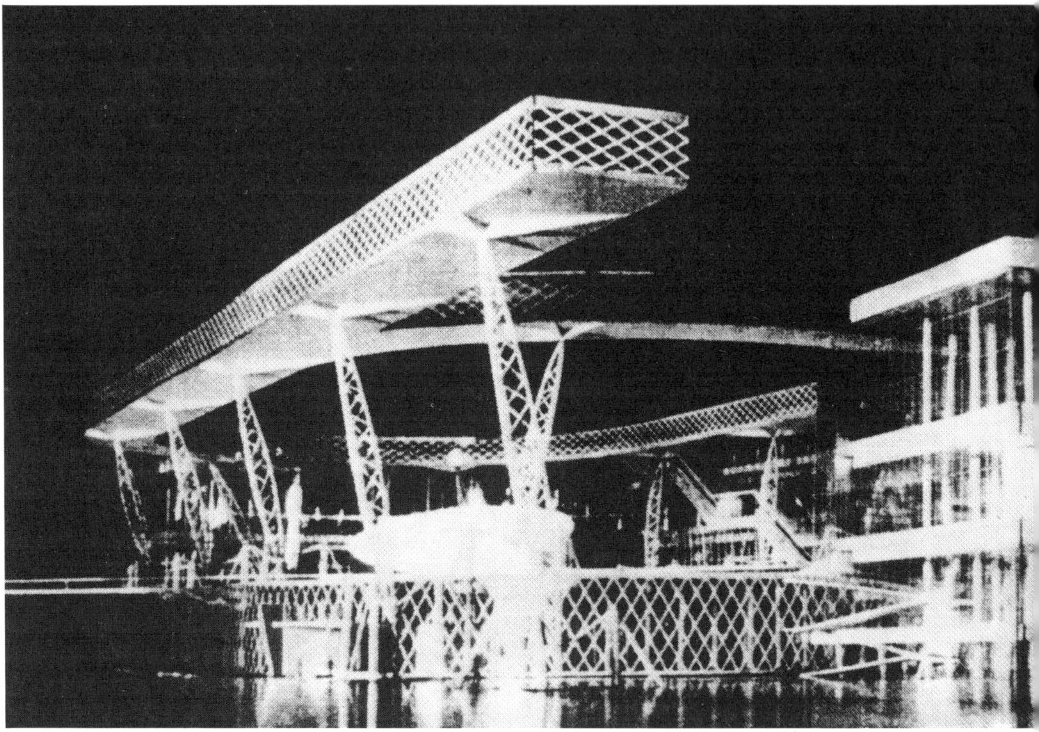

PARIS
333

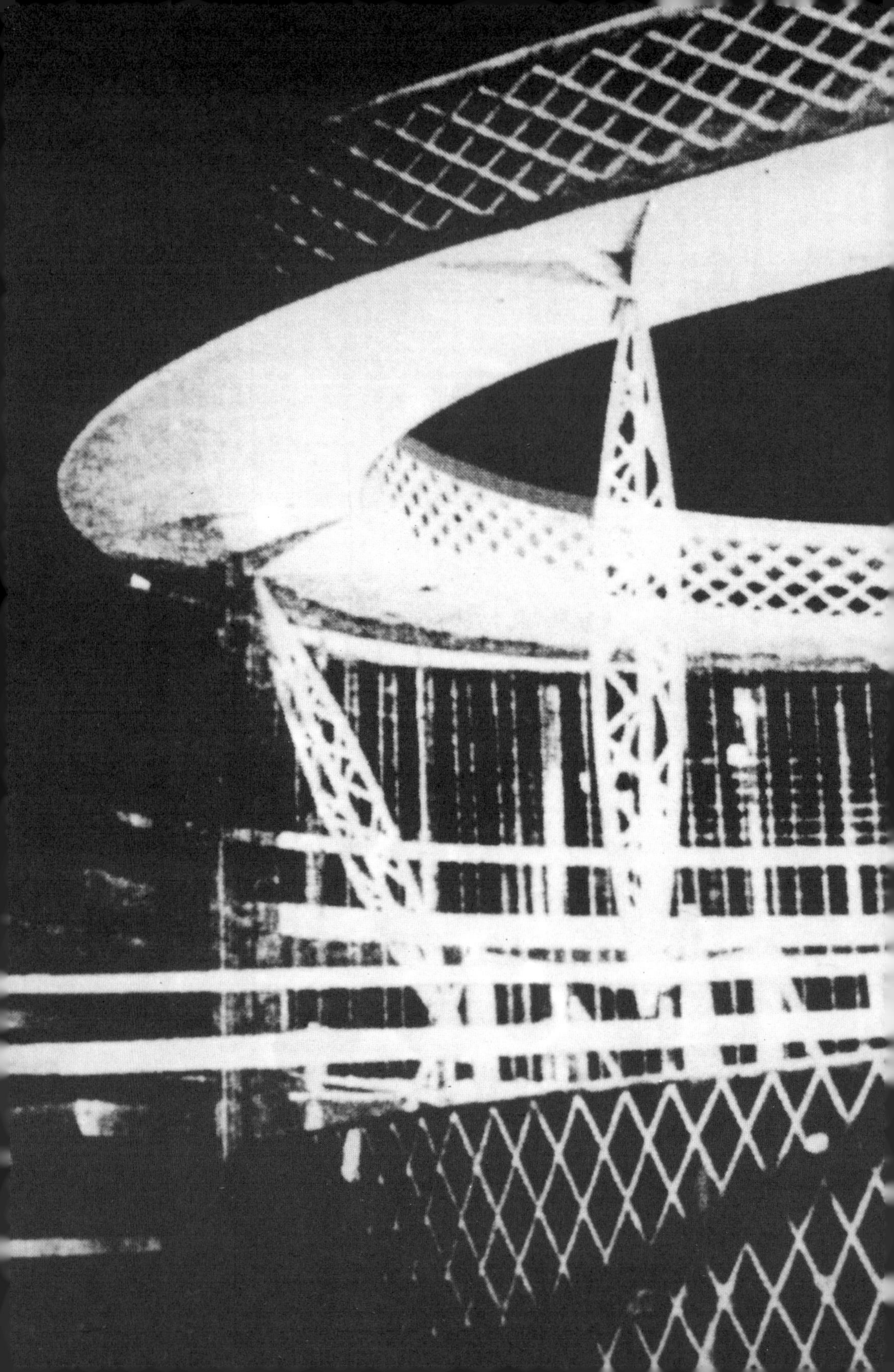

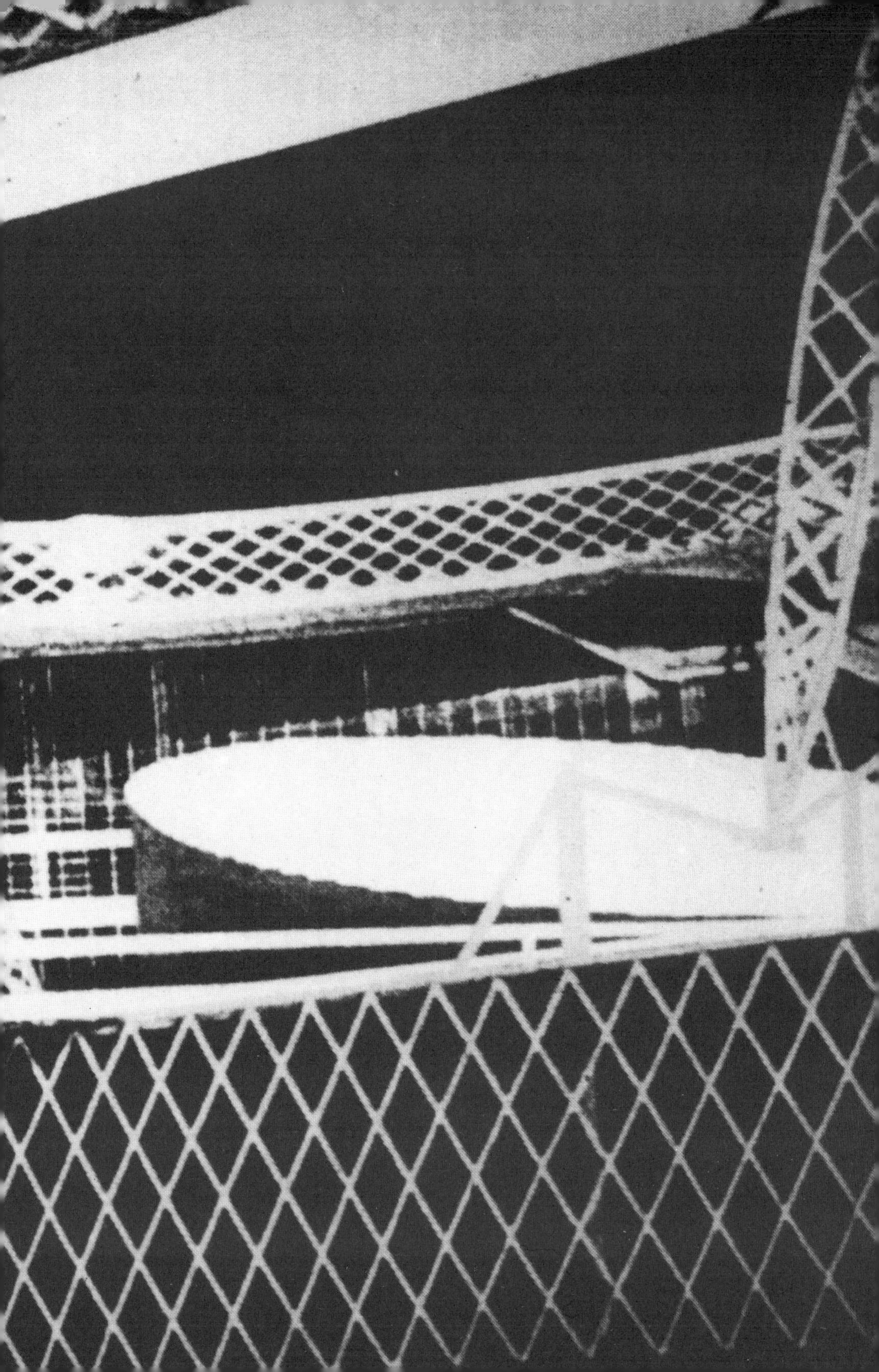

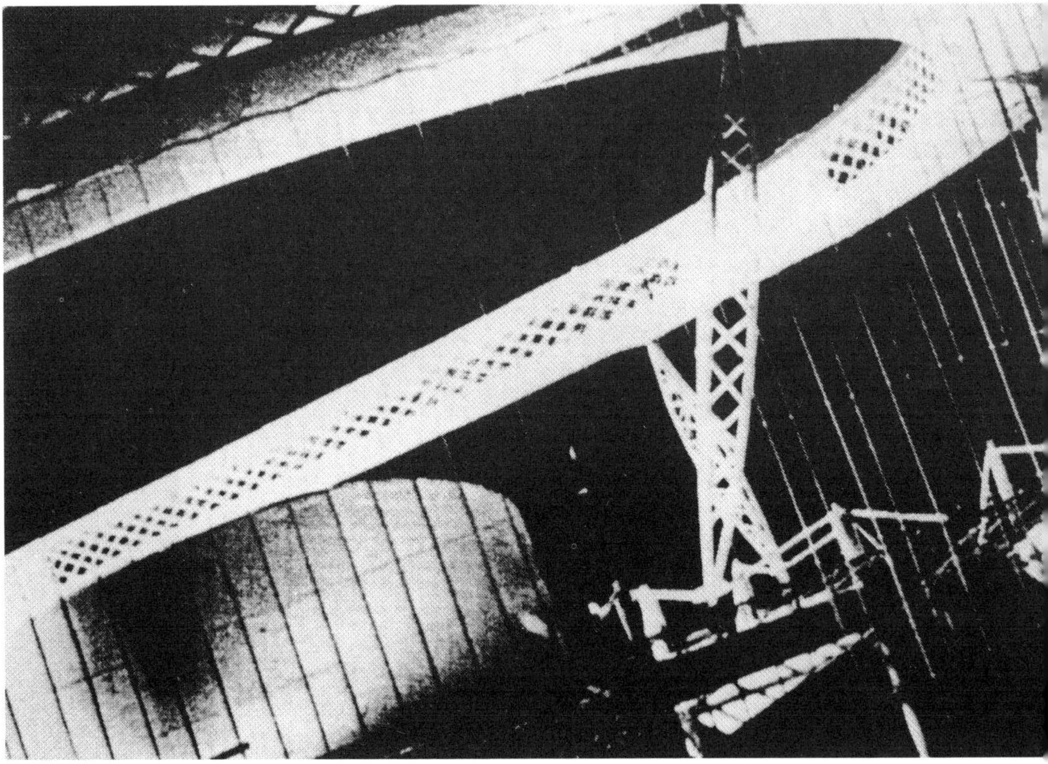

PARIS
337

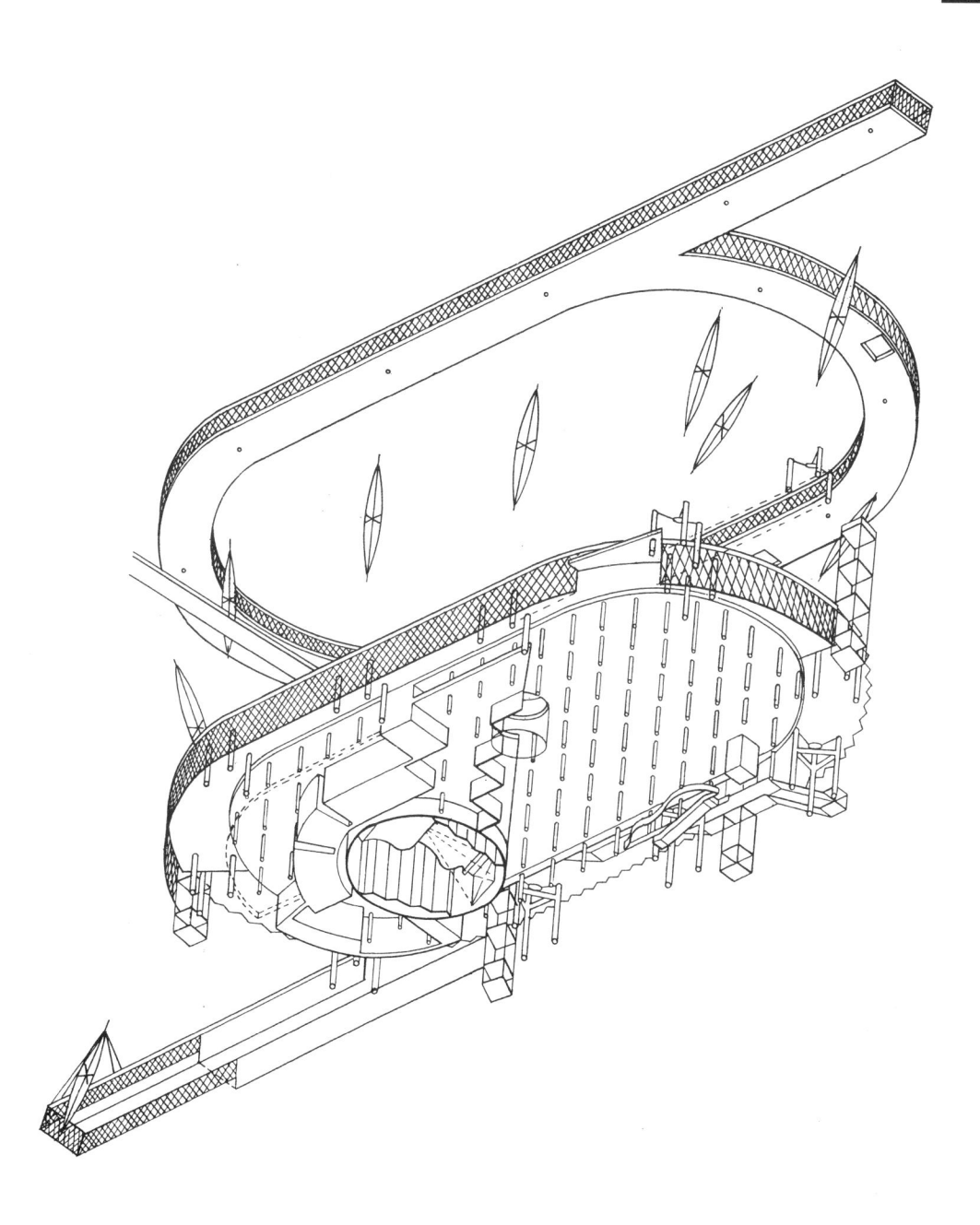

Public circuits

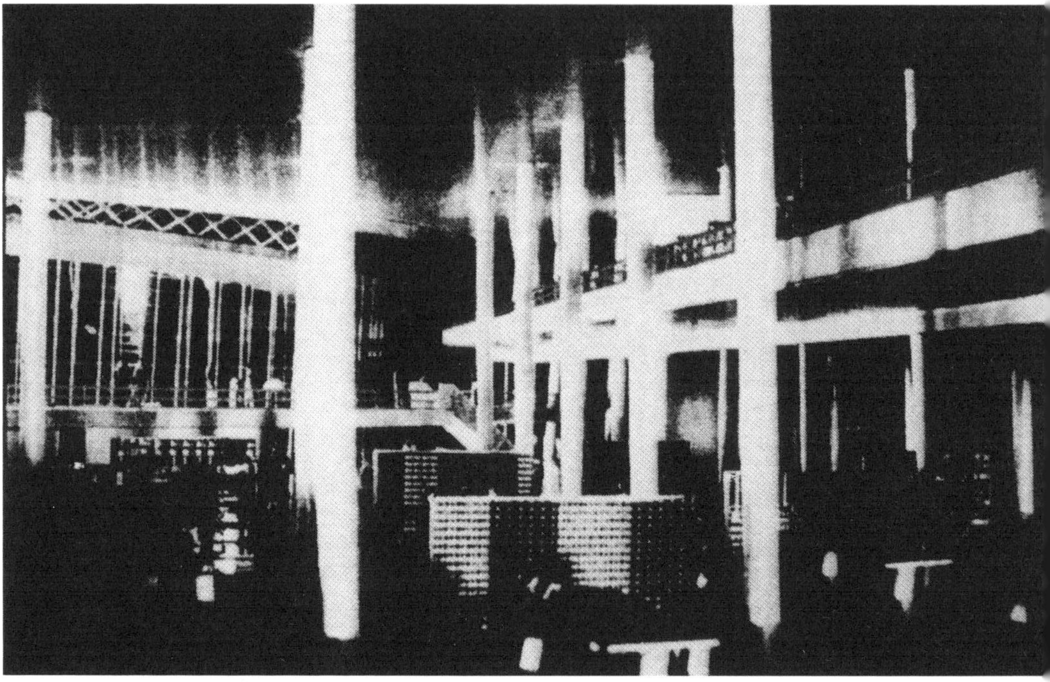

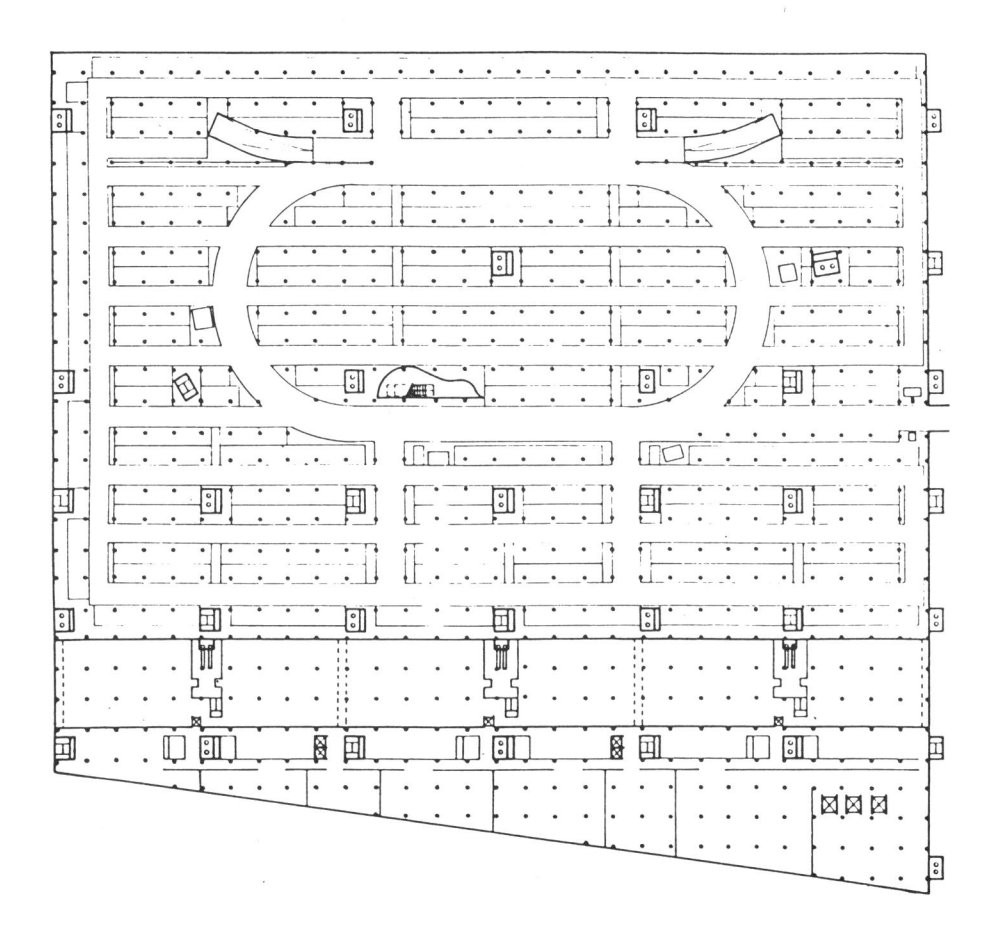

Level -3.00: parking, mechanical spaces, bookstacks

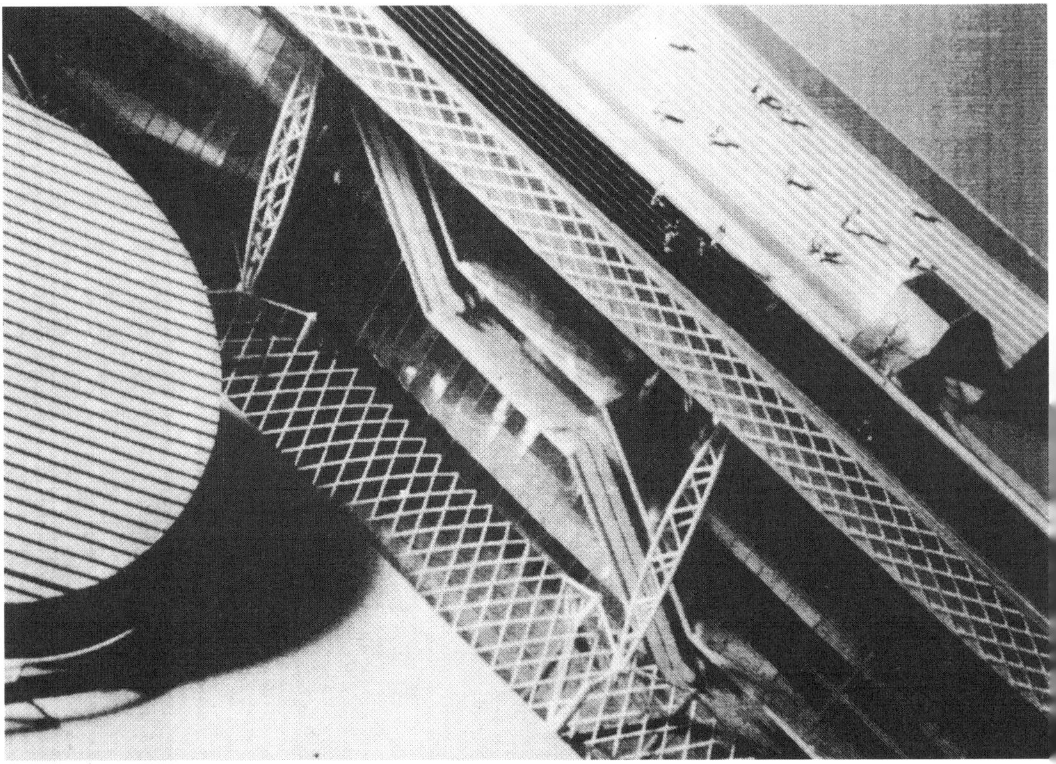

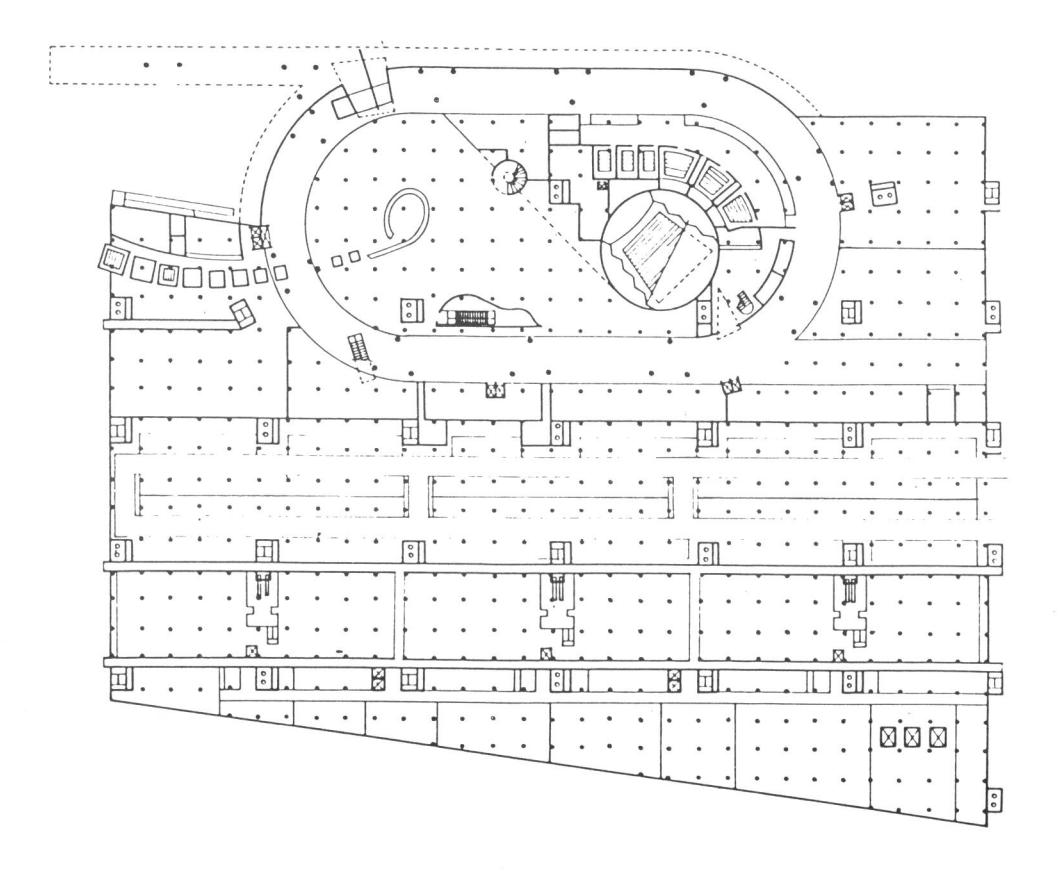

Level +0.00: visitor entrance, information, exhibitions, lobbies, conference center, cinema, children's library, newspaper reading room, sound and video library, parking, bookstacks, maintenance area

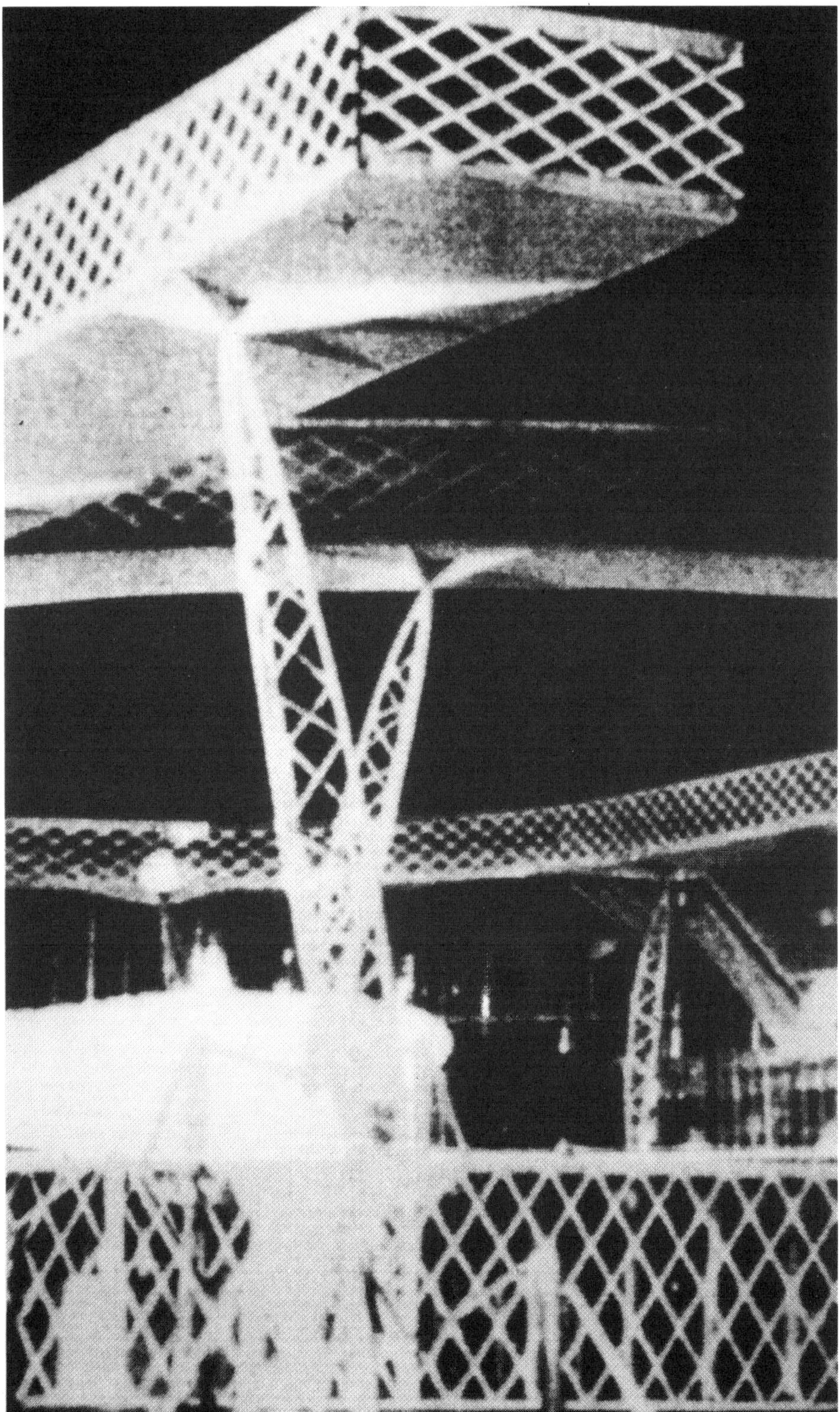

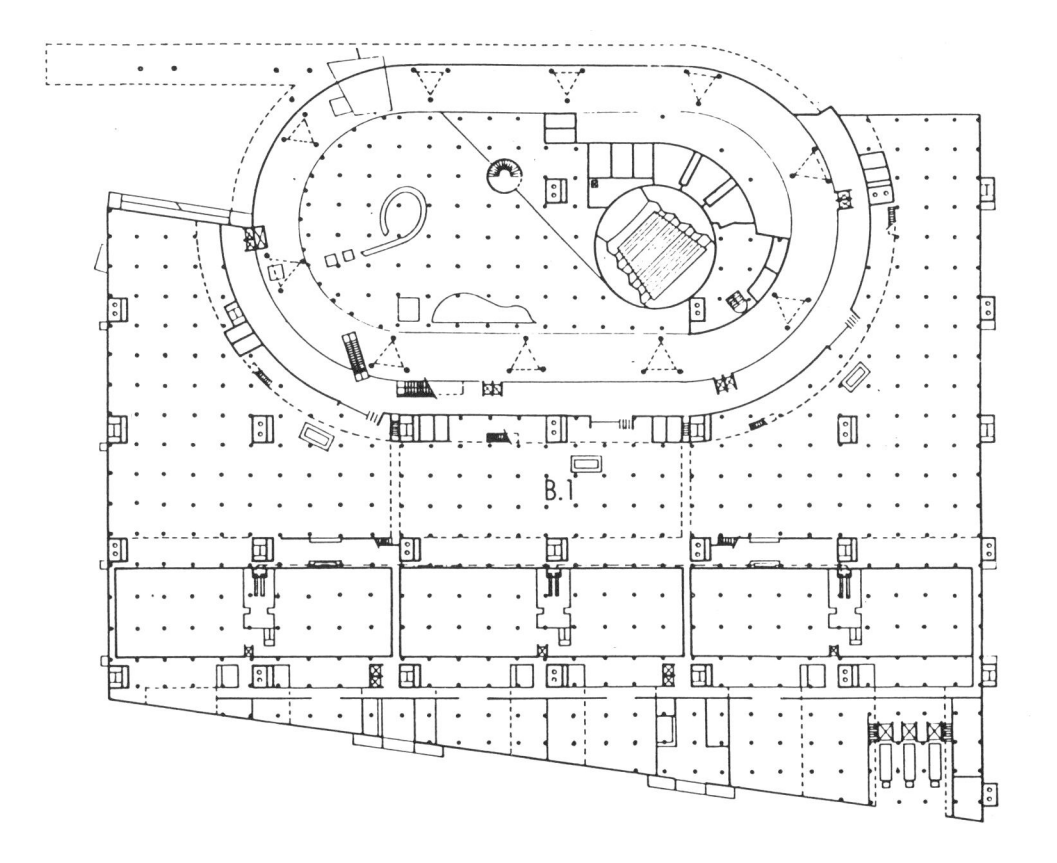

Level +3.60: main public library, bookstacks, administrative offices

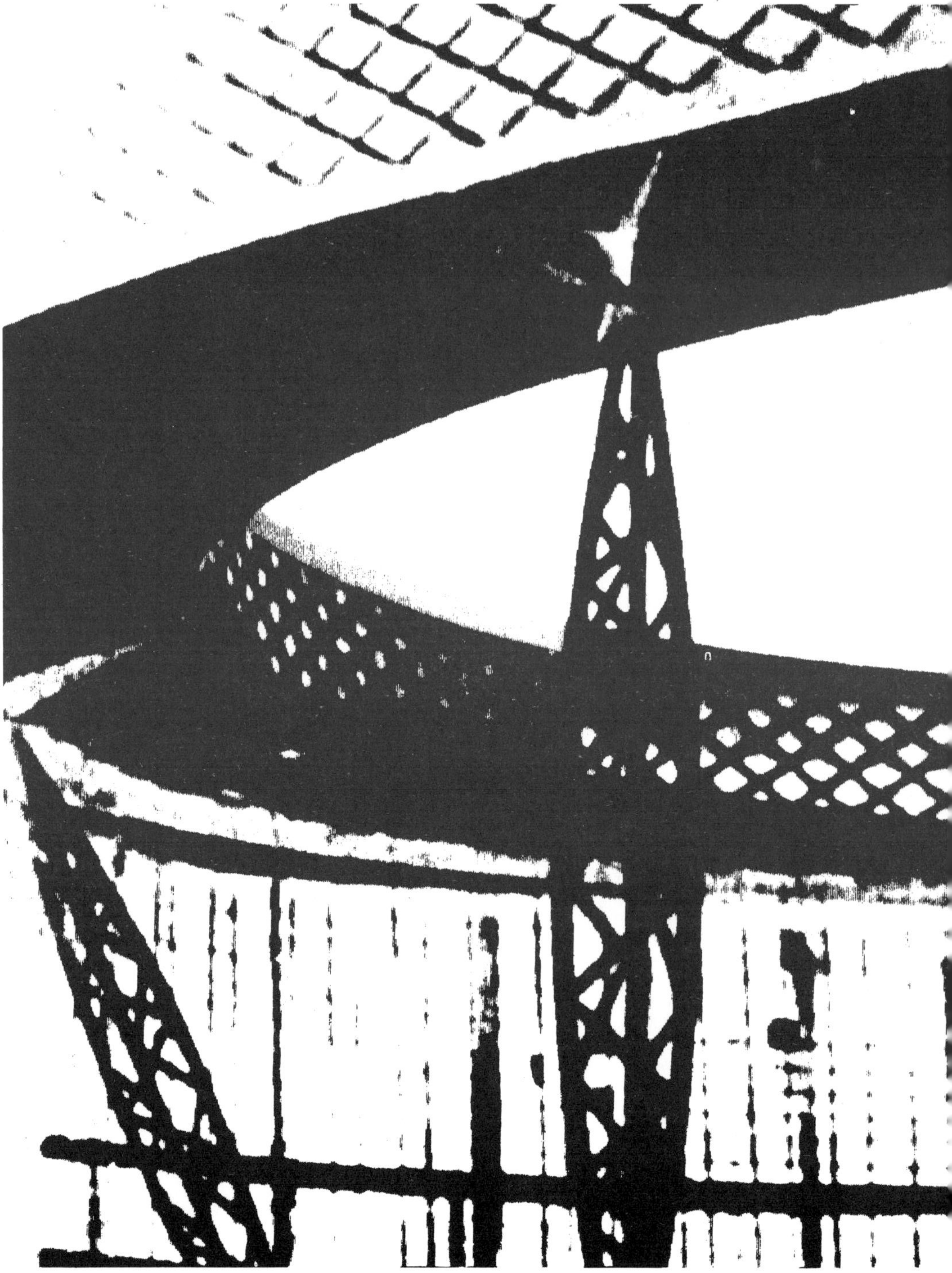

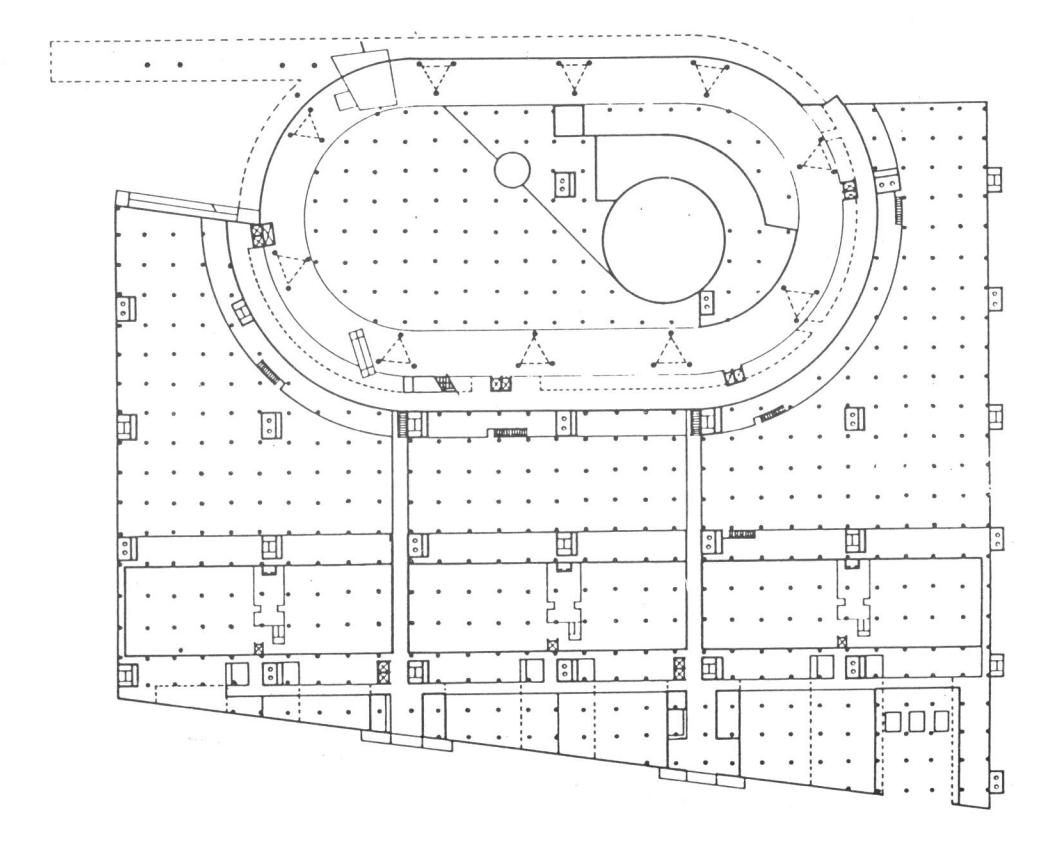

Level +6.50: main public library, mezzanine, bookstacks, administrative offices

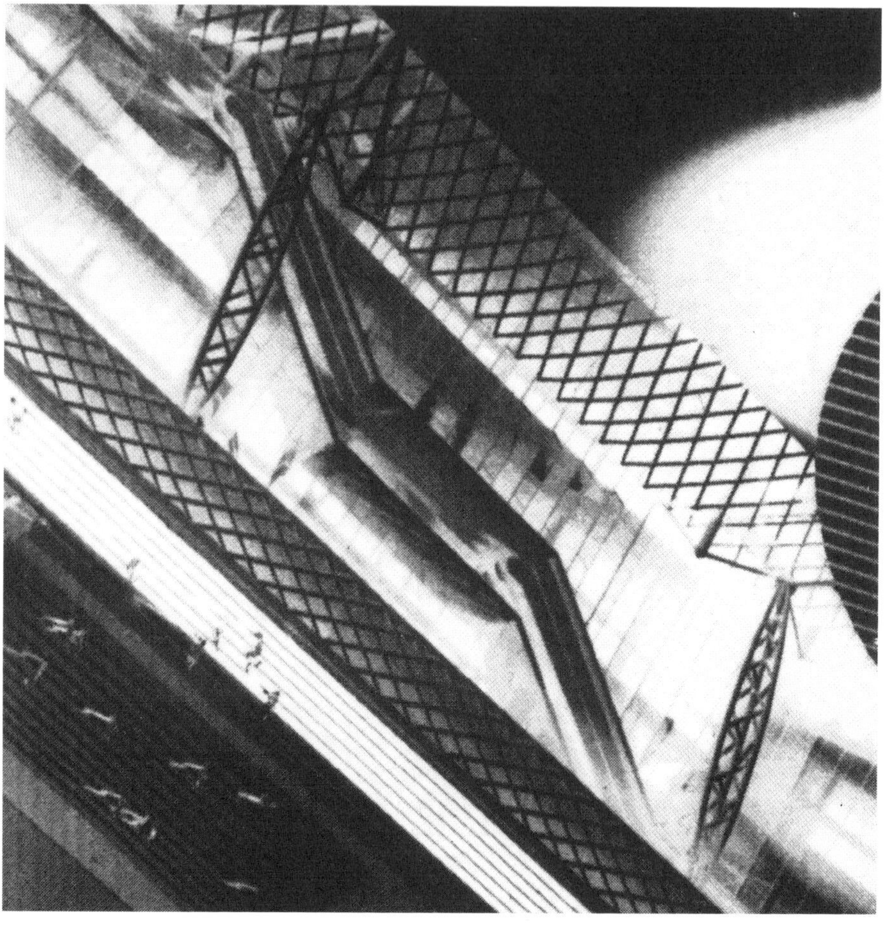

PARIS
347

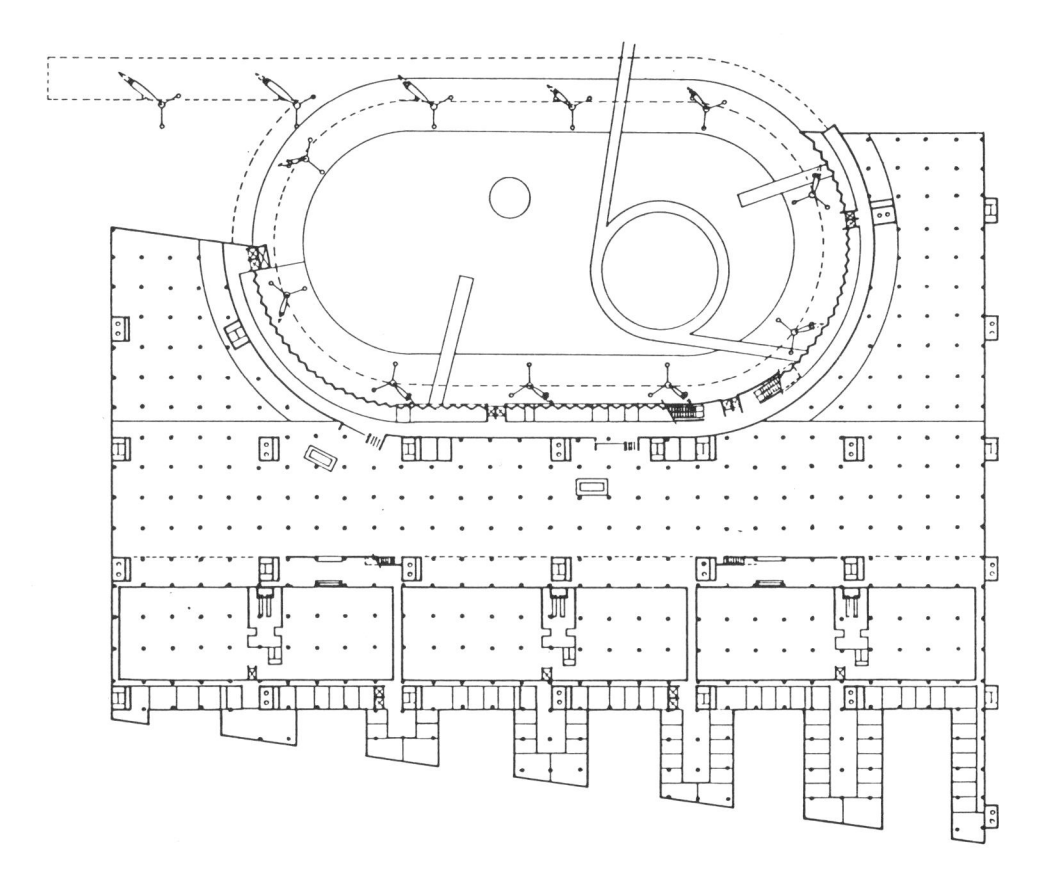

Level +25.20: indoor running track, exercise rooms, scholar and research libraries, bookstacks, administrative offices

An architectural sequence that is strategically disjunctive: the running track in the library

PARIS
349

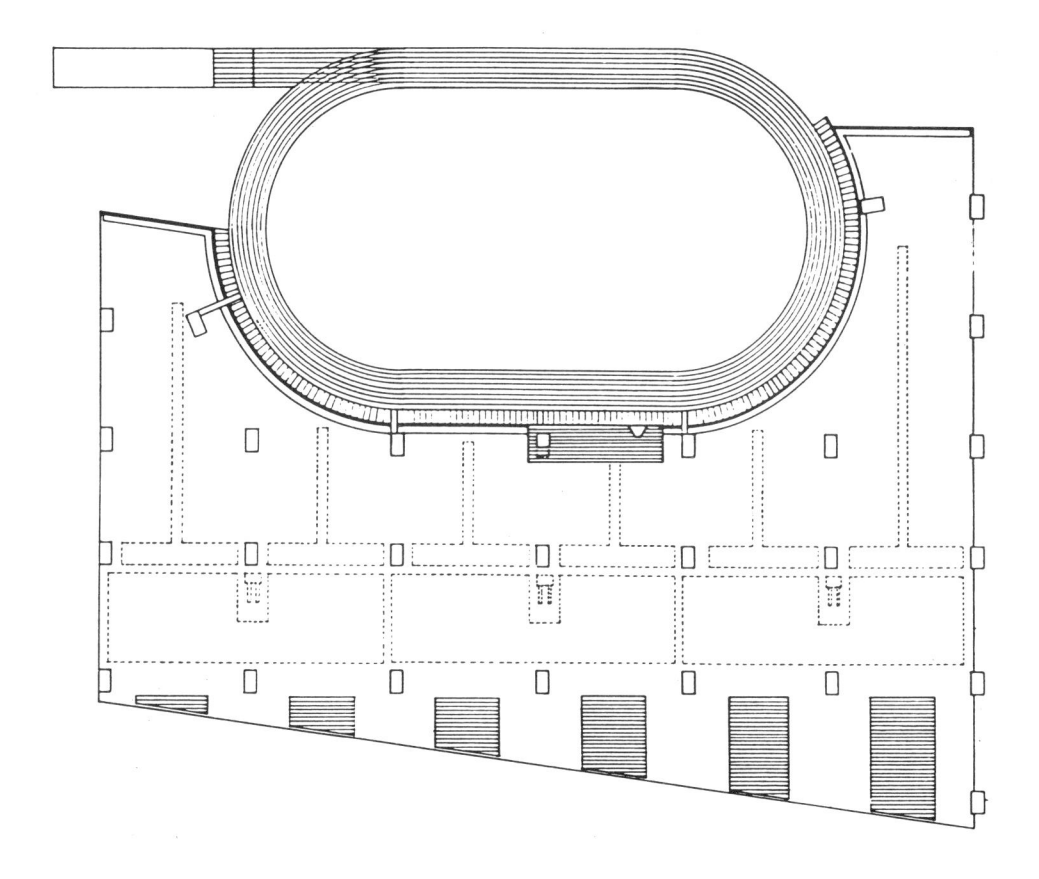

Level +32.40: roof; outdoor running track, sports facilities and playgrounds

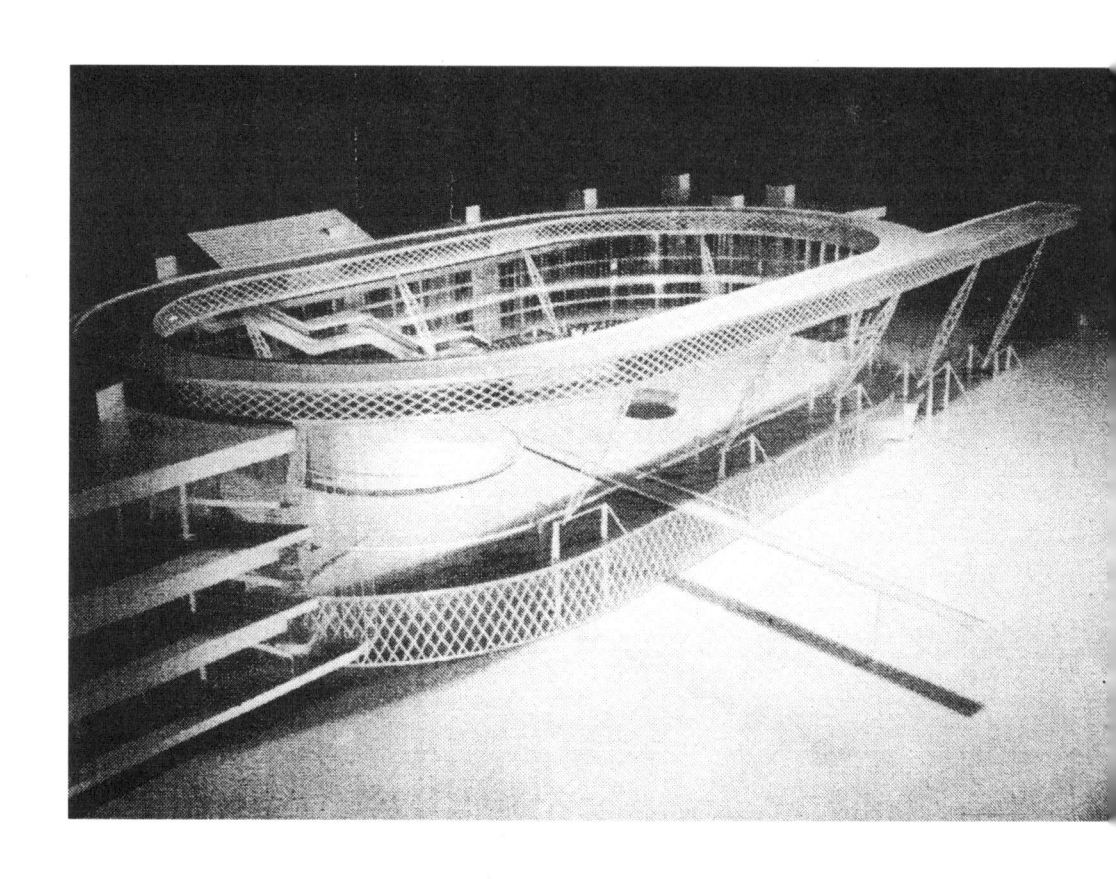

Programs fall into three categories: those that are indifferent to the spatial sequence;
those that reinforce it; those that work against it

PARIS
351

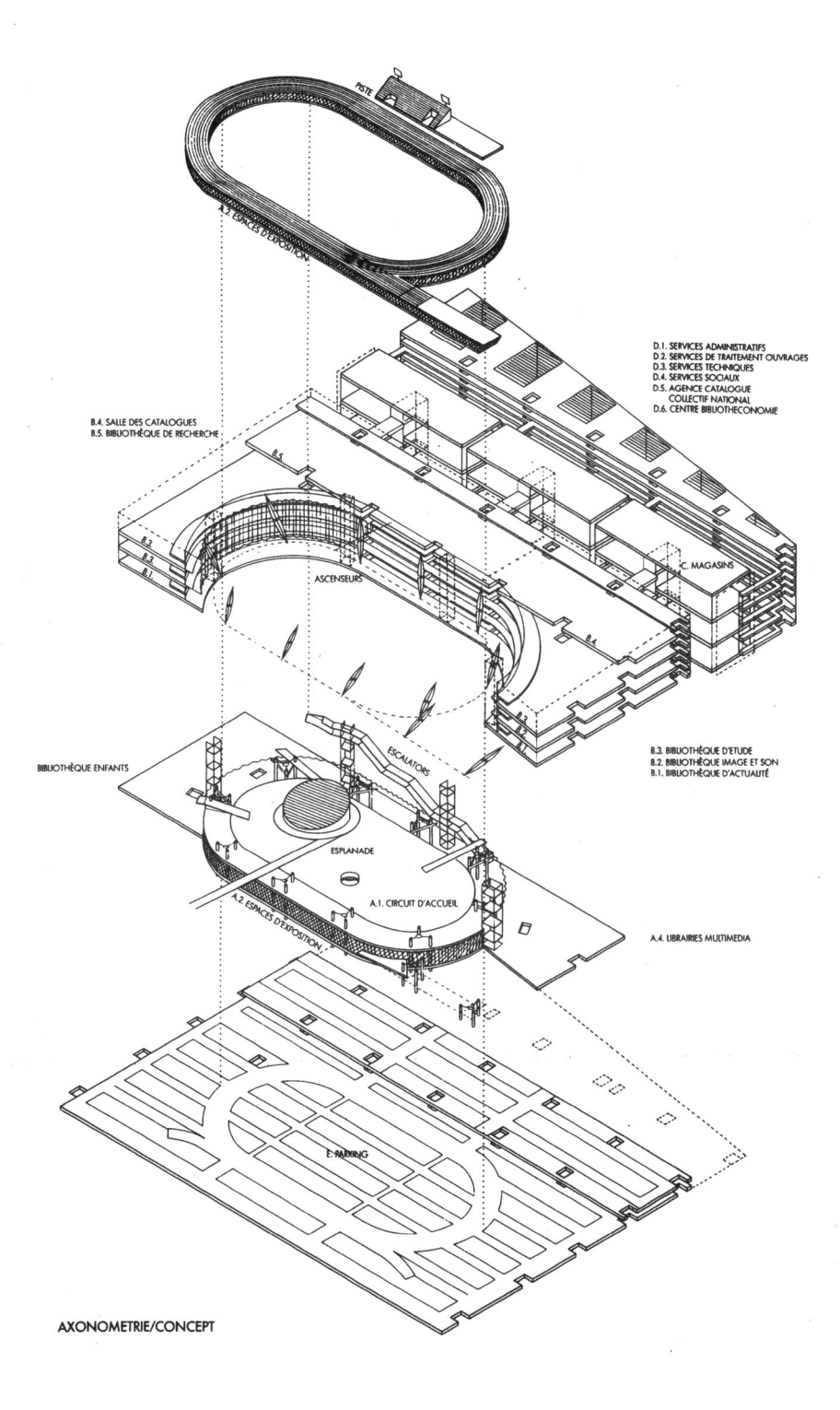

PISTE

A.2 ESPACES D'EXPOSITION

D.1. SERVICES ADMINISTRATIFS
D.2. SERVICES DE TRAITEMENT OUVRAGES
D.3. SERVICES TECHNIQUES
D.4. SERVICES SOCIAUX
D.5. AGENCE CATALOGUE COLLECTIF NATIONAL
D.6. CENTRE BIBLIOTHECONOMIE

B.4. SALLE DES CATALOGUES
B.5. BIBLIOTHÈQUE DE RECHERCHE

C. MAGASINS

ASCENSEURS

BIBLIOTHÈQUE ENFANTS

ESCALATORS

B.3. BIBLIOTHÈQUE D'ETUDE
B.2. BIBLIOTHÈQUE IMAGE ET SON
B.1. BIBLIOTHÈQUE D'ACTUALITÉ

ESPLANADE

A.2. ESPACES D'EXPOSITION   A.1. CIRCUIT D'ACCUEIL

A.4. LIBRAIRIES MULTIMEDIA

E. PARKING

AXONOMETRIE/CONCEPT

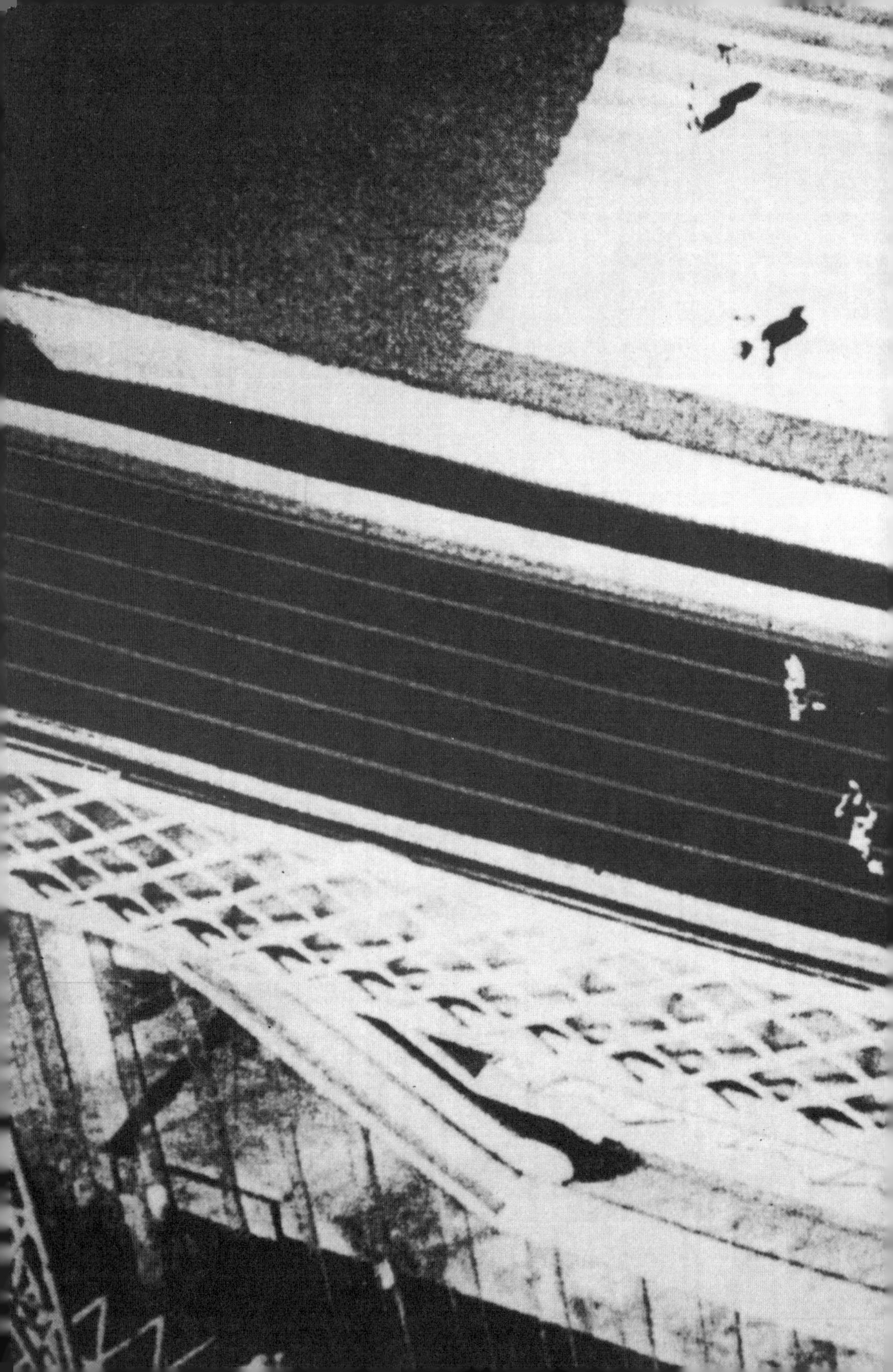

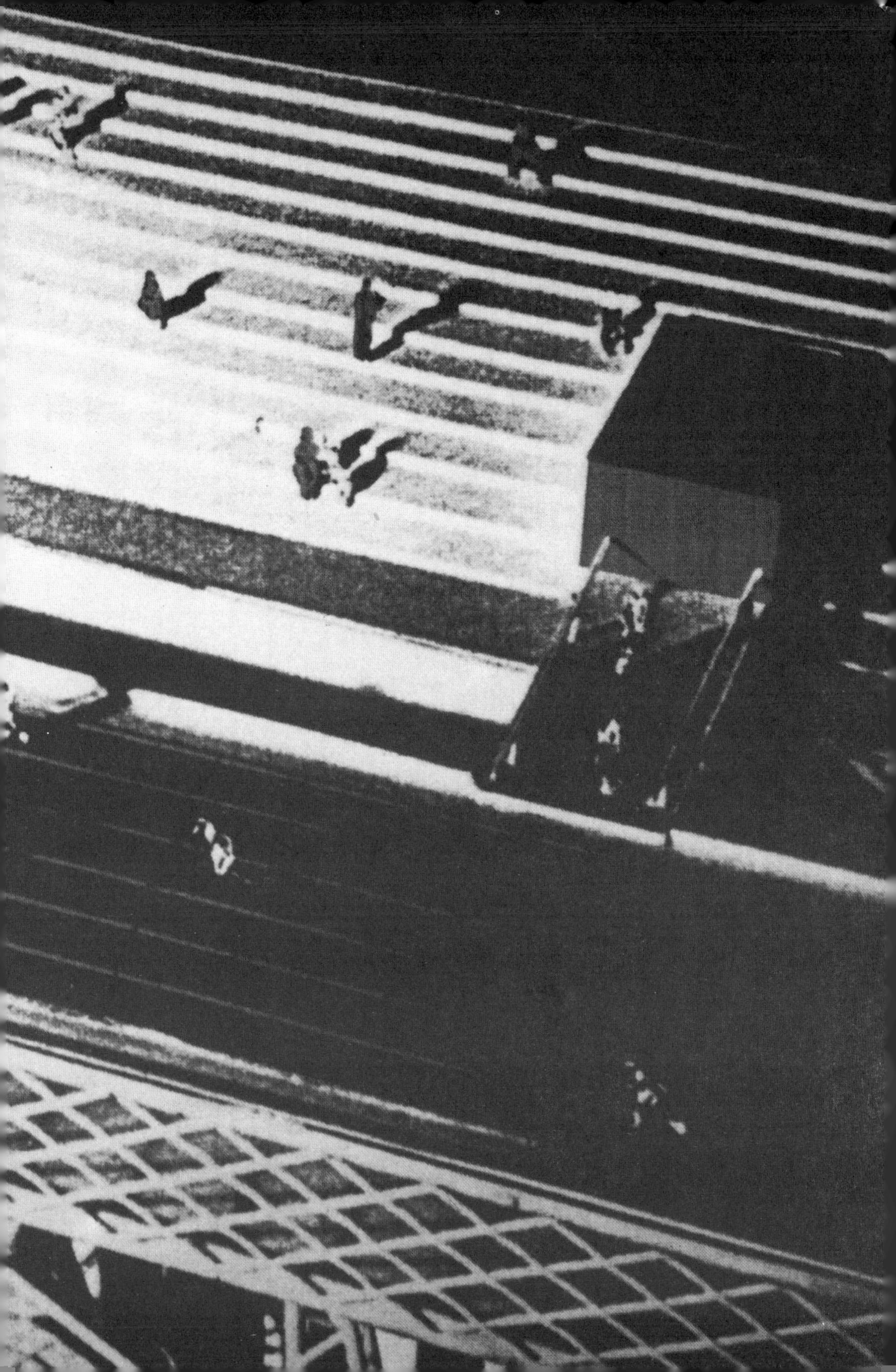

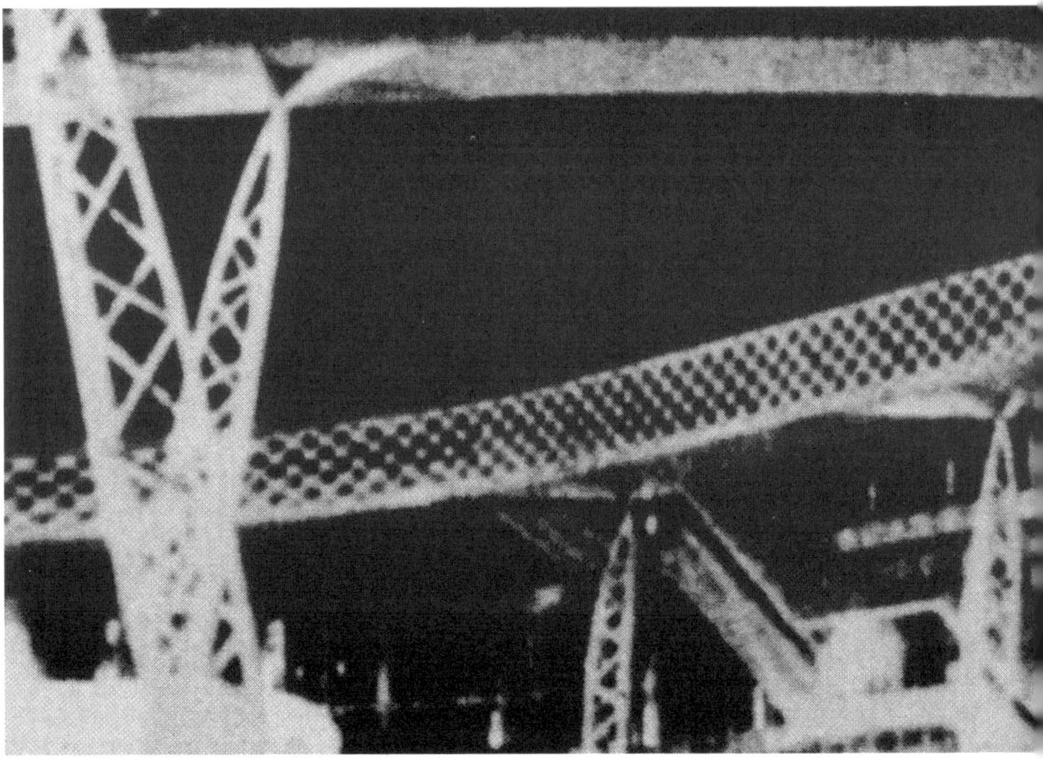

PARIS
355

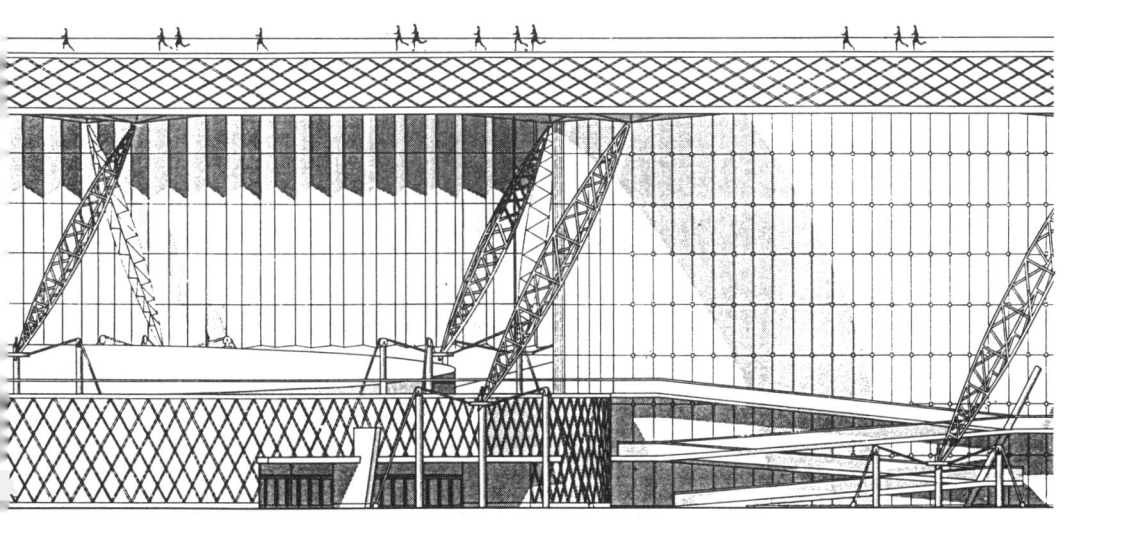

Elevation facing the Seine with the running track: the movement of the body coincides with the materiality of the space

Skylons

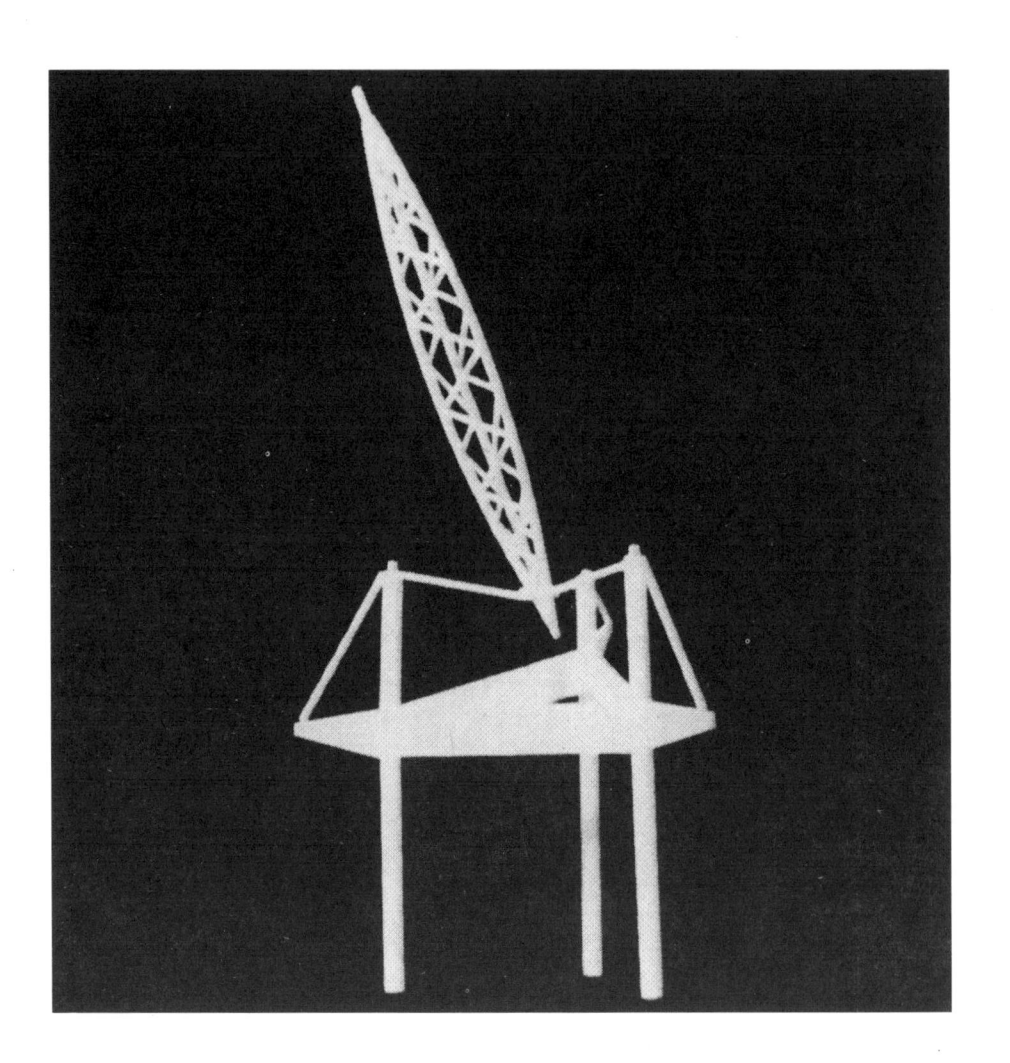

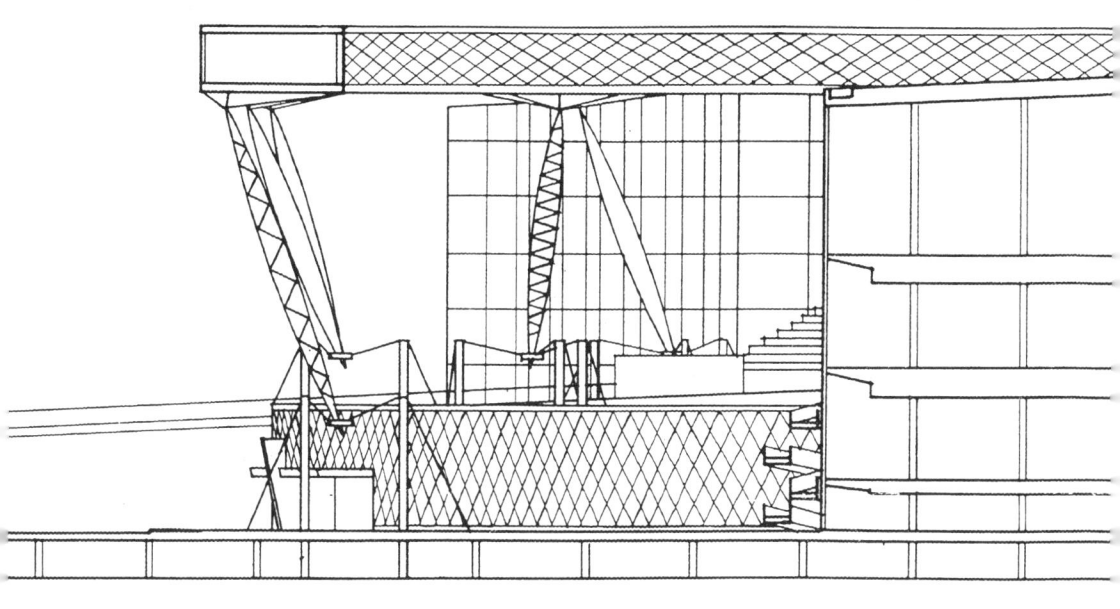

Section detail: ring structure and eccentrically placed columns

Running track and scholars' esplanade

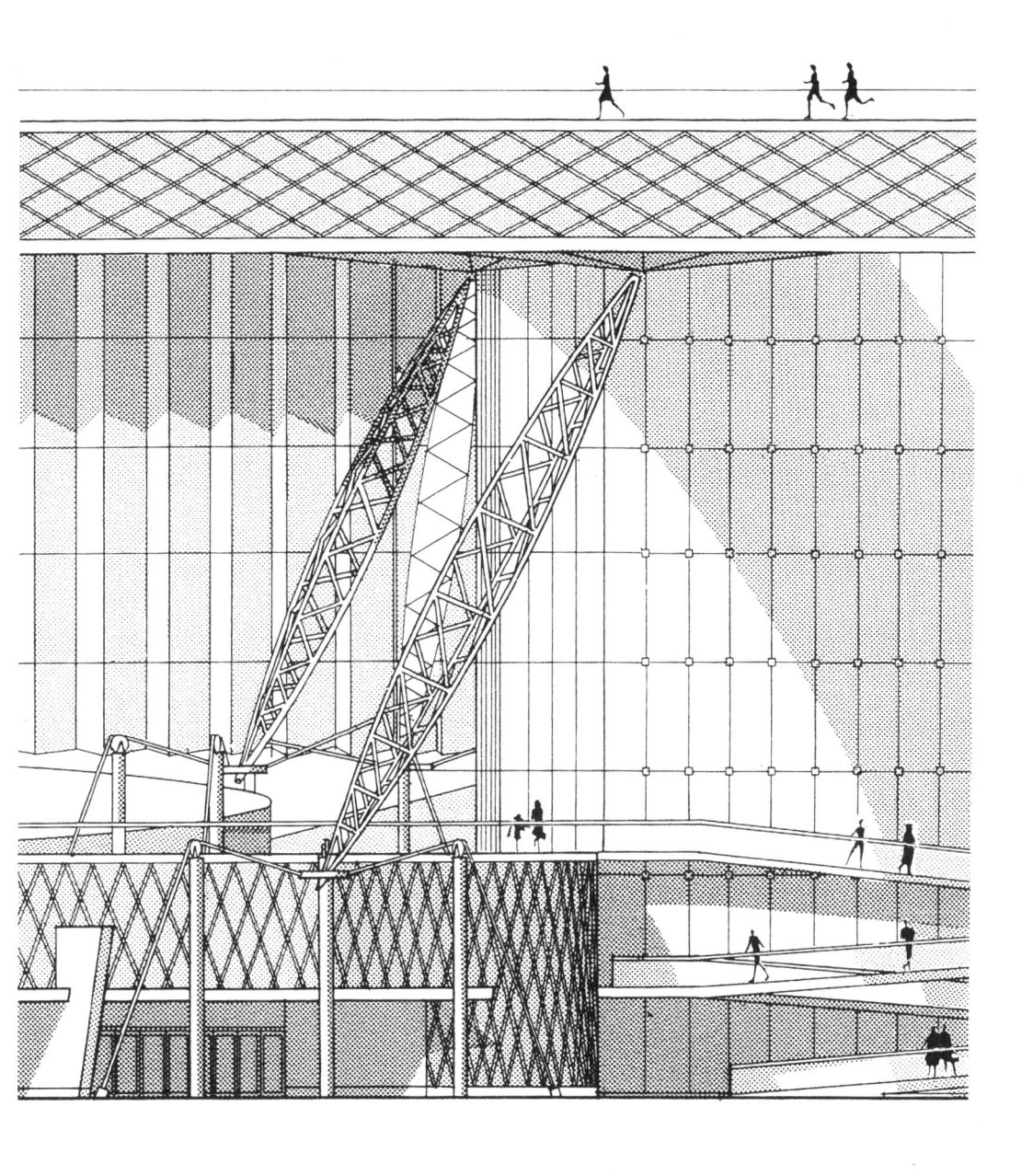

Circuits: the athlete of the 21st century and the perpetual pursuit of knowledge

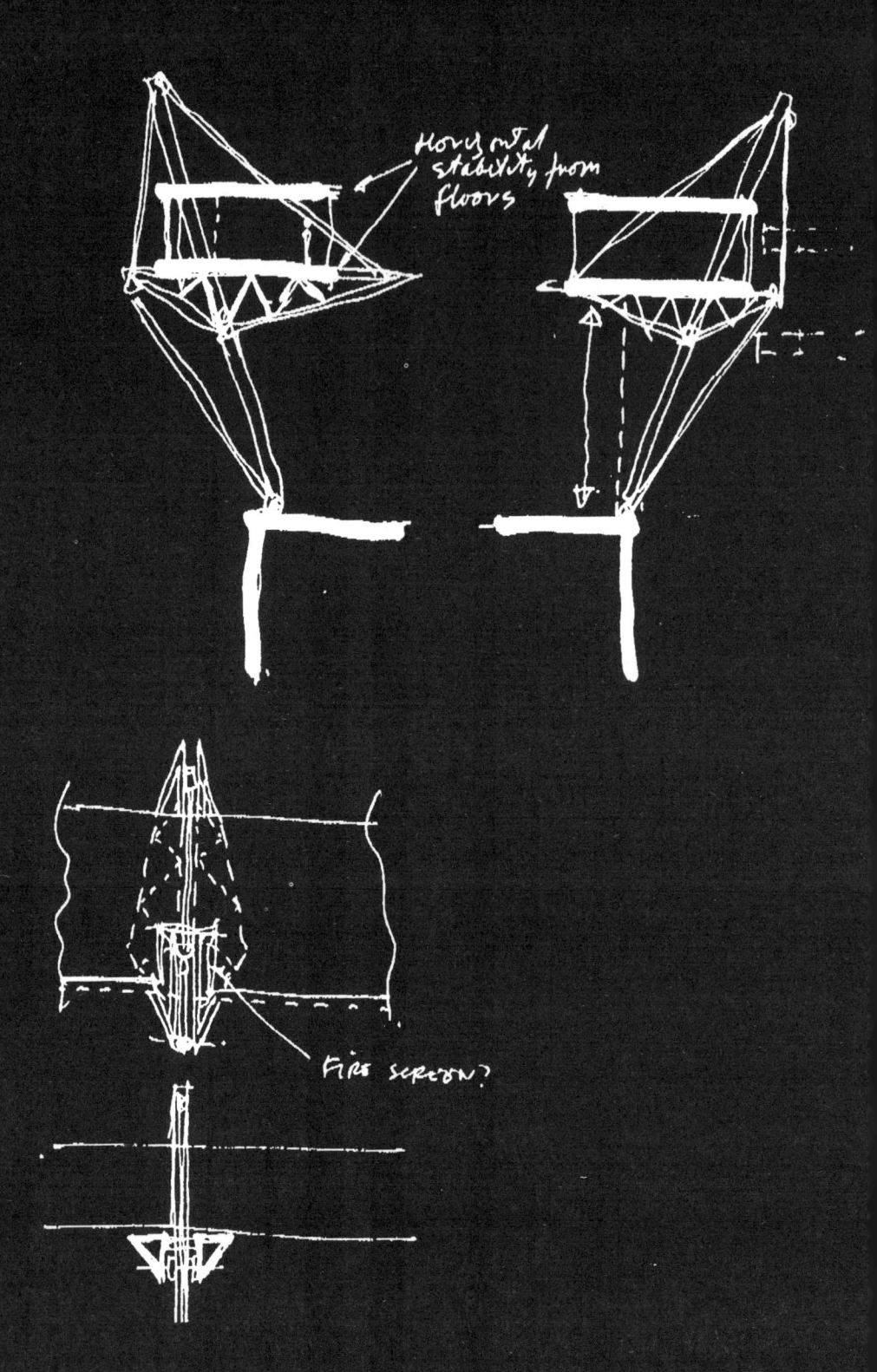

Horizontal stability from floors

Fire screen?

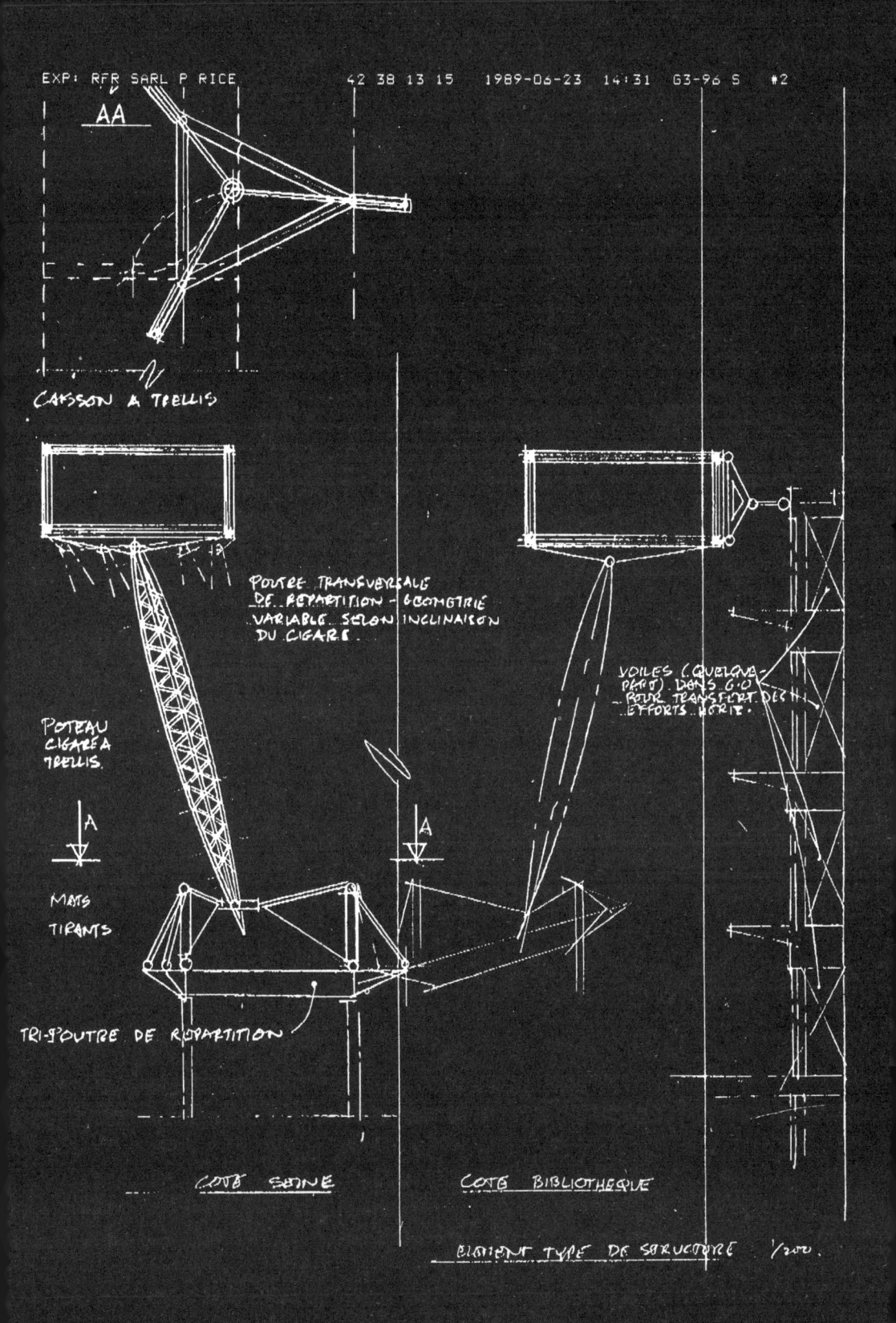

EXP: RFR SARL P RICE   42 38 13 15   1989-06-23 14:31   G3-96 S   #2

AA

CAISSON À TRELLIS

POUTRE TRANSVERSALE
DE REPARTITION - GEOMETRIE
VARIABLE SELON INCLINAISON
DU CIGARE.

POTEAU
CIGARE À
TRELLIS.

VOILES (QUELQUE-
PART) DANS G.O.
POUR TRANSFERT DES
EFFORTS HORIZ.

↓A

MATS
TIRANTS

TRI-POUTRE DE REPARTITION

COTÉ SEINE   COTÉ BIBLIOTHEQUE

ELEMENT TYPE DE STRUCTURE   1/200

Karlsruhe, Center for Art and Media (ZKM), 1989

Unstable Images

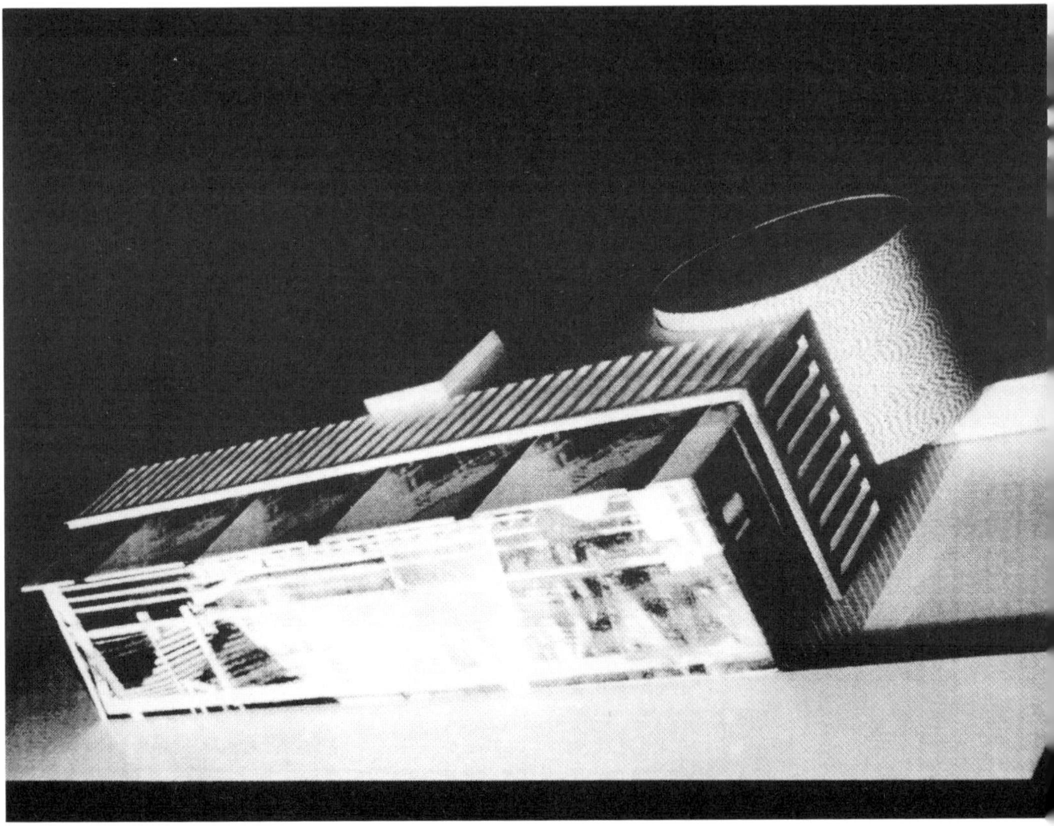

At the end of the twentieth century, architecture and urbanism are undergoing profound changes closely intertwined with the broader questions of society, art and technology. Karlsruhe, Germany and its proposed Center for Art and Media Technology (ZKM) are characteristic of that process, which solicits the following four questions:

1. How can the boundaries of a historically centralized, preindustrial city survive the inescapable transformation into a decentralized, postindustrial twenty-first-century territory? How can limits be turned into a line of exchange?

2. How can institutions dedicated to specialized research and to the development of ideas provide information and excitement to a larger public, the public mediatization of specialized research?

3. How can one construct a building at a time when the technology of construction has become less relevant than the construction of technology?

4. How can architecture, whose historical role was to generate the appearance of stable images (monuments, order, etc.) deal with today's culture of the disappearance of unstable images (twenty-four-image-per-second cinema, video and computer-generated images)?

Our proposal for the ZKM reflects these questions in four components:

1. The urban line of exchange: we suggest a new linear public passage of intense interchange and communication as an alternative to the concentric baroque Karlsruhe. This line provides a new urban system at the historical edge of the city, luring the old limit into a new line of exchange.

Note: the underground passage through the railway station is animated by banks of closed-circuit television monitors, controlled by ZKM.

2. The linear core: at the center of the building, we propose a linear public space of maximum visibility and excitement. This linear core and its balconies give access to all parts of the ZKM. Its ground floor provides most performance, exhibition and seminar spaces. Giant video screens, suspended *passerelles* and stairs, a tensile glass elevator and two rooms floating in midair activate an extensive and colorful foyer for the general public. This linear core allows for the public mediatization of specialized research.

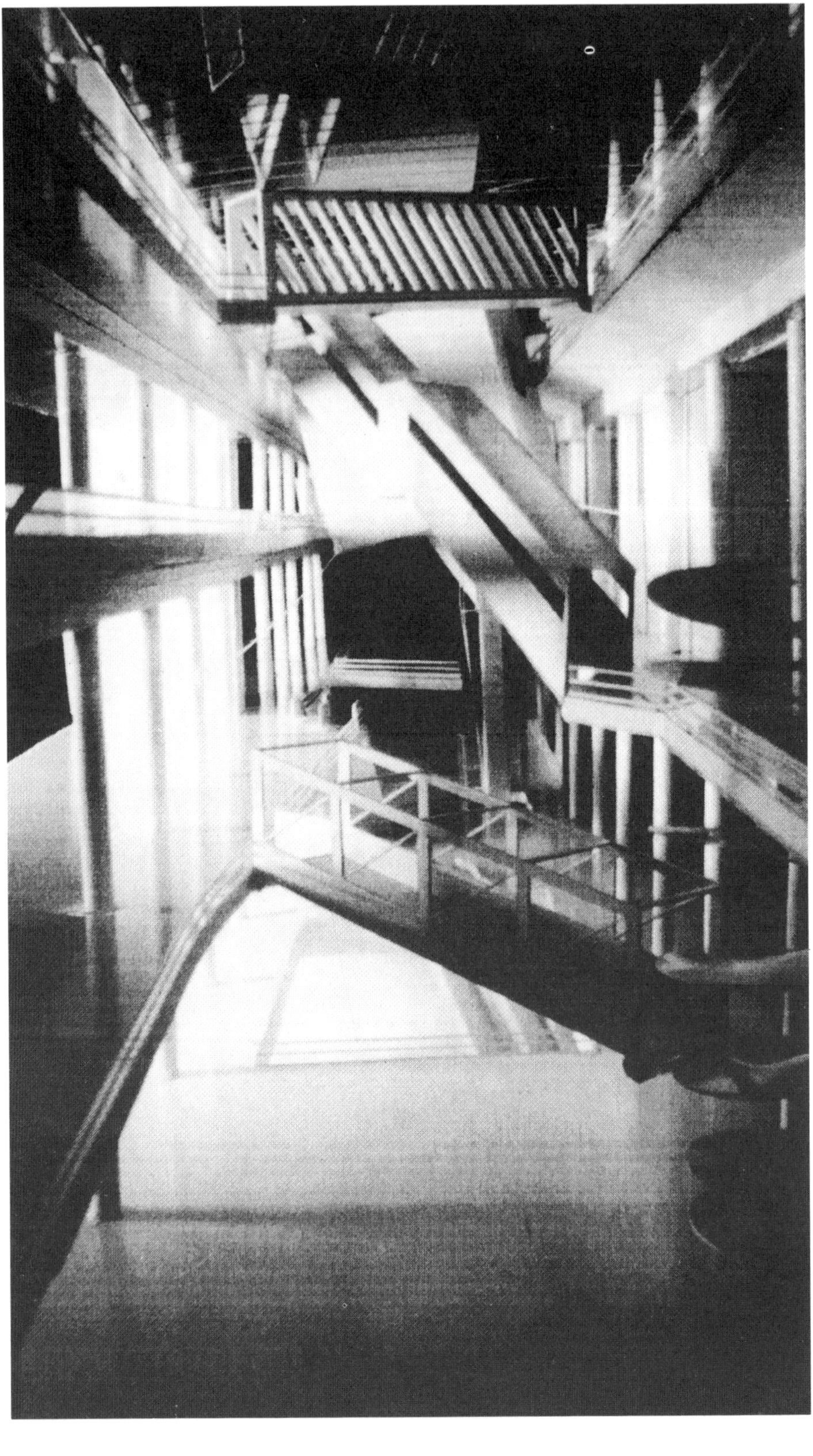

3. The two compartments: on each side of the linear core are simple compartments for all specialized functions. The compartment on the north side contains most of the larger spaces such as the media theater, the museum of contemporary art and the large studio (ellipse). The southern compartment contains most of the smaller spaces such as laboratories, offices and artists' studios, as well as the media gallery. On both sides, the more public spaces are located on the lower floors, the more specialized spaces on the upper floors.

The functional and constructive systems of the two compartments are intentionally simple: repetitive cells on a regular concrete structure. The building's simplicity and sobriety suggest that at ZKM, emphasis is placed on the development of new media, on the construction of technology (rather than on the technology of construction).

4. The casing: the tight functional structure is enclosed on the south side by an ever-changing photo-electronic, computer-animated double-glazed skin that reacts to external light and sound variations. The skin emerges from a protective, perforated stainless steel enclosure (north side), with a copper-clad ellipse (containing the multipurpose studio).

The digitized facade of the casing reminds us that if, once upon a time, architecture generated the appearance of stable images, today it may reveal the transience of unstable ones.

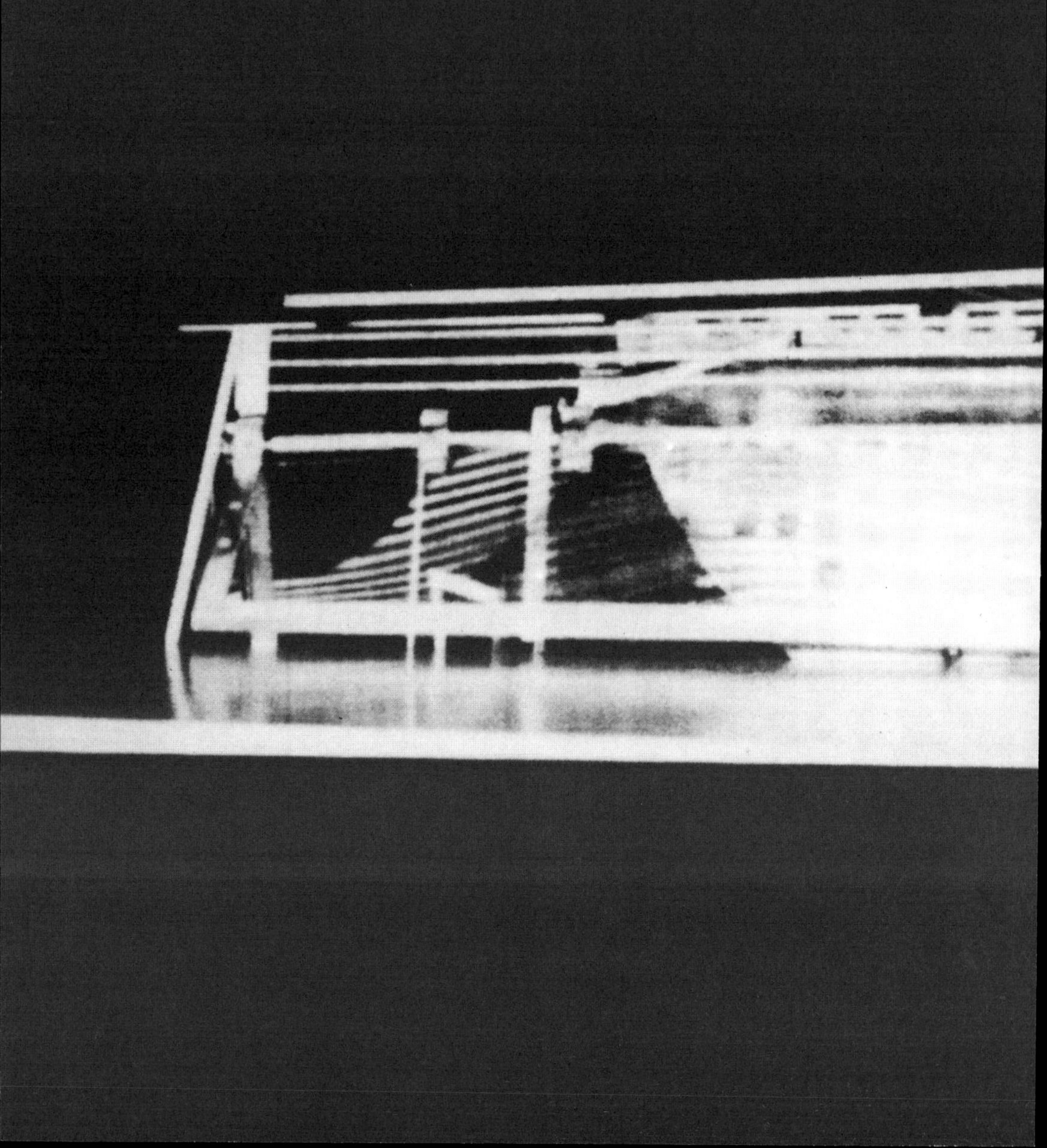

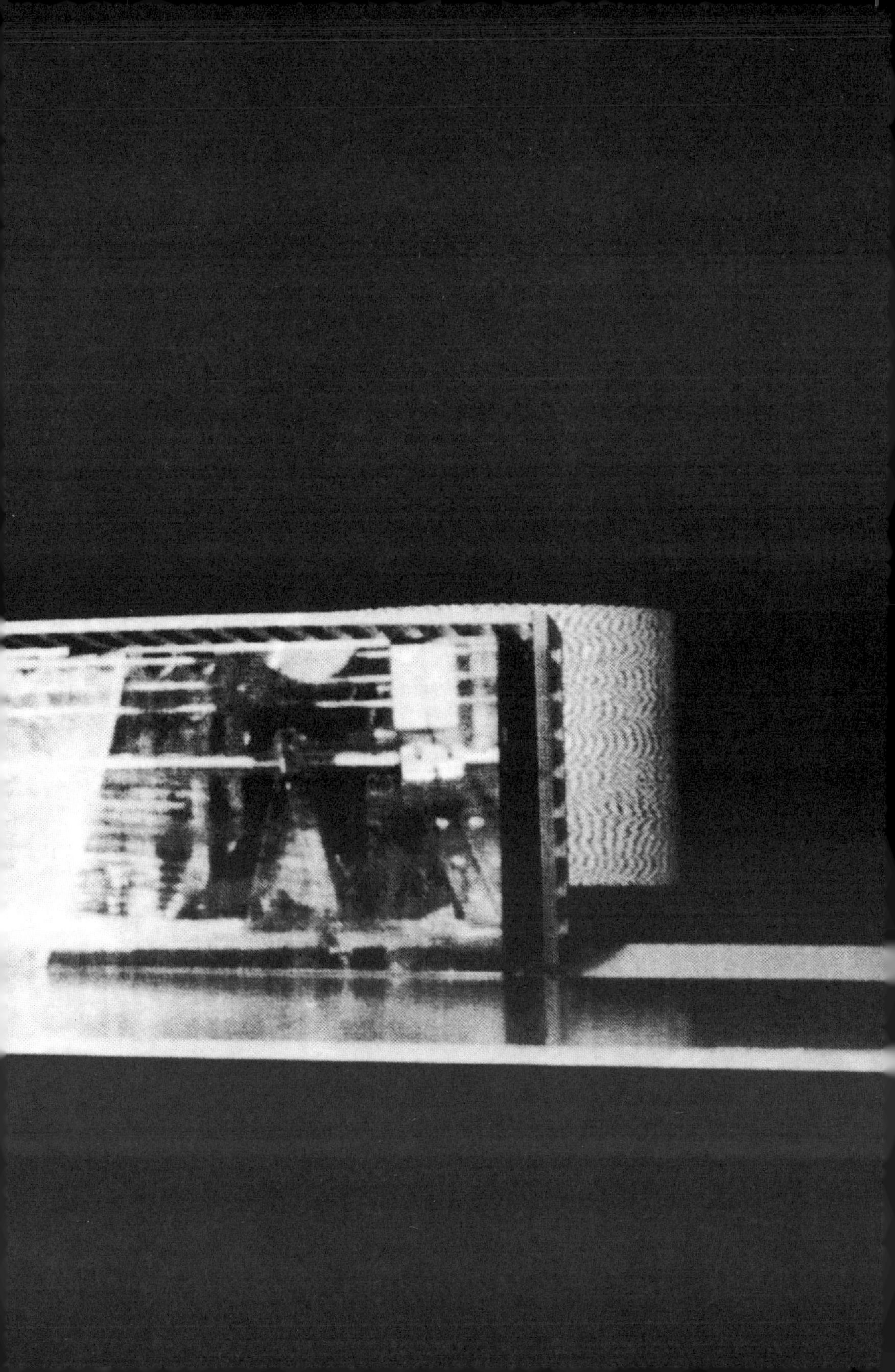

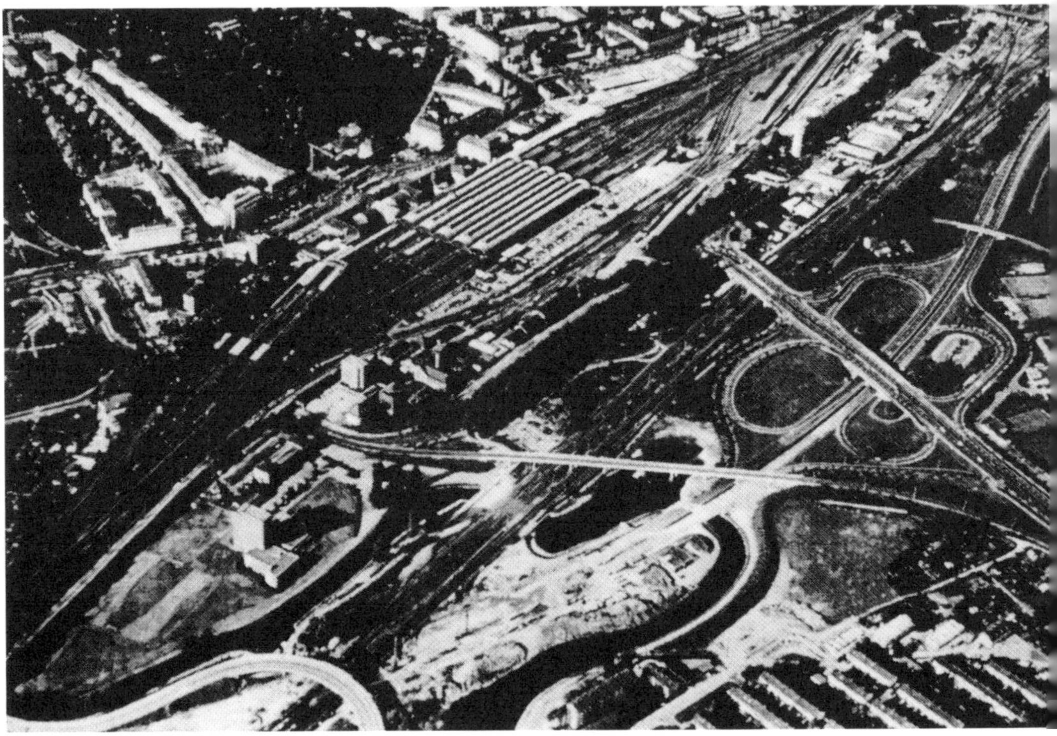

KARLSRUHE
373

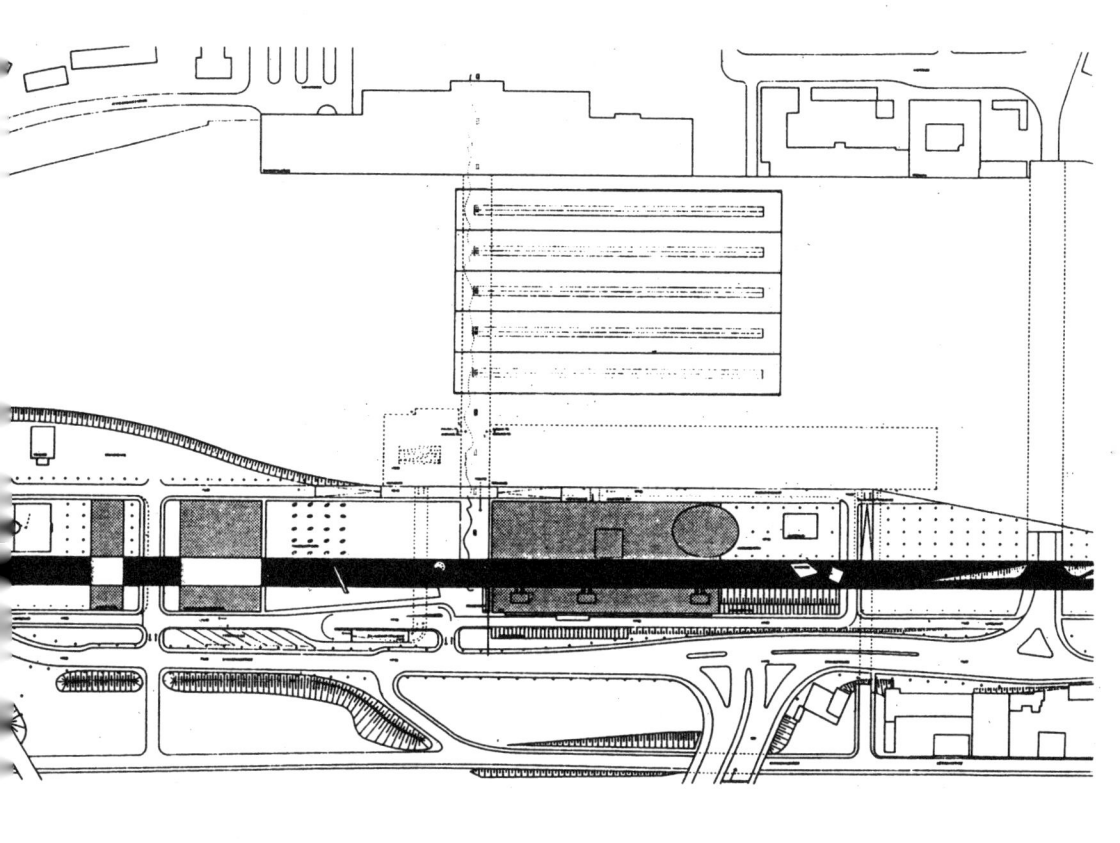

Line of exchange and communication opposed to the concentric baroque city:
composite of visible and invisible systems

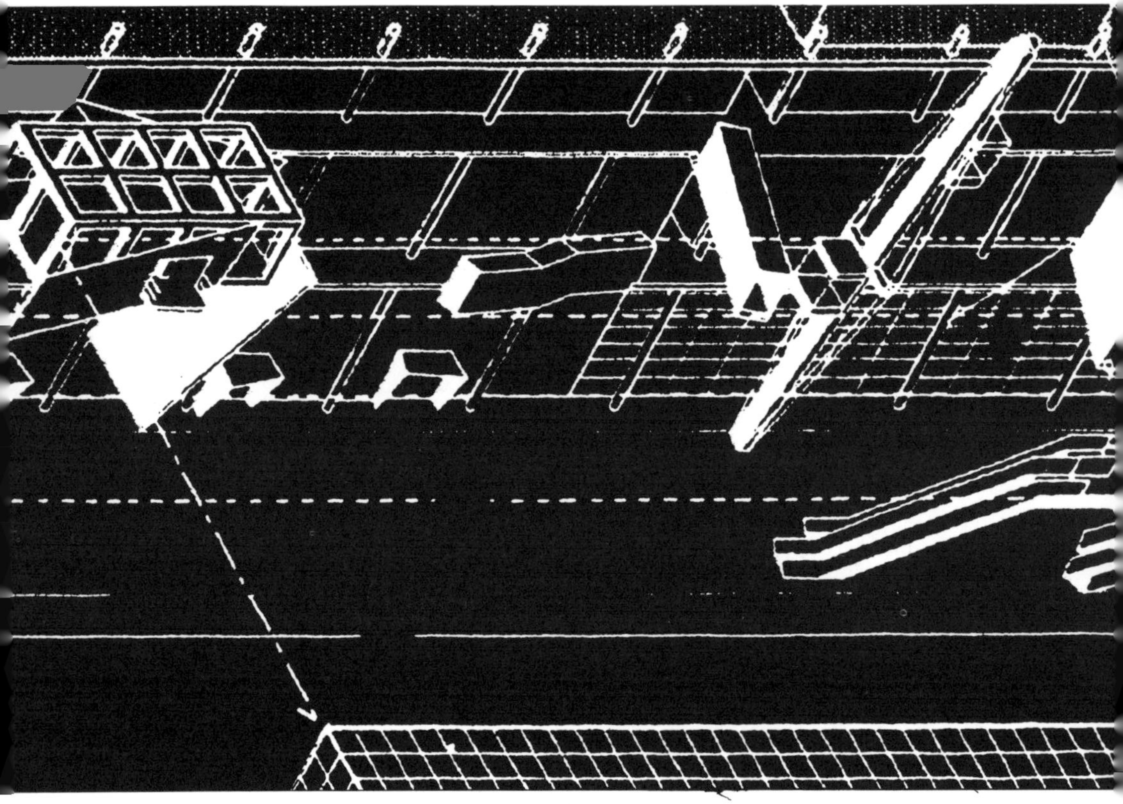

KARLSRUHE
375

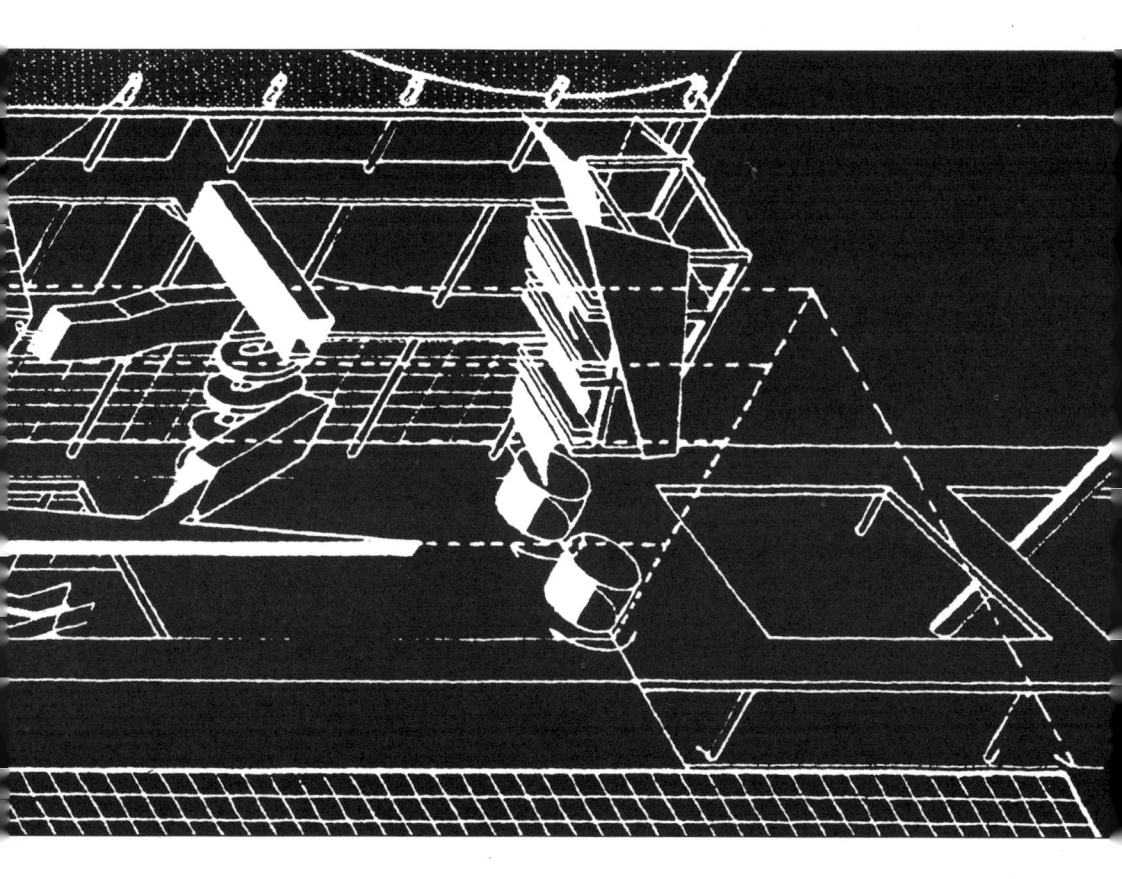

Programmatic vector: the inevitable confrontation between space and use means that architecture is constantly unstable, on the verge of change

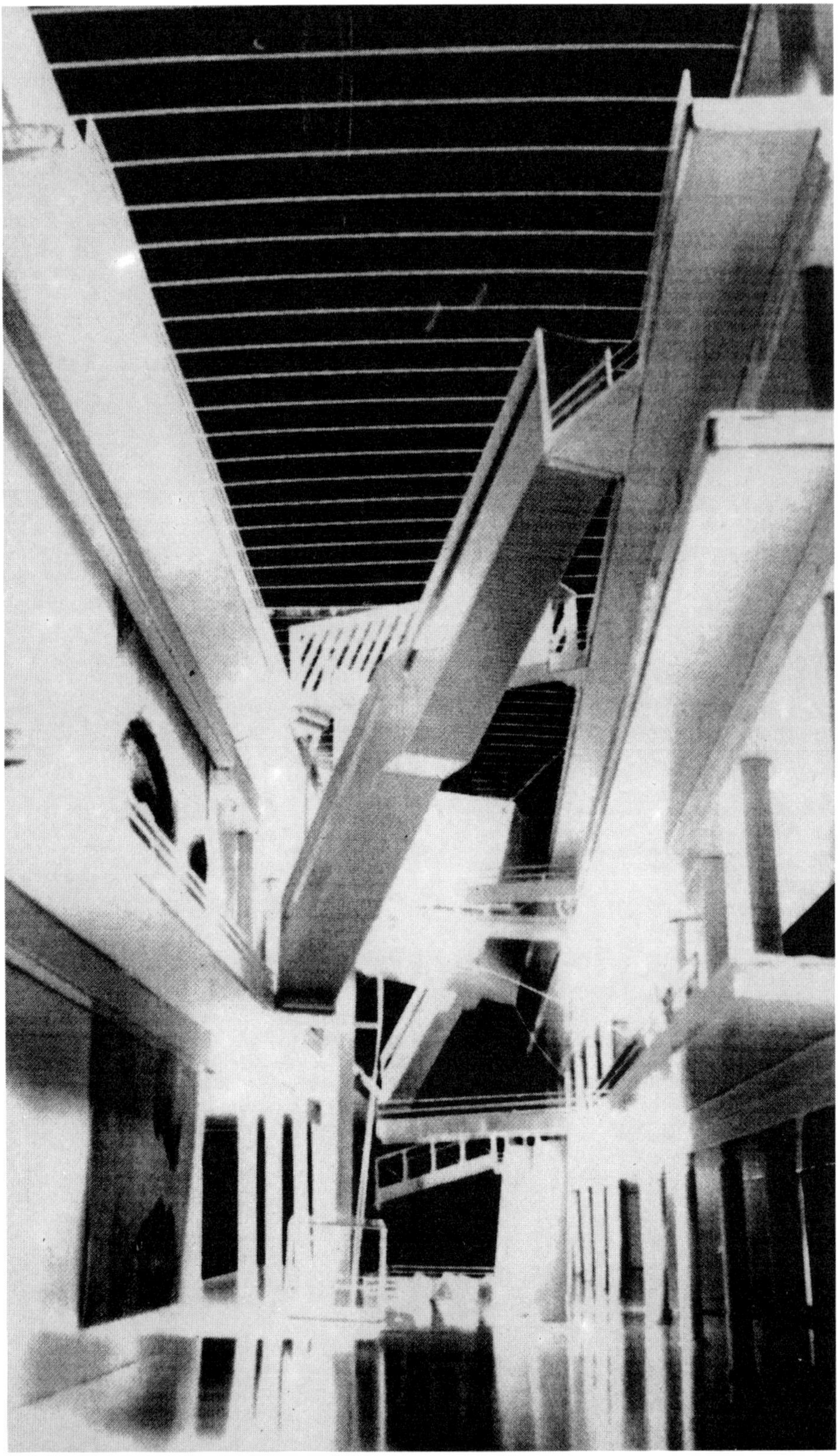

KARLSRUHE
377

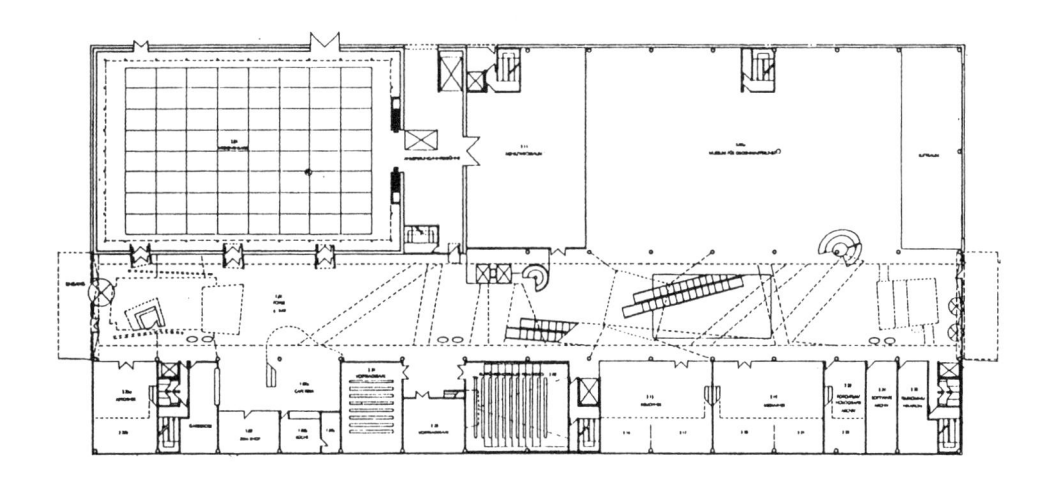

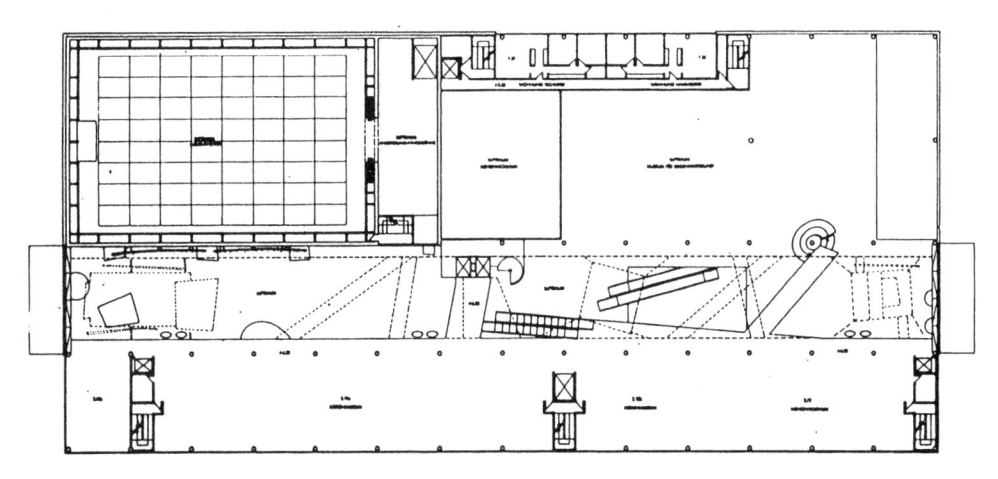

Level +0.00

Level +6.50

Linear core, theater and conference rooms, museum of contemporary art, multipurpose spaces

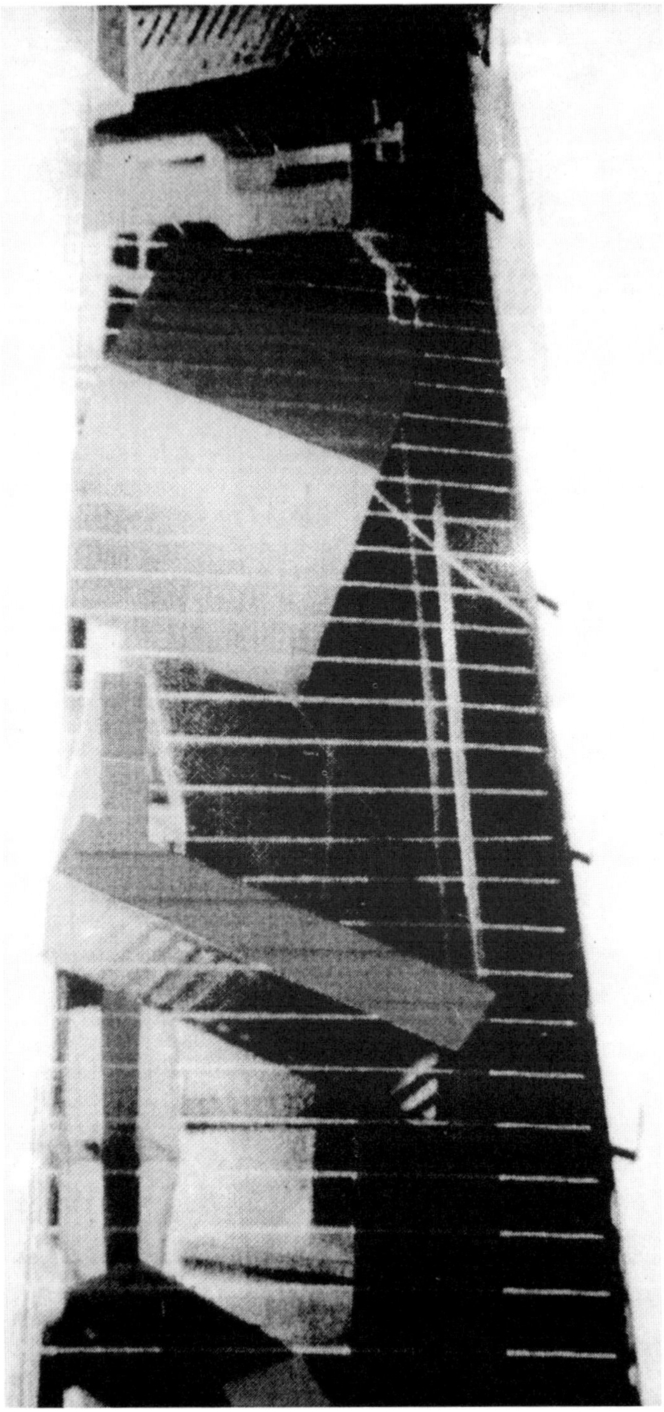

KARLSRUHE
379

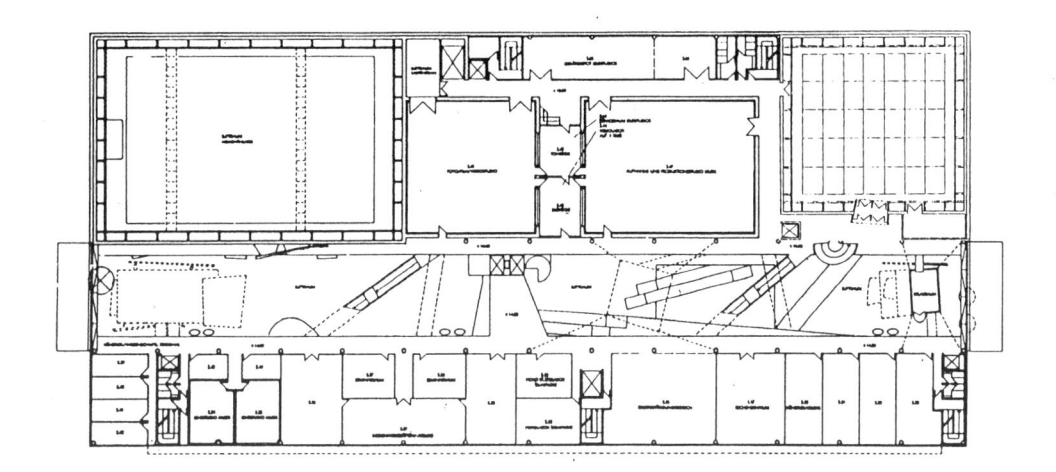

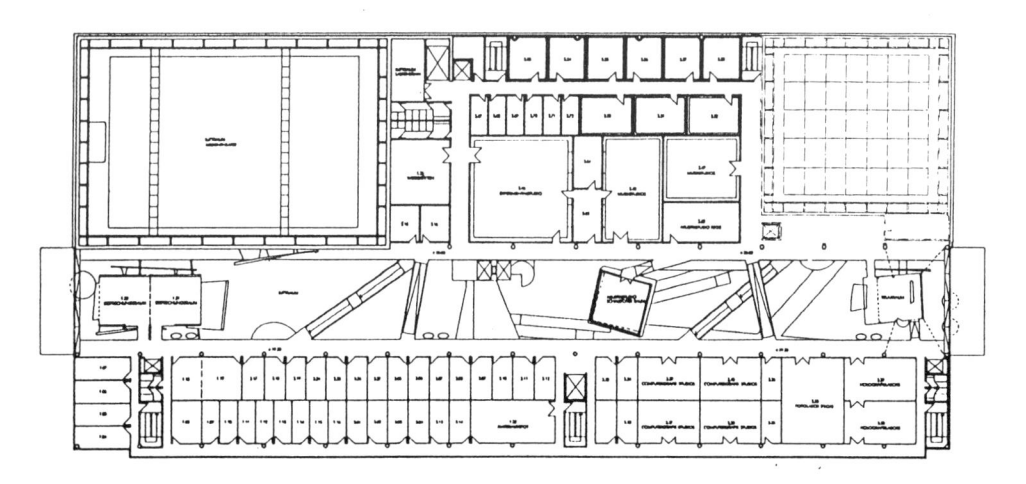

Level +14.00

Level +19.50

Linear core, sound studios, anechoic chamber, artists' workshops, auditorium

EBENE 0 ± 0.00

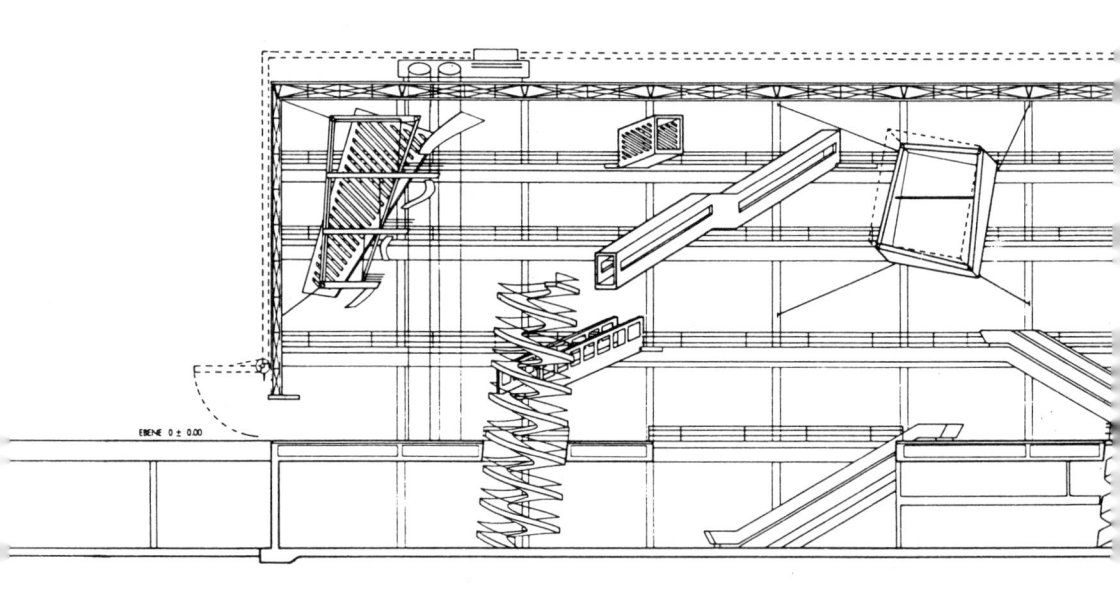

KARLSRUHE
381

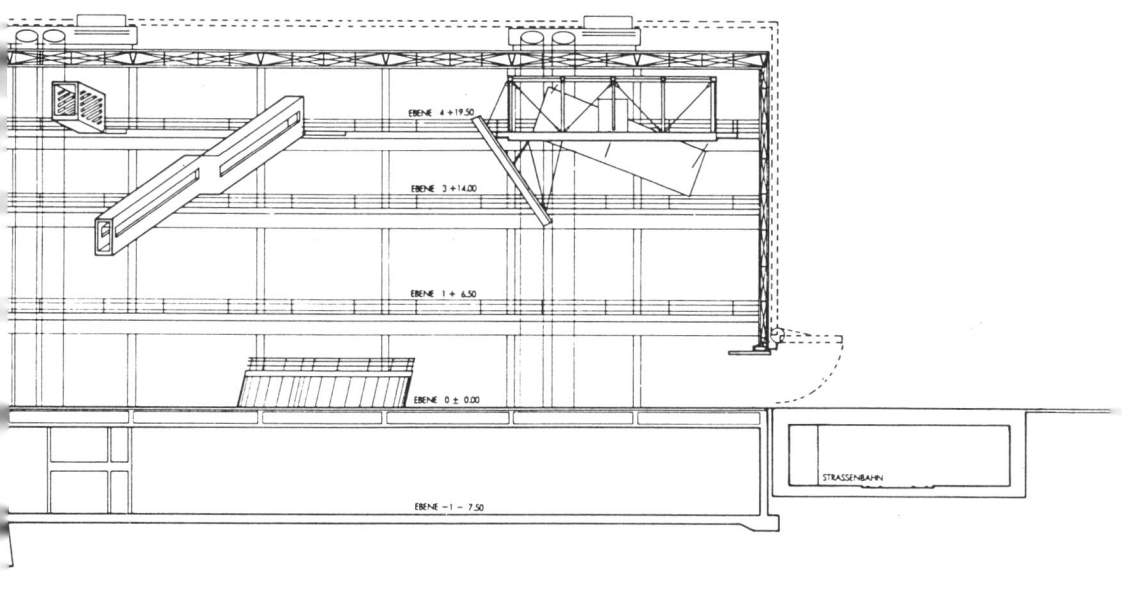

Programmatic and volumetric events in the linear core or in-between:
Suspended anechoic chamber and lounge, meeting rooms, ramps, stairs and escalators

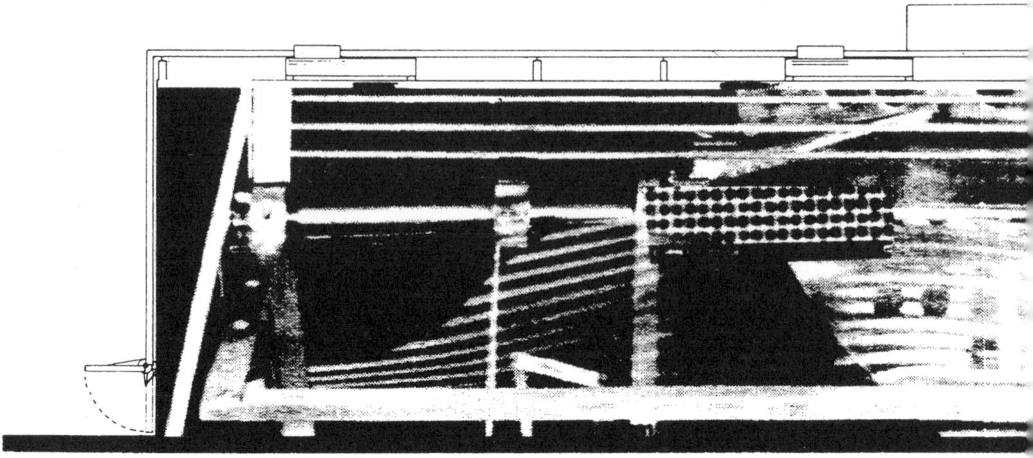

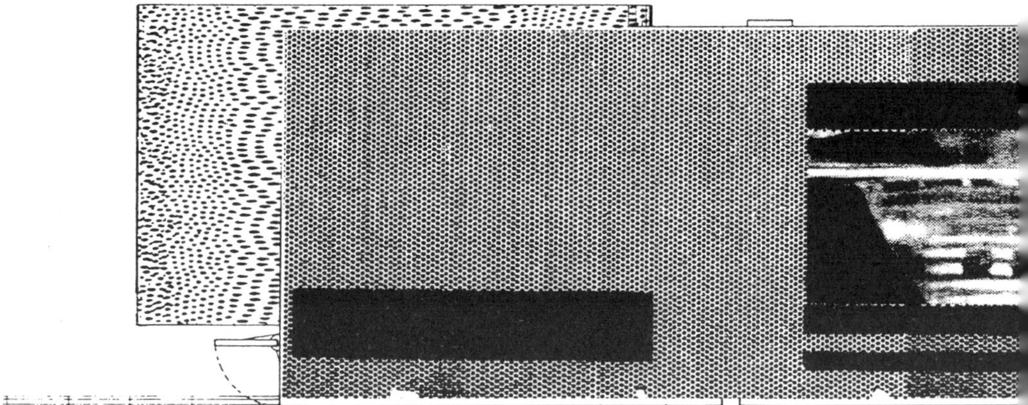

KARLSRUHE
383

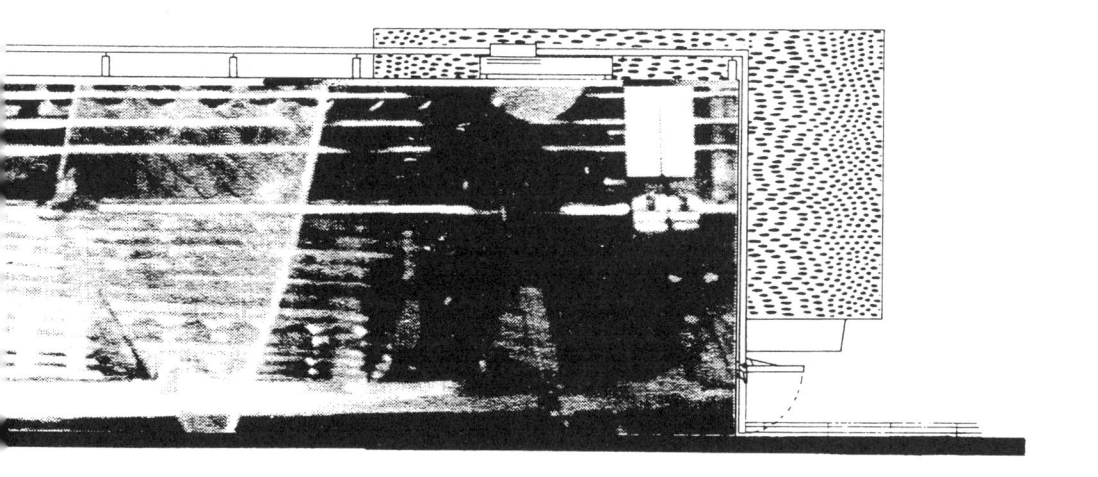

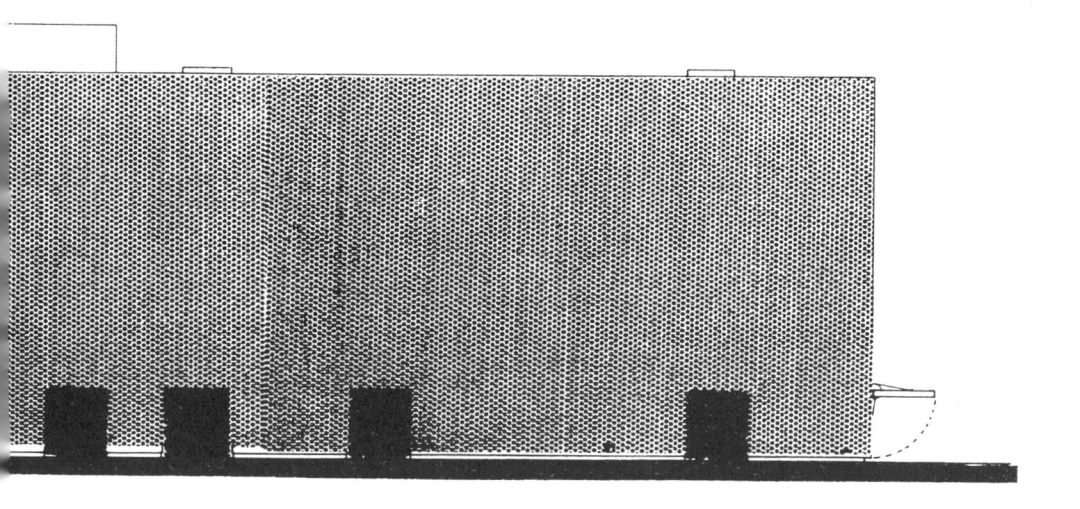

Unstable images: the appearance of permanence (perforated steel) is challenged by the immaterial representation of abstract systems (television, digital facade)

Mezzanines overlooking linear core: removing the hierarchy between frame and image

KARLSRUHE
385

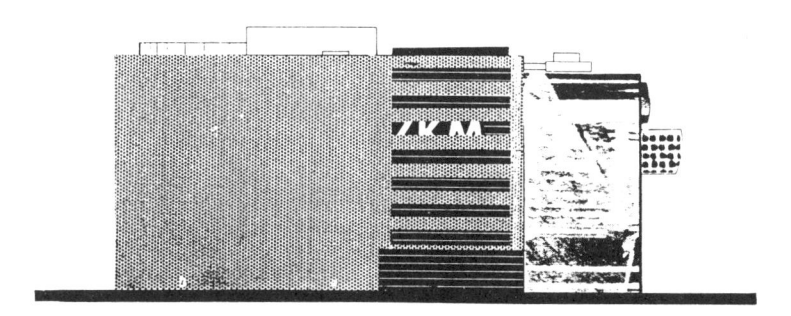

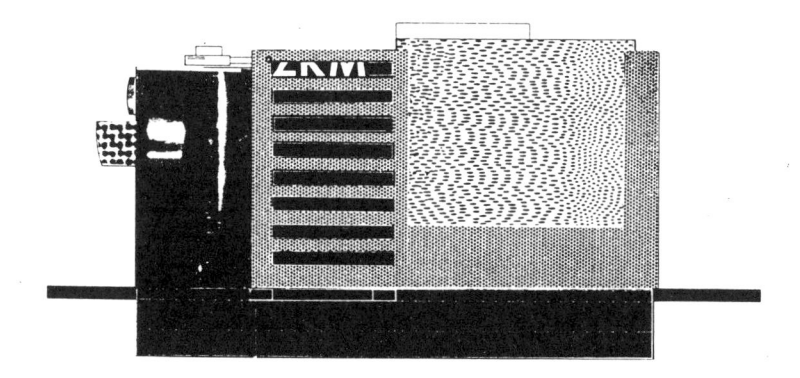

East and west elevations: no cause and effect relationship between the building and its use

Electronic facades can be both enclosure and spectacle

15 cm
15 cm

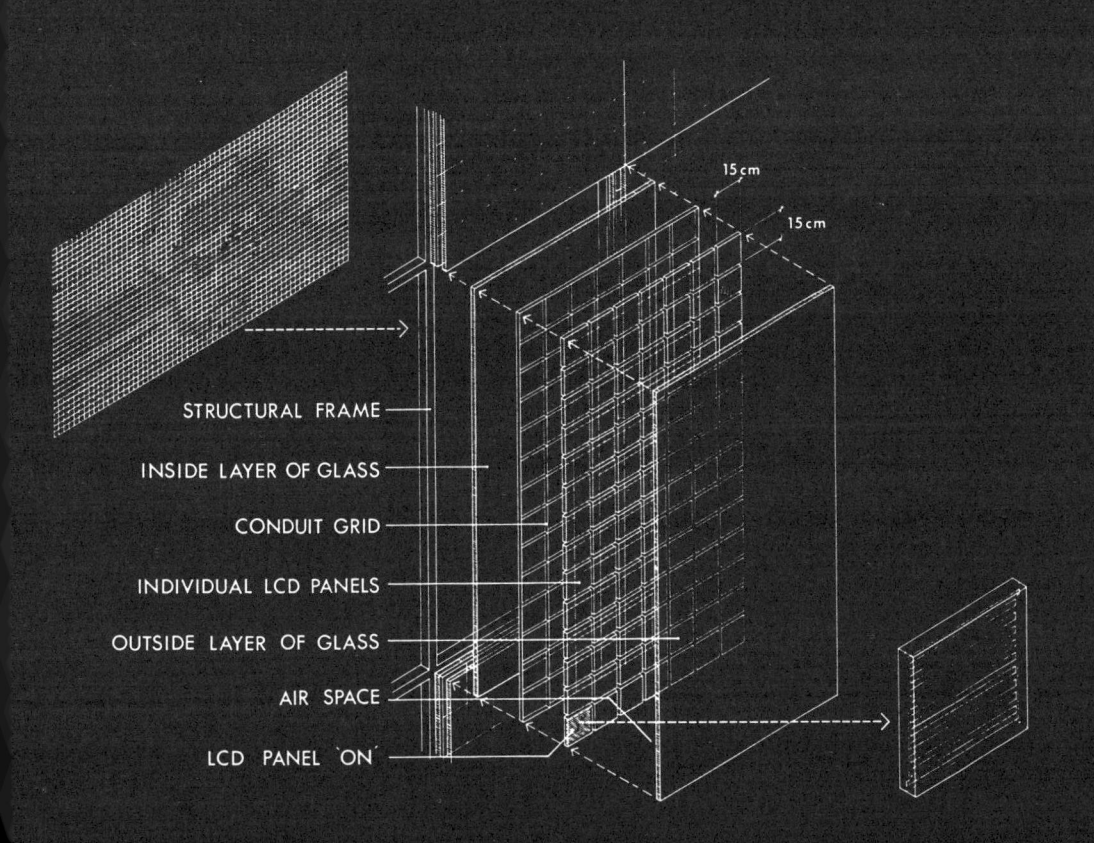

STRUCTURAL FRAME
INSIDE LAYER OF GLASS
CONDUIT GRID
INDIVIDUAL LCD PANELS
OUTSIDE LAYER OF GLASS
AIR SPACE
LCD PANEL 'ON'

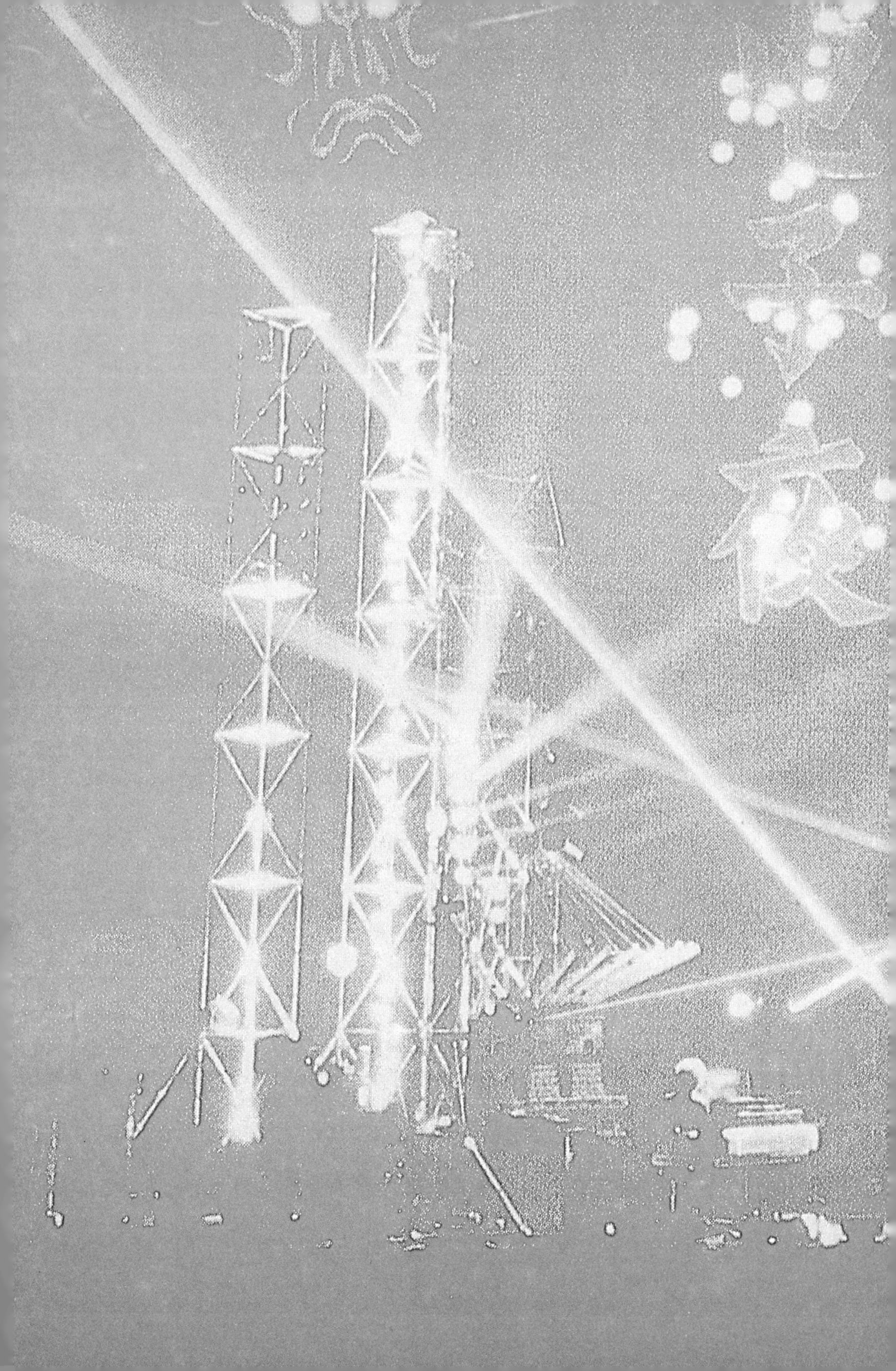

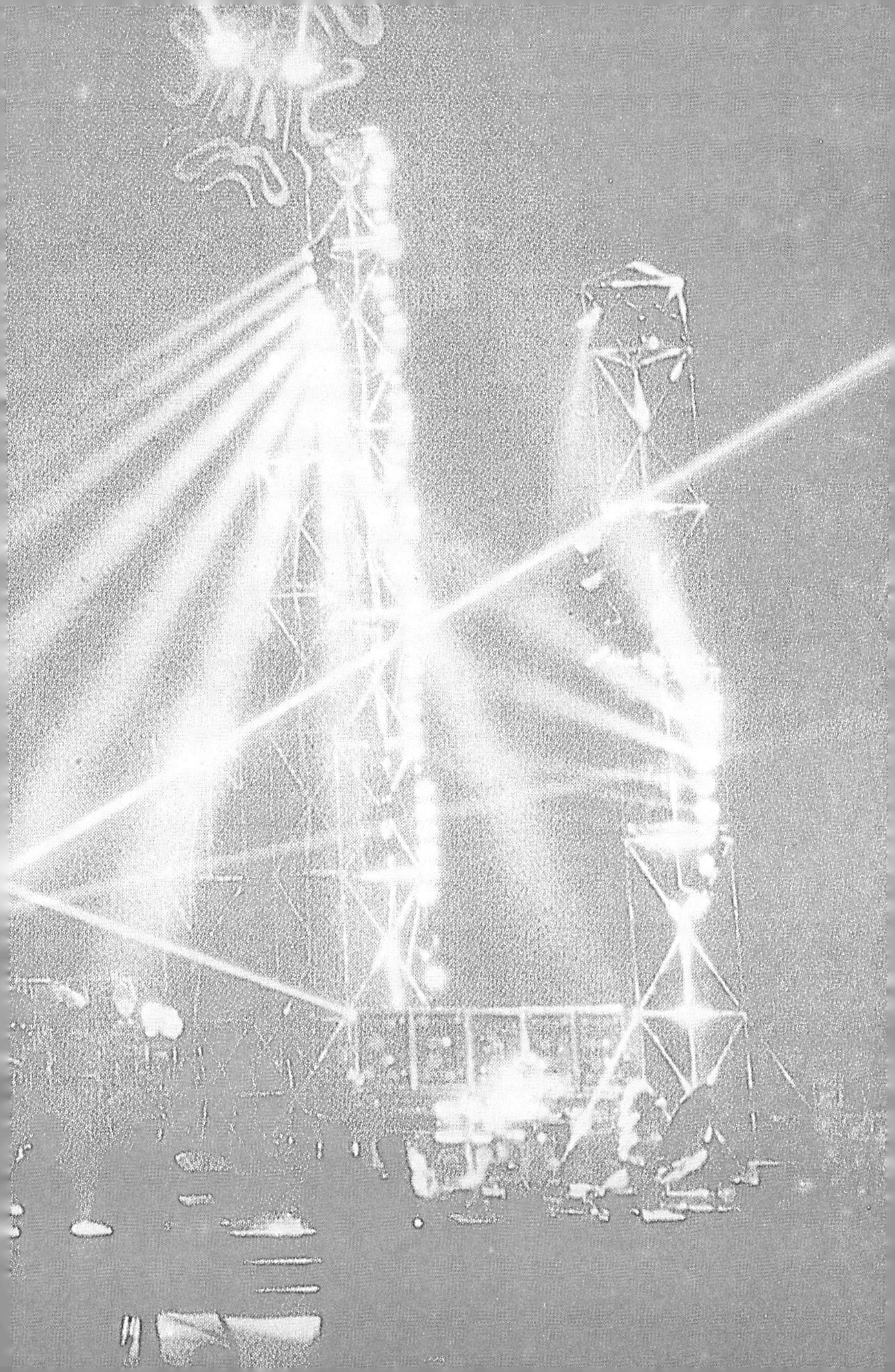

Tourcoing, Le Fresnoy National Studio for Contemporary Arts, 1991–

Strategy of the In-Between

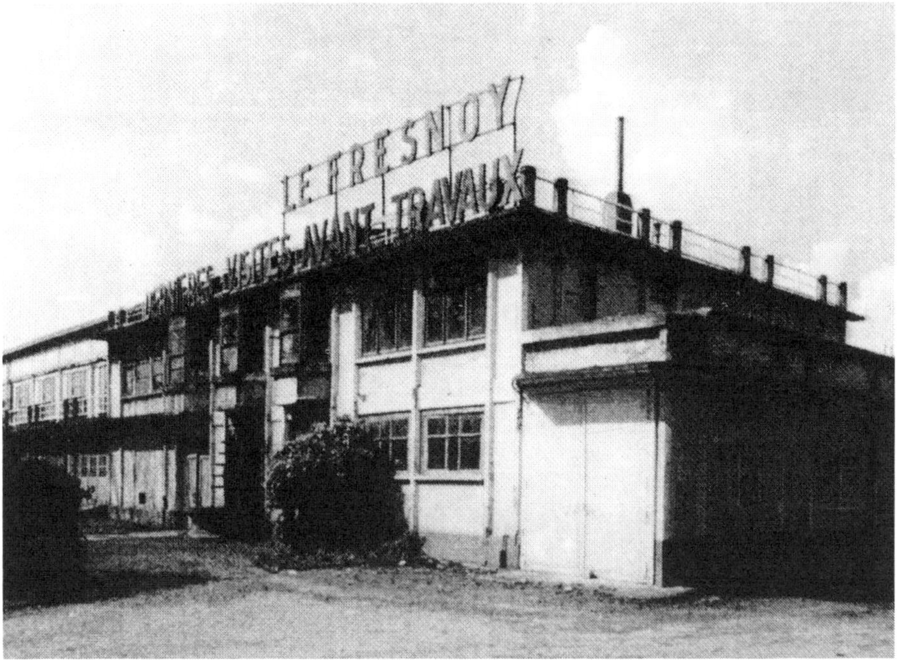
LE FRESNOY
VISITES AVANT TRAVAUX

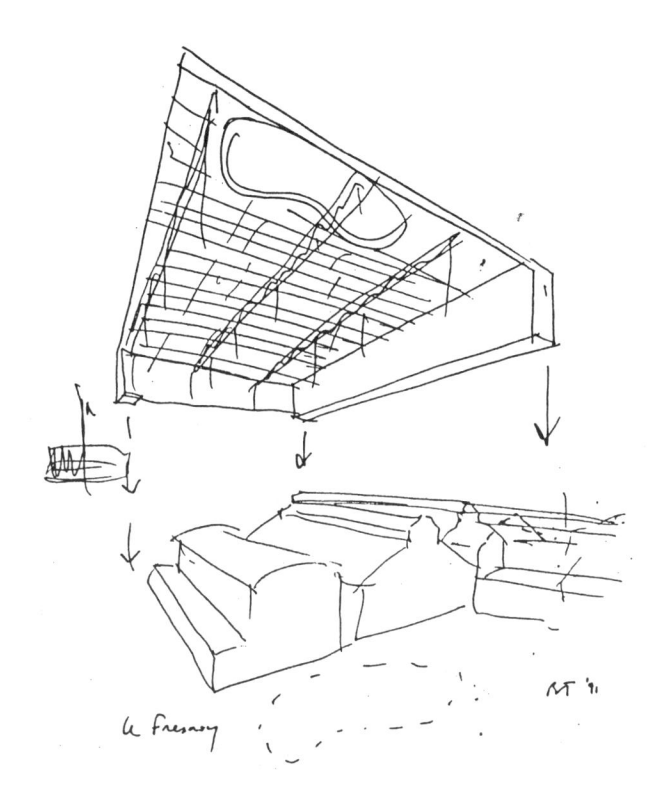

TOURCOING
393

Le Fresnoy

NT '91

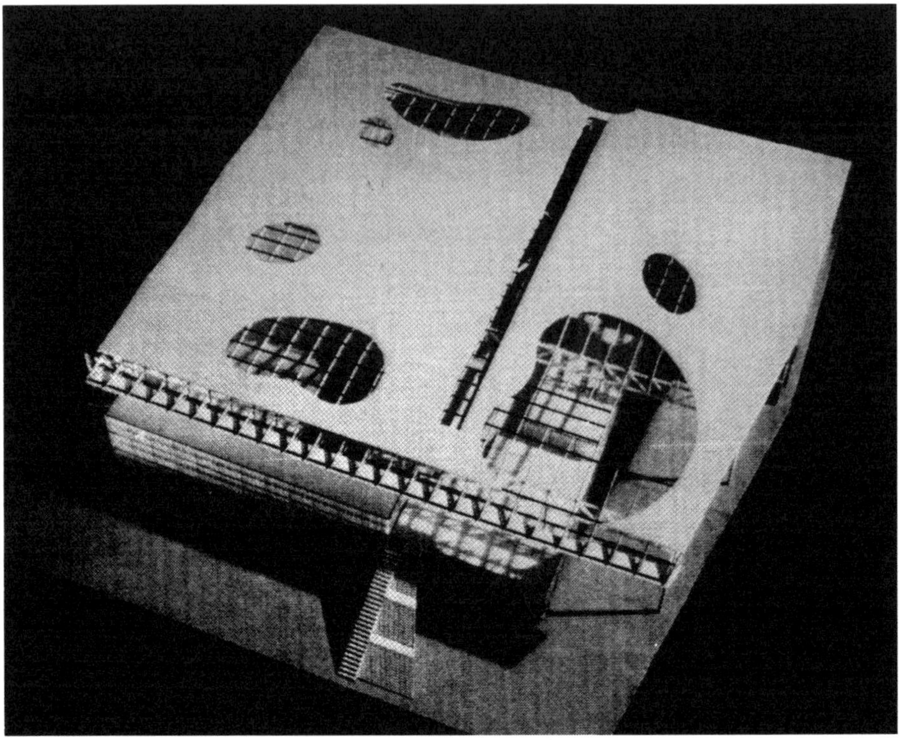

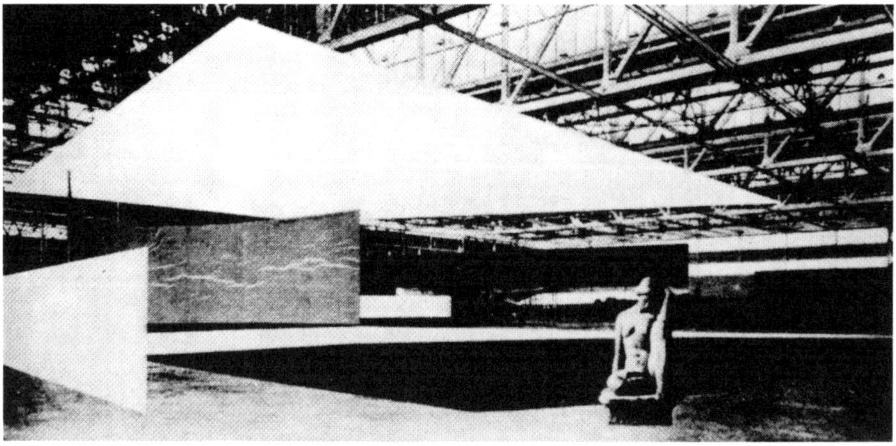

Eight thousand square meters of an international center for the contemporary arts will be inserted into Le Fresnoy, in Tourcoing, France. A school, a film studio, a *mediathèque*, spectacle and exhibition halls, two cinemas, laboratories for research and production (sound, electronic image, film and video), administrative offices, housing and a bar/restaurant: this is the multiple and expansive program of the new center.

The Fresnoy site is exceptional because it integrates the buildings of an old leisure complex of the twenties that included cinema, ballroom dancing, skating, horseback riding and other activities. The artistic and pedagogical project is unique and absolutely innovative; the architectural project has to be equally innovative. Through combinations of old and new, development and production, artists and the general public, the building's image will incorporate a model dimension.

Our first preoccupation was the condition of the existing buildings. Serious doubts about the solidity and waterproofing of the edifices, specifically walls, timber work and roofs, led us to the following analysis:

We could either demolish the parts that were most affected by time—among others, the beautiful vaulted hall to the south of the complex—and thus lose a large part of the magic of the site; or we could, faithfully and at great expense, restore all parts weakened or susceptible to further deterioration; or we could radically protect with a big roof the most spectacular parts of Fresnoy, thus sheltering them from bad weather while installing on the underside of the roof all necessary technical installations (ductwork, air-conditioning, stage mechanisms).

After a study of the cost of each one of these options, the last solution appeared by far the most satisfactory, from the financial but also from the architectural, programmatic and technical points of view.

Conceptually, we see the project as a succession of boxes inside a box.

1. First is the rectangular solid of modernity, ultratechnological, whose north side is closed. The other sides remain open and provide a view of the old and new buildings. The upper horizontal surface is a rectangle of approximately eighty by one hundred meters pierced with large openings and comprising, in its structure, all of the technical ductwork for heating, ventilation and air-conditioning, the vertical branches of which extend down into the spaces they serve.

2. Under the large electronic roof are the boxes of the existing building, most hereafter sheltered from the bad weather. The only parts demolished were a strip of the north facade and a construction situated in the southeast corner of the site (old technical spaces and keepers' quarters) whose ruinous condition did not justify a restoration. We replaced these volumes and developed a new architectural and functional vocabulary (corrugated steel facade in the north and curtain wall facades in the south) that permits us, among other things, to give a resolutely contemporary and transparent image to the entrance area and the main facade of the building. At the same time, we conceived the new facilities located in the existing volumes as technically autonomous boxes while maintaining the fluidity of the Fresnoy spaces.

Not the conditions of design, but the design of conditions

A zone of economic activity (ZAE, or commercial space) is integrated into the project and becomes the equivalent of a fourth hall, in the south end of the existing vaulted hall. An underground parking lot is to be provided under the ZAE and the school/administrative offices.

3. We then developed the "in-between," the space between the new steel roof and the old tile roofs. Large horizontal windows, covered with transparent sheets of polycarbonate in the form of clouds, create an underside of the roof flooded with light and cut through by a transversal corresponding to the project's north-south axis. A large landscaped terrace in front of the bar/restaurant profits from direct access, through the grand stair, to the garden.

If the new roof acts as the project's common denominator (a large screen-umbrella), we also sought to accelerate the probability of chance-events by combining diverse elements (the meeting of umbrella and sewing machine on the dissecting table), juxtaposing great roof, school/research laboratory and the old Fresnoy, place of spectacle.

The whole is precise and rational in its conception, varied and poetic in its spatial richness. The large steel roof with its clouds of light floats above the old tile roofs. It becomes a new plane of reference (*artifi-ciel* in French). This large roof that responds to climatic, energy and information needs also generates a new type of space—the in-between.

Fresnoy students and visitors will be able to appreciate the surreal nature of this immense horizontal space, whose size and presence makes relative the notions of interior and exterior suggested by the old buildings.

Such multifunctional spaces destined to "cover" events (conventions, concerts, sports, exhibitions and their thousands of visitors) will be the urban spaces of the twenty-first-century, here reviving a building from the beginning of the twentieth century. At Fresnoy we can speak of an "architecture-event" rather than an "architecture-object." The interstitial space between the new and old roofs becomes a place of fantasies and experiments (filming and other exploratory works on space and time).

The in-between becomes a condenser of interdisciplinary investigations between teaching and research, art and cinema, music and image.

The apparently contradictory programmatic elements enrich the project: display spaces, research labs and teaching spaces, on one hand, and historic buildings and avant-garde techniques on the other create an electronic Bauhaus. Although the new roof works as the common denominator (a big umbrella), we also tried to evoke the poetry of this combination of various elements by mixing the great roof, school and research labs with the spectacle space of the old Fresnoy. The materials reflect this superimposition: metal on the underside of the great roof and the northern facade, glass curtain walls on the eastern and southern facades, restoration work only on the other sections.

Simulated night view in the in-between

Note:
A few more points about the idea of the new Bauhaus, of the hangar and of the in-between.

In the last few years, there have been six or seven competitions for so-called New Bauhauses. This suggests a desire for the perfection and coherence represented by the Bauhaus, for its globalization of various techniques and crafts. At Le Fresnoy, we were not dealing with coherent, well-defined disciplines, as the Bauhaus did, but with the disparate multiplicity of performance art, cinema, video and film production, sound studios, a school, a restaurant, several exhibition areas and industrial facilities for multimedia crafts. At Tourcoing, the site was not empty — ready for a coherent, pure design — but already populated with a rather strange and derelict entertainment center (the first cinema in northern France) that had been used for dancing, boxing and ice-skating.

We decided to play the site's inherent complexity through contemporary concepts. The new roof would act as a life-support system for the existing building while suggesting a large warehouse hangar. The "electronic" roof defines an in-between, a residual space between the impossible layers of rationalities. What interested us most was the space generated between the logic of the new roof (which made it all possible) and the logic of what was underneath: an in-between, a place of the unexpected where unprogrammed events might occur, events that are not part of the "curriculum." This is a space of residues, leftovers, gaps and margins. Within this industrial shed, myriad events may unfold. The project is full of "supplements," of undecidable areas of knowledge. By challenging the existing conditions, by filling up the site with a series of boxes (a box in a box in a box), the project allows for the possibility of an event. We recall here two Mies van der Rohe collages (for a concert hall of 1942 and a Chicago convention hall of 1953). One shows an existing structure and the other a new structure. Both stage an event. Each supplies its own history and symbolism.

Aspects of this in-between are not without precedents. We drew here on some of the forgotten heroes of the twentieth century. Frederick Kiesler's design for Karel Capek's multimedia theater production of "R. U. R." in 1923 combined theater, film and various other graphic information systems. In "Project for a Cinema" (1930), Kiesler used horizontal film screens on the ceiling/roof, celebrating another dimension of the building. Similarly, our scheme for Le Fresnoy activates an undefined area. Since this area was not included in the client's program and had no measurable cost, we were free to do whatever we wanted. Yet the charge from the program underneath the new roof literally brought into existence the in-between stage. The beams in the new roof were initially structural, housing the air-conditioning ducts, but ultimately serve only as a support for information. Concerts and film screenings will take place in the space in between the new and old roofs, in that unbelievable landscape of residual space. The new event is produced not through collage and recollage but through crossprogramming and transprogramming. This is the architecture of the event.

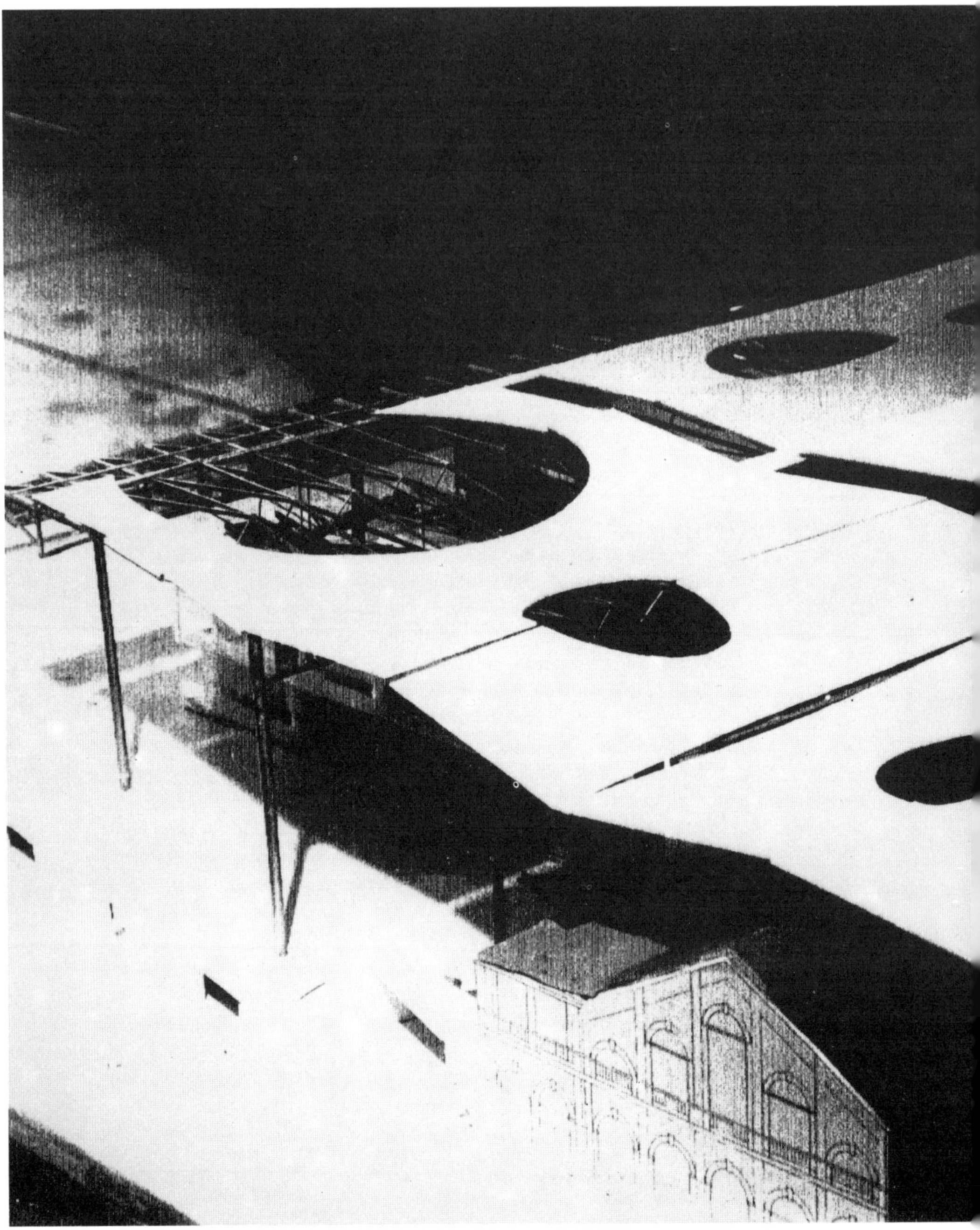

TOURCOING
401

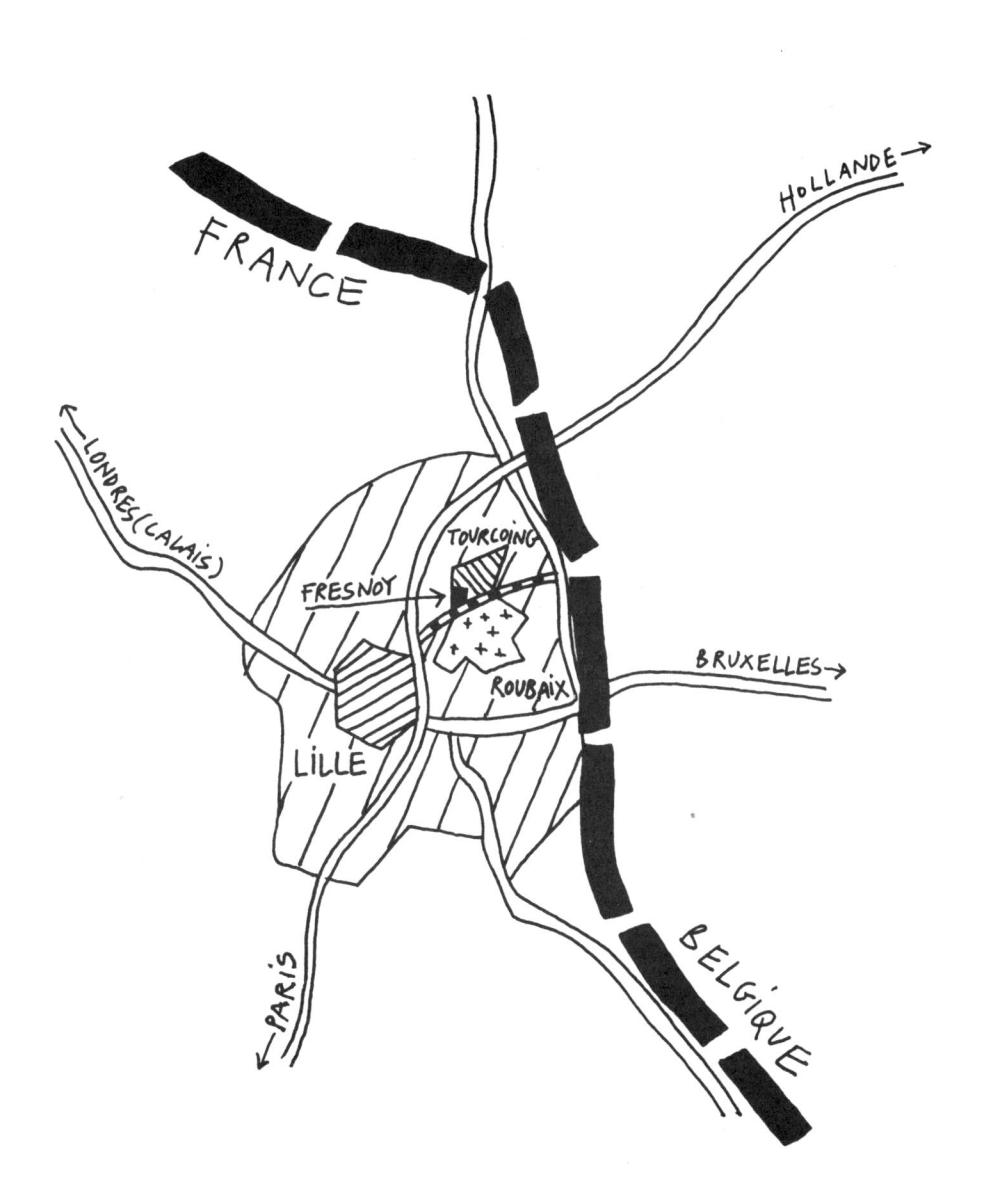

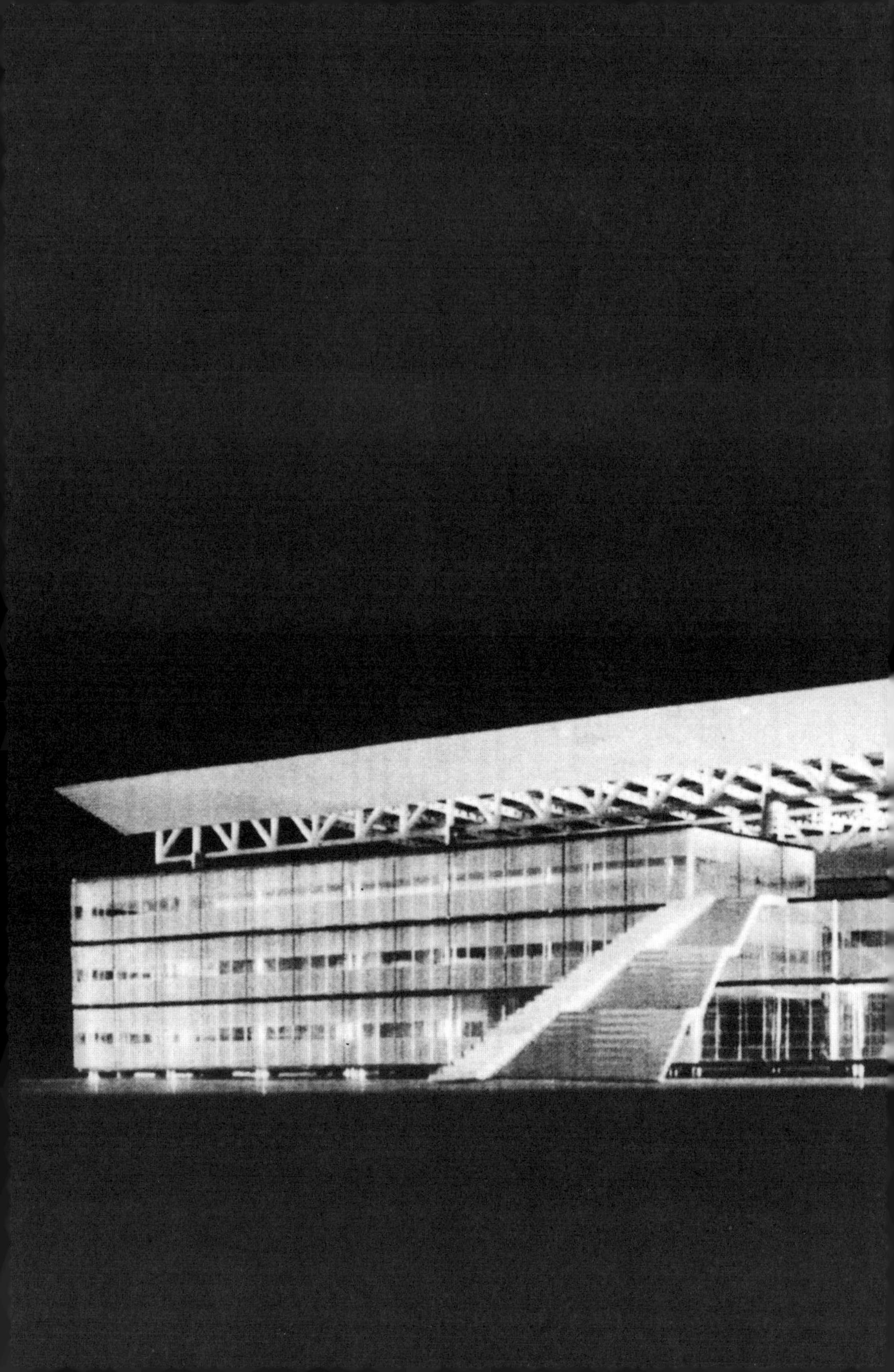

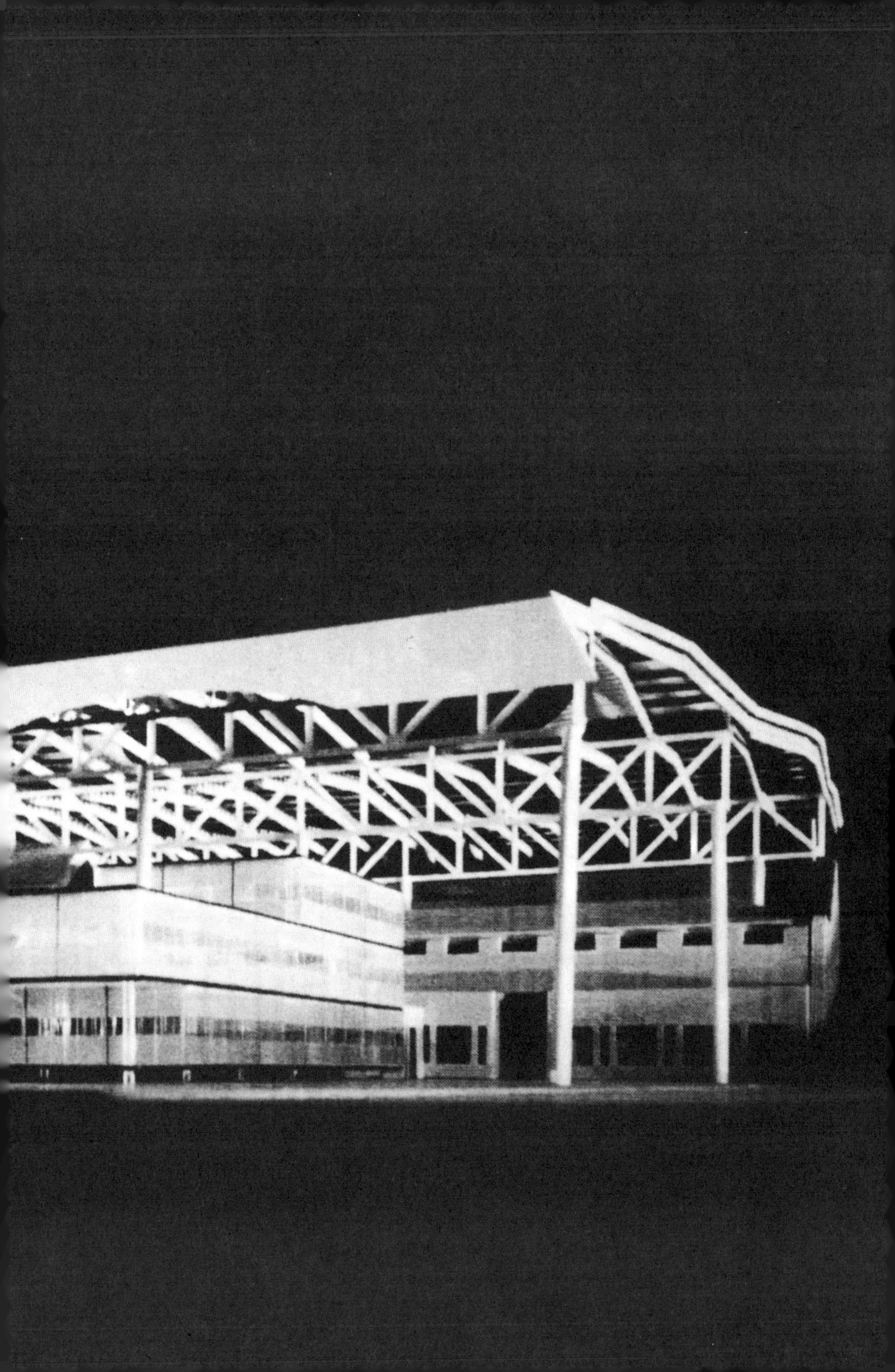

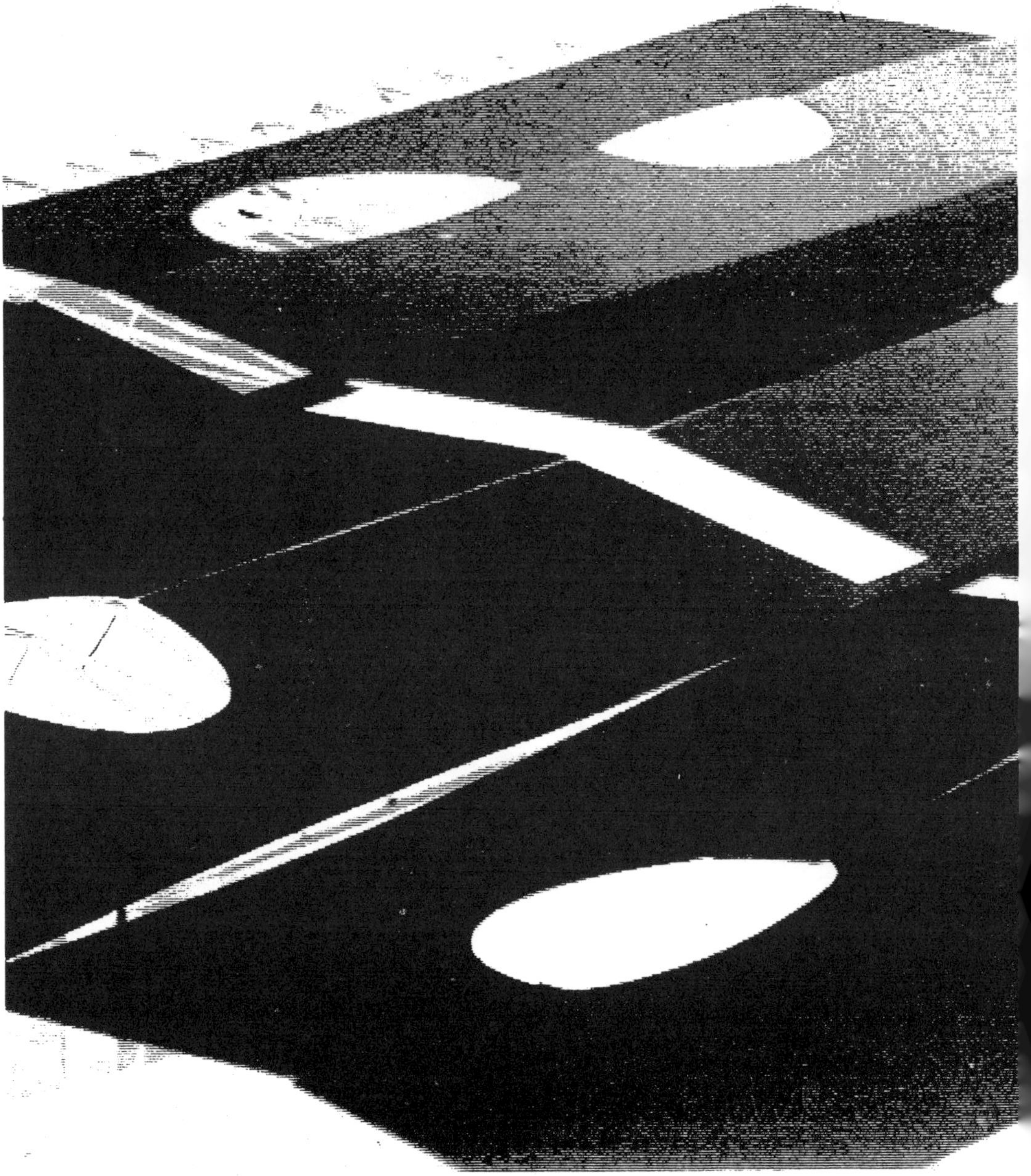

TOURCOIN
405

Decontextualization: encouraging multiple
meanings for buildings in the city

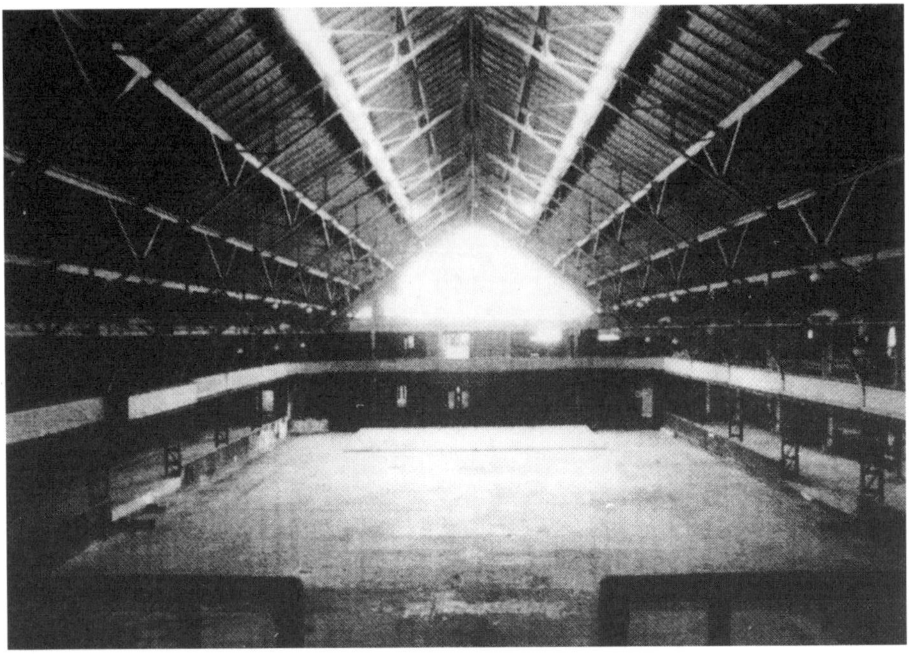

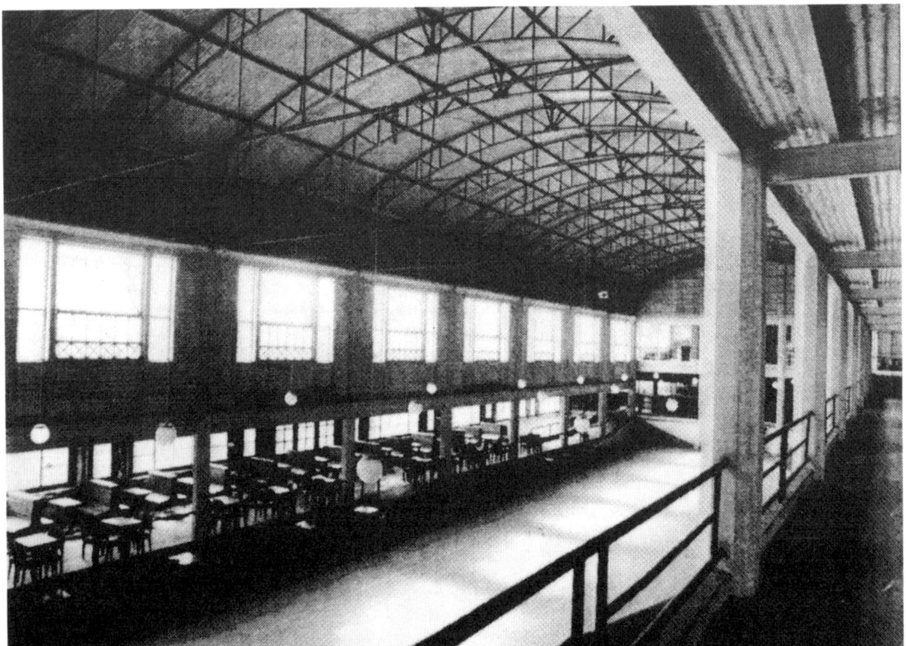

TOURCOING
407

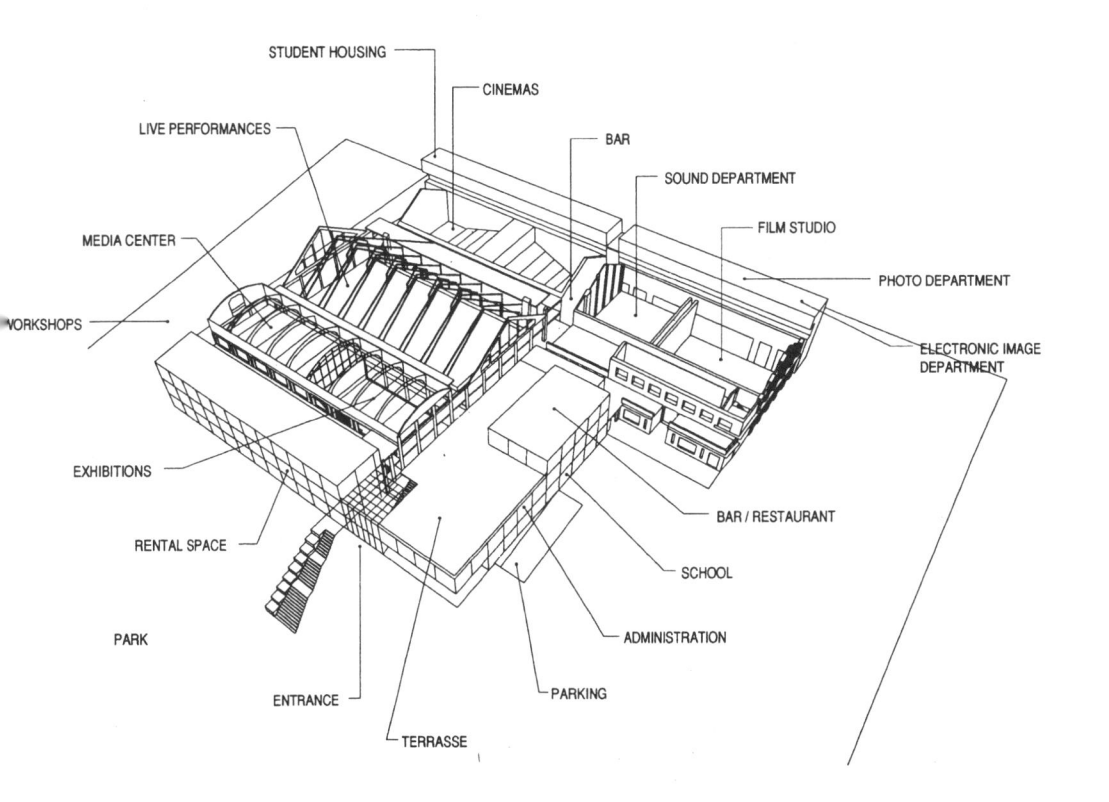

STUDENT HOUSING
CINEMAS
LIVE PERFORMANCES
BAR
SOUND DEPARTMENT
MEDIA CENTER
FILM STUDIO
PHOTO DEPARTMENT
WORKSHOPS
ELECTRONIC IMAGE DEPARTMENT
EXHIBITIONS
BAR / RESTAURANT
RENTAL SPACE
SCHOOL
PARK
ADMINISTRATION
ENTRANCE
PARKING
TERRASSE

Programs that transgress supposedly stable institutionality

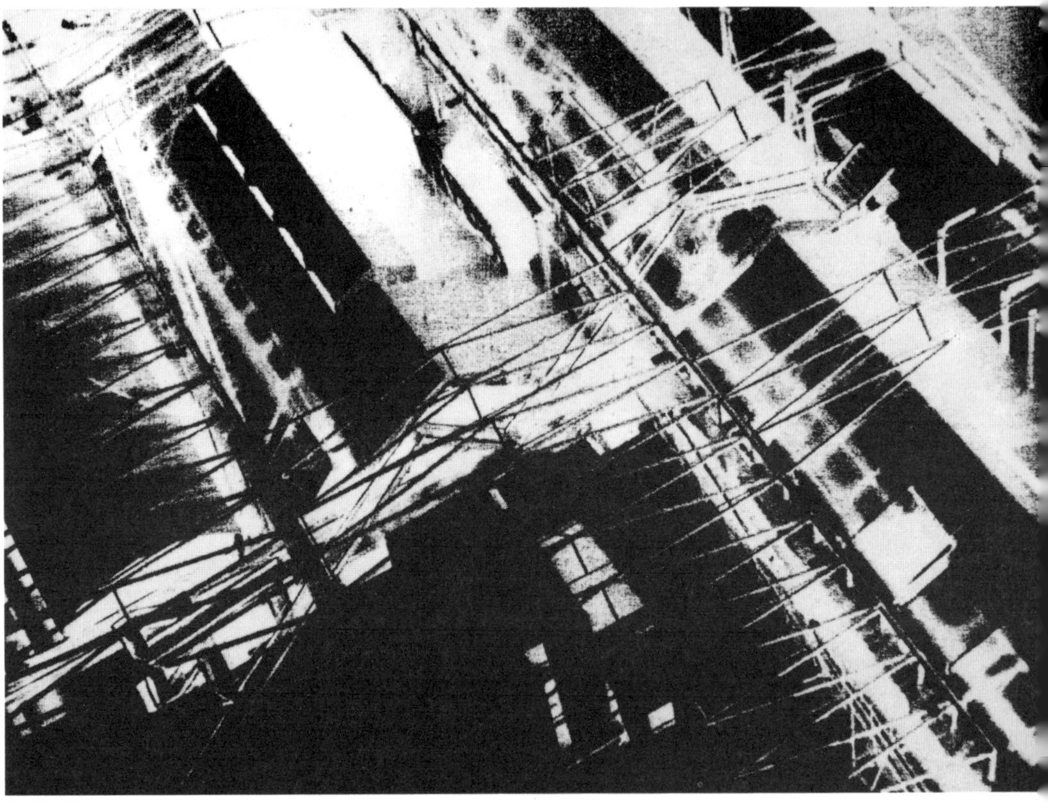

TOURCOING
409

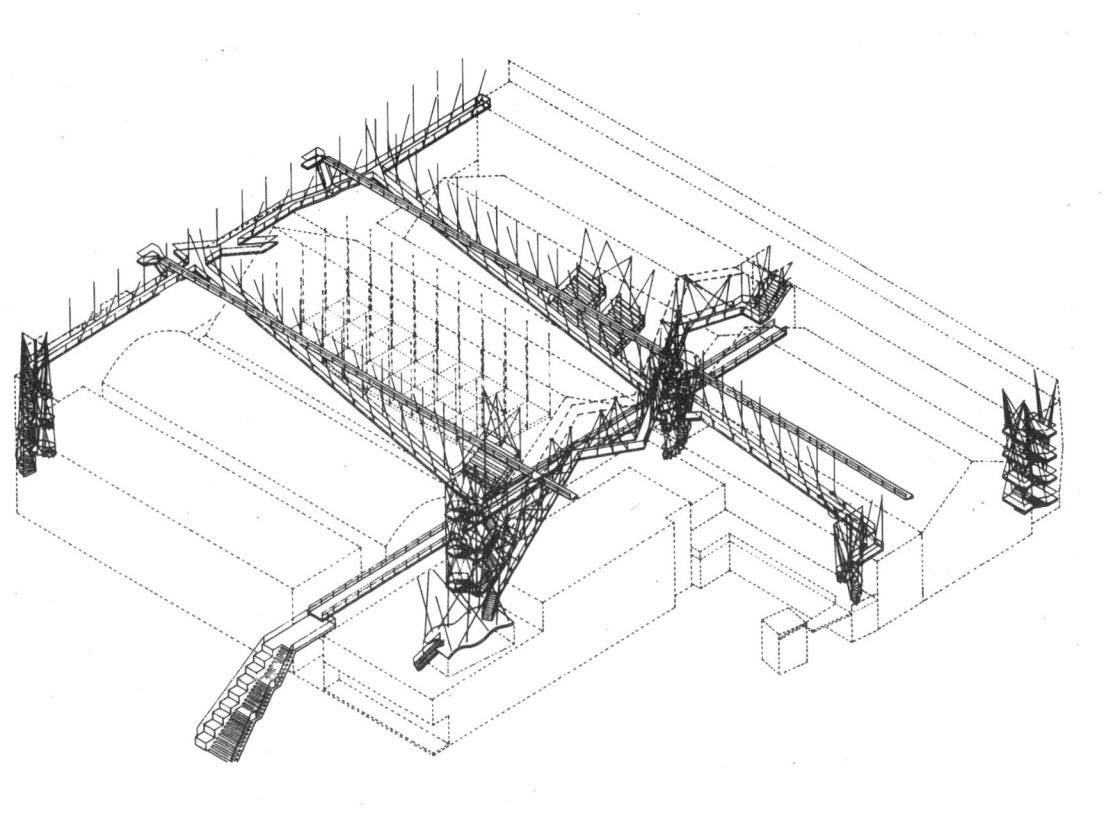

In-between: neither inside nor outside, a residual space, made of accidents --
the place of unexpected events

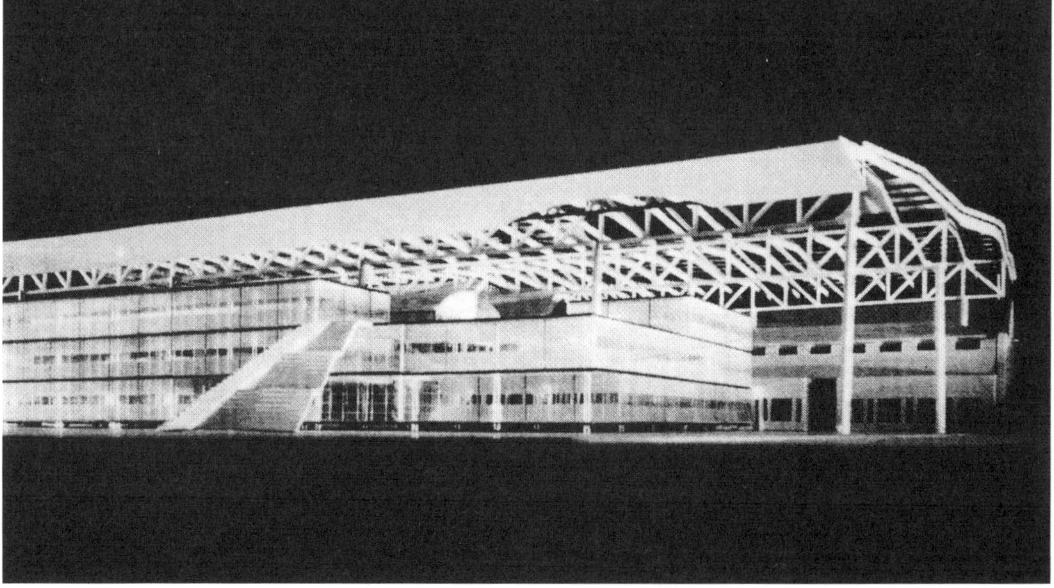

TOURCOING
411

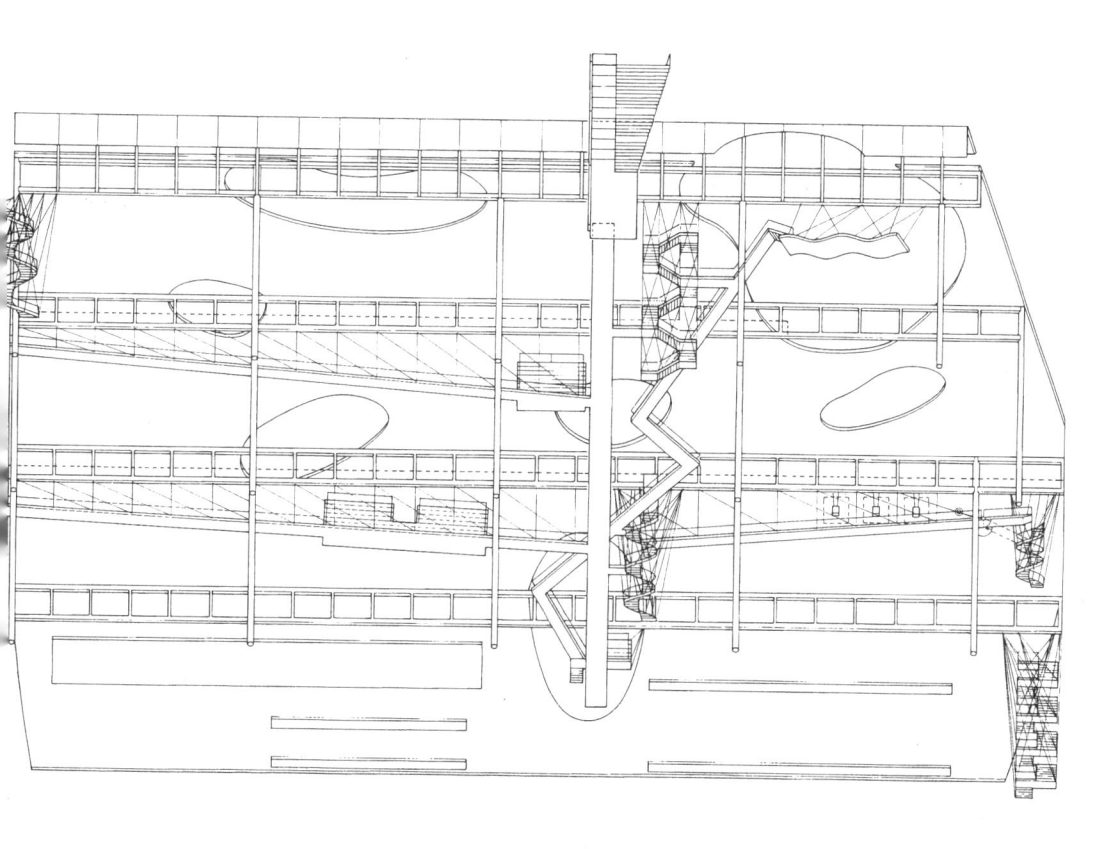

In-between. Underside of roof: exceeding any given formal configuration (catwalks, outdoor cinema, suspended garden, restaurant)

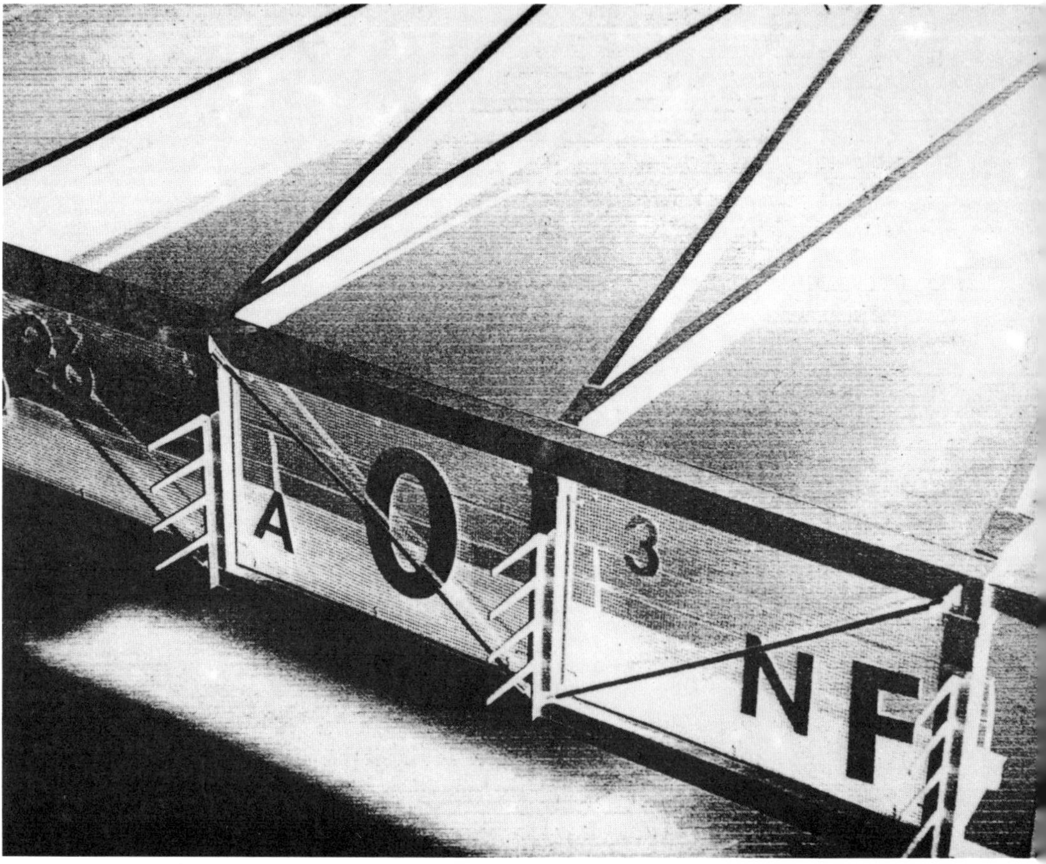
A
O
3
NF

Cinematic trusses: dematerialized structure

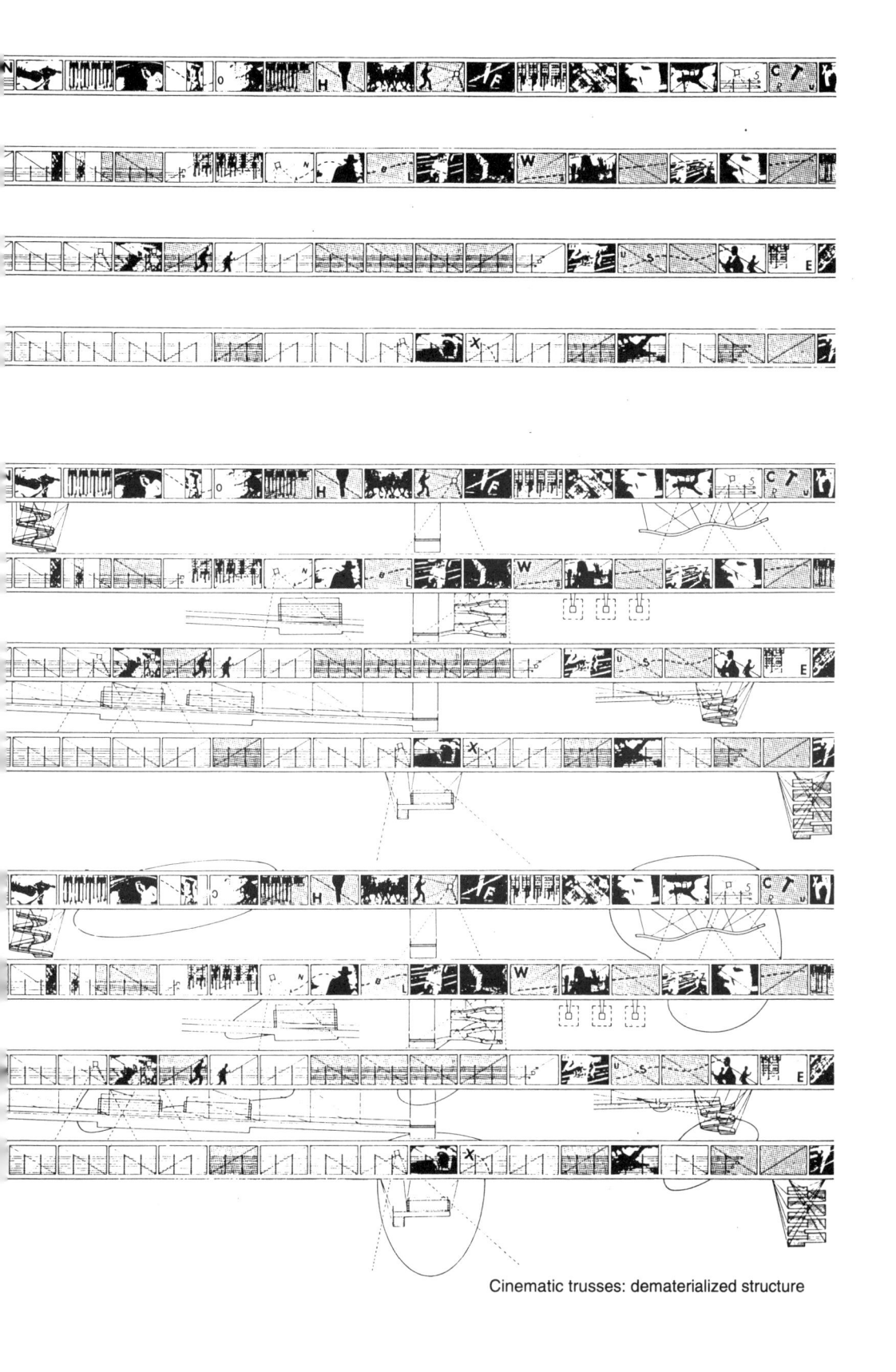

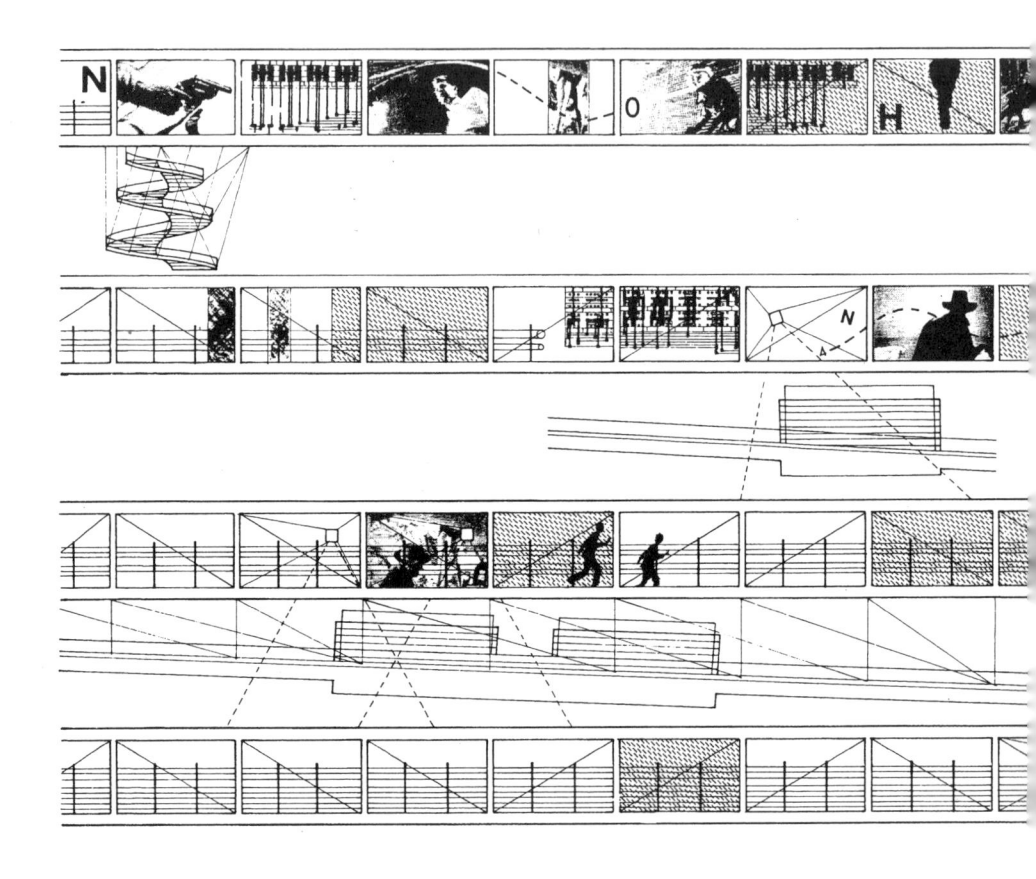

structural ->					mechanical ->

TOURCOING
415

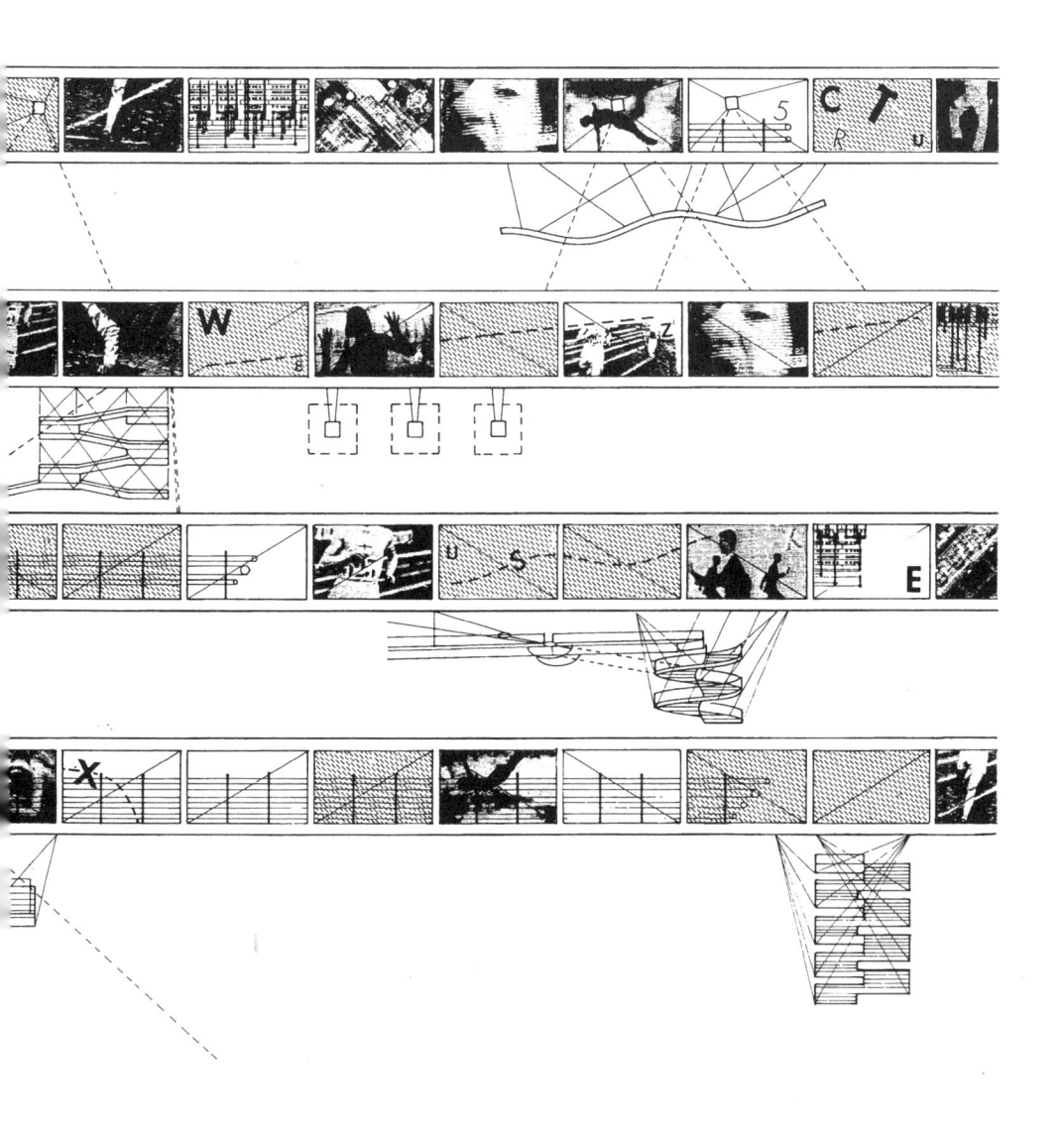

informational ->   electronic ->

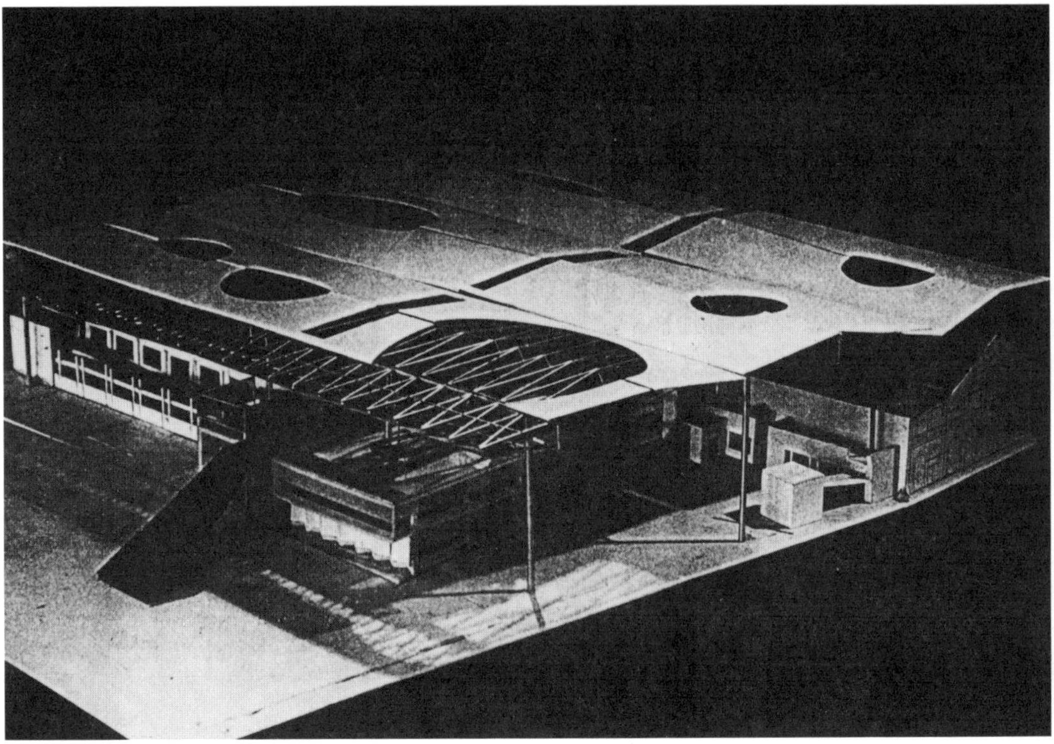

TOURCOING
417

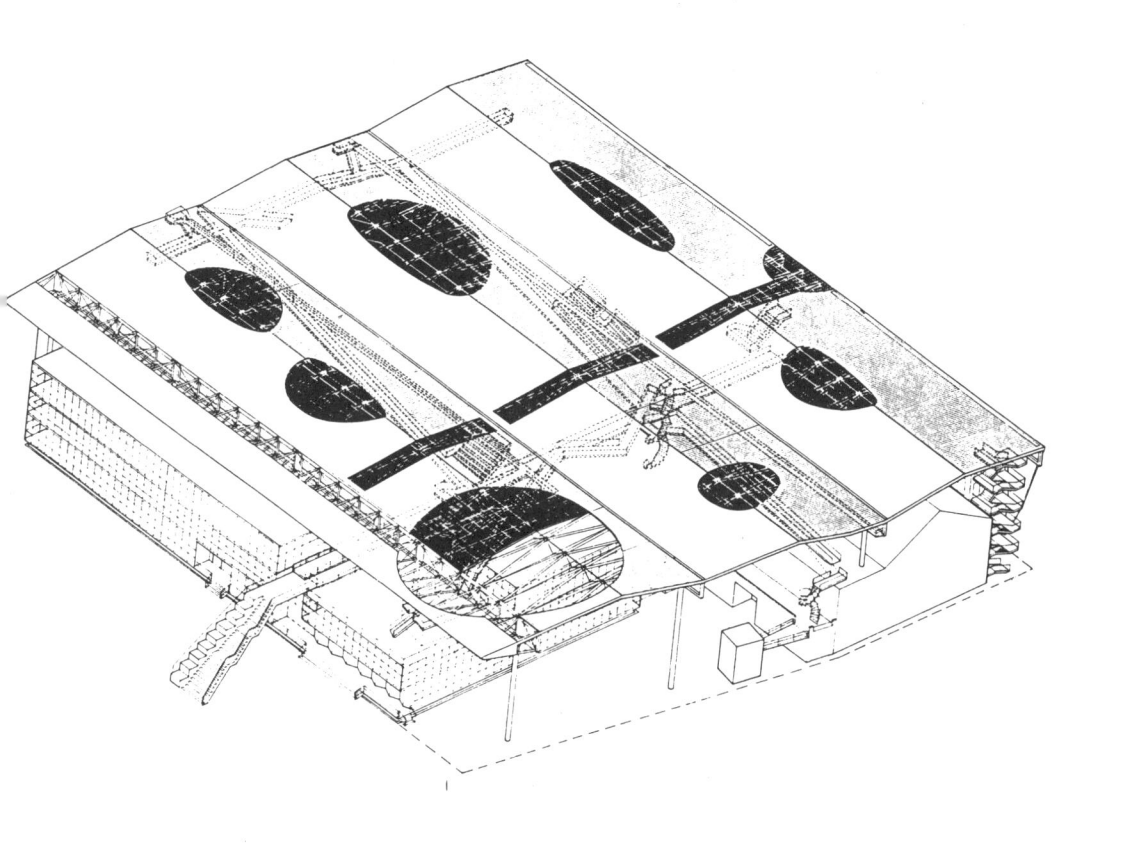

No collage, but cuts, partial enclosures, interior facades

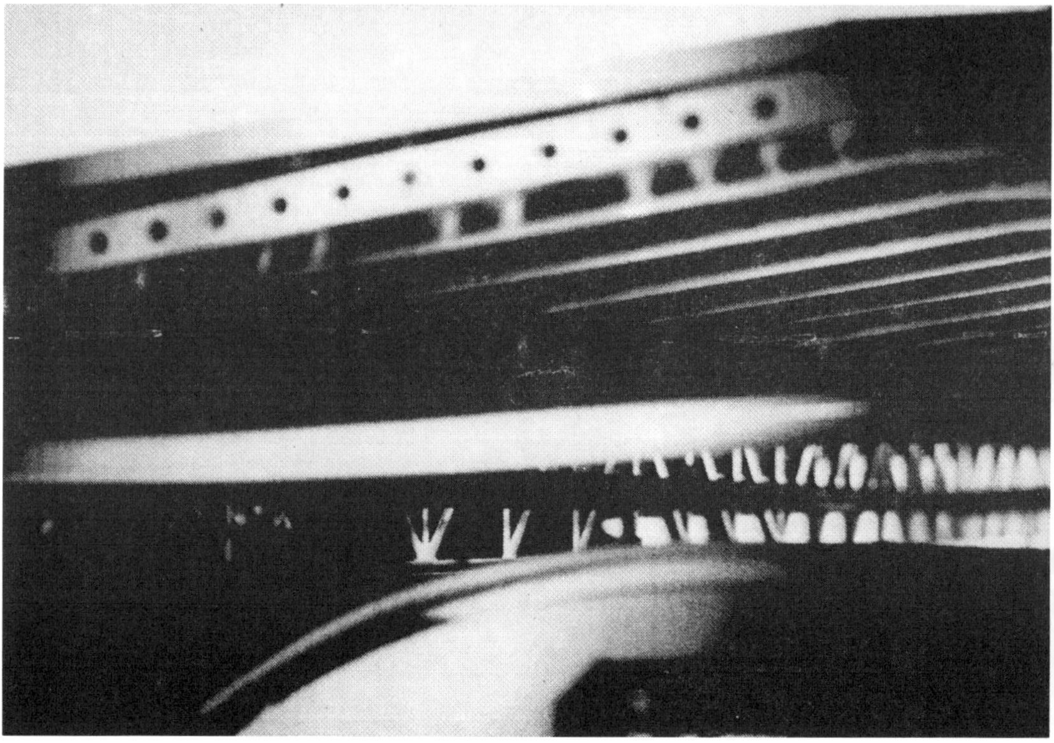

ANALOGIE VERRIÈRES
("NUAGES INVERSÉS")

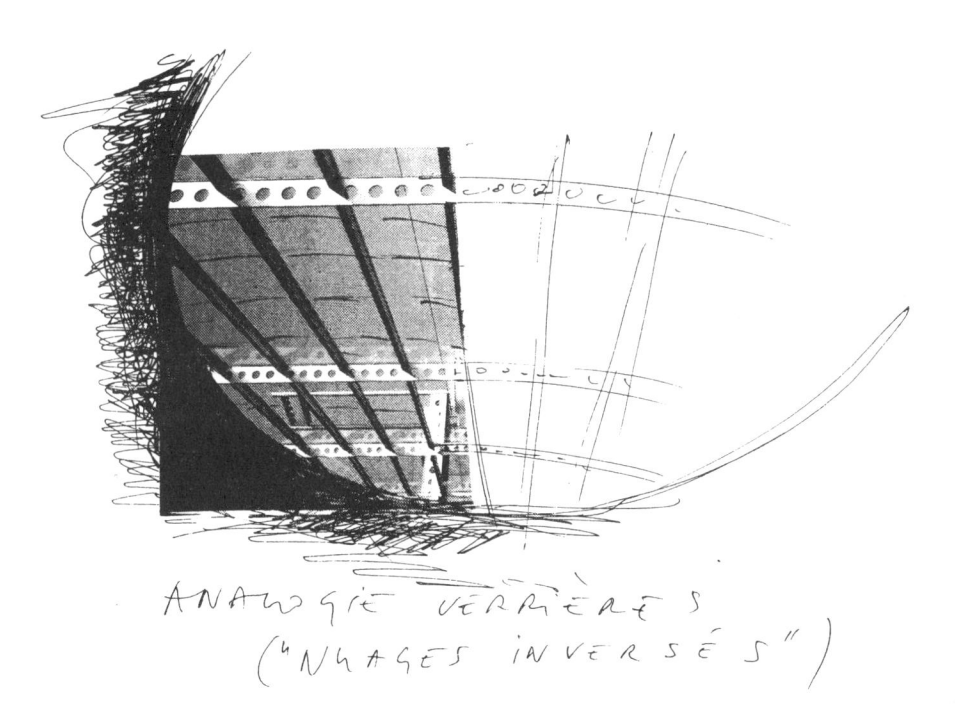

Inverted clouds: glass openings

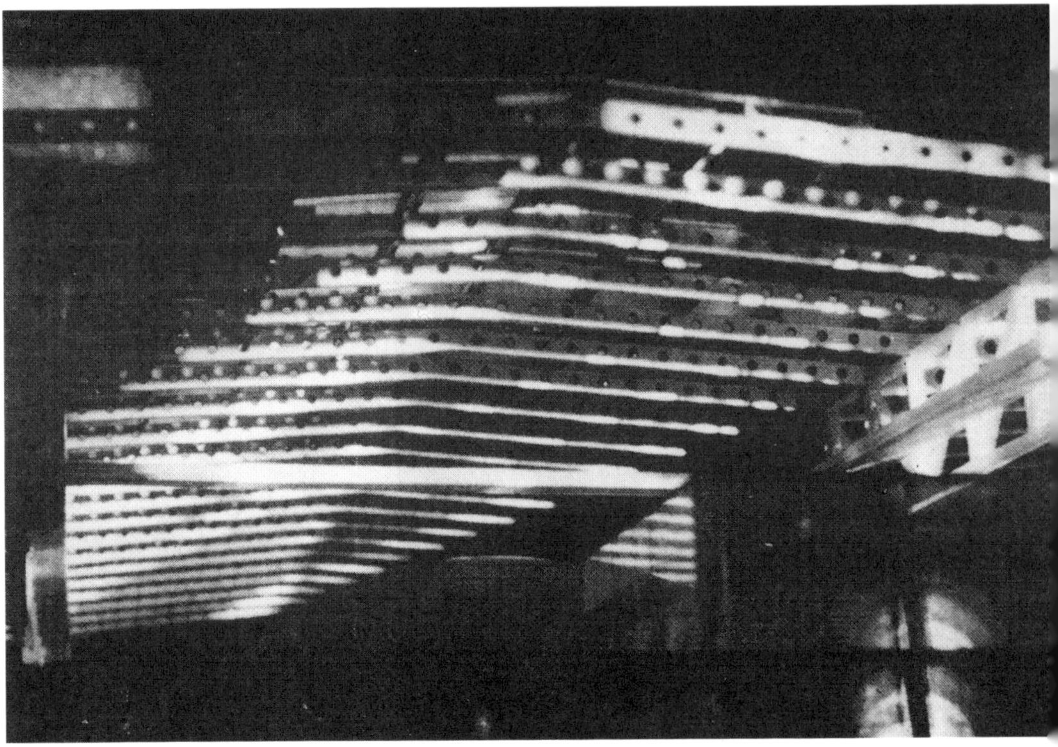

Artifi-ciel: simulated sky (Nietzsche's umbrella)

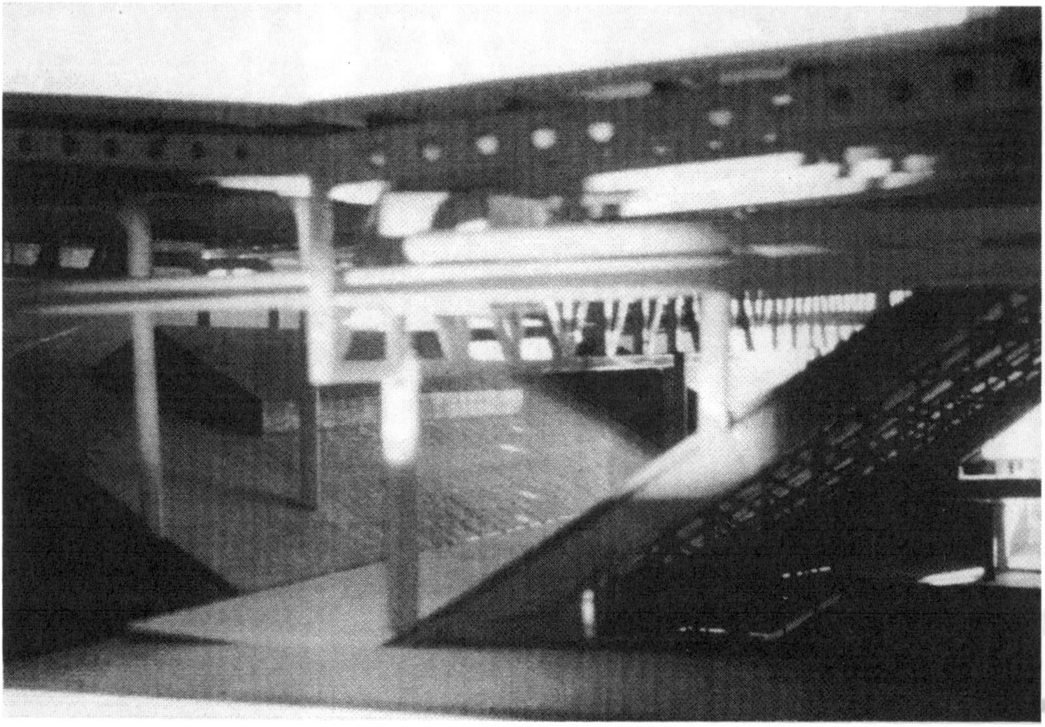

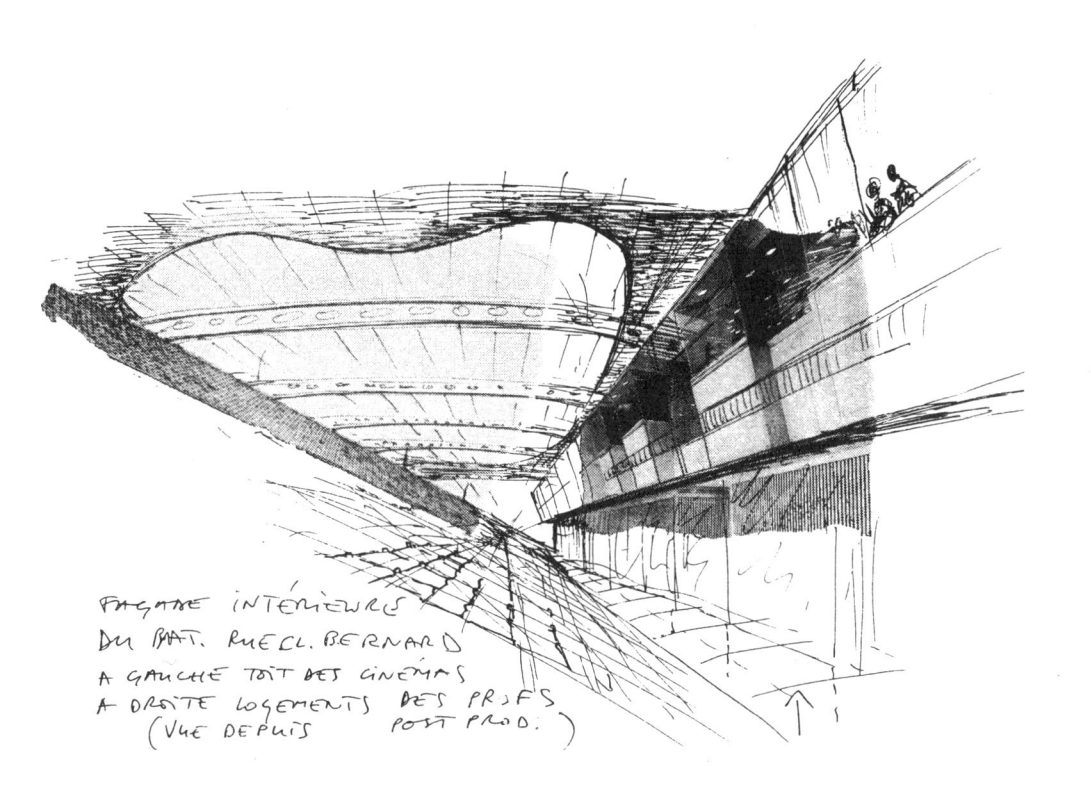

North interior facade: left, cinema roof; right, housing

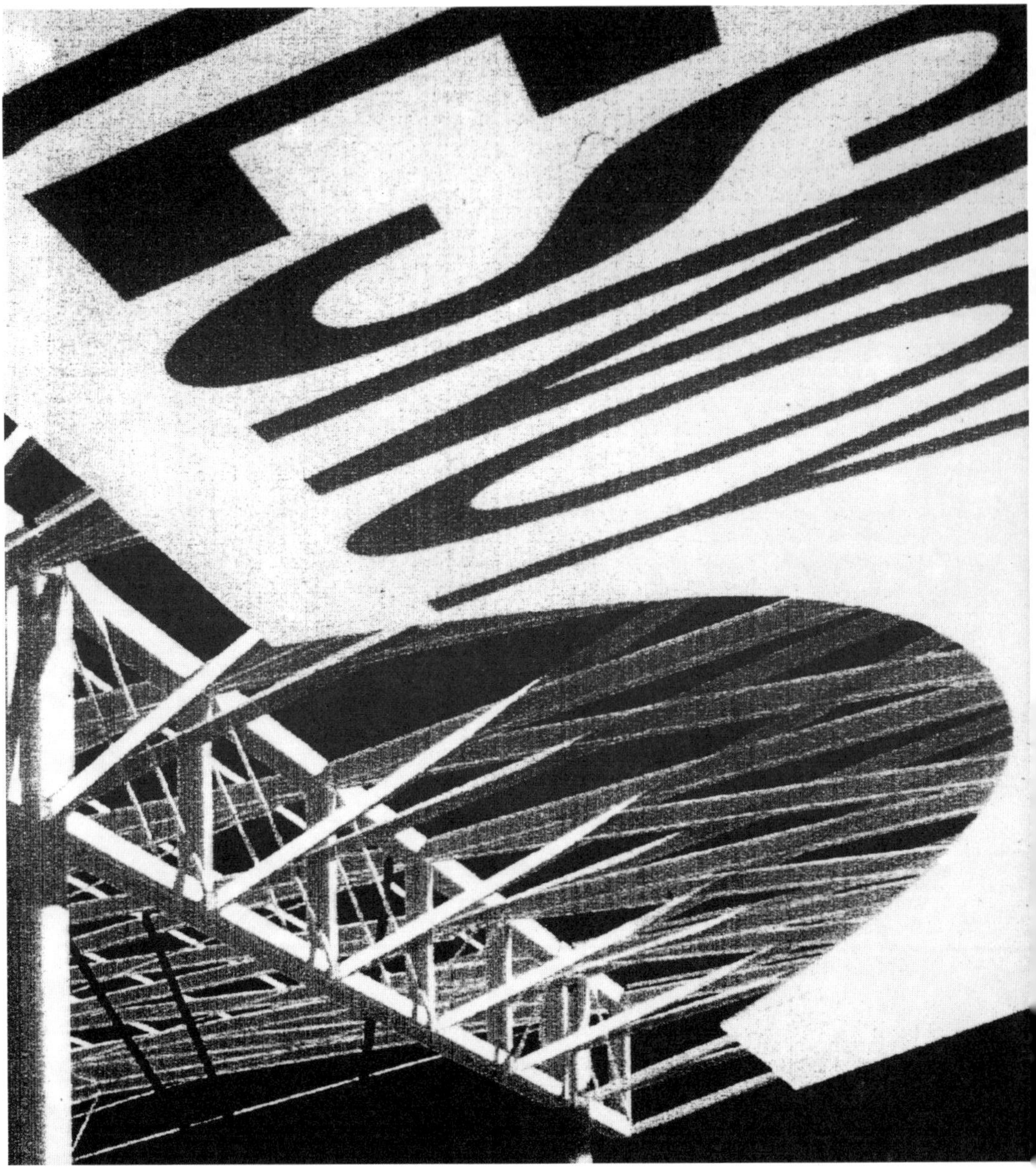

In-between: terrace and restaurant

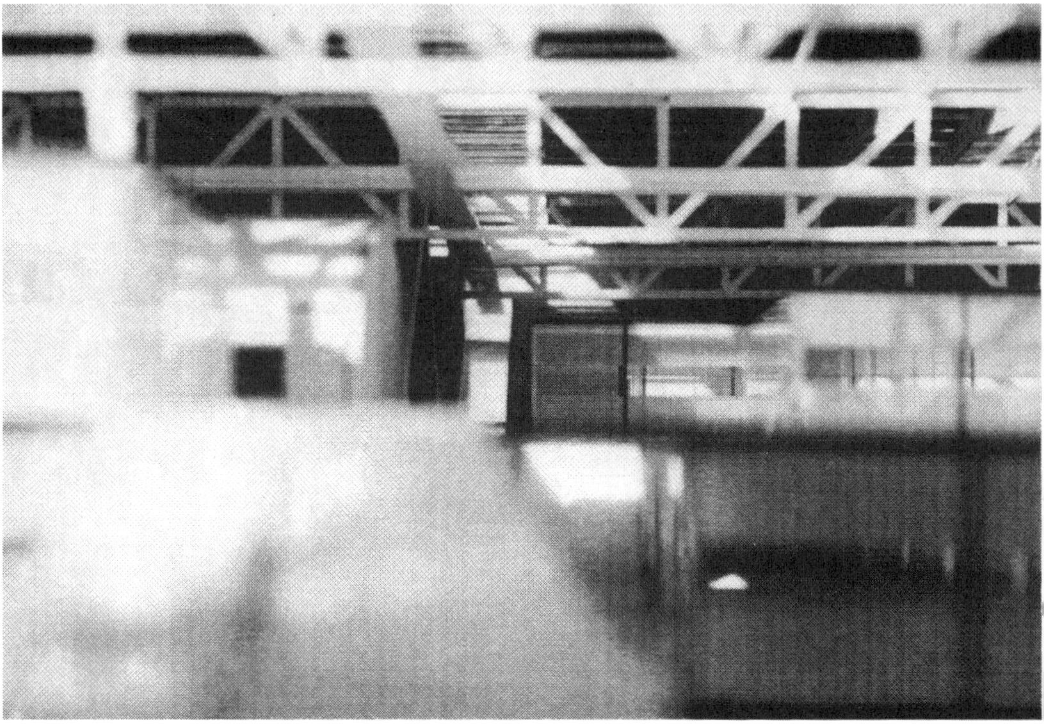

ANALOGIE
SOUS-FACE DU GRAND TOIT
GALERIES TECHNIQUES (POÉTIQUES)
ÉCLAIRAGE — TRAITEMENT D'AIR

Heating, ventilation, air-conditioning ducts, suspended walkways

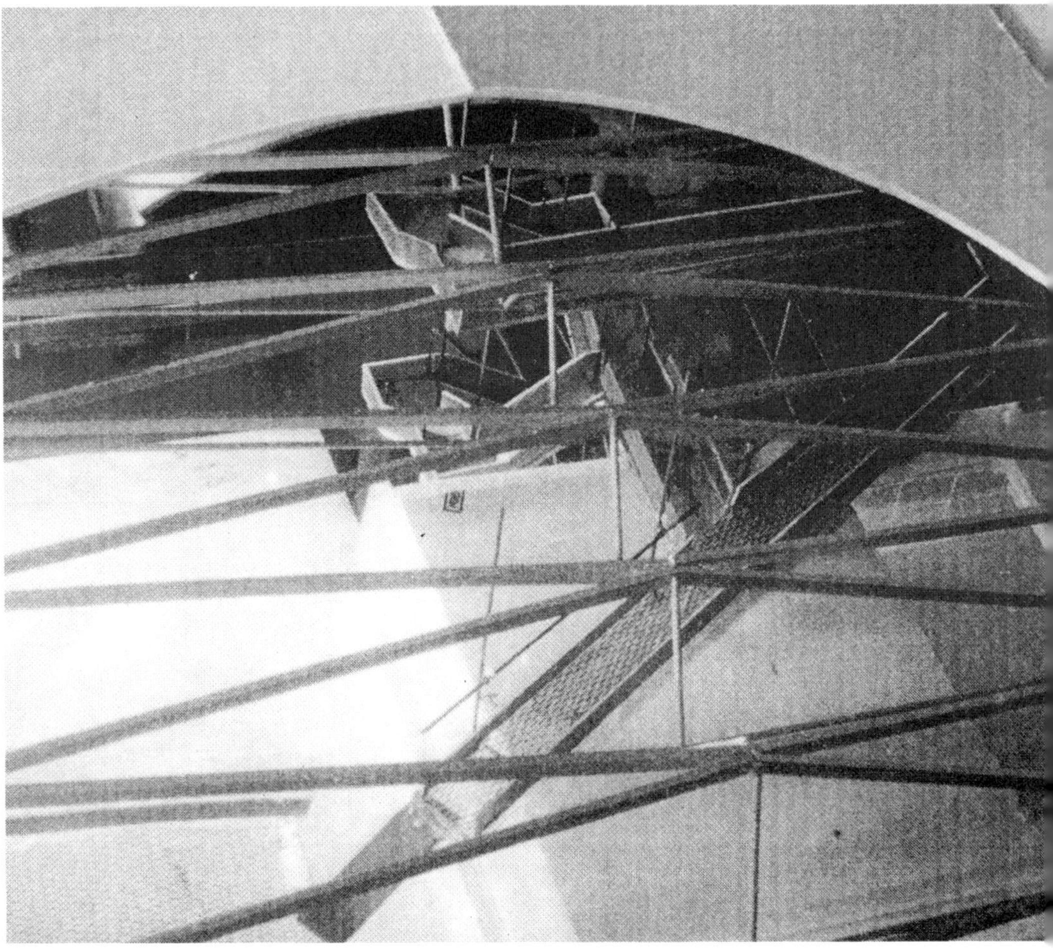

VUE VERS ENTRÉE
VERSION "BORD D'ATTAQUE" DU TOIT EN ROUGE

RUE DU FRESNOY

View towards entrance

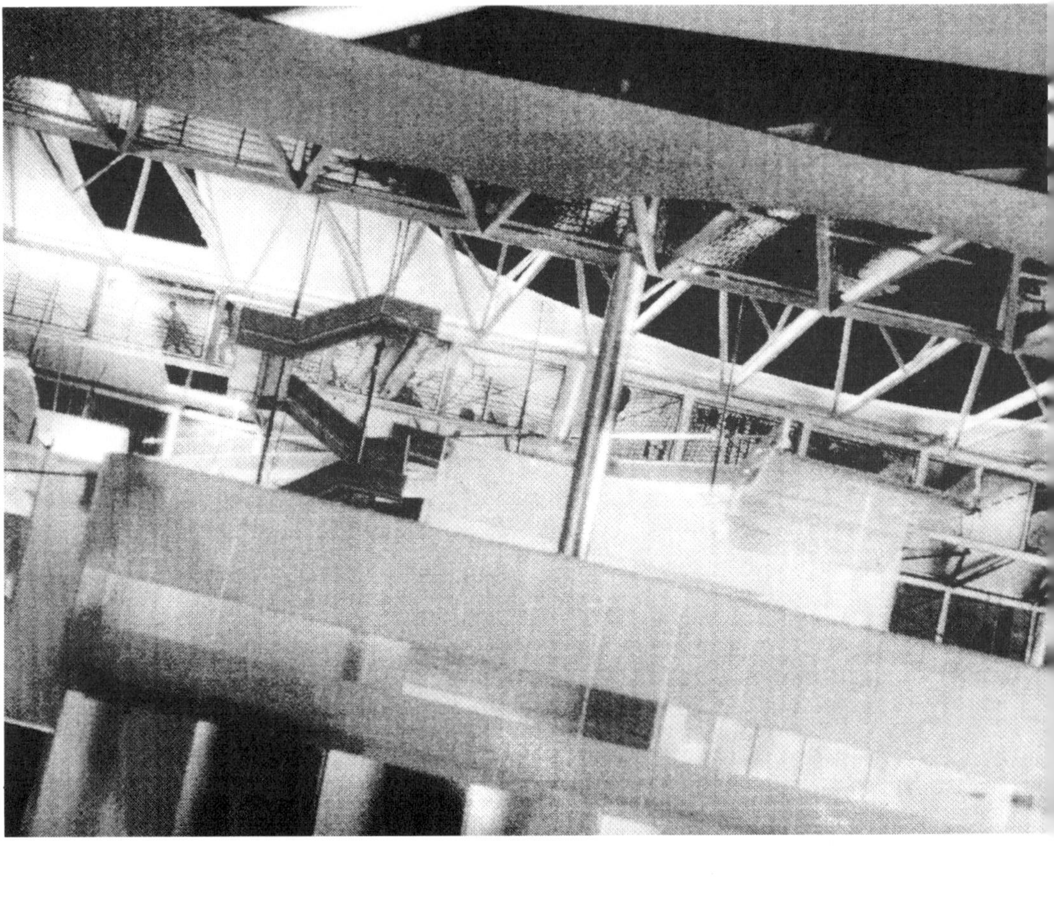

TOURCOING
431

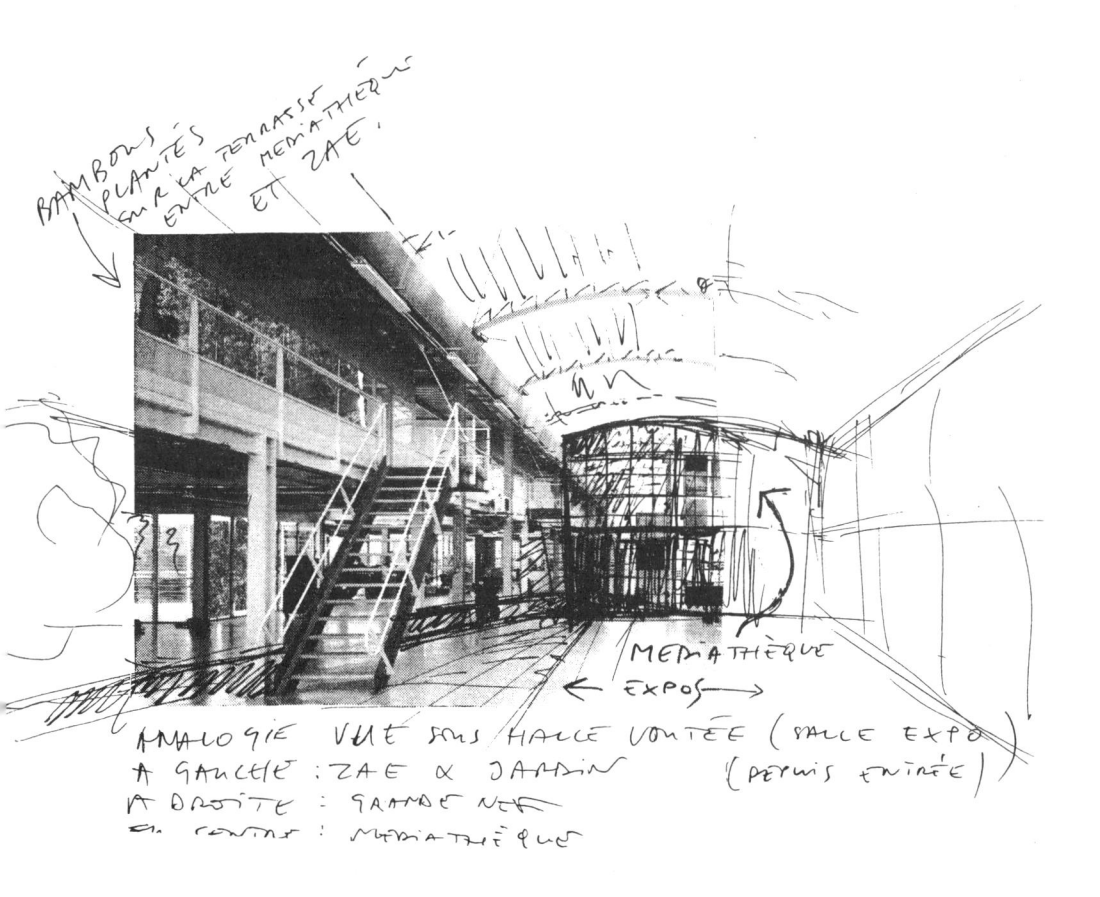

BAMBOUS PLANTÉS SUR LA TERRASSE ENTRE MÉDIATHÈQUE ET ZAE.

MÉDIATHÈQUE
← EXPOS →

ANALOGIE VUE SOUS HALLE VOUTÉE (SALLE EXPO)
A GAUCHE : ZAE & JARDIN   (PERMIS ENTRÉE)
A DROITE : GRANDE NEF
AU CENTRE : MÉDIATHÈQUE

Exhibition hall and media library

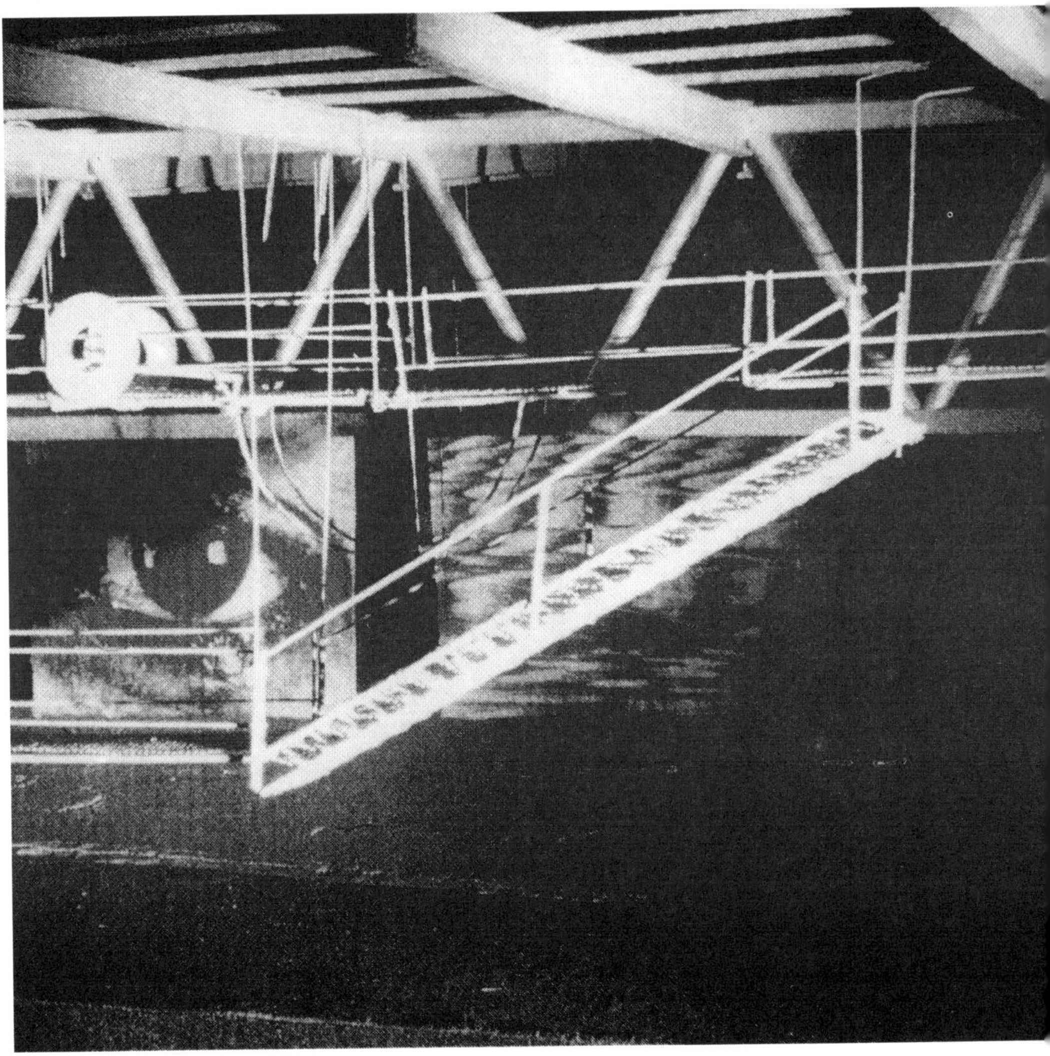

Shock of images and surprise factor: open-air cinema in in-between

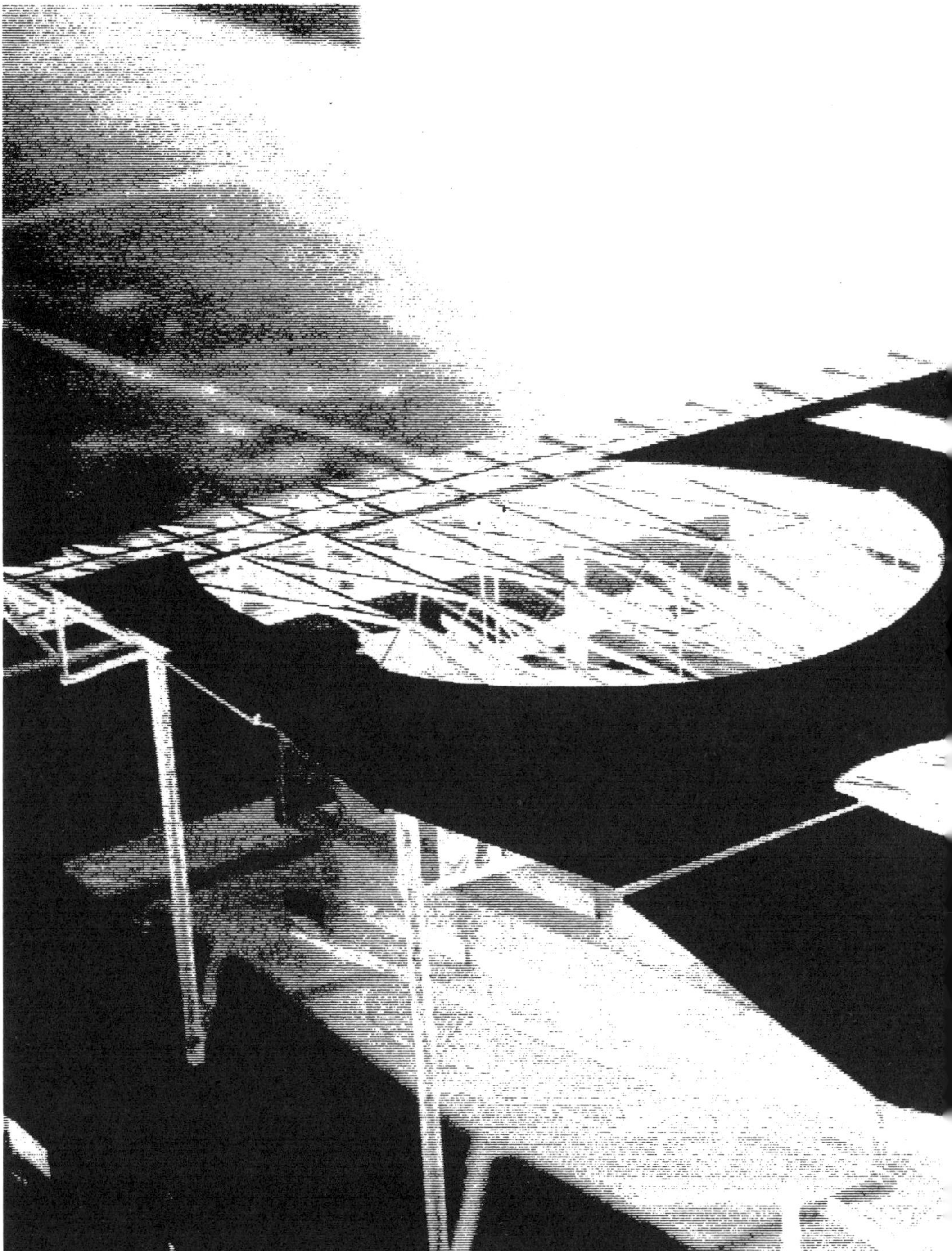

TOURCOING
435

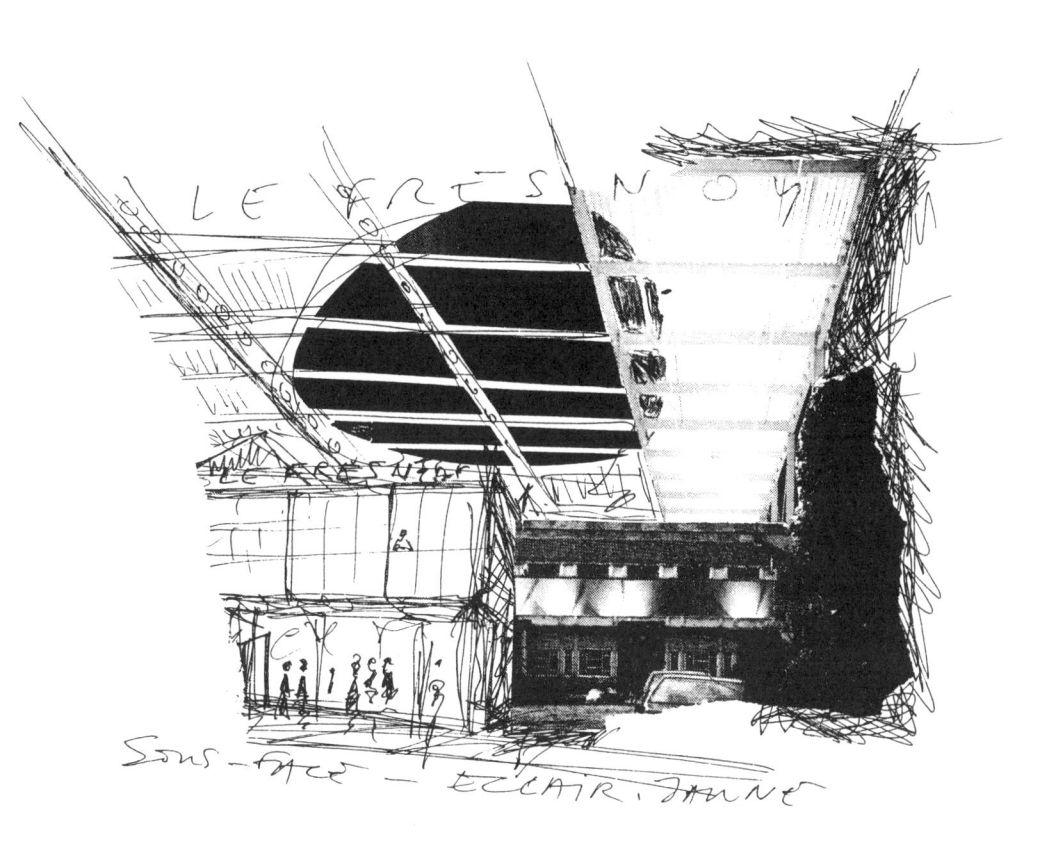

A mode of spacing that gives its place to events

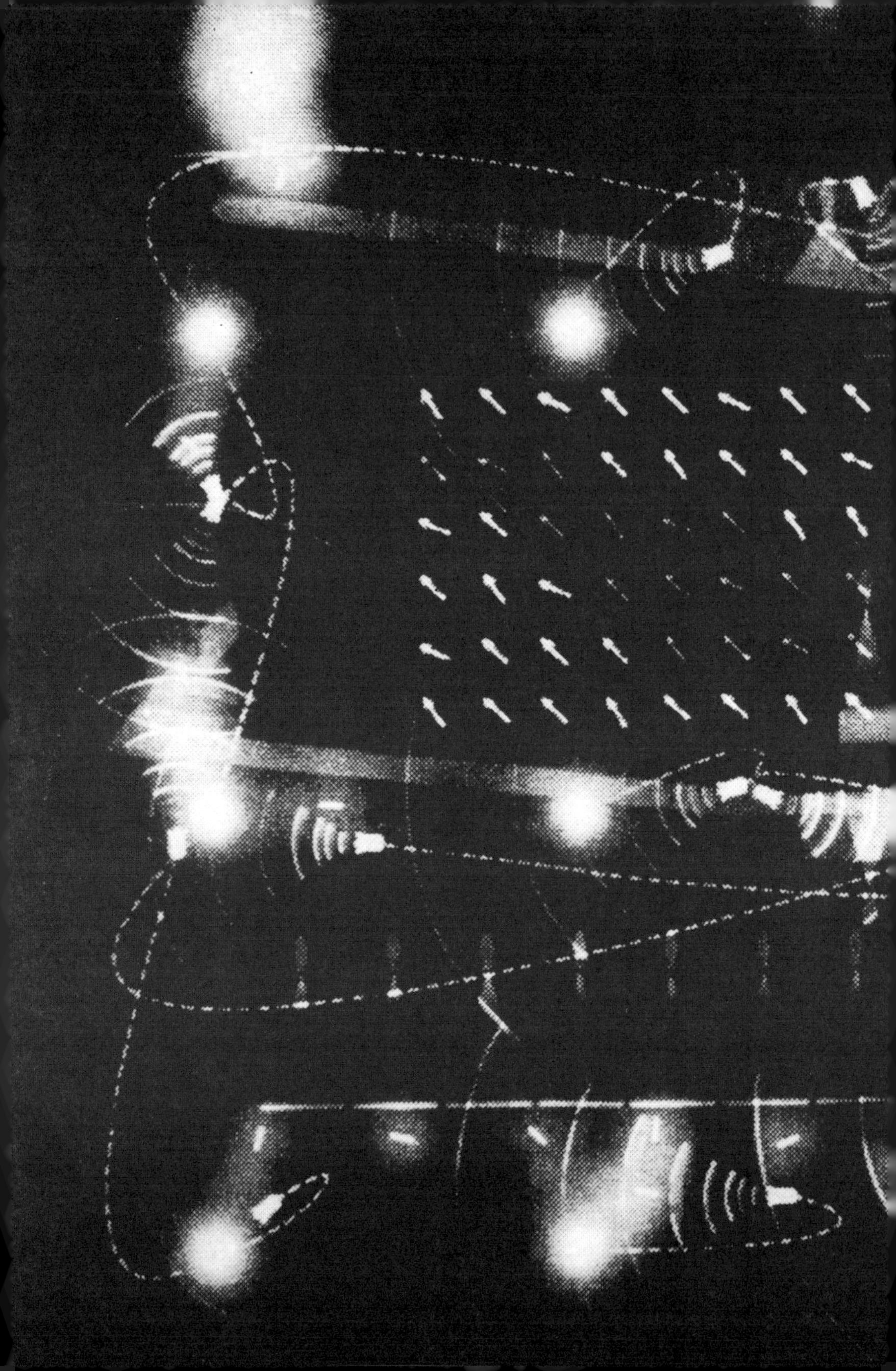

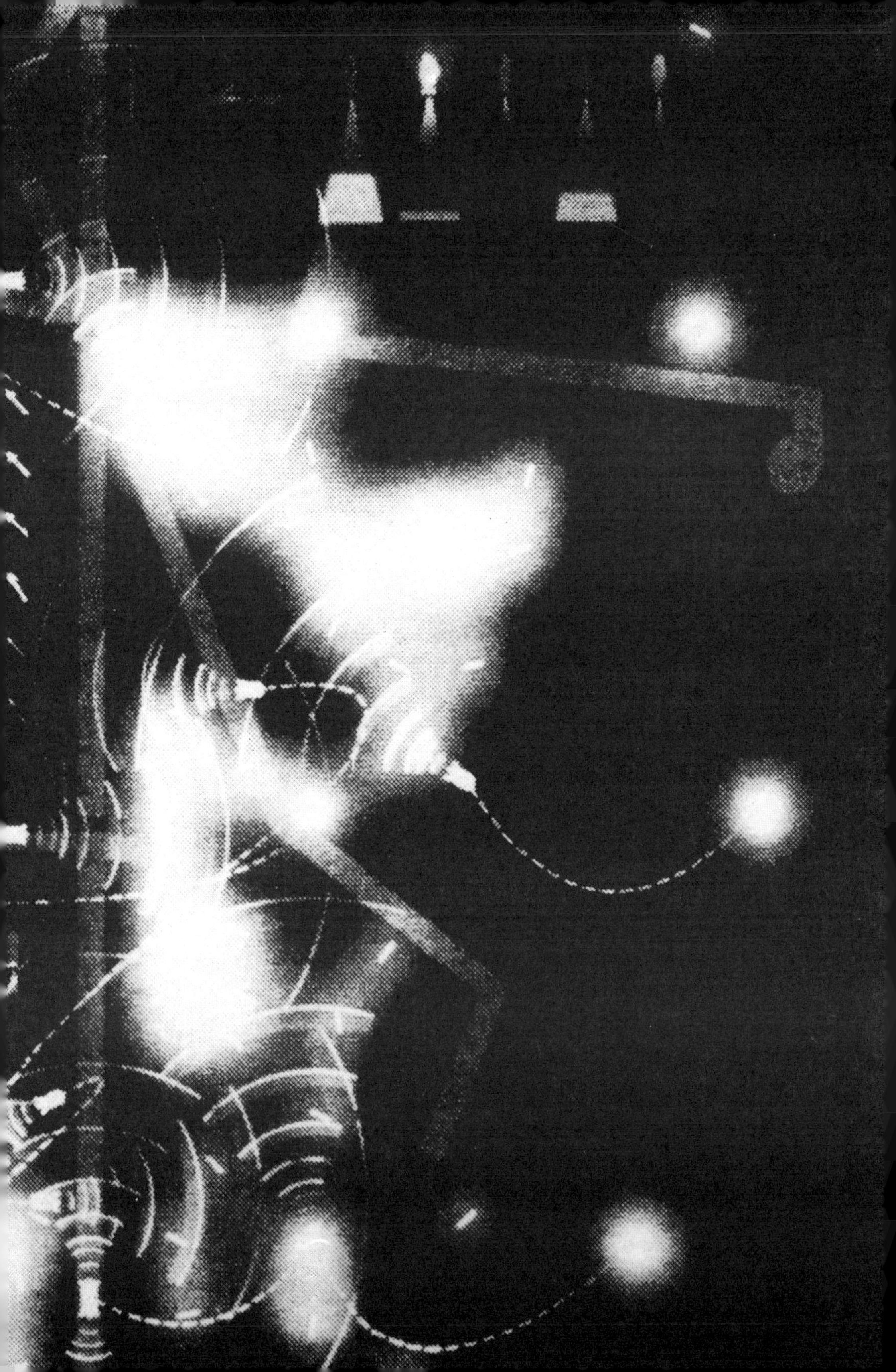

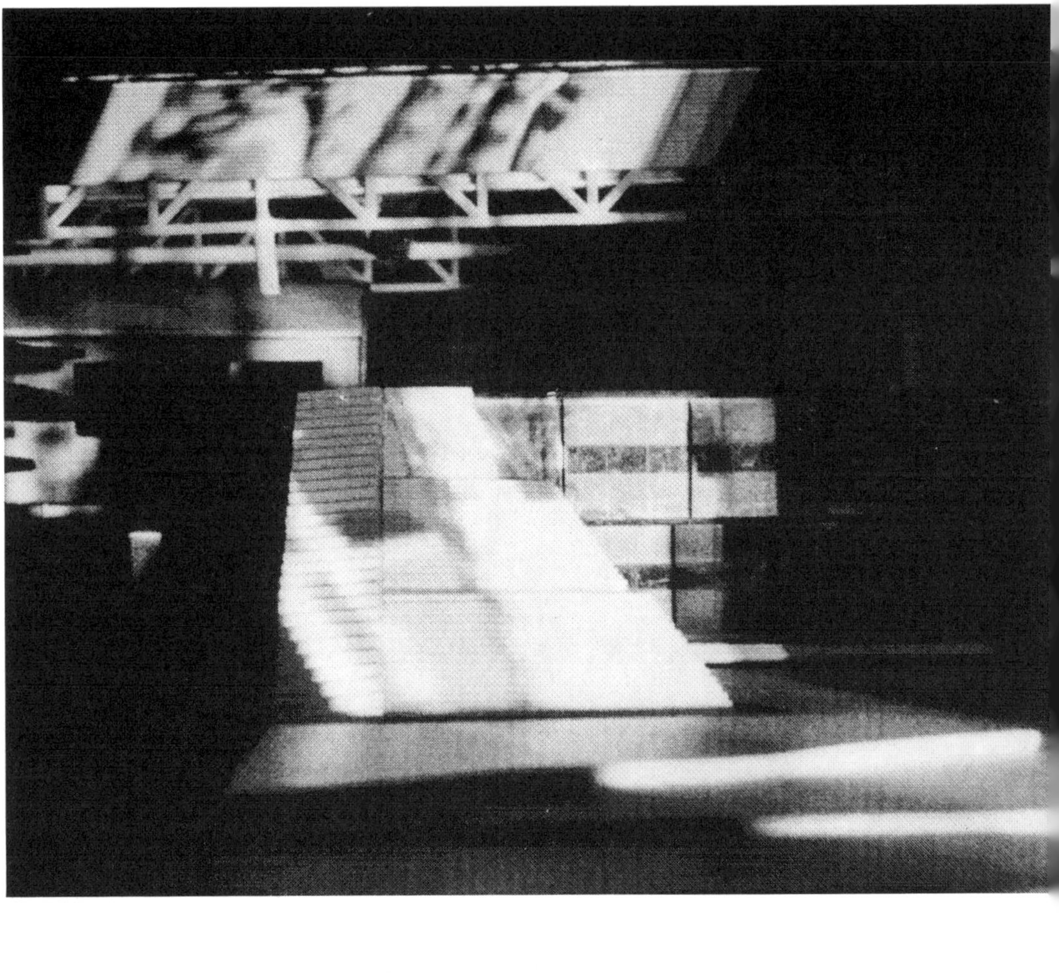

TOURCOING
439

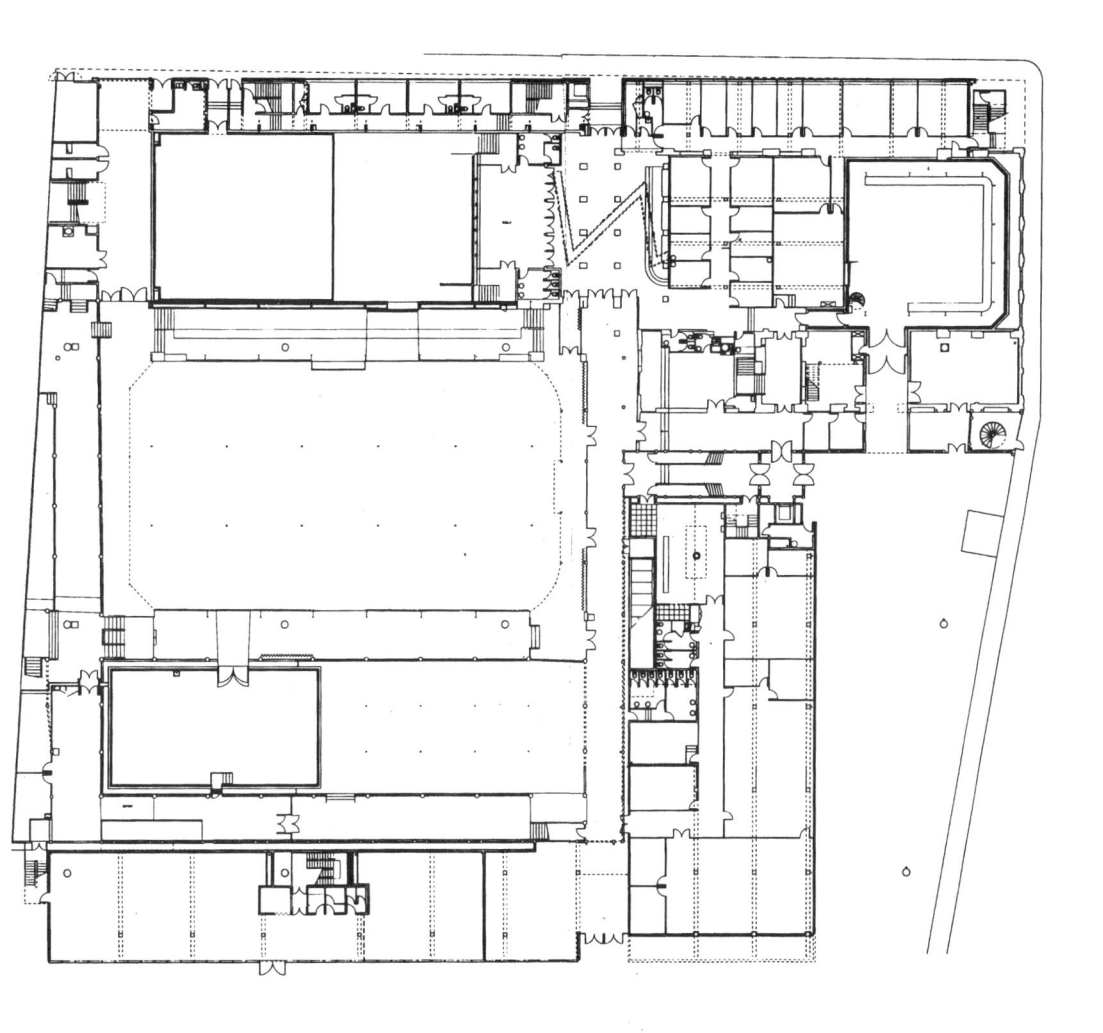

Ground level +0.00: entrance lobby, bookshop, school, exhibition hall, performance hall, workshops, cinemas, bar, video and film studios

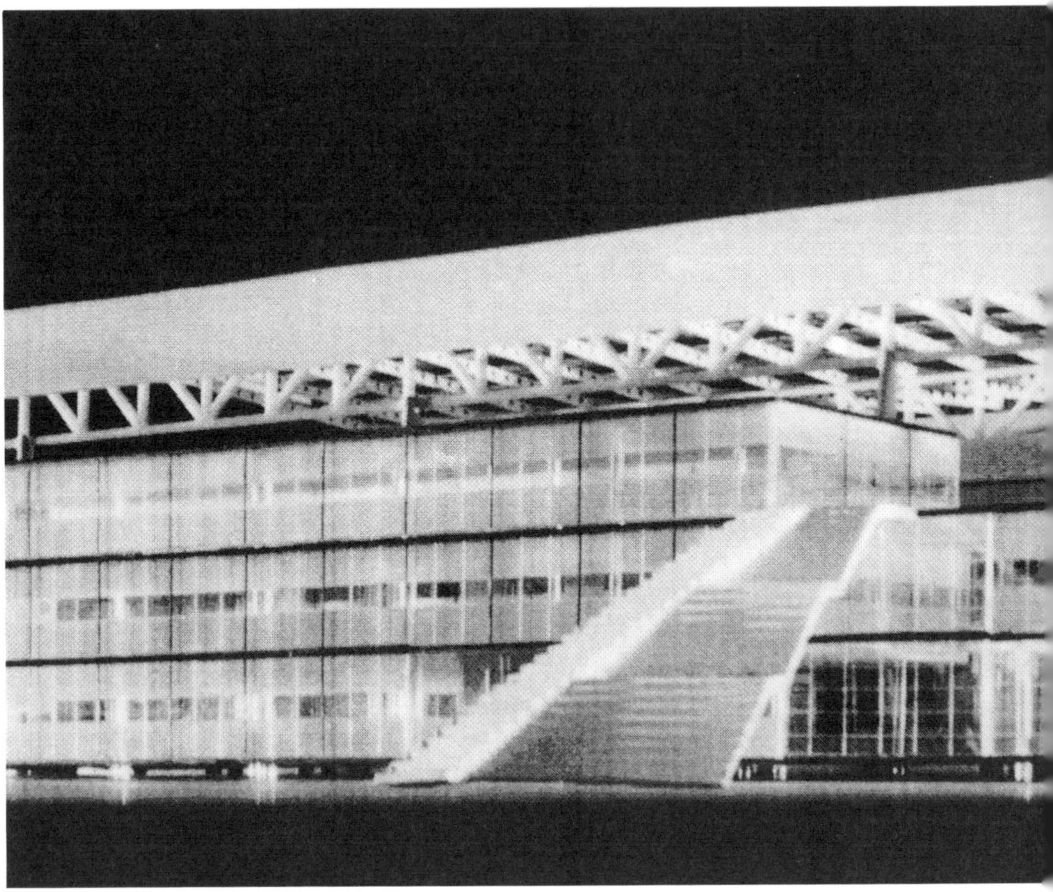

TOURCOING
441

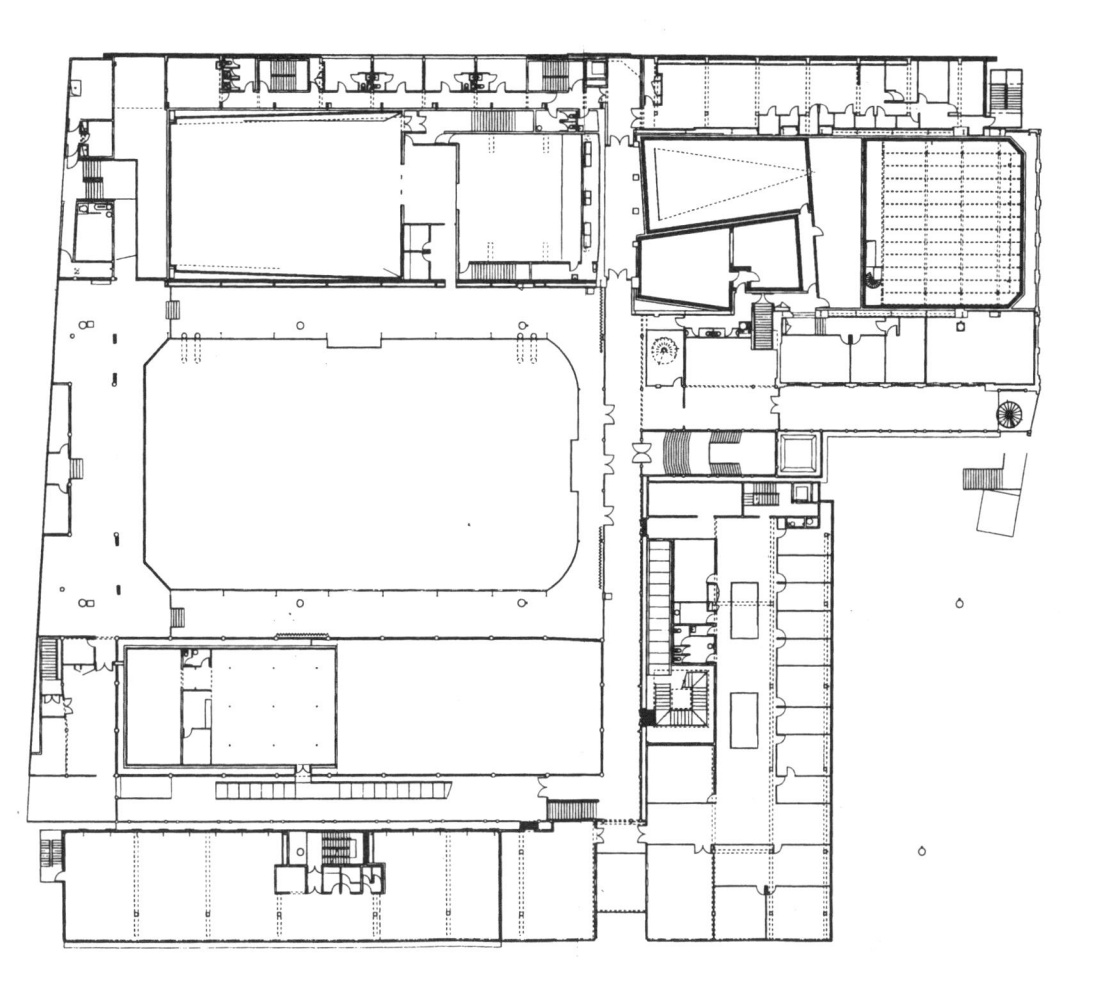

Level +3.74: media library, administration, mezzanines,
cinemas, photography studio, sound studios, cutting rooms, student housing

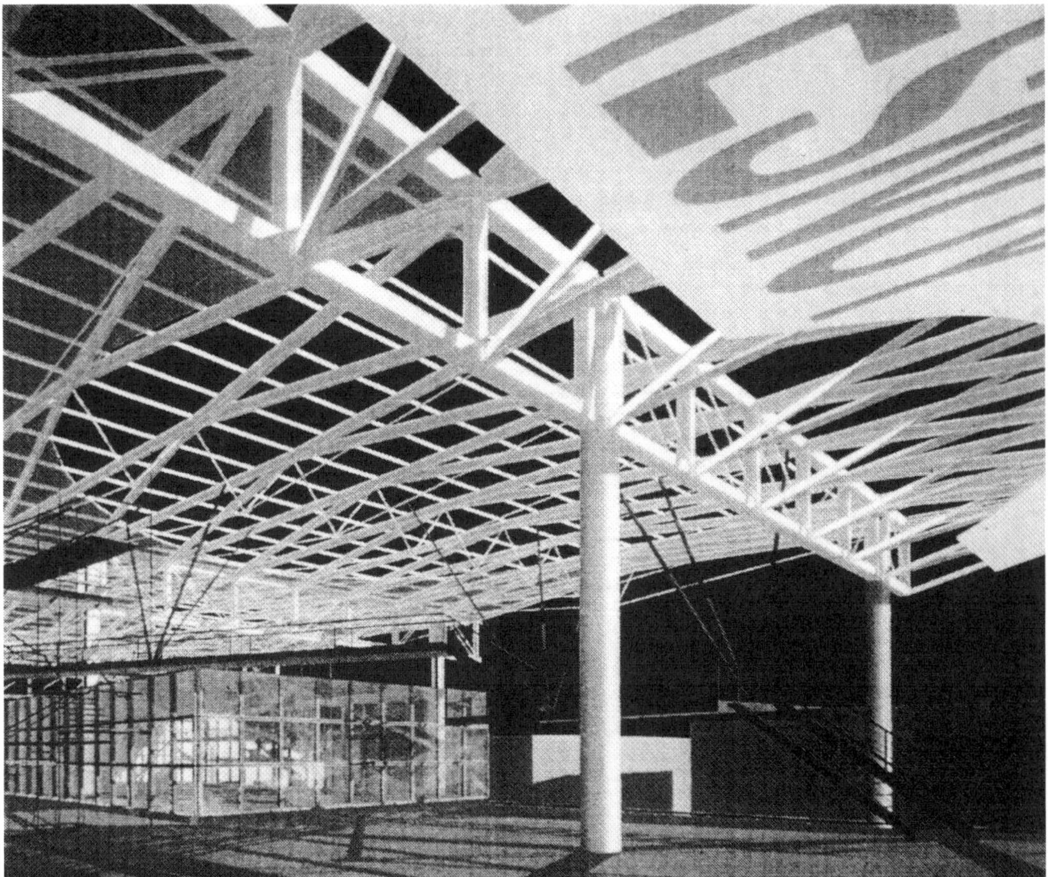

TOURCOING
443

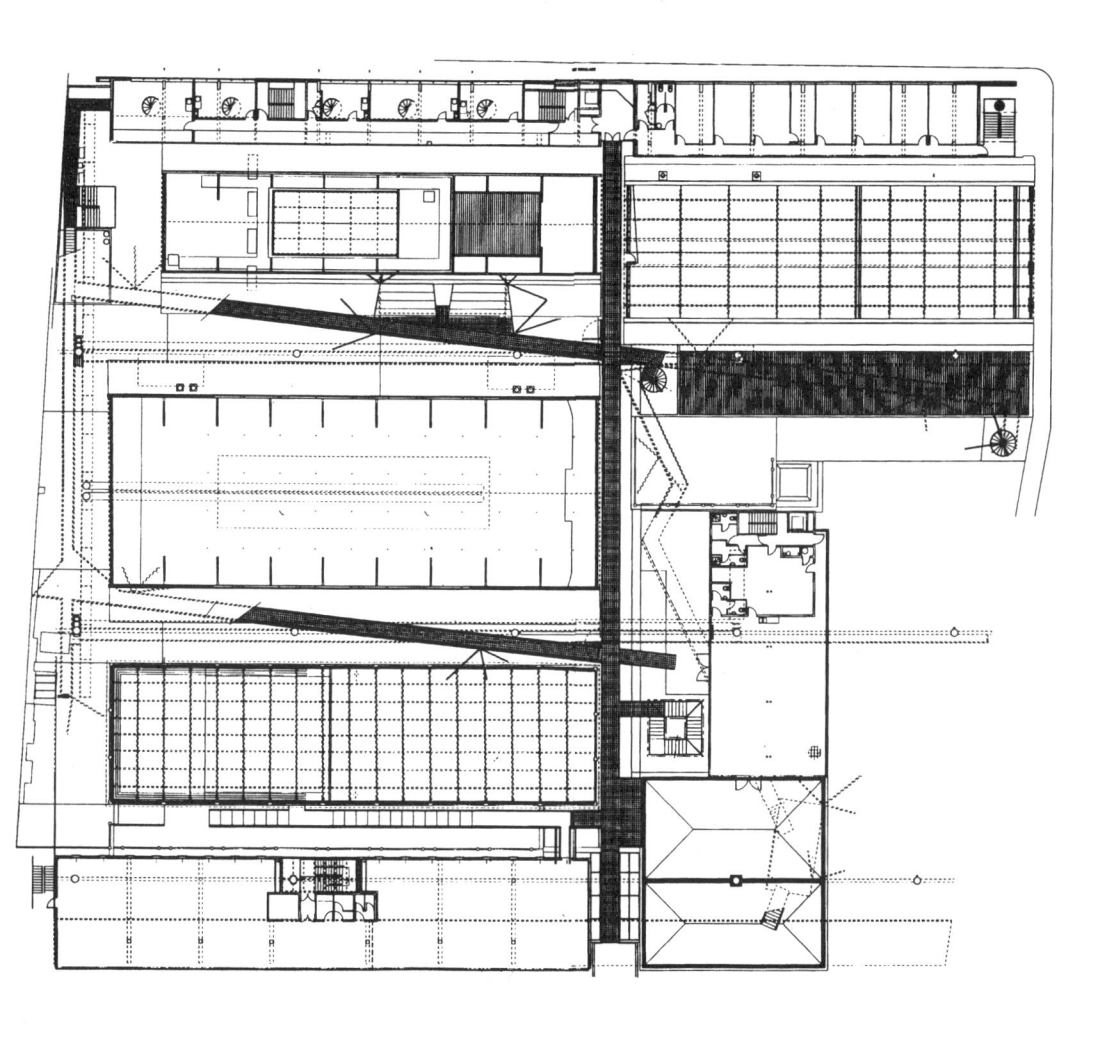

Level +7.43: in-between; restaurant, bar, exhibition spaces, open air cinema, faculty apartments

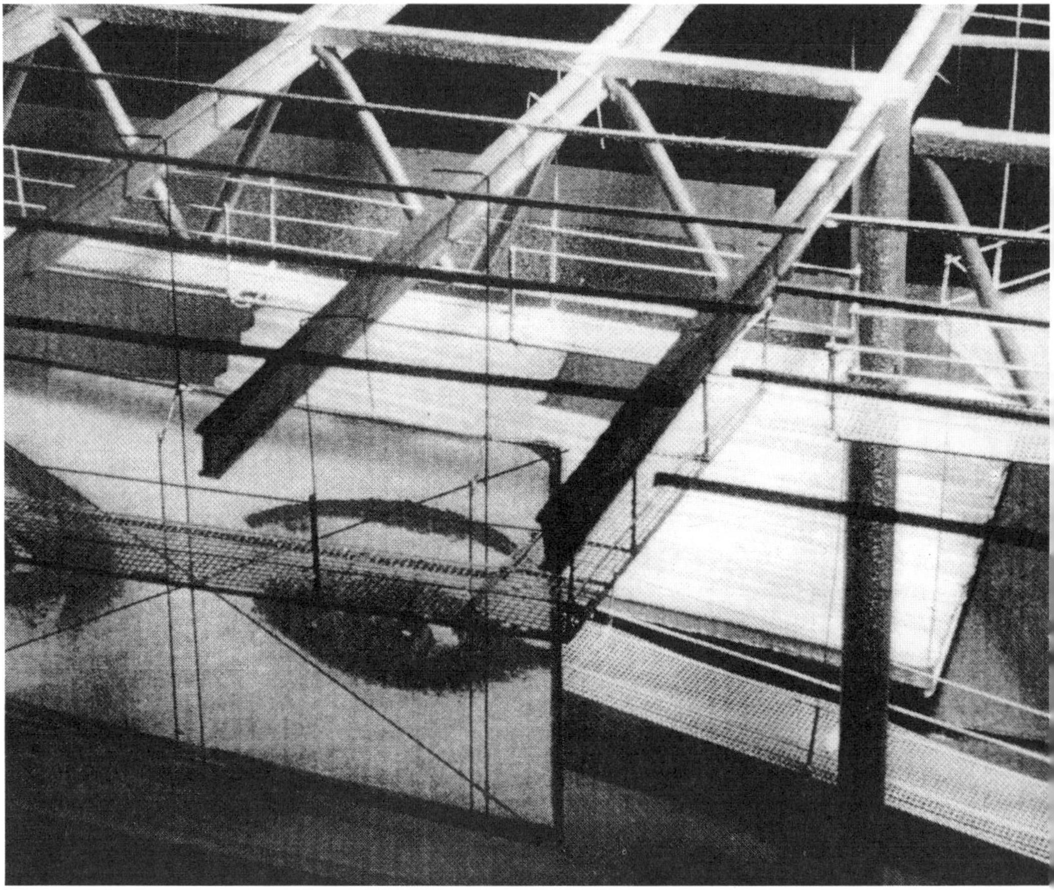

TOURCOING
445

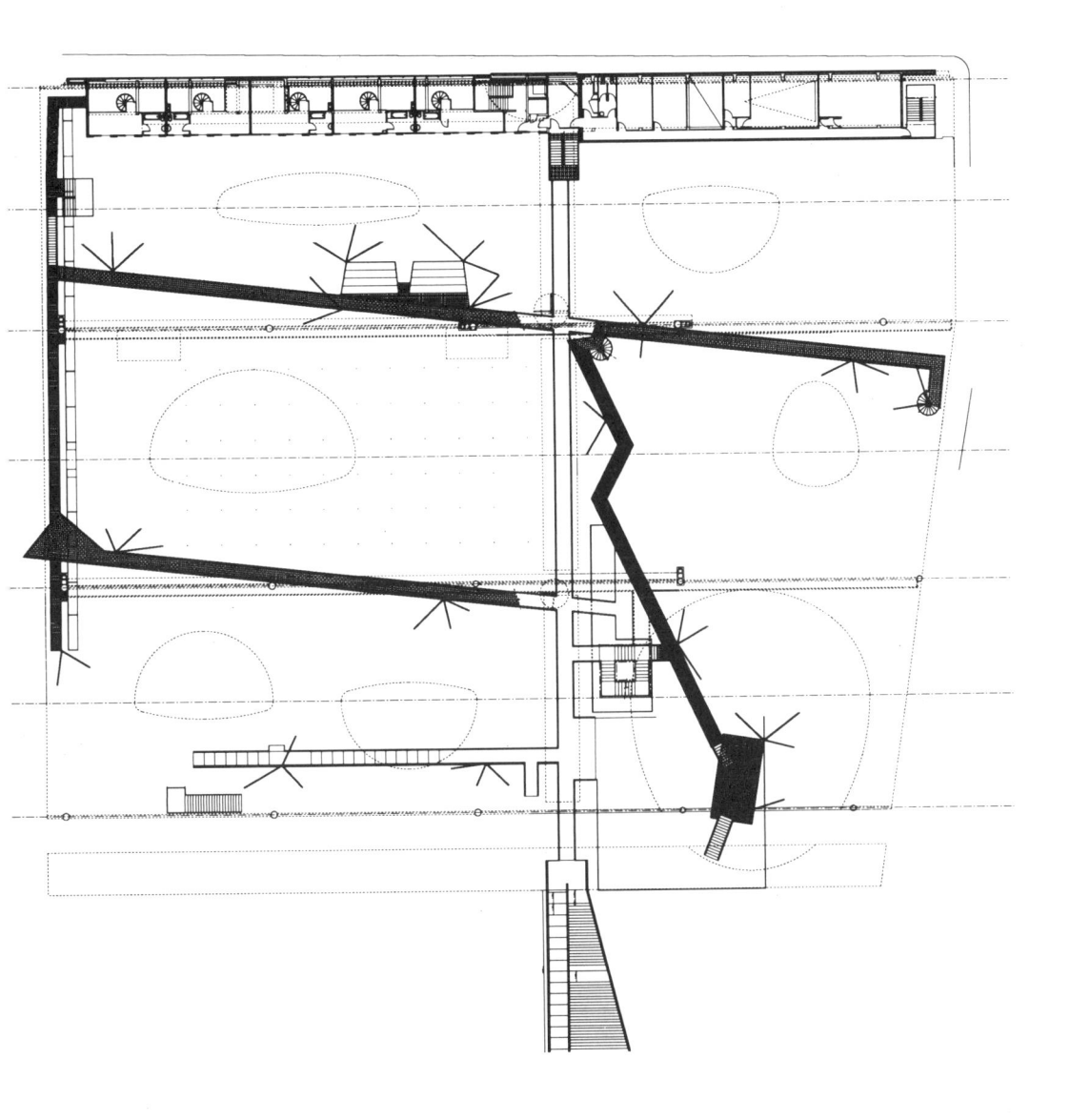

Catwalk level: in-between; catwalks, suspended video garden, suspended open-air cinema, residences and cutting rooms

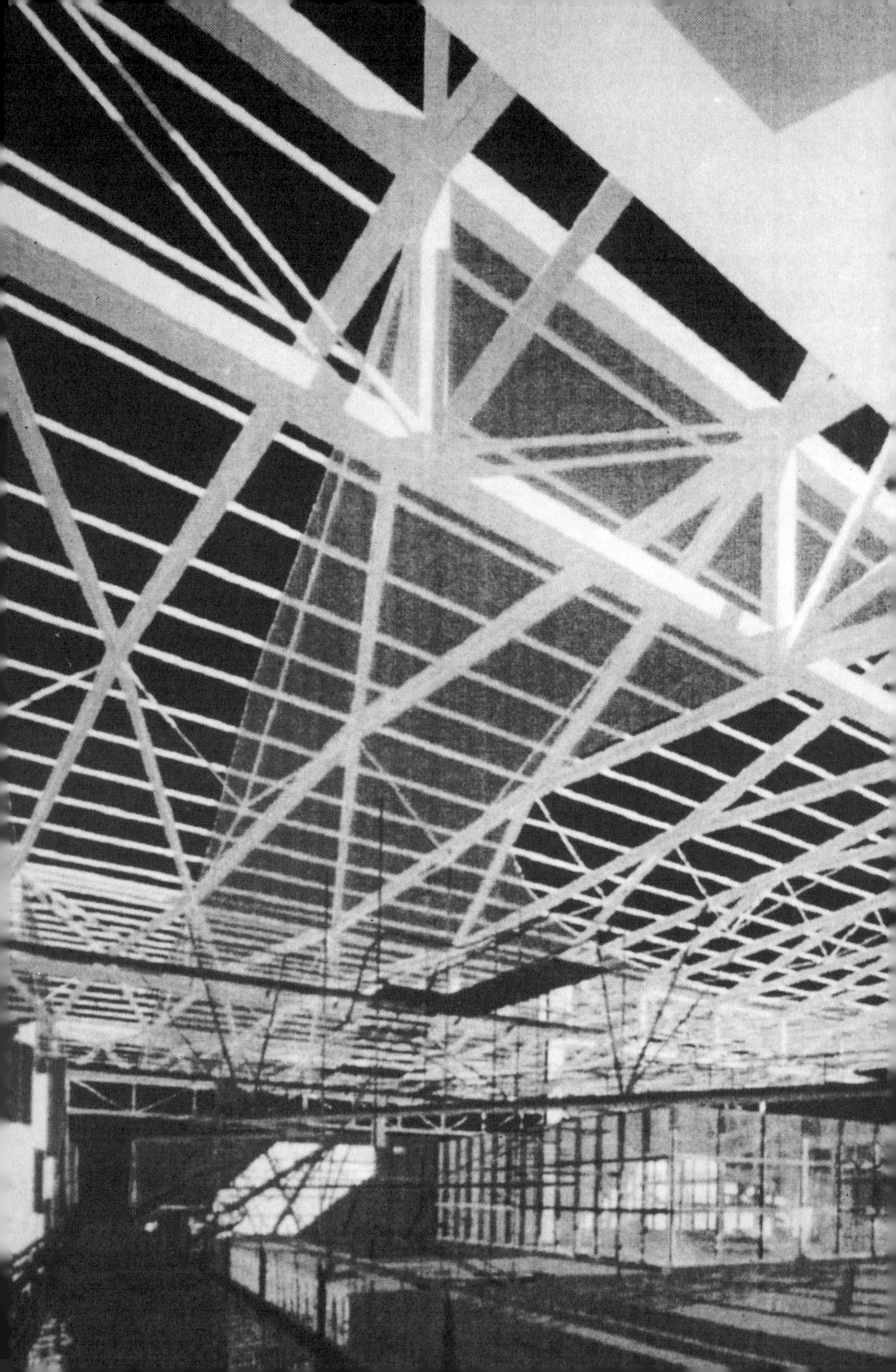

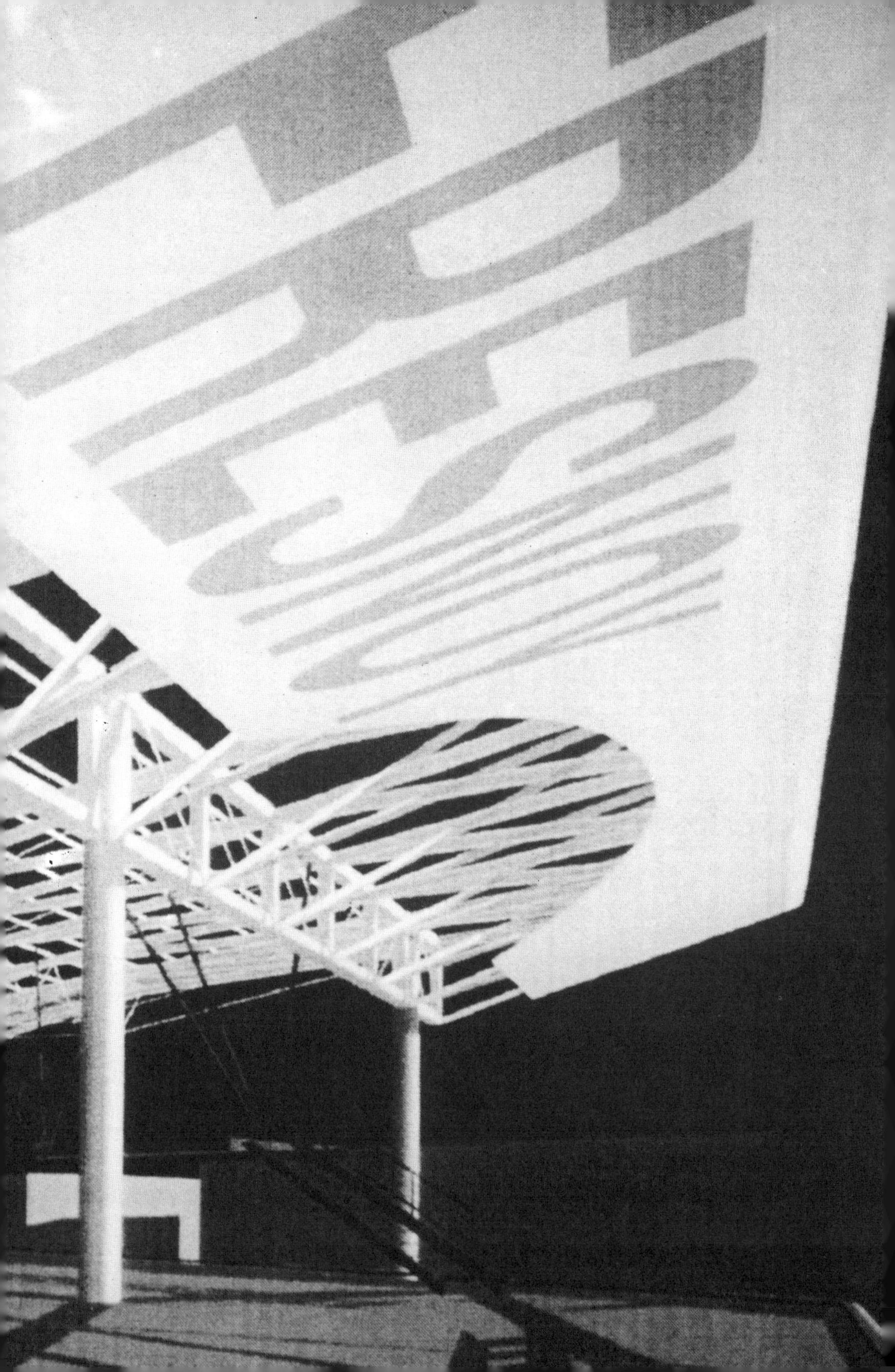

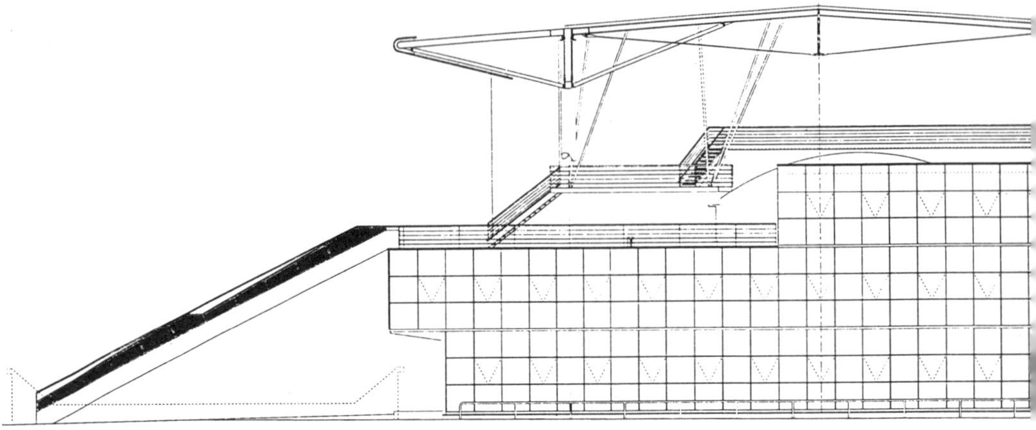

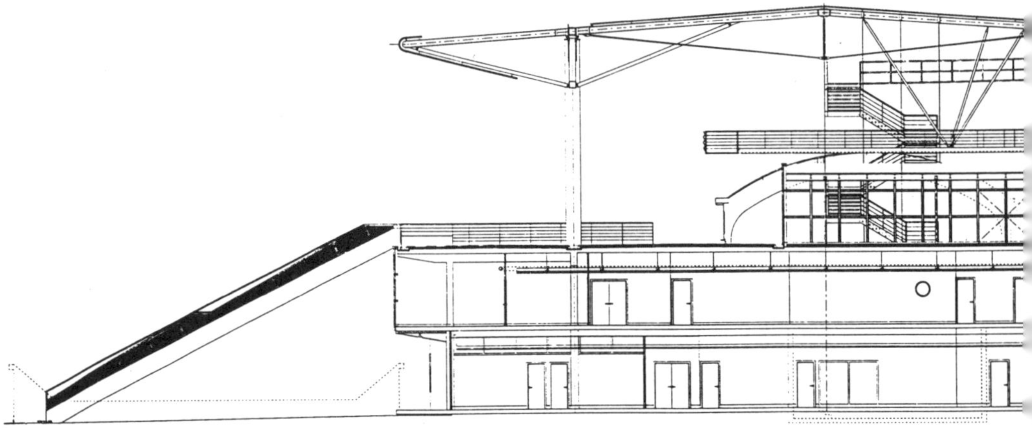

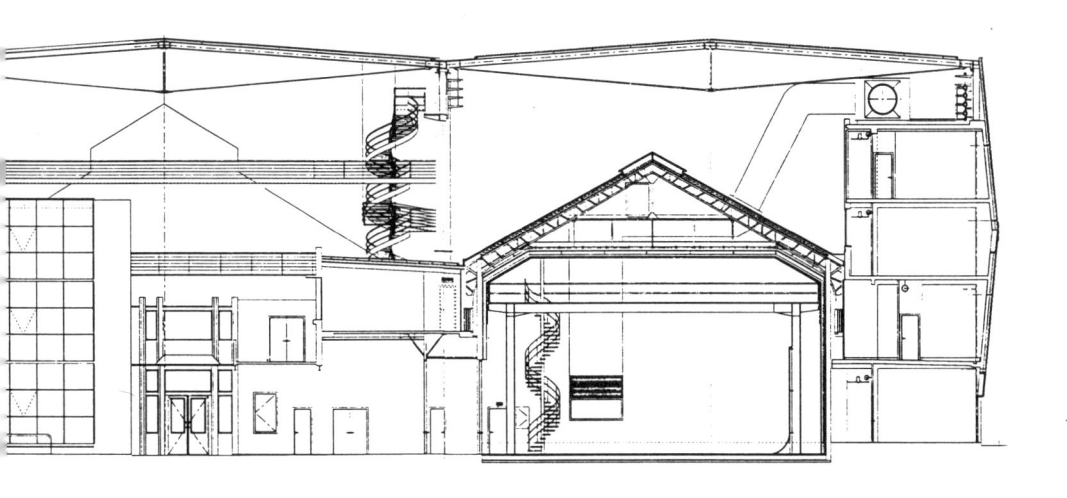

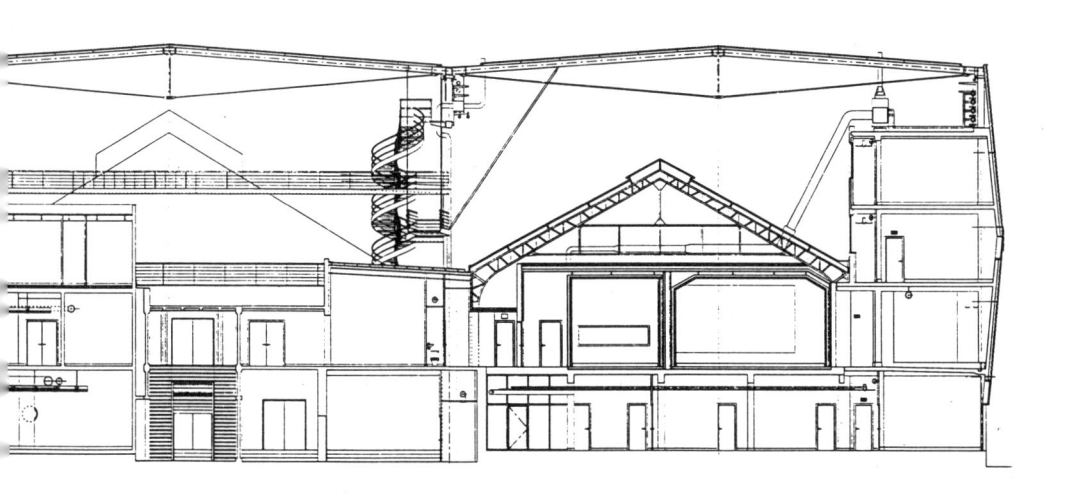

A space of constraints that may find few common denominators
Sections: school, administrative offices, the restaurant, sound studio and cutting rooms

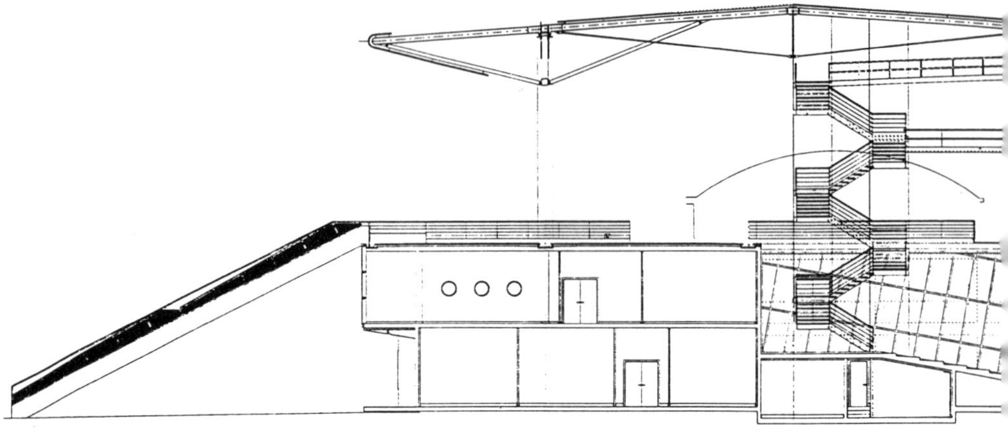

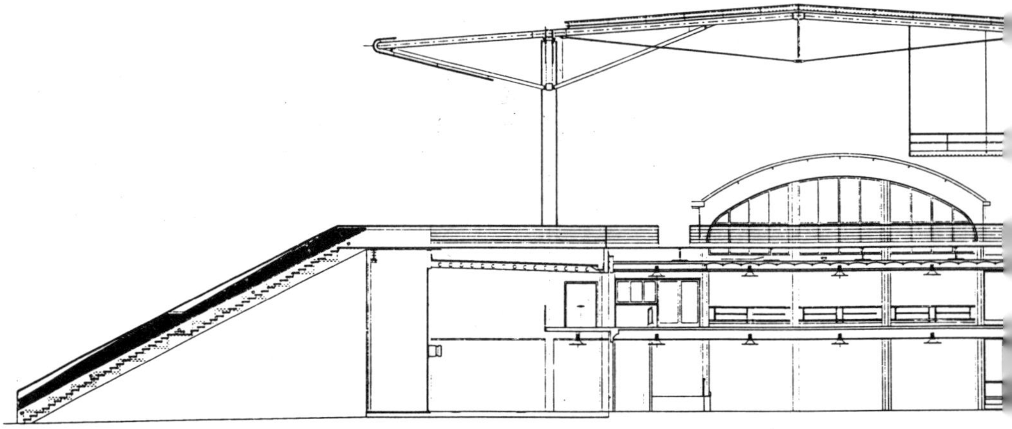

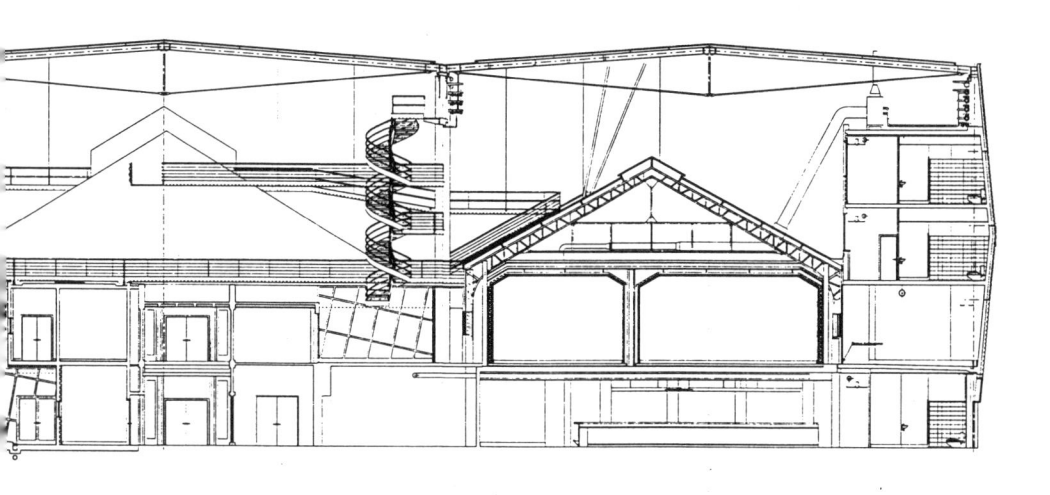

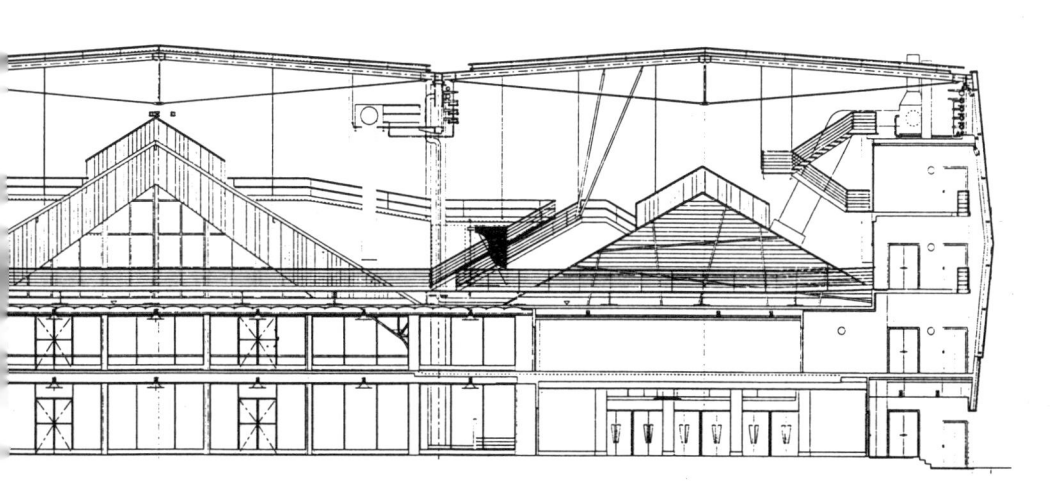

No synthesis between form and function, no homogeneous signifier
Sections: school, administrative offices, suspended staircase, ramp,
sound studio and cutting rooms

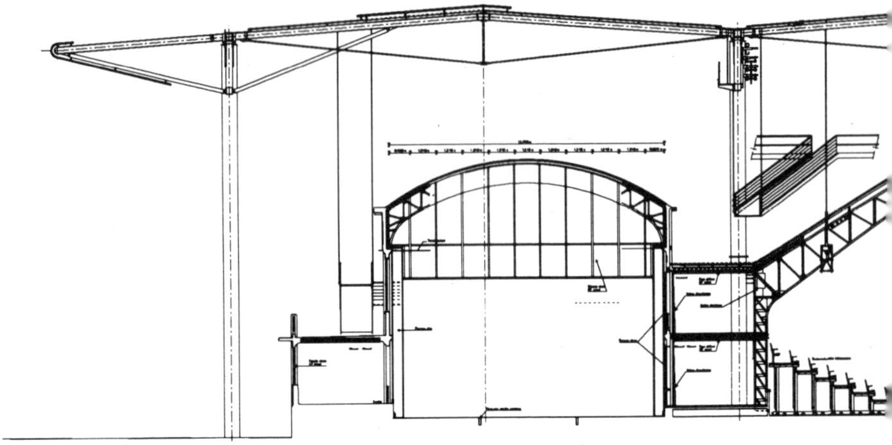

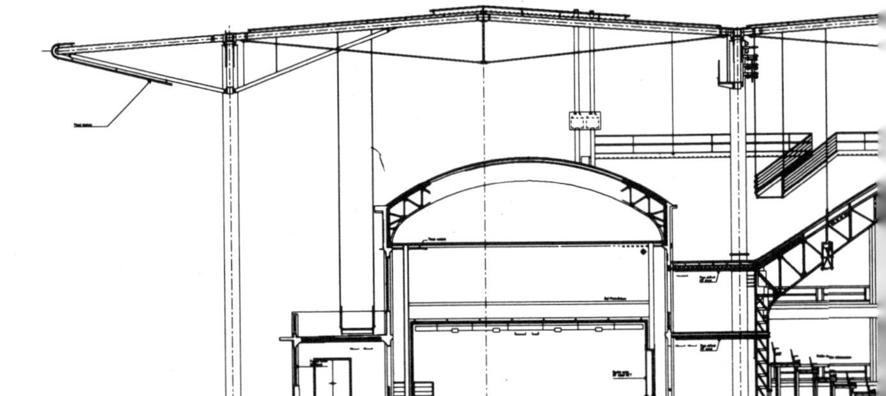

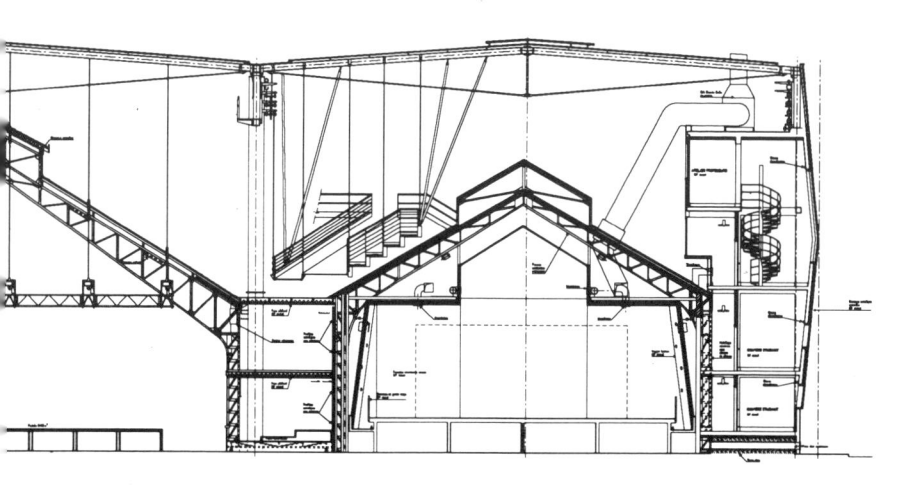

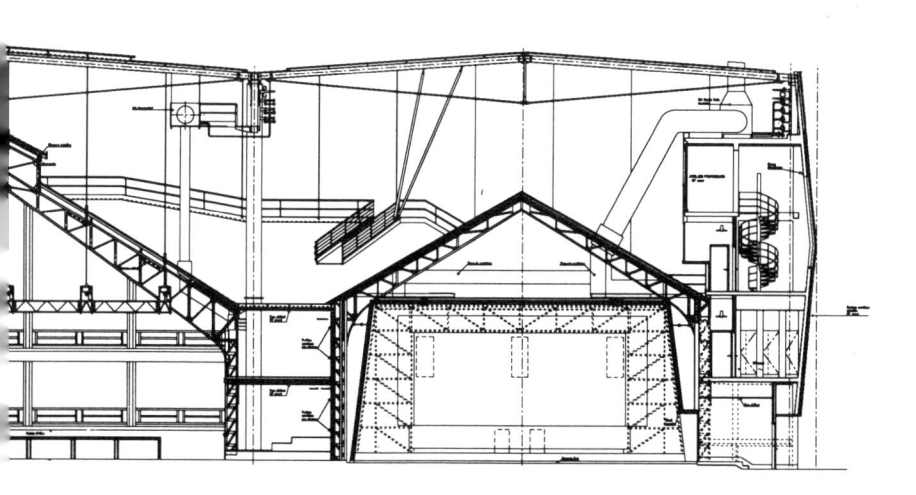

No cause-and-effect relationship between form and function
Sections: media library, large hall, 200-seat cinema, housing

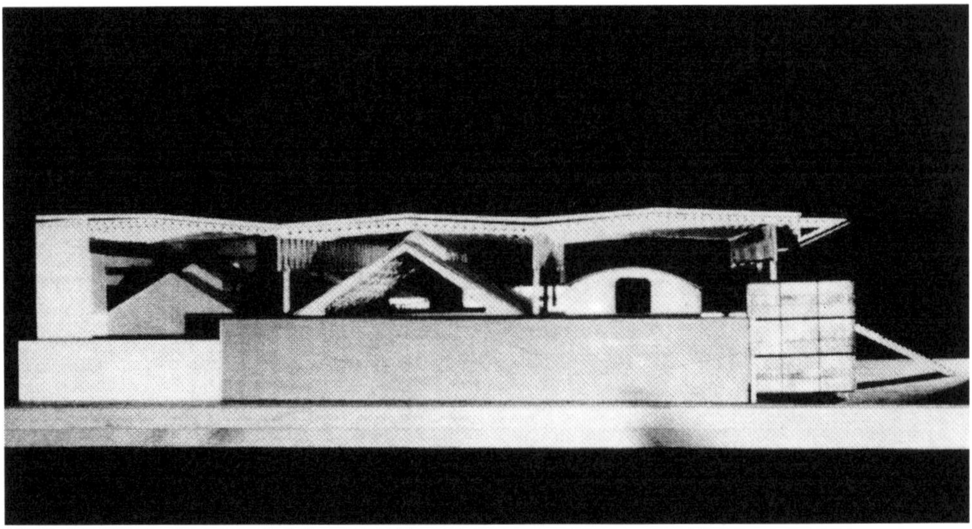

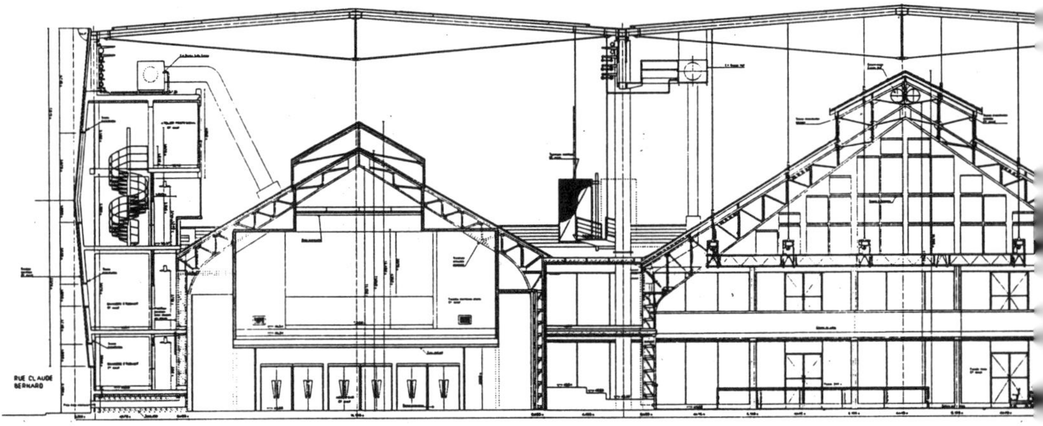
RUE CLAUDE
BERNARD

TOURCOING
455

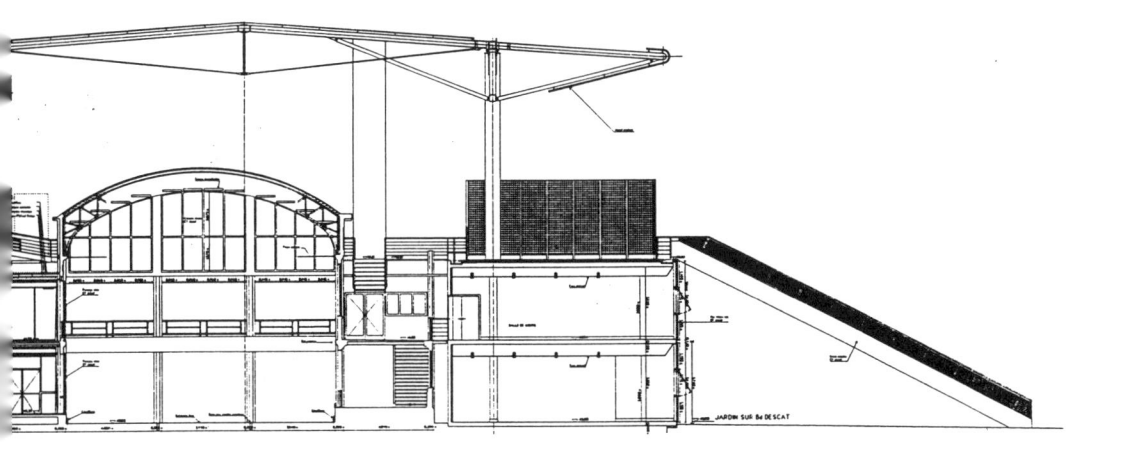

Problematizing meaning, rejecting all *a priori* signification

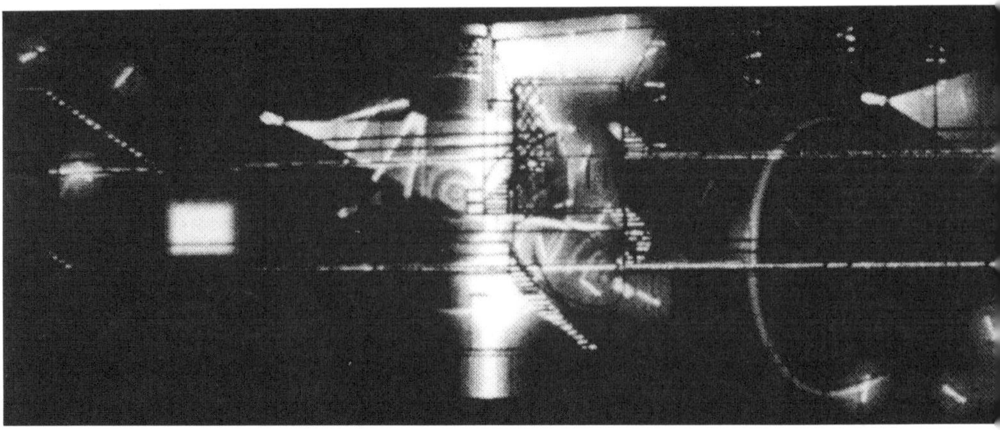

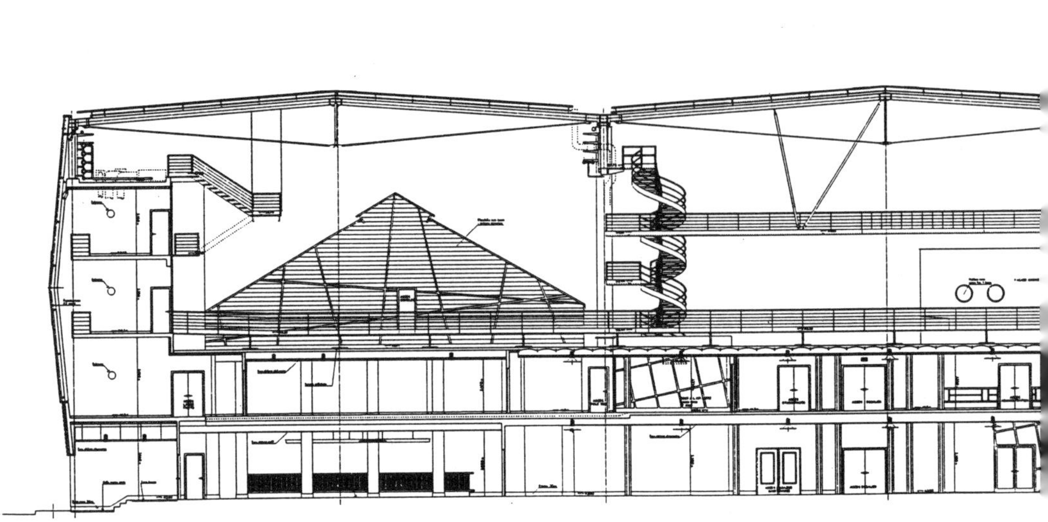

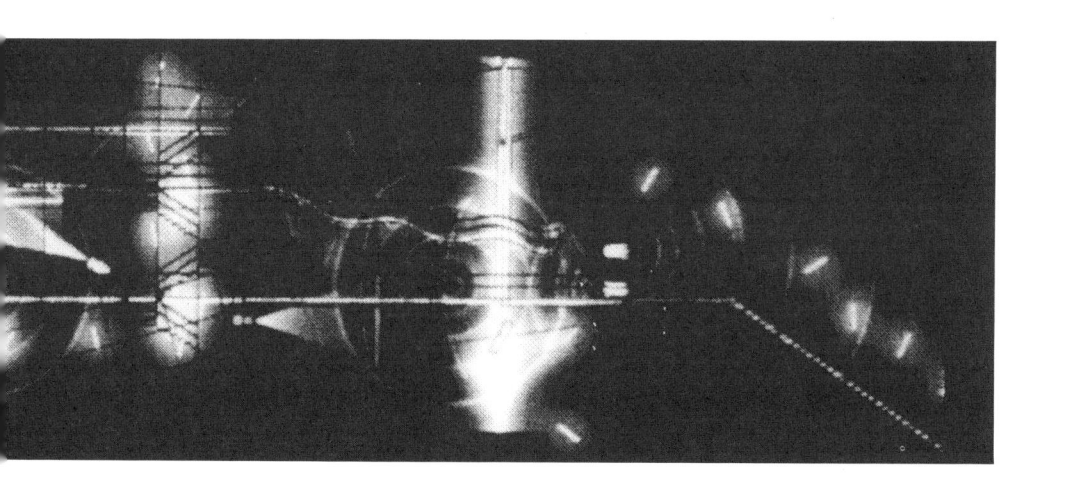

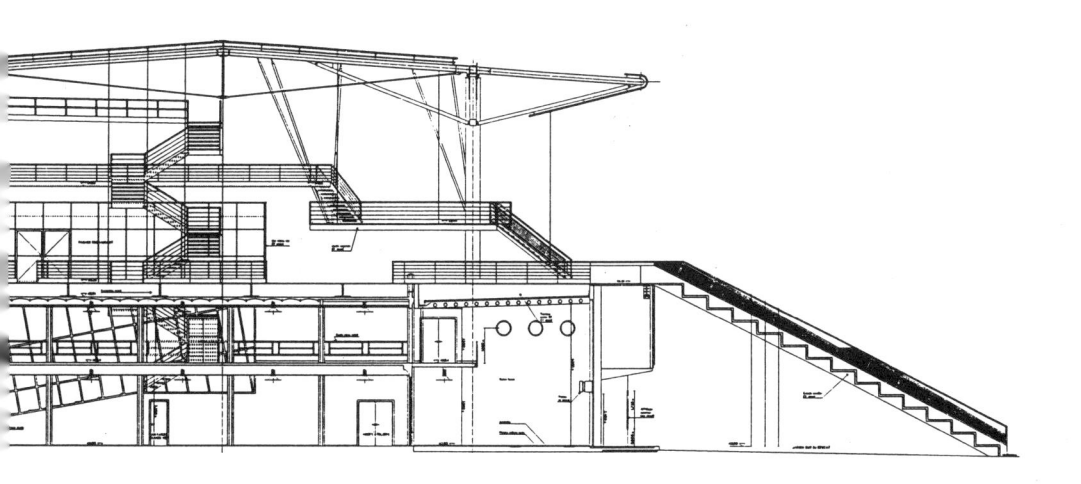

Light, space, action, movement: the heterogeneity of architecture

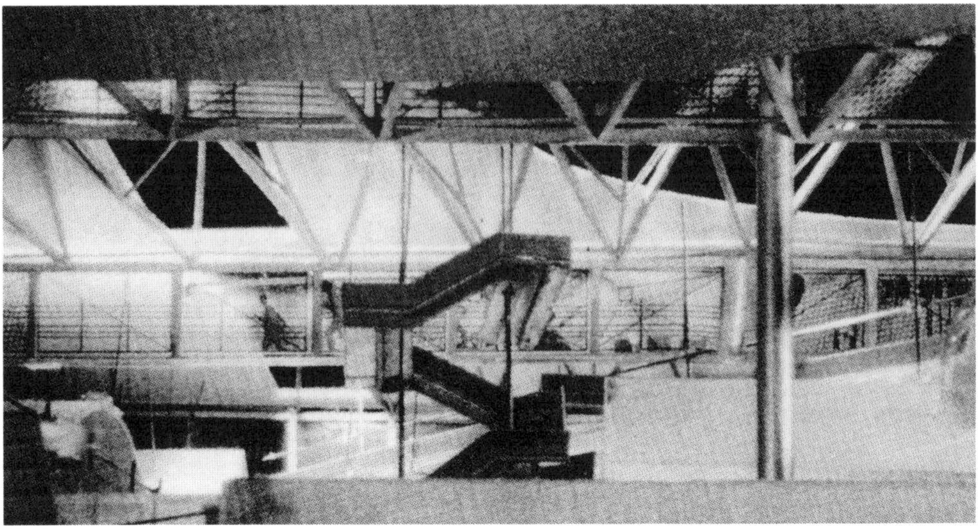

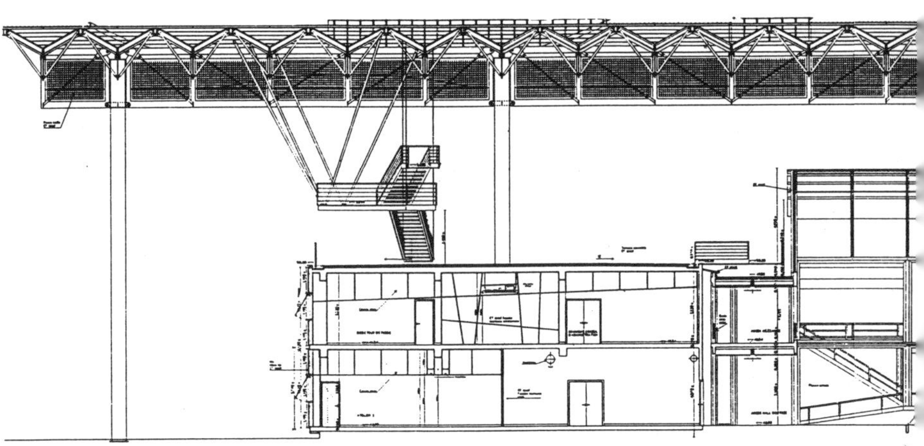

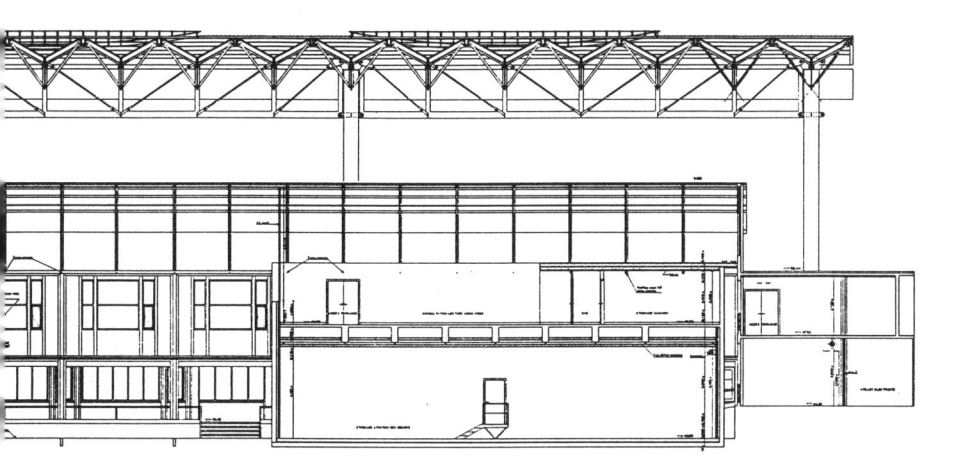

Longitudinal section: in-between, administrative offices, school, exhibition hall, media library, workshops

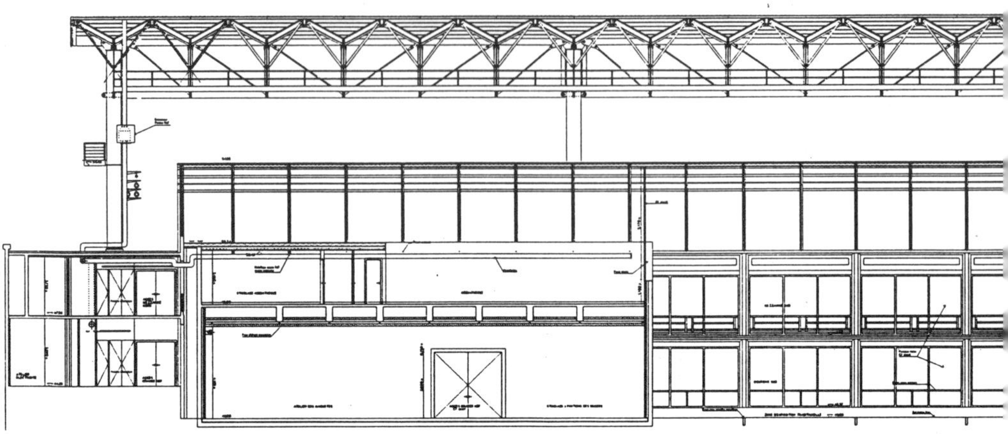

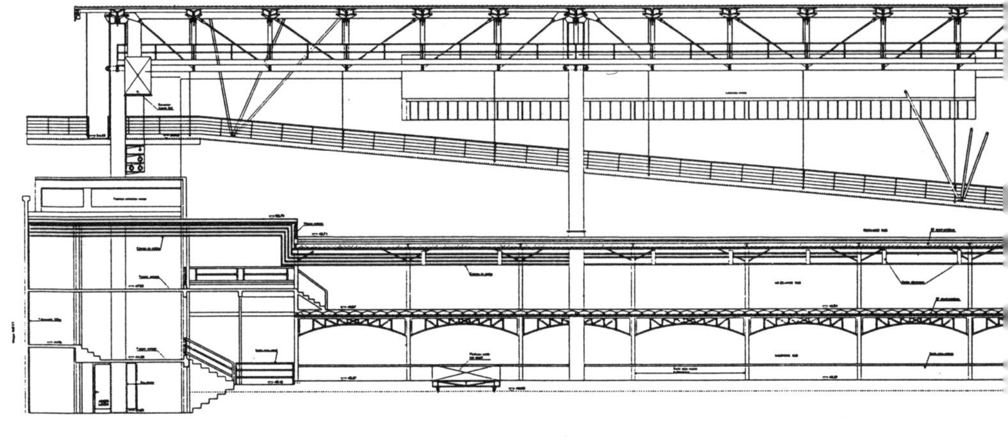

TOURCOING
461

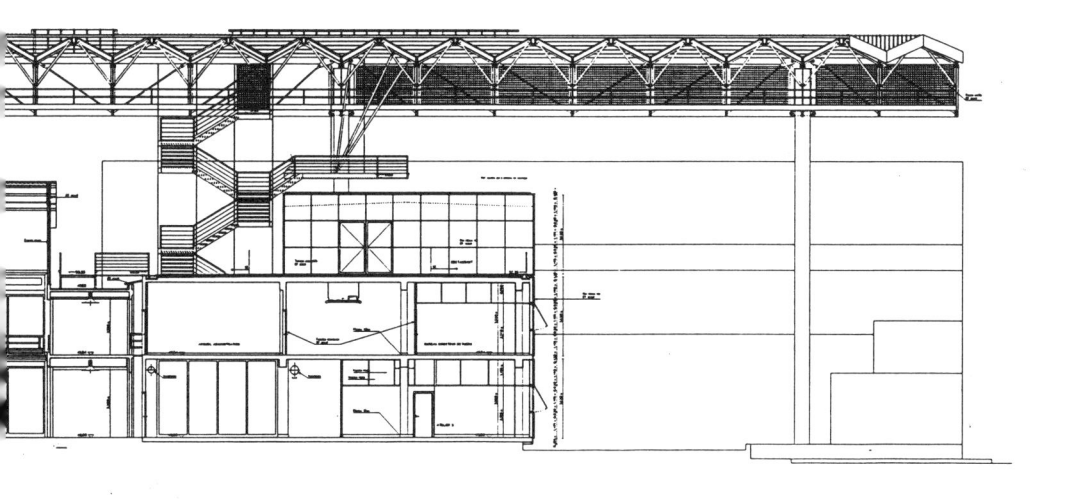

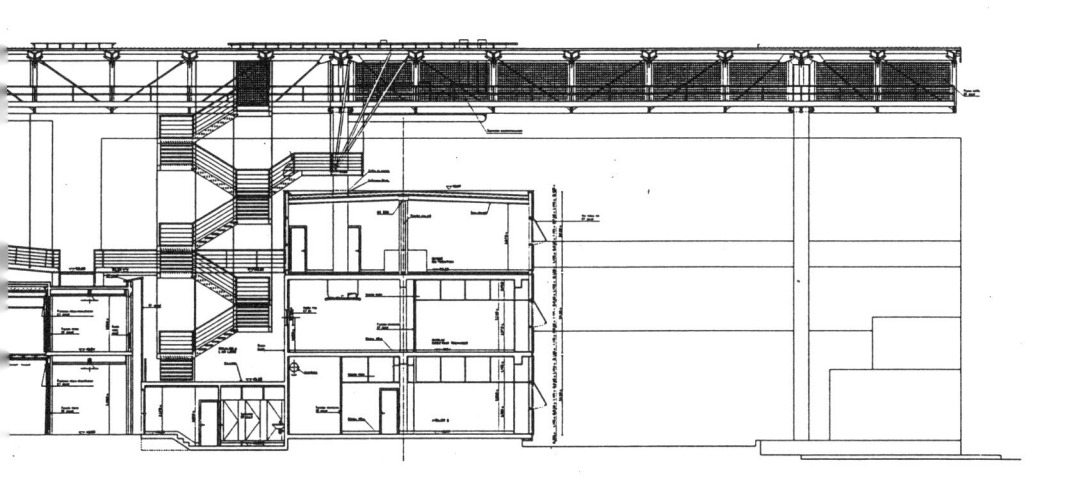

No frozen rituals of occupancy: halls, mezzanines, suspended staircase, restaurant, administrative offices and school

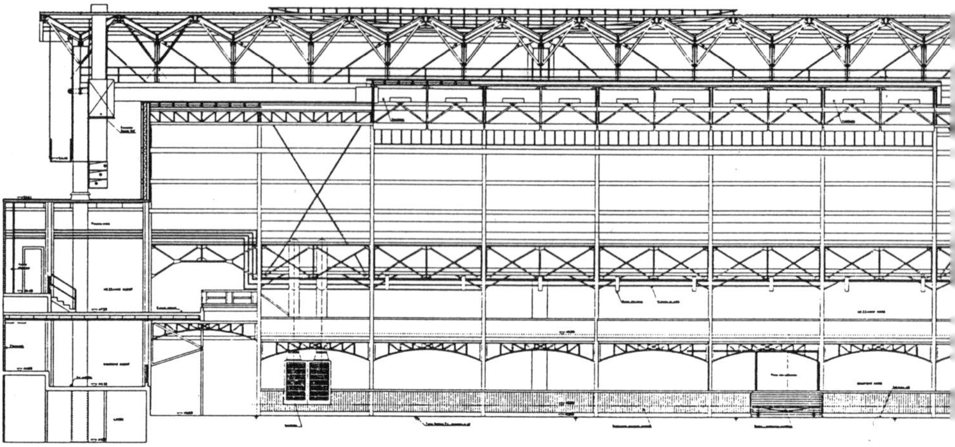

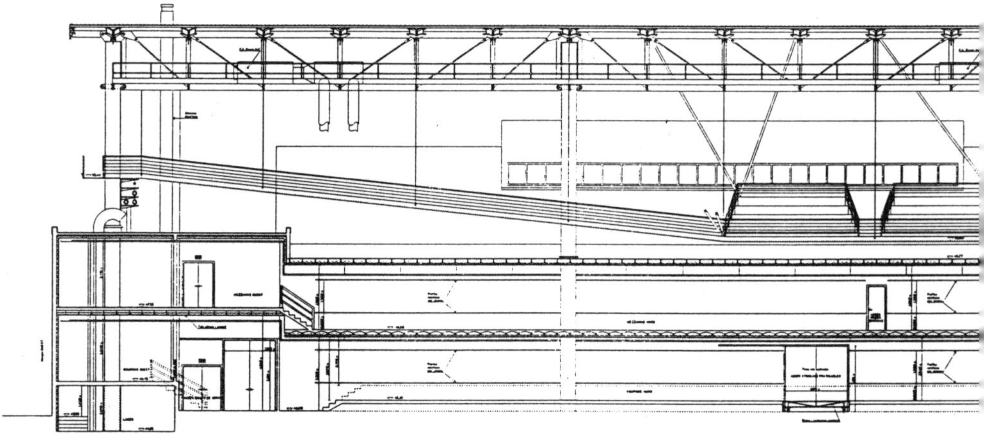

TOURCOING
463

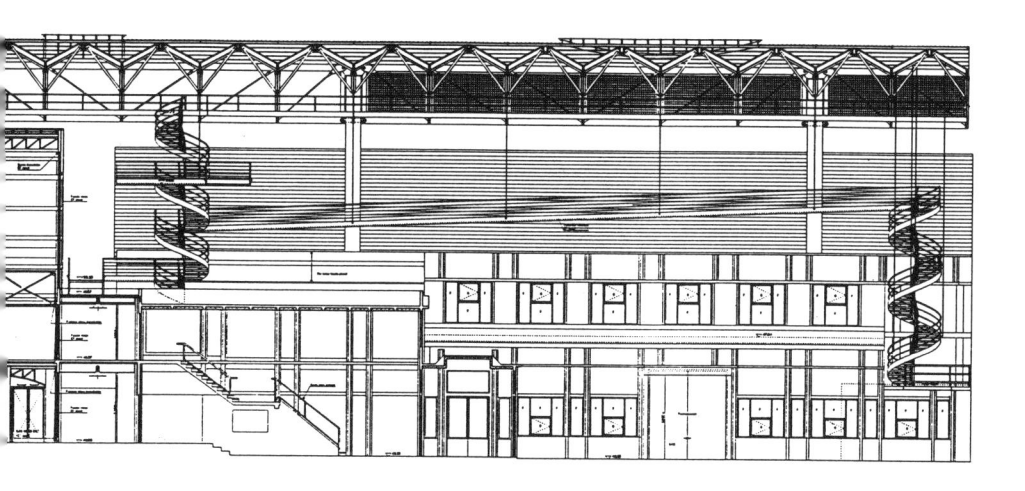

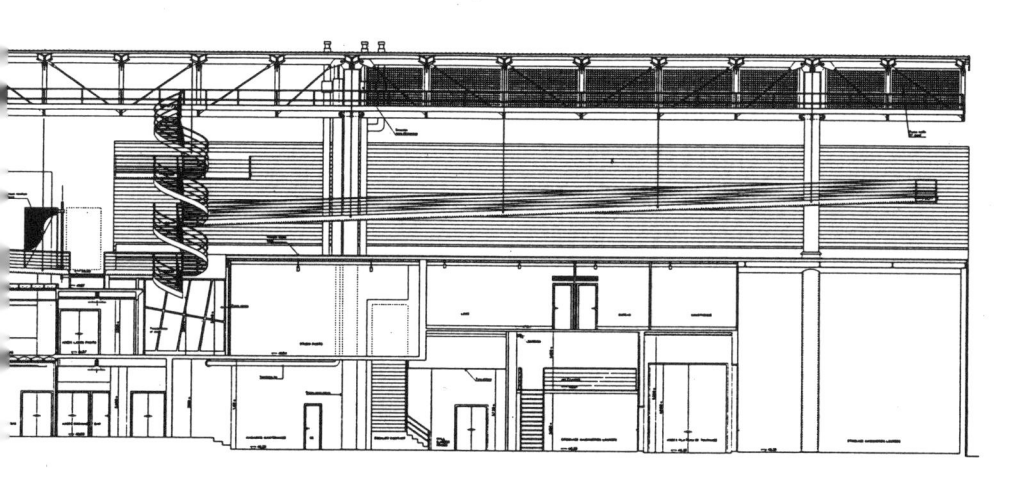

Anti-hierarchy, anti-form, anti-structure: random sections

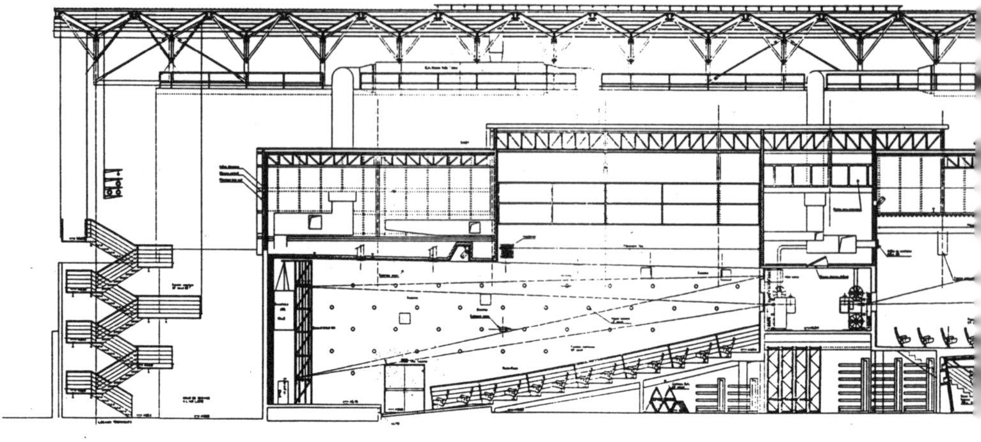

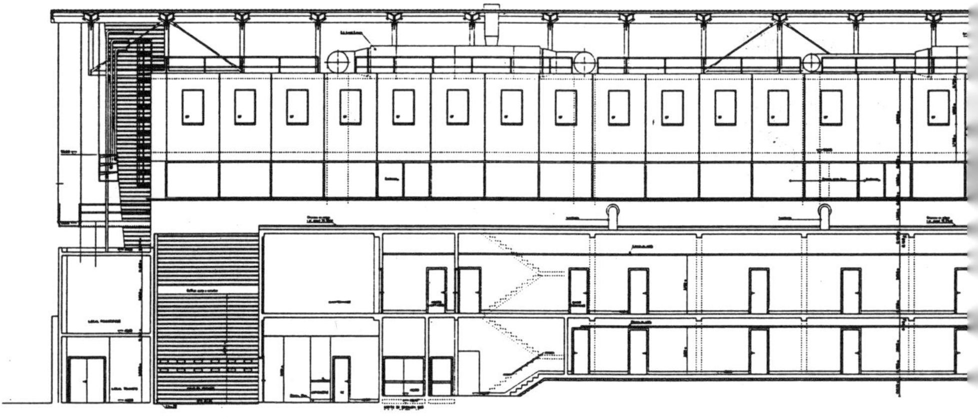

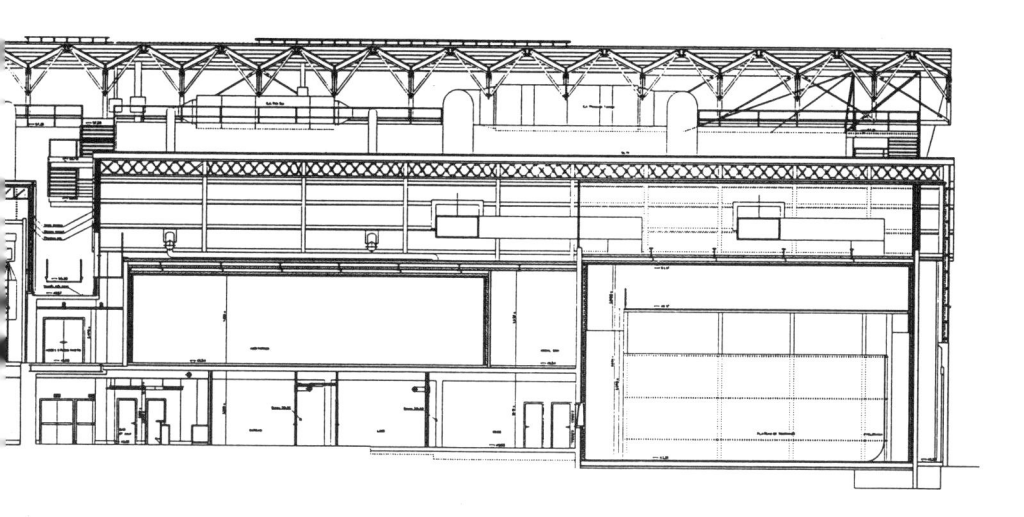

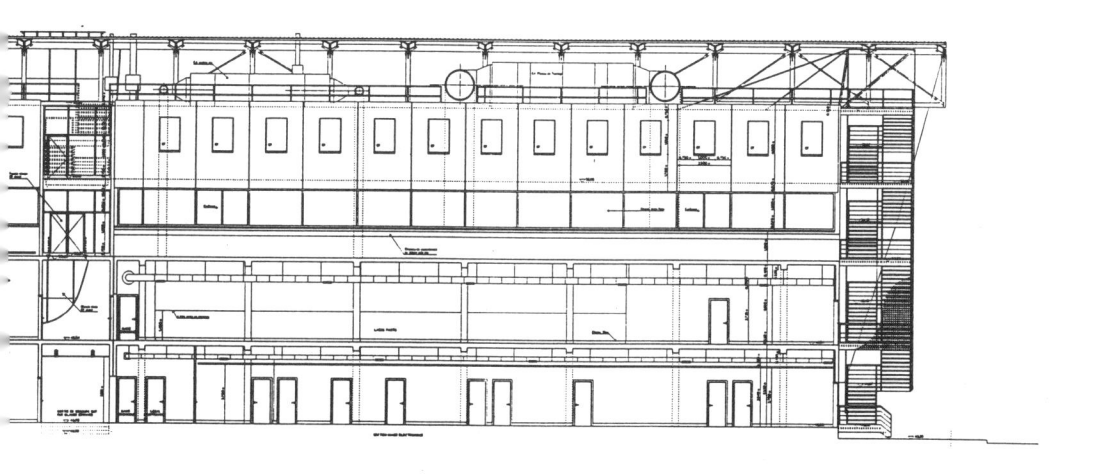

Longitudinal section: two cinemas, sound studios, offices and film studio

Interior elevation: view towards housing, cutting rooms and photography department

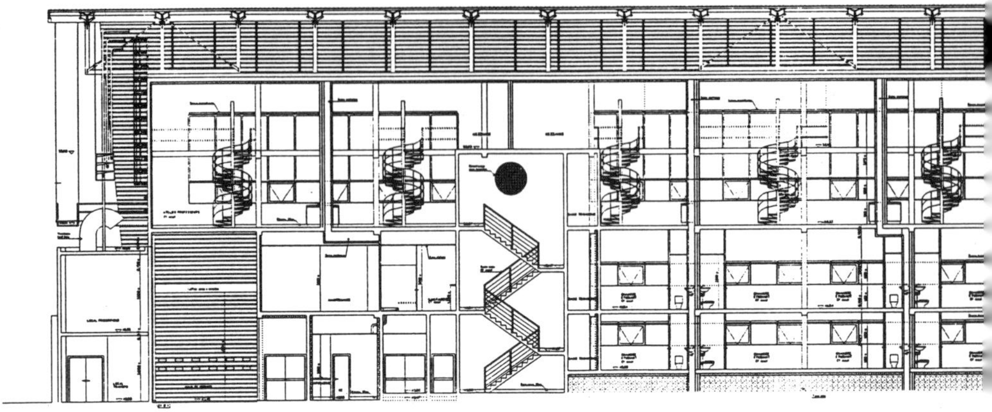

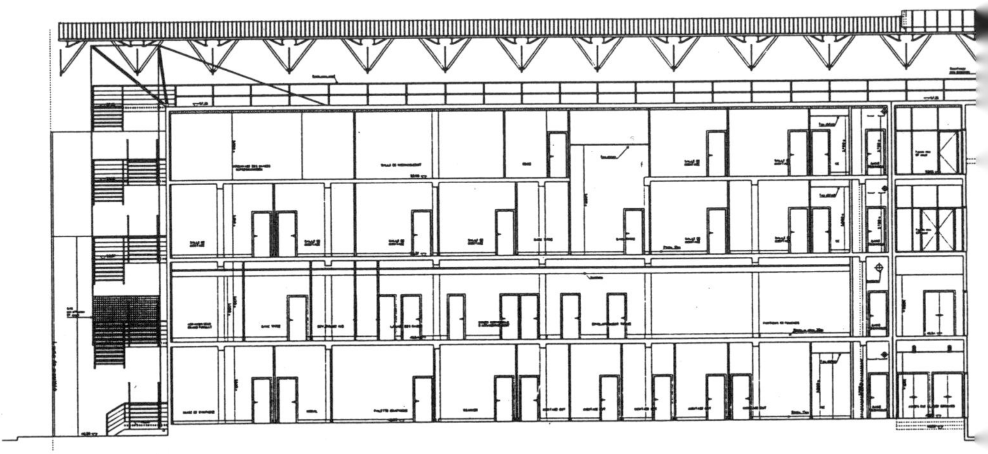

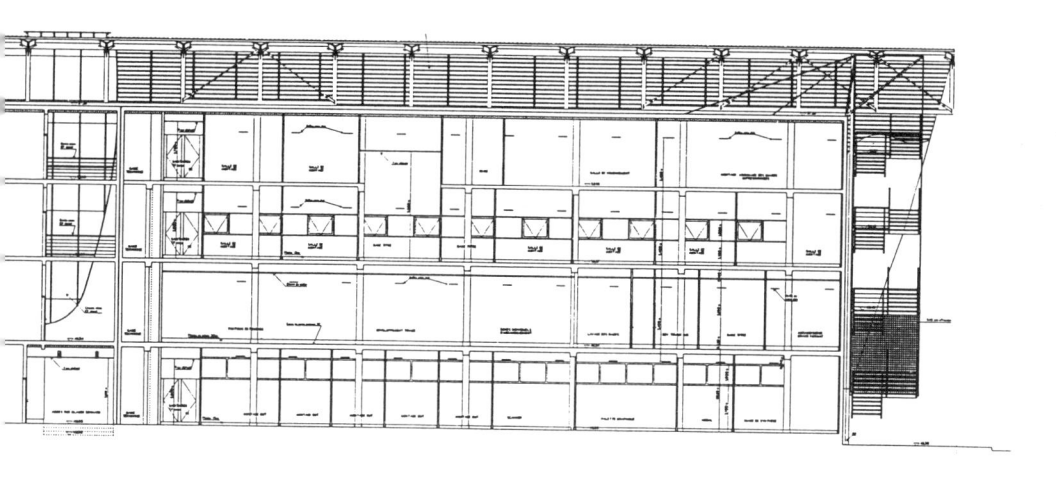

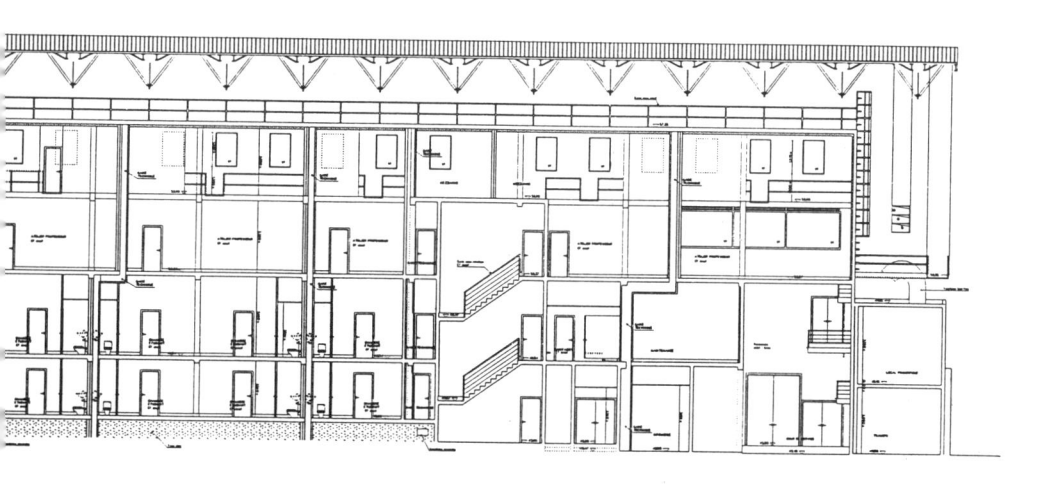

Longitudinal section: housing, cutting rooms and photography department

Longitudinal section: view towards the south

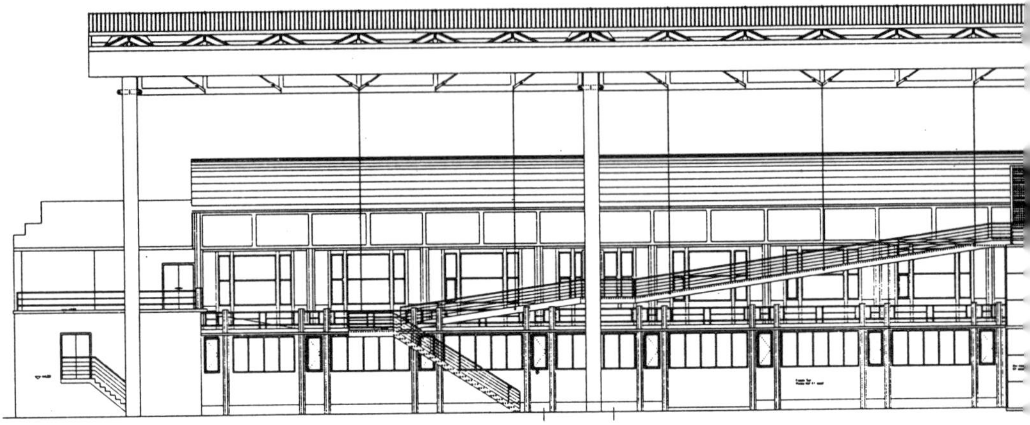

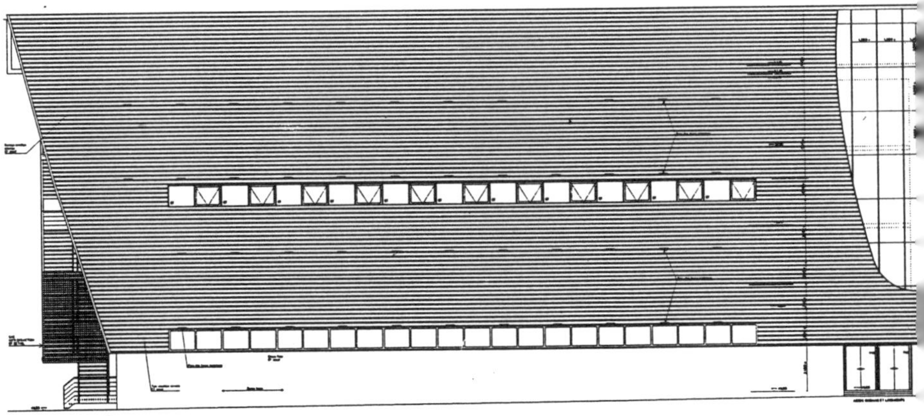

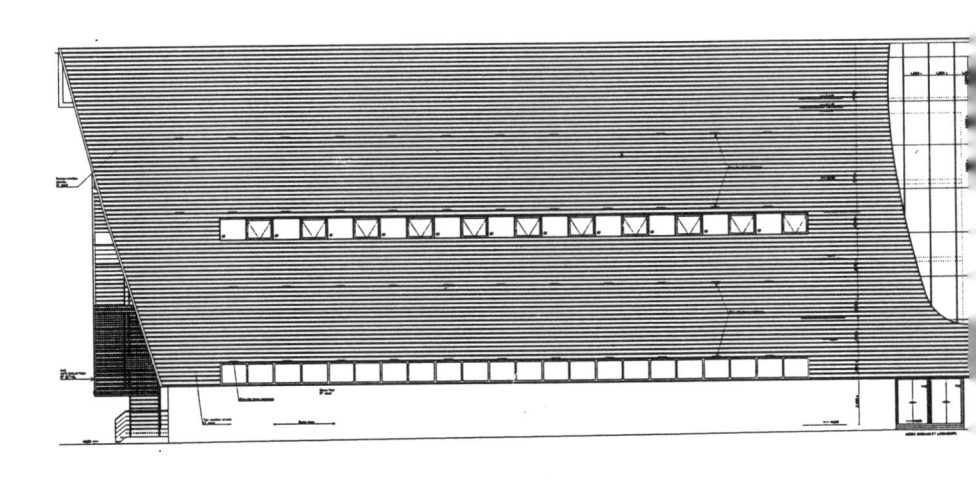

TOURCOIN
469

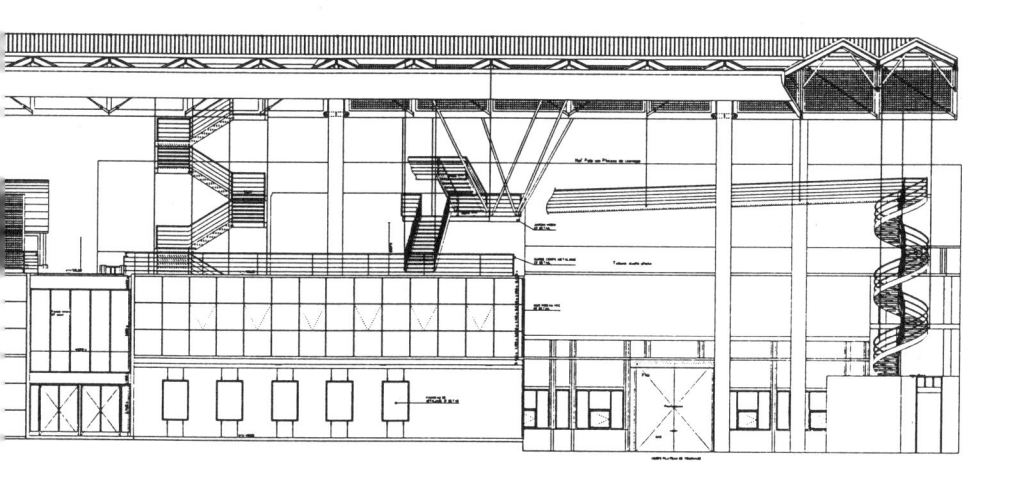

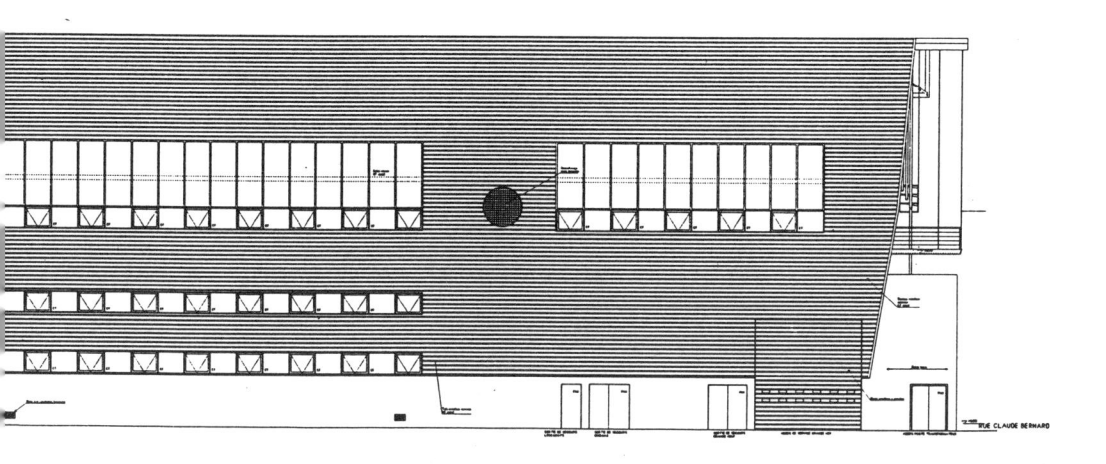

South elevation (without ZAE) and north elevation: architecture does not claim a permanence of meaning

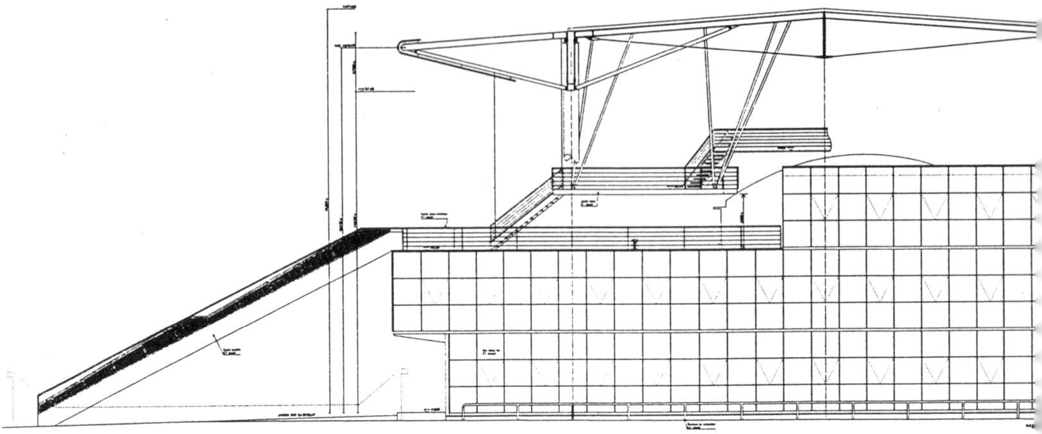

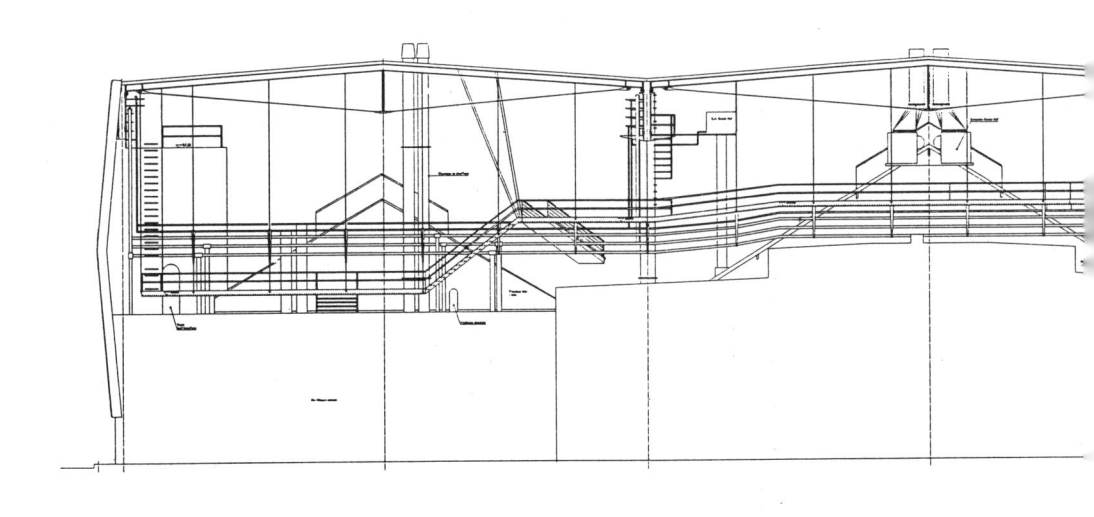

TOURCOING
471

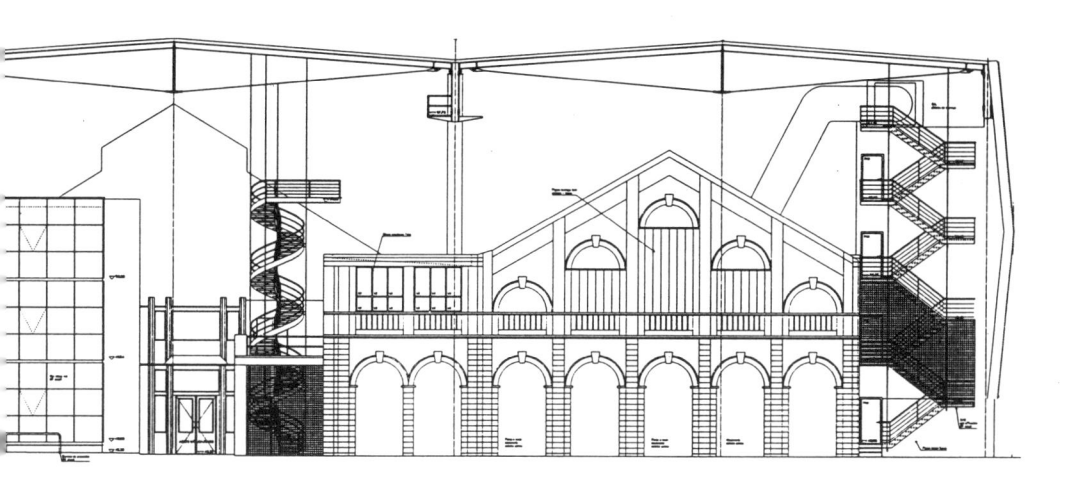

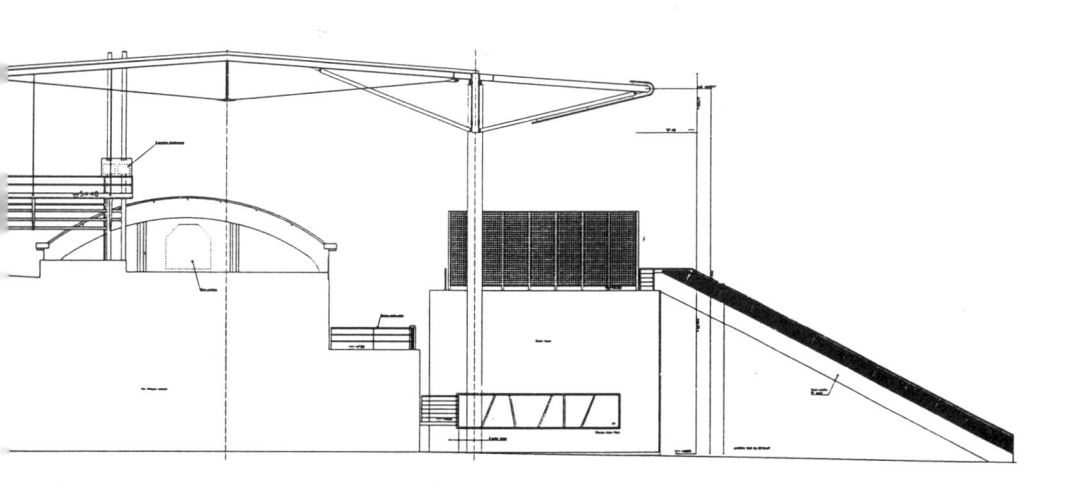

Elevations: somewhere between abstraction and figuration, a random superimposition of images that bear no relationship to one another (blurring traditional perceptions)

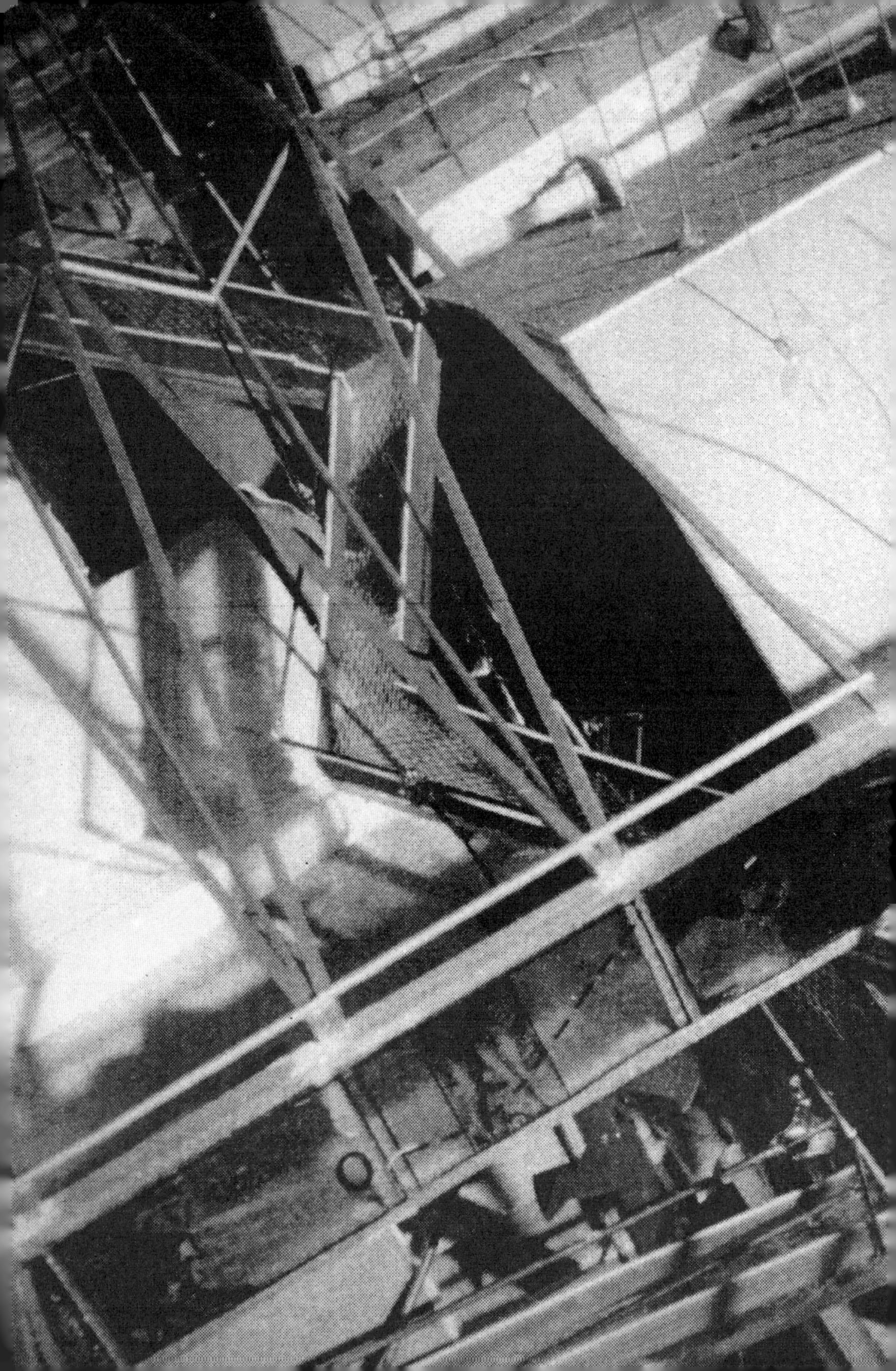

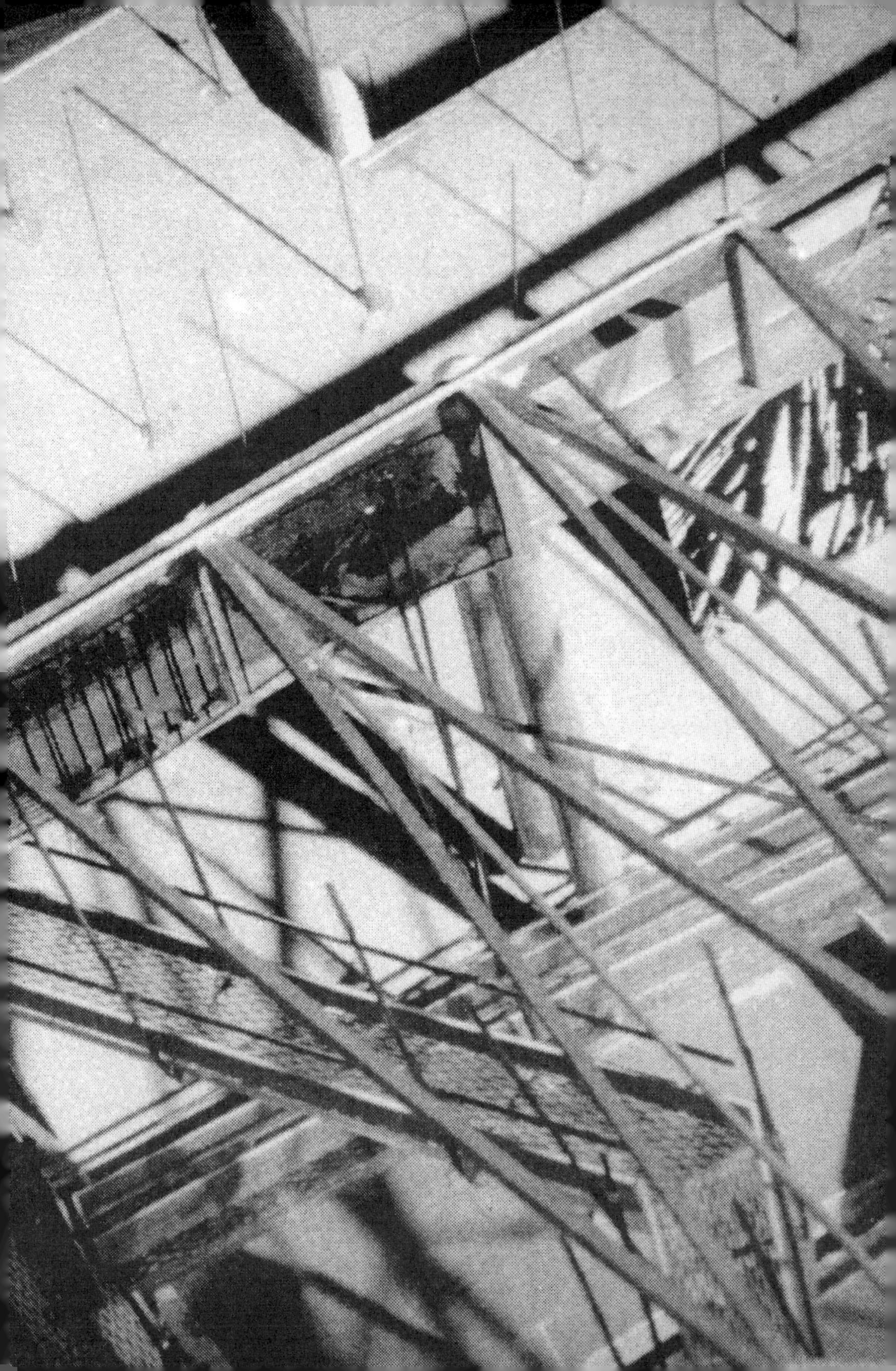

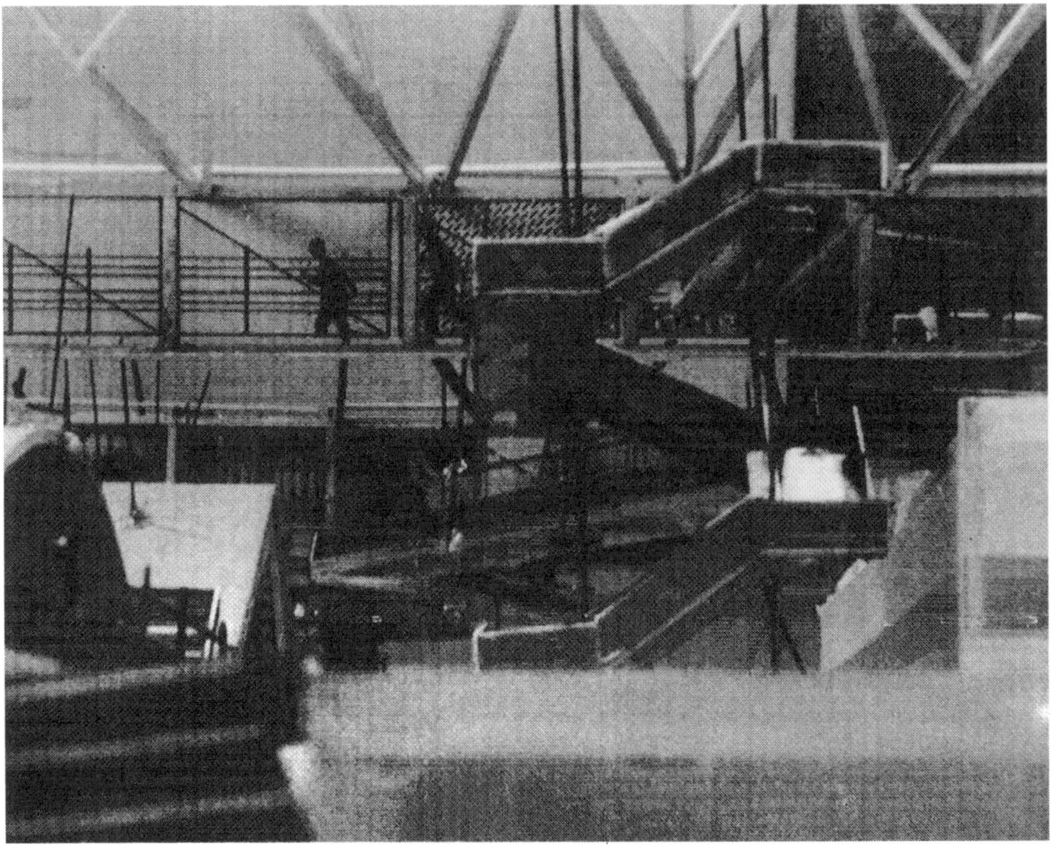

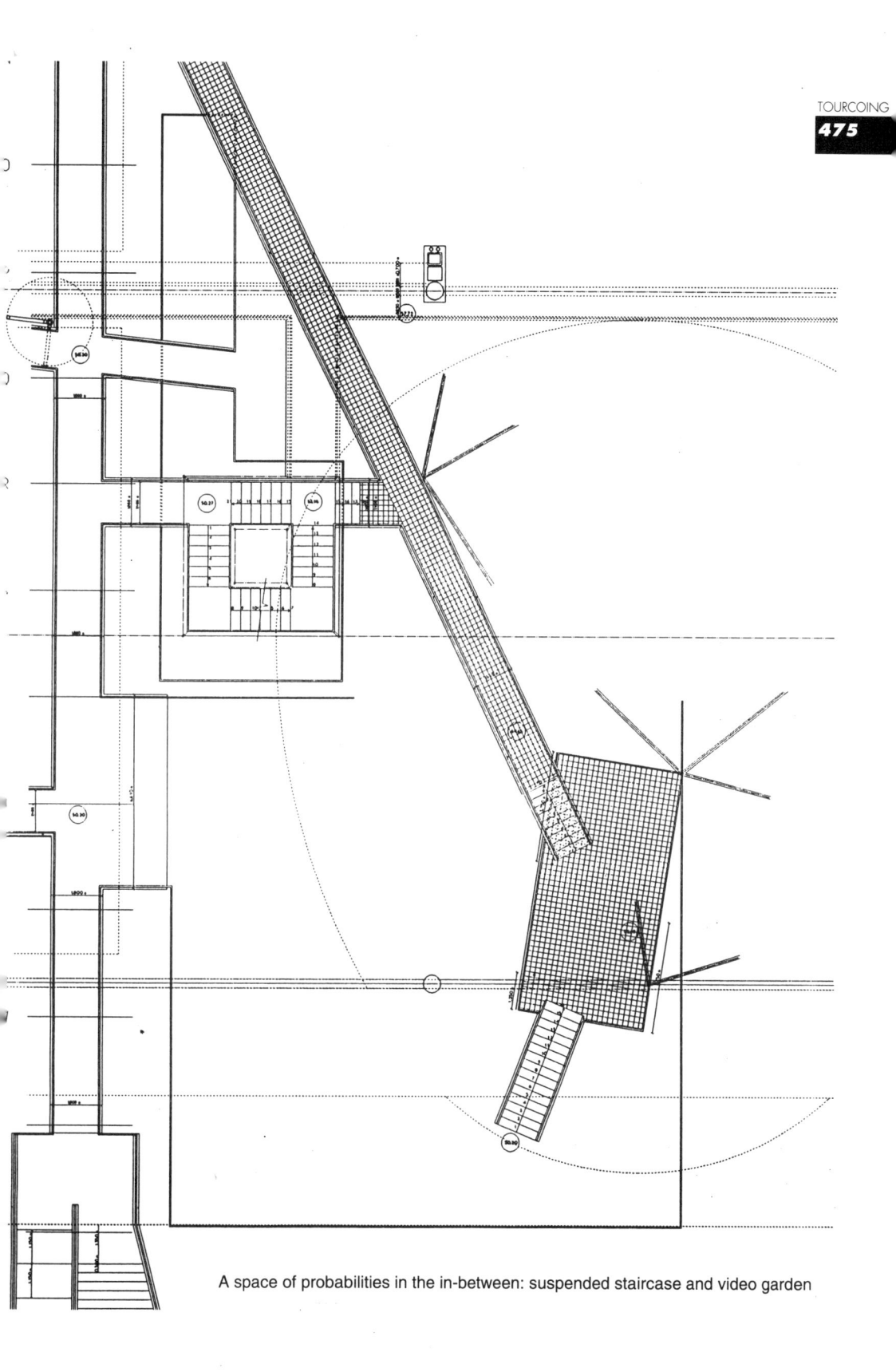

A space of probabilities in the in-between: suspended staircase and video garden

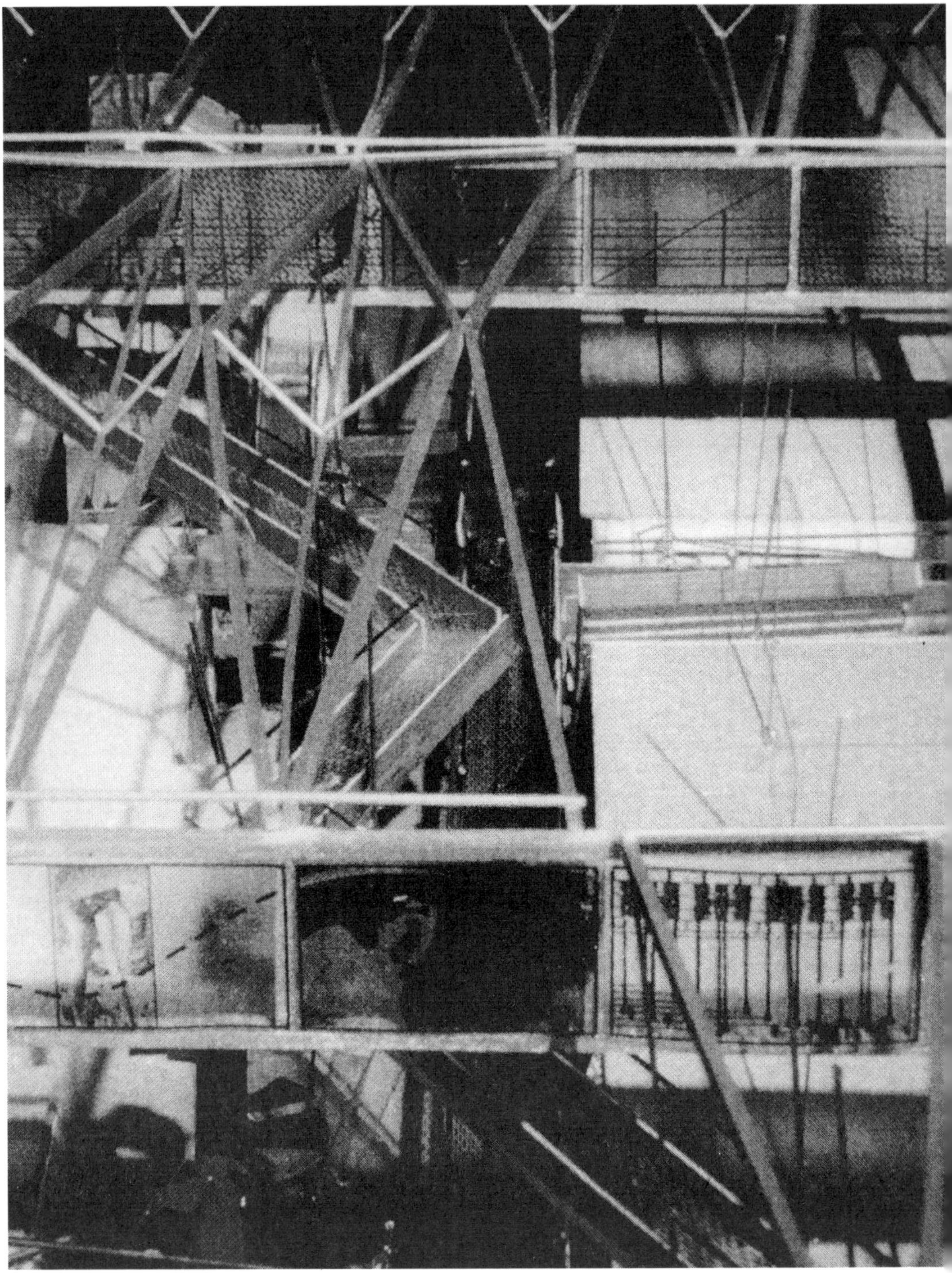

Intersection of catwalks

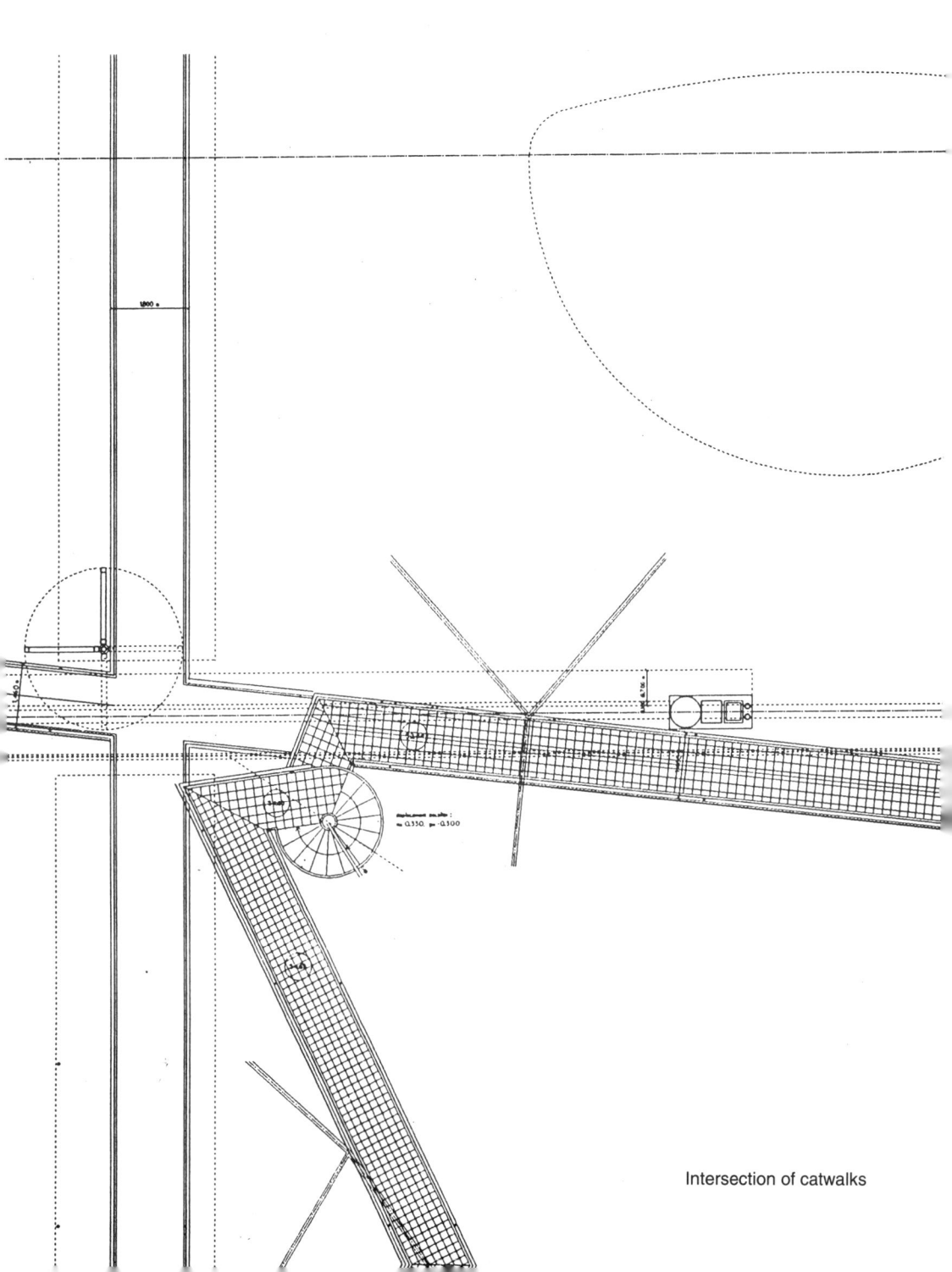

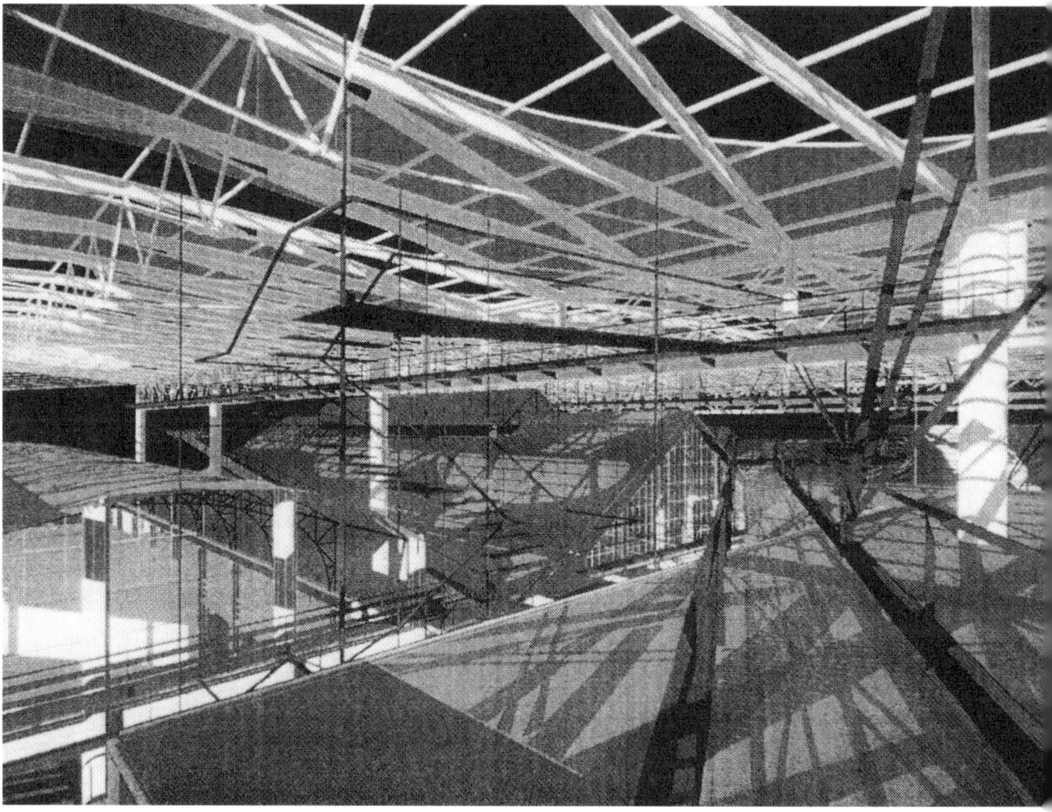

TOURCOING
479

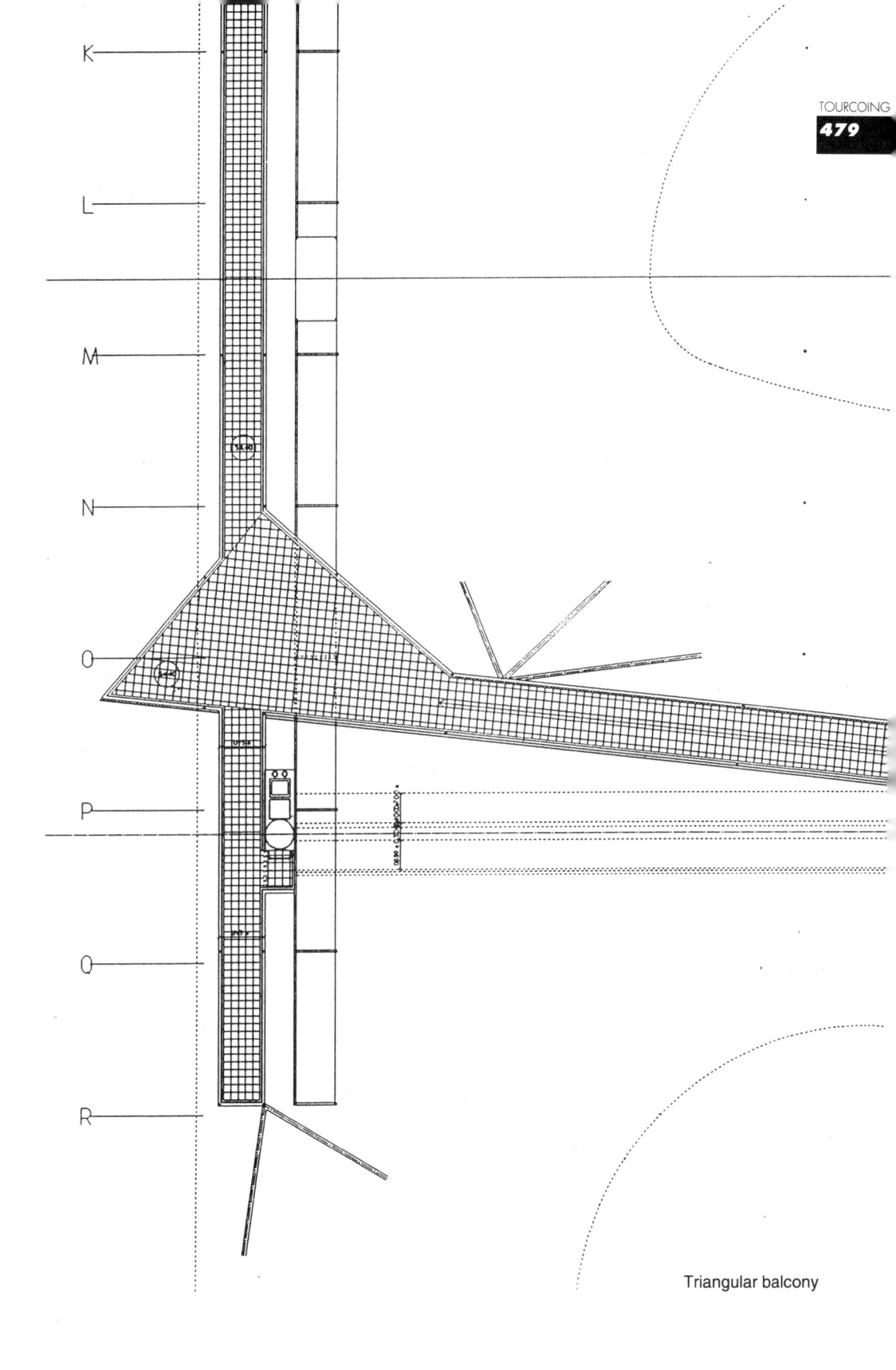

Triangular balcony

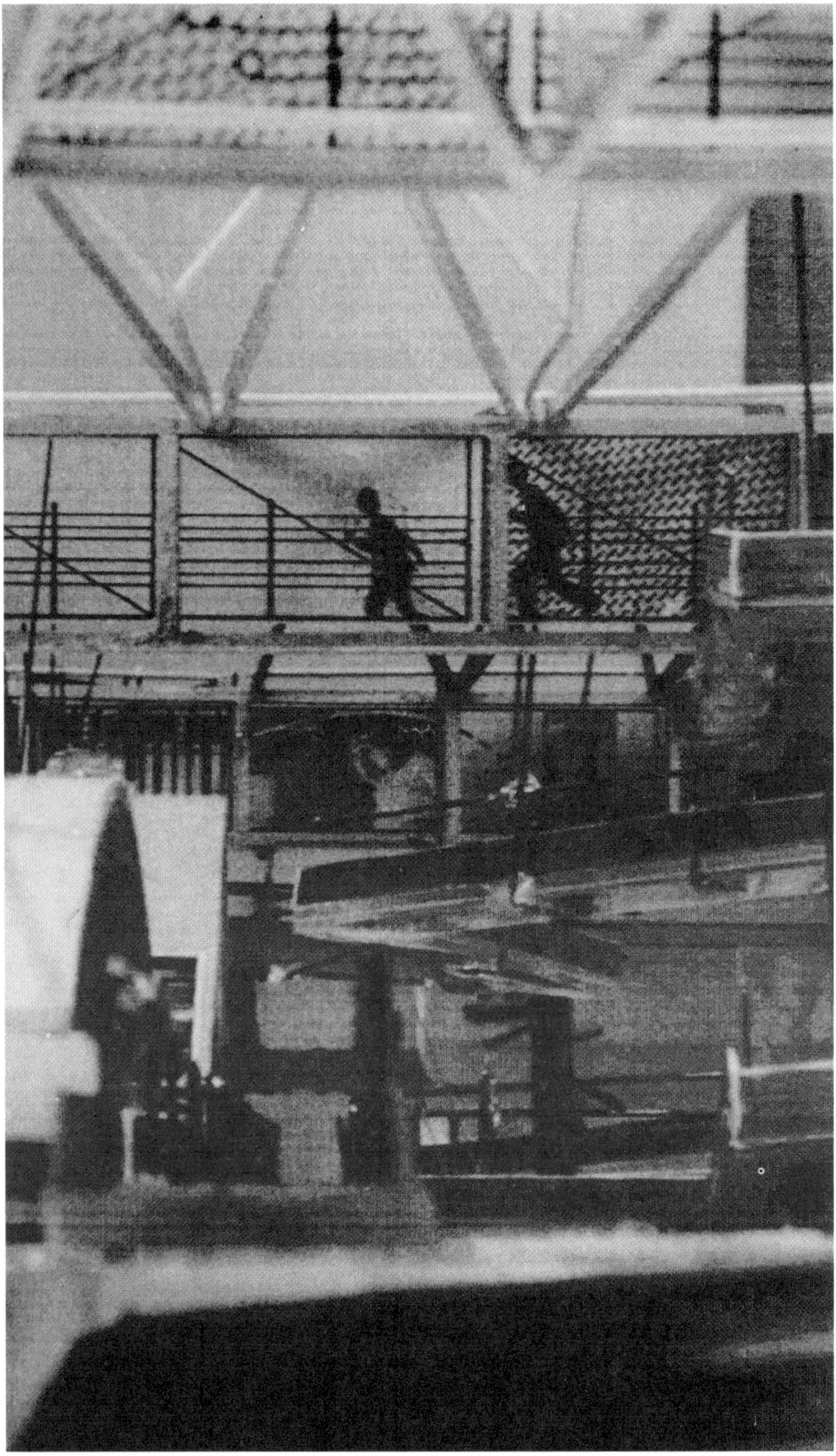

TOURCOING
481

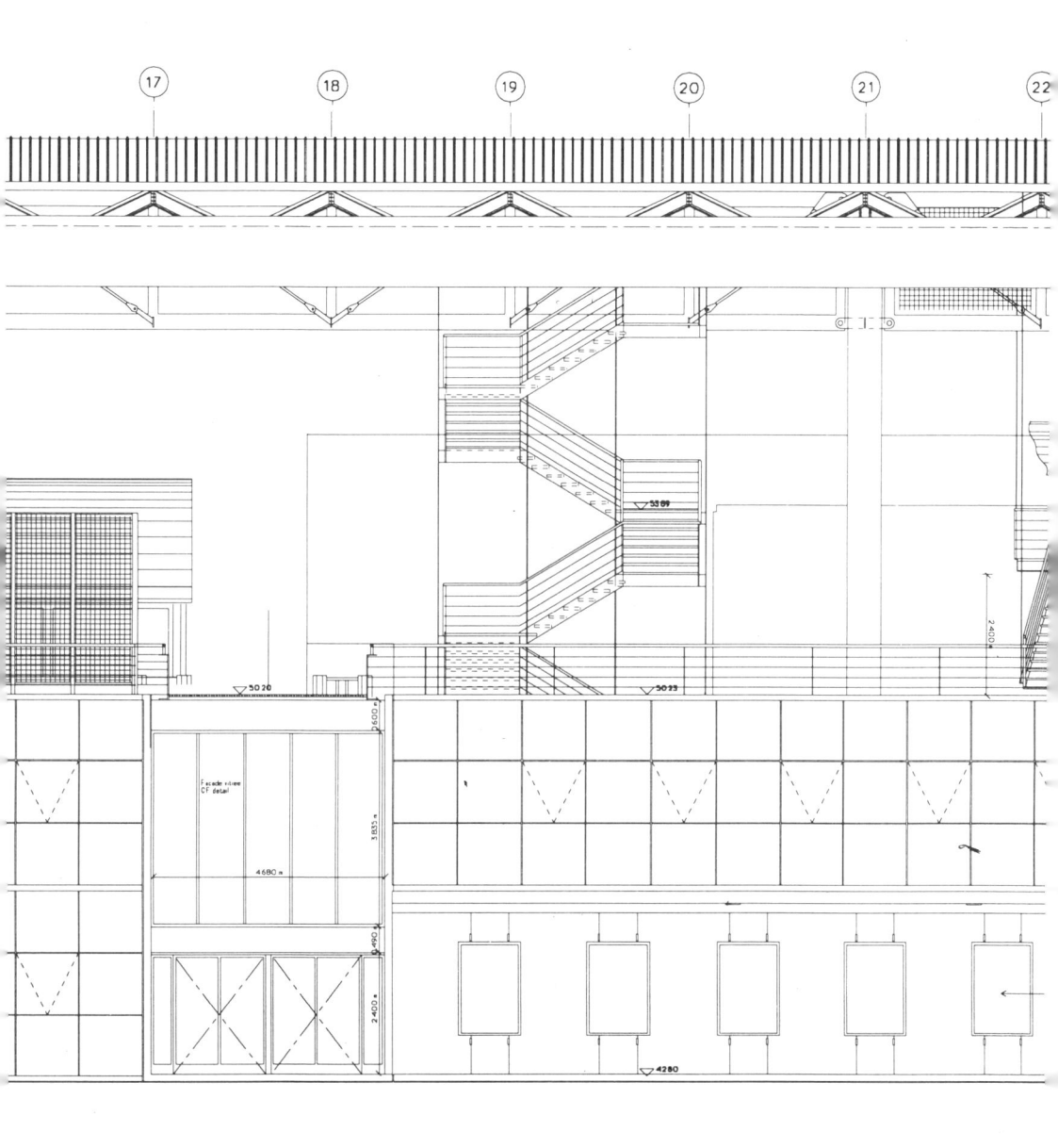

Main entry under stair awning

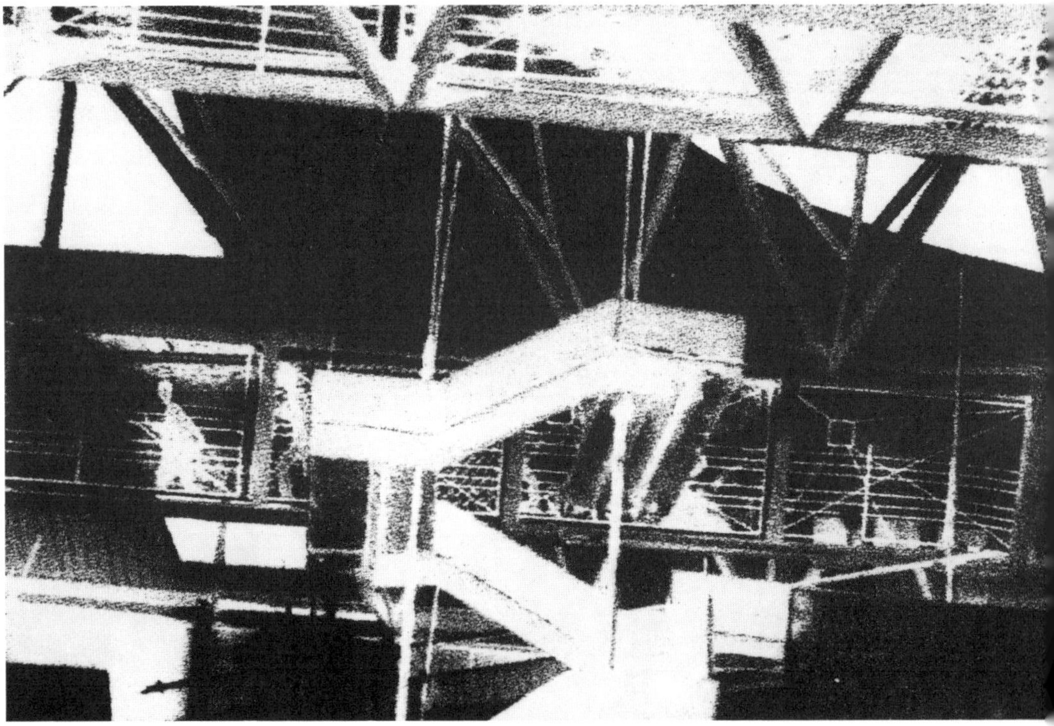

TOURCOING
483

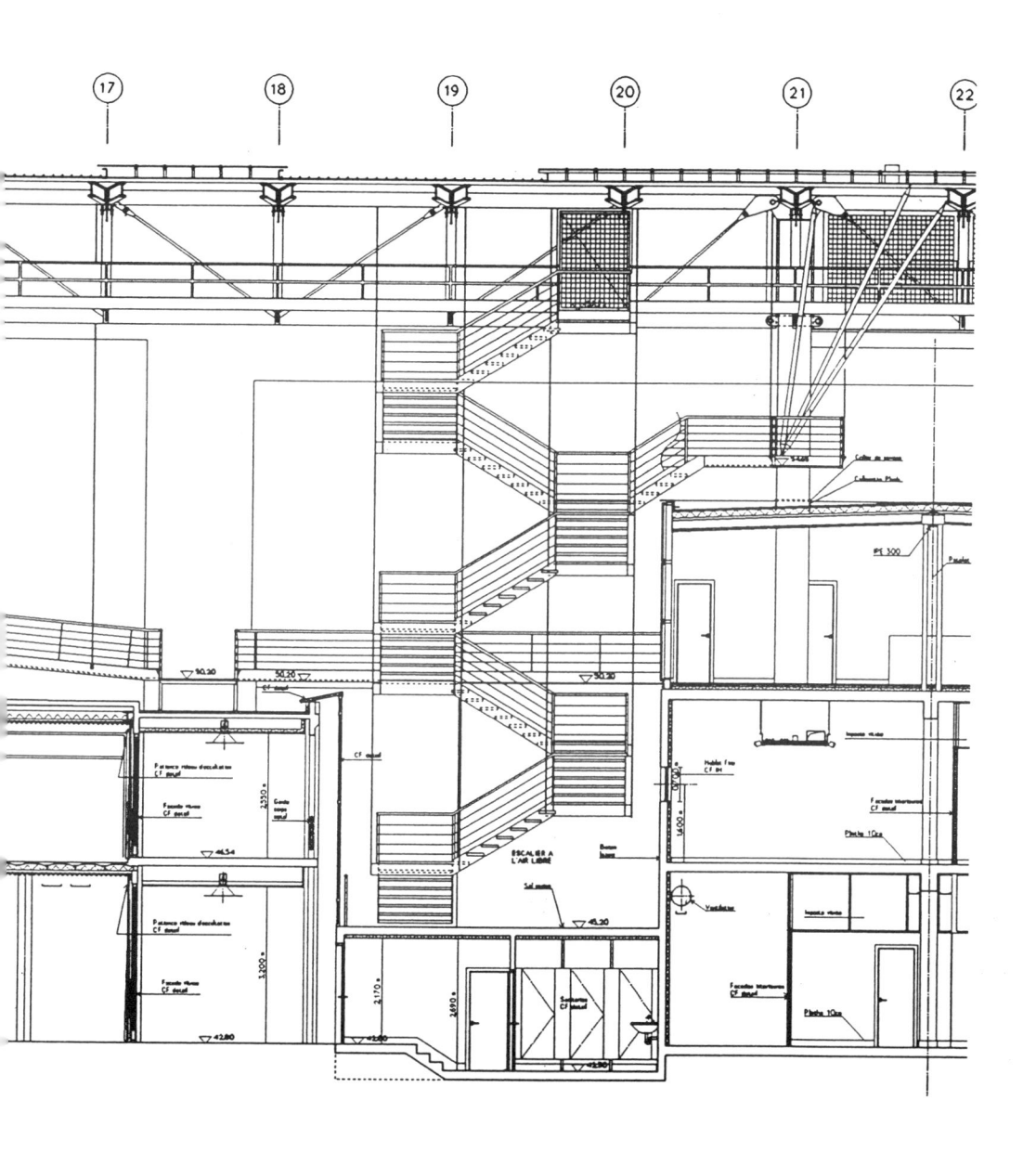

Technical catwalks, suspended staircase that interpenetrates the lower halls:
accelerating the probability of chance events in the in-between

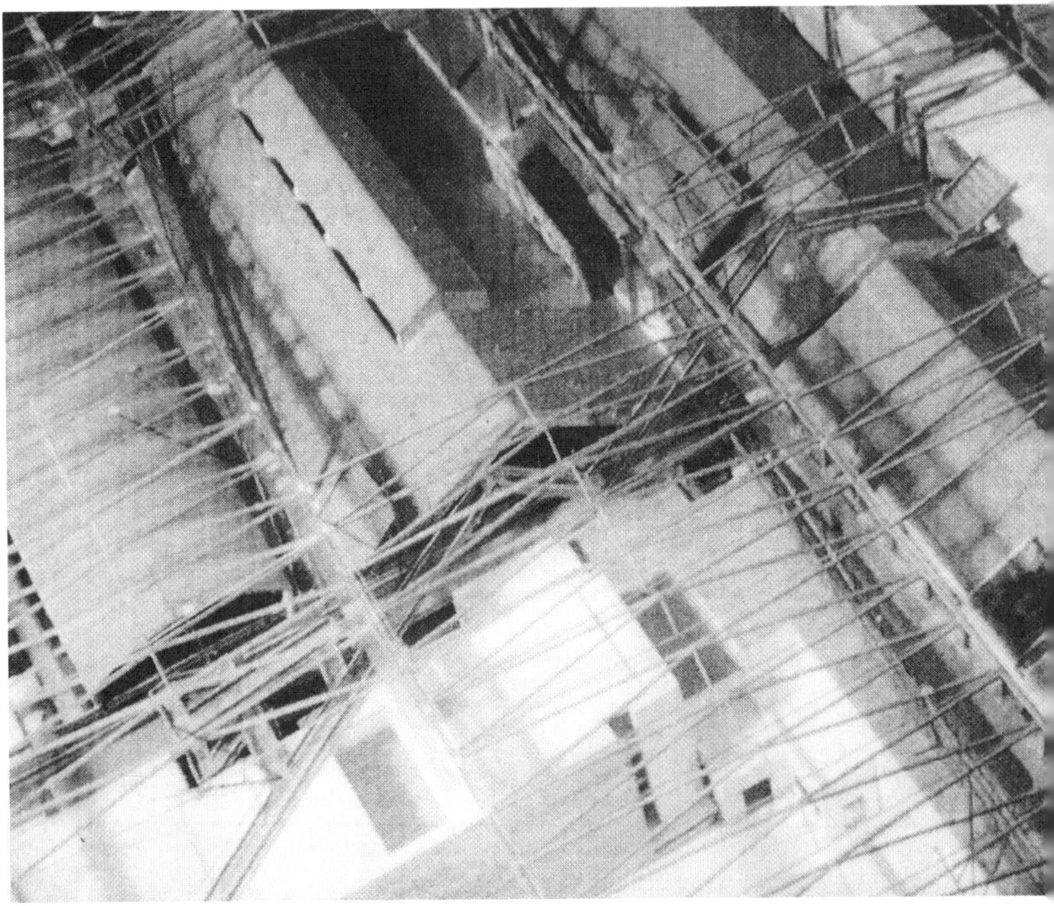

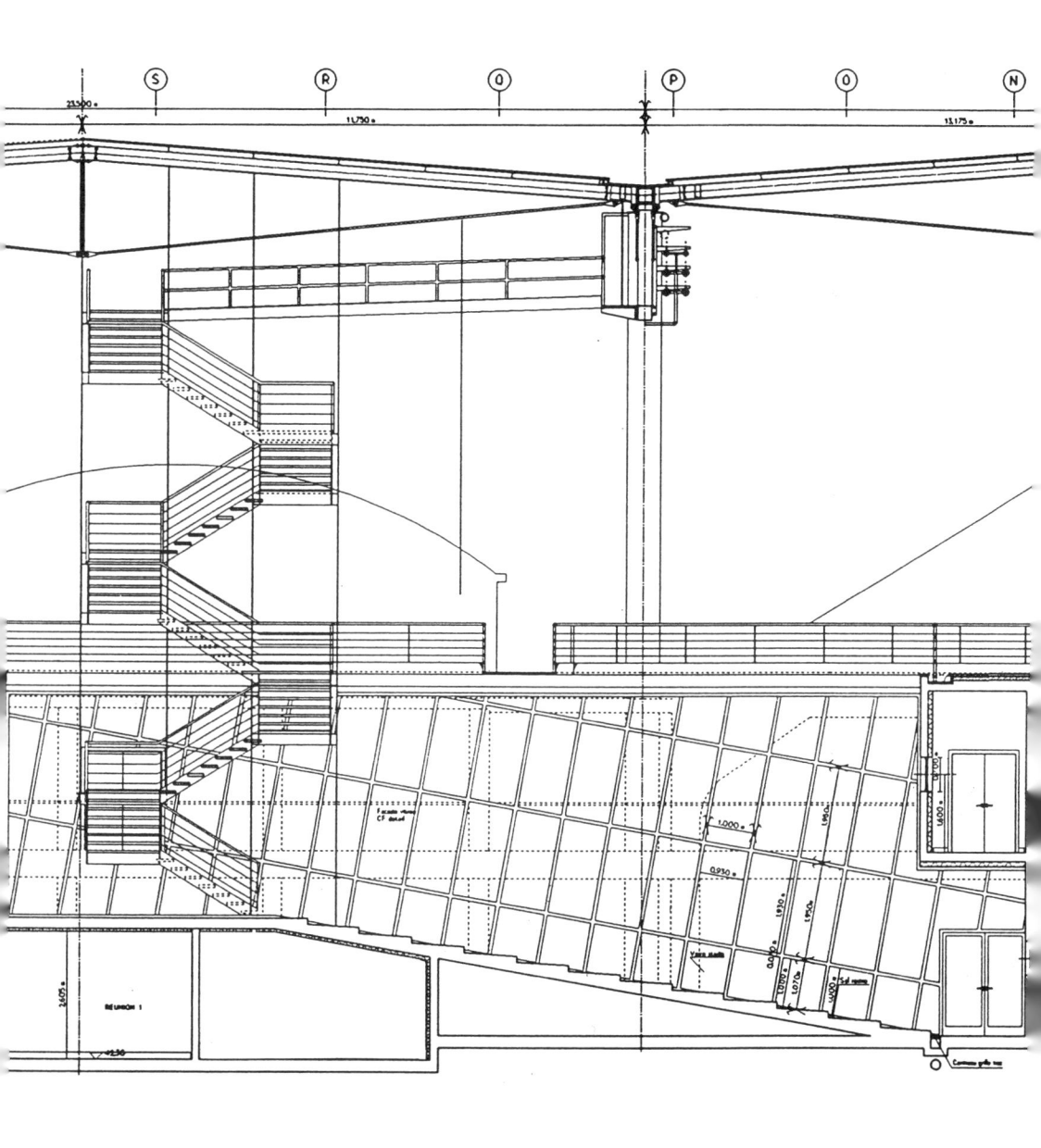

Suspended staircase and ramp: vertical interpenetration of spaces;
conjoined/disjoined condition

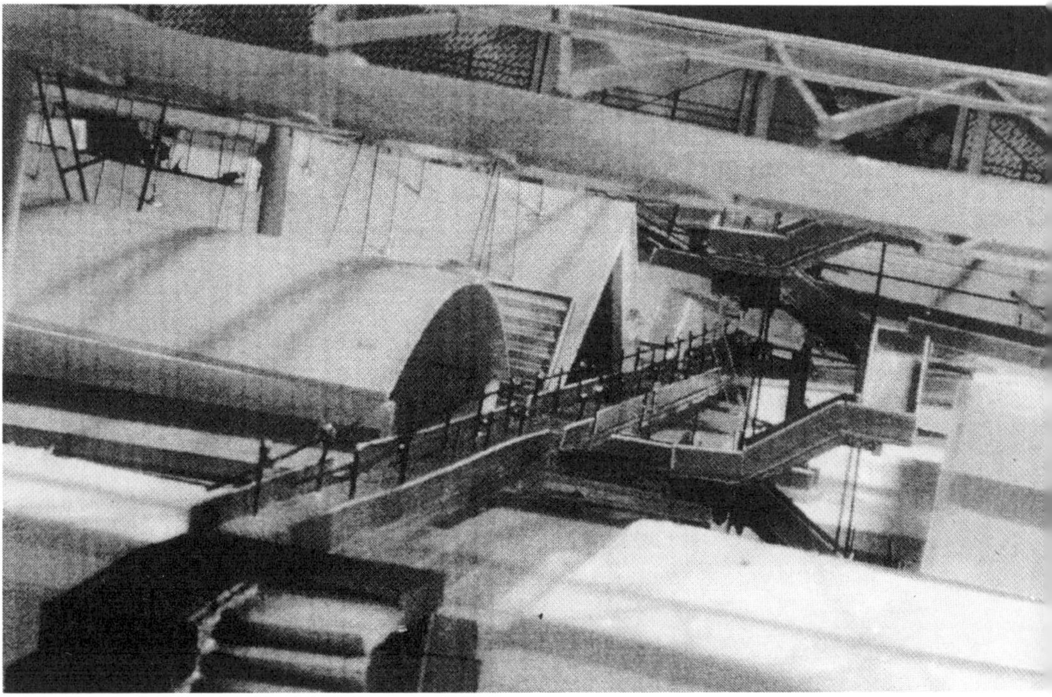

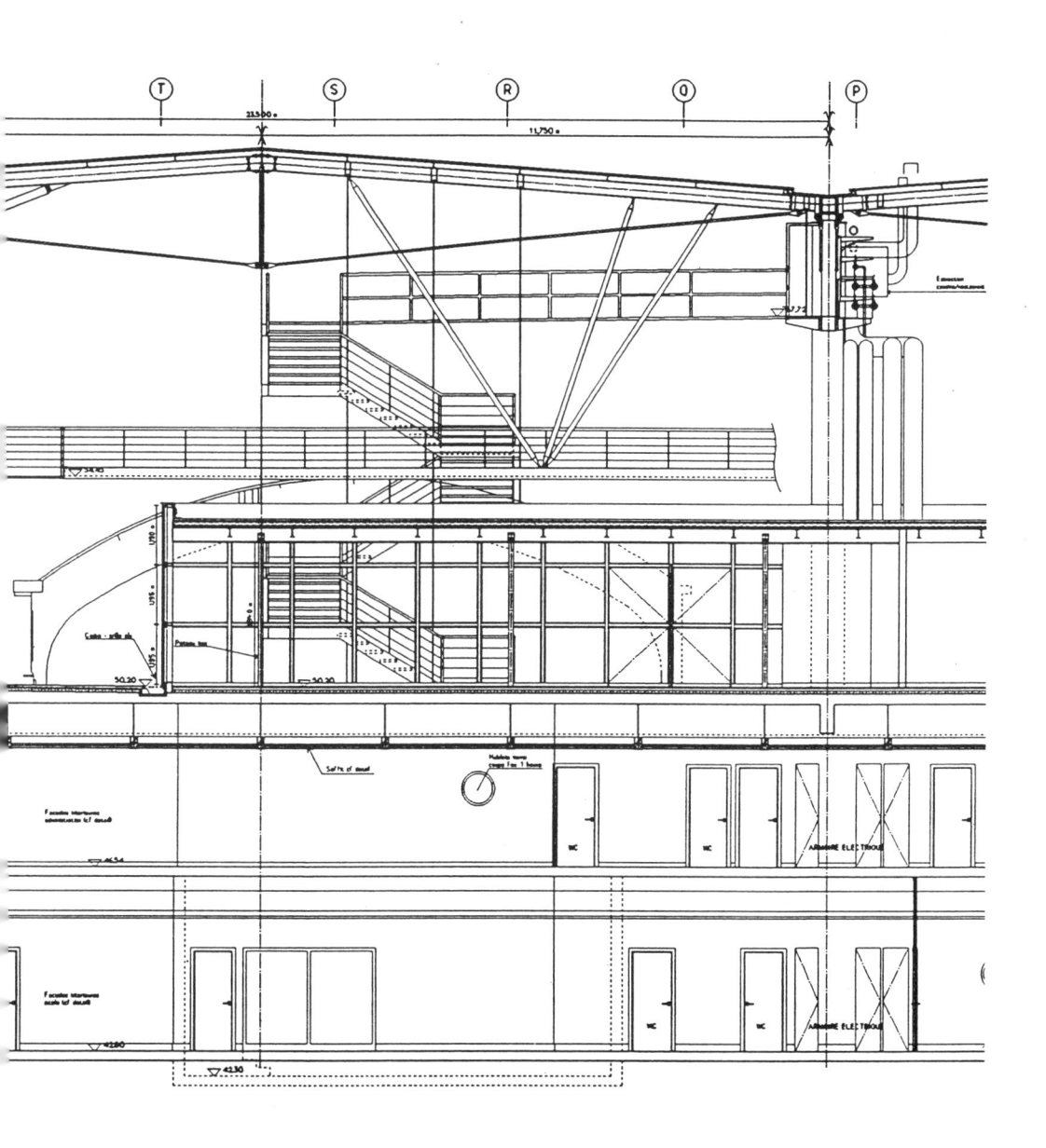

No synthesis, but a constant dissociation between space and use: new roof, restaurant, administrative offices, school

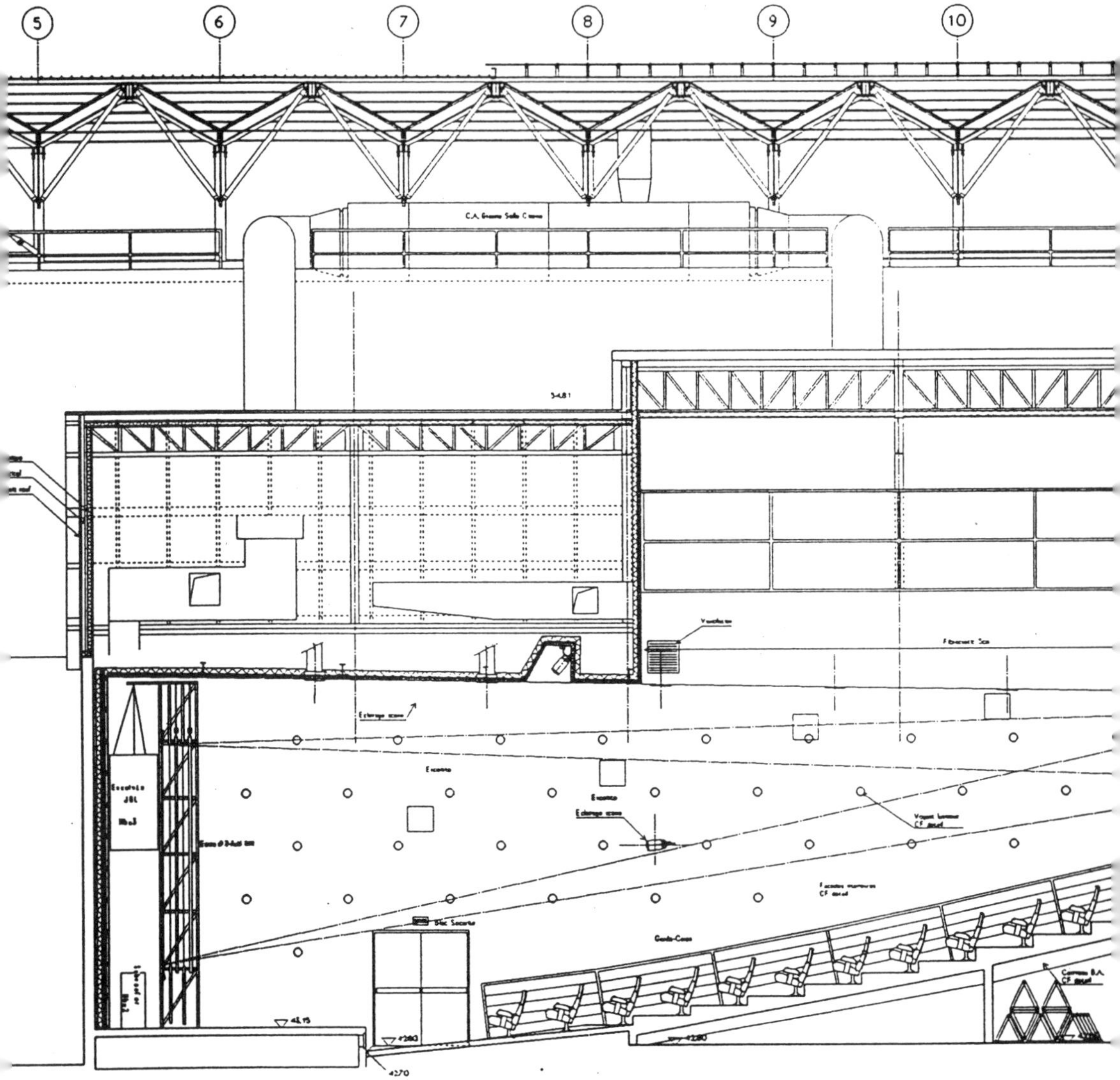
5
6
7
8
9
10

Cinemas inserted into the existing building

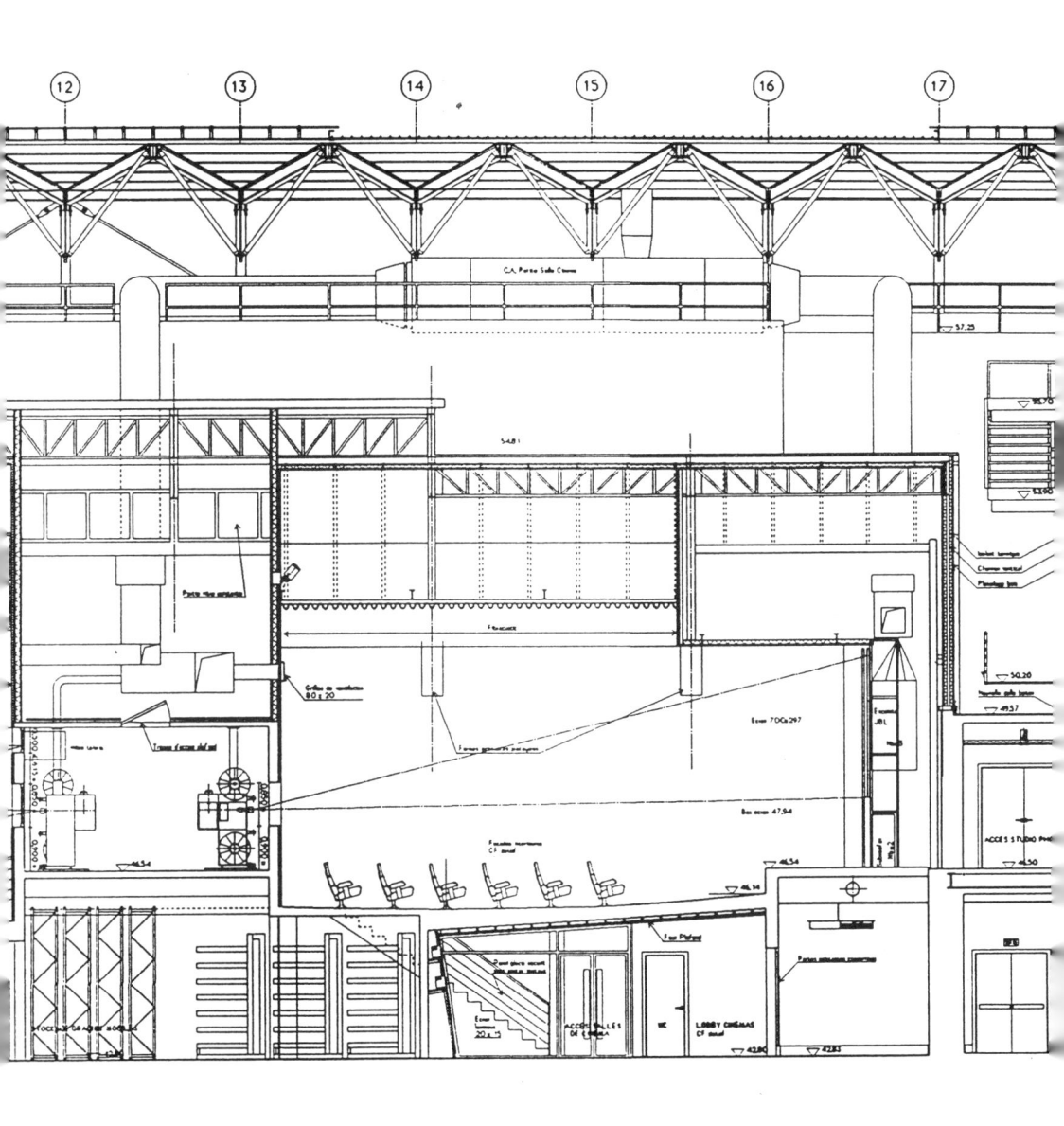

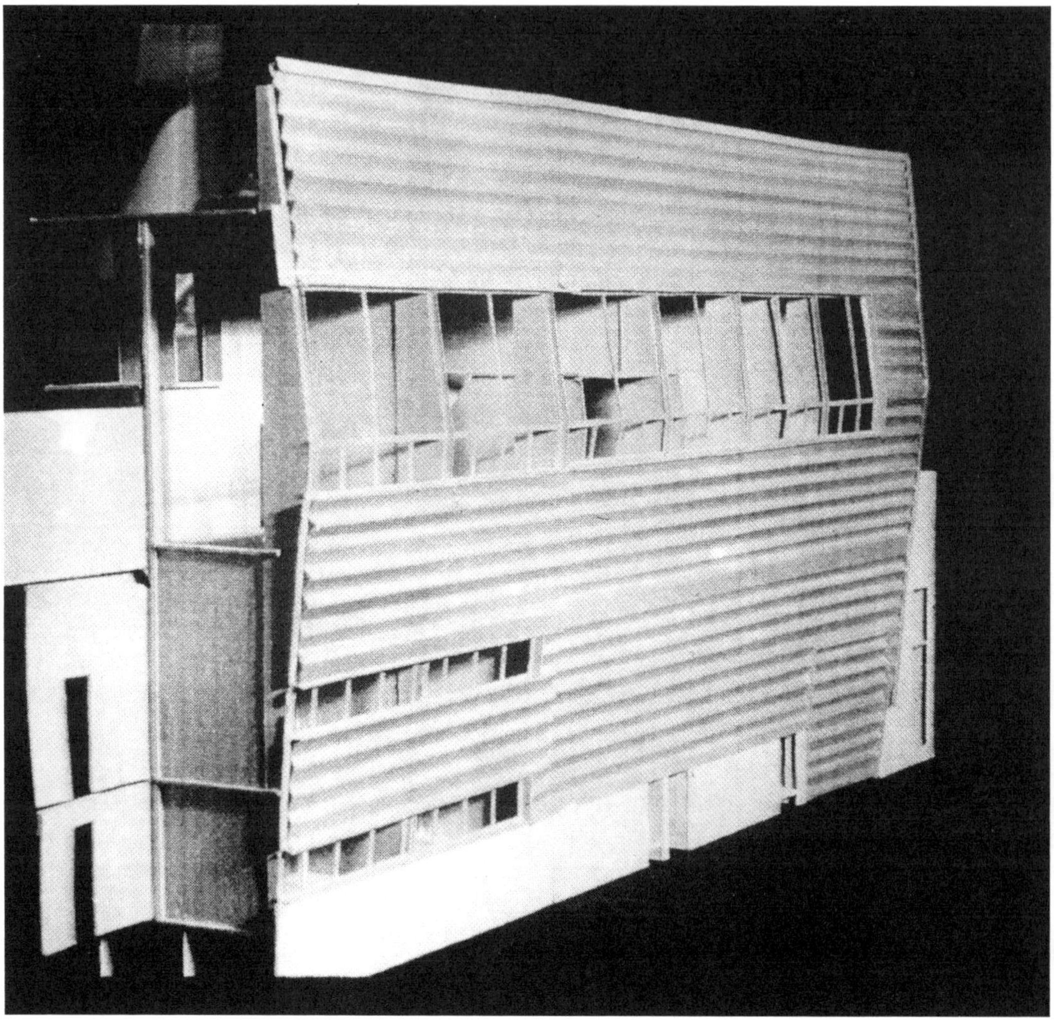

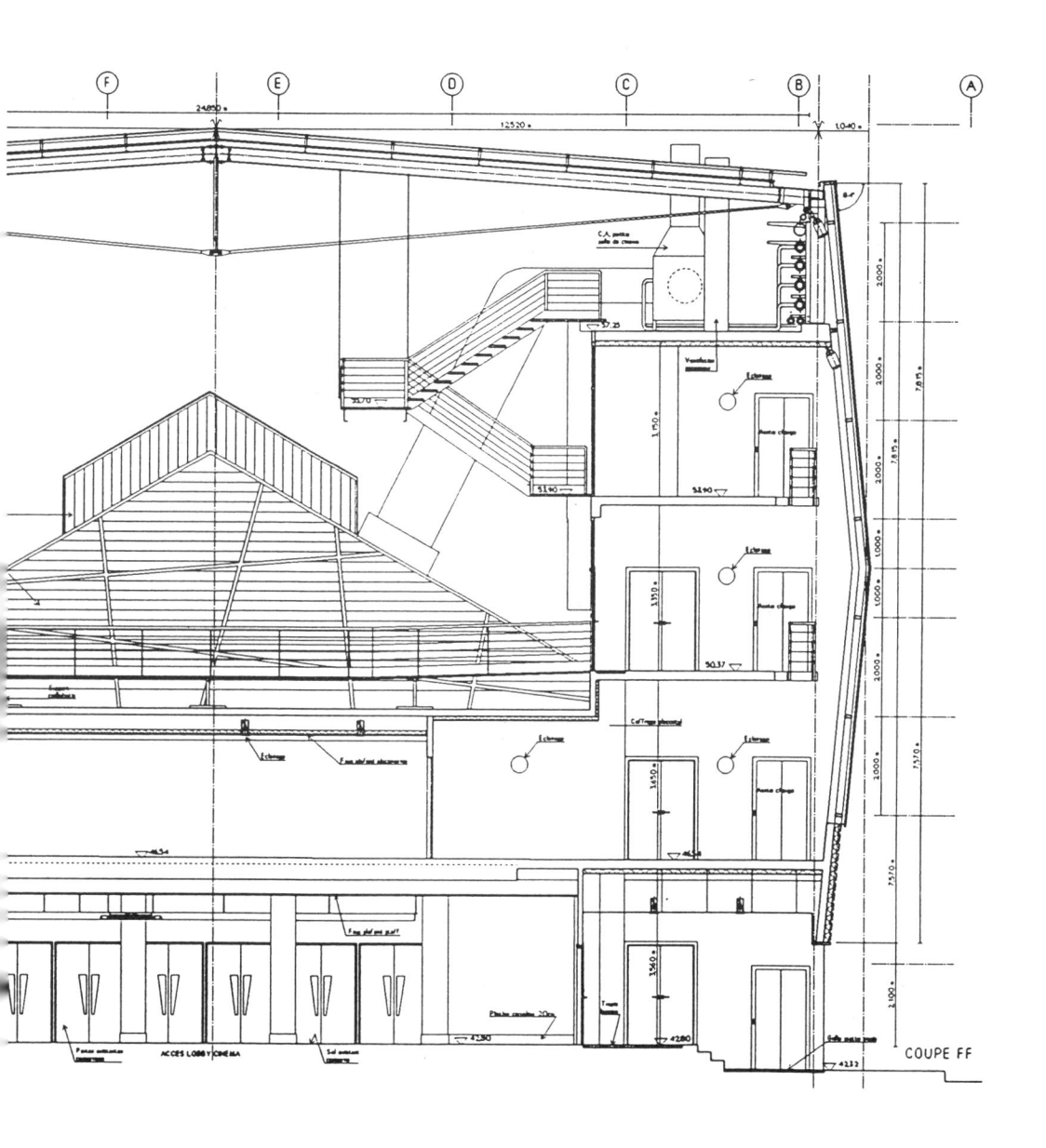

Folding: the roof turns and becomes the north facade

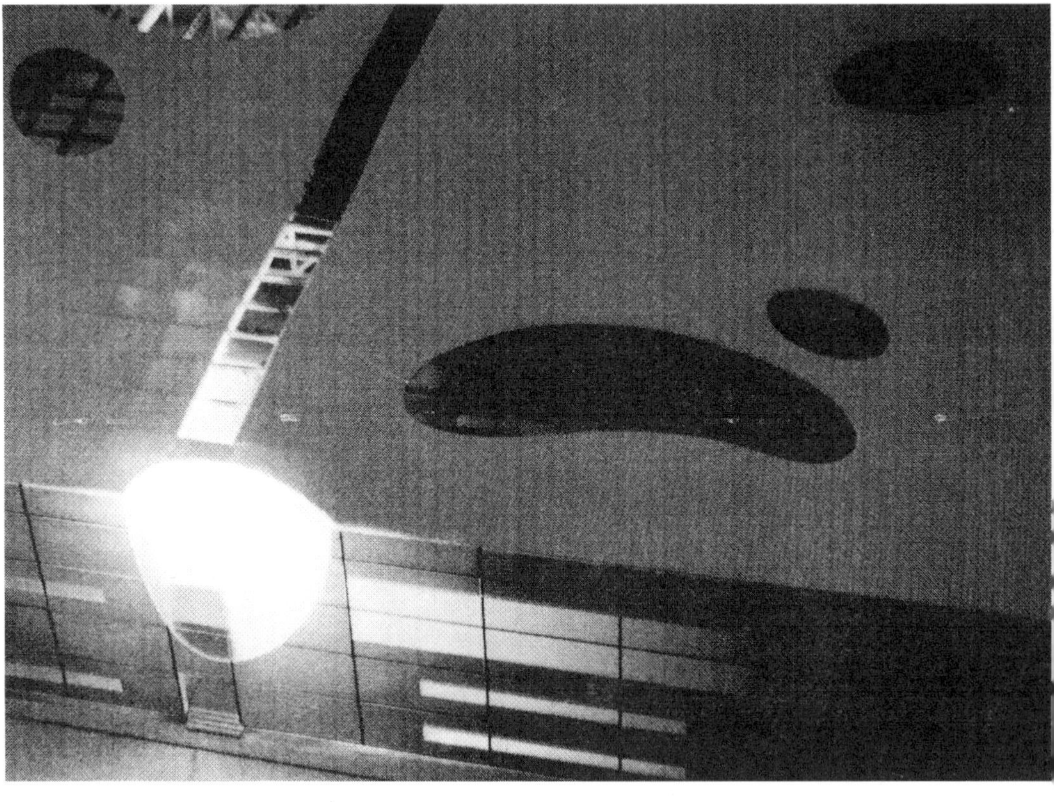

North elevation: partial view

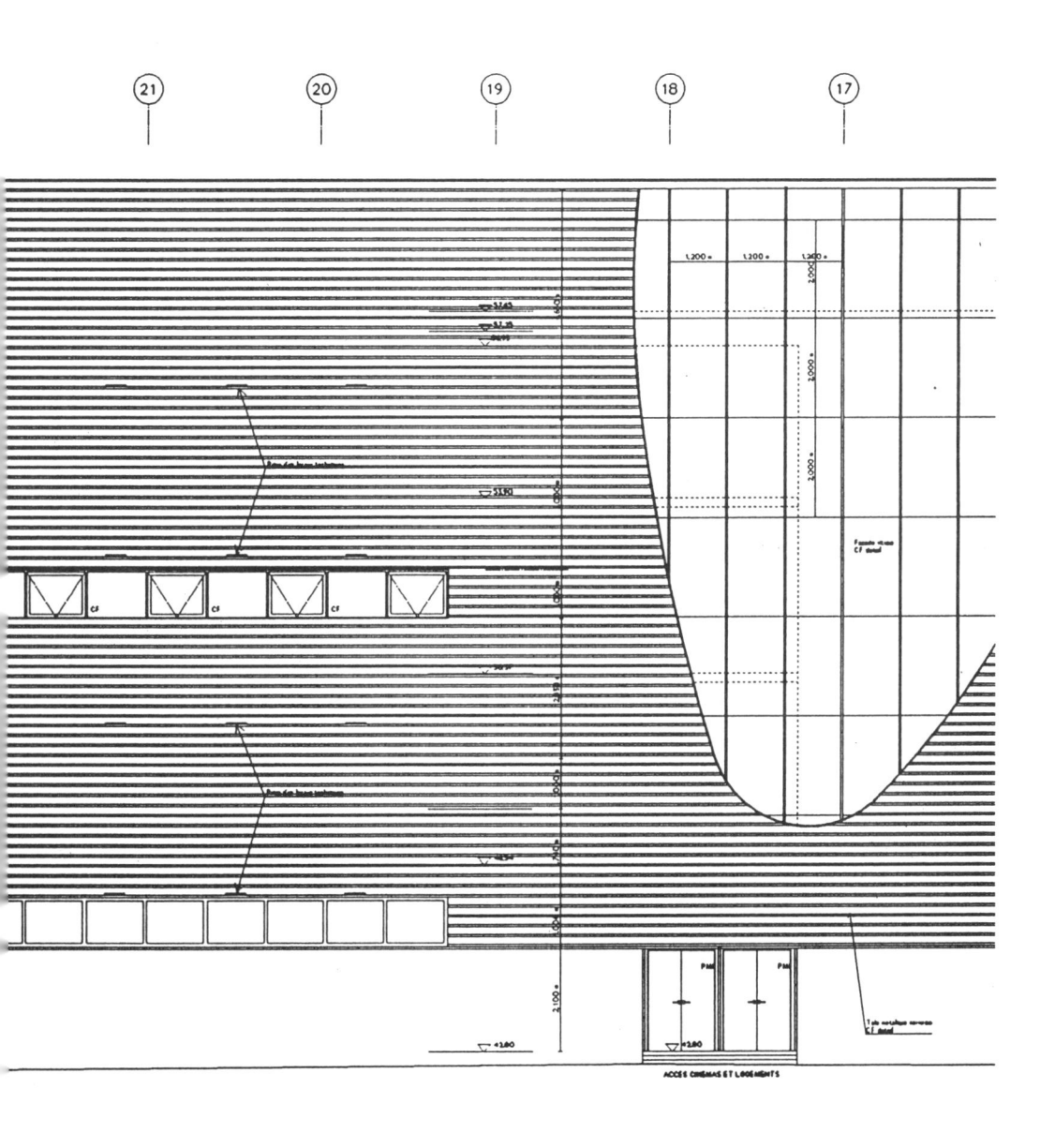

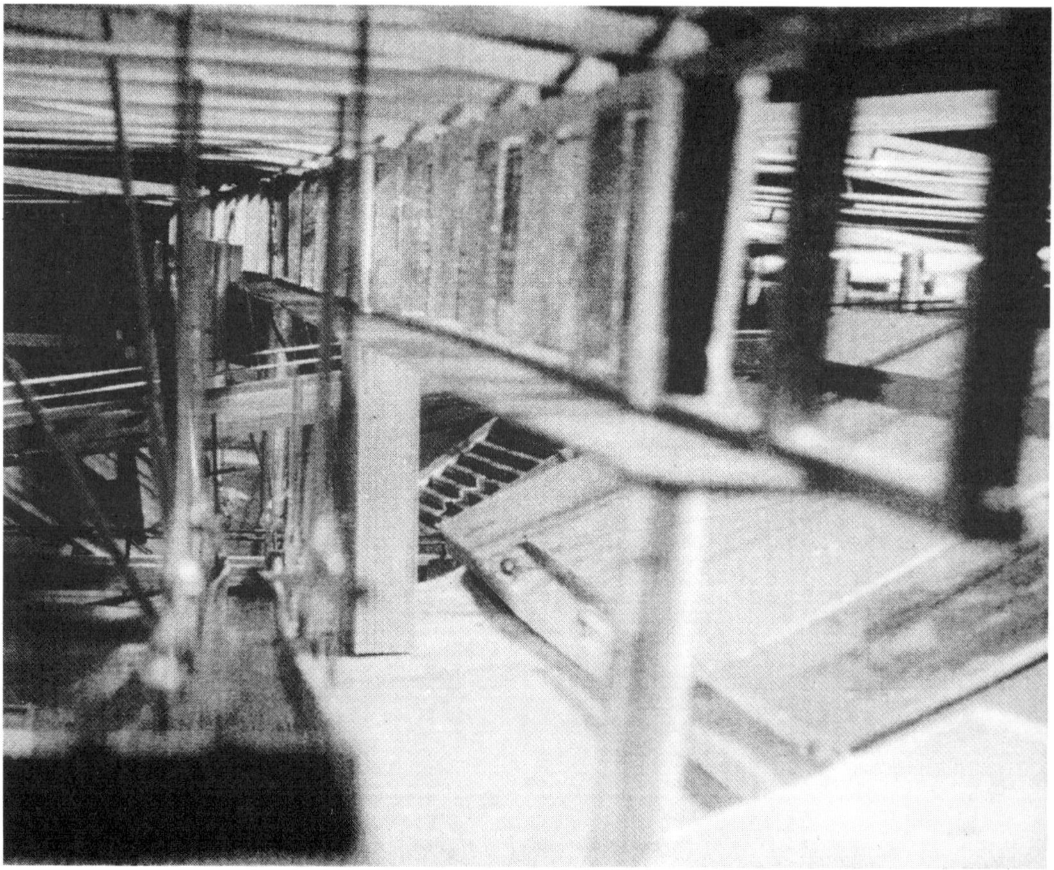

TOURCOING
495

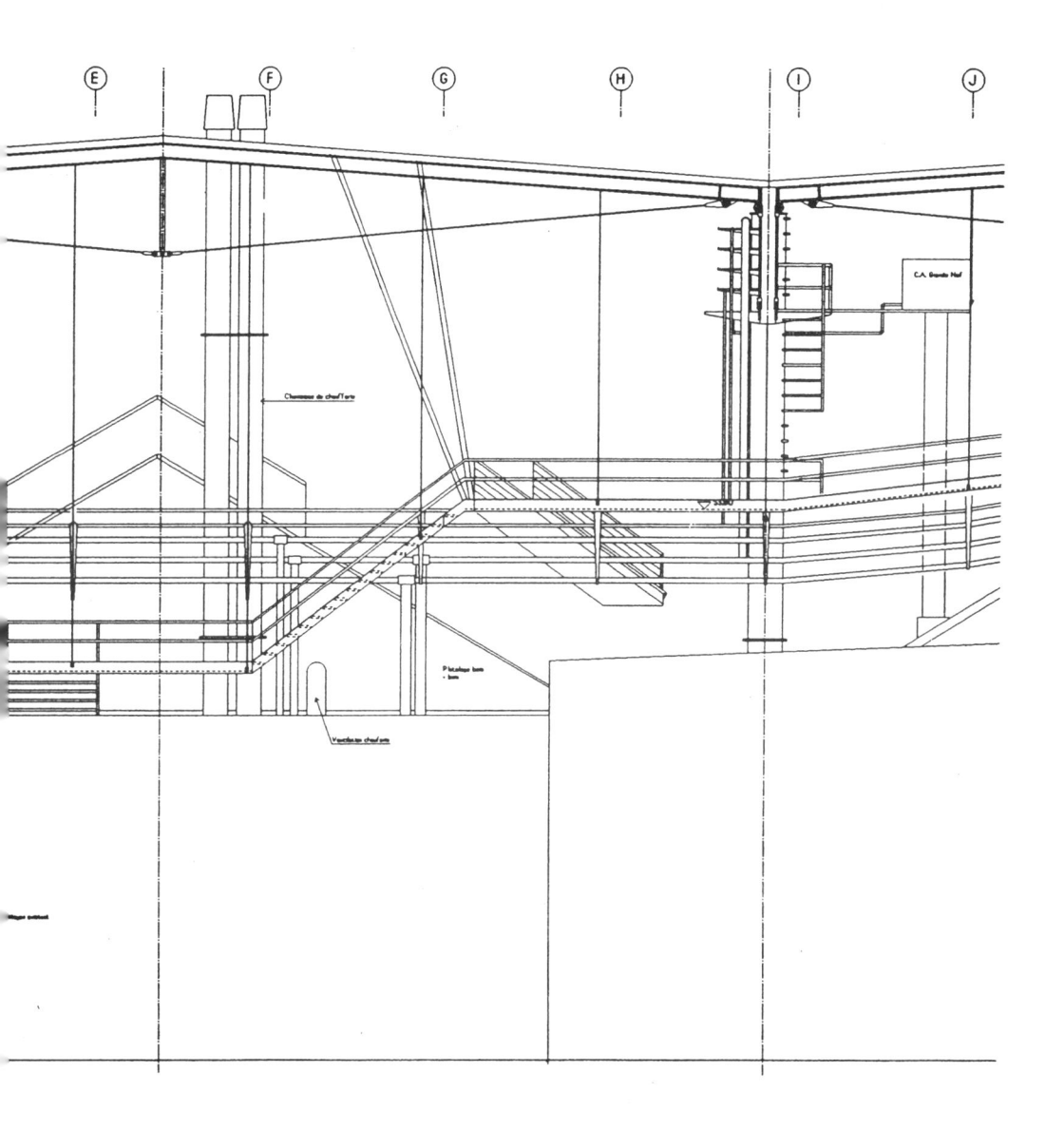

West elevation: partial view

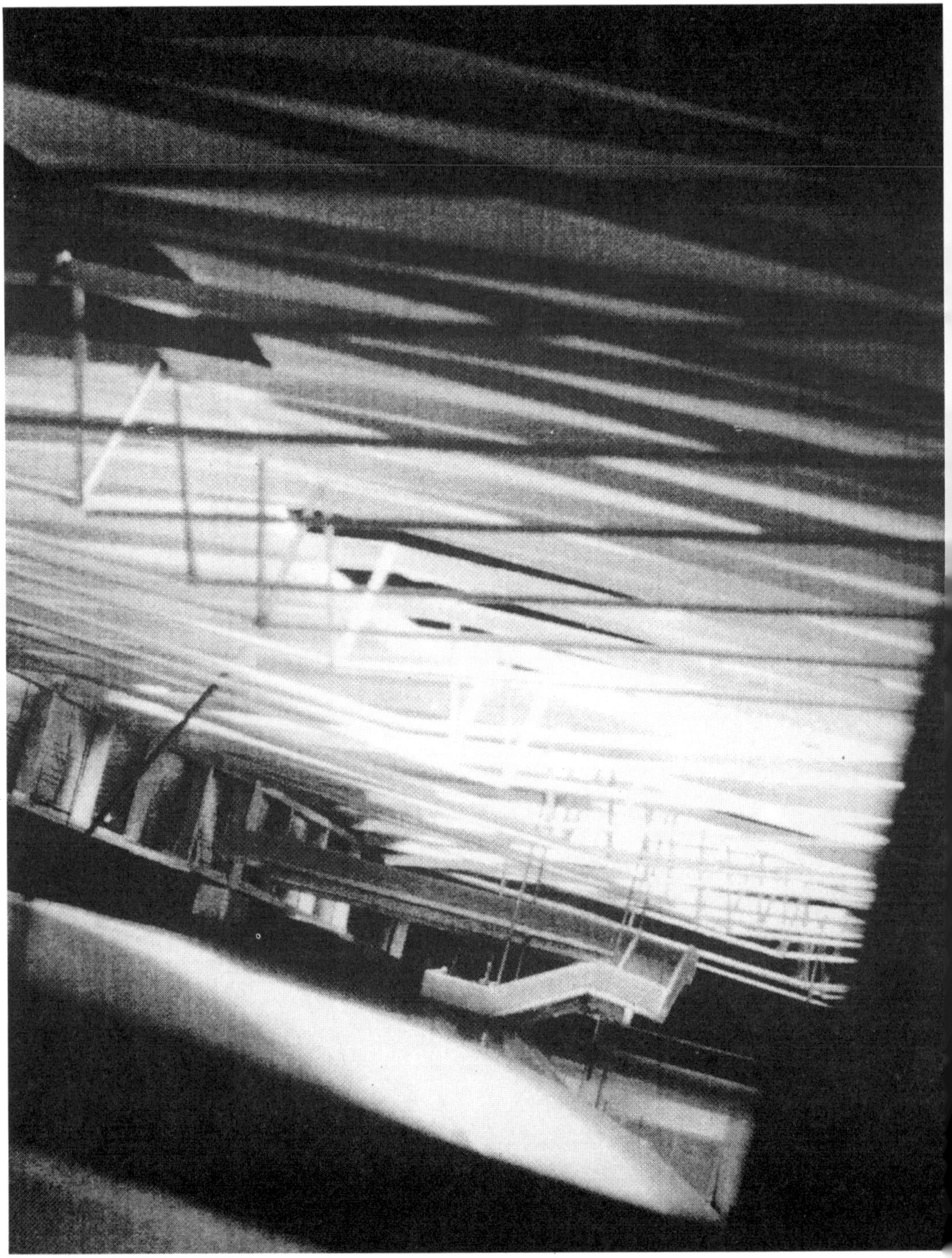

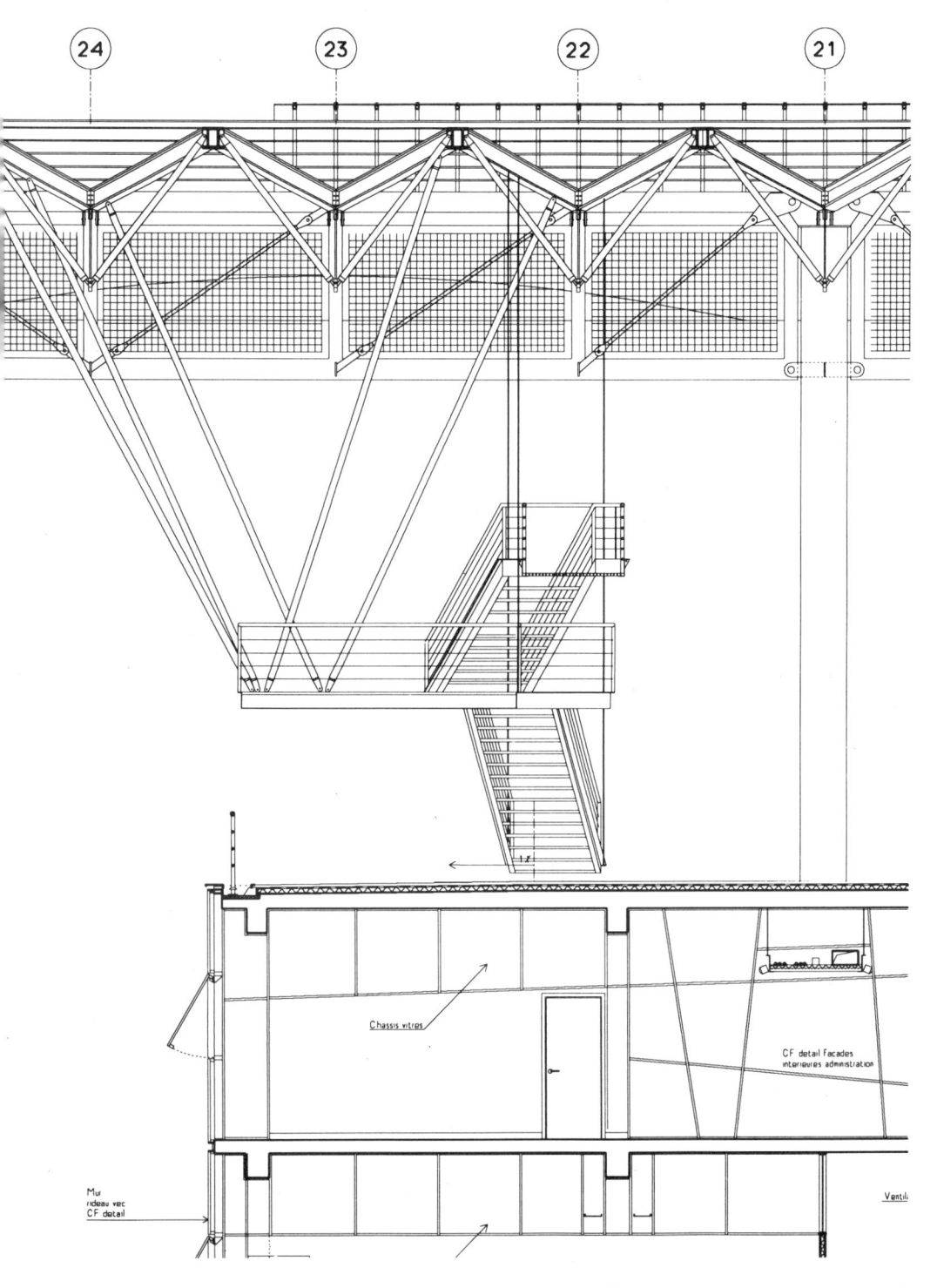

Video garden: suspended "nature"

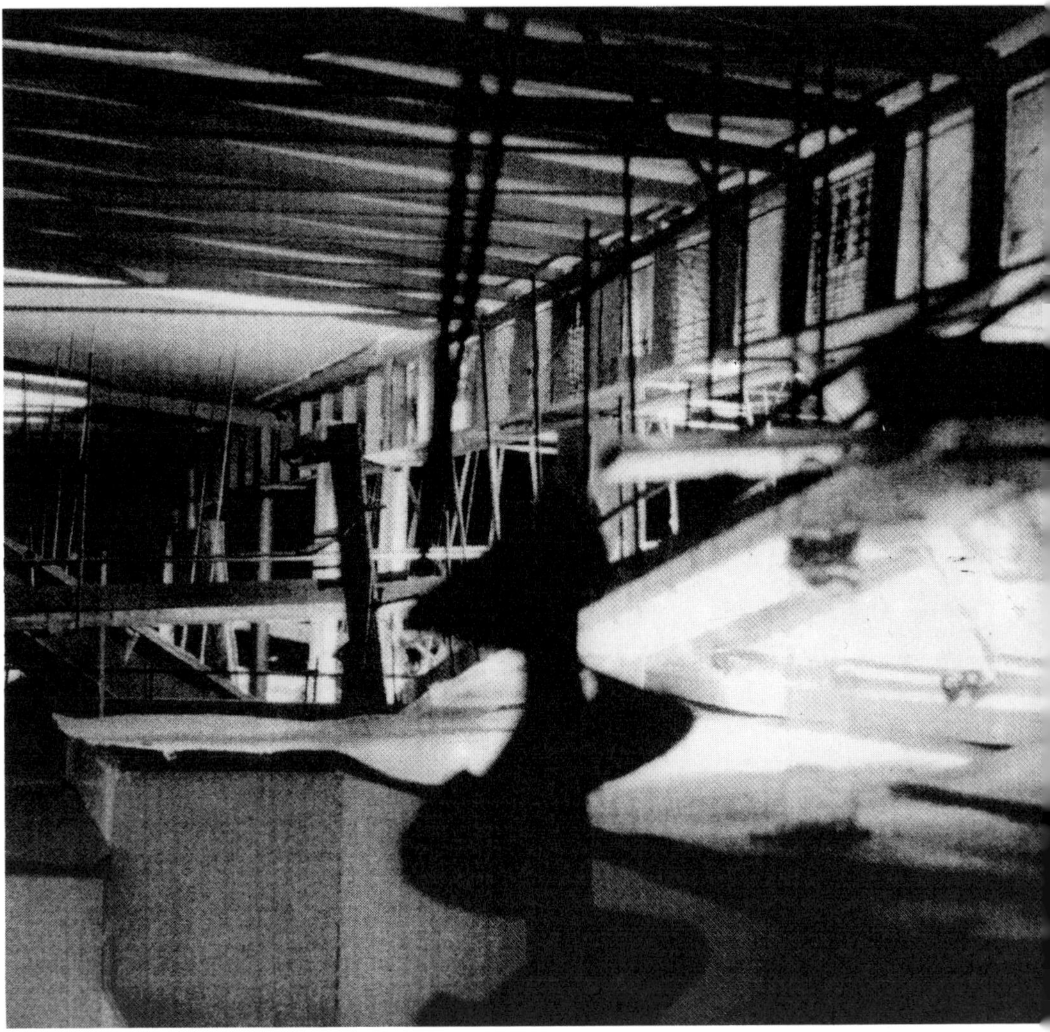

TOURCOING
499

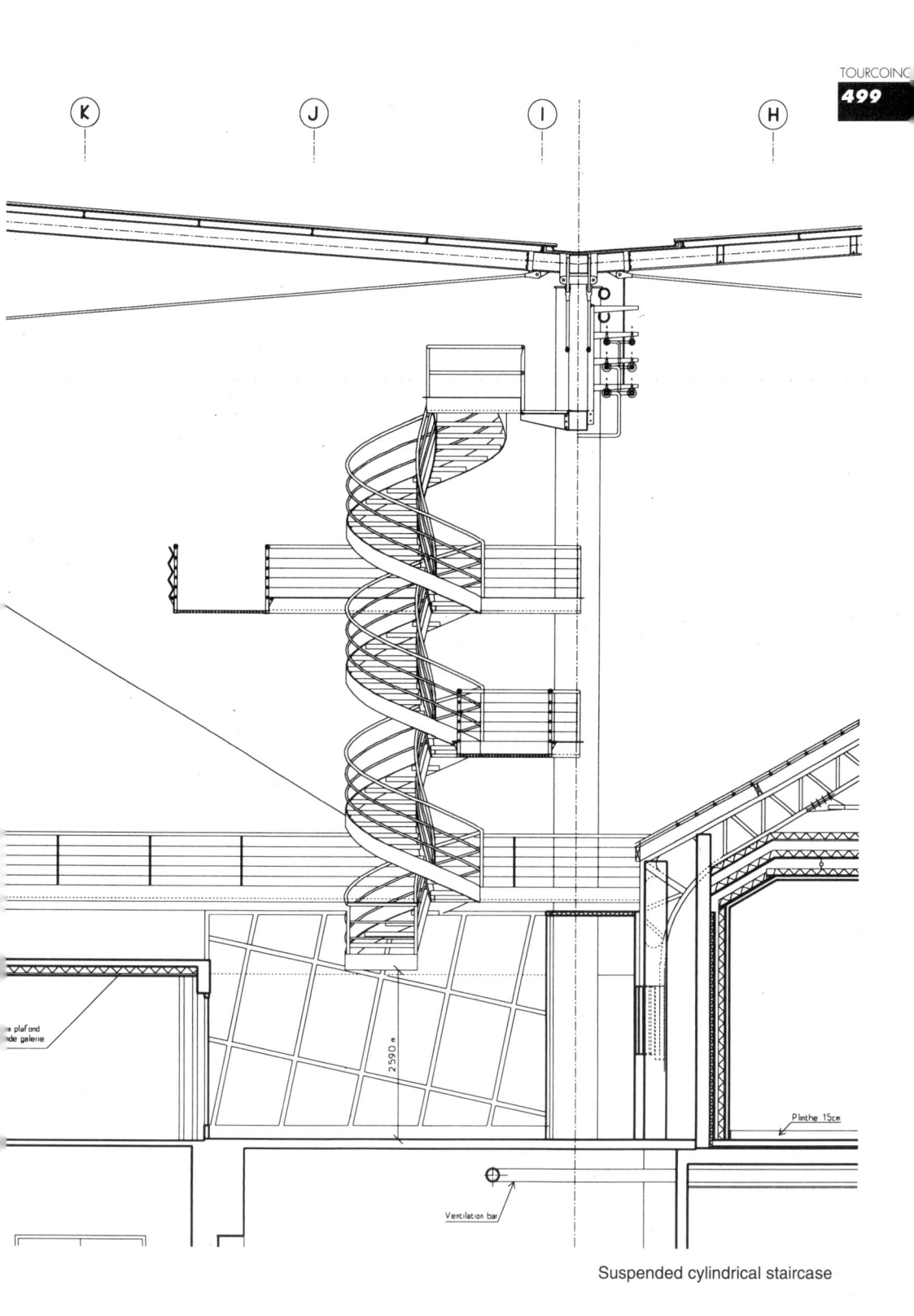

K　　　　J　　　　I　　　　H

2590 m

plafond
de galerie

Plinthe 15cm

Ventilation bar

Suspended cylindrical staircase

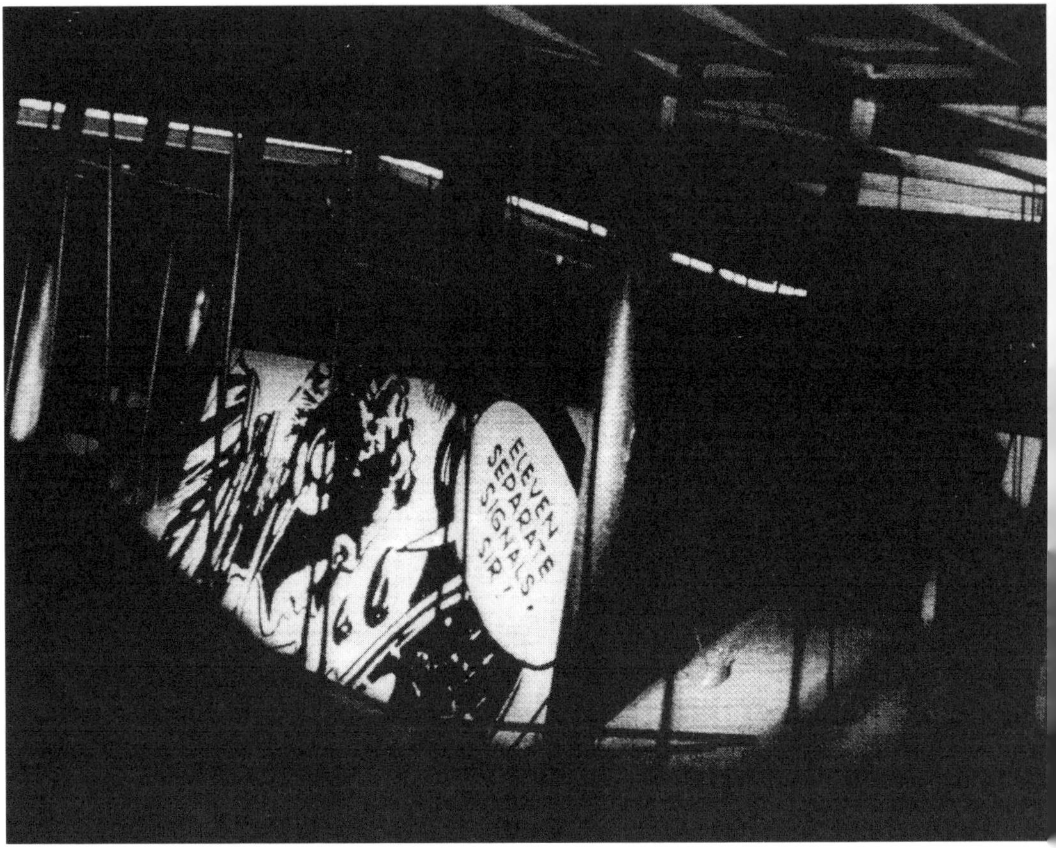
ELEVEN SEPARATE SIGNALS, SIR!

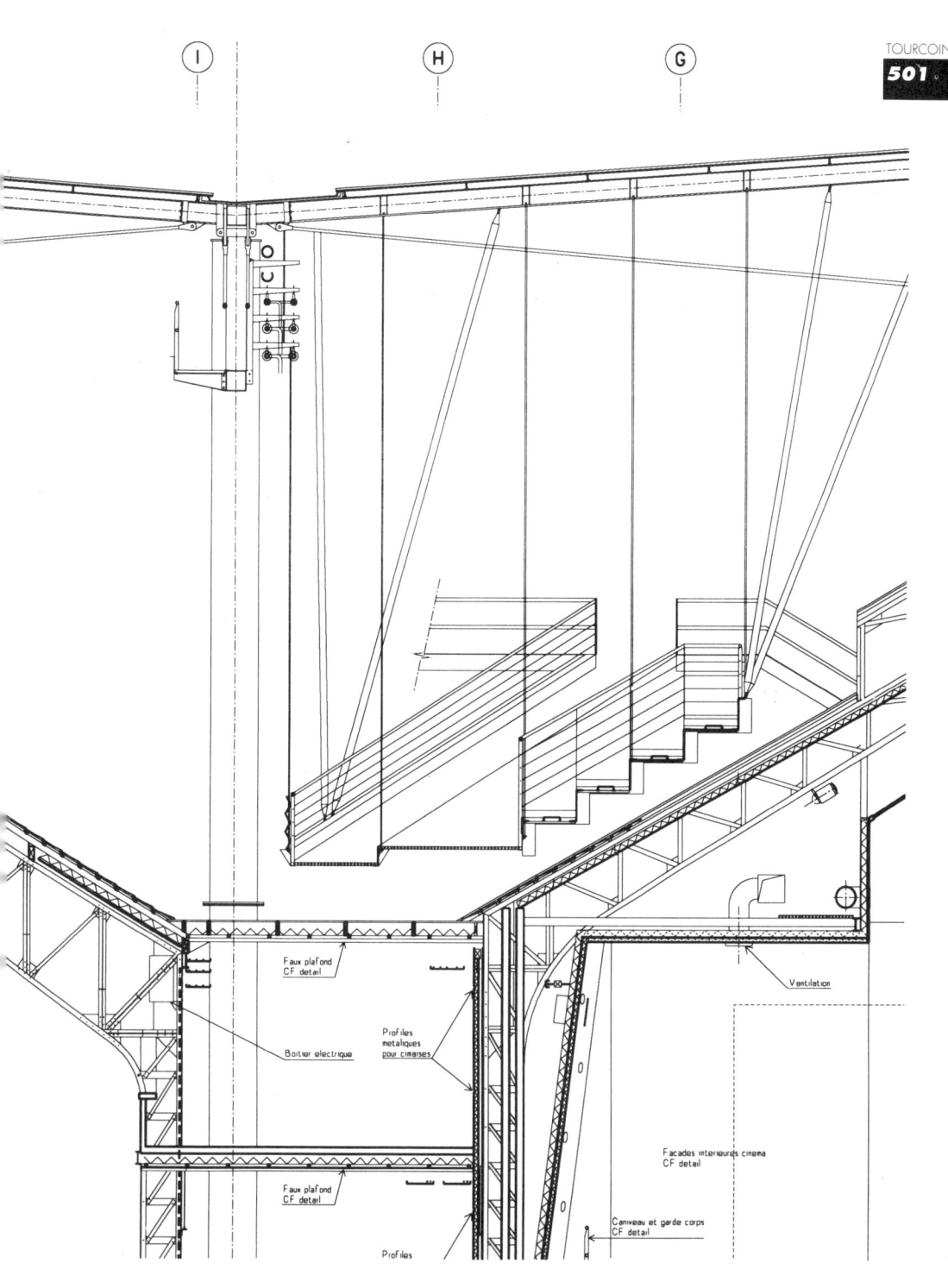

Seating of the outdoor cinema in the in-between:
against a static, autonomous view of architecture

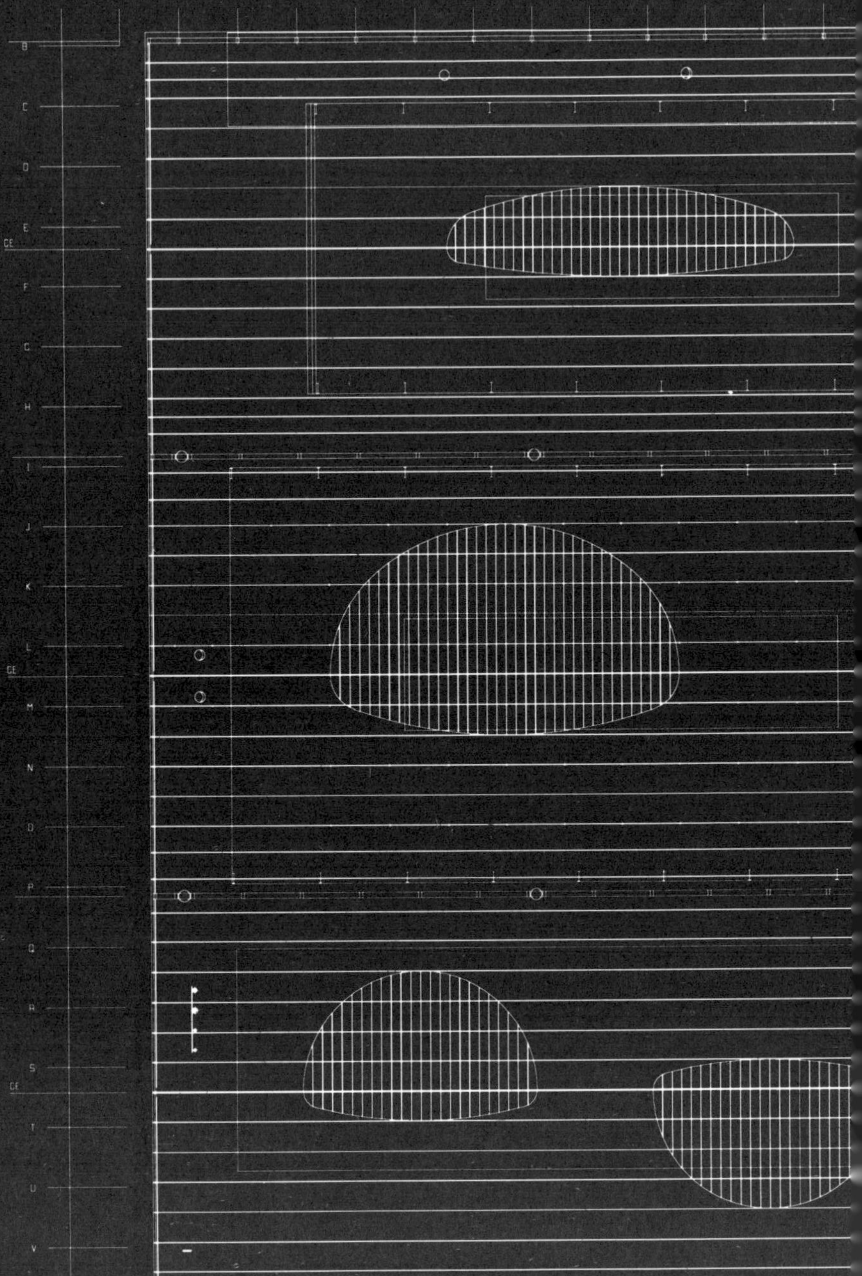

B
C
D
E
CE
F
G
H
I
J
K
L
CE
M
N
O
P
Q
R
S
CE
T
U
V
W
X
Y

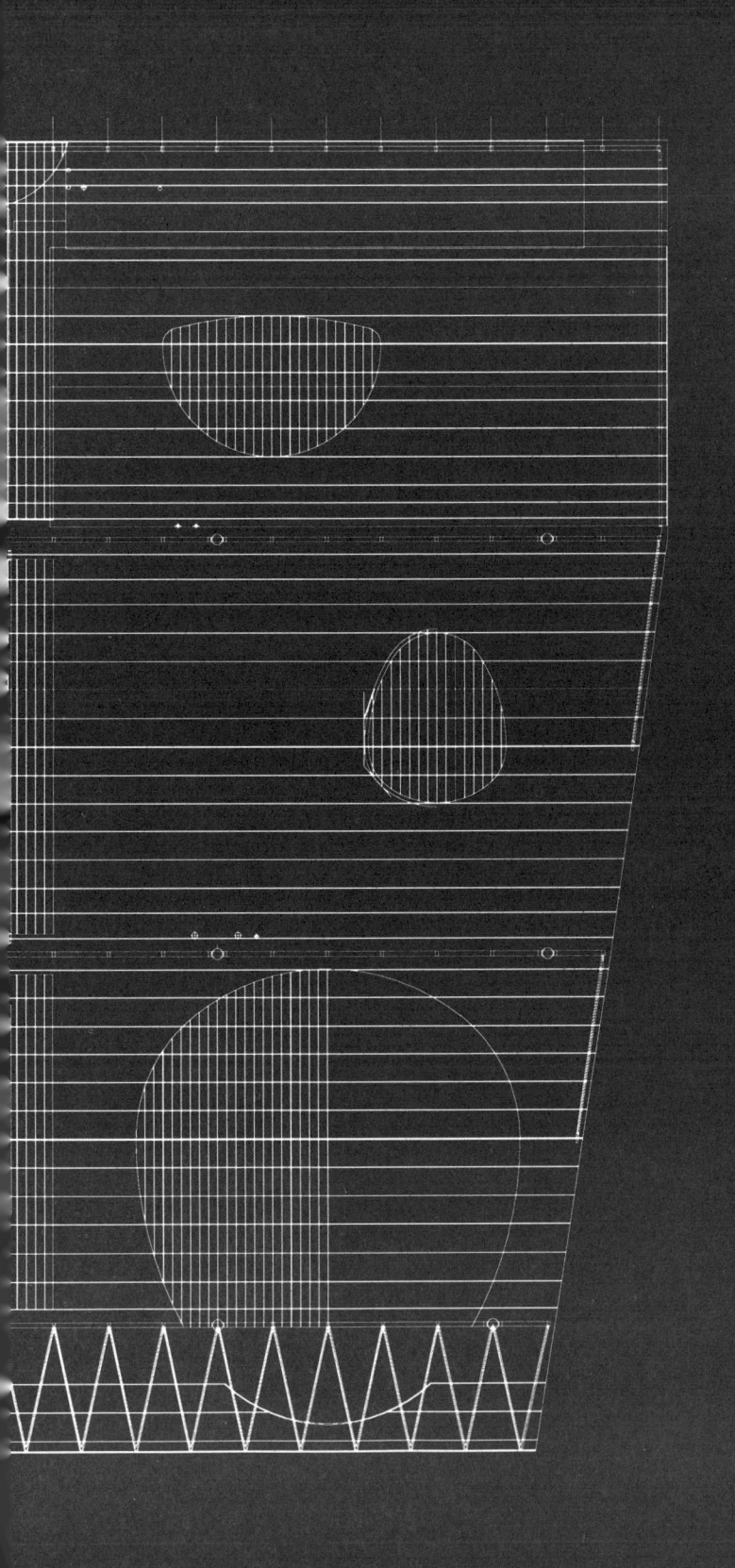

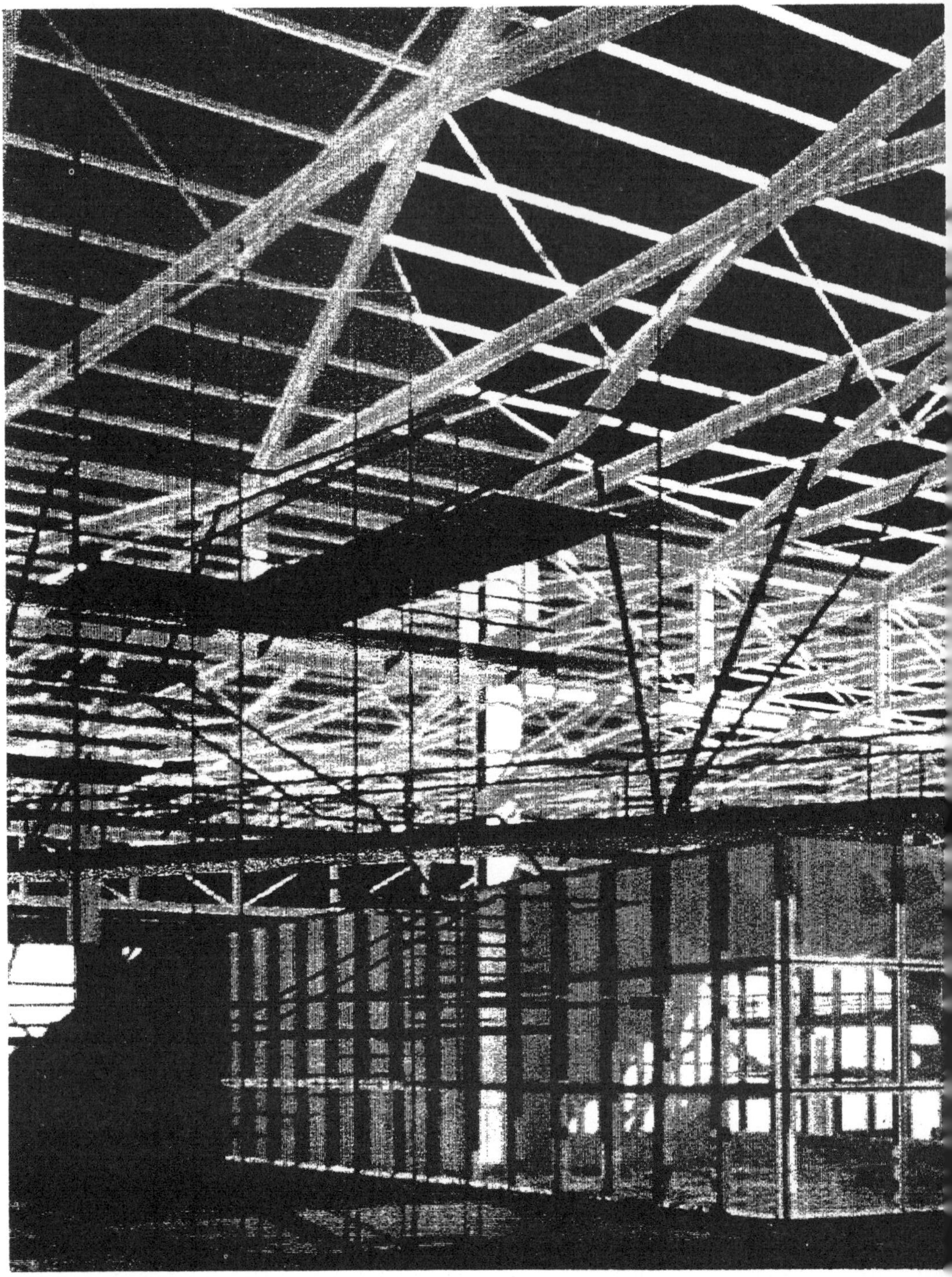

Coupe transversale

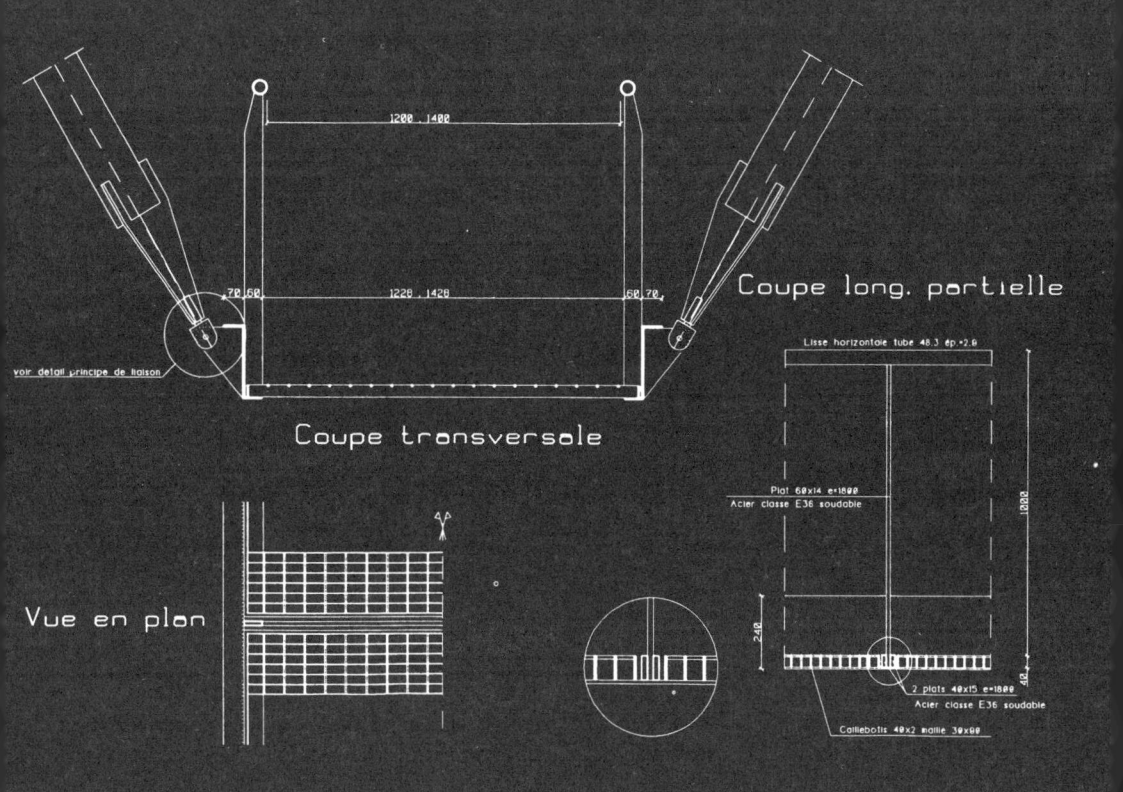

Coupe long. partielle

Vue en plan

voir détail principe de liaison

Lisse horizontale tube 48.3 ép.=2.9
Plat 60x14 e=1800
Acier classe E36 soudable
2 plats 40x15 e=1800
Acier classe E36 soudable
Caillebotis 40x2 maille 30x80

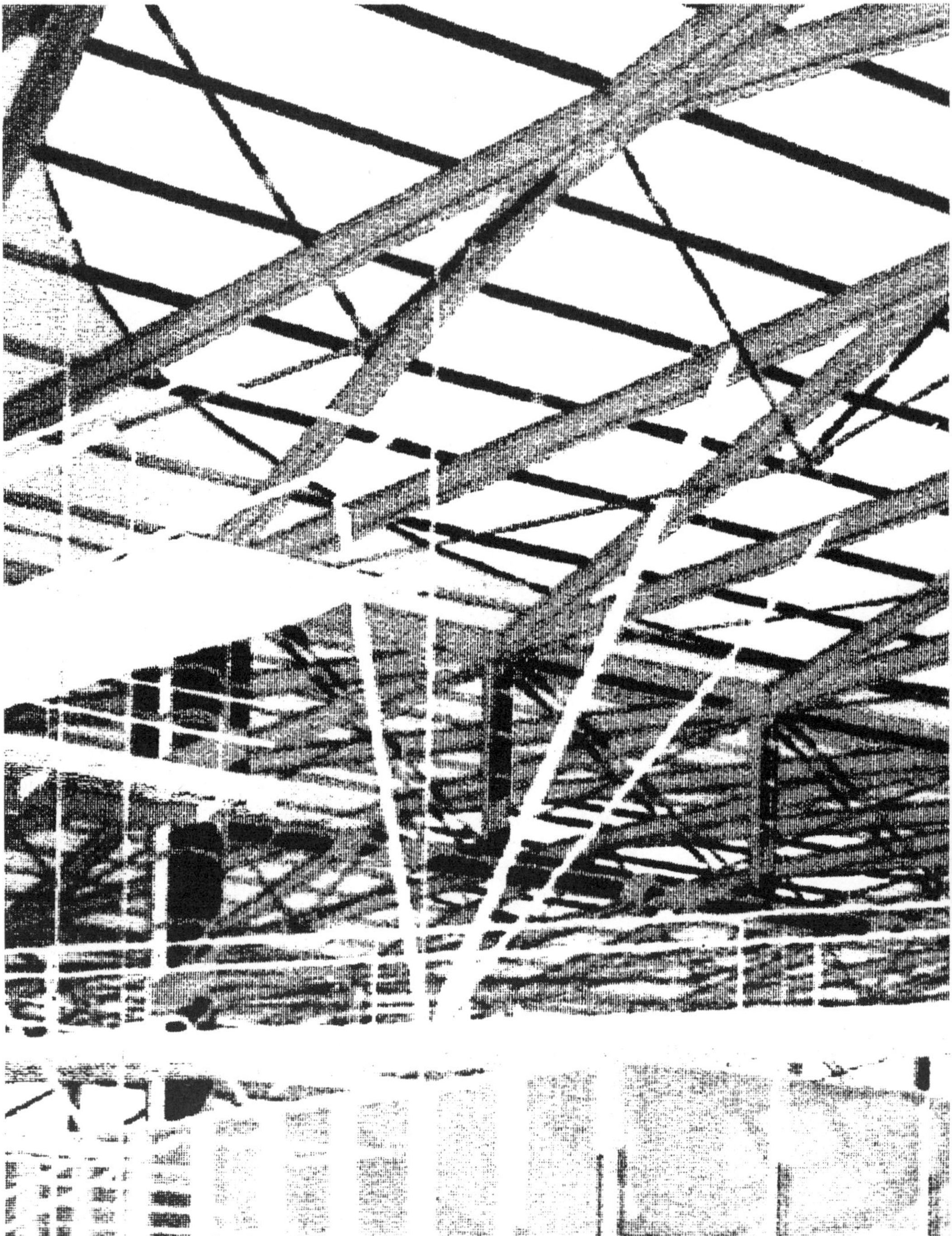

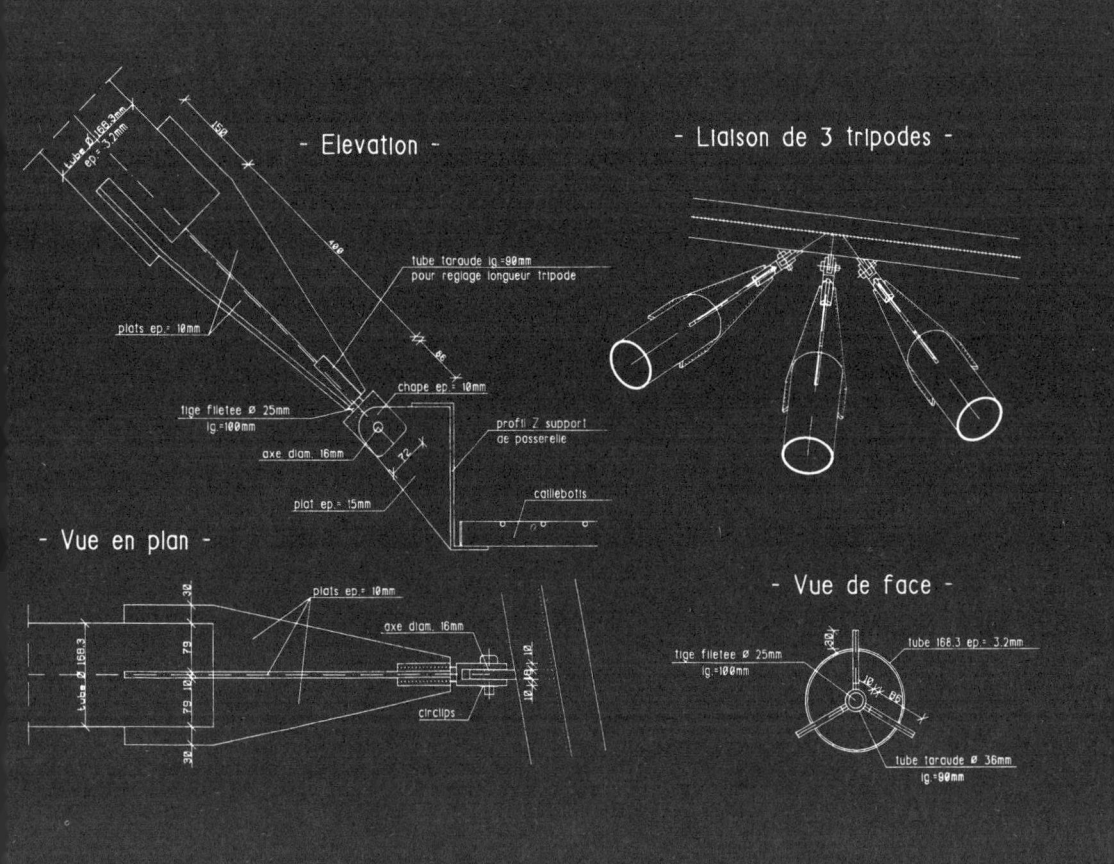

- Elevation -

- Liaison de 3 tripodes -

- Vue en plan -

- Vue de face -

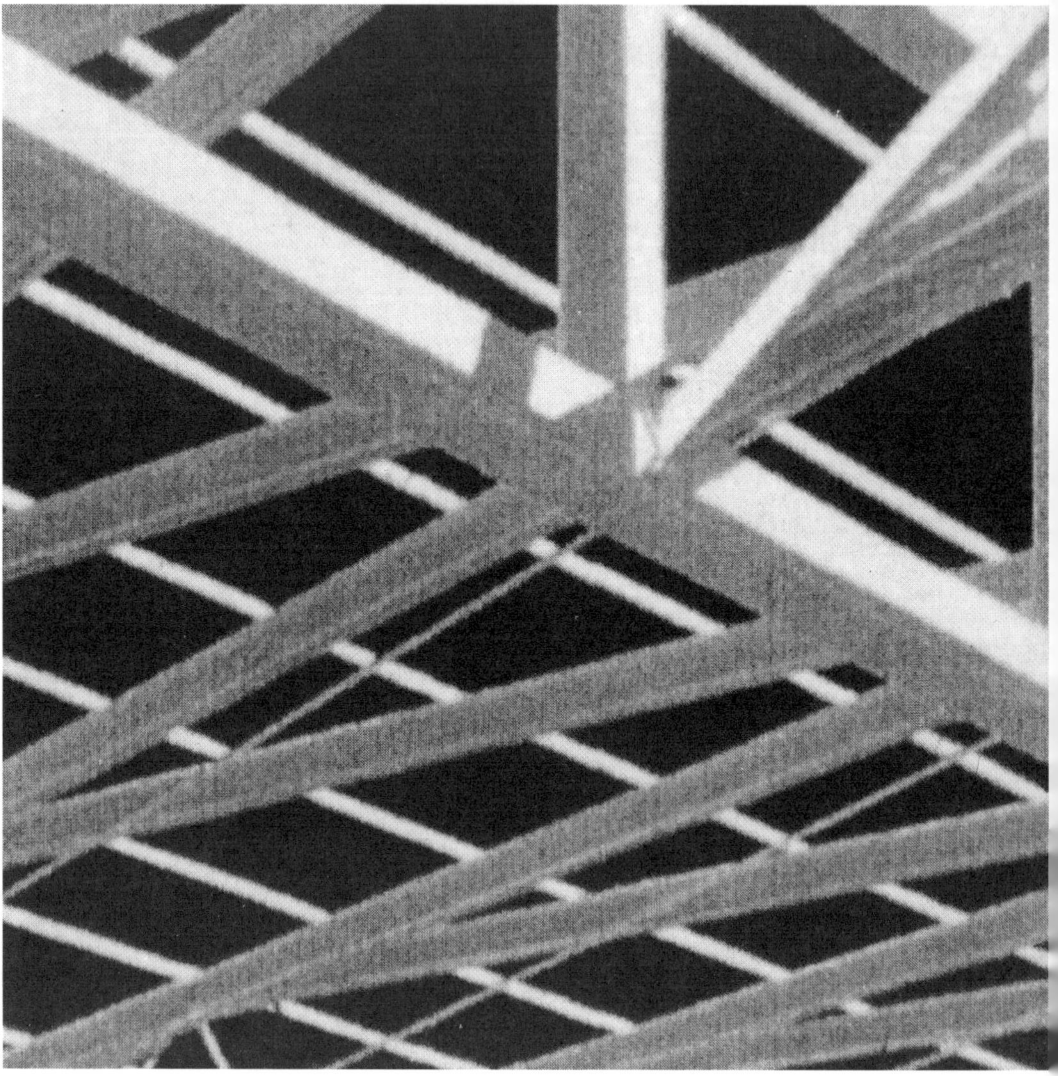

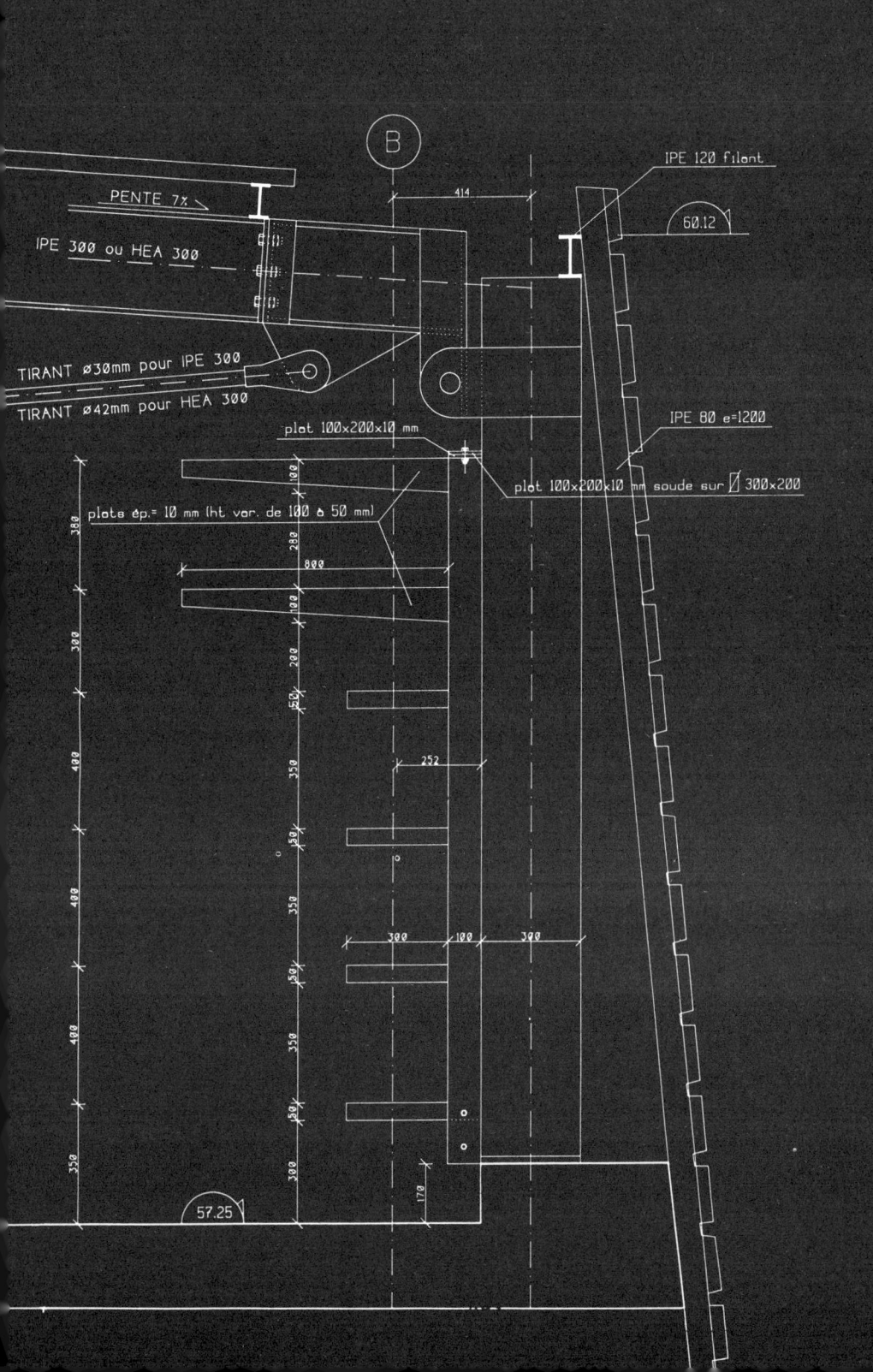

PENTE 7%
IPE 300 ou HEA 300
TIRANT ø30mm pour IPE 300
TIRANT ø42mm pour HEA 300
plat 100x200x10 mm
plats ép.= 10 mm (ht var. de 100 à 50 mm)
IPE 120 filant
60.12
IPE 80 e=1200
plat 100x200x10 mm soudé sur ⌀ 300x200
57.25

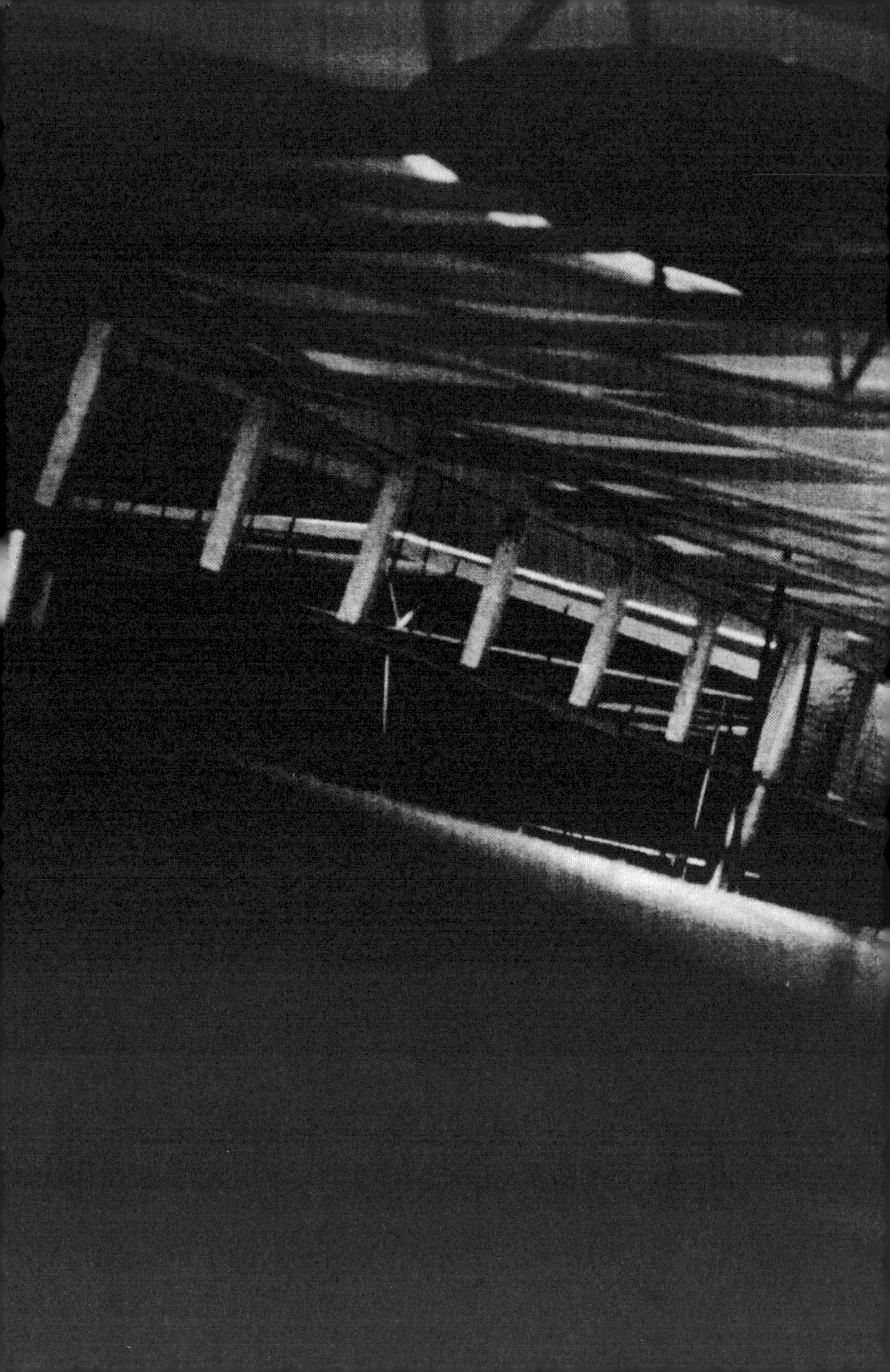

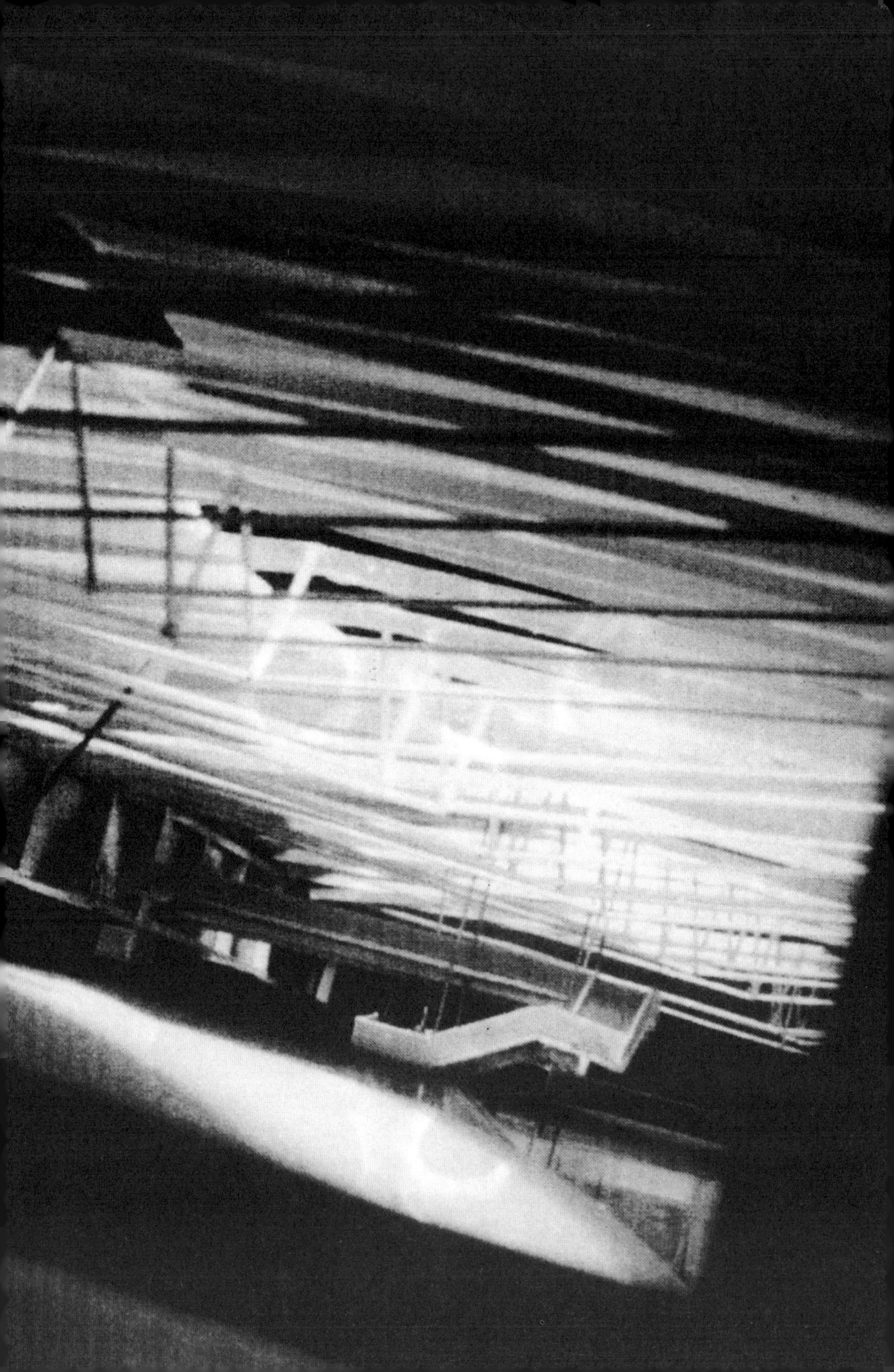

Life in the modern **metropolis**

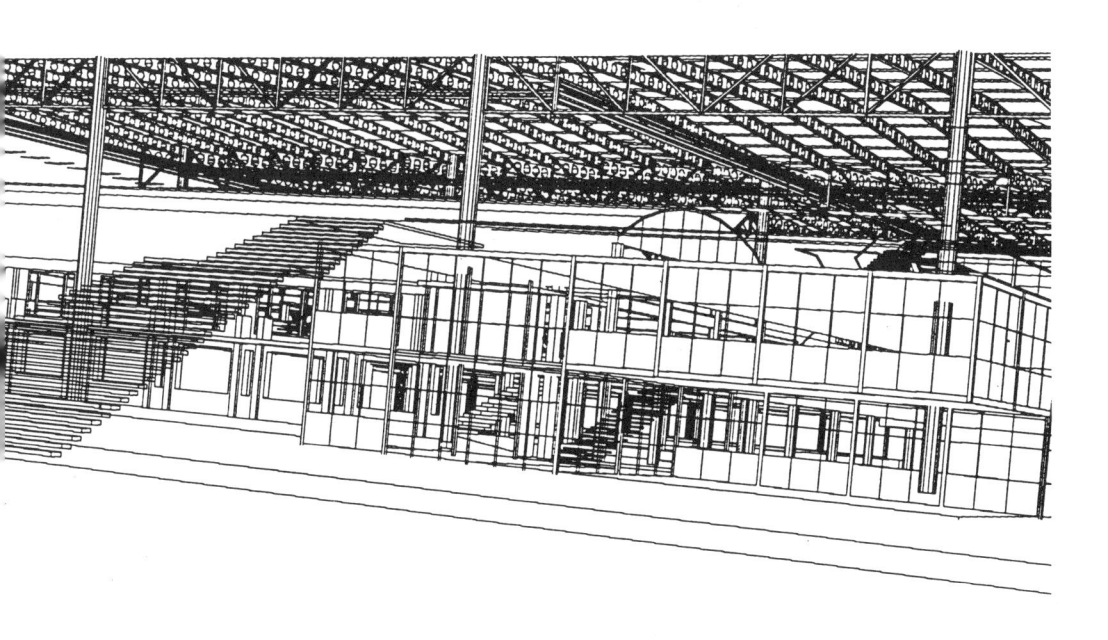

Architecture is as much about the event that takes place in a space as about the space

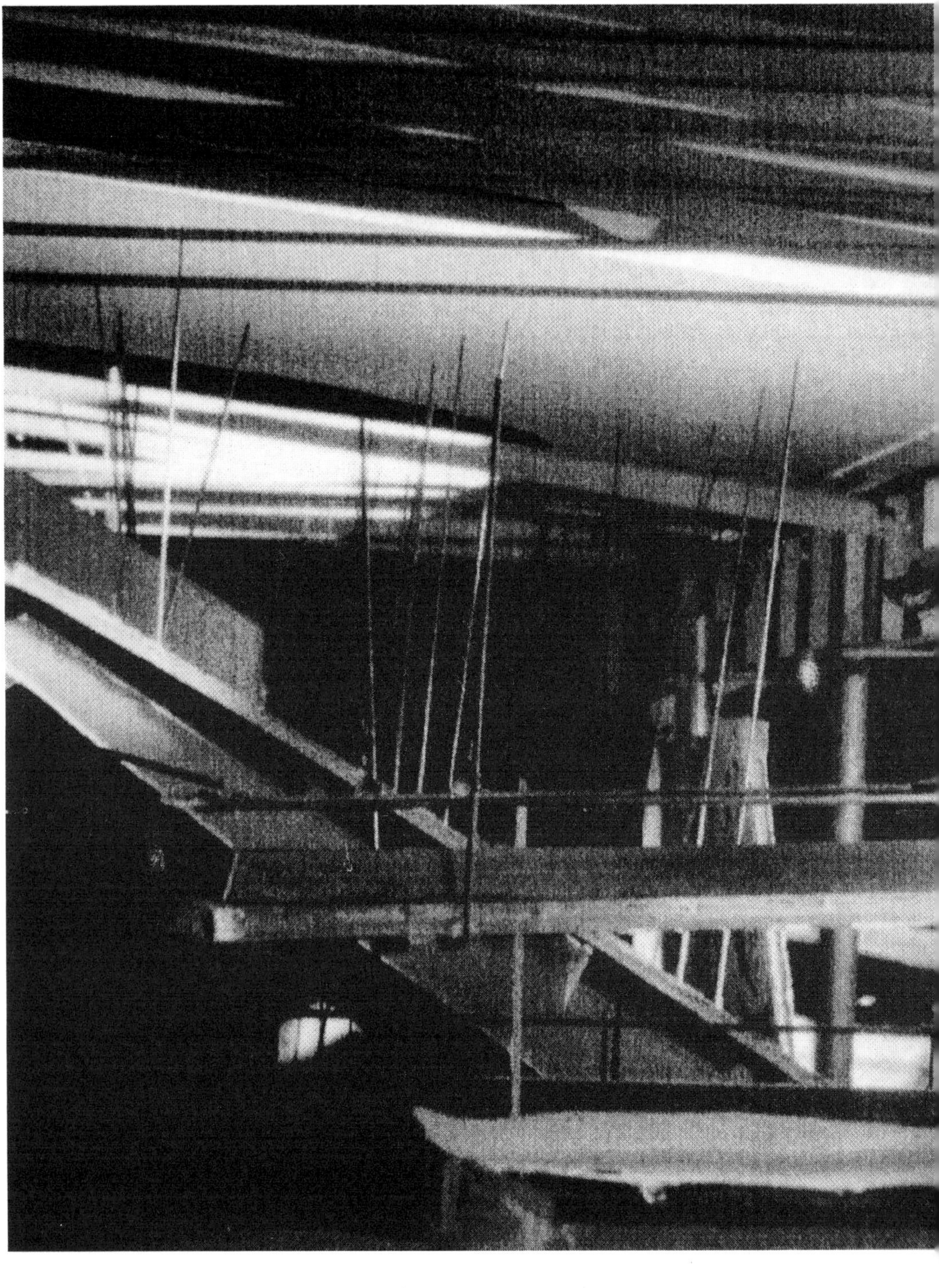

In-between: view from restaurant roof towards the large hall

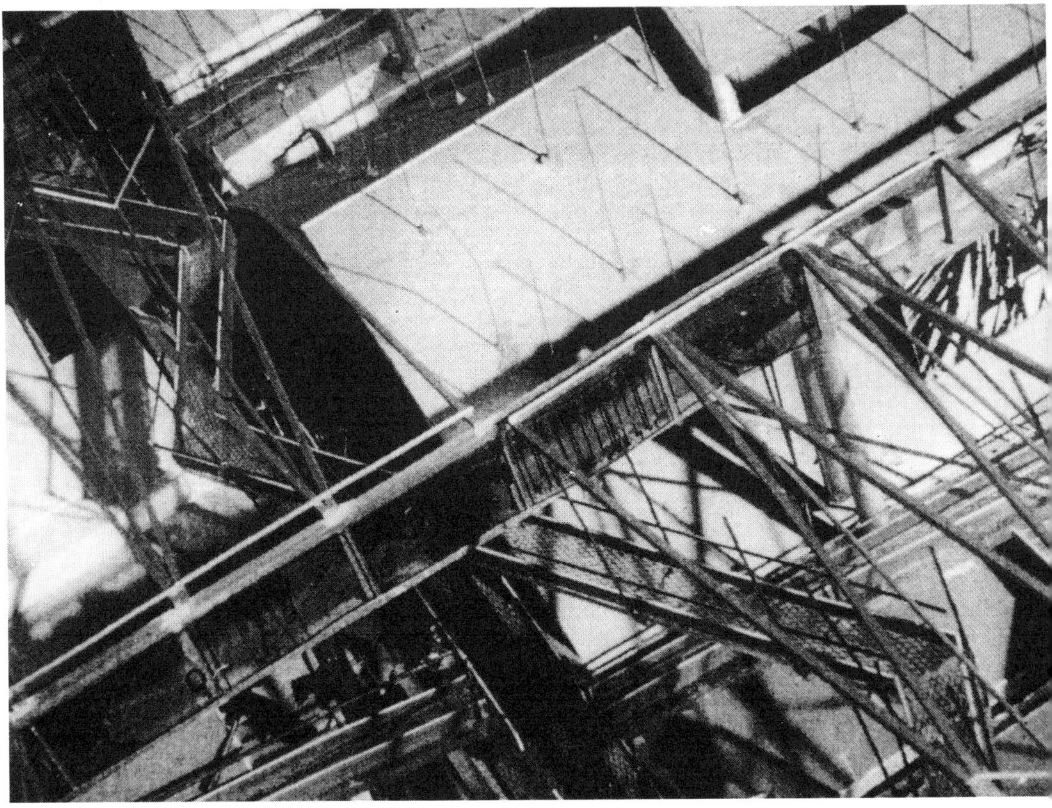

In-between: suspended garden and restaurant

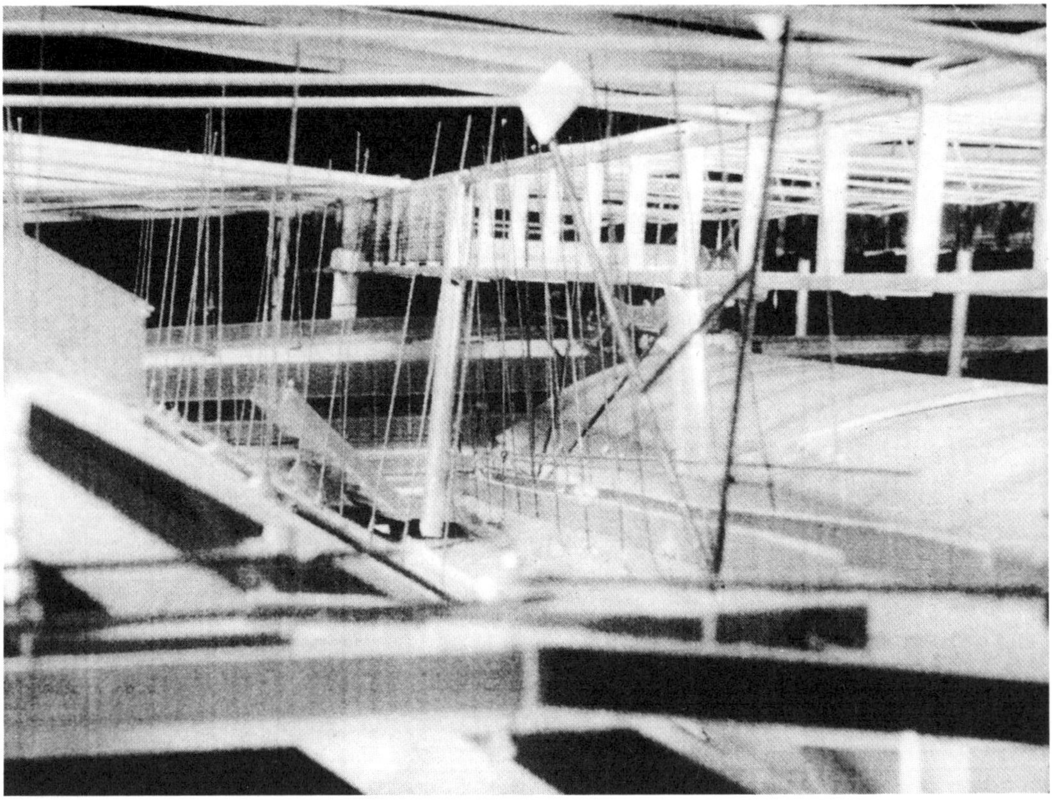

TOURCOING
519

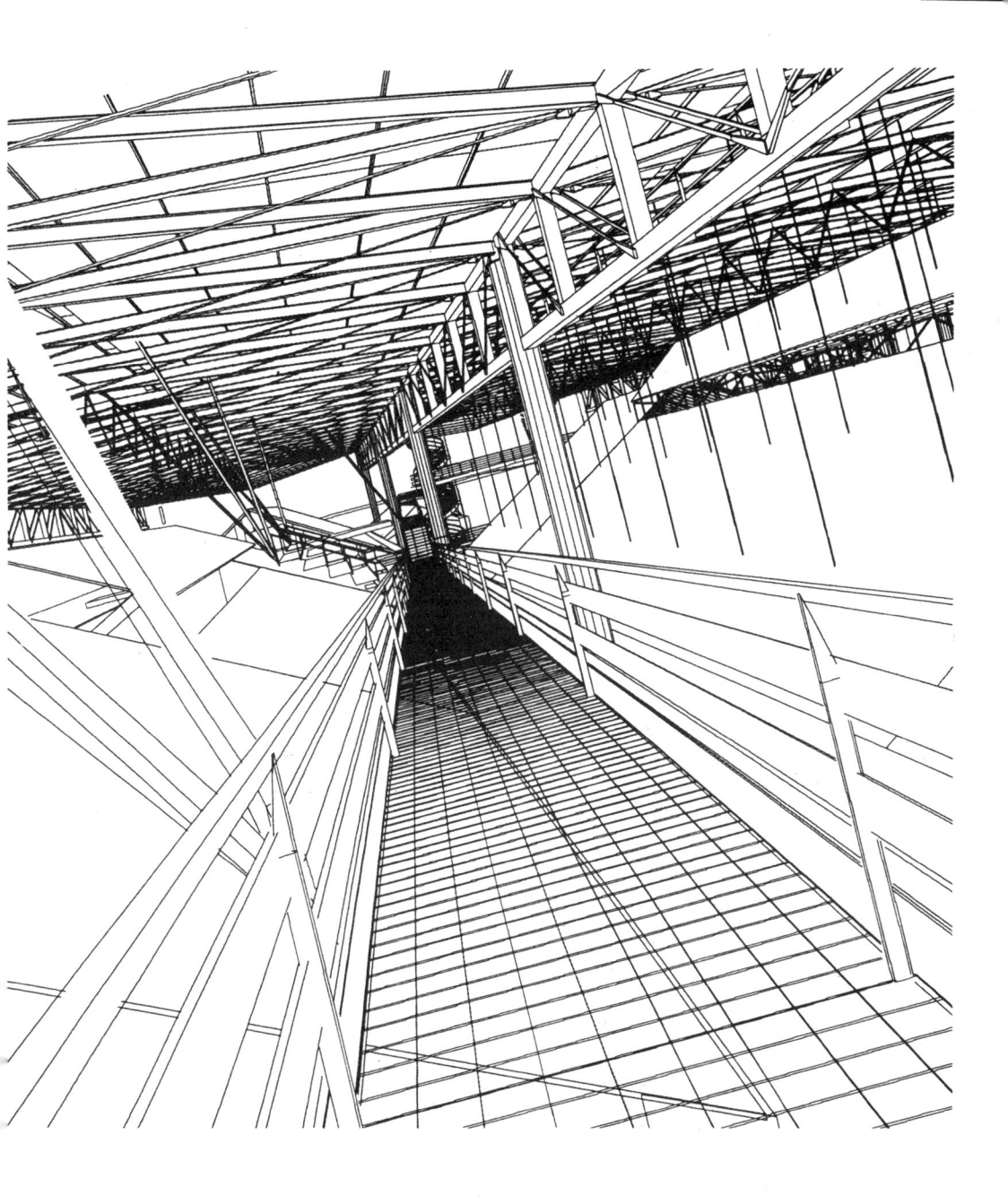

In-between: ramp between the cinemas and the large hall

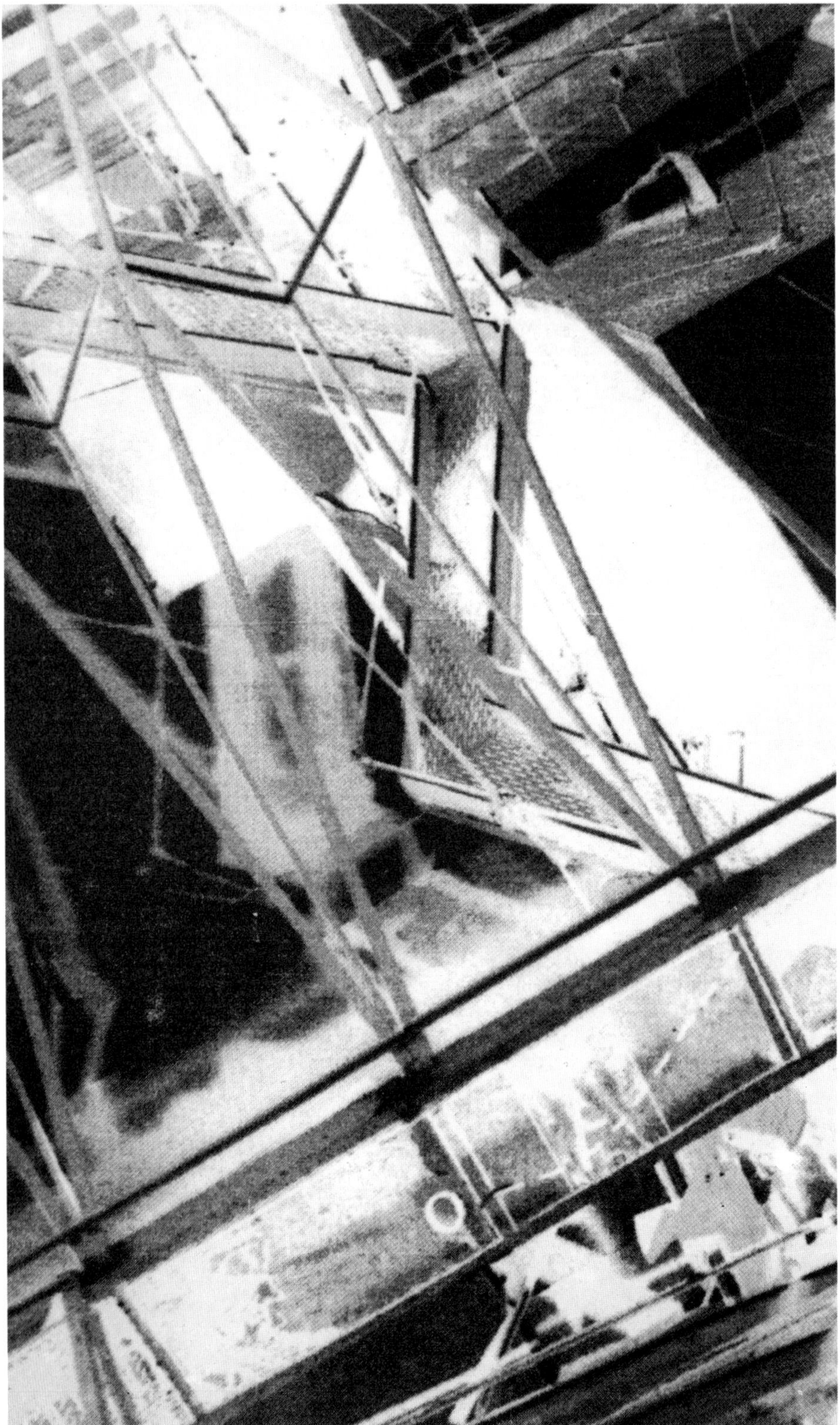

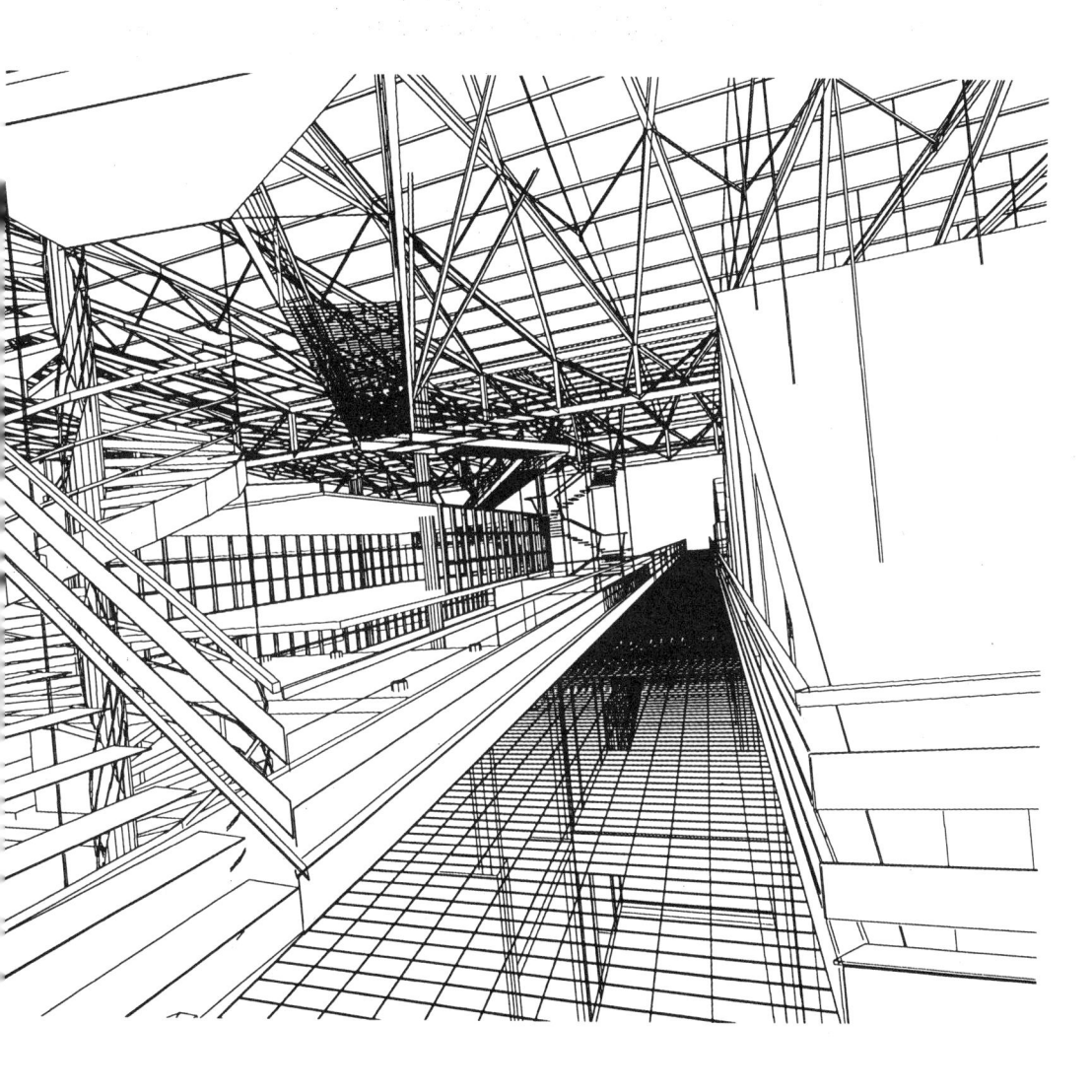

In-between: north-south catwalk and restaurant

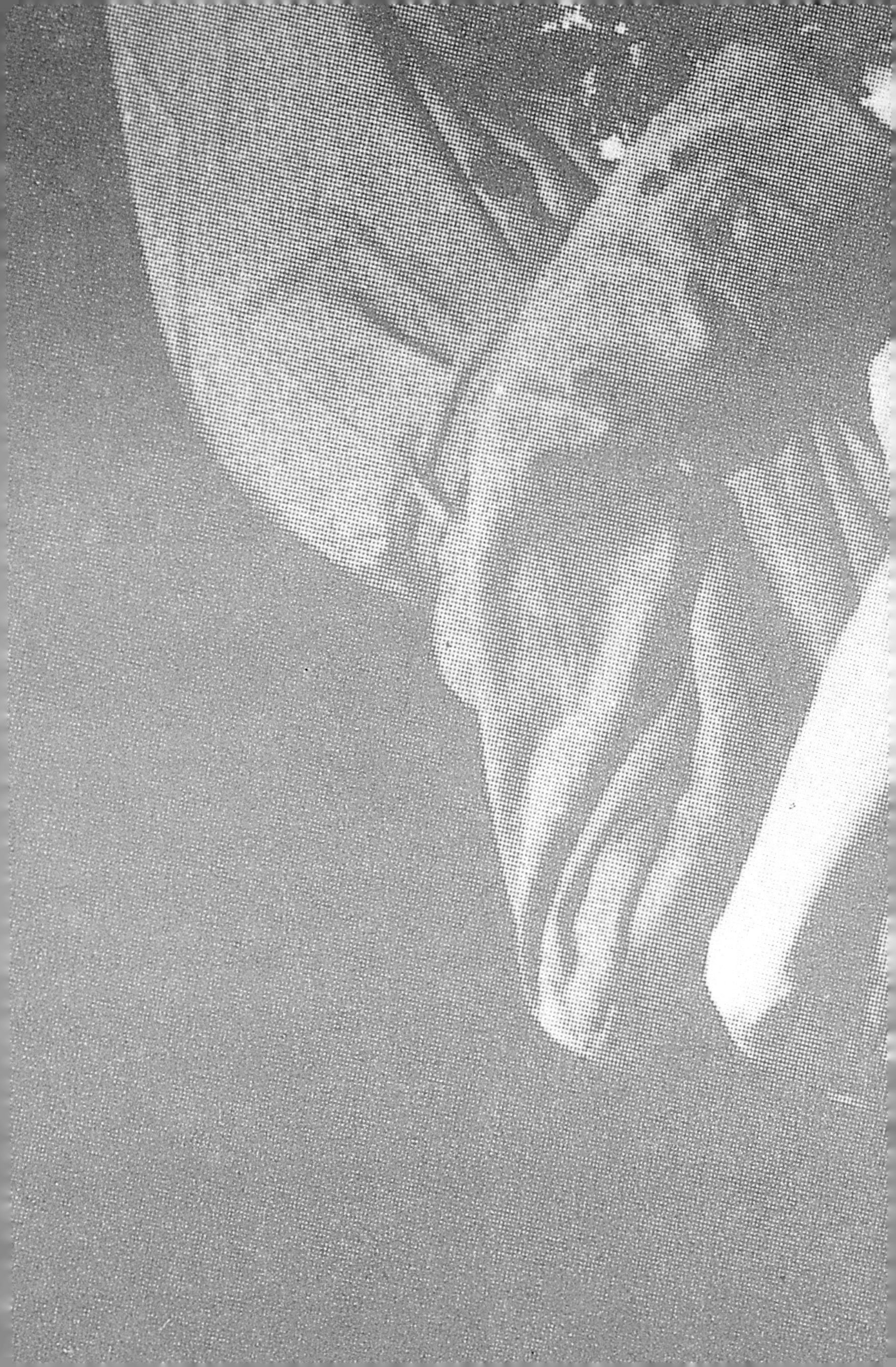

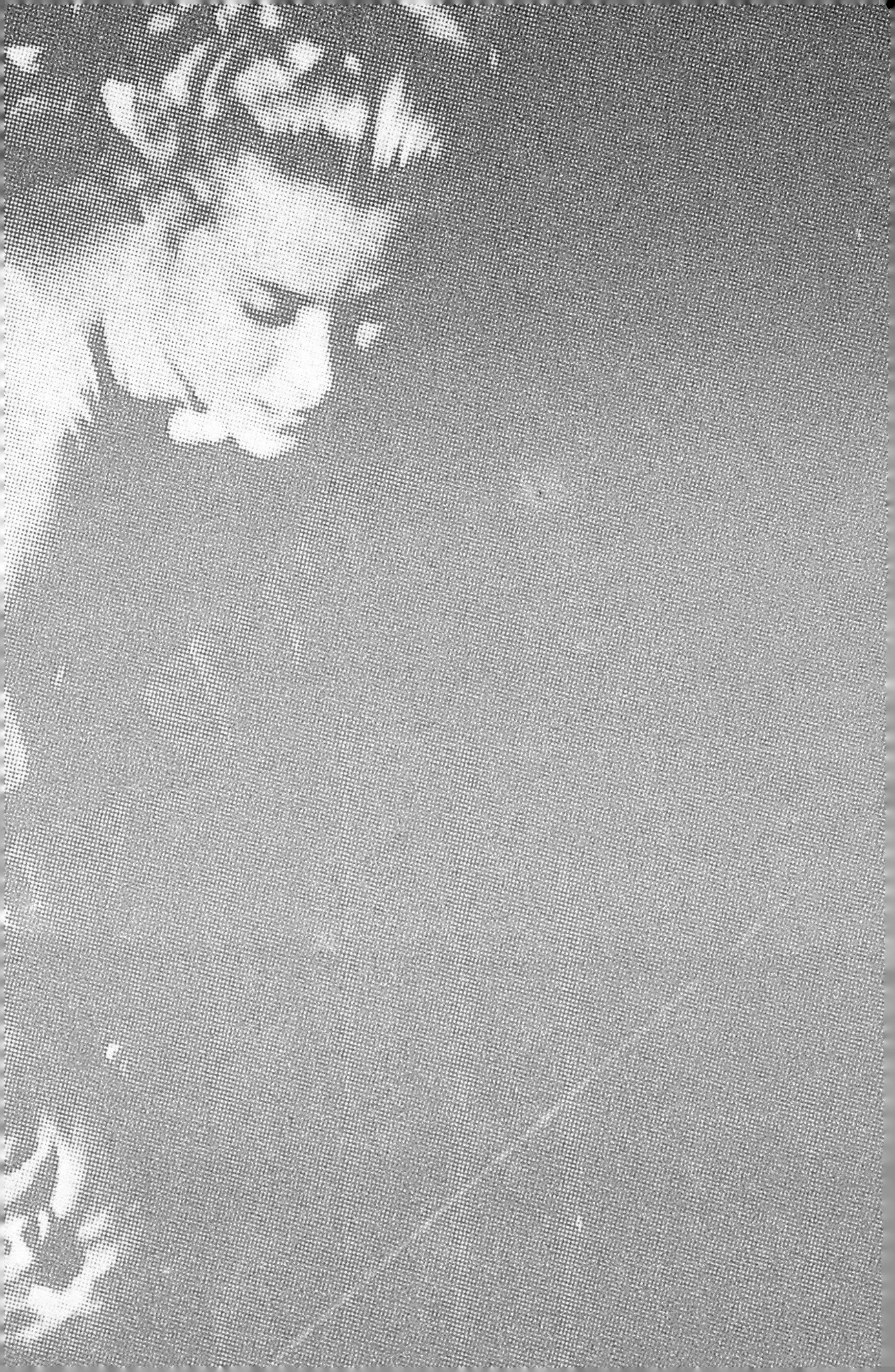

The Hague, Villa, 1992-

Domesti-City

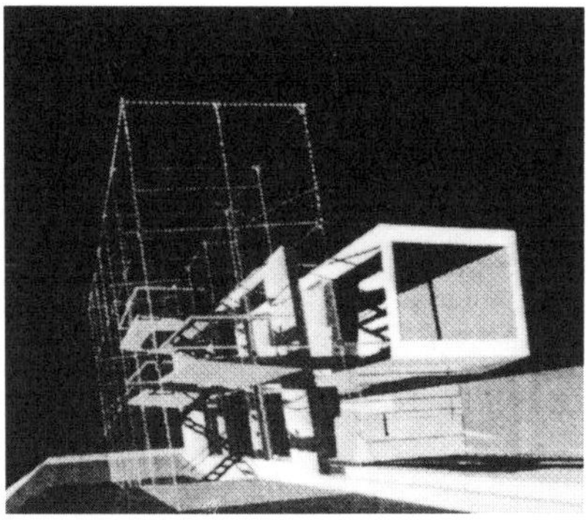

Could we expand some of the issues explored in the Groningen Glass Video Gallery (see page 556) into the domestic realm? Could the house also be the place of the "event," ever-changing in the dematerialization of its electronic contents? The invitation to design a small house in The Hague, The Netherlands became an opportunity to raise new questions about the home and related assumptions about an impenetrable private domain. We chose instead to explore some conditions of twenty-first-century living spaces.

The glass enclosure (twelve by four by seven meters) of living and work space is both transparent and translucent (printed glass). It leans away from the rest of the house, revealing an in-between, interstitial connection. The heaviest part, a concrete frame containing bedrooms, is suspended over the remaining portion of domestic space (kitchen and storage). The bathroom crankshaft locks the other elements in place.

Conceived as a series of strips placed in between a canal, a major traffic road, housing and a park, the house extends these urban events while providing a momentary pause in the digital transfer of information. The borders of the living room and work space, devoid of ornamental camouflage, expand beyond the property lines just as they are undermined by the electronic devices of everyday use (TV, fax, etc.) that they contain.

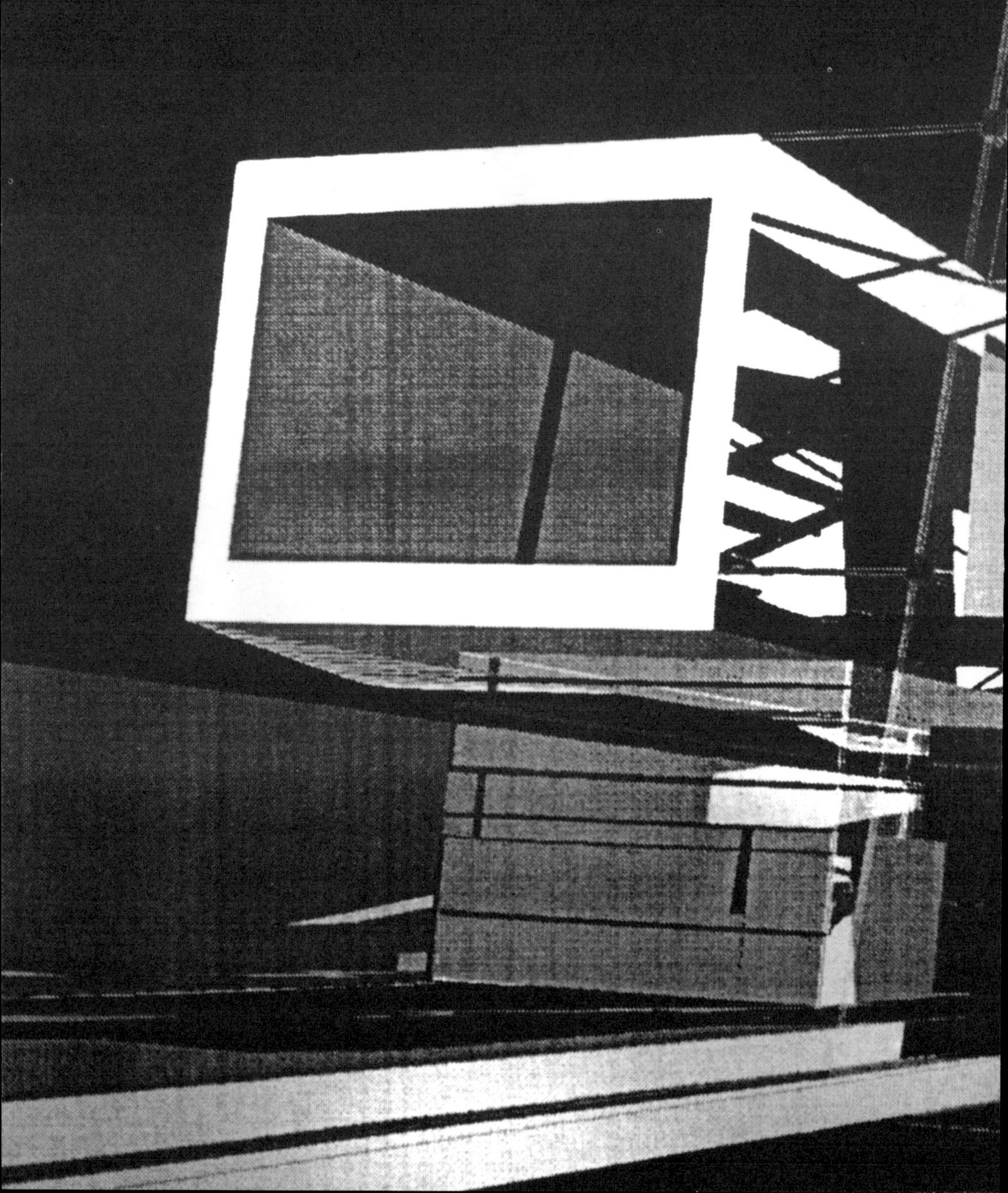

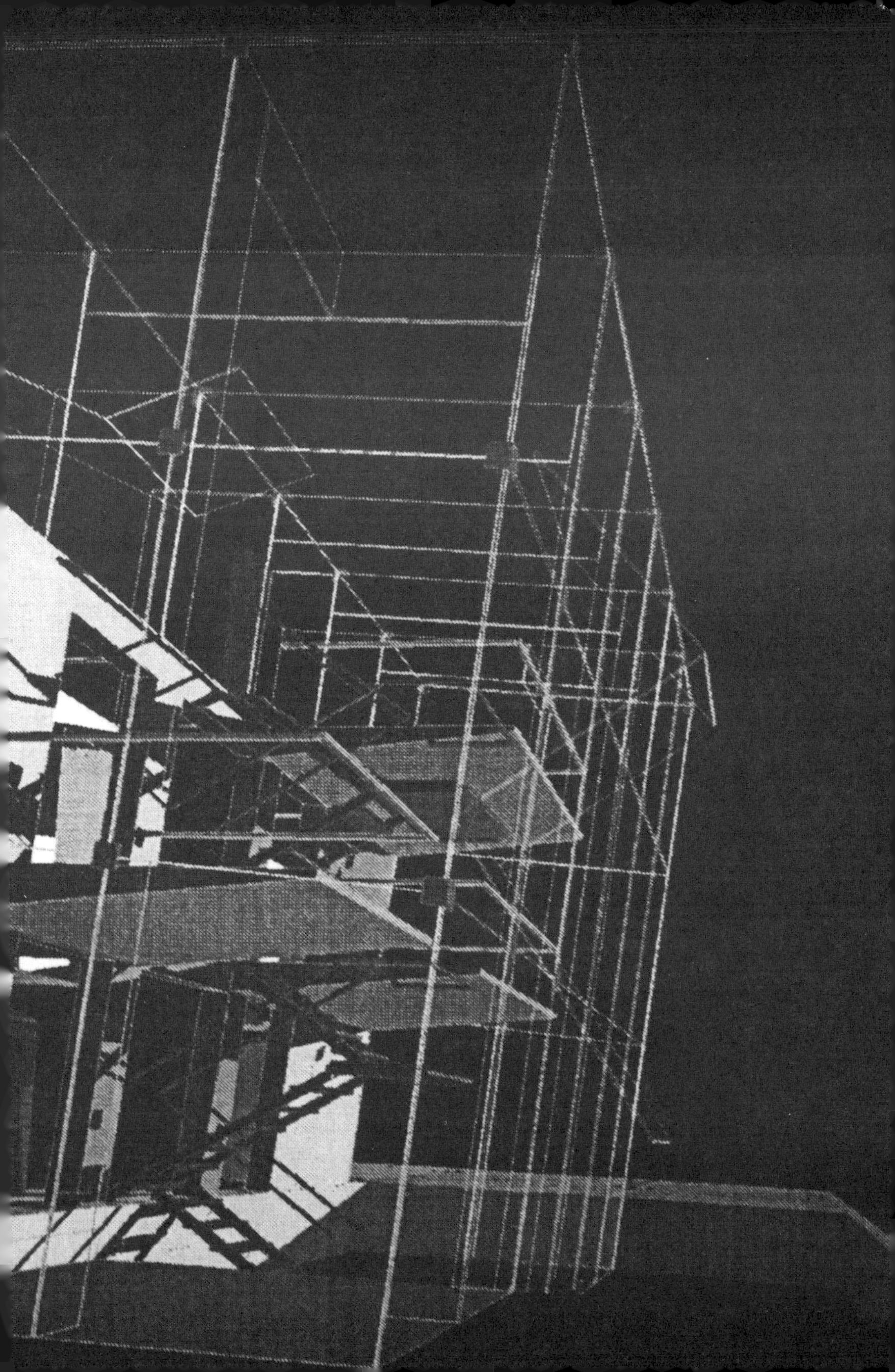

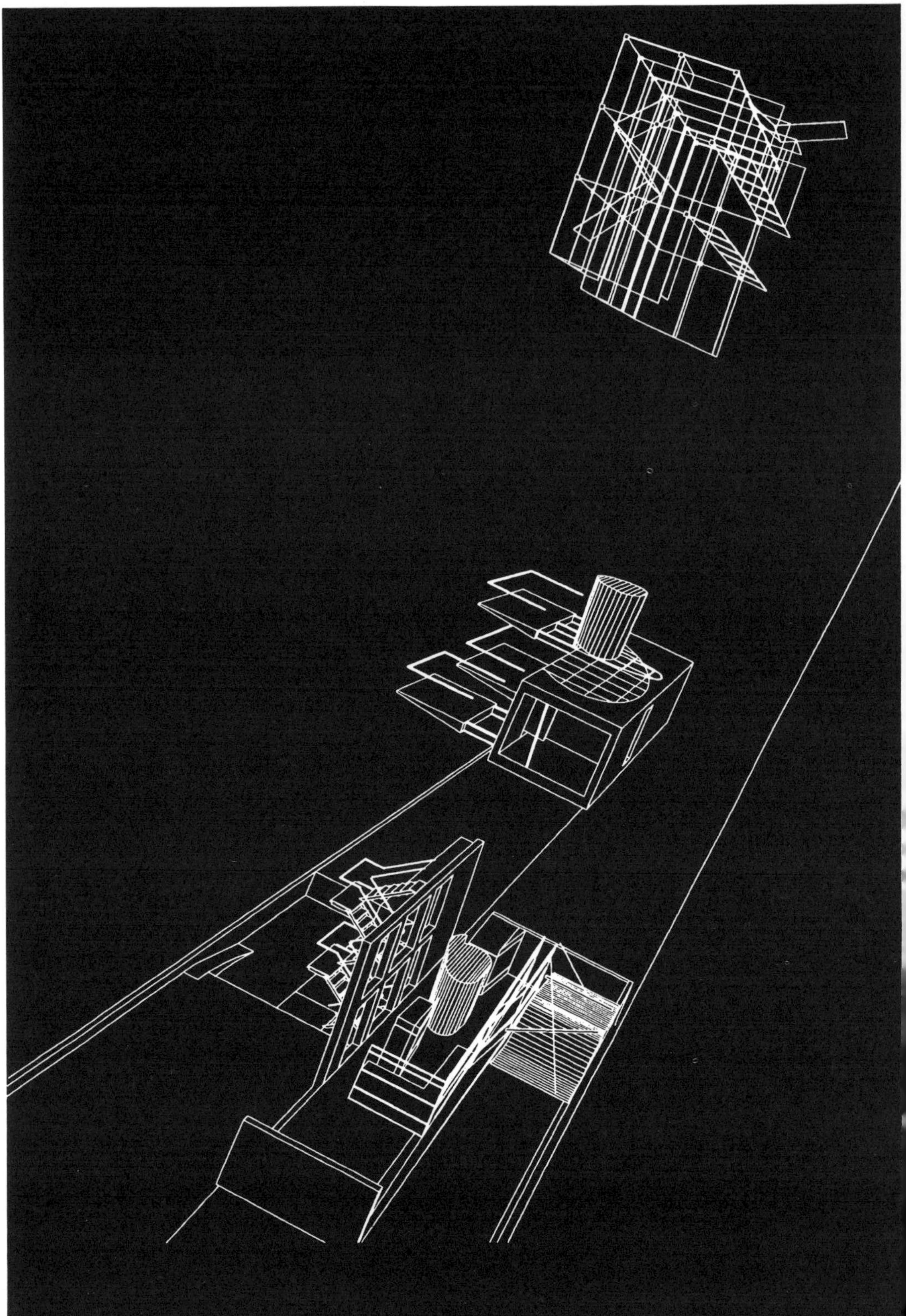

THE HAGUE
531

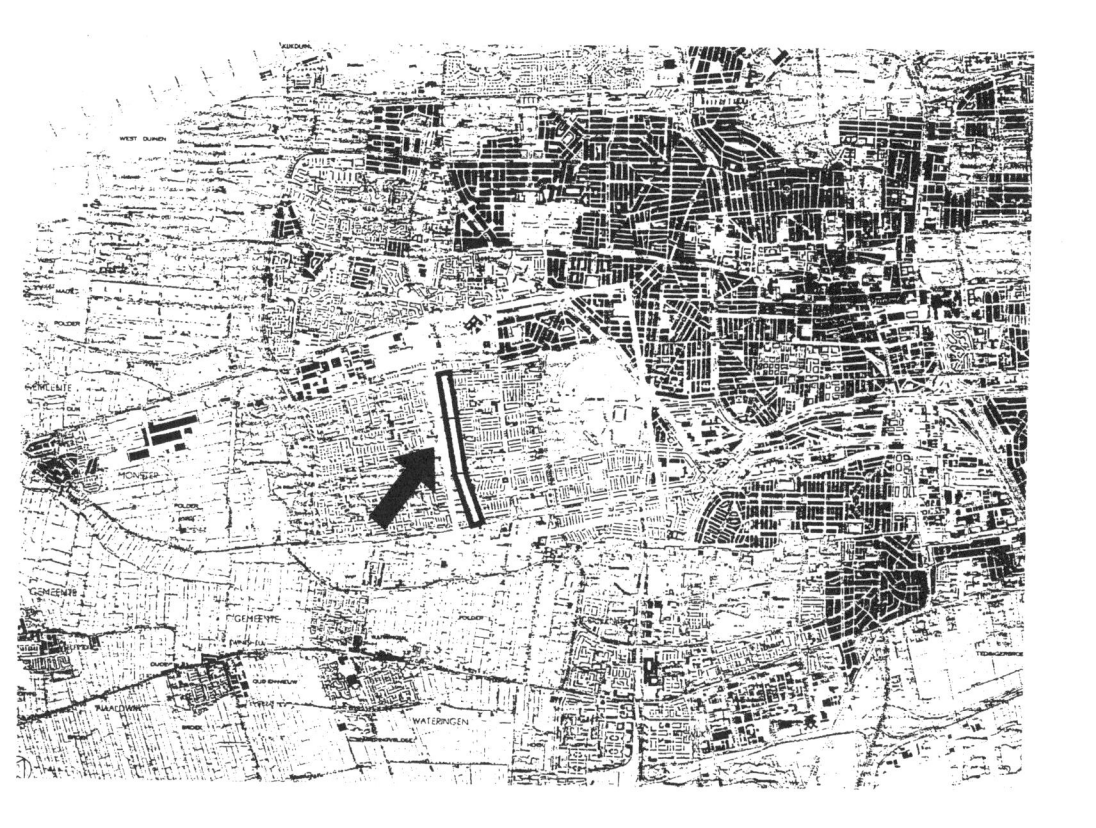

The Hague: canal

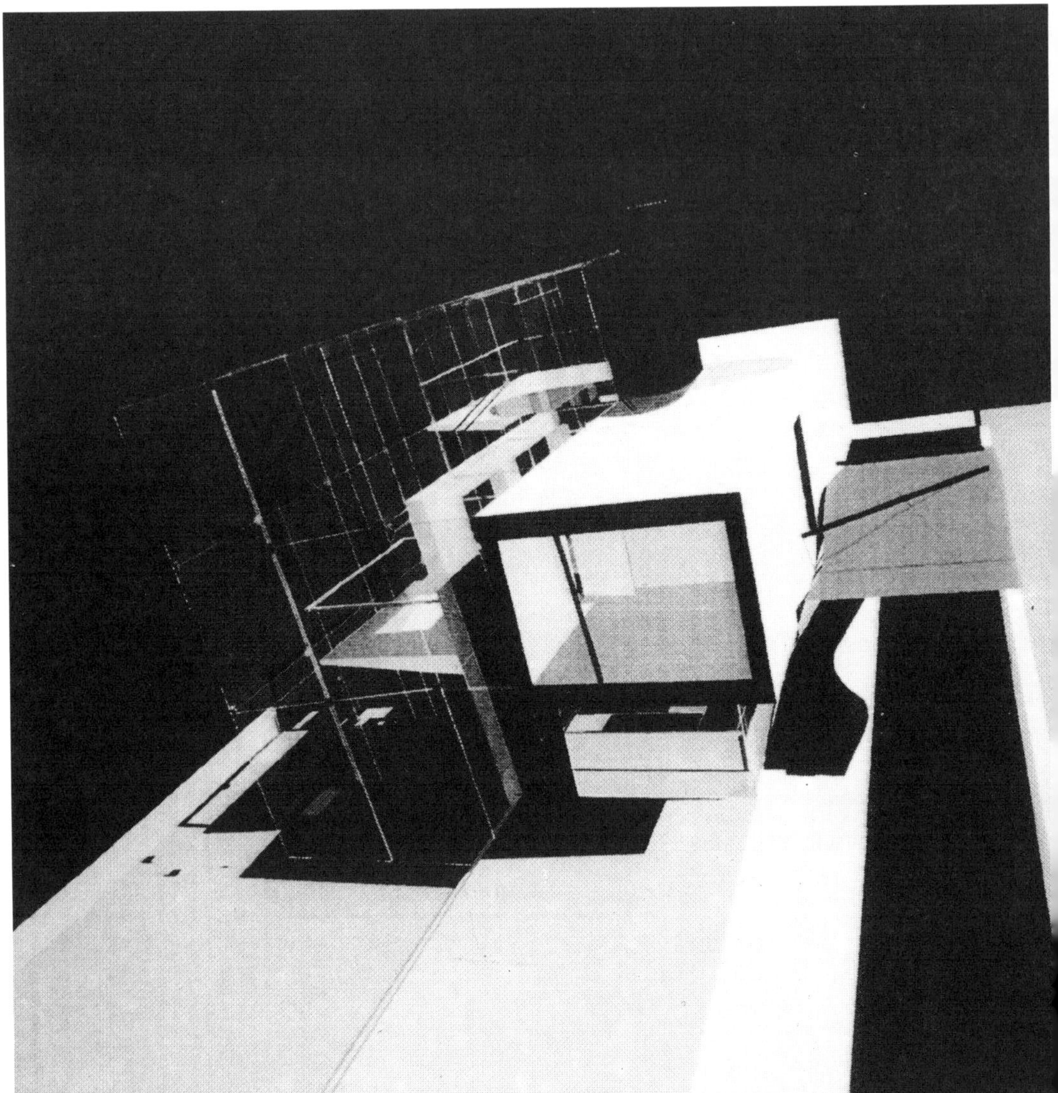

Site plan: between avenue and canal

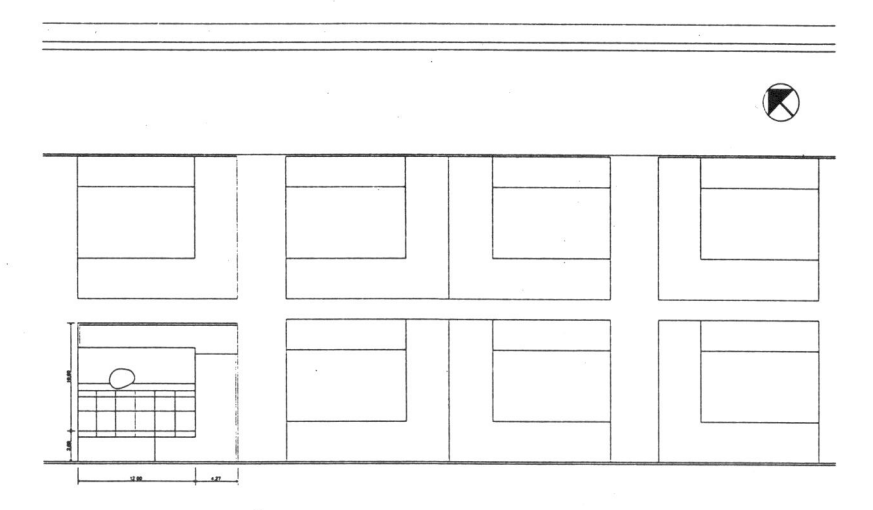

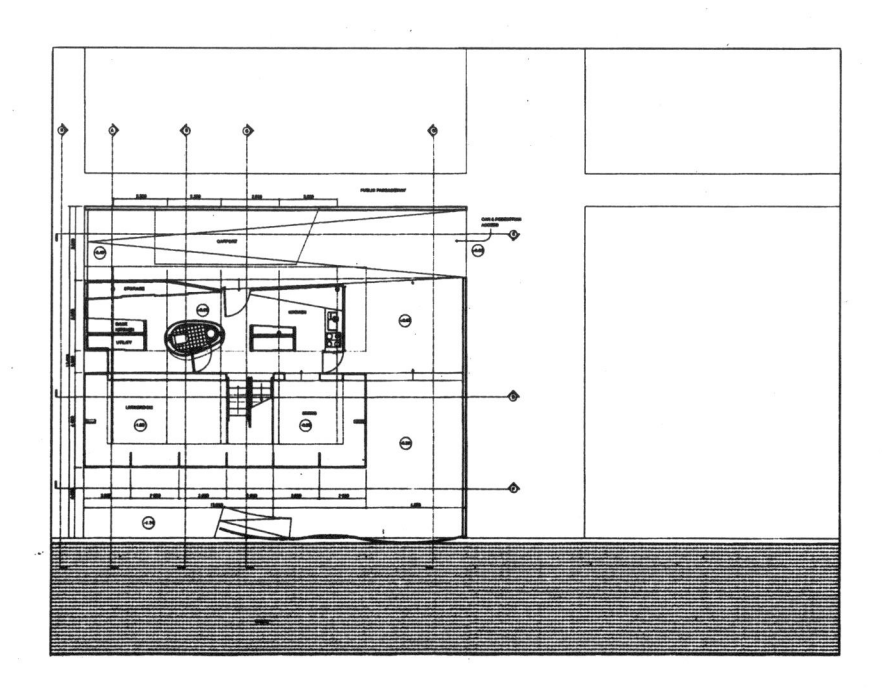

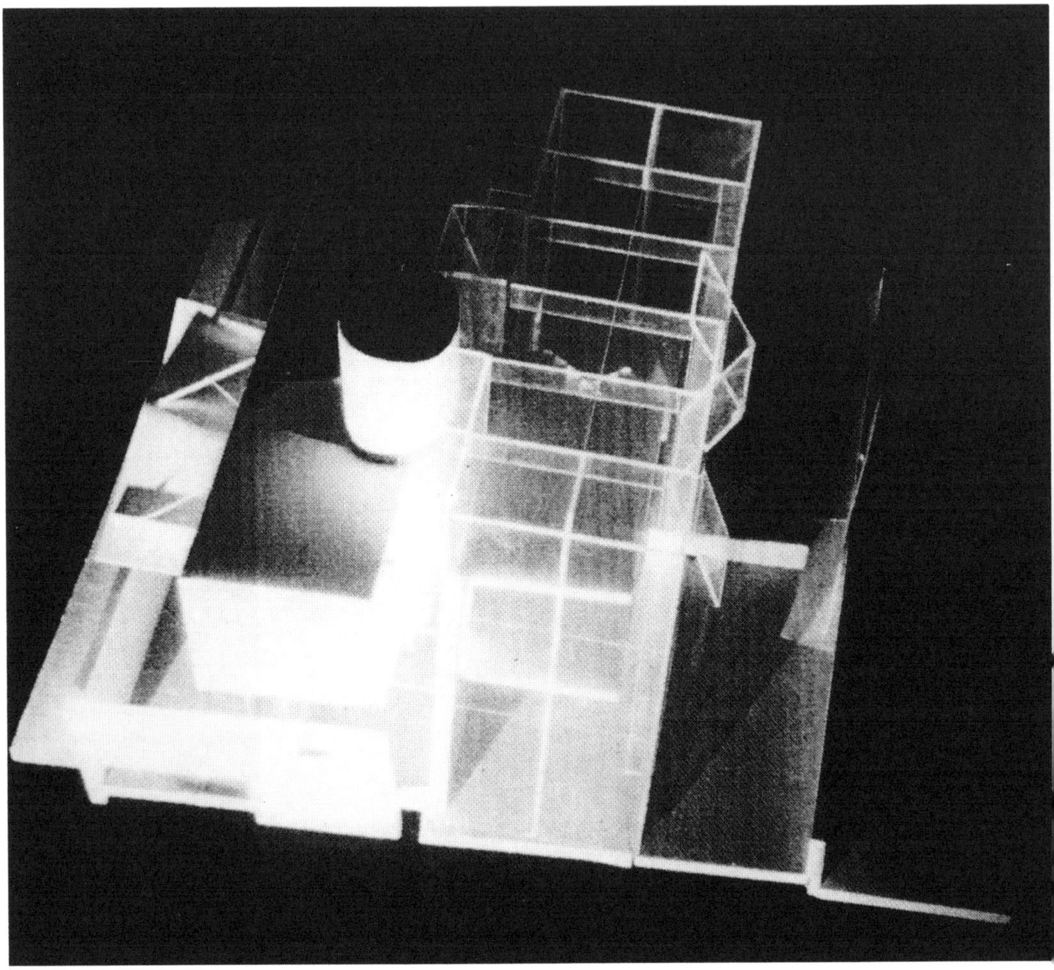

THE HAGUE
535

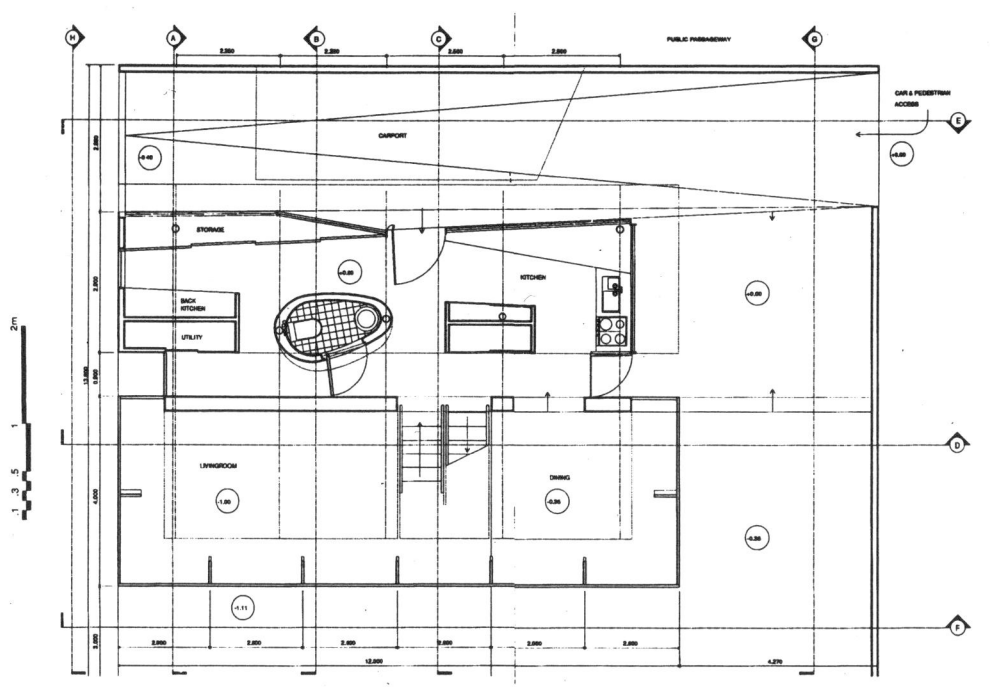

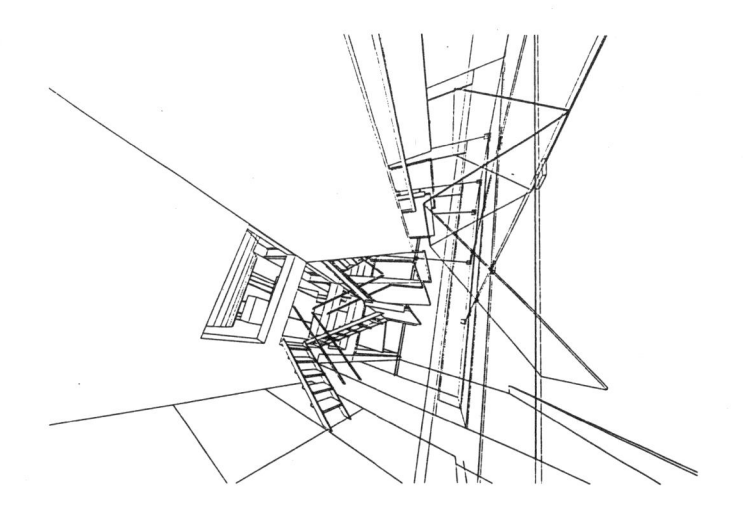

Ground level

Defamiliarization: the reversal of expectations

THE HAGUE
537

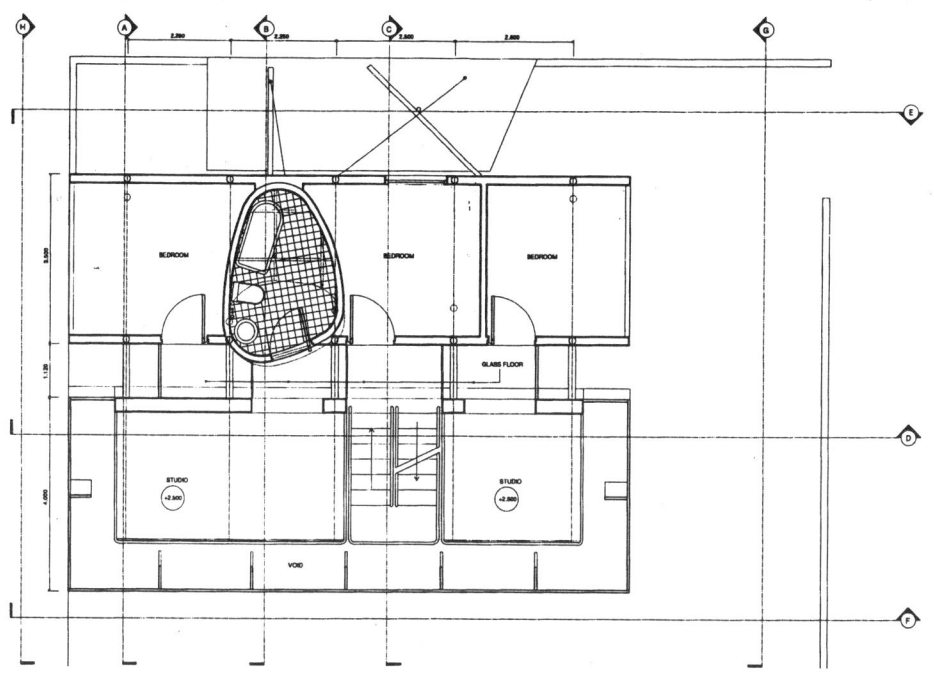

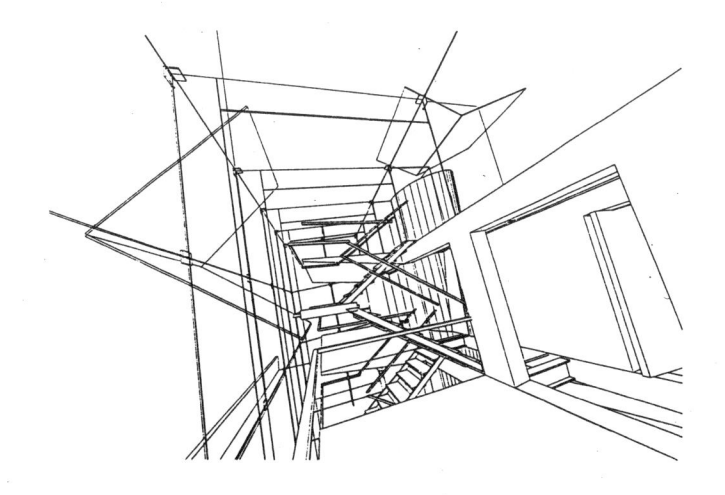

Level 1

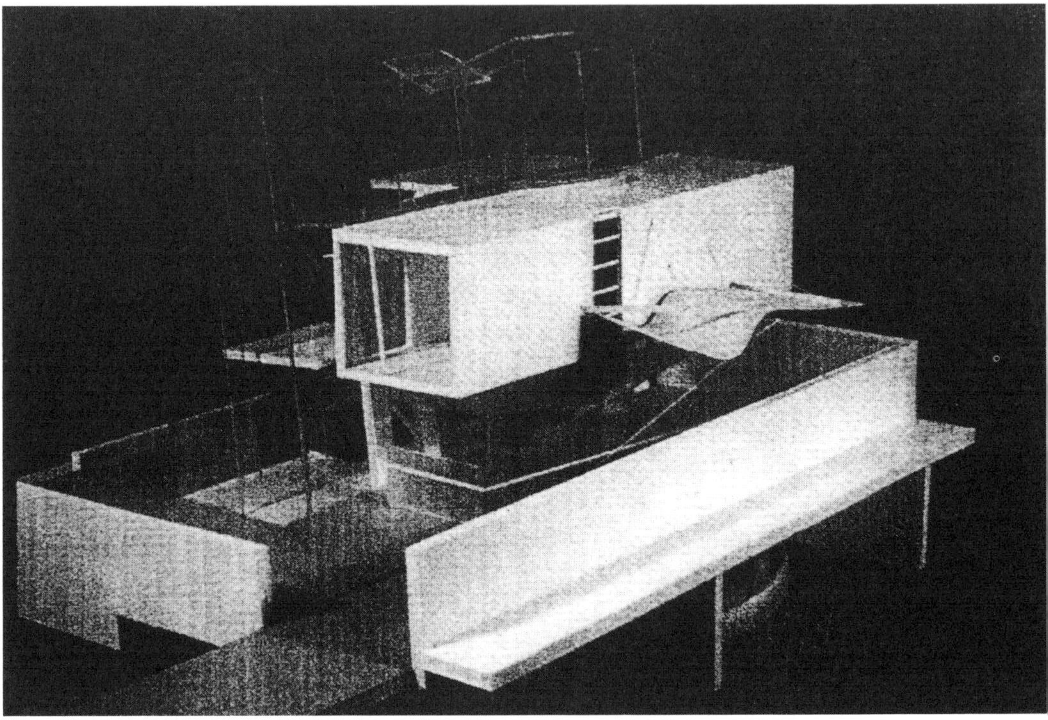

THE HAGUE
539

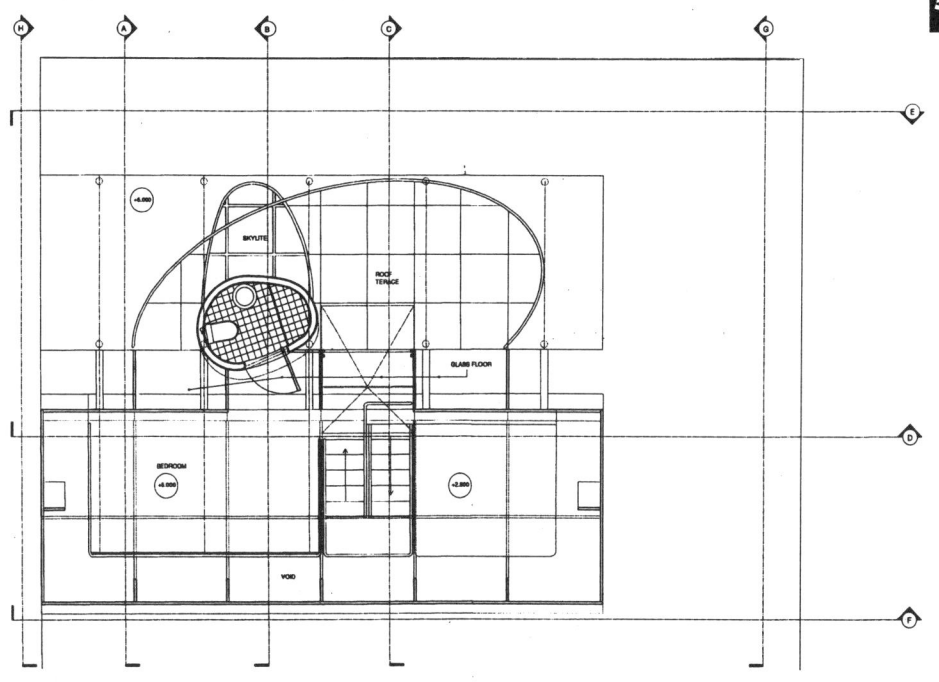

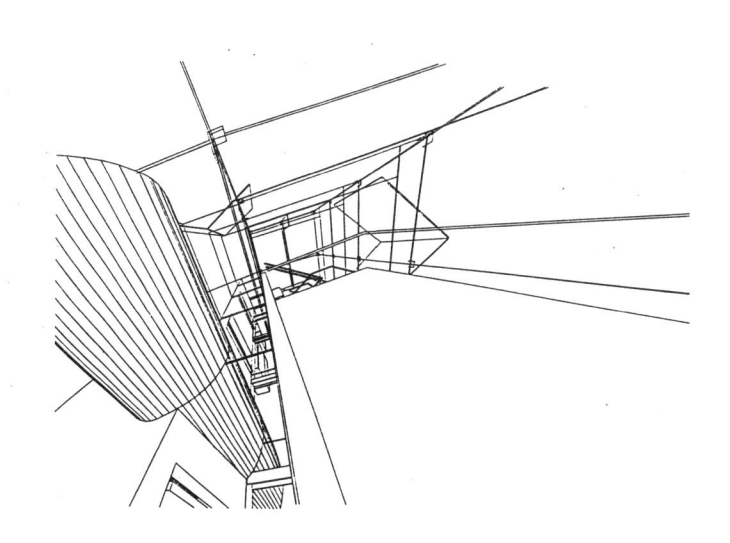

Level 2

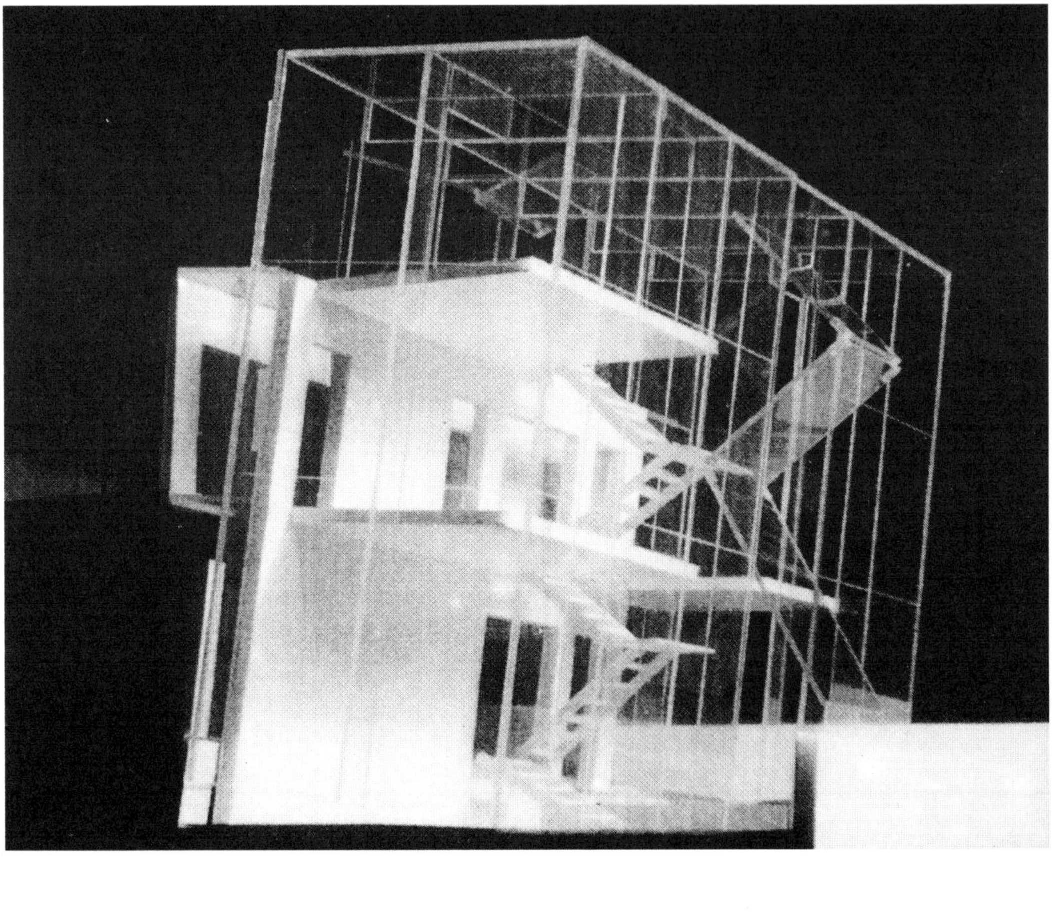

Section A

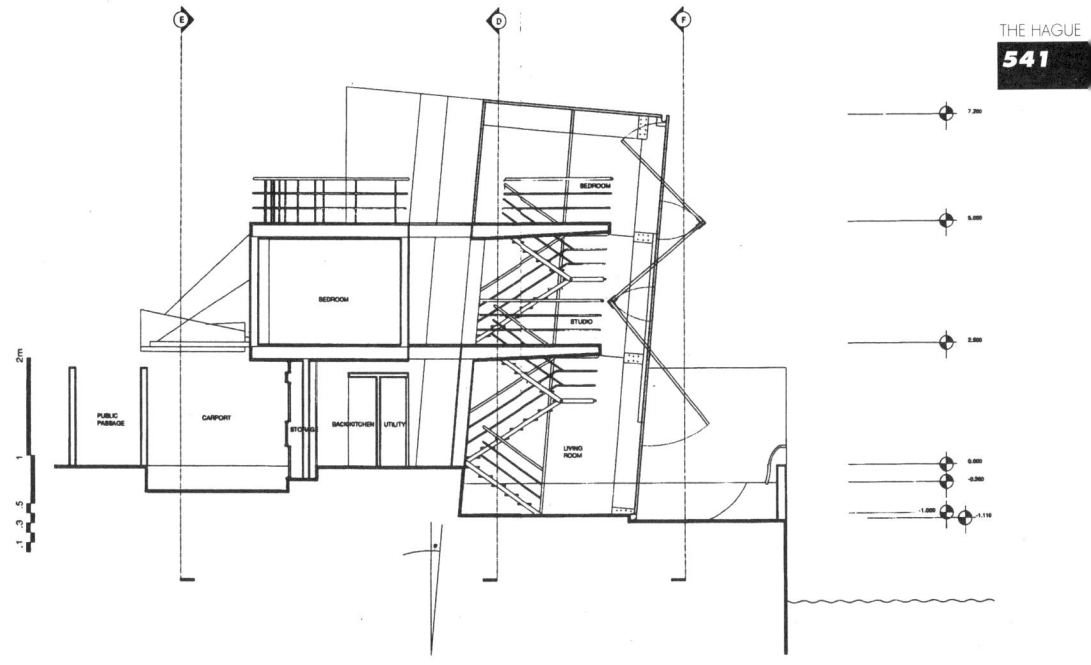

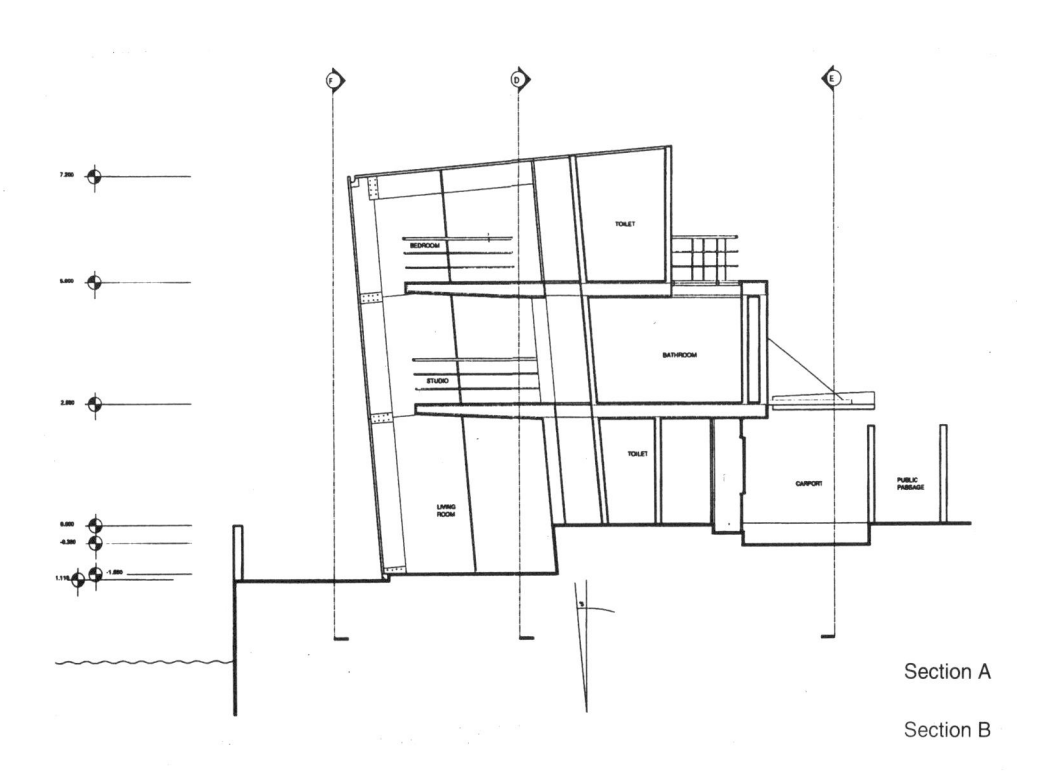

Section B

Architecture is not necessarily comforting, *heimlich*, homely

THE HAGUE

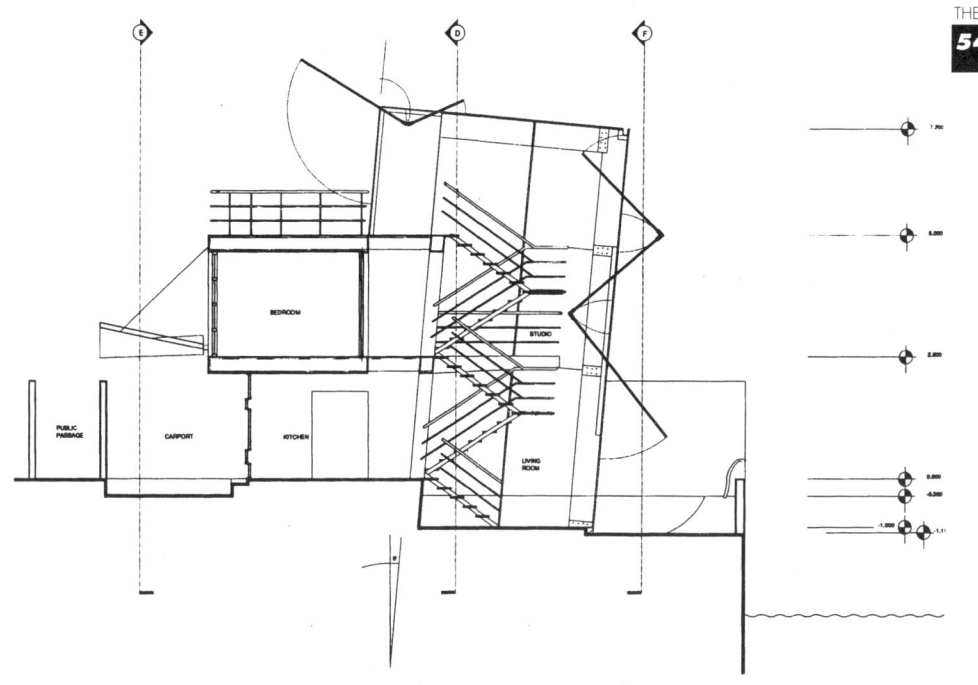

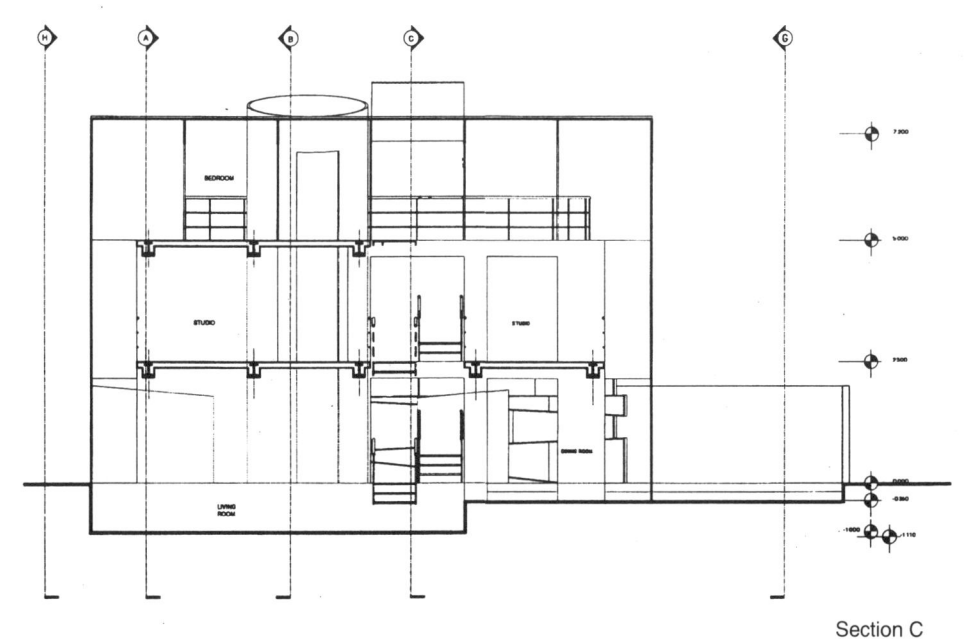

543

Section C

Section D

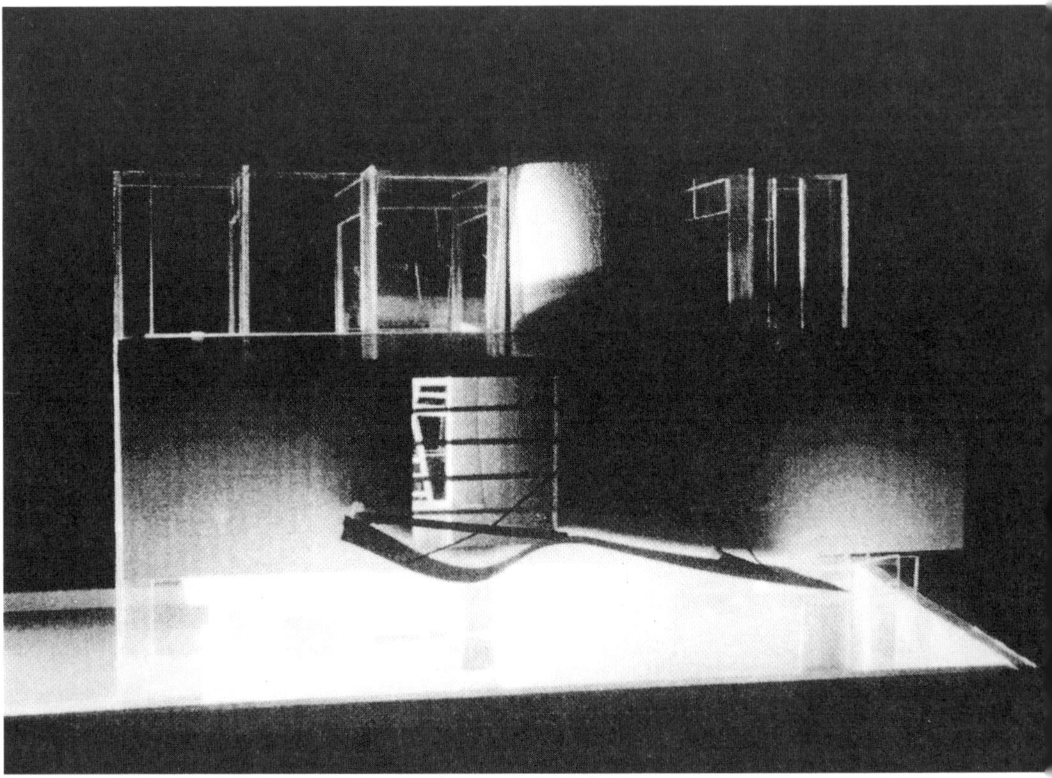

THE HAGUE
545

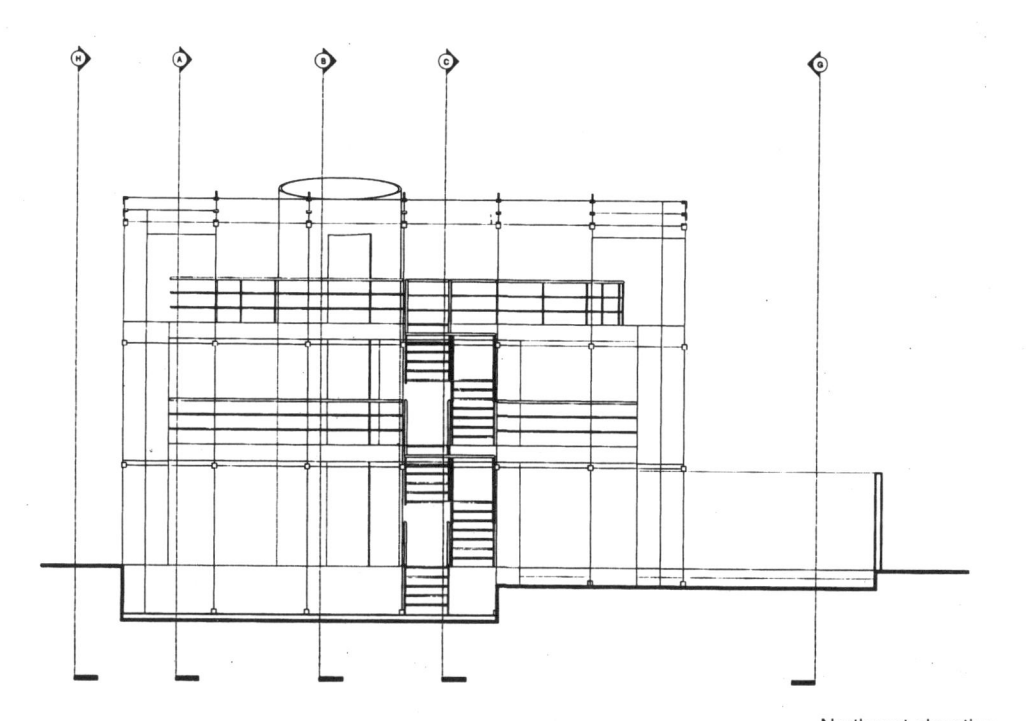

Northeast elevation

Southwest elevation

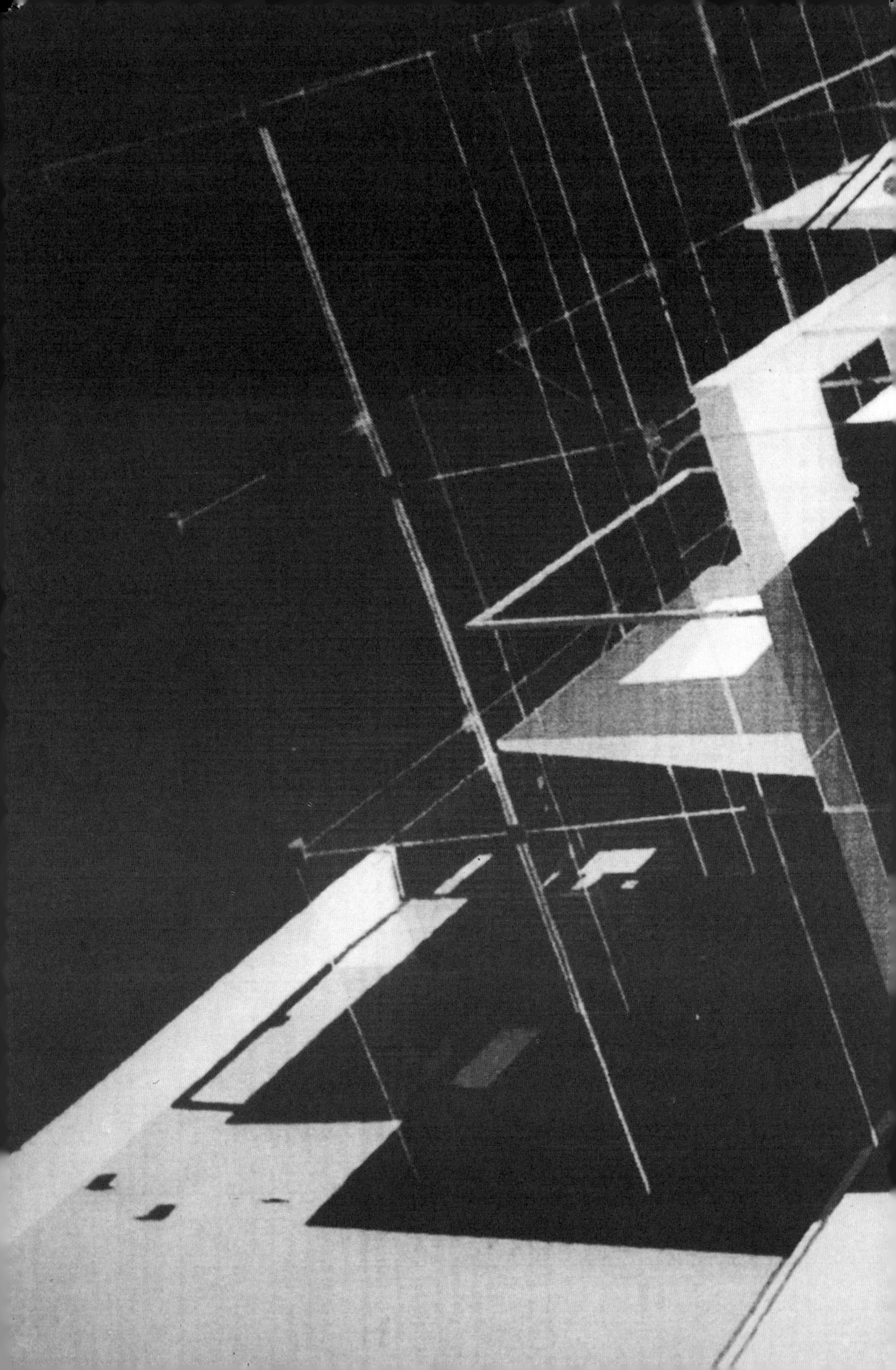

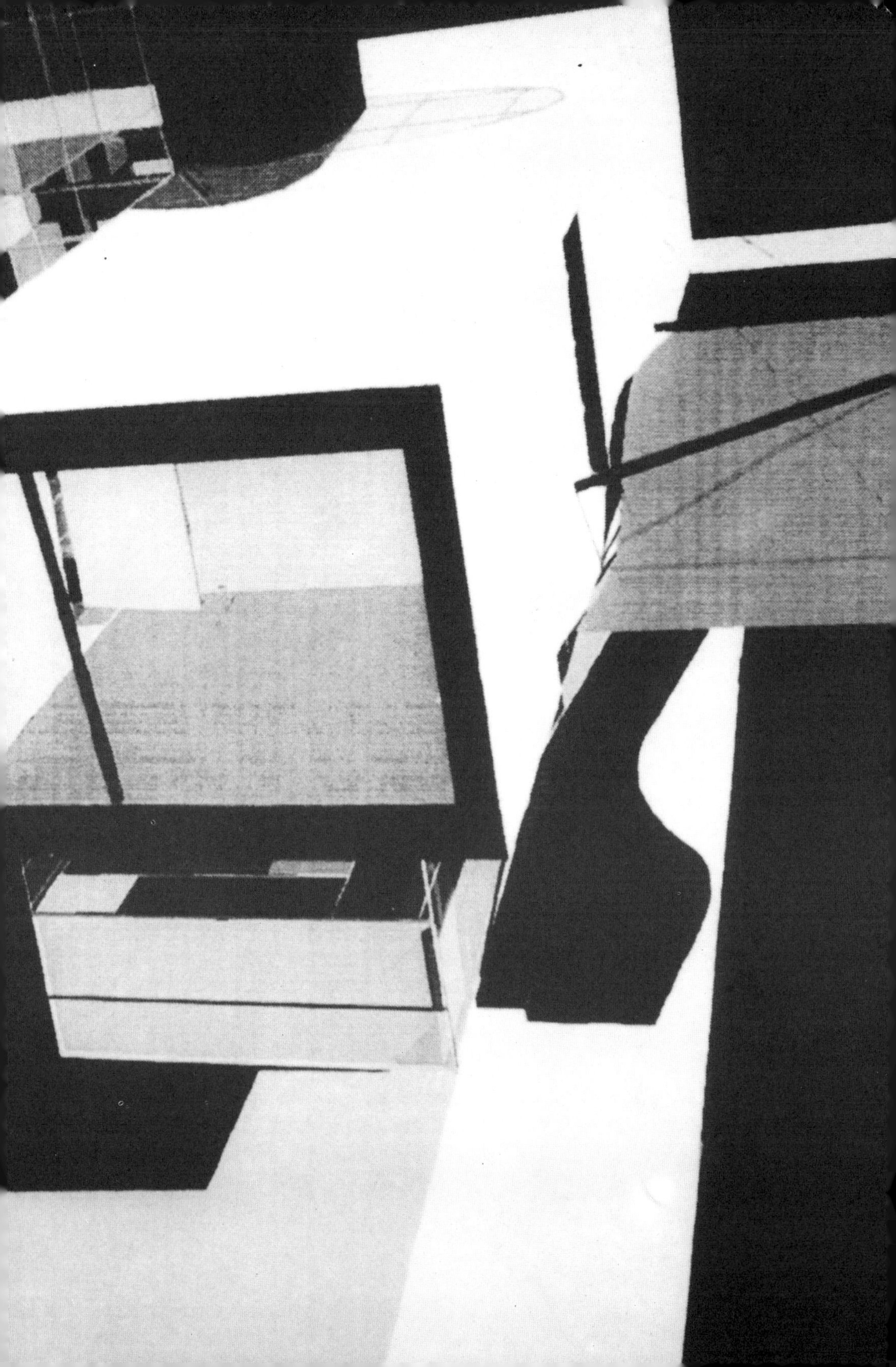

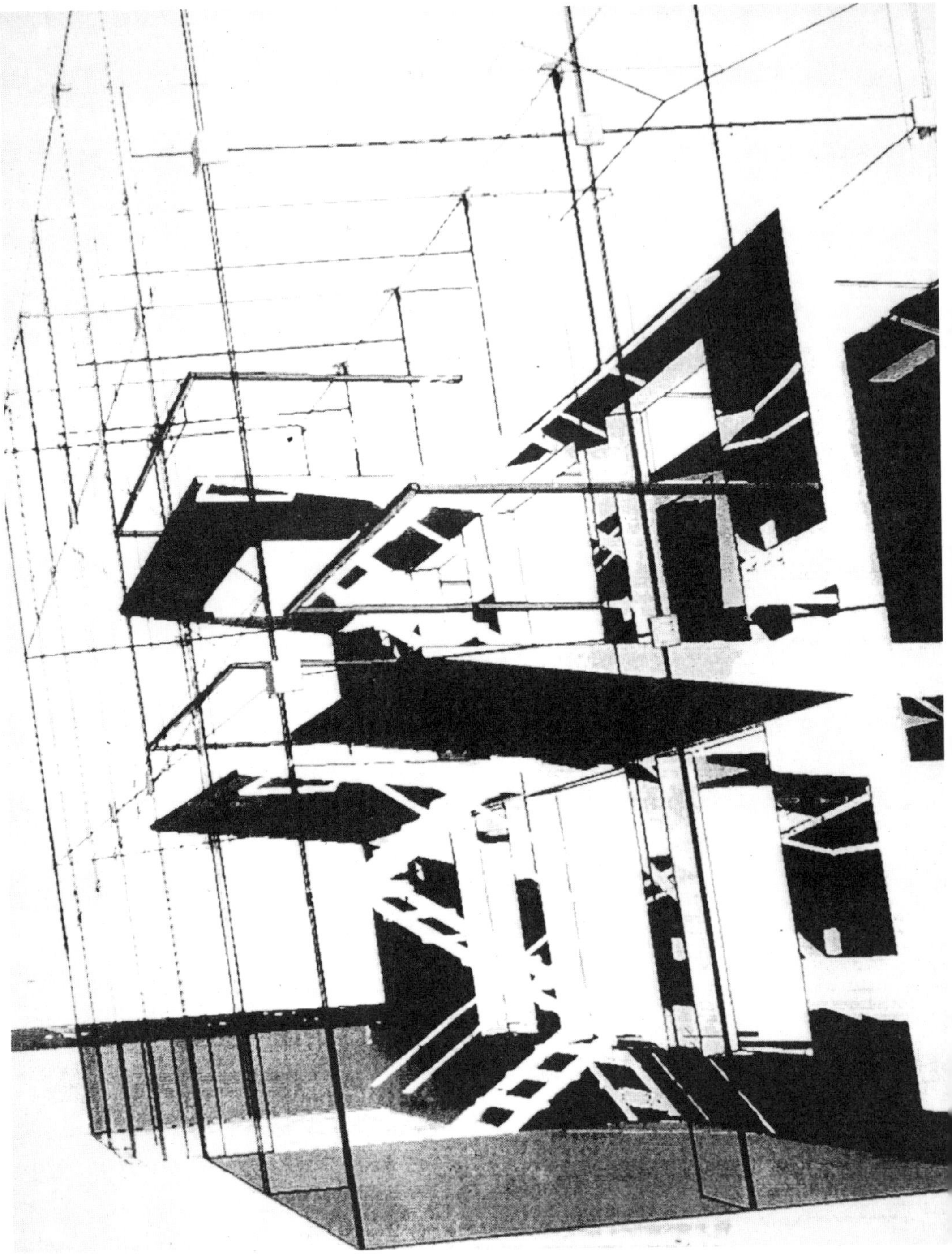

THE HAGUE
549

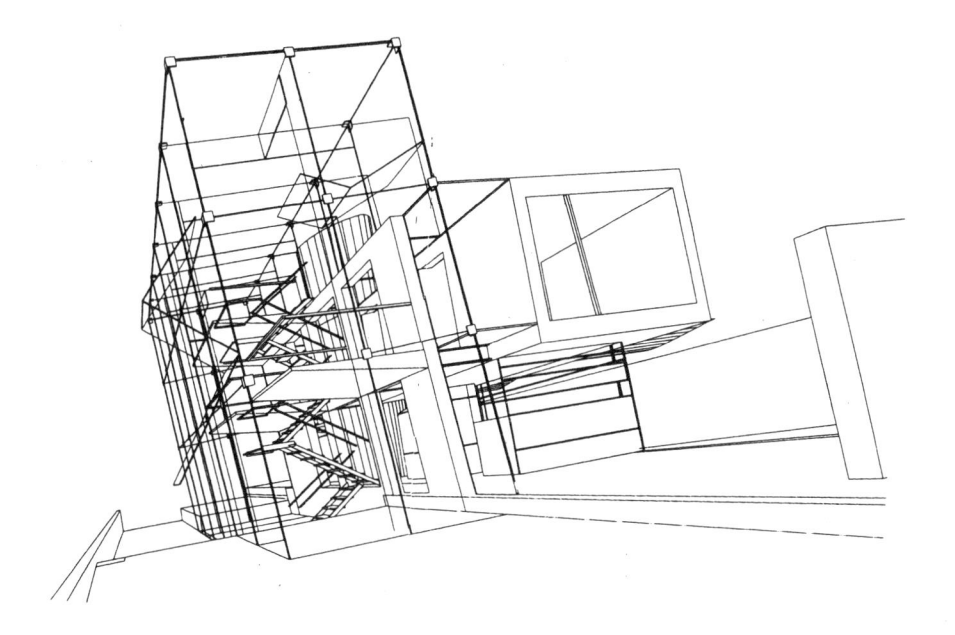

Three bands: structural glass envelope (living and work space), in-between and concrete frame (bedrooms)

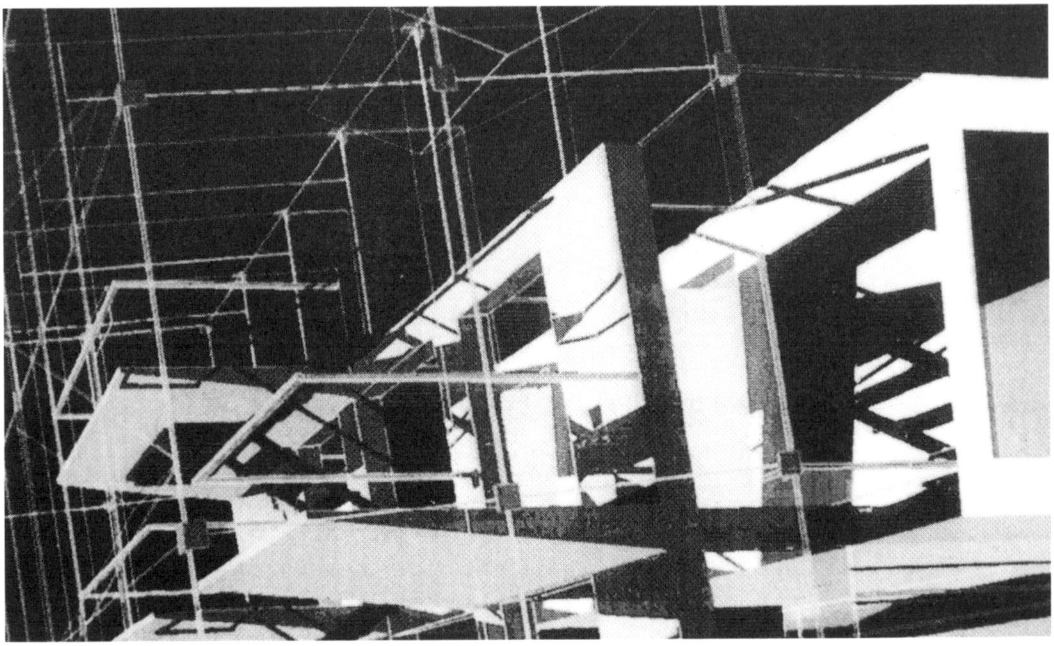

THE HAGUE
551

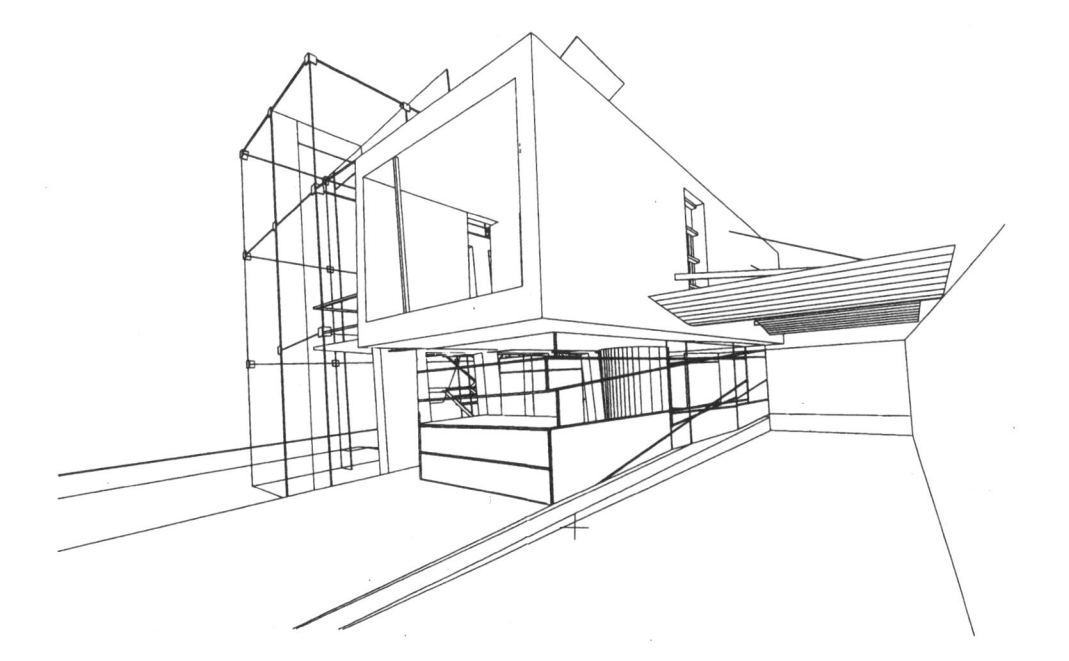

View toward entrance: keeping defamiliarization alive

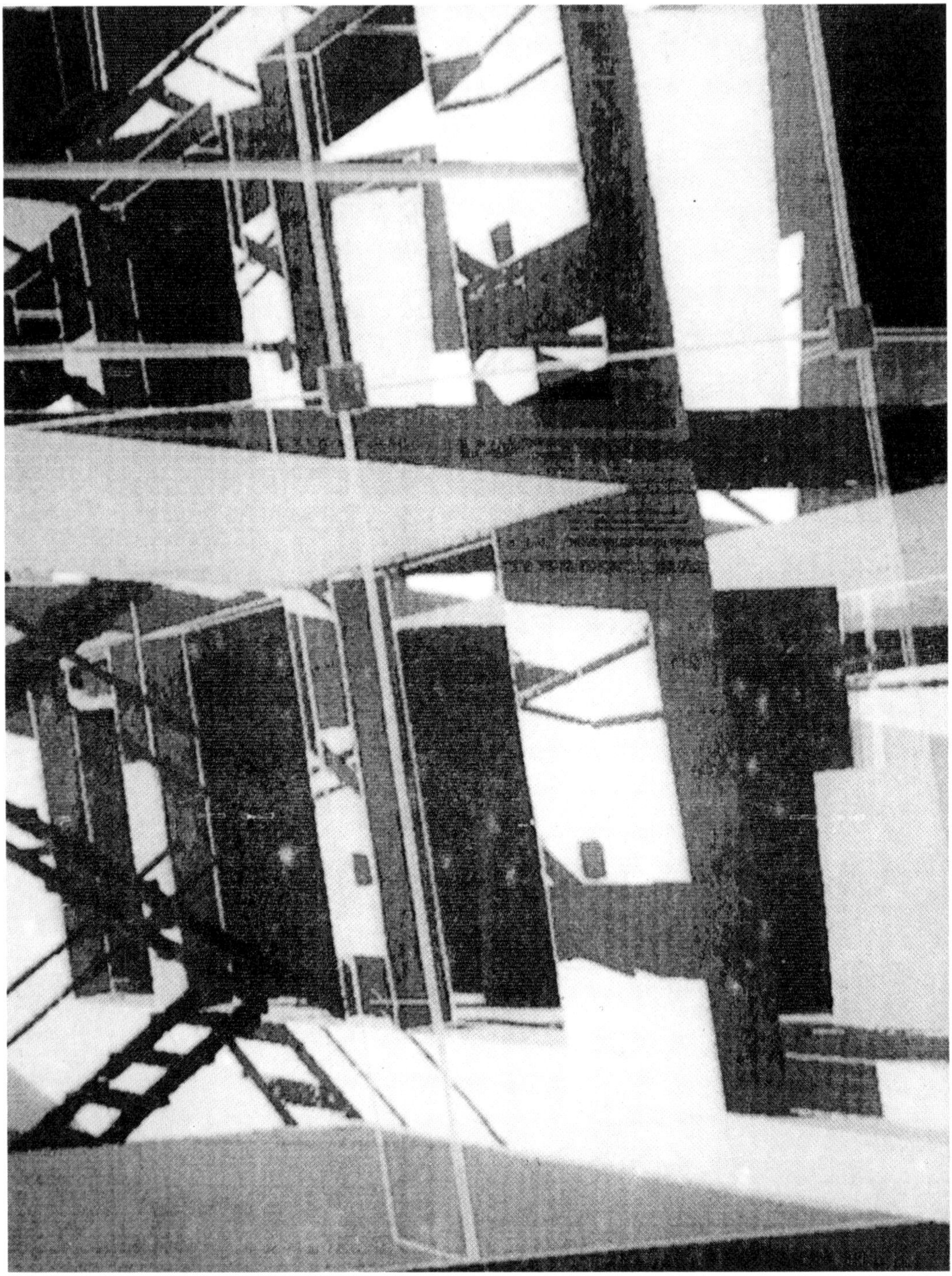

THE HAGUE
553

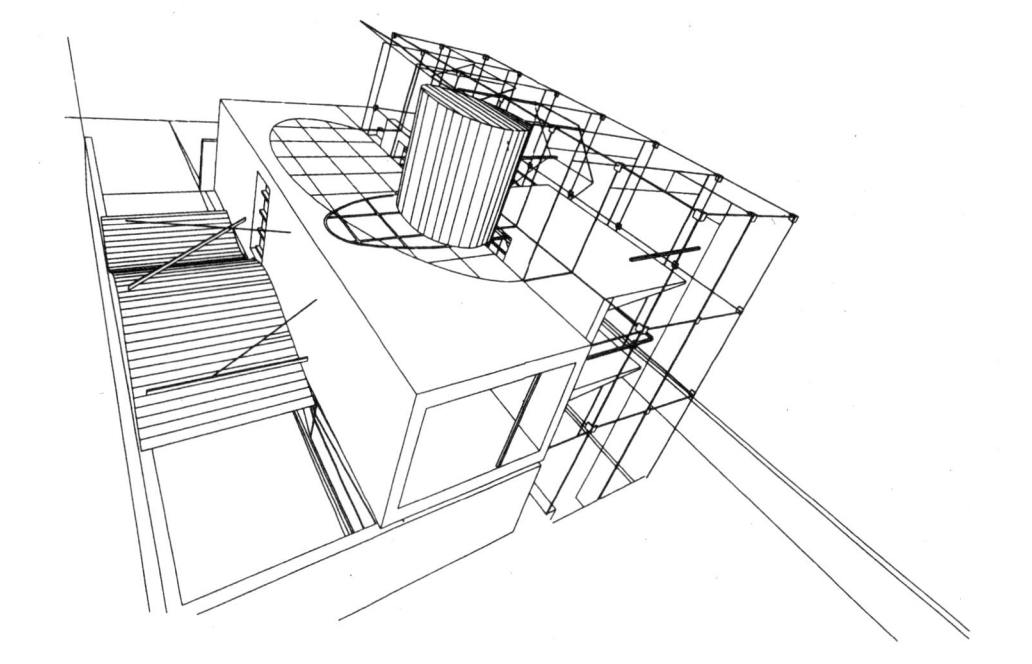

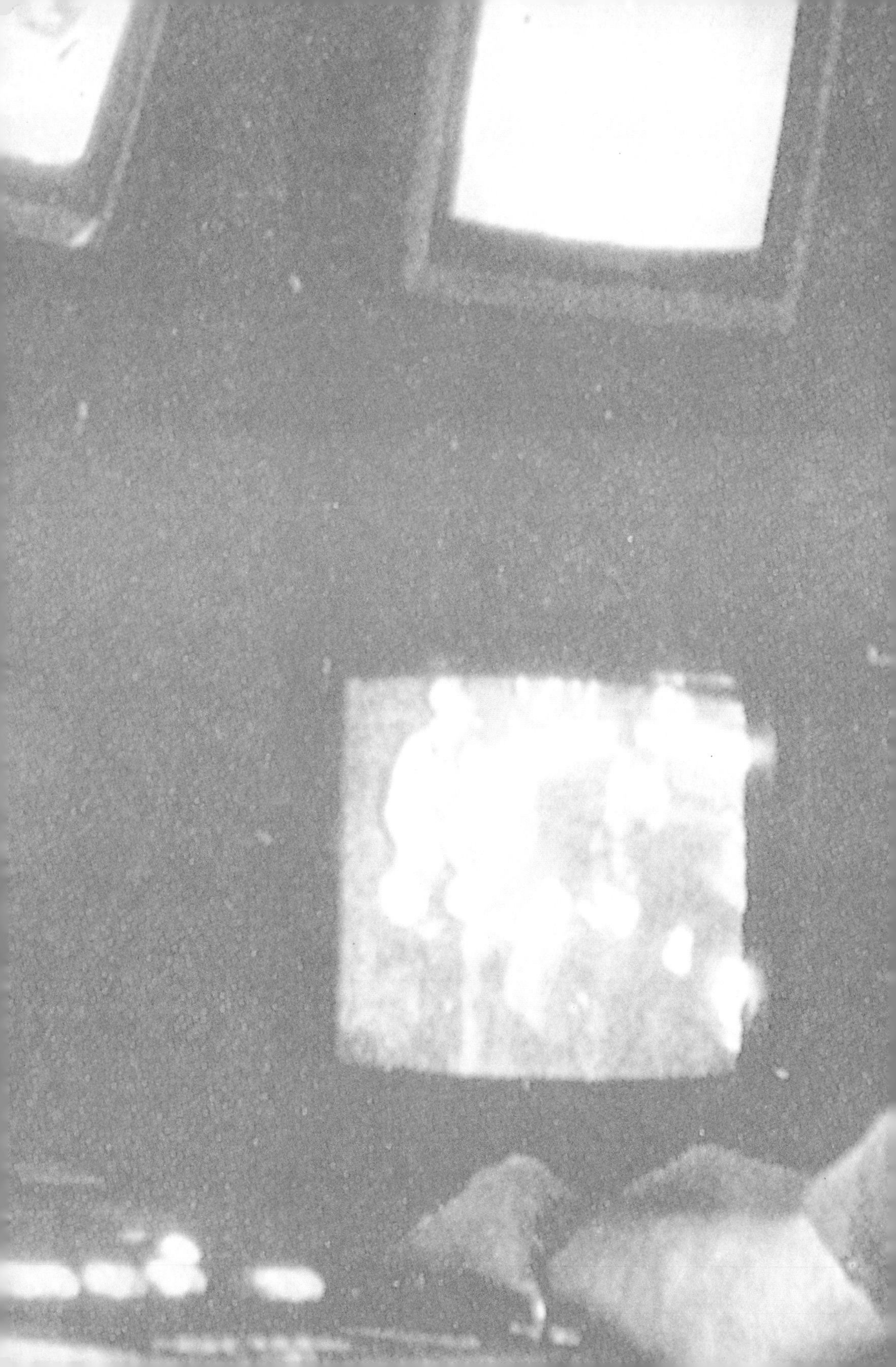

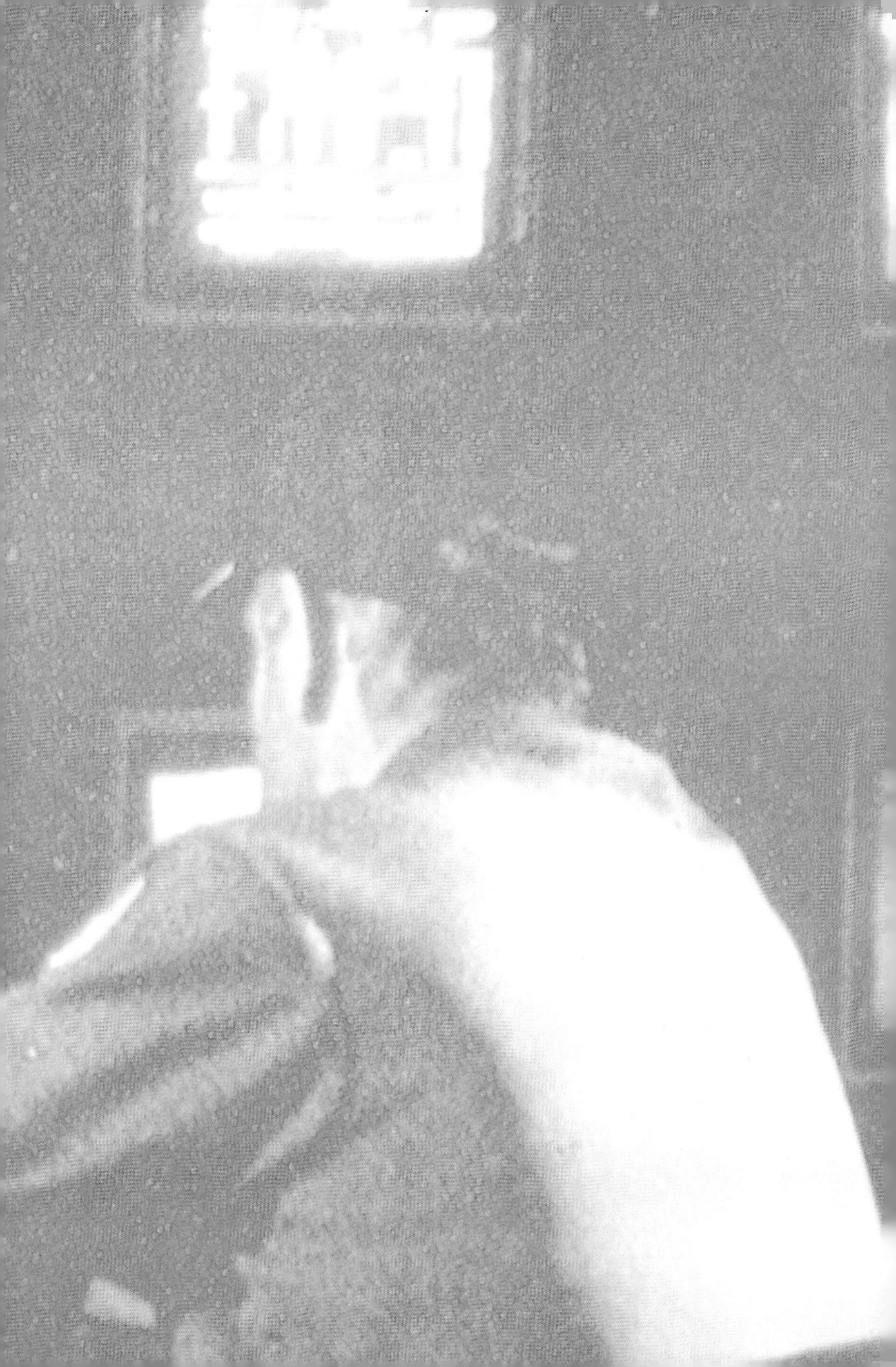

D.
Transient Events

In the transient architectures of today's cities, spatial definition changes constantly as space is activated as much by electronic as by architectonic artifacts. It is in tribute to the ephemeral nature of these inherently unstable images that the question of temporary exhibitions -- whether explicitly staged or occurring fortuitously within architectural terrain -- becomes important to the architecture of events.

Groningen, Glass Video Gallery, 1990

Immaterial Representation

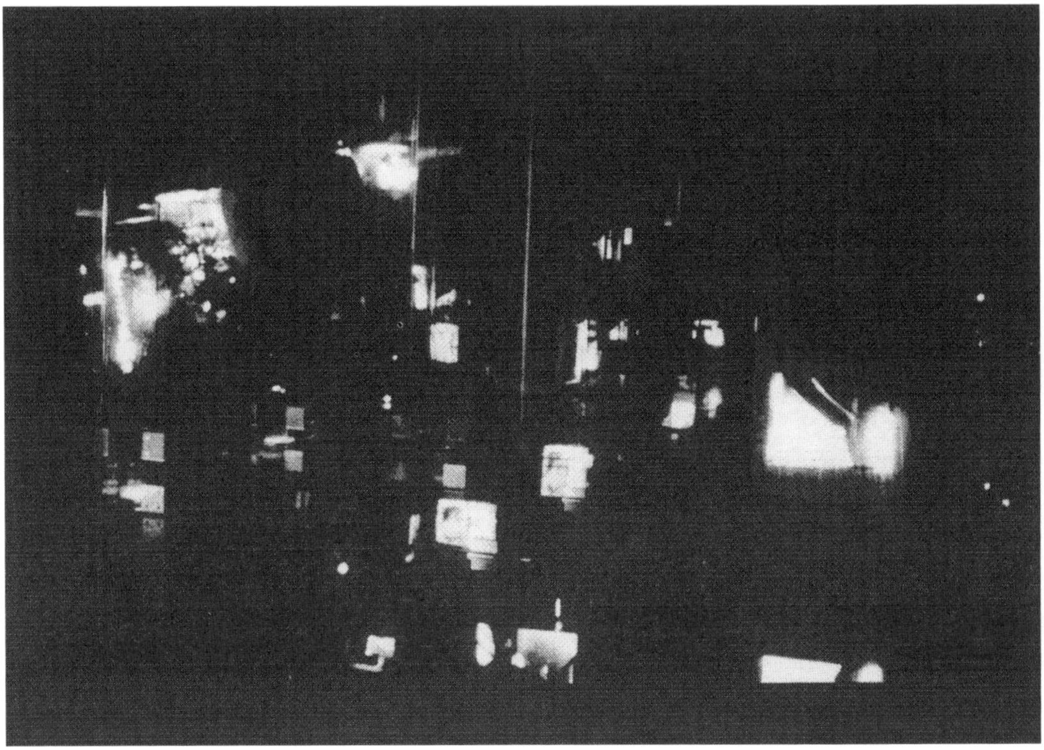

The appearance of permanence (buildings are solid; they are made of steel, concrete, bricks, etc.) is increasingly challenged by the immaterial representation of abstract systems (television and electronic images). The invitation extended by the city of Groningen in The Netherlands to design a special environment for viewing pop music videos offered an opportunity to challenge preconceived ideas about television viewing and about privacy. Was the video gallery to be a static and enclosed black box like the architectural type created for cinema; an extended living room with exterior advertising billboards and neon light; or a new "type" that brought what was previously a living room, bar and lounge event into the street by reversing expectations?

Instead of an enclosed and private space, we proposed its opposite: a glass video gallery as an inclined, transparent, glass structure. The gallery contains a series of interlocking spaces defined only be horizontal and vertical "glass fins" and by the points of metal clip connections. Located within are six banks of monitors used for screening videos. The dimensions of the glass gallery are 3.6 by 2.6 by 21.6 meters.

Placed on the tree-lined Hereplein Medallion roundabout, the gallery extends the street condition, except that in these streets borders become indiscernible—monitors provide unstable facades, glass reflections create mirages and limitless space is suggested. The gallery and urban space also contain both video objects on display and objects for displaying. They encompass monitor walls viewed through television dealership storefronts on the street while exhibiting events like those seen in the sex-video galleries of urban red-light districts.

In this new video plaza, one watches and is watched simultaneously.

Note:
The rhetorical "glass houses" of the Modern Movement often remained spatially traditional, as they were visually defined by support structures made of steel and by their solid ceilings. In the Glass Video Gallery, removing the glass means undoing the house, as horizontal beams, vertical supports, the top and the sides are all made of identical structural glass.

The oblique floor further challenges all perceptions of spatial stability. At night, the endless reflections of the video screens over the vertical and horizontal glass surfaces reverse all expectations of what is architecture and what is event, of what is wall and what is electronic image, of what defines and what activates.

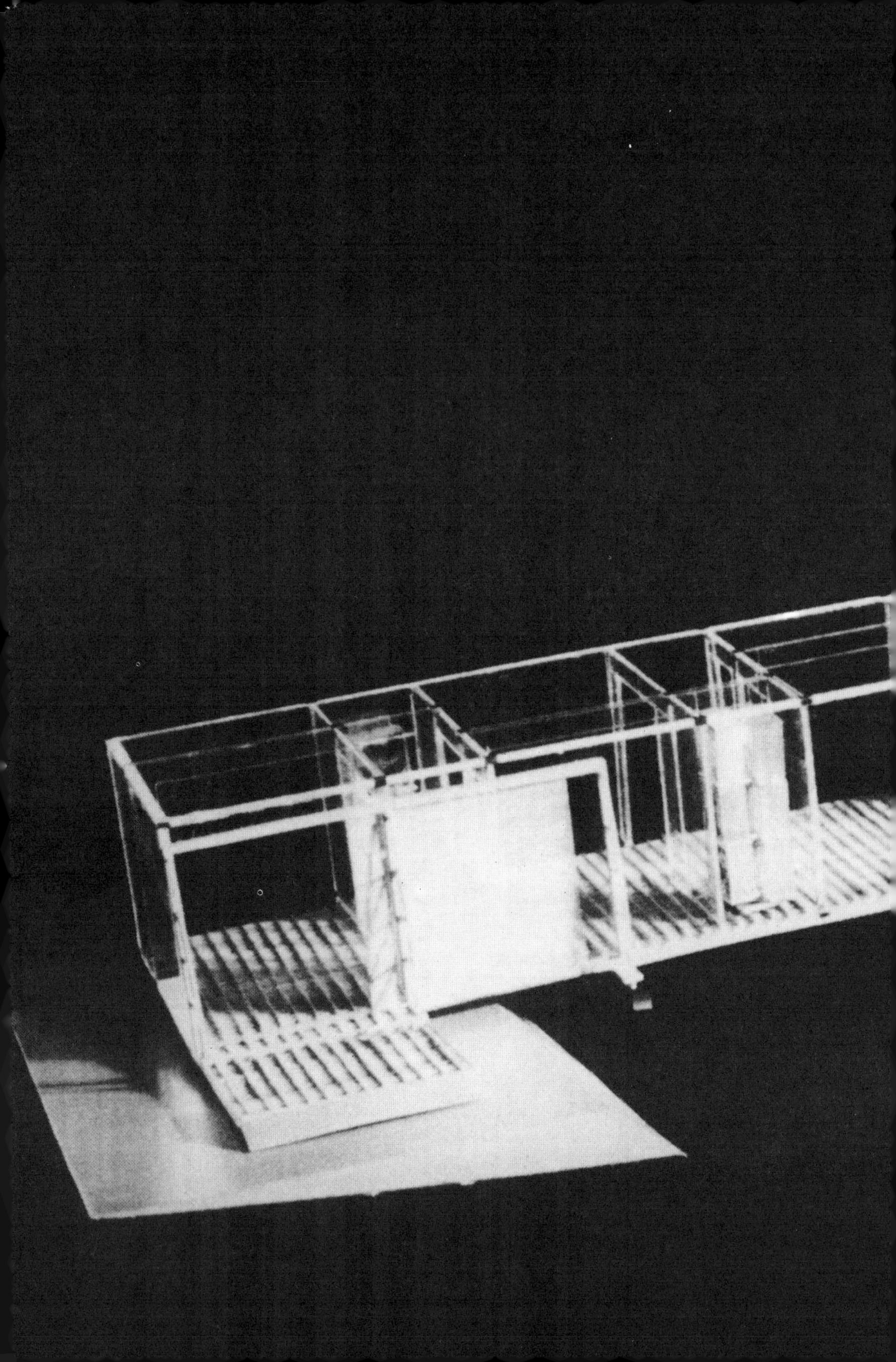

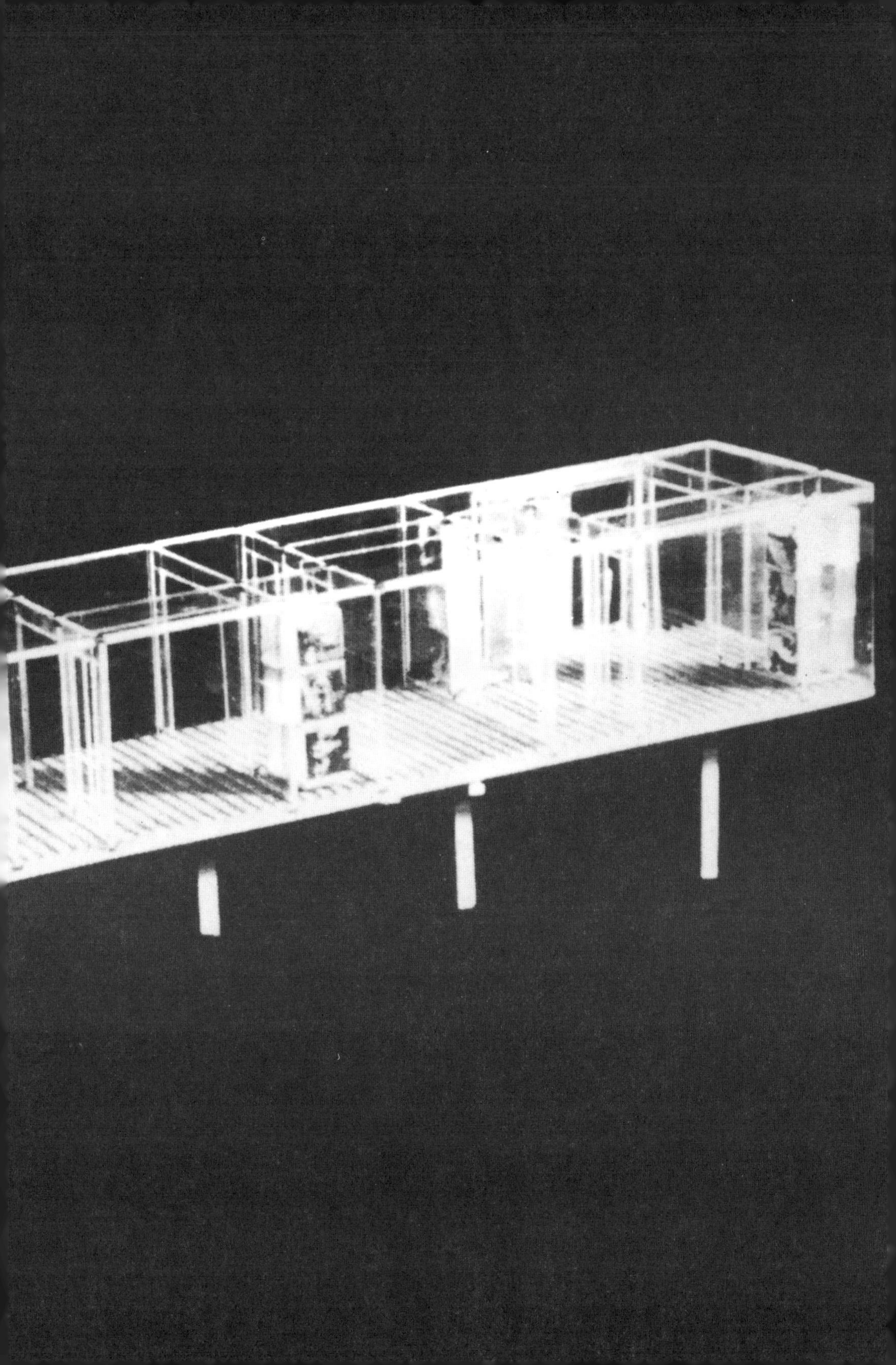

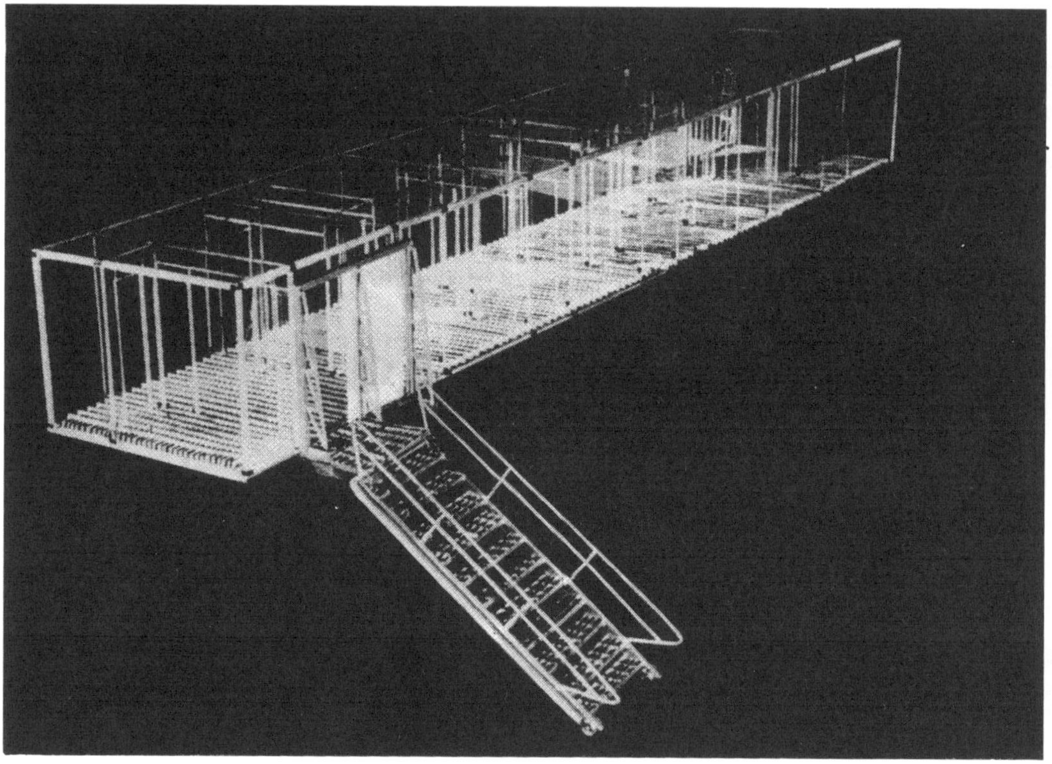

SITE OPTION 1

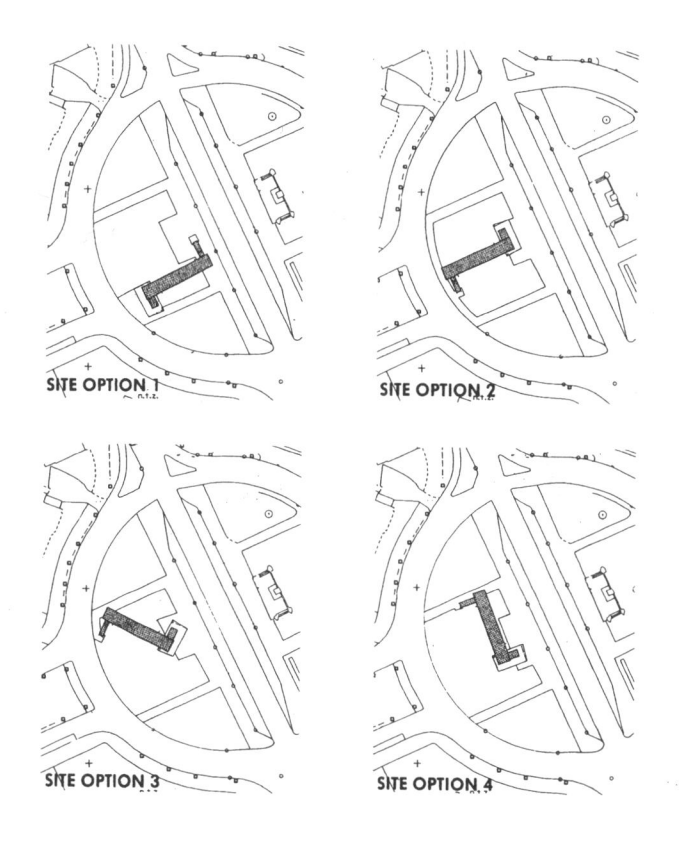

SITE OPTION 2

SITE OPTION 3

SITE OPTION 4

A randomly placed glass house

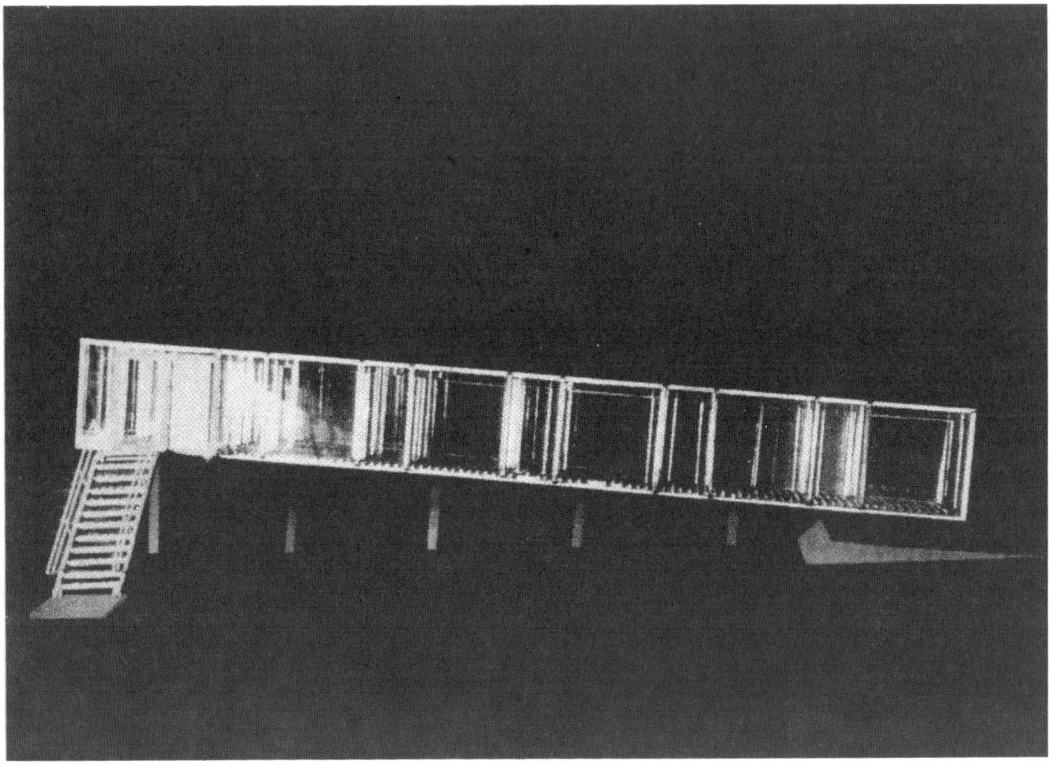

GRONINGEN
565

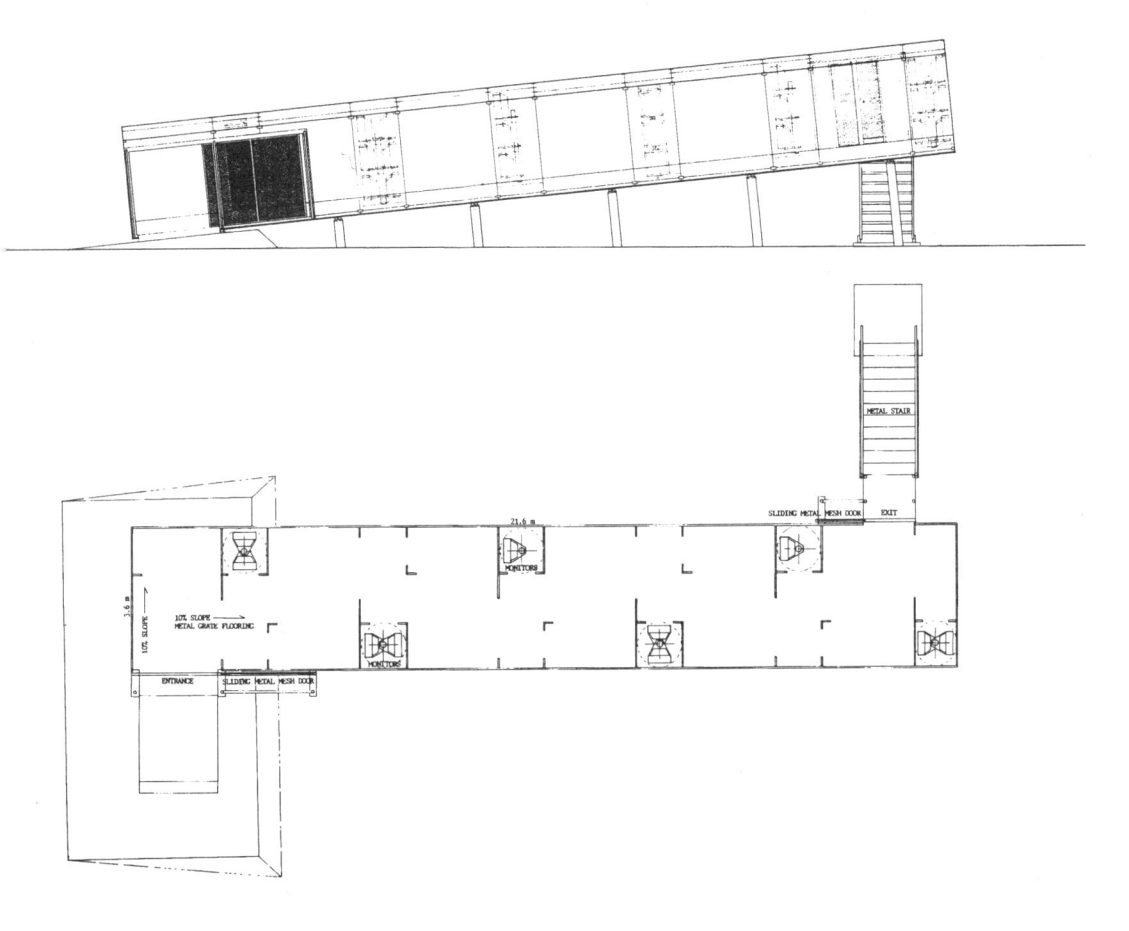

The rectangular glass construction inclines lengthwise

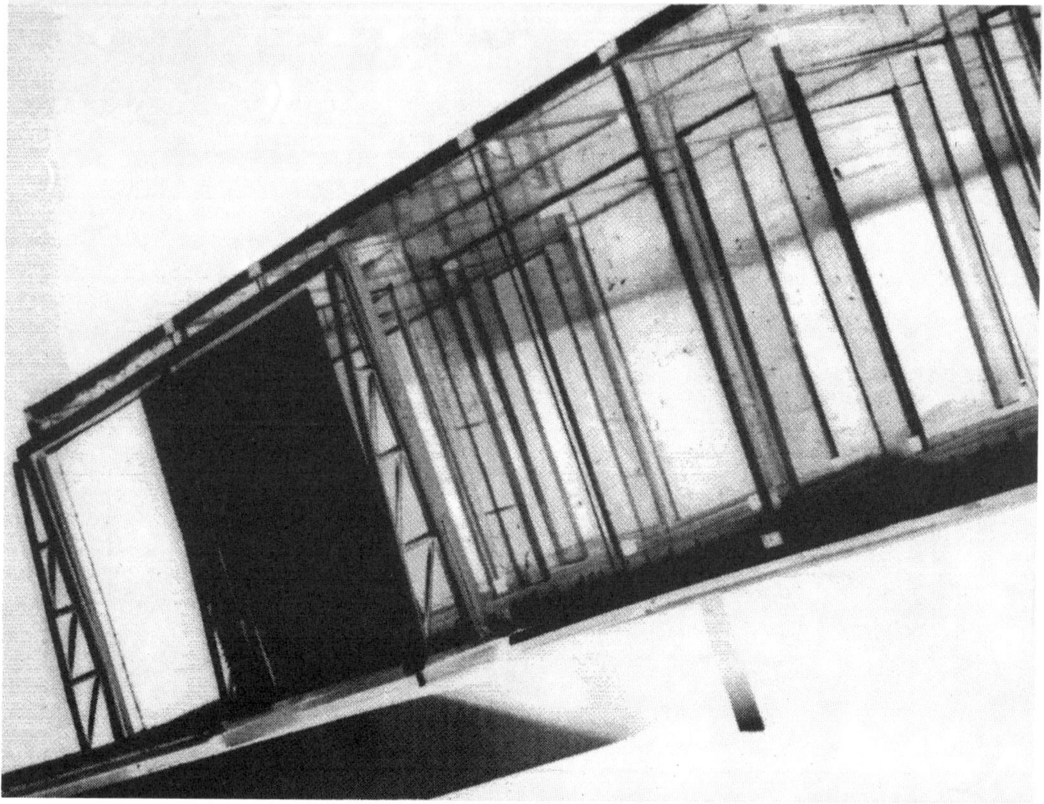

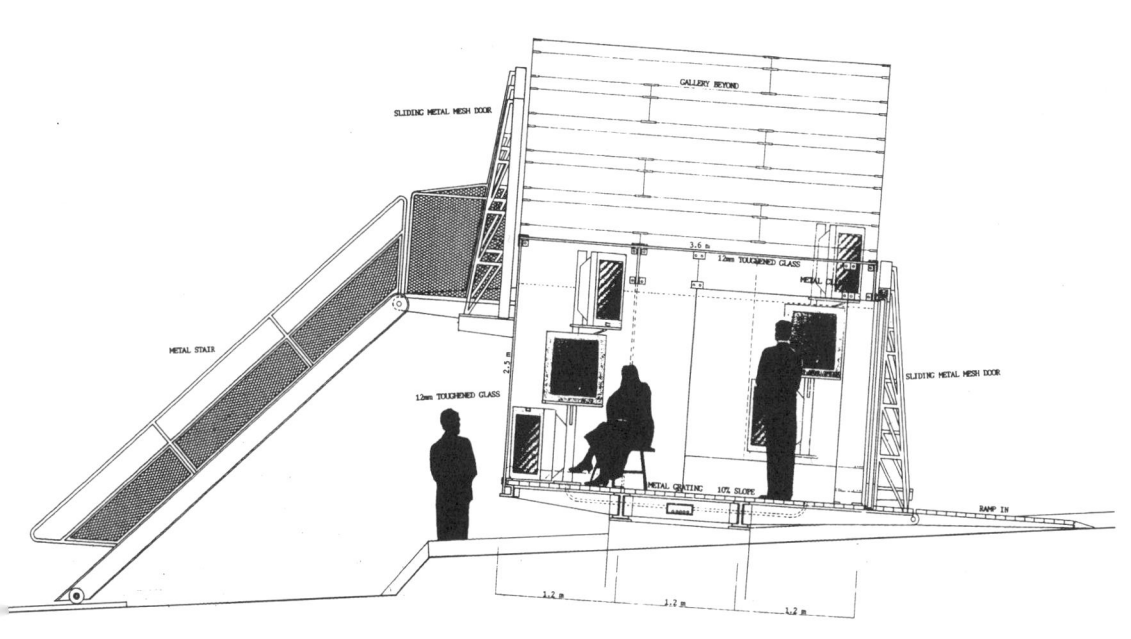

... and also sideways. The new media technology
simultaneously defines and activates space

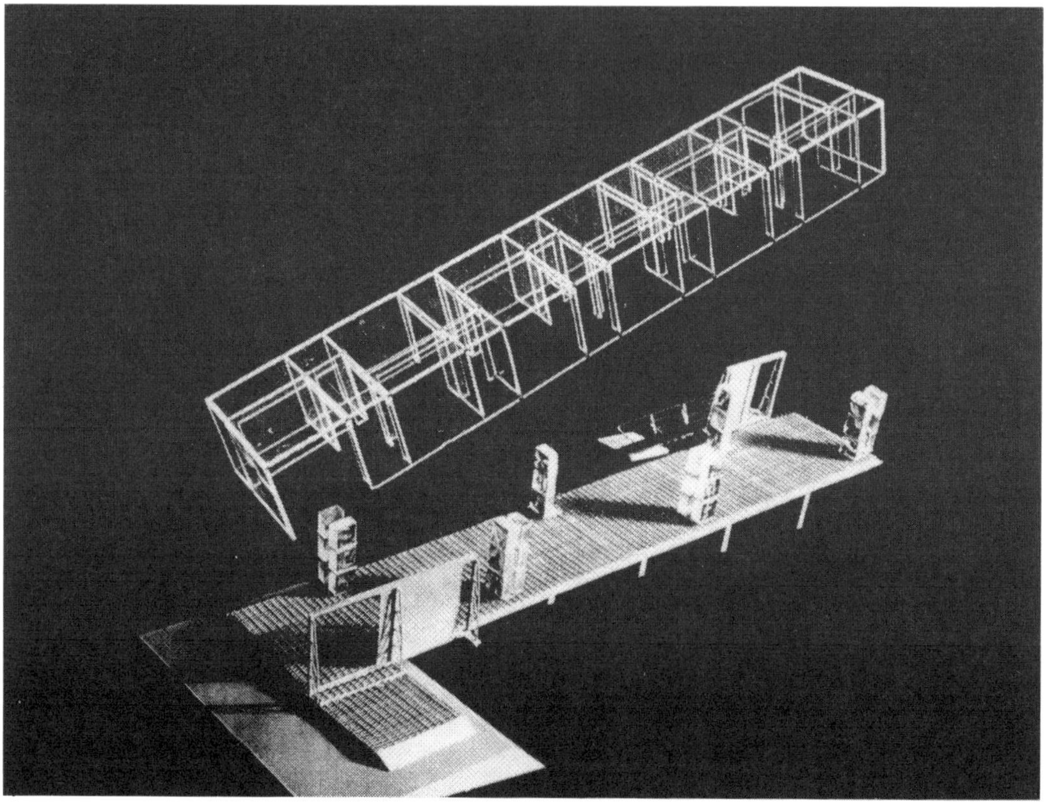

GRONINGEN
569

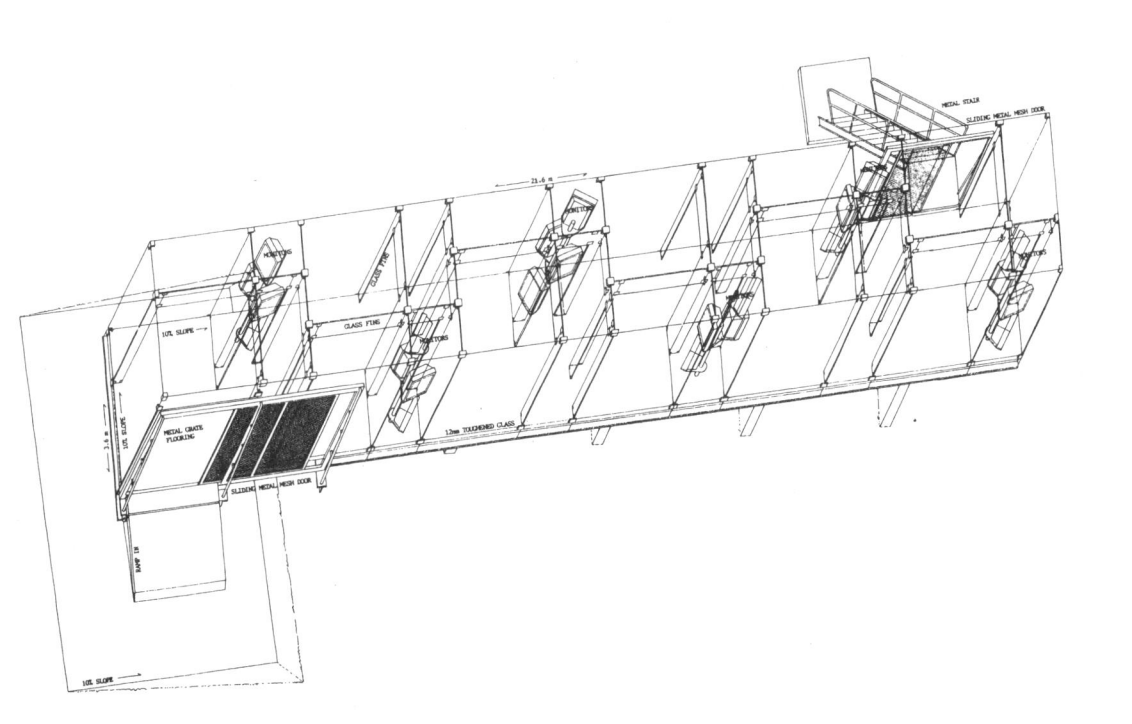

Columns, beams and roof panels are made entirely of glass

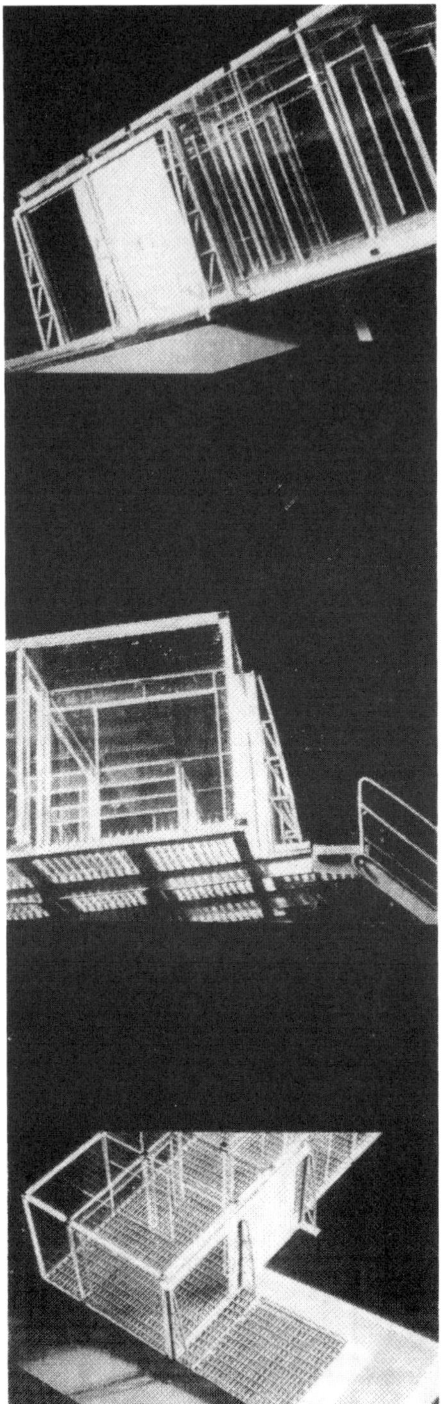

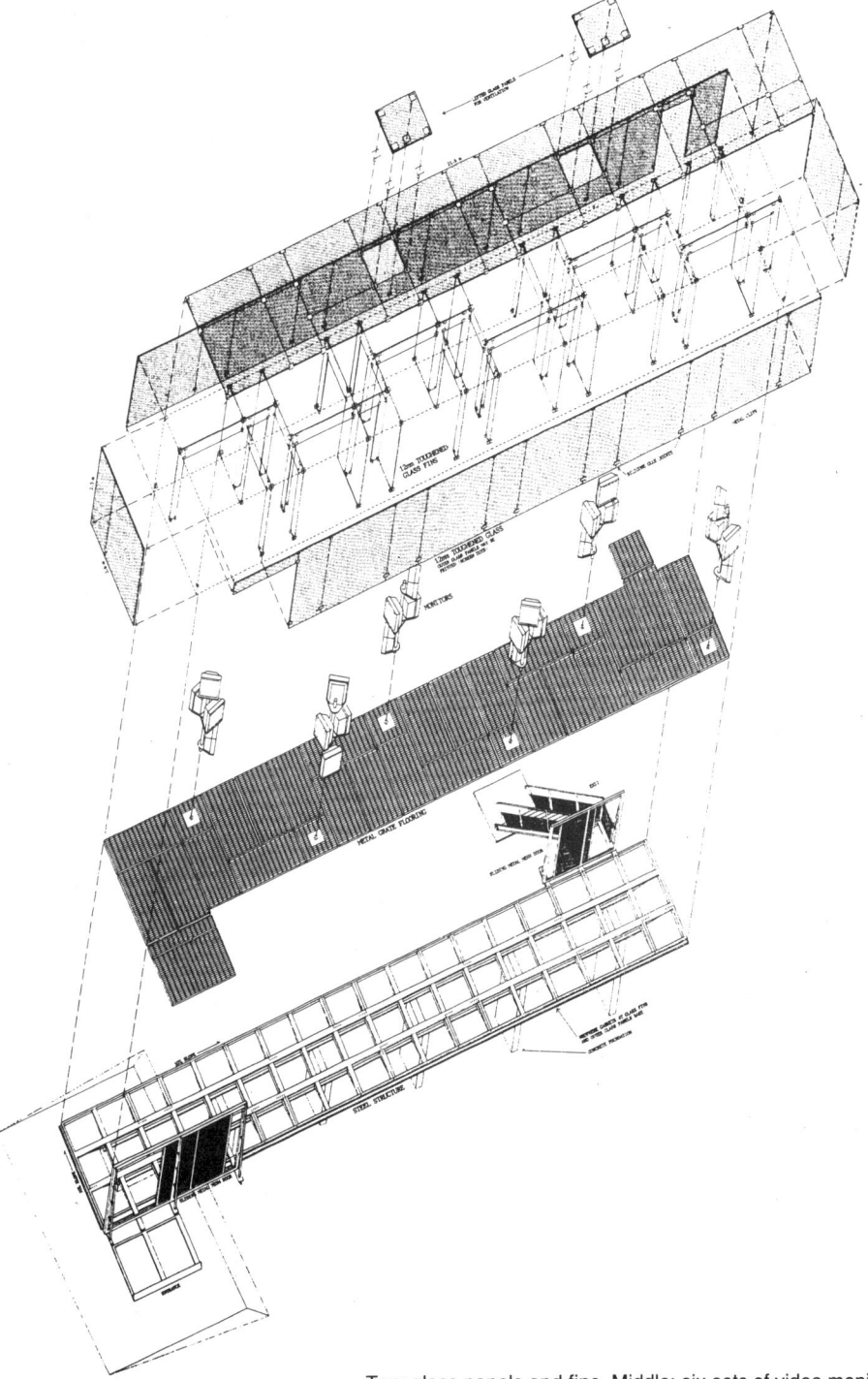

Top: glass panels and fins. Middle: six sets of video monitors
Bottom: inclined steel gratings

Daytime: hovering glass (defining space) and video monitors (activating space)

GRONINGEN
573

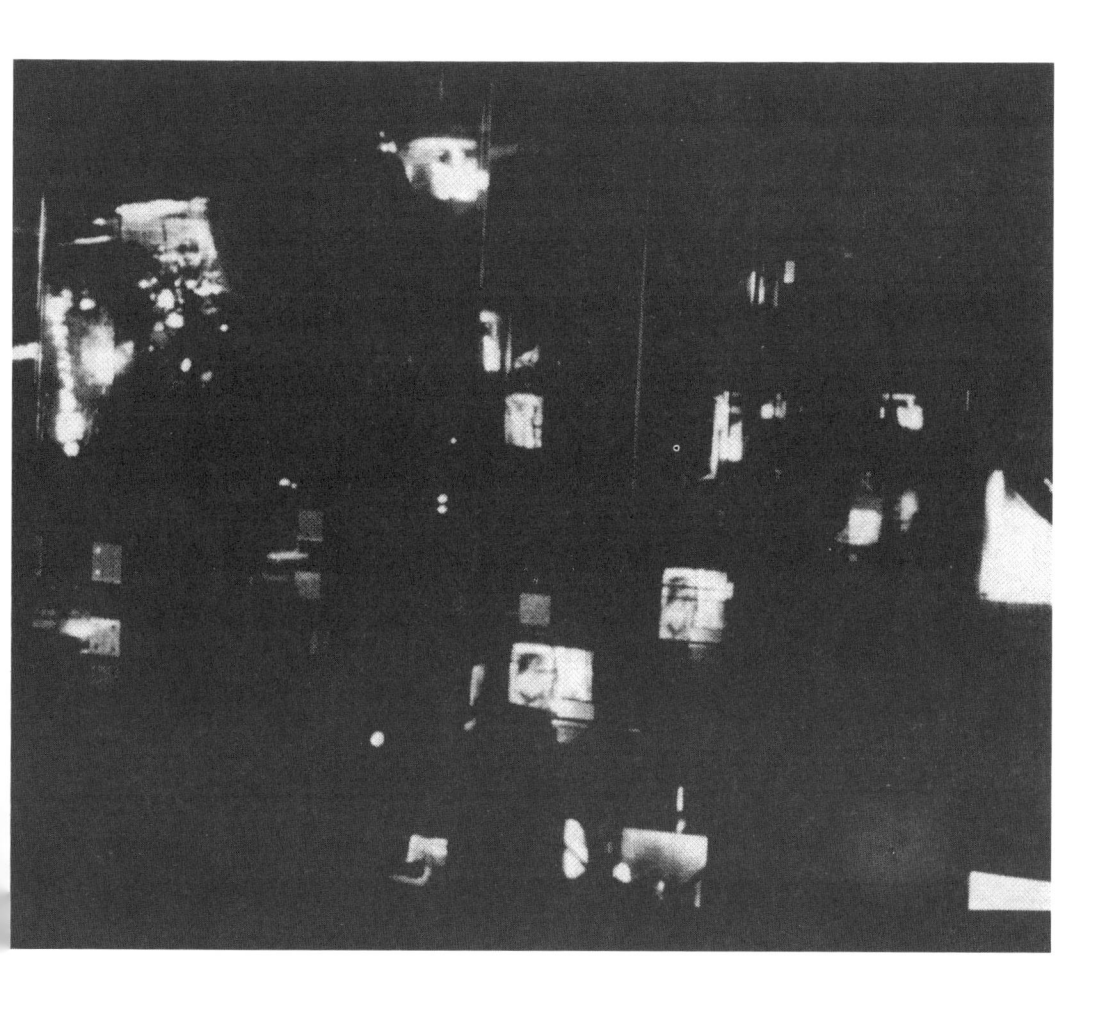

Space and events become interchangeable

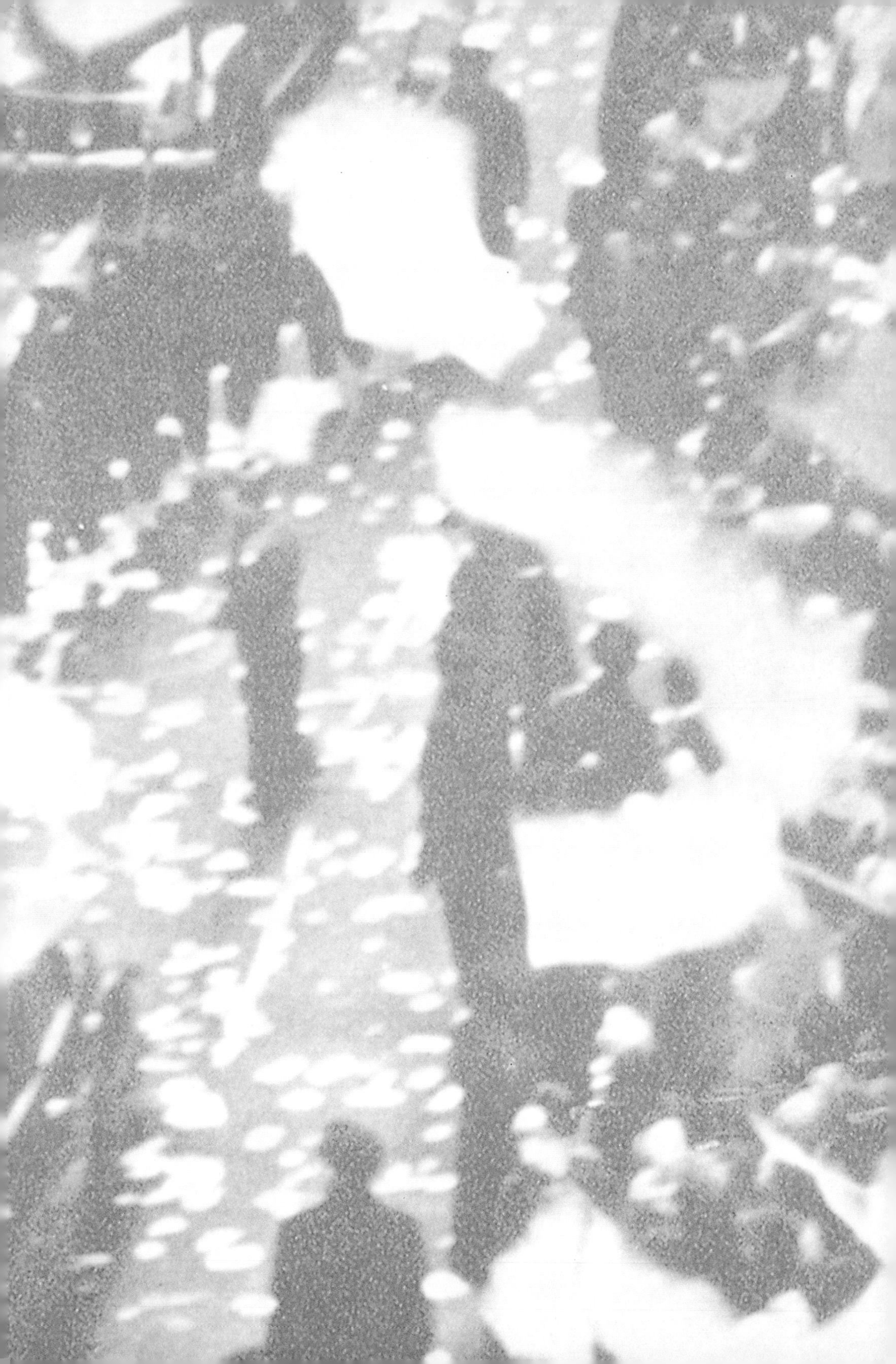

*Paris, Pompidou Center, "Art et Publicité"
Exhibition Design, 1990*

Mediation I

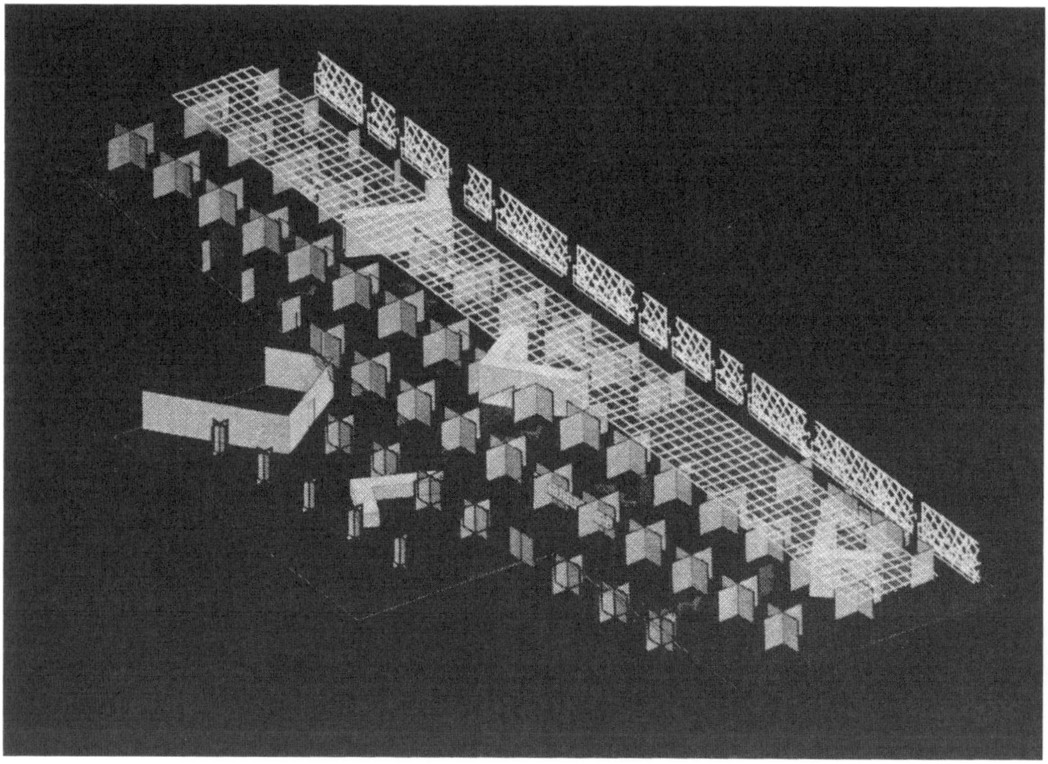

For its 35,000-square-foot fifth floor, the Pompidou Center wanted an original installation that could accommodate "Art et Pub," a major exhibition on art and advertising covering developments over the last hundred years, from Toulouse-Lautrec to Barbara Kruger and Volkswagen commercials.

The combination of extremely heterogeneous materials including, on one hand, fragile works on paper and, on the other, raucous life-size neon signs, suggested two separate parts to the exhibition, one dedicated to art and the other to advertising. However, we decided against establishing an *a priori* architectural distinction that would arbitrarily define two respective roles. We also felt that these roles were not interchangeable.

Hence we saw our installation as an architectural mediation between art and advertising. Our concept has more to do with city plans and urbanism than with the layout of interior spaces. We aimed at developing an autonomous system, independent of both the Pompidou Center structure and the programmatic content of the exhibition.

We also wanted to reveal, once again, the grand open space of the original Beaubourg plan, removing from it the enclosed "rooms" and obstructions installed over successive years. Our project plays on the idea of endless "fluid" space and on transparency: it is, indeed, rare to have the opportunity to articulate interior spaces over one hundred meters long. The exhibition concept consists of a crosslike grid, marked by sixty intersecting partitions, each 2.8 meters high (the Beaubourg ceiling height averages 4.5 meters). In plan, these partitions read as a series of crosses, each marking the angle of the spaces that they simultaneously define and activate.

Visitors move freely among the partition crosses throughout the exhibition. Semitransparent fabric panels allow some spaces to be closed while maintaining a high degree of transparency throughout the entire center. Several "sight and sound islands" and half-scale reconstructions of pavilions by Bayer and Depero, as well as a "street" fitted with neon signs and product advertising along the length of the building, explore the margins of twentieth-century art production.

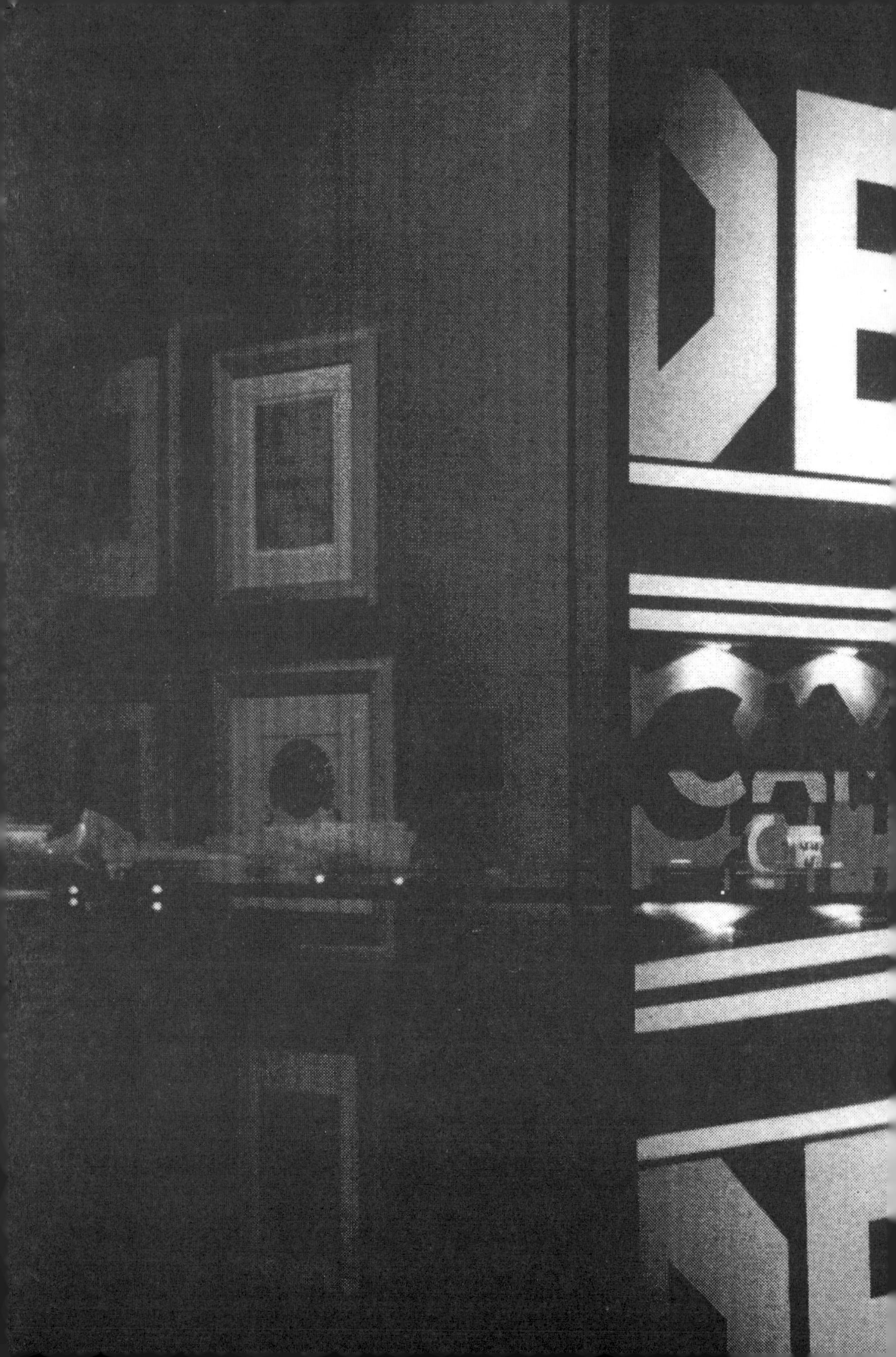

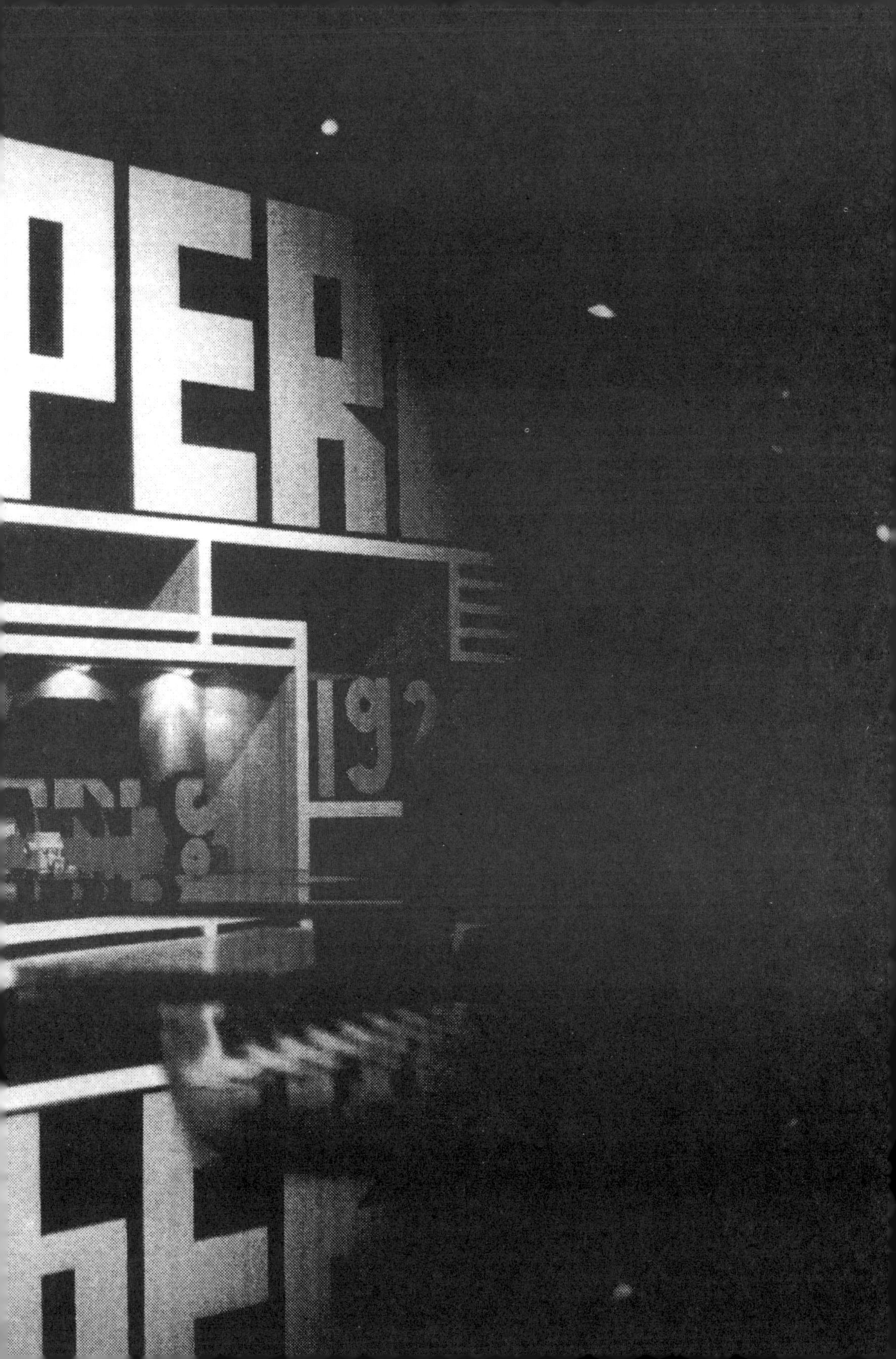
PER
19

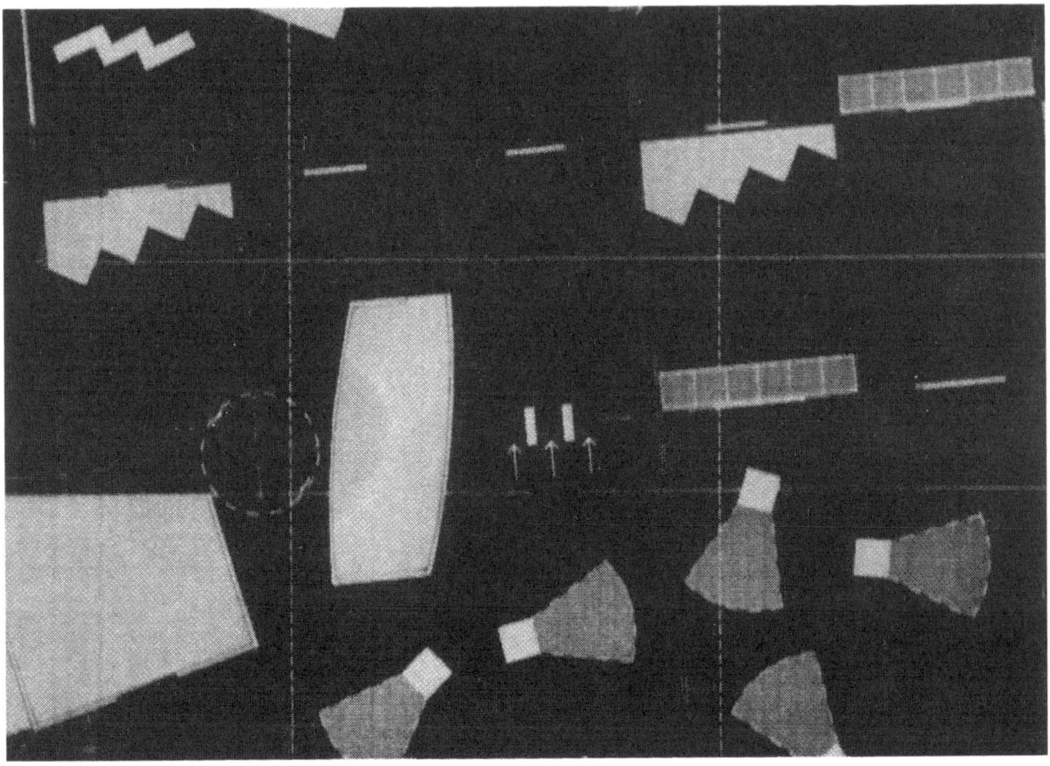

PARIS
583

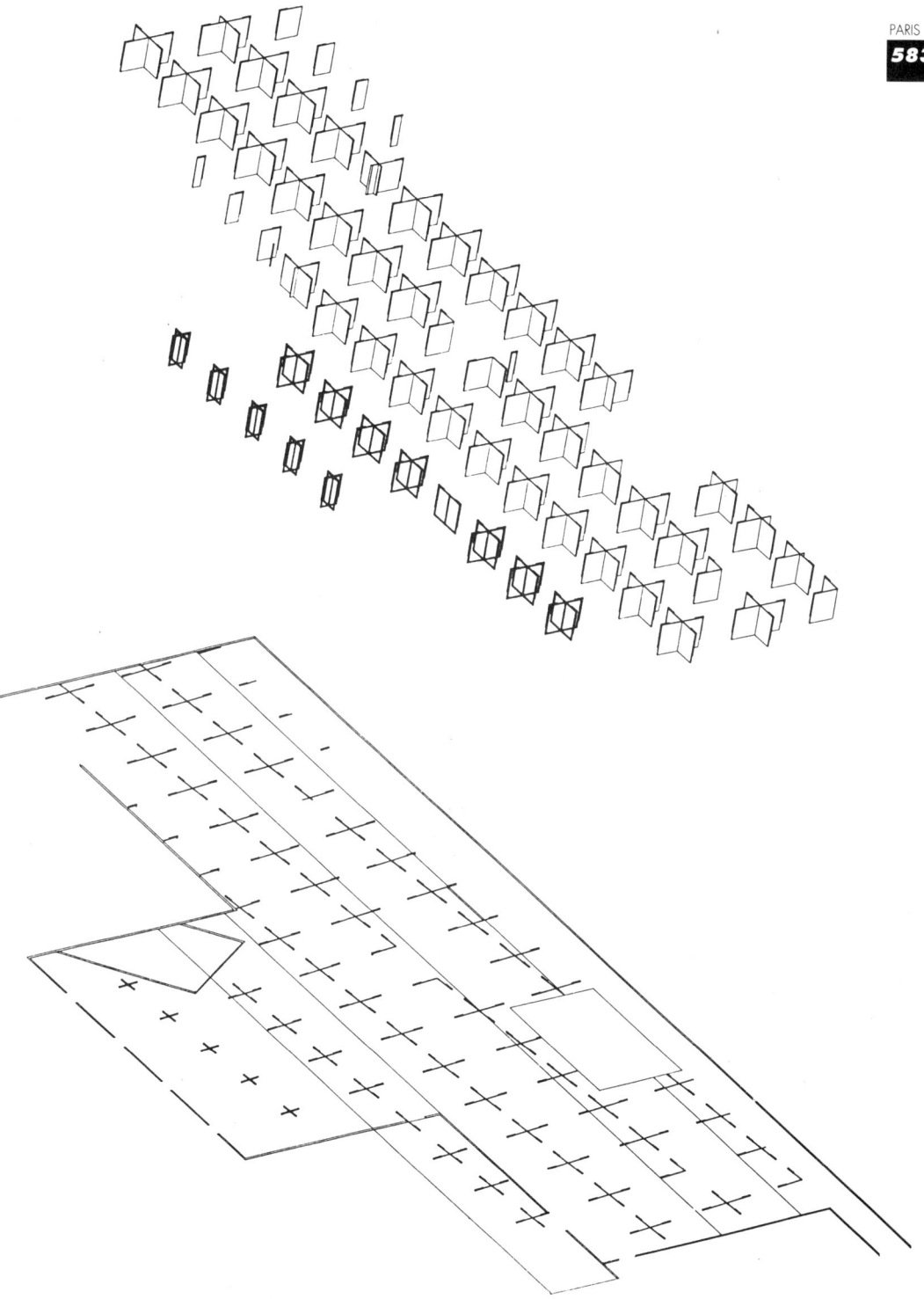

First layer: a point grid defining spaces

Space and events: two terms that are interdependent but mutually exclusive

PARIS
585

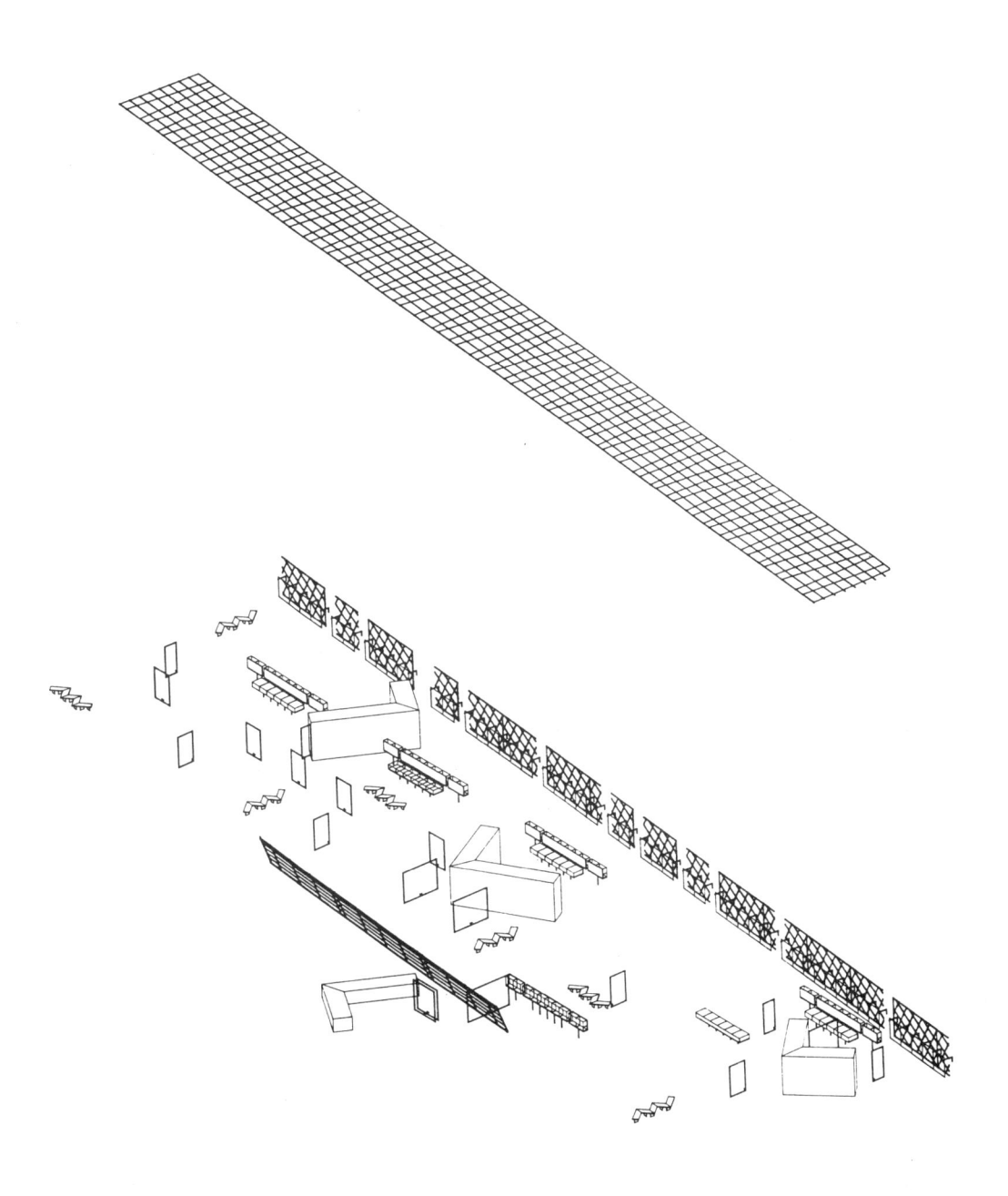

Second layer: steel mesh ceiling

Third layer: display elements, show cases, seats

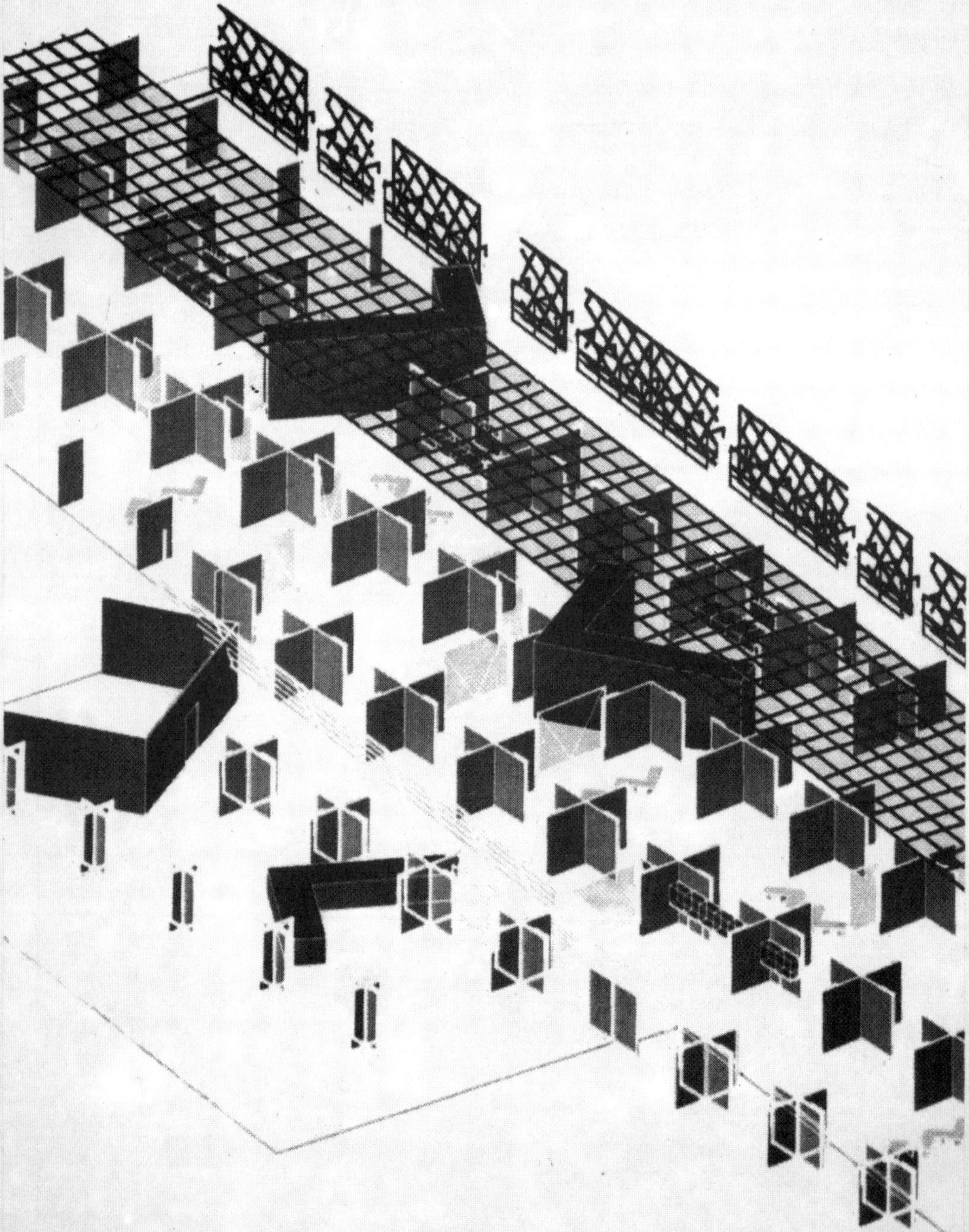

PARIS
587

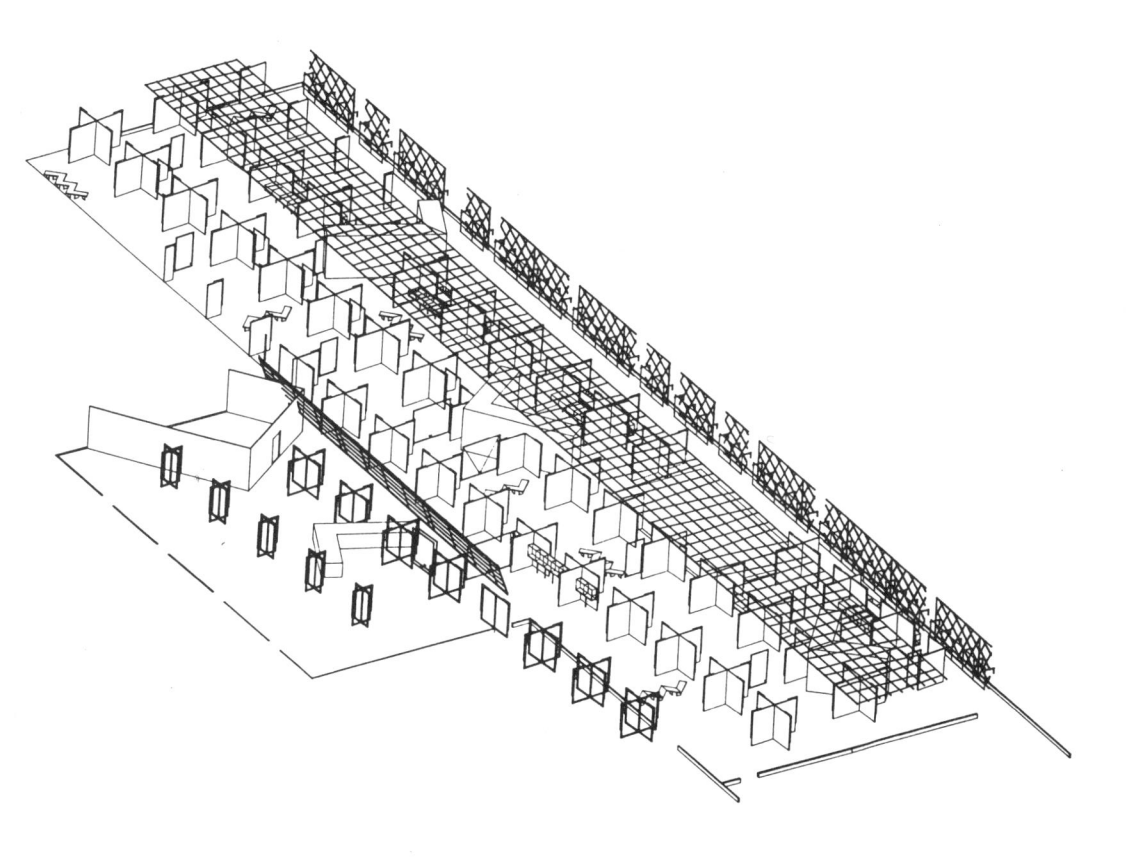

Superimposition of the three layers on an event-ual landscape

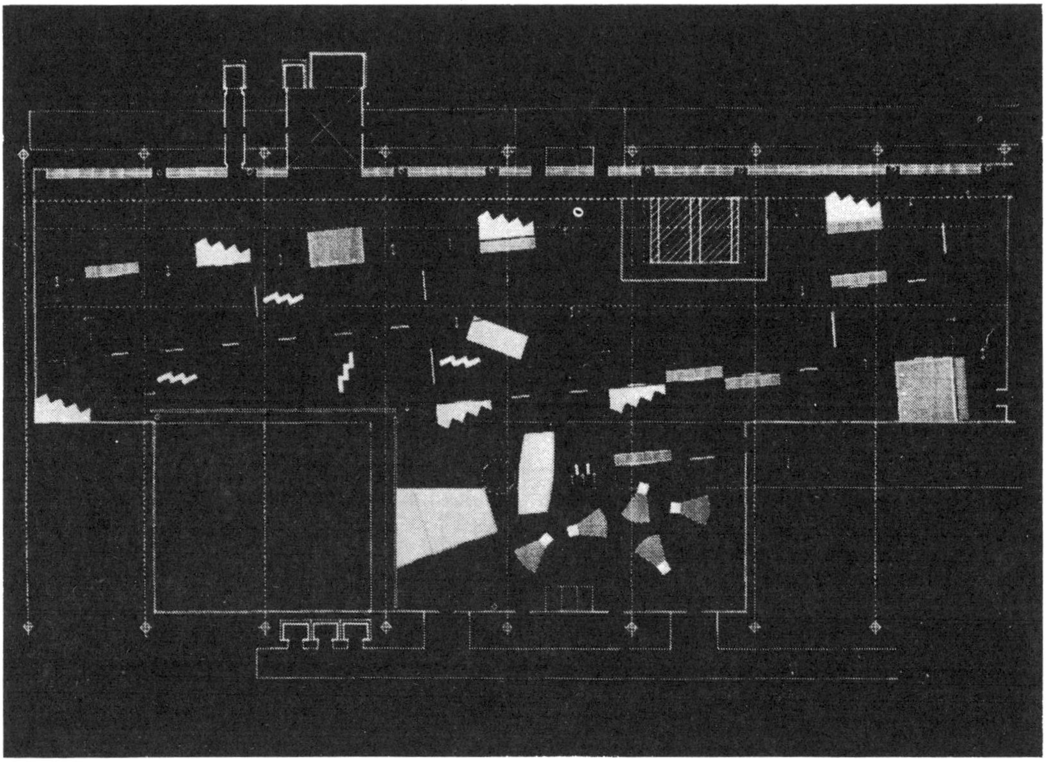

PARIS
589

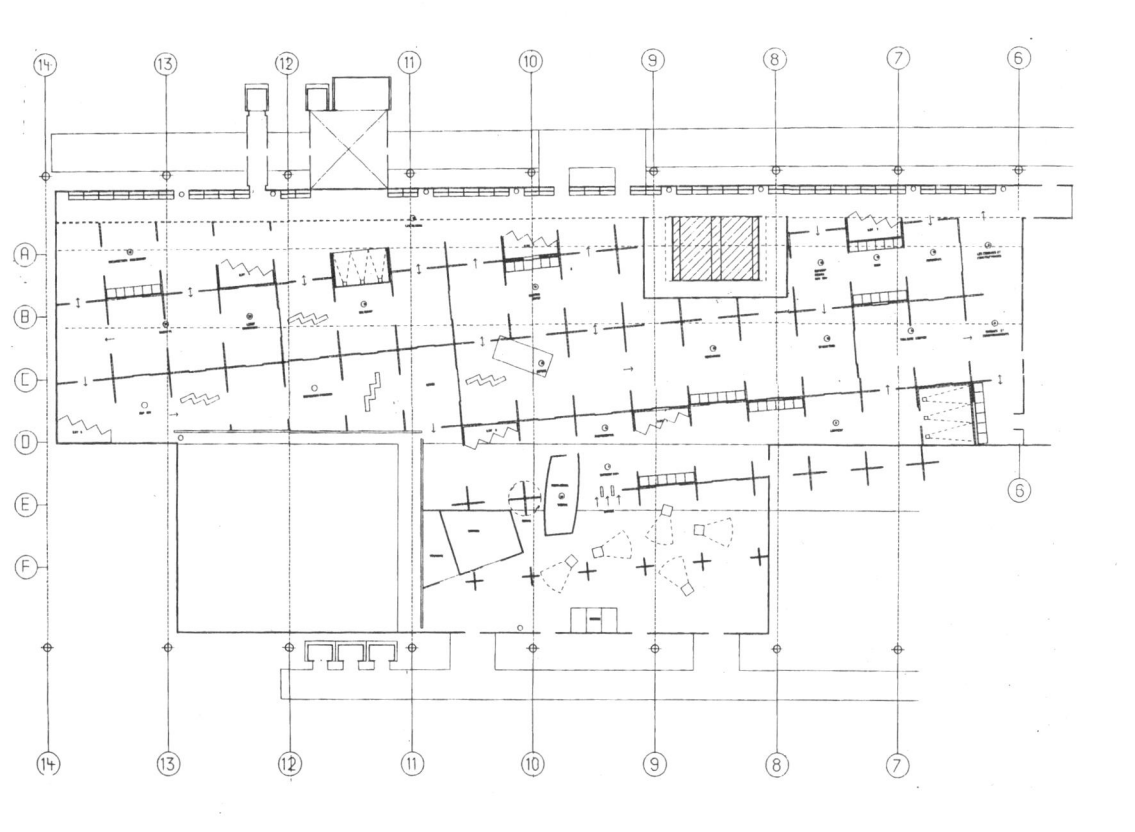

A collection of events strung along a collection of spaces

DEPERO

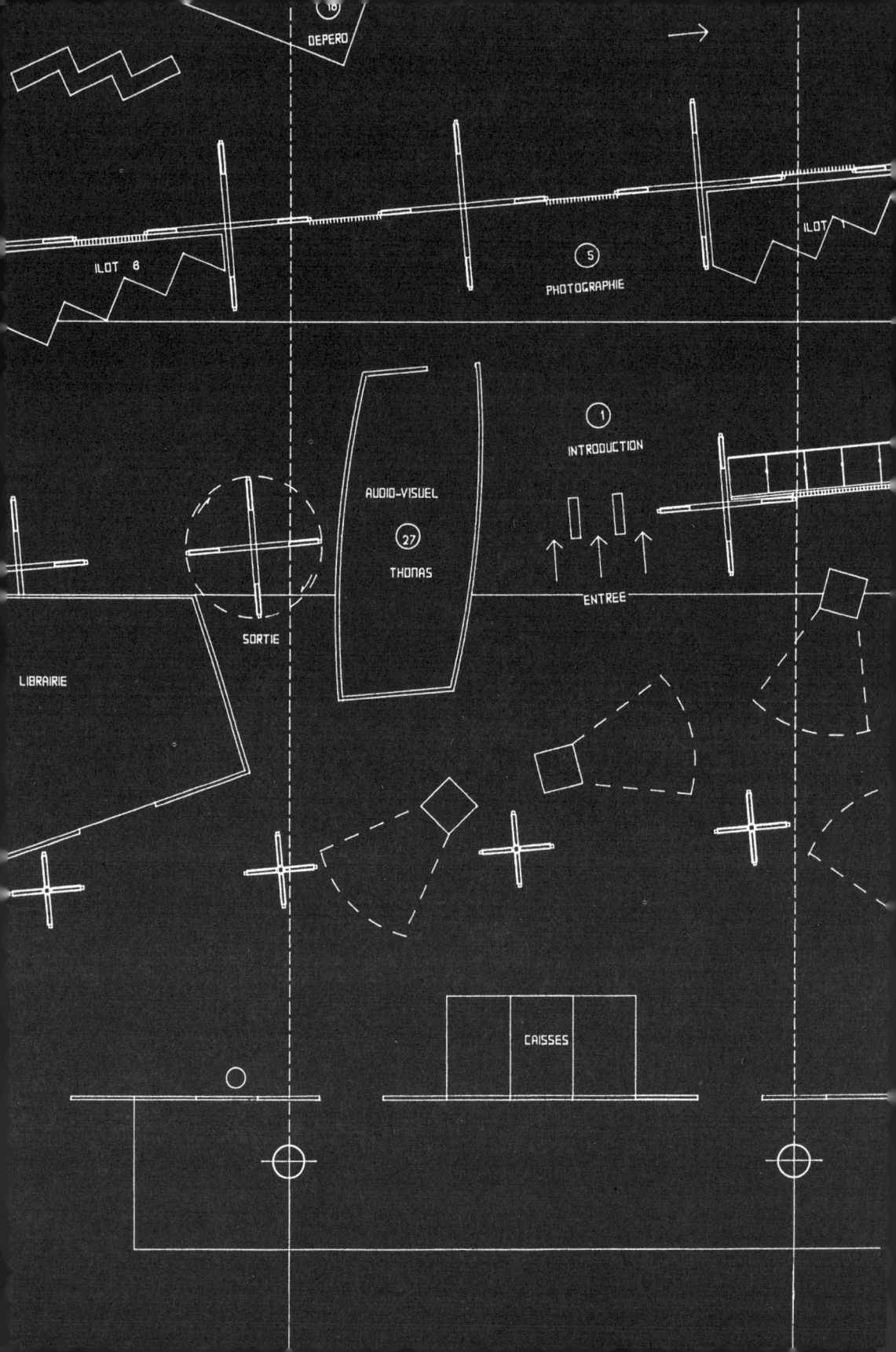

ILOT 8

⑤
PHOTOGRAPHIE

ILOT

①
INTRODUCTION

AUDIO-VISUEL
㉗
THOMAS

SORTIE

ENTREE

LIBRAIRIE

CAISSES

PARIS
591

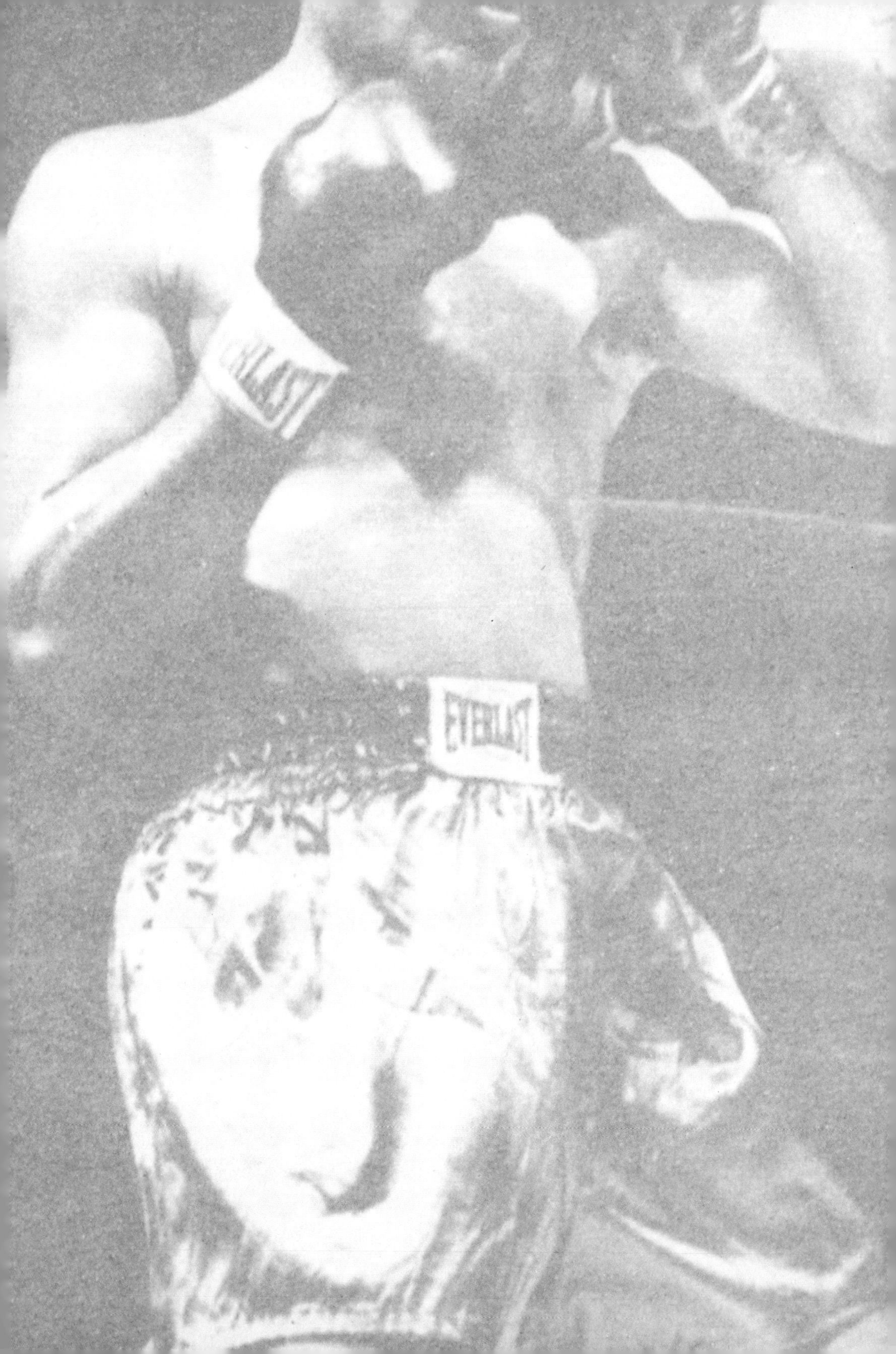
EVERLAST

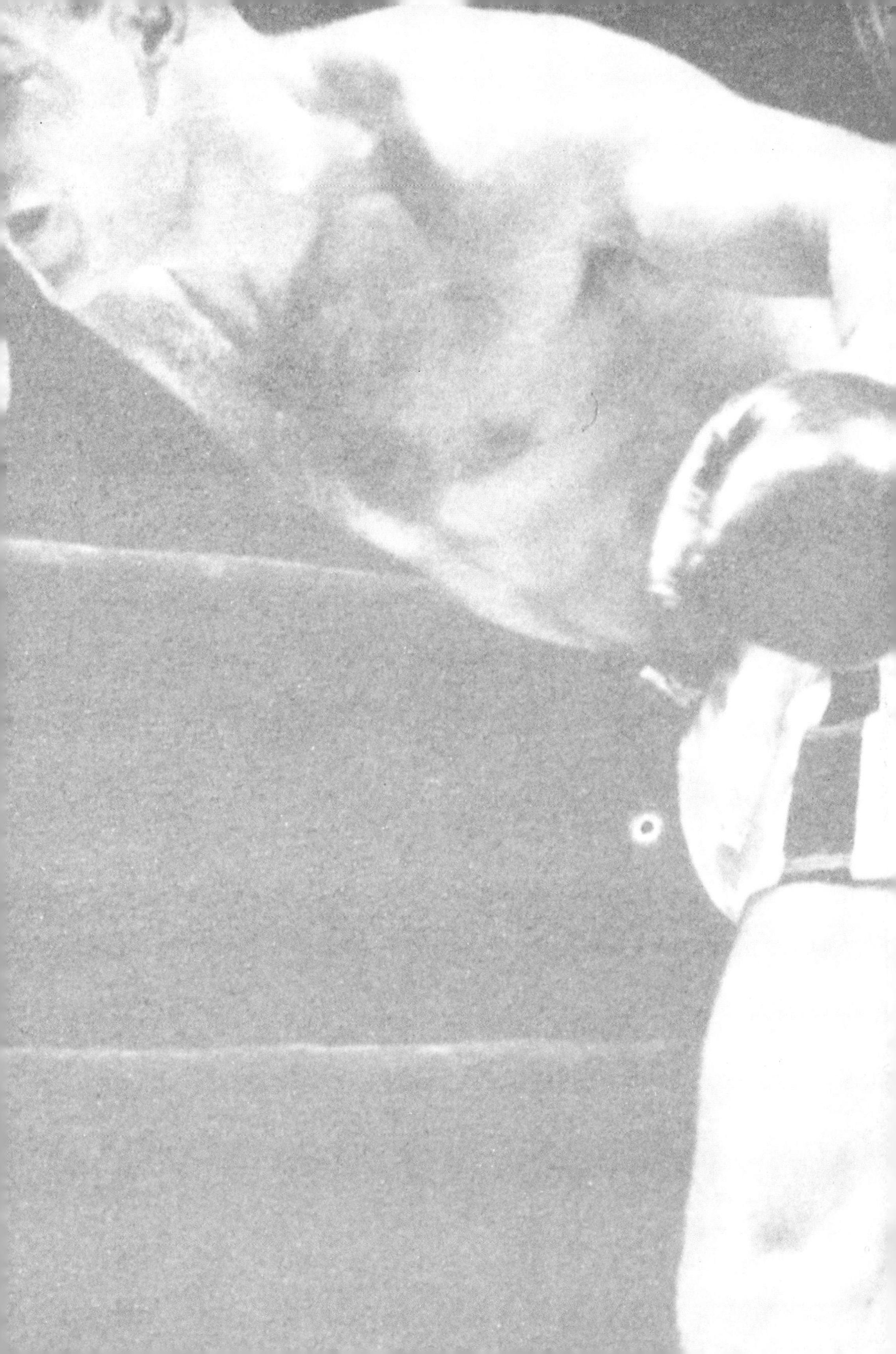

Tourcoing, Le Fresnoy, "BTA" Exhibition, 1993

Mediation II

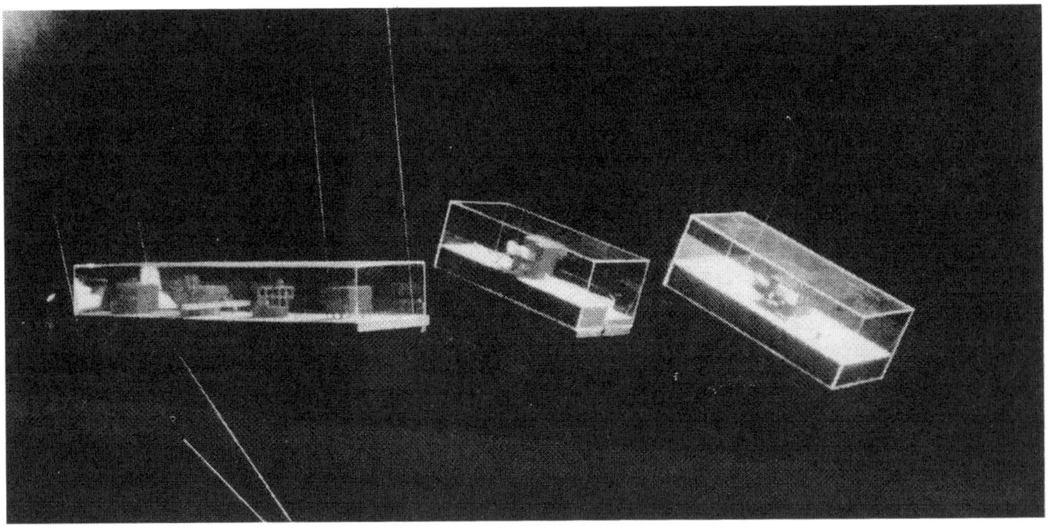

To celebrate the beginning of the construction of the new Le Fresnoy art center in Tourcoing, France and to inform the city inhabitants about the project, we were asked to install an exhibition of our recent work, more than fifteen projects and research, from the *Screenplays* (1976–82) to the Fresnoy project.

The theme of the in-between, on one hand, and the very modest budget available on the other, made us dispense altogether with the solid model bases and numerous partitions defining most architectural exhibitions.

We proposed instead a series of floating images held under tension by cables anchored to the floor and to the trusses of the existing vault structure. In order to provide spatial intimacy for the smaller works on display, two trapeze-like enclosed spaces (one red, one black) were also added. Highly focused lighting was directed towards the suspended models and drawings as the overall space remained in the dark. Ten television monitors located against the mezzanines of the exhibition hall showed artists' films selected by a curator from Le Fresnoy.

For five weeks, an abandoned vault which used to house a skating rink and wrestling matches became an architecture center for the city.

Event = a disparate multiplicity

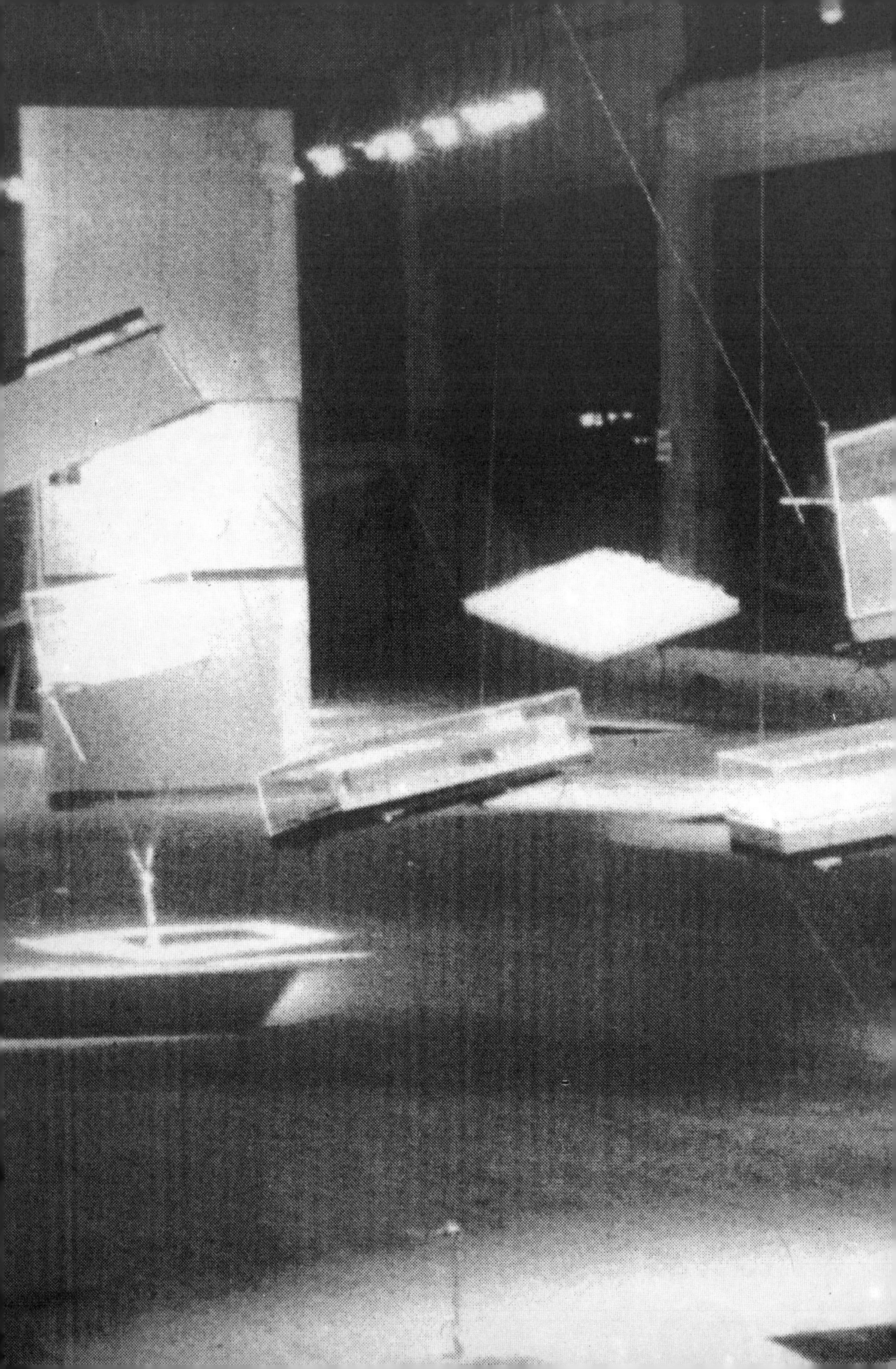

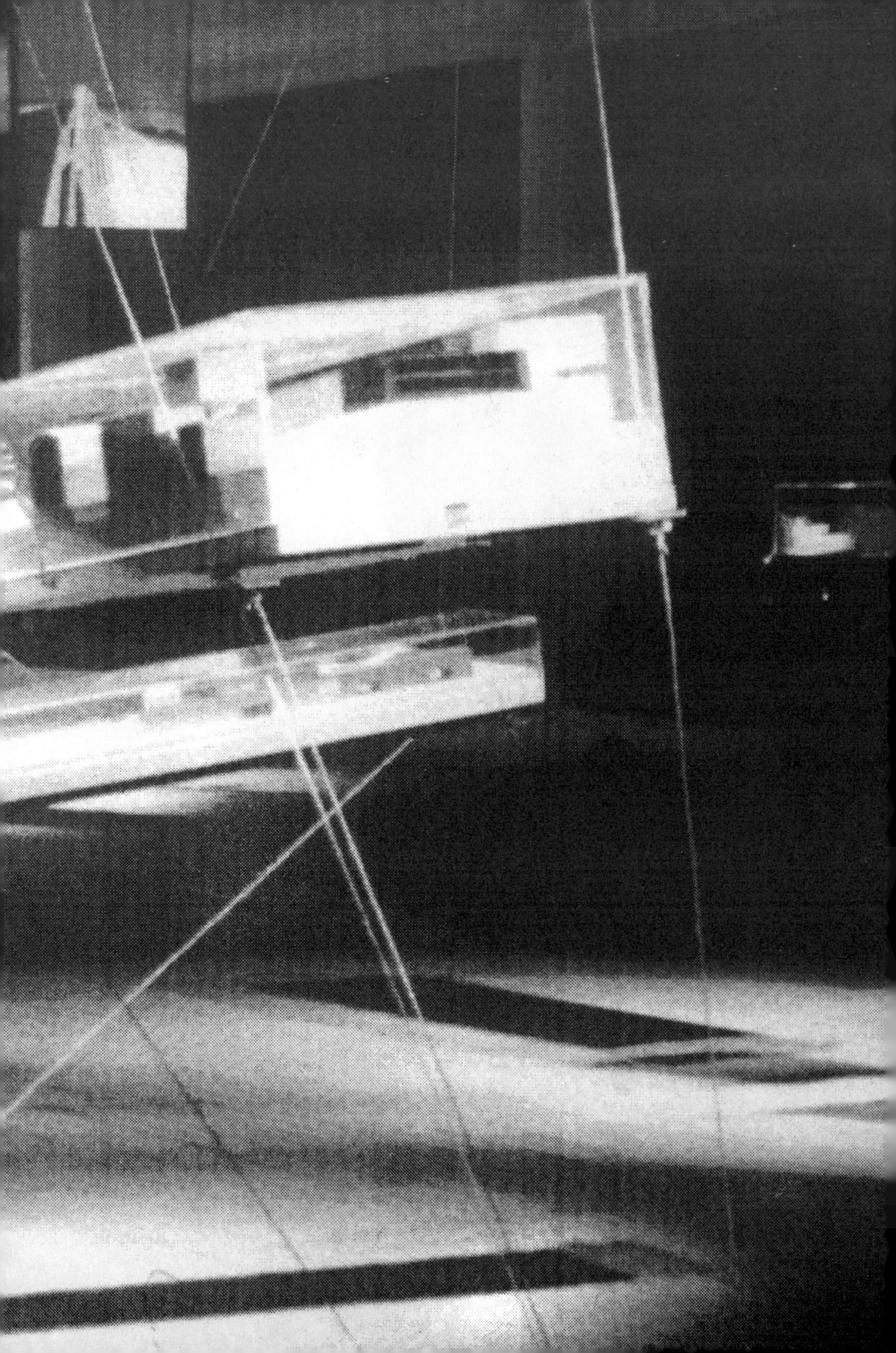

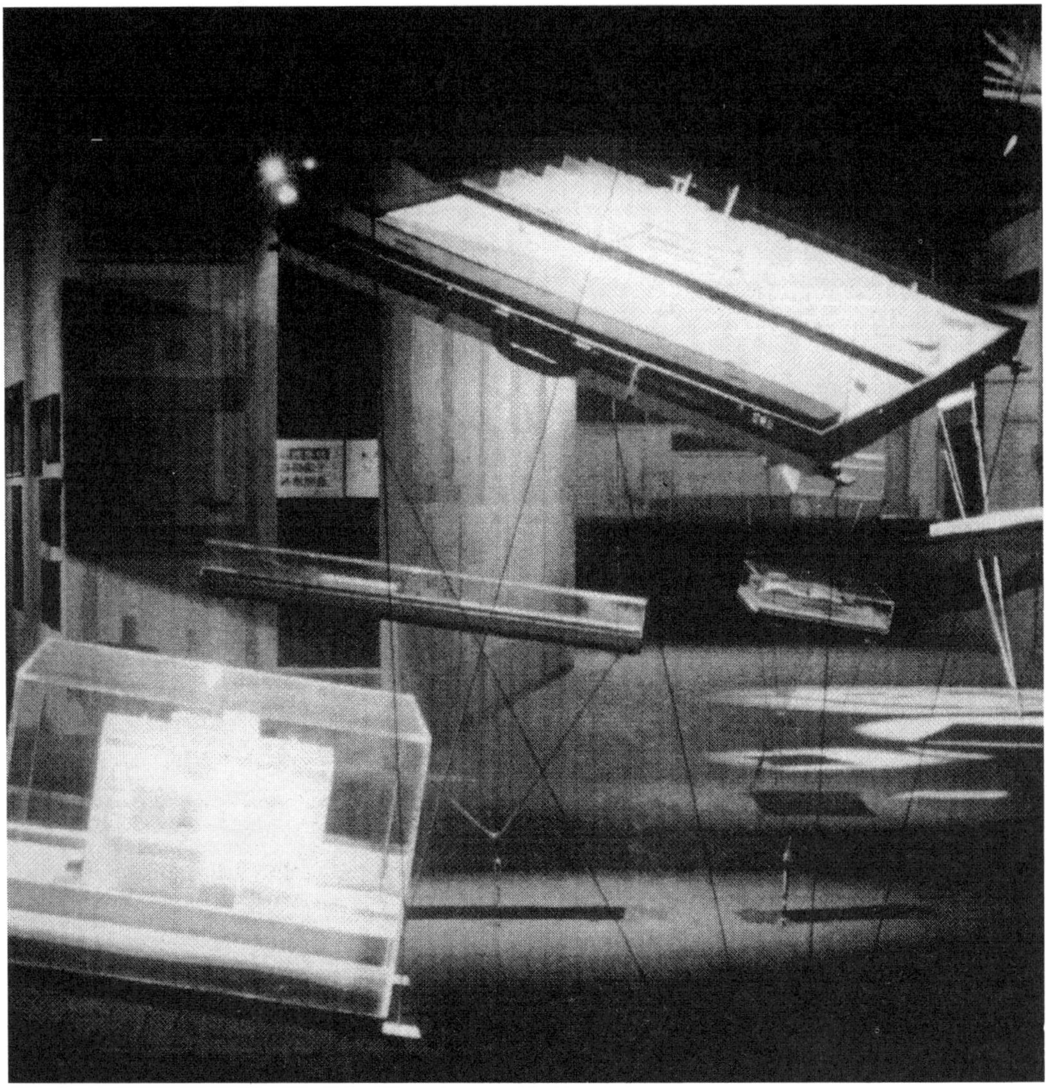

TOURCOING
601

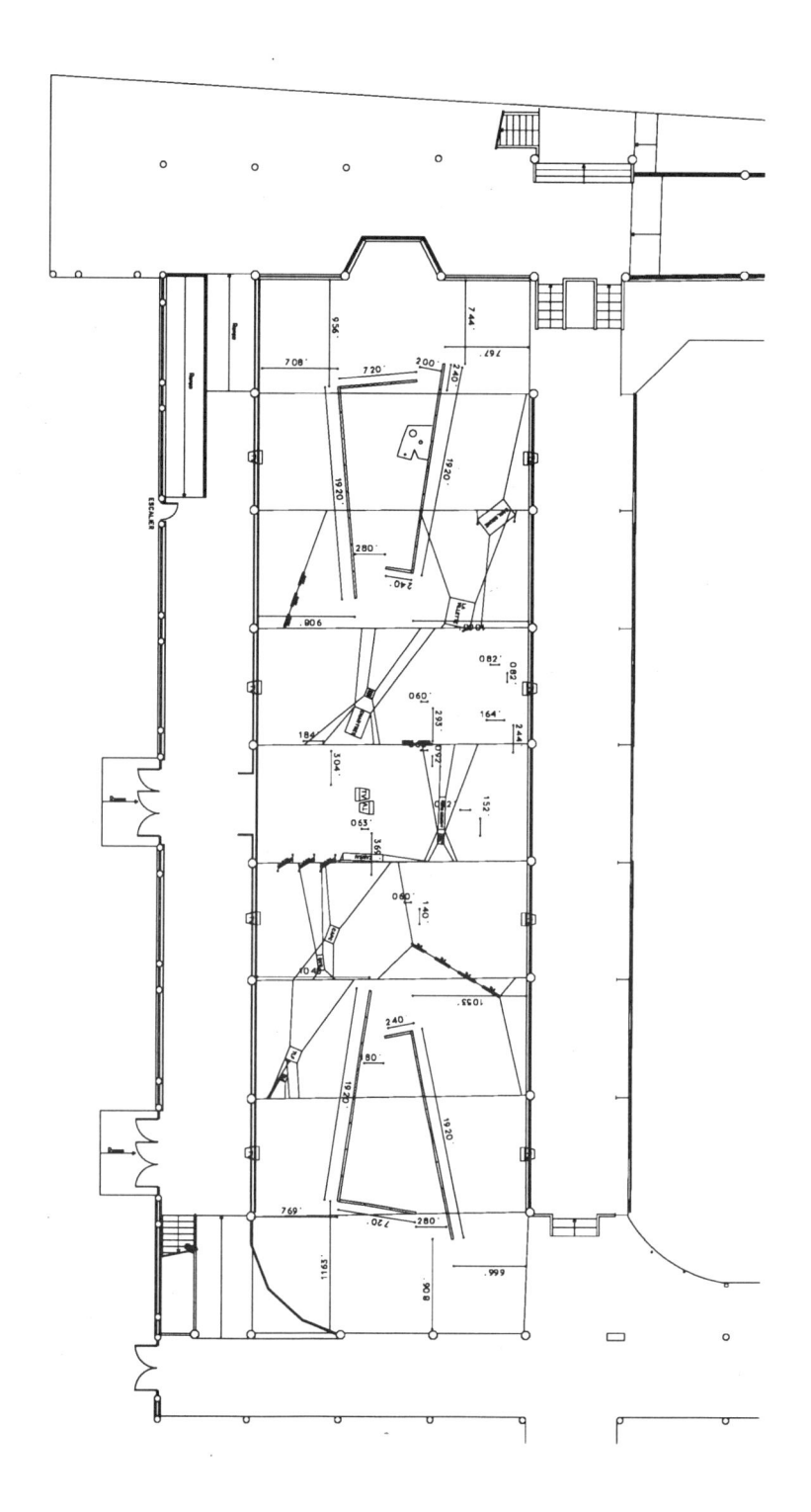

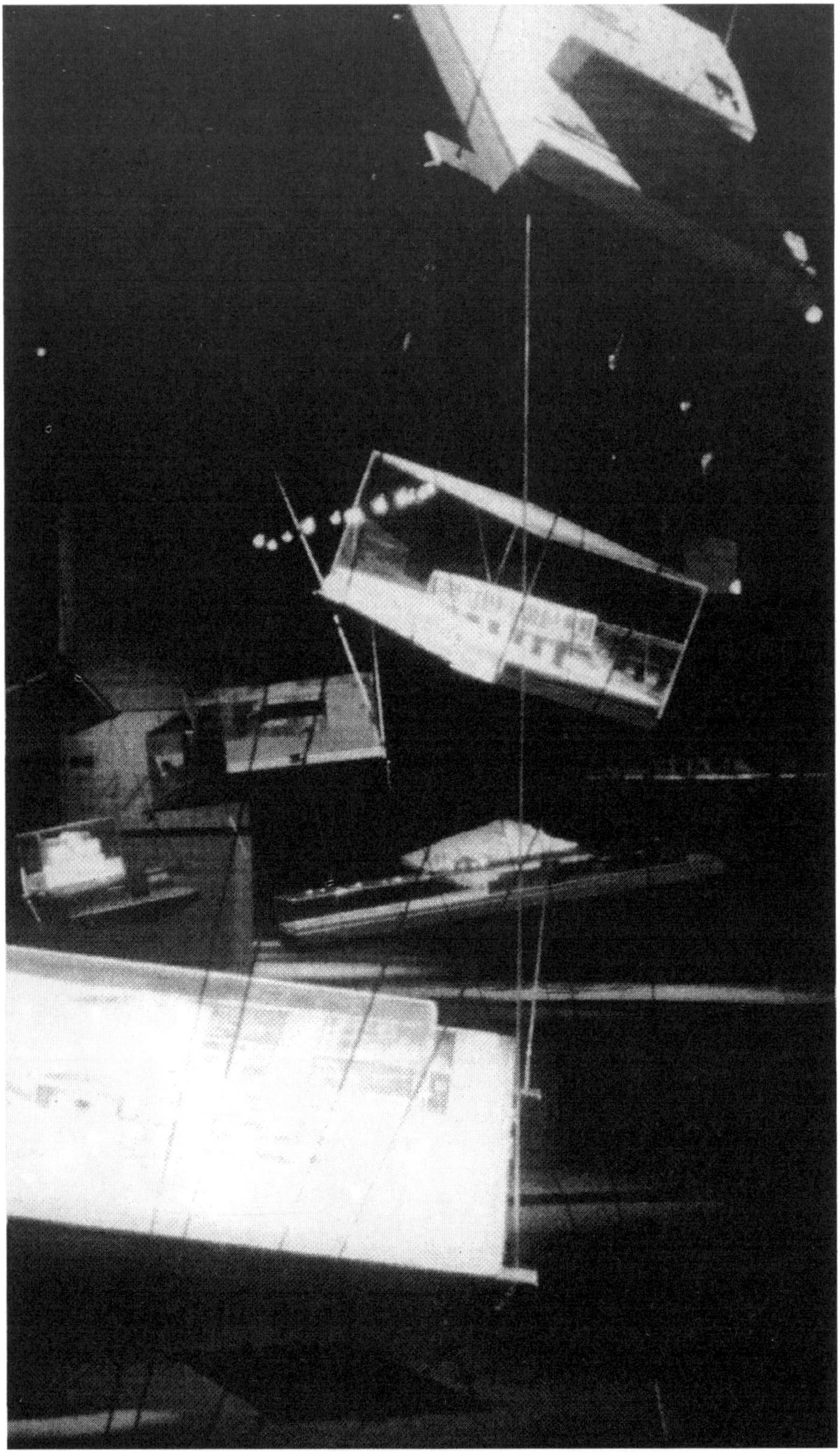

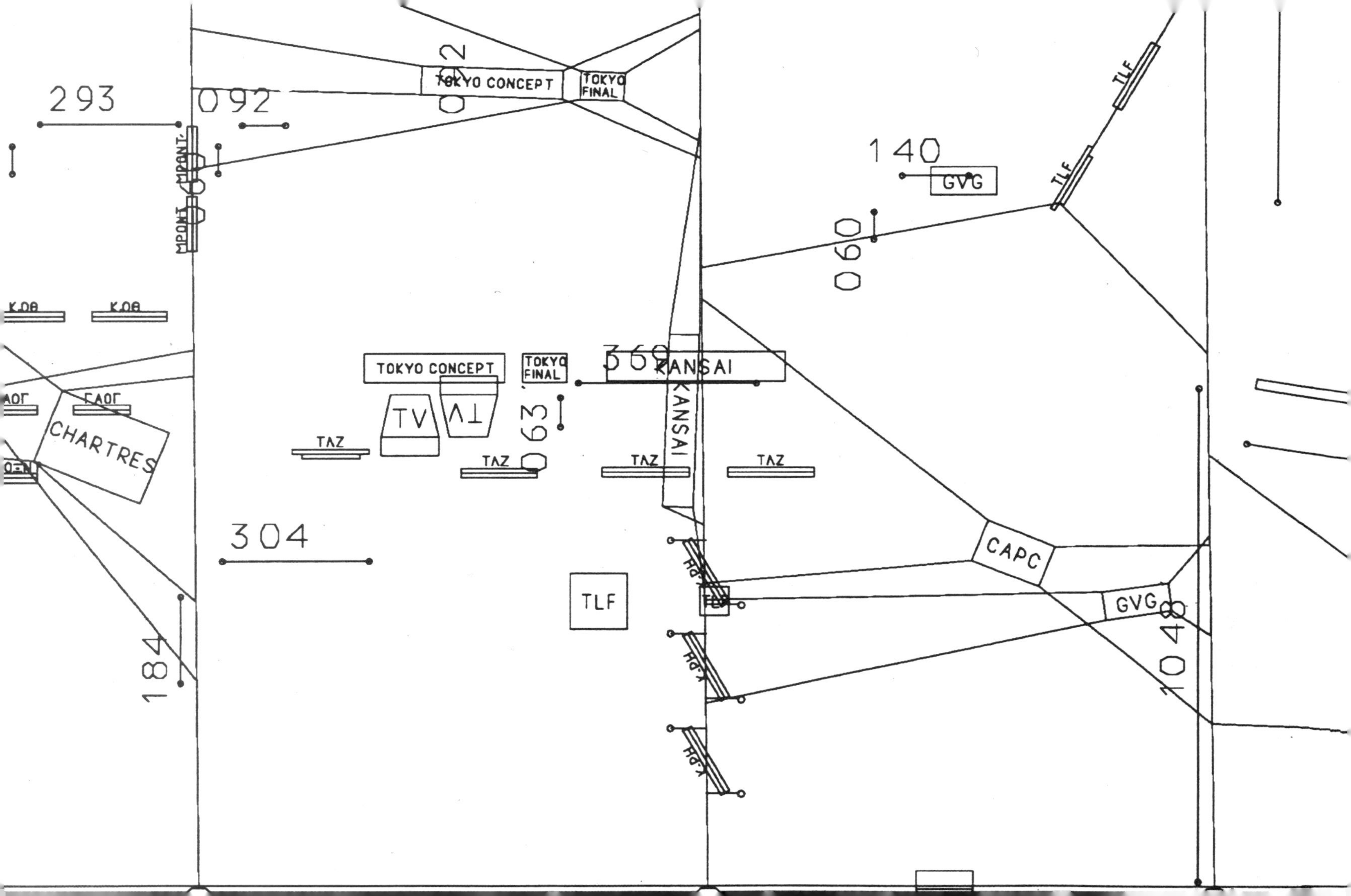
293
092
TOKYO CONCEPT
TOKYO FINAL
MPONT
K.O8
K.O8
CHARTRES
TOKYO CONCEPT
TOKYO FINAL
369
KANSAI
KANSAI
TV
TV
063
TAZ
TAZ
TAZ
TAZ
304
TLF
184
K.PH
K.PH
K.PH
140
GVG
060
TLF
TLF
CAPC
GVG
1048

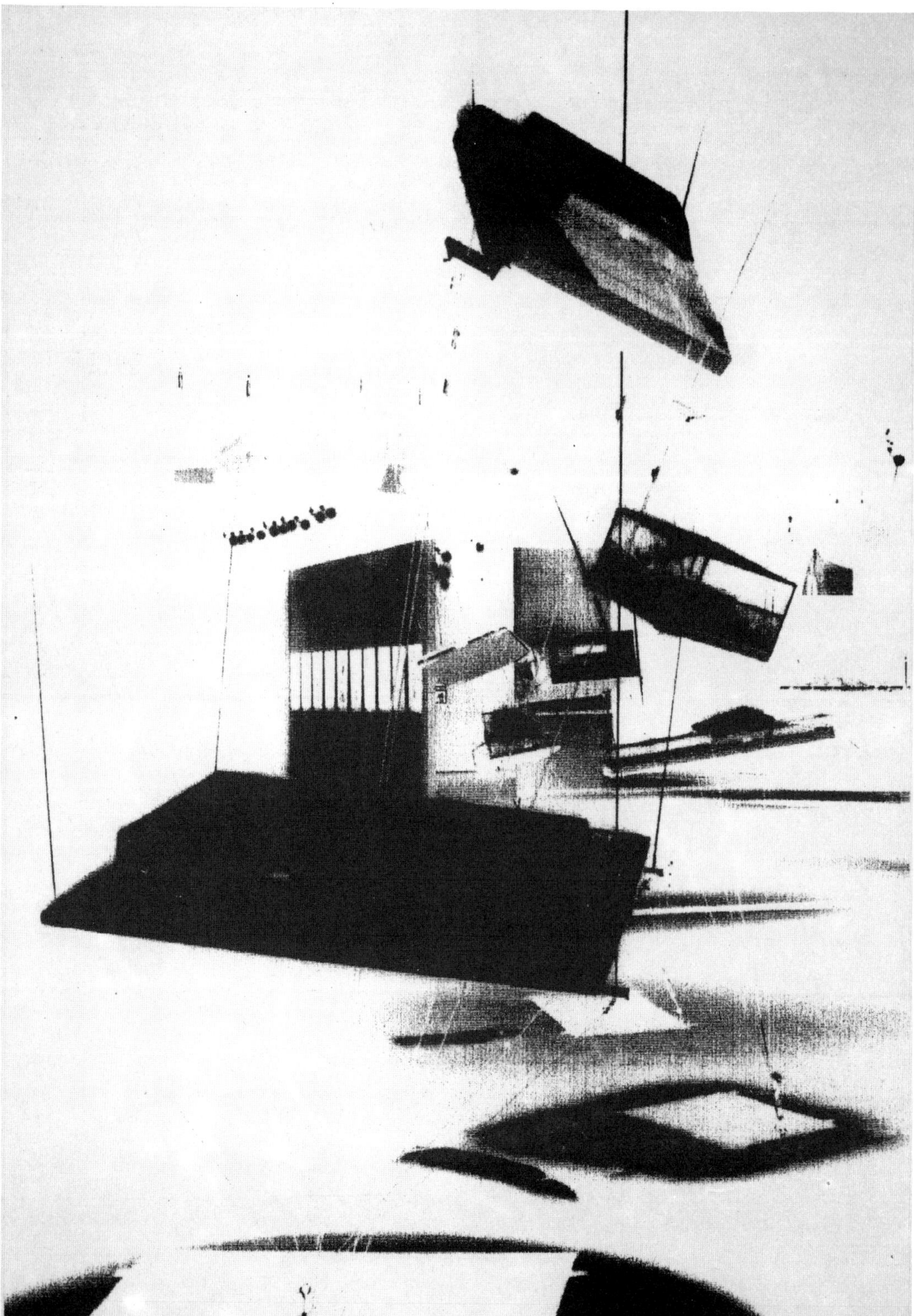

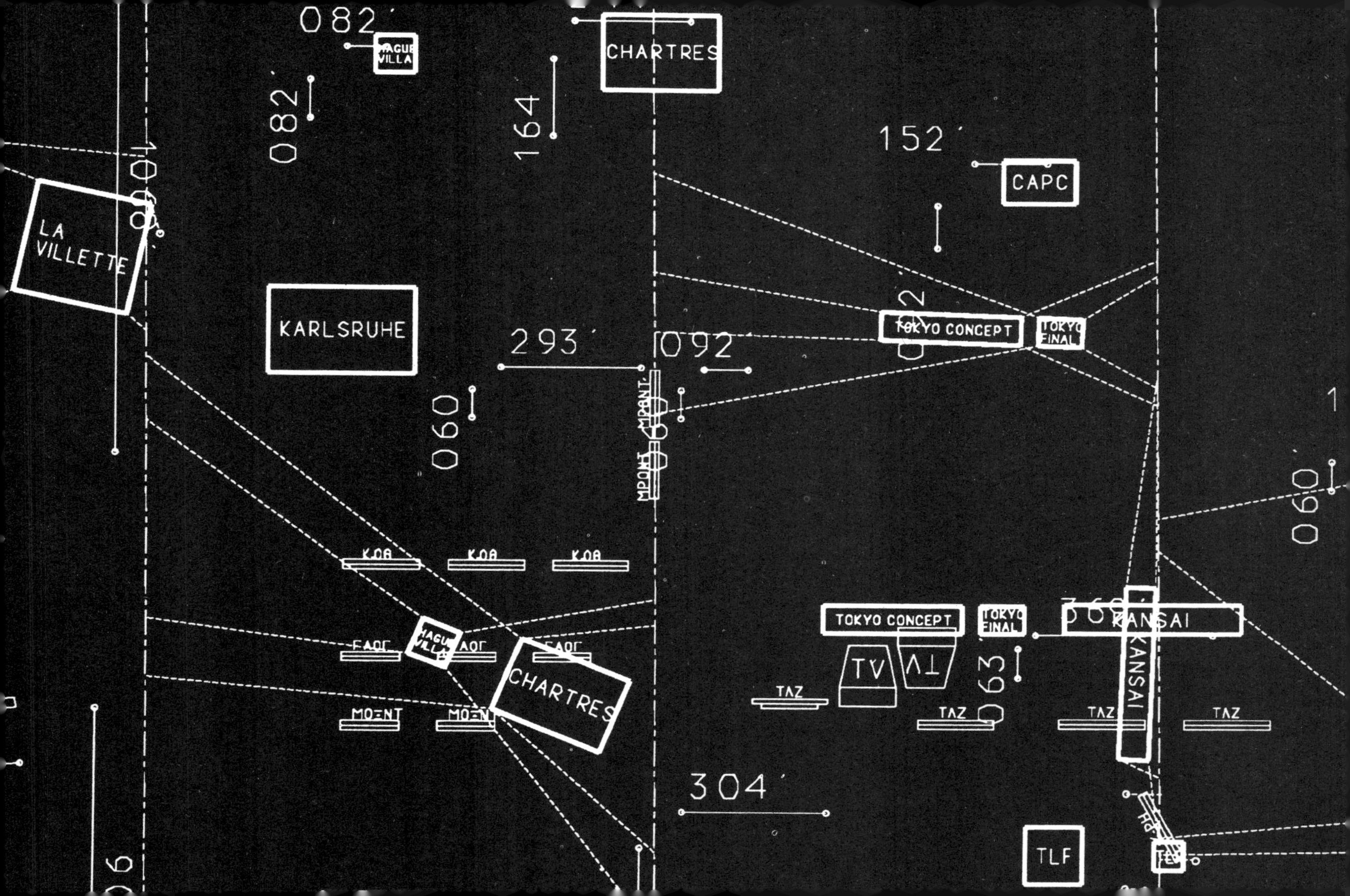

LA VILLETTE
KARLSRUHE
CHARTRES
CHARTRES
CAPC
TOKYO CONCEPT
TOKYO FINAL
TOKYO CONCEPT
TOKYO FINAL
KANSAI
KANSAI
TLF
TV
TV
KOB
KOB
KOB
EAOL
AOL
EAOL
MOENT
MOENT
TAZ
TAZ
TAZ
TAZ
MPONT
MPONT
082
082
164
152
293
092
060
060
060
304
063

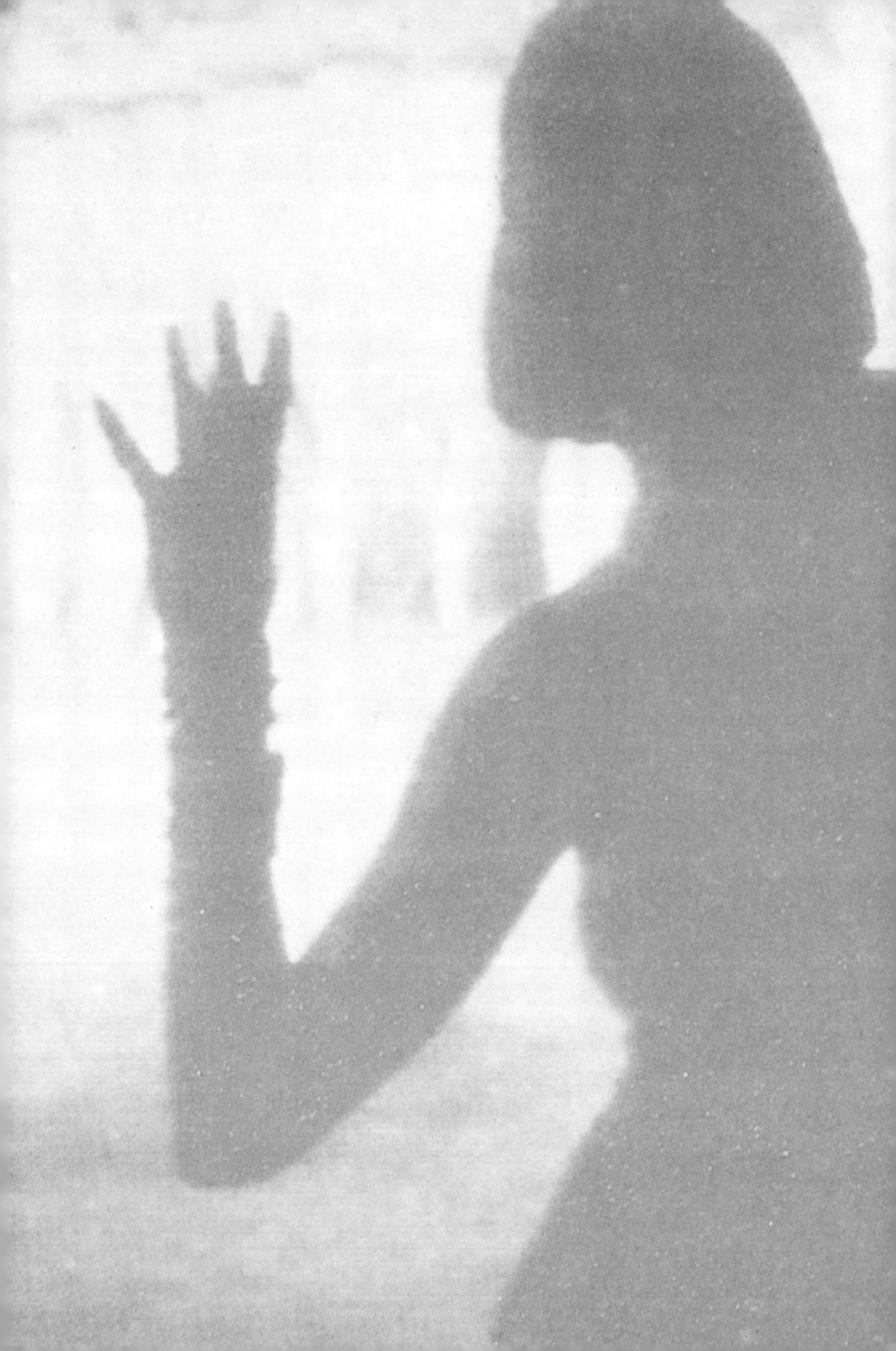

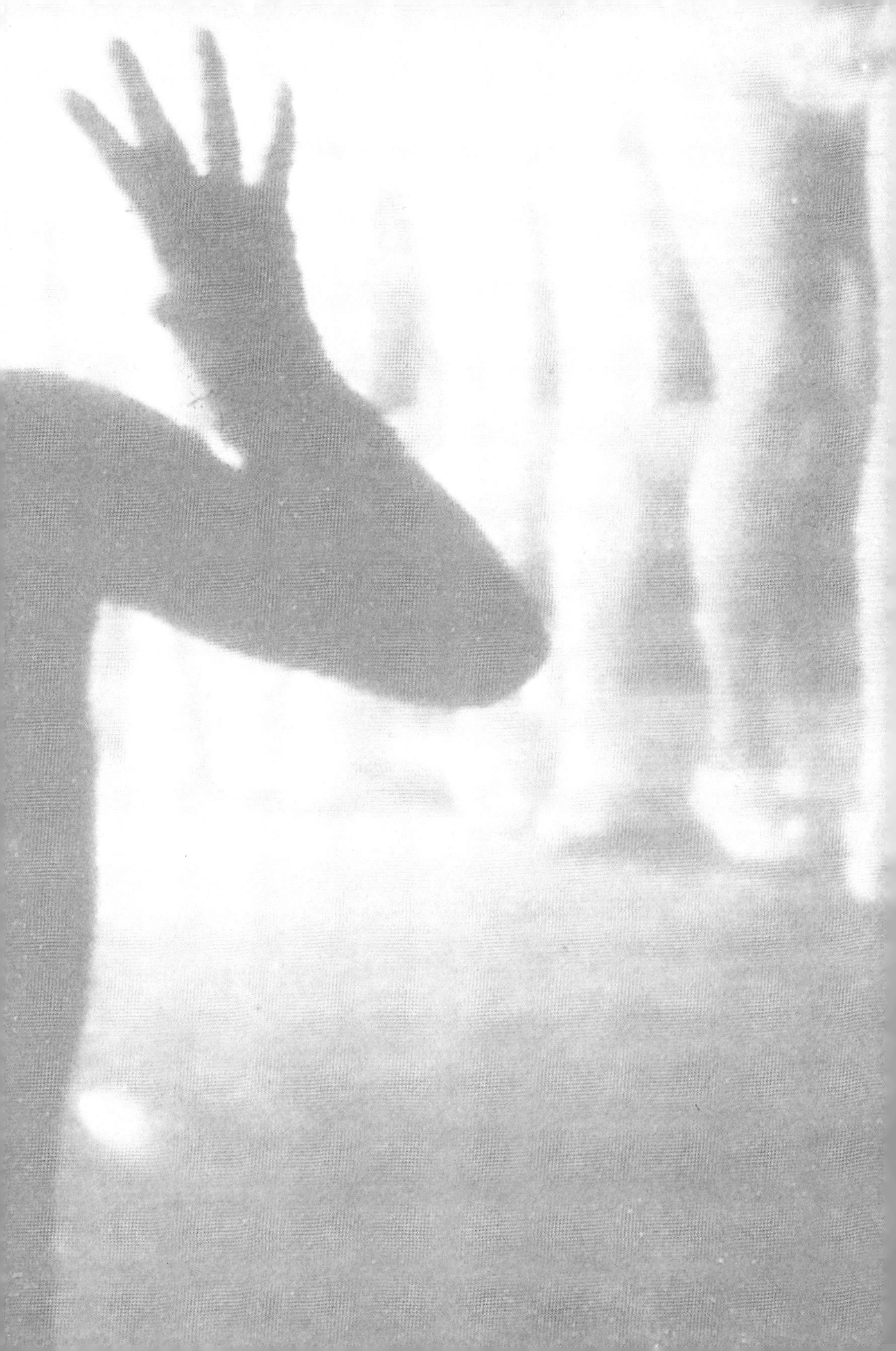

Project Teams

Parc de la Villette, Fireworks
Bernard Tschumi, Claudia Busch

Chartres, Business Park
Bernard Tschumi, Véronique Descharrières, Karen Dogny, Therese Erngaard, François Gillet, Mark Haukos, Tom Kowalski, Robert Young

Rotterdam, Railway Tunnel Site
Bernard Tschumi, Christian Biecher, Robert Young, Scott DeVere

Kansai, International Airport
Bernard Tschumi, Mehrdad Hadighi, Robert Young, Mark Haukos, Frazer Gardiner, Gilbert Schafer, Koichi Yasuda
Hugh Dutton (RFR), Stan Allen
Luca Merlini, Ursula Kurz, Christian Biecher

Lausanne, Bridge-City
Competition: Bernard Tschumi and Luca Merlini, Christian Biecher, Philippe Gavin, Ursula Kurz, Emmanuel Ventura
CAPC: Bernard Tschumi, Robert Young, Jim Sullivan
Metropont: Bernard Tschumi and Luca Merlini, Richter + Gut, Architram, Robert Young, Emmanuel Ventura, Marc Sautier, Hugh Dutton (RFR), J. H. Petignat

Kyoto, Center and Railway Station
Bernard Tschumi Architects with Nikken Sekkei Ltd.
New York: Bernard Tschumi, Koichi Yasuda, Mark Haukos, François Gillet, Robert Young, Hidemichi Takahashi, Hiroyuki Shirai, Winka Dubbeldam, Felix Jerusalem
Osaka: Kimiaki Minai, Toshinori Teramoto, Toshiro Hata, Nobuyoshi Hamada, Akira Hanajima, Masahiro Okazaki, Kazuhiro Otaka, Kosaku Maekawa, Hiroaki Ohtani, Toshihiko Azuma
Consultants: Peter Rice, Hugh Dutton (RFR); Michel Mein, Isao Nagaoka, Tom Kowalski (CAD); John Blood

Tokyo, Opera
Bernard Tschumi, Luca Merlini, Christian Biecher, Patrick Winters, Martyn Wiltshire, Alexandra Villegas, Peter Rice, Hugh Dutton (RFR), Daniel Dubos (Setec Batiment), Daniel Commins (Commins-BBM, Acoustics)

Strasbourg, County Hall
Bernard Tschumi, Luca Merlini, Christian Biecher, Neil Porter, Jean-François Erhel, Atelier UA5

Paris, Library of France
Bernard Tschumi, Luca Merlini, Robert Young, Koichi Yasuda, Mark Haukos, Frazer Gardiner, Jean-Pierre de l'Or, Ann Krsul, Philippe Gavin, Jean-François Erhel
Peter Rice, Hugh Dutton (RFR)

Karlsruhe, Center for Art and Media (ZKM)
Bernard Tschumi, Mark Haukos, Jakob Lehrecke, Jean-Pierre de l'Or, Robert Young, Midori Yasuda, Koichi Yasuda, Philippe Gavin

Tourcoing, Le Fresnoy National Studio for Contemporary Arts
New York: Bernard Tschumi, François Gillet, Tom Kowalski, Yannis Aesopos, Henning Ehrhardt, Douglas Gauthier
Paris: Bernard Tschumi, Jean-François Erhel, Véronique Descharrières, Vincent Thevenon, Paul H. Huchard, Louis Choulet, Echologos
Competition: Bernard Tschumi, François Gillet, Mark Haukos, Tom Kowalski, Robert Young, Jim Sullivan
Research group: Bernard Tschumi, Yannis Aesopos, Douglas Gauthier, Eric Liftin, Robert Moric, Sheri Olson, Jordan Parnass, Tsuto Sakamoto

The Hague, Villa
Bernard Tschumi, Tom Kowalski, François Gillet, Therese Erngaard, Robert Young, Mark Haukos, Hugh Dutton (RFR)

Groningen, Glass Video Gallery
Bernard Tschumi, Mark Haukos, Robert Young

Paris, Pompidou Center, "Art et Publicité" Exhibition Design
Bernard Tschumi, Jean-François Erhel, Robert Young, Mark Haukos

Tourcoing, Le Fresnoy, "BTA" Exhibition
Bernard Tschumi, Véronique Descharrières, Tom Kowalski, Yannis Aesopos, Henning Ehrhardt, Mark Haukos

Project List

1993
- "BTA" Exhibition, Le Fresnoy Center for Contemporary Arts, Tourcoing, France
- Federal Institute of Technology (EPFL) Extension, Lausanne, Switzerland
- World Meteorological Organization (OMM), Geneva, Switzerland
- "Spartan" Villa, The Hague, The Netherlands

1992
- Metropont, Bridge-City, Lausanne, Switzerland
- Salzburg Convention Center and Hotel, Salzburg, Austria
- Parc de la Villette Fireworks, Paris, France

1991
- Le Fresnoy National Center for Contemporary Arts, Tourcoing, France
- Business Park, Chartres, France
- Villa at The Hague, The Netherlands
- Quartier des Etats-Unis, Lyon, France
- Center for Contemporary Visual Arts (CAPC), Bridge-City, Lausanne, Switzerland
- Large Capacity Halls I & II, Tours, France

1990
- Kyoto Center and New Railway Station, Kyoto, Japan
- "The New Berlin," Berlin, Germany
- Hall for Spectacles, Nancy, France
- Cultural and Leisure Center, Carquefou, France
- Grand-Cours, Five Programmatic Squares, Echirolles, France
- " Art et Publicité" Exhibition Design, Pompidou Center, Paris, France
- Watermill House, East Hampton, New York
- Glass Video Gallery, Groningen, The Netherlands
- ARBED Headquarters, Esch, Luxembourg

1989
- New "Cité Industrielle" Planning Study, Völklingen, Germany
- Tokyo International Forum, Tokyo, Japan
- Center for Art and Media Technology (ZKM), Karlsruhe, Germany
- National Library of France (Bibliothèque de France), Paris, France
- Old Port of Montreal, Quebec, Canada

1988
- Bridge-City, Lausanne, Switzerland
- New Kansai International Airport, Osaka, Japan
- Moabiter Werder, Berlin, Germany
- Amerika-Gedenkbibliothek (AGB), Berlin, Germany
- Railway Tunnel Site, Rotterdam, The Netherlands
- Hollywood Hotel, Euro Disney, Marne-la-Vallée, Paris, France

1987
- Future Park, Flushing Meadows-Corona Park, Queens, New York
- 227 West 17 Street Loft, New York, New York

1986
- New National Theater and Opera House, Tokyo, Japan
- County Hall, Strasbourg, France

1983
- La Défense International Communication Center, Paris, France

1982
- Folie 7: Wave Hill, The Bronx, New York
- Folie 6: Kassel, Germany
- Parc de la Villette, Paris, France (completion date: 1995)

1981
- Sequential House, Princeton, New Jersey
- Folie 5: Broadway Gate, New York, New York

1980
- Folie 4: Middelburg, The Netherlands
- Folie 3: Dag Hammarskjold Plaza, New York, New York

1979
- Staircase for Scarface, Castle Clinton, New York, New York
- The Table, Architectural Association, London, England

1977
- Advertisements for Architecture

1976
- The Manhattan Transcripts (1976-1981)
- Joyce's Garden
- Screenplays (1976-1981)

1974
- Manifesto 1: Fireworks

Books and Selected Articles by Bernard Tschumi

1975
"Preface." *A Space: A Thousand Words*. Milan and London: Dieci Libri and Royal College of Art, 1975 (exhibition catalogue).

"Questions of Space: The Pyramid and the Labyrinth (or The Architectural Paradox)." *Studio International* (London),190, no. 977 (September–October 1975), pp. 136-42. (Reprinted in *Space Design* (Tokyo), no. 161 [February 1978].)

1976
"Architecture and Transgression." *Oppositions* (Cambridge, Massachusetts and New York), 7 (Winter 1976–77), pp. 55-63.

"Le Jardin de Don Juan ou la Ville Masquée." *L'Architecture d'Aujourd'hui* (Paris), no. 187 (October–November 1976), pp. 82-83. (Reprinted in *Formalism, Realism, Contextualism*. Tokyo: Shokokusha, 1979.)

1977
"The Pleasure of Architecture." *Architectural Design* (London), 47, no. 3 (March 1977), pp. 214-18. (Reprinted in *A + U* [Tokyo], no. 117 [June 1980].)

1978
"Advertisements for Architecture." *Space Design* (Tokyo), February 1978.

Architectural Manifestos. New York: Artists Space, April 1978 (exhibition catalogue).

"Architecture and its Double." *Architectural Design* (London), 48, no. 2–3 (April 1978), pp. 111-16.

1979
Architectural Manifestos. London: Architectural Association Press, January 1979 (exhibition catalogue).

"Manifestos." *Art Monthly* (London), 26 (June 1979).

1980
"Architecture and Limits I." *Artforum* (New York), 19, no. 4 (December 1980), pp. 36-44.

"Bernard Tschumi: Architectural Manifestos/Three Spaces." *A + U* (Tokyo), no. 117 (June 1980) (special issue).

"The Burrow in the Earth." *Domus* (Milan), no. 610 (October 1980).

"'Joyce's Garden' in London: A Polemic on the Written Word and the City." *Architectural Design* (London), 50, no. 11–12 (1980).

"On 'Delirious New York': A Critique of Critiques." *International Architect* (London), 1, no. 3 (March 1980), pp. 10-12.

1981
"Architecture and Limits II." *Artforum* (New York),19, no. 7 (March 1981), p. 45.

"Architecture and Limits III." *Artforum* (New York), 20, no. 1 (September 1981), p. 40.

"Episodes of Geometry and Lust," *Architectural Design* (London), 51, no. 1–2 (1981), pp. 26-28.

The Manhattan Transcripts: Theoretical Projects. New York/London: St. Martin's Press/Academy Editions, 1981.

Sequences. New York: Artists Space, 1981 (exhibition catalogue).

"Violence of Architecture," *Artforum* (New York), 20, no. 1 (September 1981), pp. 44-47.

1983
"Architecture, Limites et Programmes." *Art Press* (Paris), no. 2 (June–July–August 1983), pp. 41-42.

"The Discourse of Events." *Themes* 3. London: Architectural Association Press, 1983.

"Illustrated Index: Themes from *The Manhattan Transcripts*." *AA Files* (London), 4 (July 1983).

"Sequences." *The Princeton Journal: Ritual* 1 (1983). (Reprinted in *Vive l'Architecture: Revue Autrement* [Paris],1984.)

"La Villette: An Urban Park for the 21st Century." *International Architect* (London), 1 (1983), pp. 27, 31.

1984
"Espaces de communication" (with Colin Fournier). *Urbanisme* (Paris), no. 203 (August–September 1984).

"Madness and the Combinative." *Beyond Style: Precis* (New York, Columbia University), 5 (Fall 1984), pp. 148-57.

1985
Textes Parallèles: des Transcripts à La Villette. Paris: Institut Français d'Architecture, 1985 (exhibition catalogue).

"La Villette Park Competition." *The Princeton Journal: Landscape*, 2 (1985).

1986
La Case Vide: Folio VII. London: Architectural Association Press, 1986.

"La Ville Eclatée." *Ville, Forme, Symbolique, Pouvoir, Projets*. Liège: Mardaga, 1986.

1987
Cinegramme Folie: Le Parc de La Villette. Princeton and Paris: Princeton Architectural Press/Champ Vallon, 1987.

"Competition Entries: National Theatre, Tokyo/County Hall, Strasbourg." *AA Files* (London),13 (Autumn 1987).

"Disjunctions." *Perspecta* 23: *Yale Architectural Journal* (New Haven), 1987. (Reprinted as "Disjonctions" in *Mesure pour Mesure: Architecture et Philosophie*. Paris: Editions du Centre Pompidou/CCI, 1987.)

Disjunctions: New National Theater, Tokyo. Berlin: Galerie Aedes, 1987 (exhibition catalogue).

"Littera al Direttore." *Domus* (Milan), September 1987.

"Travaux de Bernard Tschumi." *AMC* (Paris), 12 (October 1987).

1988
"The Block: Manhattan Transcript 4." *Wiederhall 9: Autographical Architecture*. Amsterdam: Stichting Wiederhall, 1988 (exhibition catalogue).

"La Case Vide: La Villette." *Form • Being • Absence: Pratt Journal of Architecture* (New York), 2 (Spring 1988).

"N. Y. Loft." *10 on 10: The Critics' Choice*. New York: Princeton Architectural Press, 1988 (exhibition catalogue).

"Parc de la Villette, Paris." *Architectural Design: Deconstruction in Architecture* (London), 58, no. 3–4 (1988).

1989
"Bernard Tschumi: Bibliothèque de France." *Architectural Design: Reconstruction/Deconstruction* (London), 59, no. 9–10 (1989).

"De-, Dis-, Ex-" in Barbara Kruger and Philomena Mariani, eds. *Remaking History*. New York and Seattle: Dia Art Foundation and Bay Press, 1989. (Reprinted in *Archithese* (Zurich), 19, no. 1 [January-February 1989].)

"Folies in the Garden." *Monographias de Arquitectura y Vivienda* (Madrid), no. 17 (1989).

"Non-Sens/Un-Sinn" and "Zu einer Theorie der Disjunktion in der Architektur." *Archithese* (Zurich), 19, no. 2 (March–April 1989), pp. 39-40.

"Ponts-Villes." *Archithese* (Zurich), 19, no. 1 (January–February 1980).

1990
Questions of Space. London: Architectural Association Press, 1990.

"Winners in the 1989 Shinkenchiku Residential Design Competition 'Disprogramming': Judge's Comment." *The Japan Architect* (Tokyo), no. 395 (March 1990).

1991
"Event Architecture." *Architecture in Transition.* Munich: Prestel Verlag, 1991. (Printed in German as *Architektur im AufBruch.* Munich: Prestel Verlag, 1991, pp. 134-41.)

"Extract from University Lecture, Columbia University, 13 February 1991" in Peter Noever, ed., *Architecture Rising.* Vienna: Osterreichisches Museum fur Angewandte Kunst, 1991.

"Isozaki's Hors-Textes." *Space Design* (Tokyo), no. 326 (November 1991), pp. 52-55.

"Photograms." *Ottagono: Programme-Projets* (Milan), 98 (March 1991), pp. 73-88.

1992
"The Architecture of the Event." *Architectural Design: Modern Pluralism—Just What Exactly is Going On?* (London), 62, no. 1–2 (January–February 1992), pp. 25-27.

"Thèmes tirés des Manhattan Transcripts." *Architese* (Zurich), no. 5 (September–October 1992).

1993
Guiheux, Alain, et al. *Tschumi. Une architecture en projet: Le Fresnoy.* Paris: Le Fresnoy/Editions du Centre Pompidou, 1993.

Le Fresnoy: Studio National des Arts Contemporains. Paris: Le Fresnoy/Massimo Riposati Editeur, 1993.

Praxis: Villes-Événements. Paris: Le Fresnoy/Massimo Riposati Editeur, 1993.

"Six Concepts." *Columbia Documents of Architecture and Theory* (New York), 2 (1993), pp. 73-97.

"Ten Points, Ten Examples." *ANY: Architecture and the Electronic Age* (New York), no. 3 (November–December 1993), pp. 40-43.

1994
Architecture and Disjunction. Cambridge and London: MIT Press, 1994.

Selected Criticism and Reviews on Bernard Tschumi

1978
Linker, Kate. "Bernard Tschumi: Architecture, Eroticism and Art." *Arts Magazine* (New York), 53, no. 3 (November 1978).

1979
Shane, Graham. "Crime as Function: Bernard Tschumi Reviewed and Interviewed." *Architectural Design* (London), 49, no. 2 (February 1979).

1980
Goodwin, Bruce. "The Architecture of the Id." *A + U* (Tokyo), June 1980.

1983
"Bernard Tschumi et les 'Folies' de la Villette." *Le Monde Dimanche* (Paris), 20 November 1983.

Buchanan, Peter. "La Villette Park—Bernard Tschumi." *Architectural Review* (London), 174, no. 1040 (October 1983), pp. 72-73.

Chaslin, François. "Paysage après la bataille." *Nouvel Observateur* (Paris), 963 (April 1983).

Fillion, Odile. "Bernard Tschumi: Portrait." *Architecture Intérieure Crée* (Paris), no. 197 (October–November 1983).

Frampton, Kenneth. "Concours international pour le Parc de la Villette: Chapitre III: Le Footballeur patine sur le Champ de Bataille." *L'Architecture d'Aujourd'hui* (Paris), no. 228 (September 1983).

Rolin, Olivier. "Les Parc des Folies." *L'Architecture d'Aujourd'hui* (Paris), no. 227 (June 1983).

"La Villette: Un Parc Urbain du XXI Siècle." *(UIA) Bulletin de l'Union Internationale des Architectes*, no. 5 (1983).

1984
Barzilay, Marianne et al. *L'Invention du Parc: Parc de la Villette, Paris*. Paris: Graphite Editions, 1984.

Lipstadt, Helene. "A Paris for the 21st Century." *Art in America* (New York), 2, no. 10 (November 1984).

Lucan, Jacques. "Bernard Tschumi: Le Parc de la Villette." *AMC* (Paris), no. 6 (December 1984).

1985
Ellis, Charlotte. "Villette Progress." *Architectural Review* (London), 179, no. 1063 (September 1985).

Goldberger, Paul. "A New Modernism." *New York Times*, 24 November 1985.

Hatton, Brian. "Close to the Madding Crowd." *Building Design* (London), 739 (17 May 1985).

"Urban Park for the 21st Century: 32nd Annual P/A Awards." *Progressive Architecture* (Stamford, Connecticut), 66 (January 1985).

1986
"Amènagement du Parc." *Architecture Intérieure Crée* (Paris), no. 209. (December-January 1985–86).

"Art on Location." *Artforum* (New York), 24, no. 8 (April 1986).

Derrida, Jacques. "Point de Folie—Maintenant l'Architecture." *AA Files* (London), 12 (Summer 1986).

Ducret, François. "Le Parc des Folies." *Femina* (Zurich), no. 8 (April 1986), pp. 14-20.

Eveno, Claude. "Séquence 6, Profession Cinéaste." *Architecture: Récits, Figures, Fictions*. Paris: Editions du Centre Pompidou, 1986.

Pimienta, Guy. "Les parterres de la modernité." *Des Arts* (Paris), no. 2 (1986).

"Tschumi: les stries du parc." *Urbanisme* (Paris), no. 215 (August–September 1986).

1987
"Architecture et Paysage: Bernard Tschumi." *Techniques et Architecture* (Paris), no. 370 (February–March 1987).

Boles, Daralice D. "The Point of No Return." *Progressive Architecture* (Stamford, Connecticut), 68 (July 1987), pp. 94-97.

Isozaki, Arata. "Dialogue Now: Interview with Bernard Tschumi." *Hermes* (Tokyo), no. 12 (September 1987).

Lucan, Jacques. "Travaux de Bernard Tschumi." *AMC* (Paris), no. 17 (October 1987), pp. 2-33.

Pélissier, Alain. "Parc Urbain: Entretien avec François Barré; Entretien avec Bernard Tschumi." *Techniques et Architecture* (Paris), no. 370 (February–March 1987).

Salvy, Eglé. "La Villette Reinauguration et Bilan." *L'Express* (Paris), no. 1893 (16–22 October 1987).

1988
"Bernard Tschumi—Parc de La Villette, Paris." *Architectural Design: Deconstruction in Architecture* (London), 58, no. 3–4 (1988).

Bolle, Eric. "Deconstructivisme: Probleem of Pleizer?" *de Architect* (The Netherlands), 19, no. 5

(May 1988), pp. 32-35.

Forgey, Benjamin. "The Assault of the Modern." *The Washinton Post*, 26 June 1988.

Giovannini, Joseph. "Breaking all the rules." *New York Times Magazine*, June 1988.

Jencks, Charles. "The Architecture of Deconstruction" in *Architecture Today*. New York: Harry N. Abrams, 1988.

Johnson, Philip and Mark Wigley. *Deconstructivist Architecture*. New York: The Museum of Modern Art, 1988 (exhibition catalogue).

LeFaivre, Liane. "El Realismo Sucio en la Arquitectura." *Arquitectura Viva* (Madrid), no. 3 (November 1988).

Lodge, David. "Deconstruction." *The Guardian* (London), 8 April 1988.

Mönninger, Michael. "Die glorreichen Sieben." *Frankfurter Allgemeine Zeitung*, 2 August 1988.

Norris, Christopher. *What is Deconstruction?* London: Academy Editions/St. Martin's Press, 1988.

Pélissier, Alain. "Jacques Derrida: La déconstruction: un projet?" *Techniques et Architecture* (Paris), no. 380 (October–November 1988).

Posner, Ellen. "Deconstructive Criticism." *The Wall Street Journal* (New York), 18 July 1988.

Sorkin, Michael. "Decon Job." *The Village Voice* (New York), 5 July 1988.

Thomsen, Christian W. "Traum vom Tanzenden Stahl." *Ambiente* (Berlin), September–October 1988, pp. 124-30.

van Dijk, Hans. "Bibliothèque de France Competition, Paris," "Competition for the Rehabilitation of the Gare du Flon, Lausanne" and "Kansai Interntional Airport Competition, Osaka." *AA Files* (London), 18, 1988.

—. "With a little help of my friends: Tschumi's Vuurproef in La Villette." *Arch +* (Berlin), no. 96–97 (November–December 1988), pp. 20-33.

Vidler, Anthony. "The Pleasure of the Architect." *A + U* (Tokyo), no. 216 (September 1988), pp. 9-68 (special issue).

"Vive la France." *Archithese* (Zurich), 18, no. 4 (July-August 1988).

1989
"Bernard Tschumi (continued)): Kansai International Airport; City Bridges; Library of France." *A + U* (Tokyo), no. 229 (October 1989), pp. 7-32.

"Bibliothèque de France." *Architectural Design: Reconstruction/Deconstruction* (London), 59, nos. 9-10, pp. 34-37.

Curtis, William. "Les Grands Projets Parisiens, Monumentalité et Machines d'Etat." *Techniques et Architecture* (Paris), no. 385 (August–September 1989).

Garcias, Jean-Claude. "Les Folies Tschumi à la Villette." *Domus* (Milan), no. 703 (March 1989).

Feireiss, Kristin, ed. *4 x Amerika-Gedenkbibliothek*. Berlin: Ernst & Sohn, pp. 110-17.

Freiman, Ziva. "A Non-Unified Field Theory" and "In Progress: Flushing Meadows Corona Park and Bridges of Lausanne, Switzerland." *Progressive Architecture* (Stamford, Connecticut), 70 (November 1989), pp. 37-38, 65-73.

Jones, Peter Blundell. "La Villette." *Architectural Review* (London), 186, no. 1110 (August 1989).

—. "Widersprüchlichkeiten." *Archithese* (Zurich), 19, no. 4 (July–August 1989).

"Kansai International Airport Competition." *Architectural Design: Drawing into Architecture* (London), 59, no. 3–4 (1989), pp. 46-49.

Klotz, Heinrich. "Zentrum für Kunst und Medientechnologie Karlsruhe." *Bauwelt* (Berlin), no. 48

(December 1989).

Lucan, Jacques. *France: Architecture 1965–1988*. Milan and Paris: Electa/Moniteur, 1989.

"The Manhattan Transcripts " and "Flushing Meadows Corona Park" in Heinrich Klotz, ed. *New York Architektur*. Munich: Prestel Verlag, pp. 230-33.

Miranda, Antonio. "Atonal y Sincopado." *Arquitectura Viva* (Madrid), no. 7 (September 1989), pp. 24-28.

Nakamura, Toshio, ed. "Bernard Tschumi." *A + U* (Tokyo), no. 229 (October 1989).

"New National Theater of Japan; New County Hall, Strasbourg. *Deconstruction II: Architectural Design Profile* 77. London: Academy Editions, pp. 12-19.

Papadakis, Andreas, Catherine Cooke and Andrew Benjamin, eds. "Bernard Tschumi: Parc de la Villette, Paris; New National Theatre of Japan, Tokyo; New County Hall, Strasbourg." In *Deconstruction: Omnibus Volume*. New York: Rizzoli International Publications, 1989.

"Ponts–Villes" *Architecture Intérieure Crée* (Paris), no. 230 (June–July 1989).

Sørensen, Leif L. "Bernard Tschumi's Park." *Arkitekten* (Denmark), 91, no. 10 (30 May 1989), pp. 241-51.

Thomsen, Christian W. *LiterArchitecture*. Köln: Dumont Buchverlag, 1989.

1990
Appel, Teri. "Inside Out: Dissolving the Limits of Architecture." *Scape* (London), June–July 1990.

Barré, François and Pasquale Lovero. "Parco de la Villette: La Proposta Mediatica." *Lotus International* (Milan), Fall 1990.

Bennington, Geoffrey. "The Rationality of Post Modern Relativity" in *Philosophy + Architecture*. London: Academy Editions, 1990.

"Bernard Tschumi Architects: Parc de la Villette, Paris, France." *GA Document* (Tokyo), no. 26 (May 1990).

Betsky, Aaron. "The Sources and Sorcerers of Subversion" in *Violated Perfection: Architecture and the Fragmentation of the Modern*. New York: Rizzoli International Publications, 1990.

Cervelló, Marta. "It's Time for Change: Bernard Tschumi." *Quaderns d'Arquitectura i Urbanisme* (Barcelona), no. 184 (January–February–March 1990).

Cook, Peter and Rosie Llewellyn-Jones. *New Spirit in Architecture*. New York: Rizzoli International Publications, 1990.

Cooke, Catherine. "Paralelas y divergentes." *Arquitectura Viva* (Madrid), no. 11 (March–April 1990).

Davis, Douglas. *The Museum Impossible: Architecture and Culture in the Post-Pompidou Age*. New York: Abbeville Press, 1990.

"ENR News: Gallery is Structurally Transparent." *Engineering News Record* (New York), 26 July 1990.

Guise, David. *Encyclopedia Britannica Yearbook of Science and the Future: Architecture and Civil Engineering*. Chicago: Encyclopedia Britannica, 1990.

Hollenstein, Roman. "Klassische Monumentalitat, Dekonstruktivismus und Neo-Moderne." *Baumeister* (Frankfurt), 87, no. 1 (January 1990).

Klotz, Heinrich. *New York Architecture 1970–1990*. Munich: Prestel Verlag, 1990, pp. 230-33.

Martin, Louis. "Transpositions: On the Intellectual Origins of Tschumi's Architectural Theory." *Assemblage* (Cambridge, Massachusetts), no. 11 (1990).

Montaner, Josep Maria. "European Architecture 1977–1990." *Documentos de Arquitectura*

(Barcelona), December 1990, pp. 58-64.

Papadakis, Andreas. *The Architecture of Pluralism.* London: Academy Editions, 1990.

"Review." *Brutus* (Tokyo), no. 218 (1 January 1990).

"Theory and Practice." *Oculus* (New York), 53, no. 3 (November 1990), pp. 6-7.

What a Wonderful World: Music Videos in Architecture. Groningen: Groningen Museum, 1990 (exhibition catalogue).

1991

"Bernard Tschumi Architects: The Glass Video Gallery, Groningen, The Netherlands." *GA Document* (Tokyo), no. 29 (April 1991), pp. 90-91.

"Consultations Urbaines." *Architecture Intérieure Crée* (Paris), October 1991.

"Future Park: 38th Annual P/A Awards (Urban Design Citation)" in *Progressive Architecture* (Stamford, Connecticut), 72 (January 1991).

Glusberg, Jorge, ed. *Deconstruction: A Student Guide.* London: Academy Editions, 1991.

Hatton, Brian. "Surface Treatment." *Building Design* (London), 25 October 1991.

Hollier, Denis. *Against Architecture: The Writings of Georges Bataille*, translated by Betsy Wing. Cambridge and London: MIT Press, 1991.

Janson, H. W. *History of Art* (fourth edition). New York: Harry N. Abrams, 1991.

Lacy, Bill. *100 Contemporary Architects: Drawings and Sketches.* New York: Harry N. Abrams, 1991.

Lampugnani, Vittorio Magnano, ed. *Berlin Tomorrow: Architectural Design Profile* 92. London: Academy Editions, 1991, pp, 88-91.

Mandrelli, Doriana O. "The Glass Video Gallery in Groningen." *L'Arca* (Milan), no. 54 (November 1991), pp. 42-47.

Naylor, Colin, ed. *Contemporary Masterworks.* Chicago: St. James Press, 1991.

Okagawa, M. "20th Century Architecture." *The Japan Architect* (Tokyo), 1991.

Papadakis, Andreas, ed. "What a Wonderful World: Music Videos in Architecture" in *New Museums: Architectural Design Profile* 94. London: Academy Editions, 1991, p. 72.

"Pavillon de la Vidéo à Groningue." *L'Architecture d'Aujourd'hui* (Paris), no. 276 (September 1991), pp. 100-101.

Rajchman, John. *Philosophical Events: Essays of the '80s.* New York: Columbia University Press, 1991.

Thomsen, Christian W. "Bernard Tschumi—Die Philosophie der Dekonstruktivistischen Arkitektur." *Experimentelle Architekten der Gegenwart.* Köln: Dumont Buchverlag, 1991, pp. 121-40.

"Tschumi Charts Chartres." *Architectural Record* (New York), December 1991, p. 13.

"Tschumi: Otro Parque en Chartres." *Arquitectura Viva* (Madrid), no. 21 (November–December 1991), p. 87.

Welsh, John. "Almost There: Kyoto Competition." *Building Design* (London), no. 1042 (5 July 1991), pp. 16-17.

—. "Worth His Wait: Theorist Bernard Tschumi Begins to Build." *Building Design* (London), no. 1055 (November 1991), pp. 14-15.

1992

Beret, Chantal. "Modern Next." *Art Press* (Paris), no. 13 (1992).

"Bernard Tschumi—The Architecture of the Event, Kyoto Station Competition, Chartres Masterplan in Andreas Paadakis, ed. *Modern Pluralism: Just Exactly What is Going On? Architectural Design Profile* 95. London: Academy Editions, 1992, pp. 24-45.

Brooker, Peter, ed. *Modernism/Post–Modernism.* London: Longman Group U. K., 1992.

"Chartres, jardin d'enterprises." *A + U* (Tokyo), no. 257 (February 1992).

Cook, Peter. "The rise and rise of Bernard Tschumi." *Blueprint* (London), September 1992.

Frampton, Kenneth. "Place, Production and Scenography: International Theory and Practice since 1962" in *Modern Architecture: A Critical History* (third edition). London: Thames and Hudson, 1992.

Lelong, Guy. *Des relations édifiantes: essai sur Asher, Le Bernin, Botta, Buren, LeWitt, Micel-Ange, Nouvel, Tschumi.* Paris: Impressions Nouvelles, 1992, pp. 110-122.

Papadakis, Andreas, Geoffrey Broadbent and Maggie Toy, eds. *Free Spirit in Architecture.* London: Academy Editions, 1992.

Perrella, Stephen. "Anterior Diagrammatics, Writing Weak Architecture." *Architectural Design: Aspects of Modern Architecture.* London: Academy Editions, 1992, pp. 8-13.

Phillips, Christopher. "Tschumi to Design French Art School." *Art in America* (New York), May 1992, p. 39.

Taylor, Mark C. "Refuse" in *Disfiguring: Art, Architecture, Religion.* Chicago: University of Chicago Press, 1992.

Vidler, Anthony. "Trick/Track," in *The Architectural Uncanny: Essays in the Modern Unhomely.* Cambridge and London: The MIT Press, 1992.

1993
"Bernard Tschumi—Center for Contemporary Arts, Lausanne." *GA Document* (Tokyo), 36 (1993).

Davidson, Cynthia, ed. "Bernard Tschumi: Modes of Inscription." *ANY* (New York), 1 (May–June 1993).

Erngaard, Terese. "Bernard Tschumi." *Louisiana Revy* (Denmark), no. 2 (February 1993).

"The Hague Villa Project." *GA Houses* (Tokyo), 37 (1993), pp. 10-13.

Hunter, Sam. *Modern Art* (revised edition). New York: Vendome Press, 1993.

Kipnis, Jeffrey. "Towards a New Architecture" in Andreas Papadakis, ed. *Folding in Architecture: Architectural Design Profile* 102. London: Academy Editions, 1993.

Loriers, Marie-Christine. "La Strategie de l'Entre-Deux: Studio National des Arts Contemporains, Tourcoing." *Techniques et Architecture* (Paris), no. 406 (February–March 1993).

Papadakis, Andreas, ed. *Theory + Experimentation: An Intellectual Extravaganza.* London: Academy Editions, 1993.

Ruby, Andreas. "Die Aktivierung des Raumes" (interview) and "Kulturzentrum Le Fresnoy." *Arch +* (Berlin), nos. 119-120 (December 1993), pp. 70-75.

Russell, Stella Pandell. *Art in the World* (fourth edition). Fort Worth: HBJ College Publishers, 1993.

Guiheux, Alain, et al. *Tschumi. Une architecture en projet: Le Fresnoy.* Paris: Le Fresnoy/ Editions du Centre Pompidou, 1993.

Thornton, Charles. *Exposed Structure in Building Design.* New York: McGraw-Hill, 1993.

Vonier, Thomas. "Non-Parallel Parking." *Progressive Architecture* (Stamford, Connecticut), no. 10 (1993).

Wigley, Mark. *The Architecture of Deconstruction: Derrida's Haunt.* Cambridge and London: MIT Press, 1993.

Biographical Notes

Architect. Born in 1944, Lausanne, Switzerland. Double nationality French and Swiss, US Permanent Resident. Studied in Paris and at the Federal Institute of Technology (ETH), Zurich. Lives in New York and Paris. Taught at the Architectural Association in London (1970-79), at the Institute for Architecture and Urban Studies in New York (1976), at Princeton University (1976 and 1980) and at Cooper Union (1981-3). Chief Architect of the Parc de la Villette, won after an international competition in 1983. Currently Dean of the Graduate School of Architecture, Planning and Preservation at Columbia University in New York. Editor of *D* (Columbia Documents of Architecture and Theory.) Member of the Collège International de Philosophie. Principal of Bernard Tschumi Architects, Paris/New York.

Photography Credits

p. **2/3** Sandy Lesberg, in *Violence in Our Time,* Peebles Press International Inc., New York, 1977 p. **14/15** Parc de la Villette, Serge Delcroix, Paris, 1992 p. **36/37** Alfred Hitchcock, film, *Saboteur,* in *Hitchcock/Truffaut,* Touchstone Simon & Schuster, New York, 1985 p. **84/85** Peter Lindbergh, *Harpers' Bazaar,* December, 1993 p. **152/53** Andreas Feininger, *New York,* Amphoto, New York, 1970 p. **218/19** Daiho Yoshida, *Yokohama,* Impression Offset Ashai S.A., Yokohama, 1985 p. **264/65** Ben M. Hall, *The Best Remaining Seats,* Da Capo Press Inc., New York, 1975 p. **300/01** Andreas Feininger, *New York,* Amphoto, New York, 1970 p. **324/25** New York News Inc., in *Fifty Years in Pictures/Daily News,* Doubleday & Company Inc., New York, 1979 p. **362/63** Jean-Philippe Charbonnier, collection of the Musée d' Art Moderne de la Ville de Paris, 1957 p. **388/89** M. Garanger, J.-M. Jarre and F. Dreyfus Music, *Rock Sets*, Thames and Hudson, London, 1992 p, **522/23** Alfred Hitchcock, film, *Dial M for Murder,* in *Hitchcock/Truffaut,* Touchstone Simon & Schuster, New York, 1985 p. **554/55** Richard J. Anobile, film, *Outland,* Warner Books, New York, 1981 p. **574/75** Andreas Feininger, *New York,* Amphoto, New York, 1970 p. **592/93** Charles Hoff in *Fifty Years in Pictures/Daily News,* Doubleday & Company Inc., New York, 1979 p. **602/03** Brian Ferry, music video, *Don't Stop the Dance* in *What a Wonderful World/Music Videos in Architecture*, Oplage Edition, Groningen, 1990. All other photographs by Bernard Tschumi Architects.

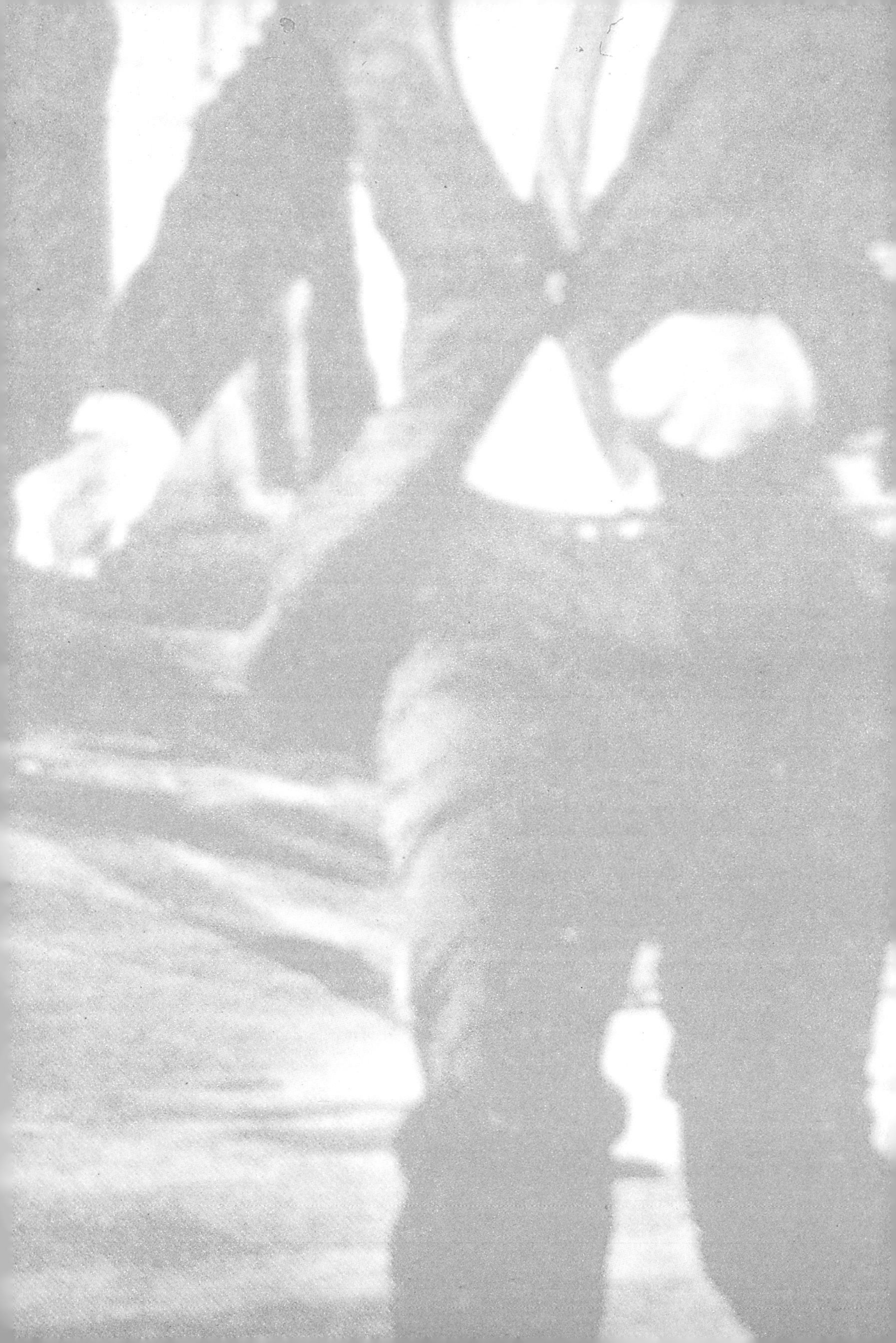